HUNDREDS OF CAN-DO ANSWERS TO A GARDENER'S TOUGHEST QUESTIONS

BY THE EDITORS OF *ORGANIC GARDENING* MAGAZINE

WINGS BOOKS
New York • Avenel, New Jersey

This 1994 edition is published by Wings Books,
distributed by Outlet Book Company, Inc., a Random House Company,
40 Engelhard Avenue, Avenel, New Jersey 07001,
by arrangement with Rodale Press, Inc.

Random House
New York • Toronto • London • Sydney • Auckland

Printed and bound in the United States of America

Illustrations by Frank Fretz and Tom Quirk
Book Design by Darlene Schneck

Library of Congress Cataloging-in-Publication Data

Q & A : hundreds of can-do answers to a gardener's toughest questions
  / by the editors of Organic gardening magazine : [illustrations by
  Frank Fretz and Tom Quirk].
        p.   cm.
     Originally published : Emmaus, Pa. : Rodale Press, c 1989.
     Includes index.
     ISBN 0-517-09304-9
     1. Organic gardening--Miscellanea. 2. Gardening--Miscellanea.
   I. Organic gardening. II Title: Q and A.
   SB453.5Q19 1994
   635'.045.84--dc20   93-28708
                                                              CIP

8 7 6 5 4 3 2 1

Contents

Part FOUR: **Beautify Your Home**

Part FIVE: **Keeping the Garden Healthy**

Introduction

The best gardeners are always the most experienced. But that experience has to come from somewhere, and most of us are far too eager to get it second-hand. For example, we know we're supposed to learn all about a plant *before* we buy it, but few of us ever do. Instead, we're inspired by a photograph or description, and we buy a young specimen or start it from seed. Either way, there are always surprises.

From the surprises grow questions. And then the search begins for that seasoned gardener somewhere who is familiar with your plant and might have a solution to your problem. Usually the plant shows signs of insect damage, or it grows too slowly. You know something is wrong—but what? Sometimes it's simply a matter of too much unruly growth: It needs pruning. So you stand before your beloved shrub or berry bush with pruning guidebook in hand, trying to decipher which limb is the one to cut. Or maybe your plant's size is twice what you expected. So now you must move it, but you need to know how this can be done without harming the roots.

For nearly 50 years, *Organic Gardening* magazine has been "that gardener somewhere" to millions of gardeners across the country. We answer questions by telephone, by mail, and through the pages of our magazine. In the last few years, our weekly mail count has reached 500 letters! From this tremendous volume, we've gathered together the questions that have come up again and again—many of which have answers that aren't easily found anywhere else—and put them into a comprehensive collection for you. From vegetables and flowers to houseplants and trees, from insect pests to soil care, we've covered the bases with detailed solutions from the experts.

We were all beginners once, and finding those first answers is a process you never forget. Discovering a plant's quirks on your own, and understanding the reasons for and the solutions to problems, build a hands-on knowledge that stays with you through all your gardening years. Your confidence grows, and you find yourself exploring, growing new and unfamiliar plants, and trying different techniques.

If you are just getting started, this book will build that foundation of garden know-how for you. And if you're one of those invaluable longtime gardeners that beginners rely on, it will be a handy reference guide to help you brush up on neglected areas. In any case, we dedicate it to the Extension agents, breeders, entomologists, and experienced gardeners who so graciously offer their advice and expertise in helping us answer gardening's diverse and sometimes complicated questions.

Stevie Daniels
Executive Editor
Organic Gardening

Part
ONE

Build a Better Garden

Chapter 1

Tips to Plan and Plant a Bountiful Garden

Planning Your Plot

Turn, Turn, Turn

Q. If you fertilize carefully, does it hurt to plant the same vegetable in the same spot each year?

A. Regardless of how well you fertilize, you should rotate garden crops every year. The more you move your crops around, the more diversified the demands placed on the soil and the more varied your cultivation practices will be. By growing one crop in the same space every year, you increase the likelihood of certain insects establishing themselves in the area. As a result, you'll see increasing insect problems in coming years. However, if you practice good rotations, you will be cultivating the same ground at a different time each year, disturbing many insects' life cycles.

Additionally, by rotating legumes with non-legumes, your fertilization requirements will be reduced because the legumes will leave nitrogen in the soil. Another advantage of good rotations is the buildup of minerals near the top layers of the soil by the roots of the different plants. While one plant may accumulate calcium in its roots, another may do the same for manganese; by rotating, you allow the crops that follow to take advantage of the accumulated minerals.

2

Small-Time Rotation

Q. As long as I use plenty of compost, is a rotation plan actually worthwhile for a small garden?

A. The smaller a garden gets, the harder crop rotation becomes. Still, there's no substitute if you want to avoid disease and pest buildup and keep soil nutrients from becoming depleted. Move your crops around the patch as much as possible.

A New Direction

Q. Should the rows of a garden be planted east to west or north to south?

A. The best advice is to orient rows and pathways according to the lay of the land. Rows should run across a slope to prevent erosion. If your land allows, however, you can choose either direction, according to your needs.

Concern with row and path orientation centers around the shading that occurs in early morning and late afternoon. During summer, the sun is essentially overhead through most of the day, so row direction has little effect on how much sunlight reaches plants. Early and late in the day, however, tall crops can cast shade on short ones. When rows run east to west, most of the shadow a crop casts falls on its own row members. When rows go north and south, all of the shadow a crop casts falls on the adjacent rows. For that reason, east-to-west planting has been the traditional recommendation. But you can use these shadows to advantage. For example, shade from corn can protect fall cauliflower transplants from the late-afternoon heat.

Battling Bolting

Q. What is meant by the term *bolting*, and what causes it?

A. Bolting is a term used by gardeners to describe the flowering of a vegetable. It refers most often to plants grown for their foliage, like lettuce, spinach, and Chinese cabbage, but can also apply to celery stalks, onion bulbs, or broccoli.

While bolting is a natural part of the plant's life cycle, it is undesirable for gardeners because it turns the edible portion of the lant bitter. In the case of onions, it keeps the bulb from developing fully and creates a woody core.

Several environmental factors induce bolting. Hot weather causes lettuce and spinach to bolt, but cold spring weather makes celery flower. Alternating periods of cold and warmth promote bolting in onions and Chinese cabbage. Onions also may bolt if exposed to drought or insect stress. These vegetables are all cool-weather crops, so they tend to do best in spring and fall. To prevent bolting in celery, don't expose the plants to night temperatures below 45°F for an extended period. Generally, careful timing of plantings will help prevent bolting.

A Well-Bred Plant

Q. I have often seen the word *cultivar* used. Could you define it for me?

A. A cultivar (short for cultivated variety) is a plant that has been selected or hybridized. It probably wouldn't be able to survive for more than a few generations outside the garden. The term was coined by botanists to distinguish cultivated varieties from natural or botanical varieties of species—those that originated and reproduce in the wild. Most garden plants are cultivars, but the term is used interchangeably with variety, horticultural variety, and garden variety in most garden publications.

Seed and Seedling Stumpers

Seed-Storing Savvy

Q. What's the best way to store seeds?

A. It's best to store seeds in a cool, dry place—a closet, for instance. The refrigerator is a good storage place, too, but don't store them in the freezer.

To store seeds in the refrigerator, keep them in a jar tightly covered with a canning lid to seal out moisture. Dehumidify the air inside the jar by covering the bottom with a layer of silica gel (about an inch per gallon jar), available from camera stores, or with 2 heaping tablespoons of powdered milk folded into a pouch of Kleenex or other facial tissue. If you use powdered milk, discard and replace it twice a year. Silica gel can be dried and reused indefinitely. Naturally, it's a good idea to use seeds as soon as possible, because no matter how well you store them, time has a way of draining seed vitality.

Germination on Trial

Q. **I have a lot of seeds left over from last year. How can I tell if they're still good?**

A. Most vegetable seeds will remain capable of germinating for three to five years if stored under cool, dry conditions. But the only way to know for sure if they'll sprout is to run a germination test.

Count out 20 seeds from the same packet. Spread them on three layers of premoistened paper towels, then roll them up carefully in the paper so the seeds stay separated. Tuck the rolled paper towels in a plastic bag and keep the incubating seeds in a warm place. If you're testing more than one batch, be sure to label each roll.

Check the seeds after two or three days, then check them every day thereafter for a week. If a root or cotyledon protrudes through the seed coat, the seed has germinated. Allow three weeks for most varieties to germinate, then calculate the rate of germination. Ten seeds out of 20 means 50 percent germination. Fifteen seeds out of 20 means 75 percent germination. Adjust the number of seeds you plant according to the percentage of seeds that germinated. For instance, if three-fourths of the test seeds germinated, sow one-fourth more of those particular seeds than you would ordinarily plant.

Toss Old Seed

Q. **I got 50 percent germination when I tested my three- to four-year-old lettuce and carrot seed. Is it OK to use the seed, as long as I sow extra thickly, or should I throw it away?**

A. When the germination percentage drops by more than one-third, it's best to throw away or compost the seed, says Dr. Jim Alston, director of research at Park Seed Company. Old seed tends to produce weaker, slower-growing and poor-yielding plants. But even if you use new seed, germination percentages will vary widely. For example, while the minimum official federal germination percentage set by the U.S. Department of Agriculture (USDA) for new lettuce seed is 80 percent, it's only 55 percent for carrot seed. Since the germination of the lettuce seed has dropped by at least one-third, you should probably discard it, but the carrot seed is OK to use.

Saving Hybrid Seed

Q. **Would you explain the difference between hybrid and regular seeds? Can you save hybrid seeds for next year's garden?**

A. Seeds described as "F-1 hybrids" are produced by crossing two pure strains, usually inbred. Often, these two strains are not particularly striking themselves, but when they are artificially cross-pollinated, the resulting plants may have more vigor and produce better than either parent. If you save seed from these varieties, the hybrid vigor is lost in the second generation, and the result will probably be unlike either of the parents. Seed from "open-pollinated" or "standard" stock, on the other hand, will stay true for generation after generation; so if you save seed, stick to these varieties and avoid hybrids.

Beware Cross-Pollinators?

Q. **Can you plant several varieties of the same vegetable (like squash) together and not have the cross-pollination affect their taste and appearance?**

A. Cross-pollination has little noticeable effect on the taste and appearance of vegetables. Only the characteristics of the seed are affected. The portion we are after—and generally call the fruit of the plant—is tissue that surrounds the seed. It is part of the mother plant, not the seed, and remains unchanged genetically by cross-pollination.

Squash, for example, cross-pollinates readily. The fruit will be true to the parent plant, while the seeds inside will be changed. Corn is the major exception. It cross-pollinates easily, and the part we eat *is* the seed. Popcorn and sweet corn planted too close together can produce poor-quality crops of both. Some of the new supersweet varieties can lose nearly all their sweetness due to cross-pollination. Peas, dry beans, and limas—because of the mechanics of their blossoms—are almost always self-pollinated.

Colorful Seed Coats

Q. **I've heard that most bean seeds sold in the North are treated by coating them with dangerous fungicides. Tell me why that is so, and where I can order untreated seeds.**

A. Actually, it appears that most of the big seed companies *don't* put fungicides on seed unless the customer requests it. The few that *do* routinely treat bean seed will sell you untreated seed if you ask for it.

The reason large seeds like bean, pea, corn, and sometimes squash, melon, and cucumber are ever treated is to protect the germinating seeds from rot if they are planted in cold, damp soil. The chemical used most frequently is captan, a fungicide that has been linked to birth defects. Seed rot is easily avoided without fungicide. Just wait until the soil has warmed thoroughly. A welldrained, friable soil helps, too.

You should be able to spot coated seed by its powdery surface, which is usually colored blue, pink, or purple. But to make sure you're getting safe, untreated seed, check in the catalog for a note explaining the company's policy. If you can't find a note, beware. Call or write the company if you're not sure.

Let's Seed
Some Identification

Q. **What is meant by *certified seed*?**

A. Certified seed is guaranteed to be true to name and uncontaminated with other varieties. State-run certification programs were begun in the early 1900s to preserve the genetic purity of new varieties, and all subscribe to the standards of the Federal Seed Act, signed into law in 1939. Today, there are about 45 programs, primarily overseeing agricultural crops and grass seed. Vegetable varieties are federally protected by the Plant Variety Protection Office and the Plant Patenting Office.

Seed potatoes (the small potato tubers that are planted instead of true seed) are also certified by state-run programs. However, the objective is to provide disease-free seed to growers. Certified seed potatoes aren't guaranteed to be free of diseases but have been spot-checked by inspectors. Seed cannot be certified if bacterial ring rot or viruses are identified. Small percentages of fungal diseases may be allowed.

Dr. Frank Manza, a potato pathologist at the University of Maine, stresses that home gardeners should always request certified seed potatoes, both to ensure a productive crop of their own and to prevent the spread of disastrous potato diseases to other gardens and commercial fields.

Confusing Calculations

Q. **Being a relatively new gardener, I'd like to ask about a problem I have interpreting the phrase "Safe Planting Dates for Vegetables in the Open." Does this mean that it's safe to plant seed in the ground, or does it mean it's safe to transplant the plant itself into the garden?**

A. Both. Basically, these dates indicate the earliest safe time for sowing seeds outdoors. They also mark the earliest times to put transplants out safely. "Safe planting date" differs from "frost-free date." For weeks after the frost-free date, the soil temperature may remain too low and the daylength too short for many tender plants to survive. Check with your county agent for planting dates in your own area.

Speeding Up Seeds

Q. **If a seed requires a minimum soil temperature of 50°F to germinate, and my soil is 45°F in the morning and 55°F late in the day, how do I know when to plant?**

A. The seed will begin germination as soon as the temperature gets above its 50-degree minimum requirement. Soil temperature affects how quickly germination takes place. In this case, when the soil temperature drops into the forties at night, the process will stop until temperatures get back into the required range.

The best way to decide when to plant is to take soil temperature readings at the planting depth for the seed. Read at sunset for the day's high and early in the morning for the low. You can plant when the daily average matches the seed's minimum requirement.

Taking soil temperatures is very easy to do. The most convenient thermometer for this reading is the long-stemmed dial type, which can be found in scientific supply catalogs. Besides being the surest way of knowing the right time for planting, soil thermometers can be used to show the effects of mulching and irrigation, or to see when the compost pile needs turning.

Give Seeds the Hot Seat

Q. Is bottom heat necessary for starting vegetable seeds?

A. It's not essential, but bottom heat is a sure way to keep the soil temperature at a steady 70° to 75°F—the best temperature for germination of most vegetable seeds. Tomato, melon, eggplant, celery, and brassica seeds do best at 70° to 75°F, while lettuce has a range from 65° to 70°F. Soil-heating cables can be used in flats indoors, in greenhouse beds, or outdoors in insulated coldframes. Although these cables maintain ideal temperatures for only pennies a day, you can also use the free heat available on top of your water heater or console television or near a radiator or woodstove. Check the soil temperature in the flat periodically with a soil thermometer. Once the seedlings are established, remove them from the heat.

Scheduling Ins and Outs

Q. What is the most desirable schedule for sowing my seeds indoors and transplanting my seedlings into the garden?

A. There is no set time for sowing and transplanting, since so much depends on climate, soil temperature, and seed varieties. You should allow six to eight weeks for germination and seedling growth indoors, so count back that much before the date you'll plant the seedlings outside. For example, cold-sensitive seedlings like tomatoes should be ready for transplanting about one week after the last spring frost date.

Most seeds germinate well at soil temperatures between 70° and 80°F, and most seedlings do best between 60° and 75°F. The temperature of your room affects seedling growth, too. If it is cold, you can expect the plants to take the full eight weeks, and then some, to reach transplanting size. If it's warm, then you can figure on less growing time.

Let There Be Light

Q. How much light do my vegetable seedlings need for a good start indoors?

A. That all depends on whether you grow them by a window, grow them exclusively under fluorescent lights, or use both. In January or February, even a south window may not offer seedlings the full 18 hours of light they require for optimum growth. A rule of thumb is to augment 6 to 8 hours of natural light with 10 to 12 hours under fluorescent tubes. If plants get no outside light, keep them under the fluorescents for the full 18 hours.

You don't need special plant-growth lights, which are designed mainly for year-round indoor houseplants. Standard fluorescent tubes designed for room lighting will produce stocky, thick-stemmed seedlings and cost only pennies a day to run. Never use common incandescent light bulbs, because they produce light chiefly in the red end of the spectrum. Such light makes plants tall and spindly, with pale, thin leaves. Incandescents also give off heat, which dries out the soil surface and the fragile plants growing under them.

A double row of fluorescent tubes provides sufficient light to grow a 16-inch-wide array of plants. One tube will illuminate a 6-inch-wide band. Because seedlings need more intense light than mature plants, keep the light tubes as close as possible to the leaves, short of touching them. Be sure to turn the flats every day to prevent seedlings at the ends of the rows from getting leggy as they stretch for more light. To make sure that seedlings get all the light they need, replace fluorescents when they reach 70 percent of their stated service life. By that time, they'll be delivering about 15 percent less light than when new.

Let It Be Close

Q. How far above my seed flats should I hang fluorescent lights?

A. Lights should be no more than 3 or 4 inches above seedlings for the first three to four weeks after germination, or they'll get leggy. In fact, veteran gardener Nancy Bubel recommends keeping seedlings as close as possible to the fluorescent tubes without letting the foliage touch the glass. As the young plants grow, raise the lights slightly (or lower the flats). For the most even growth, shift the positions of the flats every week or so, since light at the ends of the tubes tends to be somewhat weaker.

No Fungus among Us

Q. I've had trouble with damping-off disease for several seasons now. Is there any way to prevent this organically? I'd prefer not to bake my potting soil in the oven to sterilize it.

A. Damping-off is a fungal disease that causes wilting and early death of seedlings. The fungus parasites usually grow near the soil surface and enter the tiny plants at the point where they emerge from the ground.

Crowding of seedlings, high humidity, and lack of sufficient aeration all favor damping-off. If you're sowing seeds outdoors, remedial measures include thinning the seedlings, ensuring proper ventilation, drying the soil in which the seedlings are growing, and sprinkling powdered charcoal or finely pulverized clay on the ground.

To keep damping-off from gaining a foothold indoors, start with a good potting soil. Make fast compost, which heats up to 150°F or more—pasteurizing temperature. When the temperature drops to 110°F, sift the compost and store it in a tightly closed plastic bag until the time comes to mix the potting soil. Blend this compost 50–50 with vermiculite or perlite. These are both created by a high-heat process and are usually sterile. Add a little steamed bonemeal. This potting mix will be free of disease organisms.

When you plant the seeds, you can cover them with "play sand" which has already been sterilized. It is available at most lumberyards. The sand ensures that the neck of the seedling—where damping-off attacks—will be surrounded with a sterile medium that contains no nutrients to support reinfection by disease organisms via the air. Keep the area around the seedlings cool, well lit, and well ventilated. Don't plant them so thickly that they are overcrowded, and don't overwater.

One type of damping-off attacks seedlings before they break through the ground. If there are many blank spaces in your seed-starting flats, this may be your problem. The disease attacks seeds in cold, wet soils. Use bottom heat to get the seedlings up and out of the earth fast.

Hints for Hardening-Off

Q. What's the safest way to harden-off seedlings?

A. Start by giving seedlings a cool, dry week without fertilizer. The temperature should be several degrees lower than that at which the seedlings were raised. The result will be a shorter, more fibrous plant that suffers less from the transition to the outdoors.

If the seedlings have been indoors and have never had full sun, expose them to a few hours of *filtered* sun each day—in the shade of a bush, porch railing, lath house, or any improvised shelter. Daytime temperatures should range from 60° to 70°F. Gradually increase the amount of sun the plant receives until, at the end of a week or ten days, the seedling is accustomed to a full day in the sun. To protect the plants from strong and gusty winds, choose a sheltered corner for the plant's first week outdoors. Make sure to keep the soil moist enough to prevent wilting.

Although some gardeners like to soak the planting flat with a liquid fertilizer just before setting the plants in the garden, try leaving them a little on the hungry side. The roots will then put out extensive new growth in search of food when the plant is placed in its permanent home.

Working the Soil

Plowing Preference

Q. **Perhaps you can settle an argument I'm having with my neighbor. I say it's best to plow in the spring. He says it's best to plow in the fall. What do you say?**

A. Spring tilling is best. Some people plow in the fall to "roughen up" their soil to help it hold water and stem erosion, but a thickly sown cover crop of rye is far superior. Laying the soil bare to the elements over winter kills off many beneficial soil organisms in the layer that alternately freezes and thaws. The soil could be recolonized by disease organisms instead of friends. A cover crop with roots that hold the soil together, covered with mulch during the frozen months, is the best way to take the garden through the winter. The mulch and cover crop can be tilled in during the spring, adding lots of decaying organic matter to the soil.

Hop Off Those Clods

Q. **Please clarify the following statement: "Do not work soils when they are wet, especially those with considerable clay. This causes damage to the tilth, or physical structure, of the soil, which may last for a long time."**

A. The structure of topsoil is very easily destroyed, particularly when clayey soils are plowed when too wet or too dry. Wet clay soil becomes sticky and easily molded into various forms under pressure—by tiller or otherwise. The end result is that the turned earth forms hard clods when the soil is allowed to dry.

In clay soils, work around the problem by keeping cultivation to a minimum, especially in wet areas. Sand added to such soils helps. You want the soil to be left with a granular structure that is suitable for seeding yet coarse enough at the surface to resist erosion and the puddling that results from heavy rains.

Ground Work

Q. **Would you elaborate on the expression "as soon as the ground can be worked"? It appears regularly in planting instructions, but no one I've asked has a good explanation of its meaning.**

A. The soil can be "worked" when it thaws and dries enough to be plowed, tilled, or dug without causing serious compaction. In many areas of the country, the ground is saturated with water in the early spring. If turned over before it is sufficiently dry, compaction and loss of soil structure will result. The surface can turn into hard dry lumps, making it difficult for seedlings to emerge. Generally, the higher the clay content of the soil, the longer you have to wait to begin digging. A high amount of organic matter will offset this by improving drainage and aeration. On the other hand, sandy loam soils may never have a problem with excess moisture and can be worked as soon as the weather warms enough.

To see if your soil is ready, place a shovelful in a pot with drainage holes. If water seeps out the bottom, your garden is still too wet and shouldn't be worked. Another rule of thumb is to take a handful of soil and squeeze it. If it forms a ball, there's too much moisture in it. If it crumbles, however, you can get to work.

The Long and Short of It

Q. **Do fast-maturing vegetables use fewer nutrients than longer-season varieties?**

A. Generally, the total plant weight is the primary factor in determining the amount of nutrients removed from the soil. But there's no simple answer. A few varieties of short-season crops may require less fertilizer. If you grow a compact tomato that starts producing early, it may require fewer nutrients than a heavy-yielding, late-maturing variety that produces large vines.

In many cases, you will need to fertilize fast-maturing vegetables more heavily at planting time because they take up minerals at a faster rate than their later-maturing counterparts. Vegetables that begin bearing early in the season and outproduce later varieties definitely need more nutrients than ones that are slower to mature.

Mulch-Gardening

Q. Would you please explain how vegetables grown from seed sprinkled on top of the soil and covered with mulch can obtain sufficient nutrients?

A. This method of gardening is most often used for growing potatoes, as the tubers prefer a moist, cool soil and the mulch provides just that. While the plant's roots grow down into the soil, the tubers are formed in the mulch, not underground, making harvesting easier. In tests at the Rodale Research Center, researchers found that you can expect an increase of 40 percent or more in potato yield by planting in a mulch. The method they used called for tilling the plot and planting the seed potatoes in a small furrow so the eyes were just covered. Then a 6-inch layer of mulch was put on top. No weeding was needed during the growing season, thanks to the mulch.

The traditional method of mulch-planting calls for laying the seed potatoes directly on top of the soil and covering with mulch. In the Rodale test, this was not done because of the possibilities of mice eating the potatoes and of the tubers drying out before they sprouted. In other cases of mulch-gardening, the mulch is scraped away from the soil, the seeds are planted in the soil, and when small seedlings are established, the mulch is pulled up to the seedlings for the remainder of the growing season.

The Safety Factor

Pollution Solution

Q. My garden is near a road. Can auto emissions be washed off my vegetables?

A. Yes, if you use a little vinegar or dishwashing liquid in the wash water. Washing lettuce and other crops with water alone removes only a small amount of lead, the most serious hazard from auto emissions. But washing the vegetables in a dilute vinegar or soap solution removes most of the lead, according to research by plant physiologist Nina Bassuk at Cornell University in New York State. Use a 1 percent solution of vinegar (about 2½ tablespoons to a gallon of water) or half that amount of dishwashing liquid. Vegetables can also absorb heavy metals like lead and cadmium that get into the soil from auto exhaust. You can't wash them away, but a pH above 6.5 will prevent uptake of lead and cadmium. (See pages 26–28 for more information concerning pH.) If you haven't already done so, plant a hedge or erect a solid fence between your garden and the road to help shield the garden from auto emissions.

Skip the Salt

Q. The border of our property gets saturated with road salt every winter. What can we do to correct or prevent this problem for the garden plants, trees, and shrubs already located there?

A. Consider erecting a barrier, possibly of wood, to keep the salt spray from covering your garden or trees. If a barrier is impractical, a heavy mulch, such as leaves that will pack down, will provide more protection to plants than no mulch or even a light mulch. (But don't work the salt-covered leaves into your garden in the spring!) You might also bank your garden beds in the fall with a layer of black plastic mulch, sloped away from the garden but held in place by regular mulching materials.

Recyle
Washing-Machine Water?

Q. I am a gardener in Arizona and wonder about the effects of washing-machine water on the vegetable garden. Does it matter whether I use nonbiodegradable or biodegradable soaps? Water is expensive in this arid climate, and almost daily watering is necessary.

A. The common problem with soaps and detergents is that they both contain sodium, an element that, in excessive amounts, is harmful to soils (it destroys soil aggregation) as well as to plants (it induces tissue burn). The best strategy is to use as little soap as possible and to choose soap flakes or biodegradable soaps rather than detergents.

Avoid softeners that are rich in sodium-based compounds, minimize or eliminate bleach, and absolutely stay away from boron-based (borax) detergents. Low-phosphate detergents are preferable because they generally contain less sodium.

If you want to recycle your washing-machine water, the key is to direct the water onto the soil via a soaker hose or to run the water out the end of the hose to flood the soil. Do not spray recycled water on leaves! At the end of the hose you may want to attach a cloth bag (cotton or canvas) with a hose clamp to intercept particulates and soap residues.

If at all possible, collect the water in a 55-gallon drum after it is flushed from the washing machine. Make sure the drum has a valve for water to escape. This method enables the higher concentration of soap in the first washing cycle to become diluted by later rinse cycles.

Septic Tank Garden?

Q. **Would it be advisable to plant a vegetable garden over our septic field?**

A. Because there's a chance of pathogenic organisms in the soil (especially if sewage does find its way to the surface occasionally), it's better to plant food crops in other areas where direct contact with effluent is not possible.

Walnuts at 50 Paces

Q. **Last spring we set out our tomato transplants 30 feet from the base of the black walnut tree in our yard. Still, they all died by mid-July. How far away must tomatoes be planted to escape any of the tree's toxic effects?**

A. Your tomatoes should be safe if planted at a distance equal to 1½ times the height of the tree. Black, Persian, and Japanese walnut roots release a potent toxin called juglone. So do the roots of butternut, a close relative. The allelopathic effect extends through the area occupied by the tree roots. Peppers, alfalfa, apple trees, peonies, blackberries, mountain laurels, and red pines are all hurt by the toxin. It remains effective for a year after a walnut tree is removed.

Grains and other shallow-rooted plants are not hindered. Kentucky bluegrass and black raspberries actually seem to benefit from being planted near walnuts. As yet, plant pathologists haven't been able to explain why.

On the Lighter Side

Q. **To prevent burglaries, many people around here keep their backyards lighted all night. What effect does the constant light have on garden plants and fruit trees?**

A. Almost none. Most security lights are either high-pressure or low-pressure sodium lamps. The intensity of light they produce is too low to endanger the fruiting or growth of nearby plants. In addition, many common fruits and vegetables are day-neutral—their growth and fruiting are neither harmed nor helped by longer photoperiods.

Gardening with Tires

Q. **Are tires safe to use in the garden? I'd like to use some as coldframes for my melons but am concerned that tires may contain harmful chemicals.**

A. Yes, they're safe. In past years, we've recommended not using tires, but new information shows they will not harm plants. While tires contain some iron and zinc from the manufacturing process, these are actually essential plant nutrients, explains agricultural engineer Dr. A. Higgins of Rutgers University, who has studied the use of shredded tires in sludge composting. The amount of lead from car exhaust that may be on the surface would not be enough to cause concern, according to Higgins and USDA lead specialist Dr. Rufus Chaney.

Asbestos Woes

Q. **I have a vegetable garden next to an old barn with an asbestos-shingle roof. Could the rainwater running off the roof onto my vegetables cause a health hazard?**

A. As long as the shingles are in good condition, the asbestos fibers will remain tightly bonded and the chance of any getting on your vegetables is slight, says Stephen Schanamann, environmental protection specialist with the Environmental Protection Agency's Asbestos Action Program.

If the shingles are showing signs of wear, like breakage, cracking, or cupping, the risk of exposure to fibers is greater. Consider replacing the roof or channeling the runoff to deep drains.

Rubbish to Radishes

Q. If I incorporate kitchen scraps into an area of my garden, how long should I wait before planting vegetables there? Will the scraps attract animals?

A. The best way to compost directly in your garden is to dig a 1-foot-deep trench down the center of a bed or in between two rows. Each time you put kitchen scraps into the trench, cover them with 2 to 4 inches of soil. Vegetables can be planted over the filled-in trench at any time. Animals generally won't bother compost that is covered with soil, but if they do, try burying it a little deeper or cover the spot with several inches of mulch.

The Right Vermiculite

Q. Is it safe to substitute insulation-grade vermiculite for horticultural vermiculite in potting soil?

A. No. Insulation-grade vermiculite contains high amounts of magnesium limestone and can have a pH as high as 9.8. It makes potting soil too alkaline, leading to micronutrient deficiencies. Horticultural vermiculite is mined in Georgia, has a nearly neutral pH (7.0 to 7.5), and doesn't tie up micronutrients.

Plastic Potting Soil

Q. Can polystyrene packing materials be shredded and safely added to potting soil in place of vermiculite?

A. Polystyrene is safe to add—it doesn't biodegrade or release toxic substances into the soil—but it replaces perlite, not vermiculite. Unlike vermiculite, which absorbs large amounts of water, perlite and polystyrene hold water only on their surfaces, promoting fast soil drainage.

Polystyrene beads or flakes are harder to wet and hold less water than perlite, causing the soil to dry faster, according to researchers and commercial growers who have compared the two materials. Polystyrene is also lighter than perlite, making it more difficult to mix with soil and more likely to float to the top with heavy watering.

To make mixing easier, moisten the soil before adding polystyrene, then water from the bottom or gently from the top until plants are established. Because polystyrene melts at high temperatures, it must be added after the soil has been sterilized.

Projects

Barn Cloche

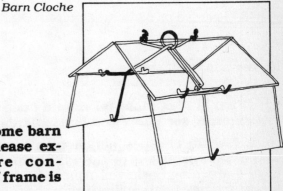

Barn Cloches

Q. I'd like to make some barn cloches. Could you please explain how they are constructed? What kind of frame is required?

A. Four pieces of 12-by-24-inch glass are held together by a set of bent heavy-gauge wire. Although single-strength window glass will work, it is better to use thicker glass (at least ⅛ inch) double strength.

Good to the Last Drip

Q. My husband and I are interested in installing a watering system for a vegetable garden and 40 fruit trees. What type do you recommend?

A. A drip-irrigation system has several advantages over sprinkler irrigation and may suit your needs. It uses one-third to one-half less water, reduces weed growth, and eliminates moisture stress.

These systems come as kits with five parts: head, filter, header, laterals, and emitters. The head, with a filter to prevent clogging, is attached to the water source. Then the header, a hose that carries water to the garden, is attached with laterals connected to it that run along beds or rows. The emitters, flexible tubes with a tiny hole in the end of each tube for water to drip out slowly (1 to 4 gallons per hour), extend from the laterals to the base of each plant. (For very closely spaced plants, substitute a drip tube for the emitters. It allows water to seep out along its length.)

To decide how many feet of each part you need, plot your garden's and orchard's dimensions on graph paper and plan the irrigation layout. Since the lines, made from polyethylene or PVC, will degrade in sunlight, they should be covered. The orchard section can be buried, allowing enough slope to drain the water if you live in an area with hard winter freezes. In the garden, cover the hoses with mulch and for longest life, store in a protected place over the winter.

Homemade Capillary Mat

Q. **What kind of material should I use to make a capillary mat for watering seed flats and houseplants from below?**

A. Use the cheapest acrylic blanket you can buy, advises Tom Seiler, past president of the Philadelphia chapter of the Indoor Light Gardening Society of America. Many light gardeners prefer them to commercial capillary mats, he says. Capillary watering will work only if there is direct contact between the mat and the potting soil, so don't cover drainage holes with crockery. When you place a container on the mat, water it from above the first time to start capillary flow. Thereafter, keep the mat moist.

Compost-Heated Hotbed

Q. **How do I build and use a hotbed?**

A. First, dig a pit to accommodate 2 feet of compost. Then fill the pit with composting materials and let it sit about a week or until it starts to heat up. Cover the compost with a foot of rich soil and plant your crops in it. In a week to ten days, the soil should be well warmed.

Hot compost below a coldframe can raise soil temperatures ten degrees higher than normal, but after about seven weeks, the hotbeds cool off to soil temperature. Thus, hotbeds are more practical in the spring, providing moderate, steady heat early in the season, while it's coldest outside. (In fall, you can always force the cold-hardy, leafy-green vegetables to mature earlier. Hotbeds are less useful in fall because the compost is working while the weather is warmest. Before the vegetables can mature, the compost will have stopped heating and the weather will have turned cold.)

Chapter 2

Soil and Soil-Building Basics

Secrets of the Soil

Keys to Soil Colors

Q. Could you give me a basic explanation of soil color? I've always been curious about the different colors of the soil and wondered how to interpret them.

A. The changes in soil color that you see from one area to the next usually mean that there was a difference in mineral development sometime along the way. Mineral deposits create characteristic colors and consistencies. Here are a few of the signals:

• Whitish colors usually indicate that a heavier concentration of salts and lime deposits are present in the soil.

• A dark color indicates a high level of organic matter. Black soil can mean good humus content, but it may mean nothing more than manganese-bearing rock particles.

• Reddish soils usually have a high iron content.

• "Spotty" soil that shows different colors, particularly shades of rust, reveals a problem with insufficient aeration. This type of soil goes through periods during the year when it cannot get enough oxygen.

• Blue, gray, or greenish subsoil suffers from periodic waterlogging.

• Tan, light gray, or light bluish-gray usually indicates poor soil, but subsoils of these colors often contain good supplies of minerals.

Indicator Plants

Q. I'm thinking of buying some property. What can I tell about the soil from the plants that grow there?

A. Plants can tell you a lot about the soil they grow in. An obvious example is the cattail. Cattails thrive in wet, marshy soil—which is far from ideal for a garden. Other plants that like wet soil include marsh marigold, nutsedge, porcelain vine, skunk cabbage, pin oak, red maple, swamp white oak, sour gum, weeping willow, honeyset, starwort, winterberry, and buttonbush. If you see tiny mosses that give the soil surface a greenish tinge that persists into the summer, this area is also too wet for gardening. But it can be reclaimed for gardening if it is tile-drained.

If you are looking for an ideal spot for your garden, look for burdock, pigweed, lamb's-quarters, and purslane. They flourish in well-drained, fertile soil with lots of organic matter. You'll almost always find good-sized walnut trees on rich ground—often in well-drained river or creek bottom soil. Stay away from areas with sorrel, mayweed, broomsedge, and chamomile, unless you are willing to work to develop the soil. These plants are usually a sign of soil that's lacking in humus and fertility.

Bluegrass and alfalfa thrive on land that is not too acid. Scrub oak, white cedar, huckleberry, hemlock, fir, azalea, blueberry, pine, mountain laurel, rhododendron, white birch, and red cedar are often signs of acid soil. If you find many of these plants on the property you're looking at, it may be more suitable for a woodland garden than a lush lawn.

The Look of Loam

Q. Gardeners frequently use the phrase "good fertile loam." Just exactly what does that mean?

A. Good loam soil has lots of silt in it, as well as enough clay and sand particles to give it good texture and structure. It also has plenty of organic matter. The secretions of earthworms, slugs, and snails, plus decayed vegetation, a host of bacteria, and fungi in the soil, all combine to create loam. You can tell good loam by touch. If the soil feels soft and oily when you rub it between your fingers, it's probably fertile loam. Squeeze fertile loam soil and it will hold together for just a minute in a loose lump; however, it will fall as crumbly bits when you drop it back on the ground.

Taming Tough Clay

Q. **My California soil is gray clay. I sink into it up to my ankles in winter, but in summer it gets so dry it develops wide cracks. I tried gardening in raised beds filled with topsoil, but yields were poor. How can I rebuild this soil?**

A. Stick with raised beds. To improve crop yields, it's more important to add organic matter than topsoil. You will need to add lots of it annually. The best approach is a three-part program: compost, mulch, and cover crops.

One *Organic Gardening* contributor from California, John Meeker, has done wonders with heavy clay. To start, he applied three dump truck loads of compost on 800 feet of raised beds, then tilled it in. Timing is critical, says Meeker, since there is only a brief period between wet and dry when clay soils will crumble easily in your fingers. Meeker used mushroom compost, but he recommends substituting the best locally available materials. For fastest results, the materials should be fully composted.

Always keep the soil covered, either with mulch or with cover crops. The mulch keeps soil and compost moist so the plants can make the most of it. As the mulch rots, it adds more organic matter. Cover crops trap the nutrients you have added, and they add more organic matter. Their roots break up heavy soil. Plant a cover crop as soon as a patch of ground has been harvested for the season, then turn it under one week before planting. Meeker uses buckwheat in warm weather and fava beans interplanted with rye when it's cool.

Adobe Gardening

Q. **We will be moving to the Southwest this year and hope to start a garden. Having lived in a relatively moist climate all our lives, we're not sure how to prepare the soil in that dry area. Can you help?**

A. The adobe soils of the Southwest tend to be heavy clay that is often rich in minerals but almost entirely deficient in humus. Sometimes they are a mixture of clay and silt. Of all soil types, adobe is one that benefits most from organic gardening methods. Since it's heavy, it requires aeration. In its natural state, this soil will contain no earthworms, and it will probably be alkaline. The pH will register at 7.5 or above. Because of this, some essential nutrients, such as phosphorus and iron, will be unavailable to your plants.

You can minimize all of these problems by adding humus. Then the soil will become easier to till and will retain moisture. Add earthworms to the humus and they'll flourish. Since humus is a neutralizer, it will bring the alkalinity down to a suitable level for many garden plants. This will free iron and phosphorus for your vegetables. Supplement these nutrients by using ground phosphate rock and acidic organic materials such as peat moss, sawdust, and oak leaves if your soil is still iron-deficient.

Double-Digging Duty

Q. I have double-dug my garden about 2 feet deep every fall for the past several years. Could I do it every other year without any loss in productivity?

A. Usually yes, but it depends on the amount of rainfall received, the crops grown (shallow- or deep-rooted), and the soil type, according to Stephen Gliessman, director of the Agroecology Program in Santa Cruz, California. If you grow mostly shallow-rooted crops in clay soil in an area with heavy rainfall, the soil will compact faster, and you might need to double-dig every year. The productivity of your crops is the best indicator. If you've seen no increase in growth or yield after several years of double-digging, try skipping a year. You don't need to redig until you observe a check in top and/or bottom root growth.

Footprint Fiasco

Q. How can I keep my soil from compacting? Since my whole family has taken an interest in the garden, I worry that the increased foot traffic will cause problems.

A. The obvious way to prevent soil compaction is by providing paths—either around the beds or between the rows. With growing beds, the number of plants subjected to root zone compaction is greatly reduced, because four or five rows of plants are put into one bed—instead of five rows flanked by six paths. Once you cultivate and mark off the areas you will be growing in, stay off them and limit your movement to established paths.

Salty Soil

Q. Our first year at this house, nothing grew in our garden. A soil test showed toxic levels of salt. We were told the only way to solve the problem was to put down drainage tile and leach out the salt. Can you offer a less expensive solution?

A. Up to 95 percent of the salts in your soil can be leached out with water. Unless the water table under your garden site is very high (less than 4 to 5 feet), drainage tile shouldn't be necessary. If you dig a 5-foot-deep hole and haven't hit water, you're probably OK. To leach your soil, irrigate the garden twice with at least 2 inches of water each time (measure with a rain gauge).

Once the salts (mostly calcium and magnesium) have been washed down below the plants' root zone, it's essential to keep the soil moist. If it dries out, the salts will be carried right back to the surface, and you'll have to start all over again. A thick layer of mulch over the entire garden is important in keeping salinity at bay. Incorporating lots of organic matter will also help your soil stay moist. But if you've got manure, Dr. Jack Goertzen of the U.S. Salinity Laboratory recommends that you compost it first, because it is high in salts. Acidic materials such as pine needles, leaves, and peat moss are preferred because they help to lower the soil's pH, which is often around 8.0 when high salt levels are present. Continue to water the garden during the winter and plant a cover crop like winter rye. As long as you keep a constant vigil on your soil's moisture level, you should be able to garden successfully.

Solarize Your Soil

Q. I've heard I can rid my soil of wilt-causing organisms by heating it. Can I do it right in my garden?

A. Soil solarization kills both fusarium and verticillium wilt-producing fungi, while it greatly reduces nematodes and weeds. During the process, soil is pasteurized by the sun to a depth of 12 to 18 inches. To solarize garden soil, thoroughly soak the plot with water. This soaking increases the soil's ability to conduct heat and is necessary because moist heat kills organisms at lower temperatures than dry heat. Next, cover the plot with clear polyethylene plastic (not black mulching plastic) 1 to 4 mils thick, and bury the edges in a trench dug around the plot. Leave the plastic in place for three to four weeks. Plastic laid during the hot summer months, when the light intensity is greatest, can heat soil to 140°F—high enough to kill pathogens but leave beneficial soil microorganisms unharmed.

Microwaved Soil

Q. Can a microwave oven be used to sterilize potting soil?

A. Yes. Plant pathology researchers at the University of Kentucky use a home microwave oven to sterilize up to 10 pounds of soil at a time. The soil should be moist and crumbly, not squishy— if it's dry enough to work, it's dry enough to microwave, says Dr. R. S. Ferriss, who developed the technique. Place the soil in a plastic bag (polypropylene bags, the kind used for baking, are less likely to break than polyethylene bags) or in a large, loosely covered microwave-safe mixing bowl. Give the top of the bag a twist, but don't seal it or it might explode as steam builds up, cautions Ferriss.

With the oven turned to full power, heating a 2-pound batch of soil for 2½ minutes or a 10-pound batch for 8 minutes will kill most pathogens. If you've had problems with damping-off or other soil-borne diseases in the past, you can extend—even double—the heating time without ill effect, says Ferriss. Doubling the treatment time may be necessary to sterilize compost or leaf mold. The high water content and myriad pore spaces of these organic materials are slow heating. After sterilization, let the soil stand uncovered until cool, then store in sealed containers.

pH Posers

Soil Test
Kit

Problems with pH

Q. Last year, my soil tested acid, so I limed it. Is it necessary to test it again this year?

A. You should test your soil again this spring. In fact, one of the best ways to safeguard your garden's productivity is to test it at least *twice* a year—before planting and in the middle of the season. Your soil's acid-alkaline standing (called pH) can change from one planting to the next—and from one place to another in your garden. If pine needles—which have a very low pH—fall on part of your garden, that section will gradually become more acidic. Certain crops will also affect the acidity or alkalinity of the plot on which they grow. Acid rain, a result of industrial pollution, lowers the pH of soil dramatically.

Soil test kits and test meters offer a fairly precise reckoning of soil pH. Test kits use colored papers or solutions to chart changes in soil pH. Meters are compact and fast-acting. All you do is insert the probe in soft, moist soil, wait a minute or two, and read the needle on the gauge. It gives a direct reading on a numerical scale. (A pH of 7.0 is neutral; lower readings, from 6.0 to 1.0, indicate increasing acidity, while higher readings, from 8.0 to 14.0, indicate increasing alkalinity.) For a small fee, state Agricultural Experiment Stations provide a soil analysis service. Although it is the most complete analysis available to home gardeners, a lab soil test is also the most time-consuming and expensive.

Sweet Water Is OK

Q. The well water at our new home has a high pH—8.0 to 8.5. Will it harm our azaleas or vegetable garden if we water with it?

A. No. Even acid-loving plants such as azaleas won't be affected. Soil has a high "buffering capacity." As soon as the alkaline water soaks into the ground, its pH will become the same as that of the soil. Alkaline water can sometimes be a problem when used to irrigate potted plants over a long period of time. With potted plants, include acid humus, peat moss, and leaf mold in the potting mixture and, if possible, use collected rainwater in place of well water.

Aloha Soil

Q. I garden in Hawaii. What can I add to my soil to make it more acidic? The soil has a pH of 7.0 to 7.5, and I'd like to get it down to 6.5.

A. A pH of 7.0 to 7.5 isn't excessively high for most vegetables. Since rainfall in your area is fairly low, the high soil pH is probably due to accumulated salts. (Beans, carrots, onions, peppers, and lettuce are most vulnerable to salt buildup.) Building up the organic matter in the soil with compost, mulch, or leaf mold will help to buffer the effects of your pH. You can also lower the pH with elemental sulfur. University of Hawaii soils extension agent George

Nakasato recommends applying 2.25 pounds of sulfur per 100 square feet. Check the pH annually and apply sulfur as recommended by the test results or your county agent.

Fertilizers, Soil Builders, and More

Fertilizer Figures

Q. **My county agent recommends a 5:10:10 fertilizer for vegetable gardens. What organic materials can I substitute?**

A. The numbers "5:10:10" mean that the fertilizer contains 5 percent nitrogen (N), 10 percent phosphorus (P), and 10 percent potassium (K). A 100-pound bag would contain 5 pounds of N and 10 each of P and K. The other 75 pounds are mostly fillers. If, for example, you applied 25 pounds of 5:10:10 per 1,000 square feet, you'd actually be applying 1.2 pounds of N, 2.5 pounds of P, and 2.5 pounds of K. With a little figuring, you can substitute almost any organic fertilizer. For instance, suppose chicken manure is the nitrogen source that's easiest for you to get. Although the analysis of chicken manure can vary widely from sample to sample, an NPK rating of 3.63:1.54:2.64 is the amount found in several samples of broiler litter.

How much fertilizer does your 1,000 square feet need to get 1.2 pounds of N? Simply divide 1.2 (the recommended amount) by 3.6 percent or 0.0363 (the percentage in the organic source), which yields 33. So, 33 pounds of chicken manure will do it. Next, figure out how much P and K is in the manure—multiply 33 by the percentage for P and do the same for K. It turns out that 33 pounds of chicken manure provide about 0.5 pound of P and 0.87 pound of K. To get more P and K, look up other organic nutrient sources, like rock phosphate and wood ashes, that are high in P and/or K and very low in N, and repeat the calculations. But don't get swamped with figures. Fertilizer recommendations are guidelines, and with organic materials, if you apply a little more or a little less, you'll still have healthy plants.

The Phosphorus Factor

Q. **How does phosphorus actually function in plants?**

A. Phosphorus plays an important role in photosynthesis—the process by which plants use light energy to synthesize carbohydrates (food) from carbon dioxide and water. This element also produces good flower and fruit growth. Its major influence is in helping plants mature.

Pulling Up Phosphorus Levels

Q. **I recently moved to a new home. Soil tests show that the soil on my proposed garden site is low in phosphorus. What can I fertilize with that will make phosphorus readily available this year?**

A. To ensure an adequate supply of phosphorus for your plants this season, feed them every two weeks with a liquid fertilizer such as fish emulsion or manure tea. Poultry manure is especially high in phosphorus in a form readily taken up by plants. Dried blood is another source of phosphorus that becomes available soon after application. Incorporate rock phosphate into your soil this spring, too, even though your plants won't be able to use much of it this year. By next season, as long as your soil's pH is below 7.0, the rock powder will begin to release a slow, steady supply of phosphorus to your garden. Adding manure or compost to your soil along with the rock phosphate may increase availability of the phosphorus as much as 200 percent. Humic acids in organic matter convert insoluble phosphorus to a form that plants can use. Organic matter also "fixes" other elements, such as calcium and iron, which can tie up phosphorus in the soil.

A Piece of the Rock

Q. **What's the difference between rock phosphate and superphosphate?**

A. Superphosphate, a chemically processed fertilizer, has high levels of immediately available phosphorus and calcium. When the high concentrations of minerals are released into the soil, the pH of the area around the fertilizer is lowered to 1.0 or 2.0. This extremely acidic condition kills any microbes in the area and can also harm insects and earthworms. The high acidity also releases soil manganese and aluminum at levels that can burn root tips. Naturally occurring rock phosphate is a good source of phosphorus for your garden. The phosphorus is released slowly, and it doesn't have a drastic effect on pH. Follow the application rates recommended by your soil test.

Great Greensand

Q. People tell me that greensand is a good fertilizer and will improve my sandy soil. What can you tell me about it?

A. Greensand is excellent for building and conditioning both hard and sandy soils. This undersea deposit, also called glauconite, contains most of the elements found in the ocean. It has been used successfully for soil-building for more than 100 years and is a fine source of potash. The best greensand deposits contain as much as 6 to 7 percent potash, 50 percent silica, 18 to 23 percent iron oxide, 3 to 7½ percent magnesium, small amounts of lime and phosphoric acid, and traces of 30 or more other elements—most of which are important for plant nutrition. Part of greensand's benefit is its ability to absorb and hold large amounts of water in the surface layer of the soil where plant roots feed. It slowly releases the potassium necessary to stimulate photosynthesis, and it stirs up helpful soil organisms.

Greensand is so fine that it may be used in its natural form with no processing. However, it should be dried if the material is to pass through a fertilizer drill. Because it is versatile, greensand may be applied directly to plant roots (it never burns) or left on the surface as a combined mulch and compost. Combining it with a manure-phosphate rock mixture is often recommended. Apply no more than ¼ pound of greensand per square foot of soil at any time of year. Rodale Research Center gardeners have also used it to give special soil conditioning treatments to grapevines, fruit trees, and filbert bushes.

Gradual Granite Dust

Q. Is granite dust a good source of potash?

A. No. Granite dust, a by-product of the tombstone industry, contains about 5 percent potassium (potash) and smaller amounts of most micronutrients needed by plants. Since it is a rock product, its nutrients are locked up in complex minerals like feldspars and silicates and aren't readily available. Win Way, soils professor at the University of Vermont, points out that granite's resistance to breakdown by natural forces is the reason it's such a popular material for gravestones. To supply your plants with a reliable source of potassium, use manure, compost, and, for a quick fix, wood ashes.

Two Limestones

Q. **What is the difference between dolomitic and regular limestone?**

A. Regular (calcic) limestone contains calcium. Dolomitic limestone contains a rich supply of magnesium as well as calcium. They are equally effective in raising the soil pH. All plants need calcium and magnesium to perform vital functions, and dolomitic limestone could be used to provide the extra magnesium. Not all soils are deficient in magnesium, however, so a good soil test should be your guide when determining which limestone to apply. Hydrated lime and quicklime are also sold, but these forms of lime have undergone chemical processes that tend to adversely affect soil microorganisms instead of providing the favorable conditions ground limestone does.

Something Fishy

Q. **I have access to a huge amount of fish tailings from a local hatchery. Would adding these tailings, mixed with sawdust, give fruit a fishy taste? What about vegetables?**

A. The fish could provide many of the nutrients needed for the growth of your fruits and vegetables, agrees Dr. Homer Buck of the Illinois Natural History Survey. To get the best results, compost the fish with sawdust, leaves, or other organic debris. Under proper conditions, the fish will be quickly reduced to usable form. Fruit wouldn't have a fishy taste, since it doesn't touch the ground; only the mineral and organic content would be absorbed.

The Seaweed Bonus

Q. **Since I live along the coast, seaweed is always easy to come by. What should I know about putting seaweed into my garden?**

A. Seaweed is an asset to the compost heap, since it decomposes quickly and helps the pile heat up. As for its fertilizing value, fresh seaweed is nutritionally similar to barnyard manure, but it contains twice as much potassium. Because it is high in iron, zinc, and potassium and contains some iodine, seaweed is an excellent food for citrus fruits and roses. If you're using large amounts of seaweed, don't let it heap up while you wait for it to decay. Nutrients leach out easily during the decaying process, so dig the seaweed into the soil quickly. Many gardeners wonder if it's necessary to wash the salt off seaweed before using it in the garden. It really isn't necessary, since the amount of salt that might cling to the plants is minimal.

Dracula's Delight

Q. How is dried blood beneficial in the garden? What does it contain?

A. Bloodmeal and dried blood contain 15 and 12 percent nitrogen and 1.3 and 3 percent phosphorus, respectively. Bloodmeal also has 0.7 percent potash. These materials may be used directly in the garden, or they may be added to the compost pile. They should be used sparingly because of their high nitrogen content—a sprinkling is enough. Both are excellent in the compost pile, since the nitrogen in them stimulates bacterial action on woody, fibrous materials.

What a Grind

Q. How do I make my own bonemeal?

A. To grind your own bonemeal, you need a very heavy-duty grinder (a hammer mill or gristmill), butcher bones, and time. A new mill powerful enough to grind bones will probably be quite expensive. Regular grain and cornmeal grinders are not durable enough to break down bones. A shredder's blades are not strong enough either. Start by boiling bones to extract the fat that surrounds the marrow. Then dry the bones thoroughly in the oven at low heat. Finally, pulverize them in the grinder. There's a better way to use bones in the garden without making bonemeal, however. Burn them in a woodstove or hearth and add the ashes to your compost pile. Your garden needs only 2 pounds per 100 square feet each year.

Compost Is Best

Q. What is the best substance for maintaining the organic content of the soil?

A. Compost is the best all-around substance, but animal manure is the most popular. Compost is high in organic matter, and its organic matter is fairly stable. But compost must be made, which takes time and effort. Manure, on the other hand, is usually available in large quantities at minimal cost, and it contains more soluble nitrogen and potash than compost. So many gardeners apply manure for basic soil maintenance and use their precious compost where it's most needed. Green manure crops, especially legumes, are also very effective, but to grow them, you'll need space for two gardens—one plot in vegetables and the other in green manure for rotation every second year.

Peat Particulars

Q. I notice that there are different kinds of peat. How do the differences affect my gardening?

A. There are usually two types of peat for sale, peat moss (or sphagnum peat) and sedge peat (aquatic grasses). Peat moss is partially decomposed sphagnum or other mosses, which decay more slowly than aquatic grasses. Peat moss is usually coarser, lighter-colored (brown to reddish), and much more water-retentive than sedge peat. For potting mixes, milled sphagnum (finely ground) is best. Cold water will run off milled sphagnum, but hot water soaks right in. For tilling into the garden or mulching, use the cheaper, coarser stuff that comes in bales. A 6-cubic-foot bale will cover about 300 square feet 1 inch deep. Sedge peat, made up of decomposed aquatic grasses like reeds and sedges, is usually dark and thoroughly decayed. It looks like very fine, black soil and is a good ingredient in potting mixes. Sedge peat is often sold slightly moist in plastic bags under the names humus peat and Michigan peat.

Both of these peats are good soil conditioners. They lighten and aerate clay soils and help sandy soils hold water longer. Sphagnum peat is more absorbent and breaks down more slowly than sedge peat. Peat is quite acidic. That's good for plants like blueberries and azaleas. If you don't have compost for potting soil, use peat. In potting mixes, peat is best used with pasteurized topsoil and a little bonemeal, both of which help raise the pH.

The Trouble with Wood Chips

Q. Last fall, I tilled in 3½ inches of wood chips and manure (bedding material from a barn) throughout my garden. I have been told that wood chips will use up the nitrogen in my soil. Do I need to add anything else to the soil before I plant this spring?

A. Although you supplied some nitrogen when you added manure along with the wood chips, it won't be enough. You will have to add more nitrogen this spring, and probably for several years, until the wood chips have broken down. (They've broken down when they can be easily crumbled when rubbed between the palms of your hands.) If you don't add nitrogen, it will be taken from the soil and used to break down the wood rather than feeding your plants. Sources of nitrogen include bloodmeal, cottonseed meal, grass clippings, and manure. Watch your plants for leaf yellowing or stunted growth—indications of nitrogen deficiency. If you recognize these signs, side-dress your plants with compost or manure tea or with a weak bloodmeal solution.

Azobacter Blues

Q. **I recently saw an inoculant called azobacter in one of my garden catalogs. What is it, and does it have beneficial effects in the garden?**

A. Azobacter are soil-dwelling bacteria that fix nitrogen and produce growth-stimulating, hormonelike substances. Because of these two activities, they are helpful to plants. They are usually present in healthy soils that contain some organic matter. But buying these beneficial bacteria would be a waste of money. Soil microorganisms are highly competitive and will generally attack any intruders into their environment. Research studies have shown that when cultures of azobacter are added to the soil, their numbers decline rapidly. Where some azobacter existed before, the population usually drops to the original level. Soils that don't contain azobacter obviously don't have the right conditions to support them, and if added to such a soil, the bacteria will die. The best way to encourage azobacter and other beneficial soil organisms in your soil is to provide them with a steady diet of organic matter.

The Safety Factor

Aluminum Soil

Q. **I've been using greensand as a source of potash for my garden. I understand now that greensand contains aluminum. Is there any danger of adding too much aluminum to my garden soil?**

A. No. Although greensand does contain measurable amounts of aluminum—a mineral that can be toxic to plants—it is bound up in a form unavailable to plants. Greensand contains less aluminum than most garden soils, anyway.

No Joy in Gypsum

Q. Local nurseries advise me to use gypsum to break up clay soil. Can you advise me about gypsum from the organic standpoint? What are alternatives?

A. Gypsum, a hydrated calcium sulfate, does improve aeration and drainage, but at the price of putting extra sulfur in the soil. Gypsum causes an imbalance in most soils, which already contain sufficient sulfur. If your soil is heavy, use organic matter—peat moss, leaves, hay, straw, wood chips, chopped stalks, compost, or wood ashes—to break up the clay while improving soil structure. Earthworms, lured by the incorporation of organic materials, also help. Turning your clay soil into a friable planting soil will take work in both fall and spring, and it usually is a three-year process. If this is the first time you've worked with clay soil, consider adding the organic matter in selected places, such as planting holes or trenches. A good cultivation after wet spring weather, during that brief period when the soil is drying and crumbles easily, helps, too.

Chlorinated Soil

Q. Is it safe to use chlorinated water to irrigate my garden?

A. Yes. Dr. William Cooper of Florida International University, a specialist on the complex chemistry of chlorination, says there is minimal risk involved. Here's what happens: When you water your garden, some of the chlorine compounds escape as gases. Those that remain are washed into the soil, but according to Cooper, it is unlikely that they would be taken up by plants. Chlorine compounds break down when exposed to light, so the chlorine in water droplets on plants or near the soil surface degrades quickly on a sunny day. The soil can destroy chlorine that percolates through it much as an activated carbon filter does, preventing it from forming compounds with soil minerals.

Cadmium Concerns

Q. What's the story on cadmium these days? "Organic" sludge is available in my city, but I'm concerned about the effects it may have on the cadmium level of my soil.

A. Cadmium can be toxic to plants and animals, although it is innocuous at the very low levels normally present in the soil. High cadmium test levels usually come from the addition of cadmium-contaminated wastes, so the sludge should be tested for zinc and cadmium by the municipality. If the city is giving out untested sludge, don't take it! The safety factor is the ratio of zinc to cadmium. As long as the sludge contains at least 100 times more zinc than cadmium, the zinc content will be high enough to kill vegetable plants before cadmium becomes a danger to human health.

Bones Aren't *That* Heavy

Q. I have heard that bonemeal contains lead. Does this mean it's unsafe to use in my garden?

A. Lead in bonemeal is a problem only as a food supplement. Bonemeal is perfectly safe to use as a garden fertilizer. Rural soils naturally contain an average of 12 parts per million (ppm) of lead, while suburban soils may contain 50 ppm, according to Dr. Rufus Chaney, U.S. Department of Agriculture heavy metals specialist. Lead in gardens doesn't become dangerous until it reaches 500 ppm, when the blood lead levels could be increased in children who might get contaminated soil on their hands and transmit it to their mouths.

Arsenic and Old Cottonseed Meal

Q. Our county agent told us that cotton is defoliated with arsenic, so cottonseed meal may contain up to 220 ppm of the poison. Must we stop using this organic fertilizer?

A. Cottonseed meal is safe to use in your garden. In fact, it's a great source of nitrogen. It's especially beneficial for citrus and azaleas because it has a slight acidifying effect on soils. In very nitrogen-poor soils, apply up to 10 pounds of cottonseed meal to every 100 square feet the first year. Arsenic is used as a defoliant on cotton crops in California, Texas, and Oklahoma. But the poison doesn't get into the seeds. The seeds that are ground into meal contain levels of arsenic only in the 0.05-ppm range. Normal arsenic levels in soil are higher—in the range of 5 ppm. The high levels of arsenic that your county agent probably is referring to are those found in cotton "trash," the leaf and stem by-products of the ginning process, which uses arsenic as a drying agent. Cottonseed meal is produced in a completely different way, using no arsenic.

Softened Water
Hard on Plants

Q. Will watering my flowers and vegetables with softened water containing high concentrations of salt harm my garden?

A. Yes. It will put salt in your soil, and the salt can accumulate to levels that are toxic to your plants. Water softeners also remove calcium and magnesium from water, both of which are essential to plant health. If the minerals in your water are a severe problem, rather than softening your entire water supply, hook up a water softener to your hot water only. Your laundry and baths will benefit, but your plants won't suffer.

Coal's Not Cool

Q. I burn coal in my furnace. Is it OK to use the ashes in my garden?

A. No. Coal ash contains a number of toxic trace elements. Although the amounts vary widely, depending on the source of coal, heavy metals including lead, arsenic, mercury, and cadmium may be present. Coal ash also contains boron and alkaline salts, which are detrimental to plant growth. In addition, some samples of coal ash were recently found to contain small amounts of dioxin, a powerful carcinogen.

Barbecued Soil

Q. Are the ashes from the charcoal I use in my barbecue safe to add to my garden?

A. No. Briquets are composed mostly of wood but also contain coal with corn or wheat starch as a binder. The problem is in the coal. Some coals have toxic levels of sulfur and/or heavy metals which are taken up by plants (see "Coal's Not Cool," above). Sulfur combines with water to produce sulfuric acid, which lowers soil pH.

Danger in Plywood Dust

Q. Can the sawdust from plywood and particleboard be used in the garden?

A. No. It's best to avoid both kinds. The glues used in plywood and particleboard are formaldehyde-based. Softwood plywood contains a phenol-formaldehyde resin, hardwood plywood has a urea-formaldehyde resin, and particleboard a mixture, depending on the wood scraps used. Although the amount of glue is small (6 percent in particleboard and less in the plywoods), the formaldehyde-based resin is cause for concern. Phenol-formaldehyde takes many years to break down. The compounds will bind with organic matter and eventually be taken up by plants. The long-term effects of consuming these compounds are unknown. Urea-formaldehyde, on the other hand, breaks down quickly, releasing synthesized urea (a source of nitrogen) and formaldehyde gas. In an enclosed area, the gas is toxic to plants.

Herbicide-Dressed Garden

Q. **I would like to expand the area of my garden into a section of the lawn that has been sprayed several times with weedkiller. The last application was 12 months ago. What can I do to this contaminated area so that it can be used for growing food?**

A. Chances are, since there has been a 12-month lapse since the weedkiller was applied, that the chemical residue is no longer harmful. But just to be safe, you can start to improve the soil condition by rounding up organic fertilizer materials, which help detoxify soil. Some, such as commercial compost mixtures and dried manures, can be worked directly into your soil to increase its humus content. Others, such as hay, sawdust, and cocoa hulls, should be set aside for later use as mulches. Plan to start your own composting immediately. (To learn how, see "Composting 101" on page 39.) In less than a month's time, you can have a high-grade organic compost that will create a better-quality soil in your new garden area.

Chapter 3

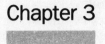

Your Customized Compost Pile

Composting Quandaries

Compost 101

Cross Section of a Compost Pile

Q. Last summer I made my first compost pile. I used a starter and put all of my garbage, shredded papers, cardboard boxes, and everything else available into the pile. Nothing happened. How about some entry-level composting information?

A. Sure. Behind composting, as we know it today, lies the original Indore method, developed by the father of organic gardening, Sir Albert Howard. The Indore method is still the most widely used, and it is still practical and productive.

Howard found that by layering different organic materials, their decomposition took place more quickly and more completely. He first placed a 5- or 6-inch layer of green matter (such as grass clippings), then a 2-inch layer of manure (bloodmeal, bonemeal, sewage sludge, or other high-protein material may be substituted), and a layer of rich earth, ground limestone and phosphate rock, then repeated this layering process.

What you want to do is mirror Sir Albert's method in your backyard. There are many variables in compost-making, so let's go through them, and you should be able to see where you made mistakes.

- Timing: Compost is best started in fall, when ample plant material is available. In the summer, piles may dry out, while in the winter, extremely cold temperatures will slow down the composting process. During the winter, add extra manure to the heap to keep the temperatures high, and insulate it with a layer of plant material (such as straw).

- Ventilation: Ventilation is crucial to a good compost pile. The soil organisms that break down the plant and animal residues and convert them into compost must have oxygen to carry on their activities. If your pile does not allow oxygen to reach the inside, the process will not work. In fact, unpleasant odors may develop. One way to get oxygen into your pile is to prop wooden sticks or posts vertically like a teepee in a tall pile and build your compost heap around them; later you can remove the sticks, leaving air passages in the pile.

- Turning: If you turn your pile regularly, you'll be sure to have plenty of air in it for ventilation. Turning also mixes the ingredients to make sure all items are exposed to the highest heat in the center of the pile, so they compost faster.

- Watering: Your pile should be quite moist during the initial stages of composting. Later in the process, the pile may be somewhat drier but should never dry out. If you're not sure how much water to use, check to see that the inside of the pile doesn't get dry and powdery or become so wet that it mats together.

- Carbon:nitrogen ratio: Most plant matter contains high amounts of carbon. Soft green plant material, such as grass clippings and kitchen scraps, and animal matter, such as manure and bloodmeal, contain nitrogen. You need the right mix of carbon and nitrogen to get your pile to heat up. For a good working pile, you should have 20 to 25 parts of carbon (in the form of dried leaves, newspapers, straw, and so forth) for every 1 part of nitrogen (in the form of manure, bloodmeal, and so forth). The more you stray from this ratio, the more problems you are likely to have. Apparently your pile, with its shredded papers and cardboard boxes, was much higher than 25 parts carbon, and the pile never really started composting. If circumstances dictate that your carbon:nitrogen ratio must be off, make sure you have more nitrogen than needed, never less.

- Avoid meat: To keep rodents, cats, and dogs from wreaking havoc with your pile, don't include meat, bones, or fat. As an added precaution, cover the top layer of garbage with soil every day.

Cool Compost

Q. **My compost pile doesn't heat up. I've been using aged wood chips, horse manure, and cottonwood leaves. All of the materials are dry. Is it possible that there is not enough moisture? What do you recommend?**

A. If you have not added water to your compost pile, lack of moisture could very well be your problem. Water the pile thoroughly and evenly until it's as wet as a wrung-out sponge, but not so soggy that you can squeeze water from it. Covering the pile with black plastic will keep the moisture in and prevent nutrients from being leached out by rain.

If the compost pile still doesn't heat up, it lacks nitrogen, which the composting bacteria need. The manure you've been using may not be fresh, or you may not have added enough. To every 4 inches of leaves, add about 2 inches of fresh manure, mixing in enough wood chips to aerate the pile. Wood chips are not the easiest material to compost, but they will break down eventually and in the meantime will keep the other materials from clumping up, making turning easier.

Lawn clippings, vegetable wastes, and coffee grounds are other good sources of nitrogen, and they're usually free. If none of these is available, bonemeal or bloodmeal can be added to the pile.

Compost Concoctions

Q. **What is a recipe for compost to use in a potting mix for starting seedlings? Should I add manure or other nitrogen-rich organic fertilizers to the mixture?**

A. Any compost that undergoes a hot rot (above 140°F in the pile's center) will be free of disease organisms. A good recipe is four parts plant matter to one part fresh manure. Mix well and keep moist but not wet. Turn every week or so until the temperature comes down to 110°F. Screen and bag the compost immediately for later use. For your potting mix, make a blend of one part vermiculite and one part compost.

There is enough plant food in this mixture without adding manure or other fertilizers high in nitrogen. Used too soon, these can cause young plants to grow too rapidly and become spindly.

Shredder Shortcut

Q. I shred fruit and vegetable scraps, dry cow manure, and dry leaves, run it all through our trusty shredder, toss it with a small ash shovel, and pour the mixture into our cinder block bin. Is it necessary to layer soil into a compost pile?

A. While not absolutely necessary, layering of materials is the simplest way to ensure that you've mixed all the ingredients in your pile and to spread helpful microorganisms throughout, which encourages heat and decomposition. With your shredder, you've accomplished the mixing before you've made your pile. You still should throw a shovelful of garden soil into your newly shredded materials every so often to introduce soil bacteria and fungi throughout the pile for even decomposition.

A Good Pit
Makes Good Neighbors

Q. Gardening in my city yard is a challenge. I wonder, for example, how I can keep my compost heap alive and hot throughout the winter months without creating a backyard eyesore for my neighbors.

A. The best way to keep your compost heap active and out of view is by making it in a pit. During the winter, the pit sides keep compost warm and accelerate the decaying process. Even such resistant materials as ground corncobs and leaves will be ready for soil-building use by late spring with this method, especially if earthworms do the mixing.

The pit can be 3 feet deep, with the length and width about 4 feet. After placing the materials in the pit, cover them with soil, burlap bags, canvas, straw, or something similar to retain heat and moisture for faster decomposition.

Compost Minus Manure

Q. Living in the city, I don't have easy access to manure. Is it really necessary in making compost?

A. You don't need animal manures to make compost successfully. You can get by using nitrogen-rich sources like grass clippings or cottonseed meal. One easy method is to cut or shred fresh plant materials as finely as possible in order to expose a maximum amount of surface to the organisms of decay. As soon as the heat has subsided, the heap of finely ground plant materials may be given a nutritional boost by introducing some redworms and branding worms bred especially for the compost heap. These animals will supply the manure needed. You can also add such animal residues as bonemeal, dried blood, dried fish, and, if possible, dried manure to the heap.

Aerobicize Your Composter

Q. I built a barrel composter but find it doesn't work well. Why?

A. All compost needs air. A barrel composter, if filled to capacity, doesn't allow air to mix with the compost material when the composter is turned. Fill your composter only half to two-thirds full and see if that helps it to work better. To ensure good aeration, try turning the composter three to five times a day. Too much moisture, which can be a problem in barrel composters, will also slow decomposition.

Rotary Compost

Q. I gave my drum composter several turns a day, but two to three weeks later, the compost was still not finished. What went wrong?

A. Drum composters work best when the compost material is finely shredded. You can use one of the larger-size, heavy-duty shredders or, if you have only small amounts of materials, try one of the newer, smaller-scale models. And remember that bulky matter—long stems and clumps of organic debris—doesn't mix very well.

If bulk wasn't the problem, maybe lack of adequate nitrogen was. Fast compost requires a 25:1 carbon:nitrogen ratio. Many combinations of organic materials come close to the ideal proportions. For example, you can mix equal parts of garden debris, kitchen scraps, and leaves; half straw and half manure; or equal amounts of straw, grass clippings, and garden refuse. Layer the ingredients, wetting them down as you go, until the drum is almost full. The mixture should be as damp as a wrung-out sponge, not dripping wet. Turn the drum five times a day and add more water if the compost starts to dry out. In two to three weeks, it will be dark, crumbly, and ready to use.

Shred with Your Mower

Q. What is an easy way to convert my lawnmower into a shredder for compost material?

A. The easiest thing to do is not to convert your lawnmower at all. Just run the mower over your piles of weeds, leaves, straw, and manure, and your compost material is ready. It is helpful to do this job near a wall, which can prevent the cuttings from spreading out too much.

When shredding material with a rotary mower, it is best for two people to work together. One moves the mower back and forth over a given spot, while the other feeds material in front of it. You can tackle larger piles by tilting the mower back on two wheels, positioning the blades until they are directly over the pile, and then lowering the mower gradually.

Compost on Hold

Q. Can compost be saved for several years and still retain its value?

A. Yes, as long as you keep the pile covered. You can make a cover of weighted-down plastic sheeting, metal roofing, or wood that will keep rain and snow from leaching out water-soluble nutrients. However, no matter how it's stored, compost is still a valuable soil conditioner, improving the soil's tilth and its ability to hold water and oxygen.

Don't Rock Fast Compost

Q. I want to make fast compost with leaves and pure horse manure (not bedding). What's the best ratio to get a good hot mix? Will rock phosphate and other additives help speed up the composting process?

A. The best way to get the proper ratio for fast, hot compost with leaves and fresh horse manure is to alternate 3- to 4-inch layers of leaves with 1- to 2-inch layers of manure. The pile should be at least 3 feet square and 3 feet high to retain heat properly.

Mineral additives like rock phosphate, basalt rock, and bonemeal are more for compost enrichment than activation. They won't speed up the composting process, but they won't hinder it either. These substances increase compost's nutrient content, but they are not necessary. If your soil is low in phosphorus, for example, adding raw pulverized phosphate rock will give you compost with a slightly higher phosphorus level. Add these rock powders or bonemeal to compost only if a soil test indicates your soil needs boosting.

Keep the Lime Out

Q. Should I lime my compost pile? If so, do I still have to lime my garden?

A. We recommend that you don't add lime to your compost pile. Even if you put very acid materials like oak leaves or sawdust into your pile, the composting process will almost always turn out an end product with a pH of about 6.5—slightly below neutral.

Lime in the compost pile can also cause the formation of ammonia gas, resulting in a loss of valuable nitrogen. So lime your garden but not your compost.

Bacterial "Starters" for Compost Heaps

Q. I have recently started my first compost pile. I have read many ads for compost makers, tablets, powders, and liquids that claim to add beneficial bacteria to speed composting. A box of Rid-X is much cheaper and claims to add beneficial bacteria to a septic tank. Is there any reason I can't add Rid-X to my compost pile? Are they the same beneficial bacteria?

A. Of course you could add a box of Rid-X to your compost pile, but we doubt it would do anything. The beneficial bacteria needed for biological breakdown of human waste in a tank of water are completely different from those needed in a compost pile. It would be a lot like trying to raise fish on a good stand of alfalfa.

There is a great deal of controversy about the value of adding bacteria to compost heaps. Rodale researchers believe that, under normal circumstances, there is no reason to use a bacterial mixture in a properly built compost heap. However, the Bio-Dynamic Farming and Gardening Association strongly believes in the use of a biological starter, or preparation, on a compost pile. Although

Rodale researchers know of no university tests on the value of compost starters, the only point they see in their favor is that they may speed up the process in some cases. In the case of a poorly built heap, this could be of value, especially in the area of nutrient preservation. However, if you build your heap right and keep an occasional eye on it, you should not need any bacterial additions.

What Makes Good Compost?

Chips Ahoy!

Q. I have access to wood chips and cow manure and would like to use them to make compost. In what proportions should I mix them?

A. Composting wood chips is usually not practical because they contain a lot of carbon and relatively little nitrogen, explains Dr. Charles Michler, a researcher at the Forestry Sciences Laboratory in Wisconsin. You would have to mix 80 to 100 pounds of manure with every pound of wood chips to compost them within a month or so.

It's better to use wood chips as a mulch for fruit, perennial vegetables, and ornamental plantings. Since the chips break down so slowly (only about 1 percent a year), they won't rob a significant amount of nitrogen from the soil, Michler adds.

Cow manure, on the other hand, is an excellent ingredient for a compost pile. By layering it about half and half with materials such as straw, leaves, grass clippings, and kitchen scraps, you'll be able to produce fast, high-quality compost.

Composting Bermuda Grass

Q. With the heat and dryness here in Yuma, Arizona, one of the few grasses that will survive is Bermuda grass. I've been saving all my lawn clippings but was recently told Bermuda grass is unacceptable as a compost material because its growing ability is not destroyed in the composting process. Is this true?

A. Bermuda grass, an important pasture grass, can be a problem for home gardeners because it spreads both by creeping stolons (aboveground runners) and rhizomes (underground runners).

If your pile is properly composted, it should become hot enough to destroy both stolons and rhizomes, and there should be no problem using the compost. You might want to monitor the pile with a thermometer (such as a meat thermometer) to determine whether you're reaching a high enough temperature. Be sure not to mulch with Bermuda grass.

Diseased Plants: Compost or Destroy?

Q. I know that diseased plant parts should always be destroyed. But do they have to be burned, or can I compost them?

A. Most diseased plant material can be safely composted. Recent research suggests that nearly all plant pathogens are killed by temperatures of about 140° to 145°F—the range a well-constructed compost pile should reach in its initial stages. (You can use a meat thermometer to monitor your pile.) To make sure the outside of the pile heats up, we recommend covering it with black plastic for the first few days or turning it consistently and thoroughly. But don't worry too much if the temperature of your compost doesn't reach 140°F, because the competing microorganisms also do a pretty good job of killing pathogens.

Be aware, however, that composting won't kill fusarium or verticillium wilt. Any plants that have succumbed to these two diseases should be burned. If you're not sure of the disease, or if you compost by the "slow" method, burning diseased material will ensure destruction of all plant pathogens. You can then use the ashes in your garden.

Sawdust Savvy

Q. I'd like to use some sawdust in the garden. Most of it is from walnut and cedar trees. Will using it be a problem?

A. There should be no problem from the cedar sawdust. But you are right to be concerned about sawdust from walnut trees. Walnut wood contains a toxin called juglone that can kill or stunt your vegetables. A year's composting will break down the juglone, making the sawdust safe for the garden.

All sawdust should be composted before being added to the garden anyway. Because it is a high carbon/low nitrogen material, raw sawdust can cause a nitrogen deficiency in the soil as it breaks down. If you must put it directly on the garden, be sure to add a rich nitrogen source like bloodmeal, cottonseed meal, grass clippings, or manure.

Compost on Ice

Q. What's the best thing to do with kitchen scraps in the winter?

A. In regions that freeze during the winter, it's best to store the scraps until spring. Store them outside in a covered container. The scraps will freeze, and in the spring they can be composted. One *Organic Gardening* staff member uses a covered 30-gallon plastic trash can and finds it keeps all the scraps two adults and two children produce from December through mid-March.

If you have a basement or garage that stays above 50°F, you (with the help of some earthworms) can compost your kitchen scraps in containers throughout the year.

Which Style of Sludge?

Q. I've been considering the use of sludge to fertilize my flower garden. What is the difference between digested sludge and dried-activated sludge?

A. Digested sludge is given primary treatment by anaerobic digestion (occurring in the absence of free oxygen), but it's not heat-treated. The product is usually of relatively low quality as a fertilizer compared with products from an activated system.

In flower gardens, the digested sludge should be applied to bare land in the fall and lightly dug in, or composted. It is unwise to apply this sludge to vegetable gardens or to soils that will sustain an edible crop in the same season.

Dried-activated sludge is made from sewage that has the grit and coarse solids removed. After this process, the substance is inoculated with microorganisms and then aerated. The resulting organic matter is withdrawn from the tanks, filtered, dried in rotary kilns, ground, and screened. As you can imagine, properly heat-treated, dried-activated sludge usually draws a good price.

Caution: Whichever sludge you choose to use, make sure that the specific treatment system is not also involved in handling toxic materials (heavy metals) that are coming into it from industrial plants. Make sure sludge has been tested for the absence of cadmium, nickel, and lead. Also, raw, untreated, or improperly treated sewage sludge should never be applied as a fertilizer or soil conditioner.

The Safety Factor

Compost Cat Litter?

Q. We would like to compost our cat's used cat-box filler for use in our vegetable garden. Is there a danger of introducing harmful organisms?

A. Technically, the litter can be used in compost if you are sure that your materials compost thoroughly, the compost reaches a high temperature, and a good carbon/nitrogen balance of materials is used. However, we don't recommend composting the litter for vegetable gardens because cats, especially "outdoor" cats, occasionally carry diseases that can infect humans.

Toxoplasma gondii, a protozoan, usually causes few, if any, symptoms in man and remains unnoticed. But infection of pregnant women can lead to severe birth defects, and infection of a newborn may cause blindness and mental retardation. The cysts of *Toxocara cati,* a nematode, can infect the digestive tract of humans, leading to migraine headaches and visual impairment.

All things considered, we feel there should be enough safe compost materials so that you shouldn't have to use kitty's litter. And while we're on this topic, here's one additional caution: Pregnant women should never clean litter pans.

Toxic Tomatoes?

Q. I understand there is a mild poison in potato and tomato vines and rhubarb leaves. Is it OK to compost them?

A. It's safe to compost your potato, tomato, and rhubarb refuse. In the first place, the compounds are not toxic to plants. Furthermore, they break down quickly when composted. The toxin in tomato and potato vines is an alkaloid called solanine, which can cause vomiting, diarrhea, and abdominal pain. Rhubarb leaves have high concentrations of oxalic acid, which also can cause vomiting and stomach pain. Use only the fleshy main ribs for your pies.

Barrel Cleaning

Q. I have several 55-gallon steel barrels that I would like to recycle as composters and as a barrel root cellar. However, the barrels were used in the printing industry and contained chemicals (press wash and isopropyl alcohol). Is it possible to remove these residues so the barrels are safe to use?

A. No matter how these barrels might be cleaned, it is still not wise to use them for storage containers. Since strong chemicals were previously stored in them, you can never be certain that there are no harmful residues still embedded in the metal. Your best bet would be to get hold of some wooden barrels or build some simple wooden containers yourself.

Rust in the Barrel

Q. I've started some compost in my homemade barrel composter, but the barrel is rusty. Could I unknowingly transmit something harmful to my garden?

A. If anything, the rust from your barrel will probably give the iron content of your a compost a boost with the addition of iron oxide. However, a rusty barrel won't hold up over a long period of time. If you put a lot of effort into making your composter, replace the rusty drum with a good 55-gallon drum, preferably coated with a protective layer of lead-free paint.

Toxins in Mushroom Soil

Q. I use mushroom soil in my garden. The mushroom growers get their straw and manure from large horse farms that spray their stables, and I know that mushroom growers spray, too. Will pesticides end up in my soil?

A. Most mushroom compost contains pesticides. And while all of the insecticides commonly used break down into other compounds fairly quickly (most growers spread their mushroom soil in a field in a 2-foot-thick layer for a year or more before selling it), some of the residues may be harmful. Ask the mushroom growers whether they use a preventive spray program, which involves constant use of pesticides, or Integrated Pest Management (IPM), in which sprays are only applied if an insect problem occurs.

Toxicity, however, is not the only issue. Some of the pesticide compounds used, or their breakdown products, have been proven to be carcinogenic or mutagenic. In addition, an abundance of weed seeds usually finds its way into the compost while it sits in the field. And valuable nutrients such as nitrogen and potassium will have leached out, so mushroom soil will supply primarily phosphorus, some micronutrients, and organic matter.

Sludge Safety

Q. The municipal sewage treatment plant in our community makes composted sludge available to the public free of charge. I have put it on our flower beds, and it does wonders. Is it safe to use on the vegetable garden?

A. In most places, it's still not a good idea to use sewage sludge in your vegetable garden because of the possiblity of heavy metal contamination, most of it from industry. Not all sludges contain heavy metals, but how do you make sure that the sludge you use isn't contaminated? The federal government doesn't have regulations governing giveaway sludge problems. Some states and municipalities do, but the monitoring programs vary widely.

Metals in Milorganite?

Q. If I fertilize my lawn with Milorganite, can I use the clippings on my garden without a harmful buildup of heavy metals?

A. Yes. As long as you maintain the pH of your lawn at 6.5 or above, cadmium, which is found in the sludge product in small quantities (the level, tested daily, is about 45 parts per million), won't be taken up by the grass at all. When Milorganite production first began, cadmium levels were higher, but industries in Milwaukee now remove the metal from their waste before it goes into the treatment system. According to the Milwaukee Metropolitan Sewerage District (which produces Milorganite), even if you fertilized your vegetable garden directly with Milorganite at recommended rates, it would take 200 years for the cadmium level in the soil to reach the Environmental Protection Agency's unacceptable level.

Problems in the Pile

Antsy Compost

Q. I've got ants in my compost pile. What can I do to get rid of them?

A. Ants may be using your compost pile as a cafeteria—eating aphid honeydew, fungi, seeds, and other insects in the pile. They'll also eat moldy lollipops, buttered toast, and any goodies that might end up in your pile. So store your garbage until you have enough for a layer, then cover it with a 3- to 4-inch layer of material that won't interest the ants—such as weeds, grass clippings, or straw.

The compost can also provide shelter for nests and hills. The ants, however, will remain only while the pile is relatively cool. A hot pile will get rid of the ants as well as give you faster compost. If you turn the pile and it doesn't heat up, you have one of two problems. The most common is that your pile lacks sufficient nitrogen. Mix fresh manure or grass clippings into the heap and it should heat up. Turn the pile every three to five days and it will stay hot. If adding nitrogen doesn't work, the pile is probably too wet or dry. A good compost heap is moist, not soggy. To dry a waterlogged pile, turn it every day. When it dries enough, it will start heating up again. Cover the pile with plastic bags to shed the rain and increase the temperature. Ants won't be attracted to the finished compost.

Gnats in Compost

Q. I live in a residential area and make compost with grass clippings, leaves, and kitchen scraps. My problem is that hundreds of flies and gnats hover over the pile, and I'm afraid the neighbors will complain. Any suggestions?

A. While a few insects are to be expected, if large numbers are attracted to your compost, it probably isn't aerated well enough. Mix the grass thoroughly with the leaves so that it doesn't decompose anaerobically. (A foul odor is an indication of anaerobic, or oxygen-deficient, decomposition.) The pile should also be moist, but not dripping wet. To further reduce the number of flies and gnats in the area of your pile, you can cover it with a tarpaulin. You could also make or buy a compost bin, which your neighbors may find less objectionable.

Grubby Compost

Q. I mix grass clippings and leaves to compost slowly, and every year the pile is loaded with fat white grubs. How can I keep them out?

A. Slowly decaying organic matter is an attractive egg-laying site for various species of May and June beetles. The larvae of some species feed only on decaying plant material, but others can seriously damage plant roots. Prevent egg laying by covering the compost with plastic, though grubs may still migrate in from surrounding soil. Some gardeners have controlled grubs in compost by introducing insect-killing nematodes. Recent research indicates that these nematodes can control grubs in lawns and gardens as well.

Glass Compost

Q. I've read that glass is present in municipal compost. Doesn't the presence of these tiny razor blades pose a threat?

A. Glass, passed with refuse through a grinder, is either pulverized to the consistency of beach sand or shattered into highly polished fragments that have a surface much like that of a pebble. The polishing action is due to the abrasive nature of refuse. The principal objection to the presence of this glass in compost is that it detracts from the aesthetics of the product. While it might be ideal to eliminate all glass from compost in municipal composting, its presence will not constitute a hazard.

Chapter 4

Four for Fertility

Manures, Mulches, Cover Crops, and Earthworms

The Right Stuff

Spring Manure

Q. I didn't get manure into my garden during the fall. Is it okay to manure the garden this spring, or will the fresh manure burn my early crops?

A. It's OK to put down a medium application of fresh manure (except poultry manure) if it's tilled into the soil at least two weeks before planting and rained on in the interim. If rain doesn't come, water the area deeply soon after tilling. But set a manure-free spot aside for carrots, which may branch excessively in freshly manured ground.

Keeping Up Appearances

Q. Is there any way to transform fresh manure into well-rotted manure without causing a neighborhood revolt due to smell and appearance?

A. We suggest piling the manure in an out-of-the-way corner of the yard and covering the pile with a tarpaulin or plastic sheet.

Unless there is plenty of straw already mixed with the manure, layer it with an equal amount of straw, hay, or leaves and allow it to compost for a year without turning. Surround the pile with attractive fencing for a neater appearance.

Aged, Not Composted

Q. I have access to manure from a horse barn. It's about a foot deep and has been there for some time. Is it composted manure? How should I use it?

A. Aging is not composting, so you don't have composted manure. Since it's been protected indoors, and the weather hasn't leached out the important nutrients, you can either till it into your garden four to six weeks before you plant, or layer it with other organic matter to make compost.

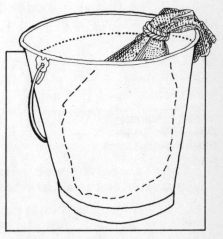

Making Manure Tea

Liquid Fertilizers

Q. I would like to know the advantages of liquid fertilizer. Does it have any long-term benefits to the soil? How economical is it? Is it a practical alternative to organic fertilizer or composting manure?

A. The liquid fertilizers that are most beneficial include "tea," made from manure or compost, or seaweed or fish emulsion extract. Organic teas and sea extracts are excellent "pick-me-ups" during the summer when plants are growing fast because the liquids move through the soil quickly and are absorbed rapidly by roots. Liquid fertilizers also boost the productivity of intensive vegetable beds. There are some liquid chemical fertilizers that are so strong they will burn your skin on contact, so you can imagine what they will do to your soil. Don't use them.

Manure and compost teas are the least expensive liquid fertilizers. To make them, scoop manure or compost into a burlap bag and suspend it in a bucket of water. Steep one to two weeks, moving the bag around every couple of days. Use full strength or dilute to the color of weak tea.

Fish emulsion, made from soluble fish-canning wastes, is high in nitrogen. Fish emulsion is potent stuff—you should never use solutions stronger than 1 tablespoon to a gallon of water, and half of that for foliar feeding. As a foliar spray, fish emulsion has been found to increase tomato yields by 16 percent.

Current research into seaweed extracts shows that they benefit plants because, while lower in nitrogen than manure tea and fish emulsion, they contain a wide range of trace minerals (often more than 60). In work at Clemson University, foliar feeding of seaweed extract enabled tomatoes to survive temperatures slightly below freezing and provided considerable protection from insects. There are also products that combine both seaweed and fish emulsion for a balanced fertilizer. Apply any foliar spray once every three to four weeks.

These products are normally diluted for use, so the total cost is not too high. But liquid fertilizers don't improve soil structure, so they are not a replacement for incorporating organic matter into your soil. If you have a good soil management system that keeps your soil healthy, you could supplement it with an organic foliar-feeding program.

Horse Manure
Takes the Cake

Q. I have access to horse, cow, sheep, and hog manure. Which one can provide the highest nutrient content in my garden?

A. As a rule, horse manure is more valuable than the manure of other farm animals, but the nutrient content varies with the amount of grain that is included in the diet. Since grains are relatively high in all plant nutrients, the more grain, the better the manure.

Horse manure is richer in nitrogen than either cow or hog manure, and it ferments more easily. For this reason, it is usually referred to as a "hot" manure. Sheep manure also falls into the "hot" category and is generally quite dry and rich. Cow manure and hog manure are relatively wet and low in nitrogen, so these manures ferment slowly and are regarded as "cold" manures.

On the Wings of a Dove

Q. **I have an old barn with a lot of pigeon manure on the floor. Is the manure a good fertilizer and safe to use?**

A. Pigeon manure is a very good fertilizer, according to Marie Rotondo, secretary-treasurer of the International Federation of American Homing Pigeon Fanciers, who uses it regularly in her garden. It's more than twice as concentrated as chicken manure; apply 4 to 8 pounds fresh or 2 to 5 pounds dried per 100 square feet of garden area. Because it is so hot, it will burn young roots and leaves if spread directly on the garden.

Droppings from domesticated pigeons are safer to use in the garden than those from wild pigeons. Breeders strive to keep their birds healthy. Wild birds, usually found in cities, may be carriers of psittacosis, a severe form of pneumonia, and *Cryptococcus neoformans*, which can cause meningitis. To be safe, always compost pigeon droppings before you apply them to your soil.

Dr. Richard Fite, an avian pathologist at the University of New Hampshire, says that because dry manure is exceptionally dusty, you should wear a tight-fitting dust mask with a rubber apron and filter to keep from breathing airborne particles.

Dog Wastes

Q. **Is it OK to use dog droppings in my garden?**

A. No. Don't use dog feces in the garden. Theoretically, pathogens and parasites in the material would be killed if it were composted thoroughly at high temperatures. But there's too great a chance that some of the material won't be pasteurized or the high temperature won't be attained. Furthermore, the dog manure is dense and will not break down as readily as livestock manures.

The feces may contain tapeworms, roundworms, and hookworms, which are parasites of dogs. In their larval stages, they also infect humans and are generally contracted from infected soil. The organisms can survive in the soil for over a year or until the ground freezes.

Zoo Doo

Q. **How safe is it to use manure from zoo animals for fertilizing a vegetable garden? The Portland Zoo sells this, and the Seattle Zoo is looking into the possibility.**

A. There is no more danger of disease being transmitted from zoo animals to humans than there is from horses or cattle, so treat zoo manure as you would any other. The U.S. Department of Agriculture (USDA) regulates zoos, and according to Dr. Keith Sherman of USDA's Animal Care Staff, any zoo that takes sheep-, horse-, or cowlike animals from foreign countries after the normal quarantine period must meet strict post-quarantine regulations. These regulations require that the manure from these animals be disposed of at the zoo, either by burning, burying, or composting. Disposal is aimed at preventing the spread of hoof-and-mouth disease, which animals may carry but not suffer from themselves.

Animals that have been born in this country have no federal restrictions on their manure, and it may be treated the same as that from any other animal in that area, according to state and local laws. Thus it may be sold—as is done in Portland with elephant manure. Under the label of "ZooDoo Manure," the elephant manure is sold to help the zoo meet its maintenance costs. Although only elephant manure is sold at the Portland Zoo, all their animals have been born in this country with the exception of one giraffe, whose waste is handled separately. The remainder of the Portland manure is sold to area worm growers for composting in worm beds.

Mulch, Mulch More

What's for Mulch?

Q. **Although we mulched our garden with decayed plant materials, we were disappointed to find a good crop of weeds throughout the growing season. Is there a recommended amount of mulch or better mulching materials that would improve our track record?**

A. Determining the right amount of mulch and what type of mulch works best for a particular garden is often a trial-and-error procedure. However, there are basic guidelines you should follow for successful mulching. The first is simply providing enough mulch so that those weeds do not appear during the growing season. In your case, a thin layer of finely shredded plant materials would have been more effective than unshredded loose material. Eight or more inches of hay, straw, or a similar loose, "open" material would also work well. So will 1 or 2 inches of buckwheat or cocoa bean hulls or a 2- to 4-inch layer of pine needles. Leaves and cornstalks should be shredded or mixed with a light material like straw to prevent packing into a soggy mass. In a mixture, shredded leaves can be spread 8 to 12 inches deep for the winter. Other good mulches include sphagnum moss, a variety of weeds, crop residues, grasses, clovers, and different types of hay.

Peanut Shells Are Perfect

Q. **Are peanut shells suitable as mulch around vegetables and flowers?**

A. Peanut shells make a great mulch. Your soil will not only get the benefits of weed control, improved moisture retention, and ground cover, it will also be the beneficiary of added nitrogen. Peanut hulls contain 1.5 percent nitrogen. They also contain small amounts of phosphorus (1.2 percent) and potassium (0.78 percent).

If the hulls are ground or broken up, they will tend to pack down after rains to form a hard crust. Adding more nitrogen in the form of cottonseed meal—not bloodmeal or dried blood, which will burn plants—to the hull mulch will help decompose the compacted layer and break it up.

Yesterday's Papers

Q. **Can household waste papers such as newspapers, paper bags, cardboard, and milk cartons be used as mulch? I recently purchased a shredder and wish to use all my waste papers as mulch, if possible.**

A. Go ahead and mulch with newspaper, paper bags, and cardboard, provided none are covered with colored ink. Stay away from slick magazine paper and any dyed material such as comics, which may contain lead dyes. Milk cartons aren't recommended because they also contain dyes. On top of that, they are usually coated with paraffin, which is a petroleum product—certainly an undesirable addition to your mulch.

It's a good idea to add a layer of straw, hay, corncobs, or wood chips over the paper to keep it from blowing away and to aid in moisture retention.

A Hairy Subject

Q. **I've been reading that the use of hair dyes can cause breast cancer in women. Is it safe to use clippings of dyed hair as mulch in the garden?**

A. The questionable compound (2,4-DAA) in hair dyes breaks down rapidly when exposed to moisture and air. Considering the rather low concentrations of the substance and the rapid breakdown, there's probably no harm in using dyed hair as mulch. If you use it in the vegetable garden, we suggest you compost it first.

Is It Straw or Is It . . . ?

Q. **What's the difference between straw and hay? Which is the better mulch?**

A. Straw is the dry stems and leaves of a grain crop like oats or wheat, and hay is cut green from fields that are usually a mix of grasses, legumes (alfalfa, clover, and so on), and weeds. Because of weed seeds, mulching a garden with hay can sometimes introduce many more weed seeds as well as new weed species. So it is better to compost hay first. Straw isn't nearly as weedy, but it generally has some weed seeds and a few grain heads.

Hay is a little higher in nitrogen—it has 1 to 2 percent, while oat straw is 1 percent and wheat straw only 0.3 percent. Wheat straw could rob your soil of nitrogen if used as a mulch. Neither hay nor straw supplies much phosphorus, and they both contain 1 to 2 percent potash.

Basically, it's a choice between potential weed problems with hay and lower nitrogen with straw. The best choice is to mulch with straw, supplemented with compost or manure to make sure it doesn't deplete the soil.

Worth Its Salt

Q. **I've heard salt hay is recommended as a mulch. Is it better than regular hay? Where can I obtain it?**

A. Salt hay comes from a grass that grows abundantly in eastern coastal marshes. Its main advantage over regular hay is that it's relatively free of weed seeds. It also doesn't mat down like hay will. Although the grass grows only in saline conditions, it contains very little salt. You can buy it by the bale at a building supply store or garden center, or you can cut it yourself if you live near the shore.

New Jersey extension agent Richard Obal uses salt hay in his garden at home. He says, "I wait for the first flush of weeds in the spring and grub those out with a hoe." Then he applies a 2- to 4-inch-thick layer of salt hay in late June, when the soil has warmed up. Any thicker, he says, and the slugs become a problem because they like a dark environment. He figures that mulching with salt hay controls up to 90 percent of the weeds in his garden.

Pines and Needles

Q. I have an unlimited amount of pine needles and would like to use them to mulch my vegetables, berry bushes, and fruit and nut trees. I've heard they make soil very acidic—is this true?

A. Pine needles make a good mulch for all the plants you mentioned. The needles are slightly acidic because the trees take up relatively small amounts of the alkaline elments (calcium, magnesium, and potassium). They also release organic acids as they decompose, but since the process occurs fairly slowly, there is only a slight acidifying effect on the soil. This effect makes pine needles ideal for blueberry bushes and other acid-loving plants, while still suitable for those requiring a neutral pH.

Between a Rock and a Hard Place

Q. Is it true that you can mulch with stone? It sounds so unusual, I wonder how it compares with hay or straw methods. How is it done?

A. Stones have most of the advantages of other types of mulches, and they even do some things better. For instance, they are particularly good for conserving soil moisture. They allow the soil to heat up quickly in the spring and, because they absorb heat, help to protect tender plants during cool nights.

The bed to be stone-mulched must be cultivated deeply, just like any permanently mulched plot. Organic matter should be disked or tilled into the soil. If leaves are available, spread a thick layer over the soil and place the stones on top of the leaves.

The stones are set in rows 2 feet wide, leaving a foot between stone paths for planting. Spaces between the stones can be filled with compost or garden loam, and the rows can be mulched with compost, straw, or other mulches. While stones help keep weeds down, note that they add nothing to the soil's organic content.

Sawdust Smarts

Q. Since I do a lot of woodworking, I have a lot of sawdust. However, some of my friends cringe when I use it as a mulch in my garden. They claim it robs the soil of nitrogen, but it always seems to work fine for me. What is right in the long run?

A. The trick to using sawdust properly is to offset the potential nitrogen shortages by adding some compost, manure, bloodmeal, or soybean or cottonseed meal to the soil before mulching. An even better alternative is to compost the sawdust with nitrogen-rich materials and then apply the mixture as a mulch. If you apply sawdust directly to the soil after one of these treatments, don't till it in unless it's completely composted.

The trouble with sawdust is that it's relatively indigestible to soil microorganisms. They use so much nitrogen in their efforts to decompose the sawdust that little is left for the plants. The plants may then turn yellow—an obvious hunger sign. Since this isn't happening to you, maybe you've been adding nitrogen-rich materials to your sawdust all along.

Cover Crop Queries

Cover Crops

Q. **The man who plows my garden suggested that I plant rye this fall as a cover crop and plow it under in the spring. What is a cover crop, and what are the benefits?**

A. More gardeners are finding that cover-cropping—using a legume, grass, or grain crop to add fertility and organic matter to the soil while preventing erosion during the winter—keeps their gardens working year-round.

Rye, wheat, and ryegrass, all nonleguminous cover crops, are probably most popular with the small gardener. Sown in the fall, these crops are incorporated into the soil in the spring to provide organic matter.

Leguminous cover crops, like clovers and alfalfa, will not only supply organic matter but will also capture nitrogen from the air and fix it in your soil—a free source of nitrogen fertilizer. For the most benefit, however, leguminous crops should grow a full year, preferably in rotation with your regular vegetables and grains.

For the small gardener who wants to put his whole garden into production each summer, ryegrass is probably the best cover crop to sow in the fall. Let it grow to about a foot in the spring, then mow before plowing it in. The mowing is a big help in speeding decomposition.

Certain cover crops are especially suited to different areas and purposes, so check with your Cooperative Extension Service for varieties and planting schedules that work best for you.

Green Manure

Q. We have a large (90-by-100-foot) garden in desperate need of manure or some other source of nitrogen. The 12 pickup loads of manure we hauled last fall were not enough. Since we are far from any source of manure, what green-manure crop could we grow? Would such crops supply all the nitrogen our garden needs, or would we have to supplement with manure?

A. Gene Logsdon, author and green-manure expert, answers: "You do not say what kind of soil you have in your garden or what its pH is. If you have put 12 pickup loads of manure on a 90-by-100-foot plot, you should be growing a fair garden even if the soil was rather poor. If the weather has been quite dry, perhaps the manure has not rotted enough to give results. Have a soil test done; perhaps there is some other deficiency in your soil.

"I would suggest before you try growing any green-manure crop (if vegetables won't grow, the green manure probably won't either) that you test the pH and treat with lime if needed. Or, if your soil is too alkaline, treat with acidifying material. Then I'd apply 200 pounds of soybean meal over the garden to build in a source of nitrogen, plus bonemeal or rock phosphate for phosphorus and potash in whatever form you can get it. If the soil tends to be alkaline, use 200 pounds of cottonseed meal instead of the soybean meal.

"Then for green manure I'd grow soybeans, broadcast and disked or raked into the soil at about the same time you normally plant bush beans. When the soybeans are grown, but before the beans mature, plow them under. You may want to shred the plants with a rotary mower first. You should still have time to plant rye and plow that under the next spring and plant clover.

"Unless you can grow clover on your garden or part of it for two years, the first year mowing the clover and letting the clippings fall to rot on the ground, and the second year plowing the clover under, green-manure crops will not supply all the nitrogen you need. Some supplemental nitrogen is advisable until you build up the soil to a high state of fertility and it contains plenty of organic matter. Then a legume green manure allowed to grow a year and plowed under a second year will help sustain that level of fertility.

"If you cannot get manure but can buy fresh-cut alfalfa (good green alfalfa hay is a second choice), you've still got a solution. Using it as a mulch or working it into the ground as a soil amendment will increase both nitrogen and potash in the soil. Dry alfalfa meal is a pretty good organic fertilizer, too."

C'est Bon Buckwheat

Q. Is buckwheat a legume? I've heard it is highly regarded as a green manure. What kind of nutrients will it make available in the soil, and when is the best time to plow it under?

A. Buckwheat is not a legume—it's actually an herb. Organic growers often refer to buckwheat as the green manure crop par excellence. It has the ability to use phosphates in the soil unavailable to most other plants, according to University of Minnesota researchers, and it produces a lot of organic matter, kills off weeds, and grows quickly.

Buckwheat is well known for its ability to loosen hard clay soils and for growing well on marginal land. These assets are due to the large amount of vegetation that can be turned under, as it does not have an especially deep root structure. As a green manure, it will make three crops in one growing season. As a smother crop for weed control, it does best in the midsummer or fall. For a grain crop, it is best harvested after a frost has killed the plants and the mature seeds have had time to dry.

Which Rye?

Q. I want to plant rye as a cover crop. Which is better, winter rye or annual rye? How late in the fall can I plant it?

A. Traditionally, winter rye (*Secale cereale*) has been used as a cover crop. This is the kind of rye grown for grain. Annual or common rye (*Lolium multiflorum*) is a temporary lawn grass, but it also works well as a winter cover. Be sure not to plant *perennial* rye (*L. perenne*)—once planted, it is very difficult to get rid of.

If your soil is poor, winter rye will be a better cover crop, as it's a more efficient extractor of nutrients. An extremely hardy plant, it can withstand temperatures as low as 40°F. You'll get the best growth by planting four to six weeks before a frost, at a rate of 2 pounds per 1,000 square feet, although later sowings will also work. Mow or scythe down the rye and till it under as early in the spring as you can. Otherwise, the stems become coarse and hard to work with. You should wait a week or two before planting to allow time for the rye to decompose.

If this lag time is a problem for you, try annual rye. It will probably winter-kill anywhere that temperatures fall below 0°F. The dead grass is easily turned under, and you can plant right away. You'll end up with less organic matter, however, and some of the nutrients may have leached out. Since some of the rye seed will lie dormant over the winter, some sprouting will occur throughout your garden in the spring, which can be a nuisance. Sow at a rate of 4 to 8 pounds per 1,000 square feet four to six weeks before the first frost. If you can't get the rye sown then, later sowings will still give you a cover.

Uncovering Cover Crops

Q. Last September, I sowed a cover crop of rye to enhance the fertility of my garden soil and protect it from erosion during the winter. What do I have to do now to prepare my soil for planting?

A. If cover crop topgrowth is heavy, it's best to chop it before working it into the soil. Use a rotary mower and cut close to help kill the rye. Then use a tiller to work the material into the soil. Or you can just spade it under.

The time to work in a cover crop is usually determined by the time you plan to plant a main crop in that section. Since so much of the value of cover crops depends upon their large fibrous root systems, which add organic matter to the soil, it's best to postpone working them in for as long as planting schedules permit. The bigger they get, the more organic matter your soil gets.

Warm-Climate Covers

Q. Which cover crops are best for warm-climate summers and winters?

A. Because it germinates and grows fast in hot weather, buckwheat is hard to beat as a summer cover crop (green manure). Buckwheat crowds out weeds and can be turned under in six to eight weeks. Field peas also grow well in hot weather, boost soil nitrogen levels, and can be harvested in the green-shell stage before the plants are tilled in.

For winter cover, try berseem clover, crimson clover, or sweet clover, all of which fix large amounts of nitrogen. If you want an edible cover crop and if overwintering insects or diseases are not a problem, you can even plant kale, garden peas, turnips, or radishes. Sow thickly and harvest some for eating, but turn under most of the crop to enrich the soil.

Annual ryegrass and cereal grains can also be used in winter, but be sure to turn them under before they grow too tall and thick for your tiller to handle. Dig or till in all cover crops before they mature their seeds, and allow two or three weeks for them to decompose before planting vegetables.

Two's Company

Q. **My garden is in Delaware. Can I successfully grow vegetables and a cover crop of annual ryegrass at the same time?**

A. Yes, you can, by using a system developed by senior extension agent Tom Jurchak for northeastern Pennsylvania vegetable farmers. The key is to time the ryegrass so it won't compete with the vegetables but will make good growth before winter. Jurchak finds that late July is the best time to overseed most crops, but you can sow annual ryegrass until September 1. Cultivate the soil, then broadcast the seed at the rate of 1 pound per 1,000 square feet. You should have a thick stand of ryegrass by frost. Till it under in early spring.

This method works well for crops like beans, brassicas, peppers, potatoes, sweet corn, and tomatoes. It's better to mulch cucumbers, melons, and other low-growing crops to avoid weed competition and make harvesting easier.

Stop That Crop

Q. **Last year I planted alfalfa in my garden as a cover crop. I tilled it under in the fall and was surprised to see it come back stronger than ever in the spring. I let it grow last summer, but how can I stop it?**

A. You were right to try to till it in, because spading often does little more than move the earth around. Dr. James Elgin of the Beltsville Agricultural Research Center recommends that you cut off the crown of the plant with a shallow tilling (about 1½ inches deep) and follow with a deeper tilling to chop up the roots. Late summer is the best time to till in alfalfa, because the soil is firm and dry then. It's difficult to do a good tilling job in moist, soft soil. For winter cover, you might want to plant annual ryegrass. It will make a good start in cool weather and protect the soil over the winter. Till it under before it heads in the spring.

Keepers of the Soil

Cool Customers

Q. In the fall when I turn my garden, I dig up earthworms. They seem sluggish, and I'm afraid they will die in the cold. Should I wait until spring to till?

A. You can cultivate as long as the temperature will remain above freezing for several hours afterwards. The worms are sluggish because they are cold-blooded and their body temperature matches that of their surroundings. With a few hours' grace, they can burrow back into the soil, eventually migrating below the frost line, where they wait out the winter. Freezing temperatures, however, will kill them and their eggs.

Come Back Little Earthworm

Q. Four years ago I turned part of my backyard into a garden. The sod I dug was full of earthworms. Last year there were none. I add manure and mulch with organic matter. My crops do well and my soil looks rich. Why have the earthworms left?

A. What time of year did you dig for earthworms? The early spring and late fall are the best times to find your worm population in the top few inches of soil. When the soil temperature is over 60°F, they burrow down to cooler regions.

Earthworms require a moist, rich soil. Your mulched and manured garden seems to fit the bill. However, earthworms are also extremely sensitive to soil pH, and garden soils tend to be slightly acidic. Most species of earthworms do best in neutral to alkaline soil (pH 7.0 or slightly above). Common nightcrawlers and field worms won't survive below a pH of 5.4. The best range for most crops is pH 6.0 to 7.5. Check your soil pH and add lime if necessary.

Burned Worms

Q. Last fall, I learned of an old gardening practice called "burning over." All garden stubble is left to dry, covered with leaves or hay, and slowly burned. Is this a valid practice? What are the benefits?

A. "Burning over" or any type of field or garden burning is definitely not a recommended practice. It's harmful to earthworms, soil organisms, and the humus itself. Soil organic matter in the top few inches can be destroyed and moisture dried out of the soil. Besides, there's no reason to burn. Those plant "wastes," once decomposed through composting and worked in, are good organic matter for building your soil.

Potted Earthworms

Q. **I've been told that earthworms can slow drainage in plant containers. Is that true?**

A. Yes. To drain well, soil in containers must be coarser in texture, with larger pore spaces, than soil in the garden, and it should be uniform in structure from the top of the container to the bottom. Earthworms can gradually destroy this desirable structure by ingesting the soil and passing the undigested remains as fine-textured castings, which can compact with repeated waterings into a soggy layer that resists drainage. This condition is most likely to develop near the bottom of the container, where earthworms spend most of their time because the soil remains cooler and more moist there than nearer the surface. A few earthworms may have little effect on drainage in a large container, but the smaller and shallower the pot, the more likely they are to cause a problem.

Wormy Compost

Q. **I'd like to make garbage-can compost this winter so I can recycle my kitchen scraps. I understand that you need earthworms to make this kind of compost. How do I do it? Do I need a special kind of worm?**

A. The best earthworms for garbage-can compost are red worms (*Lumbricus rubellus*), also called red wigglers. They are sold by commercial worm-growers and are available through mail order sources. Use either heavy plastic or galvanized cans with tight-fitting lids. Two large cans should be enough to provide compost for a moderately sized garden. Punch several holes the size of a large nail in the bottom of each can. Then, set the cans up on concrete blocks in the basement or in another place where they won't be subjected to freezing temperatures. Put a plastic pan or other container under each can to catch the liquid that will seep out of the holes during composting. (You can use this "compost tea" to water your plants.) Put about 3 inches of soil in the bottom of each can, and add 500 to 1,000 red worms per can. Layer soil, shredded newspapers, shredded leaves, or coffee grounds over each layer of kitchen scraps to neutralize odors.

A Fine Cast

Q. How do earthworm castings improve the soil?

A. Earthworm castings, composed of digested soil particles, organic matter, and secretions, contain from five to ten times as much nitrogen, phosphorus, and potassium as the surrounding soil. They also have one-third higher beneficial bacteria, which speed the breakdown of organic matter and the release of nutrients. The fine texture of castings makes them an excellent medium for plant growth—some plant stores even sell bags of pure castings, which, like top-grade compost, improve potting soil. Because earthworms refine soil size in the casting process, an earthworm-rich garden creates better soil texture as well as adding plant nutrients. And earthworms do make a substantial contribution—they can produce up to 700 pounds of castings a day per acre.

Part

TWO

Grow a Better Crop

Chapter 5

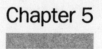

The Lively Nightshades
Tomatoes, Peppers, and Eggplant

Tomato Tactics

Tomatoes Once and Done

Q. I'd like to direct-seed tomatoes in our Phoenix, Arizona, garden. When is the best time to plant the seed, and should I use a row cover?

A. You can direct-seed tomatoes as early as the average last frost date, which is February 23 in your area, says Dr. Norman Oebker, a vegetable crops specialist at the University of Arizona. Enclosing the bed with a spunbonded polyester row cover, such as Reemay, will raise the air temperature and make the seedlings grow faster once they've sprouted. However, it won't affect the soil temperature, which should be at least 60°F for best germination. To warm the soil, cover the bed with black plastic before planting the seeds. Cut small slits in the plastic where the plants are to grow, and sow five or six seeds in the soil at each slit. When the seedlings are 6 inches tall, select the strongest one in each group and remove the others. To prevent overheating, cover the plastic with straw when soil temperatures reach 85°F.

Tomato Terms

Q. **Could you tell me what is meant by the terms determinate and indeterminate with regard to tomato plants? How can I tell the difference?**

A. These classifications refer to the growth habit of the plant. Determinate varieties include most *early* varieties. They have fairly short stems, and each stem ends in a flower cluster. Between the various flower clusters on determinate varieties there are fewer than three leaves. This growth habit leads to concentrated early set of fruit, which is usually low on the plant. Most determinate varieties tend to be bushy. They don't need staking, and they don't respond well to pruning. Determinate tomatoes tend to stop growing while the fruit sets and ripens. If you prune them, you are likely to reduce their fruit yield considerably.

Indeterminate varieties, on the other hand, have stems that grow as long as they live. They produce a flower cluster, then three leaves, then another cluster, then three more leaves, and so on. Indeterminate varieties produce later than determinate tomatoes. They respond well to staking, training, and pruning.

To Train or Not to Train

Q. **Should I prune my tomatoes?**

A. Determinate tomato varieties like 'Roma', 'Tiny Tim', and 'Floramerica' do not respond well to pruning and should not be staked. Indeterminate varieties should be staked and pruned or they become too difficult to manage. These so-called trained plants will have lower yields but will take up less space than untrained plants. By staking and pruning tomatoes, you will be able to get twice as many plants in the same area, so the final yield will be higher. The fruit size will be more uniform, with fewer small tomatoes. Pruning does not affect the rate at which the fruit ripens.

On the other hand, letting your plants sprawl also has advantages. Sprawling, viny plants that are unpruned are better protected from drying out and are less susceptible to cracking and sunscald than trained plants. Mulch well and allow the vines to ramble over the mulch.

More Tomatoes, Less Space

Q. I love tomatoes but have a small garden. What can I do to get maximum production from each plant?

A. Try varieties with an indeterminate growth habit, which yield more than determinate types, and stake the plants. Such well-known varieties as 'Beefmaster', 'Beefsteak', 'Better Boy', 'Burpee's Big Boy', 'Burpee's Big Girl', 'Early Girl Hybrid', and 'Manalucie' are indeterminate, as are the plum tomato 'San Marzano' and the cherry tomato 'Sweet 100'. Seed catalog descriptions tell whether a variety is determinate or indeterminate. Plant the tomatoes 2 feet apart in beds or at 18-inch intervals in rows set 3 feet apart. To prevent the staked plants from becoming top-heavy, they must be pruned. Pinch out all but a few stems that grow from leaf axils of the main stem. Two or more stems produce highest yields. After the soil has warmed up, mulch the plants, since staked tomatoes dry out quickly.

Setting Fruit under Lights

Q. We are trying to grow tomatoes indoors, but under our small light setup, they grow spindly and drop all their flowers. How can we get them to fruit in winter?

A. Increase the light intensity. Two 40-watt (4-foot) fluorescent tubes or a south-facing window may supply enough light to ripen a few salad tomatoes on a dwarf variety, such as 'Tiny Tim' or 'Pixie'. Four 40-watt tubes alone, or two 40-watt tubes hung in a south-facing window, will promote more fruiting. If you're interested in heavy production from a greenhouse tomato, such as 'Stakeless' or 'Starshot', you'll need eight 40-watt tubes.

To get the most from your light setup, keep the tops of the plants 6 inches or less below the tubes. If you have only a few plants, place them near the center of the fixture, where light intensity is highest. Various combinations of tubes will work, such as one cool white and one warm white or one cool white and one wide-spectrum plant light per two-tube fixture. The plants should receive light for 14 to 16 hours a day. Keep daytime temperatures between 70° and 80°F and allow a 10-degree drop at night. When plants bloom, pollinate the flowers by shaking the plants gently every day or two, or distribute pollen with a brush.

Saving Tomato Seed

Saving Tomato Seed

Q. I'm saving tomato seed. What's the best way to separate the seed from the pulp?

A. The best way is to ferment the fruit, since this also destroys tomato-canker bacteria, which can cause the plants to wilt and white spots to form on the fruit. Be sure your tomato is fully ripe, or even overripe. Cut open the fruit and scoop out the seeds and pulp. Put the mixture into a jar or glass with ¼ cup of water, and let it ferment at room temperature. Stir at least twice daily. The fermentation turns the pulp into a thin liquid and allows the viable seeds to sink to the bottom of the container. The fermentation will take four days at 60°F or three days at 70°F. At least three days are needed to destroy the canker bacteria. After the seeds have sunk to the bottom of the container, pour off the liquefied pulp and the seeds that are floating on the top. Spread the remaining seeds on newspaper or paper towels to dry. After drying, rub the seeds off the paper and store in an airtight container.

Winter Tomatoes

Q. I live in southern California and would like to grow tomatoes through the winter, since the temperature here rarely falls below 50°F. Are there any varieties that set fruit at low temperatures?

A. Even though you are in a frost-free climate, tomato plants don't set fruit well below 65°F and are injured at 55°F. However, you can harvest a crop of tomatoes during the winter by covering the row with a plastic tunnel.

Wayne Schrader, a farm advisor for San Diego County, California, suggests the following system, using 'Celebrity' tomatoes: Set out tomato plants in October or November in a row about 28 inches wide. Place 6-foot-tall stakes at 4-foot intervals down the center of the row. Tie a piece of heavy string to the row of stakes 26 inches above the ground. Then cut two pieces of 36-inch-wide clear plastic 6 feet longer than the length of the row. Lay one of the long edges of one piece along the outer edge of the row, leaving 3 feet of excess at each end, and either cover it with several inches of soil or weight it with stones or bricks. Do the same with the other piece along the opposite edge of the row. Attach the other long edges of the plastic to the string with clothespins, creating a "pup tent." Fold the excess plastic to cover the ends and secure with stones or bricks.

This row cover will increase the air temperature 6 to 20 degrees during the day and will warm the top 3 inches of soil 3 to 8 degrees at night, according to Schrader. When the interior temperature rises above 75°F, vent it by opening the ends or by removing the clothespins and pulling back the plastic. When the tomato plants flower, shake them so pollination will occur. By the time they outgrow the cover, the temperature will be warmer. Then you can remove the cover and train the plants to the stakes.

Hot Tomatoes

Q. How can I grow a good tomato in Texas? I've grown delicious tomatoes in several states, but here they all end up thick-skinned and tasteless.

A. According to John Dromgoole, an *Organic Gardening* contributor from Austin, Texas, you'll get better tomatoes if you time the planting so that they ripen before and after the hottest weather in July and August. For the first crop, start seeds or buy transplants early and grow them in milk cartons or other containers so that you'll have large plants to set out as soon as the weather is warm enough. Mulch the plants, irrigate often (thick skins indicate water stress), and work in plenty of water-holding organic matter—humus breaks down quickly during long, hot summers.

Before the summer heat ends fruit production, take cuttings of these plants to root. These vigorous replacements are ready to set out in time to produce a fall crop. If plants are in good condition, indeterminate varieties can be rejuvenated after the early crop by removing weak and broken stems and heading back the remaining shoots. A topdressing of fertilizer and regular watering should bring them back into production by autumn.

An Altitude Problem

Q. **How can I get my tomatoes to ripen earlier in our area, Idaho Falls, Idaho? We often have a frost right after Labor Day, just when the crop is beginning to turn red.**

A. Your difficulty in getting tomatoes to ripen in your area is understandable, with a 105-day growing season and an altitude of 4,800 feet. Choose the earliest varieties possible, such as 'Early Girl', 'Betterboy', and 'Better Girl'. Then add 20 days to the maturity date, because even though the average last frost occurs June 1, the soil temperature doesn't reach 50°F until midmonth, according to Bonneville County extension agent Charles Dunham.

Transplant seedlings started in early April into a south-sloping bed for maximum sun exposure, setting the stem below the soil surface to encourage more rooting. Dunham suggests covering the plants with hot caps and pinching the tops after fruit set. He's found that the Wall-o'-Water cloches help tomato plants grow faster.

Stop the Drop

Q. **What causes tomato blossoms to fall, and how can I stop them from doing so?**

A. Tomato blossom drop has a wide variety of causes. Low soil moisture with hot, dry winds will do it. A sudden shift from a hot spell to cool, wet weather is another cause. To prevent blossom drop, irrigate when the weather is hot and dry and plant tomatoes in soil that has good drainage. Certain varieties like 'Walter' and 'Floramerica' hold their blossoms better in hot weather.

The soil's mineral content also can play a role in blossom drop. Deficiencies of potassium, phosphorus, and nitrogen can all cause flowers to abort and drop off. But the most common mineral problem is *too much* nitrogen. It causes rapid, succulent growth and throws the plant's metabolism off balance, promoting blossom drop. Avoid applying high-nitrogen materials like bloodmeal or fresh manure during the early growth of the plant. If you use manure tea on your tomatoes, make sure it's weak.

Finally, both verticillium and fusarium wilt diseases can aggravate blossom drop. Many tomato varieties resist both diseases. These resistant varieties will be marked in most seed catalogs.

Sunscald

Q. Why did many of my tomatoes have papery, blisterlike patches this past year?

A. The patches are sunscald, which is caused by direct sunlight burning the fruit in hot, dry weather. The problem can also affect peppers. Plants that have lost their lower leaves or have been pruned and trellised are especially susceptible to this disorder. Sunscald first appears on green tomatoes as a yellow or white patch on the side facing the sun. The patch may remain yellow or white as the fruit matures, but usually the cells are badly damaged and the patch turns brown and papery. Often the damage opens the way for fungal infection.

Protect your plants from defoliating diseases by rotating your crops, planting disease-resistant varieties, and practicing good garden sanitation. Be sure your soil has enough nitrogen, but don't just pour on the fertilizer or it will stimulate leaf growth rather than fruit production. Plants without enough nitrogen will die back early, dropping their leaves before the fruit is mature. If the tomatoes become exposed to the sun, shade them with a cheesecloth awning or lathwork.

Green Shoulders

Q. My tomatoes won't ripen on the stem end. What do you think the problem is?

A. Most likely, the fruit is receiving too much sun, resulting in a physiological problem called "green shoulder." The first tomatoes of the season often have green shoulder because there's not enough foliage to shade them. Some staking methods tend to make the problem worse. You may want to try cages, which don't require pruning of protective foliage.

Catfaced Tomatoes

Q. Here in Florida, I have beautiful tomato plants over 5 feet high, but the bottoms of the fruits are catfaced—puckered and veined with brown scar tissue. What causes this, and how can I prevent it?

A. Catfacing results when environmental stresses during bloom cause young fruits to develop more than the usual number of cells. Exposure to temperatures below 55°F or above 85°F are the most frequent causes, but drought, high winds, and the herbicide 2,4-D can also produce catfacing. Heavy use of fertilizers high in ammonia, such as uncomposted poultry manure, may contribute to the problem.

The best way to prevent catfacing is to plant resistant varieties, such as 'Floramerica', 'Burpee's VF', and 'Big Set'. 'Floradel' and 'Floradade' are bred especially for Florida conditions.

Hounding Hornworms

Q. **My tomato patch is full of hornworms. The majority of the hornworms have white "tubes" on their backs, which I understand are the eggs of a parasitic wasp. How long does it take for the wasp to destroy the worm?**

A. The white "tubes" you see on the hornworms are the pupae of the braconid wasp, a beneficial parasite. Entomologist Bob Tetrault of Penn State University's Extension Service says that once the wasps reach the pupal stage, they've finished feeding on the hornworm and, though the worm may still be alive, its ability to destroy tomato and potato crops is basically a thing of the past. If the wasps have reached the pupal stage in your garden, let the cycle continue, allowing as many wasps as possible to reach adulthood and to continue breeding in the remaining hornworms. But if you have hornworms and see no white pupae forming, by all means, handpick the worms and destroy them immediately.

Stinkbug

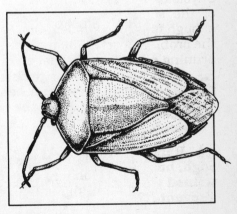

Attack of the Tomato Stinkbugs

Q. **Some of our tomatoes have small, irregular white lumps under their skins. Our neighbors have the same problem with some of their tomatoes. What's wrong?**

A. The white lumps on your tomatoes are caused by stinkbugs. Early in the season, the pest pierces the fruit to feed and leaves traces of saliva behind. The saliva in the wound breaks down the tomato tissue, causing the spots. You can still eat the fruit by cutting off the damaged part. Stinkbugs prefer damp places and generally attack the fruit closest to the ground. Control stinkbug damage by staking or trellising plants and pruning tomato suckers to avoid high humidity.

Trouble Spots

Q. Last year, tomato spotted wilt hit our area. I planted 22 tomato plants, and 11 of them turned black and died. Can you offer any help?

A. Since spotted wilt (*Lethum australiense*) is a viral disease transmitted almost entirely by tiny insects called thrips, you can control it by keeping the thrips off the plants, says Dr. Lowell Black, a vegetable disease specialist at Louisiana State University. He offers this suggestion. After you've prepared the bed in spring, cover it with black plastic. Then spray the plastic with aluminum spray paint, allow it to dry, and plant as usual. The reflective surface apparently confuses the insects as they fly over it, and most will not land on the plants. In Black's experiments, the treatment reduced the incidence of spotted wilt by 60 percent over the control.

Another effective technique, says Black, is to grow two plants per pot and set them out together. He has found that in a given area the same number of plants become infected, so doubled-up plantings yield better than conventional spacing. In areas where spotted wilt is severe, Black suggests combining the two methods.

Tomatoes Don't Smoke; Neither Should You

Q. Last year, we had a problem with tomatoes started indoors. In midsummer they were healthy with green fruit. Gradually, they seemed to die from the base up. We've been told cigarette smoke may be a problem.

A. Tobacco mosaic virus (TMV), which is highly contagious, is spread to tomato plants by people who've handled tobacco, including smokers and tobacco chewers. While it rarely kills the plants, TMV causes stunting, small fruit, reduced yields, and yellowing and curling of the leaves.

To prevent the spread of TMV, wash your hands thoroughly before you handle plants. Some TMV experts recommend dipping tomato transplants in milk before setting them out, since milk strongly inhibits the disease. Set out transplants where tomatoes have not been grown for at least two years. Remove and burn diseased plants and those surrounding them, since composting doesn't create temperatures high enough to kill the virus. Eliminate perennial weeds, and keep tomatoes away from their nightshade family relatives, including tobacco, cucumbers, and potatoes, which are possible disease carriers. Several TMV-resistant varieties now available include 'President', 'Celebrity', 'Big Pick', and 'Quick Pick'. Crop rotation will help prevent buildups of any of these diseases.

Seeing Spots

Q. My tomato leaves develop brown spots, turn yellow, and drop off from the bottom up. I believe this is early blight and wonder if the manure I got from a neighbor whose tomato plants also have this problem could be the cause.

A. Since you didn't notice any problems with the fruit, it's probably not early blight, which causes lesions in the stem end of the tomato and dark circular spots with targetlike concentric rings on the leaves. Your plants probably have septoria leaf spot (*Septoria lycopersica*), another fungal disease. Septoria thrives in warm, wet summers and usually appears just as the plants set fruit. Older leaves are attacked first, developing round spots $\frac{1}{16}$ to $\frac{1}{8}$ inch in diameter that are watersoaked at first, then turn gray with dark margins. The stalks are gradually defoliated from the ground up, and the fruit fails to mature or is spoiled by sunscald. The manure you used could have been contaminated with this fungus. Its spores are spread during watering or by contact with soil or tools.

To control septoria, buy disease-resistant varieties and practice good sanitation in the garden. Try to obtain manure from another source or compost it first, away from your garden. Septoria spores require a high moisture level for germination. If possible, water the plants with drip, rather than overhead, irrigation to avoid wetting the leaves. To enhance air movement, stake or cage the plants and prune back some of the stems. The fungus can live for at least three years on tomato refuse in the soil and indefinitely on weeds such as horse nettle and other nightshades. Burn crop residues and eliminate weeds. Finally, grow tomatoes in four-year rotations with unrelated crops.

Blighted Hopes

Q. **My tomatoes have early blight. Are there any nonchemical ways to control this disease?**

A. Yes. Use a three-year rotation with crops not in the tomato family (potatoes, peppers, and eggplant are all tomato relatives), and bury or compost all plant refuse immediately after harvest. Several resistant varieties are 'Early Cascade', 'Floramerica', 'Manalucie', and 'Red King'.

Tomato Wilt

Q. **Before my tomatoes ripen, the leaves on the plants turn yellow and die from the bottom upward. The tomatoes are small and don't taste as good as healthy ones. What is the problem?**

A. Your tomatoes are infected with a soilborne fungus called fusarium wilt (*Fusarium oxysporum* f. *lycopersici*). Although it is one of the most prevalent tomato diseases, it is easily controlled by using resistant varieties, often designated in seed catalogs and on seed packages by the letter F after the variety name.

Tomato Brown-Out

Q. **My tomatoes develop small, light brown spots that appear to be skin-deep at first, then become larger and spoil the tomatoes when they ripen. What causes the spots, and is there a solution?**

A. Round, sunken, water-soaked spots on ripening tomatoes are characteristic of tomato anthracnose, a fungal disease also called ripe rot. It attacks mainly the fruits, though you might find small dead spots with a yellow halo on the oldest leaves. The fruits can be infected when they're green but show no sign of spotting until they ripen, which usually coincides with hot, humid weather—perfect conditions for the fungus. Varieties susceptible to defoliation by leaf diseases are most vulnerable to anthracnose.

The fungus overwinters on decaying tomato vines and fruit in the soil, so clean up and burn or trash your tomato plants in the fall. Grow tomatoes on a two-year or longer rotation with other crops. When watering, soak the ground, not the plants. Since spores are spread by splashing water, overhead irrigation can greatly increase infection.

A Peck of Pepper Problems

Bitter Peppers

Q. **Last year my bell peppers were small and bitter. Could dry conditions or low organic matter in the soil (it was a new garden) cause these problems?**

A. Low organic matter combined with a dry season would mean that your peppers didn't get the two things they needed most for fruit production—a high moisture level and high humidity. Peppers are natives of the tropics, so they need warm temperatures (70° to 80°F during the day and 60° to 70° at night) and moist conditions. If stressed, the plants will never fully recover.

To avoid setbacks, young pepper plants should be set out after the soil is warm but before the plants flower. During dry periods, water them daily. Mulch and close spacing (16 inches apart is adequate) will also help maintain high moisture levels.

One other factor that can lead to plants' producing small, bitter peppers is a boron deficiency in the soil. As a safeguard, have your soil tested before you plant this year.

All Show, No Go

Q. **My bell pepper plants grow large but don't produce peppers; instead, the blossoms fall off. Can you tell me what is wrong?**

A. Temperatures below 60°F or above 80°F will cause blossom-drop, but your problem is most likely due to water stress. Large, blocky-fruited varieties like 'California Wonder' and 'Yolo Wonder' are especially sensitive to stressful conditions, according to pepper specialist Dr. Chris Wien of Cornell University. He recommends 'Lady Bell', 'Canape', 'Green Boy', 'Ace', and 'New Ace', which have somewhat smaller fruit but are more productive under stress. Make sure you mulch pepper plants and water regularly during dry spells.

Not-So-Hot Peppers

Q. I grow 'Hot Portugal' peppers. Some of the fruits are as hot as fire and some are as sweet as bell peppers, even though they were picked from the same bush at the same time. This is true whether they're picked green or red. What causes the variation?

A. Climate and, to a lesser degree, culture. Many hot-pepper cultivars produce less capsaicin—the substance that makes them hot—when grown under cool, moist conditions than they do under hotter, drier conditions. You may get more pungent peppers if you space the plants to get maximum sunlight and grow them fairly dry after fruit set.

A surer way is to experiment with cultivars until you find one that suits your climate. 'Long Red Cayenne' is consistently the hottest pepper grown at the Rodale Research Center, Kutztown, Pennsylvania. 'Sandia', a 7-inch pepper suitable for stuffing, is recommended by Dr. Roy Nakayama, now retired, a former chili breeder at New Mexico State University.

Get-Up-and-Go
Got Up and Went

Q. For the past two years my bell pepper plants have grown very slowly. The lower leaves turn pale green and fall off. I apply composted leaves to the bed twice a year. What do you suggest?

A. Acid soil, which stunts the growth of most vegetable plants, may be the problem, suggests Dr. Chris Wien, a pepper specialist at Cornell University. Have your soil's pH tested and if necessary, raise it to approximately 6.5 with dolomitic or calcitic limestone. (The correct amount to apply depends on the soil type and acidity and is usually included with the test results.)

Compost made from leaves may not contain enough nitrogen for peppers. To boost the nitrogen level of your next batch of compost, try adding some manure or grass clippings to the leaves, and cover the top of the compost pile with a tarp or boards to keep rain from leaching out nutrients. Until your compost is ready, you can sidedress the pepper plants with a sprinkling of bloodmeal after they've set several fruits.

Warped Peppers

Q. Our garden is situated in California's moderate coastal climate. Some of my bell peppers are badly deformed. What causes this problem?

A. Cold weather before or during flowering often causes peppers to be misshapen. Temperatures in the 40s and 50s or lower can damage developing ovaries or reduce pollination, resulting in undersized, flattened, or otherwise distorted fruit.

Choose pepper varieties better suited to your area. 'Golden Bell' and 'Staddon's Select' both set fruit under cool conditions better than other bell peppers. Make the most of available heat and light by planting on the south side of the house, away from the shade.

Drying Paprika

Q. My red peppers turn brown or moldy when I hang them up to dry. How can I get them to dry red and mold-free?

A. The peppers will naturally darken somewhat as they dry, but you should be able to get brighter paprika, free from mold, by drying the peppers in an oven or food dehydrator. Use only mature, sound peppers. Cut off the stems and halve the peppers. Remove the seeds and core for drying separately. Flatten the halves and place them in a single layer on trays in a food dehydrator at 140°F or on cookie sheets in a 150°F oven until they're crisp and brittle.

For the brightest color, grind the dried pepper halves alone. Adding the dried seeds will make a paler, more pungent paprika. Store in tightly sealed containers in a cool closet or the refrigerator.

Pepper Pests

Q. In my New York State garden, I find brown, pinhead-size holes in many of my peppers just before they ripen. Affected fruits rot from the inside out. What's attacking them?

A. Corn earworms are the most likely culprits, according to Dr. W. C. Kelly, a vegetable crops specialist at Cornell University. Though corn is their preferred food plant, earworms will also feed on peppers, eggplants, tomatoes (under the name of tomato fruitworm), limas, and other crops, especially in years when the pests are abundant.

In upstate New York, corn earworm moths appear in late July or early August and lay their eggs within one or two weeks. On peppers, the eggs are laid on the youngest leaves. After hatching in mid-August, the caterpillars feed briefly on the leaves, then tunnel into the fruits. Each caterpillar may damage several fruits before crawling to the ground to pupate. Tunneled fruits are quickly spoiled by bacteria and fungi, especially in wet weather.

You can avoid some damage by planting early varieties and harvesting the peppers green. If you have only a few plants, search for and rub off the eggs, which are yellowish and grooved with a flattened, spherical shape. *Bacillus thuringiensis* (Bt), a commercially available biocontrol, will kill the caterpillars, but it must be applied before they enter the fruits. Use according to directions on the package.

Since earworms vary in abundance from year to year, you can probably harvest a good crop of peppers in most years simply by watching for and culling infested fruits, says Kelly. Starting in mid-August, look for earworms in corn, which is usually attacked before peppers. As soon as earworms appear in the corn, begin to inspect your peppers for entrance holes. With only one earworm generation in the North, you can cull fruits with holes and leave sound fruits to ripen.

Eggplant Enigmas

Where's the Eggplant?

Q. Last year the blossoms on my eggplants developed, wilted, and dropped off. What caused this, and how can I prevent it?

A. The villain is probably the tarnished plant bug, a ¼-inch-long, greenish-yellow to brown insect that sucks on blossom stems and other plant parts, according to both Rob Johnston of Johnny's Selected Seeds and Dr. W. C. Kelly, vegetable crops specialist at Cornell University. Johnston offers two suggestions: Try adding more phosphorus to the soil, which will make the plants produce more flowers; and grow the eggplant under slitted row covers, which, despite the openings, will keep the tarnished plant bugs out.

Another possibility is lack of pollination due to extended periods below 65°F. Under these conditions, explains Kelly, either the pollen doesn't germinate or the pollen tube doesn't grow quickly enough. 'Dusky' is an early variety that should fare better than later-maturing varieties in cool temperatures. Using row covers will also raise the soil and air temperatures, ensuring good blossom set.

Phomopsis Phobia

Q. **Last summer, many of our eggplant fruits developed large, oval brown spots that sometimes rotted the whole side of an eggplant. What was the cause?**

A. Your eggplant had phomopsis blight, a fungal disease that attacks only eggplant and is most destructive in hot, wet summers. Before the fruits are attacked, the older leaves develop clearly defined, round gray or brown spots with pale centers. Badly infected leaves yellow and die. The fungus may also girdle the stem close to the soilline, killing seedlings and causing mature plants to fall over. Tools, insects, and splashed water spread the spores.

The fungus overwinters on seed, in diseased plant refuse, and in the soil, where it can persist for three years. In the fall, clean up all dead plants and burn, discard, or compost them in a hot pile. Grow eggplant in three-year rotations with other crops. Check seed catalogs for resistant varieties, which include 'Florida Beauty', 'Florida Market', and 'Florida High Bush'.

Chapter 6

Life with Legumes
Peas and Beans

Problems with Peas

Succession-Planted Peas

Q. Every year my pea crop seems to mature all at once. Many of the peas get big and starchy before I can pick them. Can I make succession plantings to lengthen the pea season?

A. Succession planting works well for peas only where summers are cool. Where summers are hot, later plantings will either catch up with earlier ones or the blossom-set will be poor and pods will dry up in the heat.

Instead, try planting several varieties with different maturity dates. 'Alaska', 'Maestro', and 'Sparkle' all begin bearing in about 55 days. Burpee's 'Blue Bantam' matures about 10 days later and will produce over a long period if the pods are kept picked. (All varieties should be picked every day for maximum production.) 'Wando' tolerates hot weather better than most varieties. It begins to bear 64 to 68 days after planting.

Fall for These Peas

Q. I garden in New Jersey. Last July I planted peas for a fall crop, but because of the heat, they didn't grow or produce well. Are there certain varieties to plant for late peas?

A. 'Wando' is a good choice because it is both heat- and cold-resistant. 'Perfection Dark Green' is another heat-tolerant variety. Plant breeder Dr. G. A. Marx of the New York State Agricultural Experiment Station in Geneva recommends edible-podded peas because you can begin eating the tiny pods as soon as they form, rather than waiting for the peas to develop inside. Another consideration in choosing a variety is disease resistance, especially to powdery mildew, which thrives under the cool, moist nights and hot days typical of late summer. 'Grenadier' is a good fall variety because it is resistant to powdery mildew.

The planting date for the best crop of fall peas is fairly critical. If planted too late, the flowers may be killed by frost. But if you plant too early, blossom set will be poor due to the heat. Estimate the ideal sowing time by noting days to maturity on the seed packet (the shorter a season the variety requires, the better) and then by counting backwards from your average first-frost date. Add a few extra days to account for the shorter days and cool fall temperatures. In your area, you should plant no later than the first week in August. Keep the peas well watered, and apply a heavy mulch so the soil will stay cool and moist.

Deep Worries

Q. My 'Sugar Snap' peas germinate poorly—only 60 percent of my seeds come up. Could I be planting too deeply?

A. Yes. At least 80 percent of your pea seeds should germinate, but planting too deeply could reduce the percentage significantly. Dr. Robert Becker, horticulturist at the New York State Agricultural Experiment Station in Geneva, recommends planting the seed no more than ½ to ¾ inch deep. He explains that edible-podded pea seed is smaller than English pea seed, so it has less food reserve and therefore tends to rot a little more easily if planted too deeply. Seed that is more than three years old is likely to germinate poorly.

Cowpea Curculio

Q. Every summer most of my Southern peas have little worms in them. What are they, and how can I eliminate them?

A. The worms are larvae of the cowpea curculio, a ¼-inch-long black beetle with numerous puncture marks on its humped back. Females lay eggs in the pods throughout the summer, and the larvae feed in the developing peas. The curculios also feed on related legumes, strawberries, and cotton. When disturbed, adult curculios drop to the ground and hide under litter, making them difficult to control with insecticides.

You probably won't be able to eliminate the pests from your garden, but you can reduce the number of wormy Southern peas (cowpeas) by planting resistant varieties such as 'Mississippi Shipper', 'Zipper Cream', and 'Freezergreen'. These varieties have thick, fibrous pod walls that resist puncture by the curculios. The heirloom variety 'Blue Goose' is also said to be resistant. To further control the pests, rotate crops and clean up debris in and around the garden after harvest to reduce overwintering areas for the adults.

Powdery Peas

Q. Last summer my peas were covered with a white, powdery coating. What was it, and how can I keep it from coming back this year?

A. Your peas had powdery mildew, a fungal disease that attacks many of the older home-garden varieties. Peas can become infected early in the season, but the disease usually strikes later, during the warmer and drier weather that favors its growth. The fungus is most common on mature vines whose productivity has declined. Pull up infected vines and compost them, or plow them under to control the disease. If younger plants are attacked, dust or spray with wettable sulfur. Some resistant pea varieties are 'Knight', 'Grenadier', 'Maestro', 'Olympia', and 'Mayfair'. Check seed catalogs for others.

Diseased Peas

Q. **For the third year in a row, the leaves on my peas turned yellow and died, starting at the bottom of the plant, and the pods were shorter than normal when they matured. Can you tell me what causes this?**

A. Several soilborne fungal diseases cause peas to become yellow and stunted. Plants infected with fusarium wilt (caused by *Fusarium oxysporum*) have downward-curling leaves, and if you split the stem lengthwise near the base, you'll see an orange to red discoloration. Various root rots attack peas, causing the lower stems and roots to turn brown or black. Seed catalogs list pea varieties with resistance to *F. oxysporum*. There are no varieties resistant to root rot (which can persist in soil for ten years or more); however, 'Wando' is said to be tolerant of *F. solani*, one of the most common rot organisms. Use five-year rotations and keep the soil well drained and aerated by adding plenty of organic matter to reduce infection.

If your peas showed no signs of disease, hot weather may have killed the plants before they could produce a full crop. Planting earlier will solve this problem.

Baffling Beans

What's the Right Dose?

Q. **Should I inoculate beans every time I plant?**

A. Yes. Rodale researchers recommend that you inoculate with each planting. Inoculant is made of rhizobial bacteria, which live on the roots of beans and peas and supply the plants with nitrogen. Inoculant is inexpensive, and it's insurance that your plants will be able to benefit from rhizobial nitrogen fixation. The commonly sold garden inoculant is good for green beans and related dry beans, scarlet runner beans, peas, and lima beans. There is also an inoculant for peanuts. Cowpea inoculant works just as well for adzuki and mung beans. Where cowpeas are commonly grown, you should be able to find the right inoculant at farm supply stores. Those stores often sell soybean inoculant also. Favas require their own inoculant.

Giving Treated Seeds the Treatment

Q. Can I use *Rhizobium* legume inoculant on treated seeds?

A. Fungicides, such as captan, used to treat seeds are toxic to *Rhizobium* bacteria. If you must use treated seeds, sprinkle inoculant into the furrow before planting the seeds. Roots will be colonized by the bacteria when they grow beyond the treated seed coat.

Is the Captan OK?

Q. This year I ordered some bean seed and noticed that it was treated with the fungicide captan. Is there a health question about using these seeds? Where can I get untreated seed?

A. Yes, there may be a risk in handling seeds treated with captan. Although not highly toxic, captan is known to be carcinogenic. Related to thalidomide, it has also caused birth defects and genetic damage in laboratory animals. Since you already have treated seed, wear heavy gloves when planting (captan can cause a skin irritation). Wash your skin and the gloves immediately afterward. The fungicide on the sown seeds will break down in several weeks. For other reasons not to use captan on legumes, see "Giving Treated Seeds the Treatment," above.

Untreated seed is widely available. Many of the major seed companies sell it. Most companies that treat their seed will sell you untreated seed if you request it. The advantage of treated seed is that, unlike untreated seed, it can lie in cold, wet soil without rotting. But since all beans require a soil temperature of at least 60°F in order to germinate, there's no disadvantage in waiting until the soil is warm enough before planting untreated seed.

Fishy Beans

Q. Why do my 'Blue Lake Bush' green beans curl up as they grow instead of forming straight pods?

A. Your beans produce curled pods because they are not getting enough water. Under hot, dry conditions, curled pods (called fishhooks) and pods with seeds that don't mature to fill out the pod (called polliwogs) can develop. 'Blue Lake Bush' green beans are bred for cool, moist conditions, with daytime temperatures of 85°F and 50°F at night. They need at least an inch of water every week. Curled pods are not unique to 'Blue Lake Bush' green beans, however. All beans can develop fishhooks or polliwogs if stressed.

Snap Beans

Picking Primer

Q. Can I increase my bean yields by picking the pods a certain way? My wife claims that if you allow the stem ends to remain on the vines, you'll get a higher yield.

A. Dr. Mike Dickson, a snap bean breeder at New York State Agricultural Experiment Station, says it's not *how* but *how often* you pick beans that counts. Picking the pods while they're young keeps the plants productive. Pick when they are the width of a pencil and the seeds are barely visible. Letting beans grow past that stage puts the plants' energy into seed rather than flower production, and it's the flowers that give you more beans.

Blistering Beans

Q. When is the best time to water to keep my beans from blistering?

A. Blisters—brown, papery spots on the pods and leaves of your beans—are burns due to sunlight magnified by drops of water. The best way to avoid this is to water the soil, not the plants. A drip irrigation system will keep your beans burn-free. If you do use a hose or other overhead system, water early in the morning so the droplets on the plant will have evaporated by the time the sun is strong enough to cause a problem. If the sun comes up hot where you live, you can water in the early evening. But water early enough so the leaves dry before nightfall. If the leaves stay moist through the night, they'll provide the perfect environment for diseases to develop.

Pooped-Out Limas

Q. I've direct-seeded two varieties of 'Fordhook' pole limas the past two springs with poor results. One set only a few pods, and the other produced pods that didn't fill out. Any suggestions?

A. The problem is most likely due to excessive heat, according to lima breeder Dr. Vernon Fisher. While limas require warm temperatures to set pods, if it's above 80°F for more than 12 hours a day, the pollen die, and beans won't form. Baby limas and 'Fordhook' varieties like '242' and 'Concentrator' (both bush types) are less finicky, but Fisher suggests planting all other 'Fordhook' varieties no later than the end of May. Even though the plants won't set many beans during midsummer, they'll be sturdy enough to survive and should produce a satisfactory fall crop.

Soybean Subtleties

Q. What is the difference between edible soybeans and field soybeans?

A. Edible soybeans produce green, black, or yellow seeds that are usually larger and more tender than the small, hard, yellow seeds produced by field soybeans. The most popular of the edible types are the green-seeded vegetable soybeans, which were developed for use in the greenshell stage, though they can also be eaten as dry beans. Because of their more tender texture, vegetable soybeans are easier to cook than field types. They're also milder, sweeter, and more digestible, says Dr. Yun-tzu Kiang, a soybean breeder at the University of New Hampshire. Field soybeans have a strong, disagreeable flavor and contain a higher percentage of indigestible, gas-producing starches than vegetable soybeans. The nutritional value of field and vegetable soybeans is about the same.

Growing Garbanzos

Q. After frost last September here in Utah, our garbanzo beans were still green and had flowers and pods. Should the beans be picked green and then dried, or should they dry on the vine?

A. Garbanzo beans are usually allowed to dry on the vine, but the growing season in your area may be too short or too cool and moist to mature a crop in the field. In a hot, dry climate, most garbanzo beans mature in 115 to 120 days, says U.S. Department of Agriculture (USDA) plant geneticist Dr. Frederick J. Muehlbauer, who works with this crop in eastern Washington. In a cooler, damper climate, the same varieties may take 140 to 150 days because the plants remain vegetative longer. They develop beans, but the crop won't dry. If you want dry garbanzos, you may have to pick the pods as they fill out or pull the plants late in the season (they're very tolerant of frost) and dry them on wire racks or in a dehydrator. The beans have reached full size if you can feel them when you squeeze the puffy pods. The variety 'U.C.-5' is said to be adapted to shorter, cooler growing seasons.

However, it isn't necessary to wait for the beans to mature—they're very good eaten in the greenshell stage, when they can be cooked like peas. Though not as sweet as peas, they are sweeter and much less starchy than mature garbanzo beans, and they have the distinctive garbanzo flavor, says Muehlbauer. His favorite way to eat garbanzos is to pull a plant, then shell and eat the young beans right in the field.

Adzuki Beans

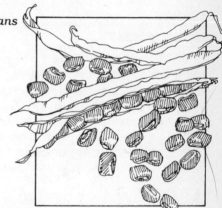

Harvesting Adzukis

Q. I'm growing adzuki beans this year. A few of the pods have dried on the vine and are shattering, but most are still green. How can I simplify harvesting—I don't want to go down the rows five or six times.

A. Most varieties of adzuki bean tend to ripen over a longer period than other dry beans. They also shatter more easily. If you want to harvest just once, wait until most of the pods have turned brown. You'll just have to sacrifice a few immature and shattered pods. Pull the entire plants and hang them in a warm, dry place.

Sprouting Mung Beans

Q. I would like to grow mung beans for sprouting. Can you tell me how to grow them and where I can purchase seeds?

A. Mung beans grow best in hot, dry weather. Maturity dates will vary with the climate. In Oklahoma, where mung beans are grown commercially and the weather is ideal, they mature in 70 days. In cooler or wetter weather, they can take as long as 95 to 100 days to mature. Mung beans can be grown as far north as Maine— though you can't expect a crop every year. Johnny's Selected Seeds of Albion, Maine, lists 130 days to maturity for northern gardeners.

Warm, sandy soils are best, but it's possible to bring in a crop in any well-drained soil. Plant the mung beans 6 to 8 inches apart after the soil warms up. Mung beans are untouched by Mexican bean beetles, which attack many other garden beans. Harvest the mature beans when the plants have died back. The pods will be slightly curved and the beans will appear olive green. They will mature at different rates. To avoid a low yield, watch the pods and pick the beans as they ripen. Once the pods get too dry, they burst open and scatter the beans on the ground.

Tepary Beans

Q. We are experimenting with arid-land crops. How do I grow tepary beans?

A. Plant the beans 2 inches deep and 2 to 3 inches apart in rows 18 to 24 inches wide after danger of frost has passed. The seeds germinate quickly and don't need irrigation. These beans do well in arid climates, producing four times as much as other beans. Teparies need little care—just shallow cultivation to control weeds until the blooms appear. The beans will mature in 60 to 70 days. The small, white teparies resemble navy beans and are native to northern Mexico, Arizona, New Mexico, and Texas.

A Bean Beetle Predator

Q. Last year my beans were destroyed by Mexican bean beetles. What's the best way to control them?

A. A small imported predatory wasp, called *Pediobus foveolatus,* is your best bet against Mexican bean beetles. Studies in Maryland and Florida found these wasps to be extremely effective against the beetles in commercial bean fields. And Dr. Robert Schroder of the USDA's Beneficial Insect Introduction Laboratory claims the wasps also work in home gardens.

When adult beetles start eating holes in your bean leaves, they're preparing to lay eggs. Then is the time to place your orders for wasps. The unhatched wasps will arrive as "mummies" (parasitized larvae of the beetles). If the mummies arrive before your bean beetle larvae are ¼ inch long, they may be held for several days outside in a cool, sheltered place (keep the lid on the container).

The nonstinging wasps lay their eggs in the beetles' larvae. The young wasps kill the larvae by eating their way out. The wasps complete a life cycle every two weeks, so there may be as many as six cycles before they're killed by frost. The wasp is not a native and can't live through the winter in most areas, so you need to release them each season. Control without predators may be achieved with extremely conscientious handpicking and with rotenone or pyrethrum sprays.

Chewing a Blue Hairstreak

Q. A ½-inch, slightly fuzzy, yellow-green caterpillar has been chewing round holes in my green beans. What is the culprit, and how can I combat it?

A. The caterpillar is the larva of the cotton square borer, also called the gray hairstreak butterfly. It is found throughout North America. The adult is blue-gray with black and orange spots and two "tails" on each hindwing. The wingspan is about 1 inch. There are two or more generations each year.

Besides beans and cotton, the caterpillars feed on apple, citrus, and several wild plants. They're seldom numerous enough to cause serious crop losses. Handpick or spray with *Bacillus thuringiensis* (Bt), a widely available biocide, according to package directions.

Weevils Hot, Weevils Cold

Q. How can I prevent bean weevils from getting into beans I grow for drying?

A. Bean weevils lay eggs on maturing bean pods in fall. Spraying with rotenone in early September will help reduce the number of egg-laying adults but will not give total control, says Dr. Art Muka, an entomologist at Cornell University. Usually only about 1 to 2 percent of the beans are infested with eggs when they come out of the field, and few adults or larvae come in with the harvest, says Muka. But if the beans are stored at room temperature, the eggs will hatch, and the weevils will grow and reproduce as long as there are beans to feed on.

Either heating or chilling the beans directly after harvest will prevent most weevil damage. To kill the pests with heat, place shelled beans in a layer 1 inch deep on a cookie sheet, heat in the oven at 120°F for 20 minutes, and then store the beans in airtight containers in a cool place. Alternatively, store the shelled beans in airtight containers in the freezer. Two weeks at −10°F will kill the weevils.

Slugging
the Slugs on Beans

Q. Last year my green beans were full of round holes, although the leaves didn't seem to be affected. I couldn't find the culprits. Any ideas?

A. Slugs probably chewed holes in your beans. You won't catch them in the act because they're nocturnal, but you might notice slime trails near the holes. You can handpick them within three hours of dawn and after dusk, when they're most active. Because they suffer from a "Dracula complex" (avoiding light), they seek out cool, moist, dark conditions, according to Dr. David Rollo, a biologist at McMaster University in Ontario. Don't mulch your beans until the average temperature is above 60° to 70°F (the ideal range for slugs), and break up soil clods, which they like to hide under. Surround the plants with a band of diatomaceous earth—the sharp crystals will pierce their soft bodies and dehydrate them.

Bean Mold

Q. The stems of my bush beans acquire a moist fungus that kills the plants at the peak of production. What is it, and how can I control it?

A. The fungus is most likely white mold (*Sclerotinia sclerotiorum*, also known as cottony rot). Plants usually look water-soaked at first and later become covered with a white fungus. At the end of summer, you'll often find black sclerotinia (the overwintering stage) about the size of a small pea on the plants or soil surface. Potatoes, peppers, lettuce, carrots, crucifers, and cucurbits are also susceptible.

Since the disease overwinters in the soil, Dr. Robert Carroll, a plant pathologist at the University of Delaware, suggests planting beans in an area where susceptible crops have not been grown for at least five years. Don't overfertilize with nitrogen, he adds, since the disease tends to attack lush growth. Space the rows 24 to 30 inches apart to provide good air circulation.

Failing with Favas

Q. Here in Florida, my fava bean plants get 8 to 12 inches high, then suddenly turn black and die. New shoots come up but they die, too. What's the problem?

A. Probably a virus, says Dr. Richard Hampton, a virologist at Oregon State University. But, since many viruses produce similar symptoms, it's impossible to say which one your plants have. Fava beans are attacked by about 20 different viruses—more than any other bean, and unfortunately, no resistant strains have yet been developed. However, Hampton adds, you may be able to get a crop by growing favas in fall or late winter in your area. Most viruses are spread by aphids, which are less active during cool weather.

Chapter 7

The Cool Cucurbits
Cucumbers, Squash, and Melons

Close Calls for Cukes

Crazy Cukes

Q. Last year my cucumber plants were healthy, but the fruit was curled up, yellow, and inedible. What went wrong?

A. Water stress often causes poor fruit formation, says Robert Mulrooney, extension pathologist at the University of Delaware. Insufficient pollination is another possibility. If bees aren't visiting the flowers, you could hand-pollinate using a small artist's brush to transfer pollen from male flowers to the stigmas of female flowers. Or plant bee-attracting plants, such as borage, thyme, or buckwheat, nearby.

**Seeing Double
(Cucumbers, That Is)**

Q. This summer I harvested a cucumber that looked like two cucumbers stuck together. Is this common? What happened?

A. "Siamese twin" cucumbers aren't unusual. The fruit of a cucumber is actually a developed ovary (the slightly swollen part beneath the female flower). When you see a double fruit, it means the plant produced a flower with two ovaries fused together. Sometimes there is a double flower as well.

A Case of Cuke Bitters

Q. How can I keep my cucumbers from tasting bitter?

A. Cucurbitacins (compounds found in cucumber leaves, stems, and roots) cause the bitterness. When the plant is stressed by hot, dry weather, cucurbitacins spread into the fruit. Since the bitterness enters through the stem, cutting off some of that end will eliminate most of the off-flavor if you harvest your cukes before they have been stressed for long. If the whole fruit has turned bitter, peeling it can help, because the bitterness is usually concentrated just under the skin.

Some cucumber varieties, such as 'Marketmore 80', have no cucurbitacins and will not turn bitter. Two other varieties with a bitter-free gene are 'County Fair' and 'Spartan Salad'. 'Sweet Slice' and 'Burpless' both produce less bitter cukes, although they don't have the bitter-free gene.

Worn-Out Cukes

Q. I planted a gynoecious (all female-flowered) cucumber along with two regular varieties. After one good picking, the gynoecious variety produced only small, curved cukes. Was poor pollination the cause?

A. The two regular (monoecious) varieties you planted should have ensured good pollination. Most likely, quality declined because the heavy initial fruit load exhausted the plants, says Dr. R. W. Robinson, cucumber breeder at Cornell University.

Because every flower can produce a fruit, gynoecious cucumbers need extra care for sustained yields. Dig plenty of manure or compost into the hills and space plants generously. Keep the soil moist all season. After fruit set, begin feeding with manure tea or fish emulsion to stimulate new vegetative growth. Pick the fruits young—once the seed coat hardens, the plants are much less likely to go on producing.

Sorting Out Squash,
Pumpkin, and Gourd Problems

Mystery Squash

Q. Last summer one of my 'Early Prolific Straightneck' yellow squash produced fruits with light green flesh and skin. Could this be a mutation?

A. It's unlikely that your green squash was produced through a mutation, according to Dr. Dean Knavel, cucurbit breeder and vegetable crops specialist at the University of Kentucky. Most probably, a seed from a green variety, such as 'Senator', was accidentally packaged with the 'Early Prolific Straightneck' seed.

Baby Zukes

Q. My first hybrid zucchini of the season grew about 3 inches long and then rotted. Later in the season, I got a bountiful harvest of normal-size fruit. Why?

A. Your early zucchini were produced from unpollinated female flowers. The blossoms of most zucchini hybrids are all female when plants first flower, explains Dr. Henry Munger, noted squash breeder at Cornell University. He recommends picking the tender young zucchini as soon as possible after the flowers open. Male flowers, which (unlike the females) have no swelling beneath them, should begin to appear within several weeks and will pollinate the females, so you can let later-developing zucchini grow as large as you like.

No Zukes

Q. Last year our zucchini squash produced lovely orange blossoms but no fruit. Where did we go wrong?

A. Squash does not set fruit when the blossoms aren't pollinated. Normally, bees carry the pollen from male to female squash flowers. But if it is too early in the season, or if your area's bee population has been decimated by pesticides, the female blossoms will wither without being pollinated. After two days, a deformed miniature squash forms. If this happens, pick the fruit immediately and compost it. Otherwise, it will drain energy from the plant.

X-Rated Seeds

Q. **We would like to use sunflower and pumpkin seeds toasted and salted, but can't find any varieties that produce hull-less seeds. Have you heard of any?**

A. Yes, but only in pumpkins. Harris' 'Lady Godiva' variety produces small pumpkins with "naked" seeds. They have no hulls and thus do not require shelling. Sorry, no hull-less sunflower seeds yet.

Bitter Pumpkins

Q. **Our 'Small Sugar' pumpkins were so bitter that we had to compost them. We planted them in March here in California and harvested after they turned orange in July. What happened?**

A. Slow growth caused by drought or insufficient nitrogen can concentrate strong flavors and lower production of sugars that normally mask bitterness, says Dr. Dean Knavel of the University of Kentucky. Water pumpkins regularly and work in manure or compost to provide slow-release nitrogen and moisture-holding organic matter.

Pumpkins need a long season of warm, sunny weather to develop high sugar content. Plant your next crop in May to mature in September, and don't harvest until the rind resists puncturing with your thumbnail, suggests Dennis Pittenger, extension urban horticulture specialist at the University of California.

Pumpkins and Corn

Q. **I planted 'Triple Treat' pumpkins in the rows of corn in my Indiana garden. They blossomed, but not one pumpkin grew. What went wrong?**

A. The most likely reason your vines didn't produce pumpkins is lack of pollination, suggests Dr. Dean Knavel of the University of Kentucky. Honeybees are generally active only between 70° and 90°F. Daytime temperatures in your area were probably in the 90s by the time the pumpkins began to flower, and they would have been even higher between the rows of corn. Since shading can also affect fruit set, interplanting pumpkins with corn should be more successful if the pumpkin seed is planted as early as possible (or even started indoors) and the corn sown several weeks later.

Drying Luffa Gourds

Q. **My wife and I grew a great crop of luffa gourds this year, but we can't find any information on how to dry them.**

A. If you want to dry luffas for sponges, place boards or something similar under the developing gourds to keep them dry. Harvest each gourd when the stem turns yellow and the skin starts to lose its green color. Green skin gives a tender sponge, but very yellow luffas are too wiry.

Cut the gourds from the vines. Slice off the larger end and shake out the seeds. Dry until the skin hardens and browns— about two weeks. Then soak the sponges overnight or longer, until you can peel the outer skin off easily in large pieces. Stand the sponges in the sun or in a well-ventilated place to dry again for several days. Then they'll be ready to use.

If you'd rather process them immediately, you can obtain a softer sponge by boiling the harvested gourds in water for several minutes. Remove the outer skin, wash out the center, remove tissues and seeds, and dry gradually in a shady place.

Gourd Birdhouse

Homegrown Birdhouses

Q. Last year I harvested only two large birdhouse gourds, and both had rotted where they touched the ground. This spring, I planted a whole packet of seed and none germinated. What am I doing wrong?

A. To keep gourds from rotting, American Gourd Society member Mary Ann Rood suggests either placing boards or straw under the developing fruit, or trellising the vines. Gourd vines usually produce more than two fruits. Perhaps you overfertilized last year, producing lush vines at the expense of flowers. However, if there were many flowers, a lack of pollination by bees could be the problem. Using a paintbrush, you can transfer pollen from the male flowers to the female flowers (the ones with a swelling where the stem meets the blossom). Your gourd seeds may have failed to germinate if you planted them in soil that was too cold. The ideal soil temperature range is between 70° and 95°F. Also, if the seed was stored improperly, it may have lost its viability.

Gourds Eternal

Q. **Is there any way to preserve the color and design on gourds and still dry them out? Mine just turn brown.**

A. Color and design always fade as gourds dry, but you can easily make dried gourds more decorative, according to the American Gourd Society. Enjoy the fresh gourds until the colors begin to fade, then put them aside in a dry place. Wipe off any mold that forms and throw out gourds that shrivel. When the gourds feel light and the seeds rattle, soak them in warm water. Scrape off the softened skins with a knife, then rub the gourds with steel wool and set them aside. When they're dry, sand lightly. You can wax, shellac, paint, or carve the dried gourds, or decorate them with woodburning equipment.

Crossover Cucurbits

Q. **If I plant squash, pumpkins, and watermelons next to each other, will they cross-pollinate? Can I plant different varieties of pumpkin on the same hill?**

A. Basically, squash or pumpkins and watermelon won't cross. Squash and pumpkins, both of the genus *Cucurbita*, will. This cross won't show up in your vegetables the first year, but it will ruin the following year's crop if you plant seeds saved from this year's plants. To keep varieties coming true from seed, separate the squash and pumpkin varieties.

The Great White Worm

Q. **A fat white worm, about ½ inch long, gets into the stems and destroys my squash and melon vines. I read that the organic way to kill the worm is to "search and destroy" with a small knife, but I end up ruining the stem as well. What is this worm and how can I get rid of it?**

A. Your worm is the larval form of the squash vine borer, a large, orange-and-black flying insect in the moth family. It lays eggs on the stems of squash vines. The larvae hatch and burrow into the stems, where they feed. A gummy, sawdustlike substance oozing from holes in stems and leaves near the base of the plant is a sure sign that squash vine borers are at work. Leaves of infested plants will droop severely on sunny days.

Slitting the stems and killing the worms (there may be three or four worms in one tunnel and two or three tunnels per plant) is in fact an effective control. Kill the worms with your knife blade or a piece of wire, then bandage the slit with tape. Other controls that don't require you to slit squash stems are injecting *Bacillus thuringiensis* (Bt), a caterpillar-killing biocide, or predatory nematodes into the base of affected stems.

Another preventive measure is to pinch off the growing point while the plant is young and before the borers attack. That forces the plant to branch out, becoming multistemmed. Then cover the stems with soil as they grow. This encourages the vine to root at the joints from which the leaves grow. Or try a delayed planting, which may miss the egg-laying moth. Earlier plantings (under cloches or spunbonded row covers) can work, too, because the adult borer doesn't begin laying eggs until July, by which time the plants are larger and much more tolerant of attack. When a plant dies, find all the larvae inside and kill them so none overwinter.

Winter squash varieties like 'Hubbard' and most summer squash varieties are severely damaged by attack. 'Baby Blue' and 'Butternut' are somewhat resistant.

Squash Bug

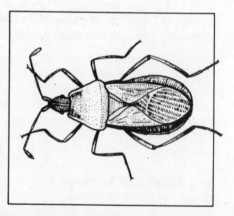

Squash Bug Strategies

Q. Every year I try to grow winter squash, but the plants are always attacked by squash bugs and die before I get any fruit. What can I do?

A. Insecticidal soap works well against squash bugs. The brownish-black, flat-backed adults fly into gardens in late spring or early summer. They suck the juices out of cucurbit leaves, causing them to wilt and turn blackish-green. After mating, the females lay yellowish-gold eggs on the undersides of squash leaves in geometric patterns. Within a few hours, the eggs darken to a bronze-brown. Green nymphs with crimson legs hatch in 5 to 14 days. They have voracious appetites and generally feed in groups.

Keep a hand-sprayer filled with insecticidal soap handy. Check the plants daily and spray the adults at their first appearance in spring. Continue watching for and spraying adults and nymphs through the season. The eggs won't be affected by the soap, so "squash" them between two hard surfaces. If you move quickly, you can also handpick or crush the adults and young. Avoid deep, cool mulches like straw and hay, which provide a refuge for the insects. After the harvest, burn or compost vines to help rid the garden of shelters for breeding and overwintering.

Banishing Mildew

Q. Every year I lose squash, pumpkin, and cucumber plants to powdery mildew. How can I curb the disease?

A. First, plant resistant or tolerant varieties. Resistant cucumbers are widely available. The zucchini varieties 'Zucchini Select' and 'Ambassador' are mildew-tolerant. There are no resistant winter squash or pumpkins, but squash like hubbard and buttercup are somewhat more mildew-tolerant than pumpkins, according to Dr. Brent Loy, a cucurbit breeder at the University of New Hampshire. In a small planting, you can slow or stop the spread of powdery mildew by pruning infected leaves as soon as the disease appears, says Loy. Don't crowd the plants, and make sure they're well fed and watered to reduce stress and stimulate early fruiting.

Researchers in Japan found that baking-soda sprays, applied weekly at the rate of a scant teaspoon of baking soda per quart of water, controlled powdery mildew on cucumbers and other crops. In the experiments, the baking soda both prevented infection by mildew spores and stopped development of the disease when it was present in an early stage.

Bringing Up Melons

Hot Soil, More Melons

Q. Cantaloupes don't yield well in my Harrisburg, Pennsylvania, garden. Do you think a black plastic mulch would help?

A. Yes. Melons need warm soil to grow well. Researchers at Virginia Tech found that melons direct-seeded through black plastic yielded earlier and twice as heavily as those planted in bare soil. The plants in the plastic mulch plots also grew faster and began running much sooner. Fruit size and flavor were identical. Black plastic absorbs heat from the sun, holds it in at night, keeps down weeds, and retains soil moisture. Clear plastic does a better job of soil heating, but weed seeds sprout. In the tests, using transplants rather than direct-seeding provided earlier fruits but didn't increase overall yield.

Bland Cantaloupes

Q. **I garden in Florida. My cantaloupes grow vigorously and produce good-looking fruits, but they taste bland, not sweet. Why?**

A. High rainfall during ripening can cause bland fruit, but sweetness is mainly dependent on variety, says Jim Stephens, extension vegetable specialist at the University of Florida. Perhaps the best choice for home gardeners is 'Planter's Jumbo', which combines sweetness and good disease resistance, says Stephens. Of the other varieties recommended by the Florida Extension Service, 'Ambrosia' and 'Smith's Perfect' are very sweet, but they're also susceptible to mildew and other diseases. Less sweet but more disease-resistant and productive are 'Hale's Best Jumbo', 'Edisto 47', and 'Super Market'.

But When Are They Ripe?

Q. **I've read that true cantaloupes like 'Charantais' don't slip from the vine when ripe. How do you know when they're ready to pick?**

A. Harvest 'Charantais' cantaloupes when the skin color at the stem end and in the ribs has changed from pearly gray-green to gold and the fruits have a strong melon fragrance, says Rose Marie Nichols of Nichols Garden Nursery, Albany, Oregon. In addition, the area around the stem will separate slightly and begin to look coarse as the fruit ripens.

Bacterial Wilt Woes

Q. **I have tried to grow cantaloupes without success. Each year beautiful vines grow, then almost overnight wilt and die. Why?**

A. Your melon vines had bacterial wilt. The disease affects all members of the cucumber family and is most common east of the Rockies, but it may also occur from Arizona to Idaho and Washington. Since striped and 12-spotted cucumber beetles spread the disease, control of wilt depends on keeping them off your plants. The bacteria overwinter in the beetles' intestines and are transferred to the plants through their feces. Bacteria enter the plant through wounds like those caused by chewing beetles.

The best protection is to keep the plants covered from settingout to harvest with spunbonded row covers such as Reemay or a tent of fine-mesh cheesecloth. Commercial growers usually plant 10 to 20 percent more cucurbits than they need, because the disease usually affects only a few plants. If you have the space and choose this strategy, simply pull up and compost dying plants. There's no need to burn them.

Melon-Patch Plague

Q. **Every year a disease shrivels my cantaloupes and Crenshaw melons when they're softball size and then kills the vines. My pumpkins develop pits in the skin and rot, but the vines survive. What's the problem?**

A. Dark pits ¼ to 2 inches across on fruits and rapidly spreading yellow or brown spots that kill foliage or leave ragged holes are symptoms of anthracnose, a fungal disease that thrives during wet summers in the East. Watermelons, cucumbers, muskmelons, and gourds are much more susceptible to the disease than pumpkins and squash. Anthracnose overwinters on dead plants, so burn all infected crop residues. Destroy wild cucumbers near the garden. Spores of the fungus are spread by insects, gardeners, and splashing water. Grow cucurbits on trellises to keep the vines and fruit dry. Control insect pests and don't work among the plants in wet weather. Also, purchase and plant resistant varieties.

Cracking Crenshaws

Q. **I like to grow Crenshaw melons, but eight out of ten crack before they are ripe. Why? How can I keep them from cracking?**

A. Crenshaws are most likely to crack when heavy rain or irrigation follows a dry spell, so the best control is to maintain even soil moisture levels through the growing season. According to Ted Torrey, director of vegetable research for W. Atlee Burpee Co., susceptibility to cracking is a genetic trait of the Crenshaw melon, and no resistant variety has been developed. Torrey recommends using black plastic to conserve moisture, control weeds, and ensure the warm soil temperatures required to grow 'Crenshaw' melons. However, you can use any mulch if you wait to apply it until early summer, when the soil has warmed.

Hollow-Hearted Melons

Q. How can I control hollow heart in my watermelons?

A. Hollow heart, characterized by a cavity at the center of the fruit, is a genetic trait, says Dr. J. D. Norton, a fruit breeder at Auburn University. You can eliminate the problem by planting varieties that don't get the disorder, such as 'Crimson Sweet', a large, early, disease-resistant variety that is widely available, or the small icebox-type watermelons 'Mickylee' and 'Minilee'. If you save seeds from your own crop, you may gradually be able to eliminate the trait by planting only seeds from fruits that don't have hollow heart.

Blossom-End Rot

Q. For the past several years my watermelons have had blossom-end rot. What can be done?

A. Blossom-end rot first appears as a water-soaked area at the end of the fruit. The area will appear dark and will spread until the fruit begins to ripen. As the patch grows, the fruit tissue shrinks and becomes dry and leathery. Bacteria and fungi may grow on the decay, causing rot or mold.

Water stress or calcium deficiency can cause blossom-end rot. Test the soil for calcium deficiency. Calcium is not available to the plants at a low pH. Watermelons prefer a soil pH of 5.5 to 6.0, but will tolerate a range from pH 5.0 to 8.0. To correct for low calcium, add lime. Dolomitic limestone is a good source, and it also supplies magnesium, an essential nutrient for watermelons. If you want to plant a watermelon crop this year, use a fine grade of limestone. The finer the limestone, the faster it breaks down in the soil and the more it raises the pH and provides calcium. For example, 100-

mesh-size particles are extremely fine, so the calcium should be available within two weeks. Most of the calcium in 40-mesh particles will become available in about a year. The grade of limestone is usually marked on the bag.

If your calcium level is OK, water stress is the problem. Watermelons need a steady supply of water, ideally an inch a week. Periods of drought or heavy rain can cause blossom-end rot. Plenty of organic matter in the soil and mulching will help maintain even soil moisture.

Chapter 8

Some Like It Not

Asparagus, Rhubarb, Cabbage, and Other Cool-Weather Crops

Cool-Weather Crop Queries

Cool Crops, Hot Weather

Q. What can be done to prevent beets, chard, Chinese cabbage, and radishes from bolting in the late spring?

A. These vegetables are basically cool-weather crops with a tendency to bolt, or go to seed, as the weather warms and the days lengthen. To get the most from these crops, always choose varieties that produce well at the time of year you want to plant them. (For instance, if you plant Chinese cabbage in spring, don't choose a variety that has been bred for fall planting.) Look for varieties that are bolt-resistant. A good technique for spring planting is to provide shade as the weather gets warmer, mulch heavily, and use floating row covers or lath, or sow on the north side of a building.

Halloween Planting
Scares Up Spring Harvest

Q. Our garden is in Iowa. What vegetables can we plant in October that will be ready to harvest next spring?

A. Northern gardeners can harvest an early spring crop of spinach, lettuce, kale, garlic, parsley, and chervil if they make their last plantings just before the cold weather hits. Protect young plants with a coldframe or thick mulch throughout the winter, and remove this protection when soil temperatures reach 40°F. Water the plants well. Southern gardeners can sow those crops throughout the winter, too. In addition, they can plant brassicas, fava beans, and peas for an extra-early spring harvest.

About Asparagus

The Crowning Touch

Q. Can you tell me how to grow asparagus crowns from seed sown outdoors?

A. Sow the seed 1½ inches deep and 2 inches apart in loose, well-drained soil in late April or early May. At soil temperatures of 70° to 75°F, emergence will begin in 10 to 20 days. When the plants are up, mulch to control weeds and keep the soil moist through the summer. After frost kills the tops, mound 3 or 4 inches of soil over the crowns to prevent freezing and waterlogging. Mulch after the ground freezes. Transplant the crown in spring about the time you set out tomato plants.

Asparagus Overhaul

Q. We are wondering how to handle our six-year-old asparagus patch, which is producing less each year. We have many pencil-size shoots and a few good thick spears. When should asparagus be cut down, in summer or fall? Should the berries be allowed to develop?

A. If you take good care of your asparagus bed, it will keep producing. Some asparagus beds are reported to be in good production more than 100 years after the original bed was established.

First, never cut the growth down in the summer or fall. Asparagus shoots grow on the energy stored in the roots by this growth during the summer, fall, and even winter. Even though the tops may look dead in fall, they are storing energy for better production next spring. In the early spring or the very end of winter, break off the dead topgrowth and add it to your compost pile. Berries should be allowed to mature on the plants. If you have too many new plants starting from the dropped berries, thin them out each year, but allow some new plants to become established and replace older plants.

A deficiency of phosphorus or potassium could be responsible for asparagus decline if you aren't feeding your patch. To combat this, you should apply a winter mulch of about 3 inches of aged manure and some compost. In the spring, after harvesting, each plant should receive a good feeding with an organic fertilizer, because the summer growth will determine how good next year's spears will be. A good organic mixture for asparagus is three parts greensand, one part dried blood or two parts cottonseed meal, and one part bonemeal. Apply this mixture at the rate of about 2 pounds per 50 square feet of bed space. This combination of a winter manure mulch and a localized late-spring feeding will give your plants both the fast-acting nutrients they need for topgrowth in summer and slow-release nutrients during the rest of the year.

Last, you should give the bed a good cultivation before harvest in spring. Apply 4 to 6 inches of a mulch that's neutral in pH, like hay or straw, during the summer to preserve moisture, keep down weeds, and prevent too many new plants from getting established. Asparagus prefers a pH of 6.5 to 7.5 (neutral is 7.0). Shallow plantings can also cause poor growth. Set crowns at least 6 inches deep.

Florida Spears

Q. I've recently moved to central Florida from Michigan. Can I expect homegrown asparagus like we had back home?

A. Yes, you can grow asparagus, but expect lower yields than you got from your Michigan garden. To produce long, thick spears, the plant needs to store carbohydrates. In the North, the plant produces and stores carbohydrates during the summer for the following spring. During the winter, cold temperatures cause the plant to go dormant. But in the South, asparagus stores fewer carbohydrates because the plant uses them more rapidly in the hotter weather. That means less energy is available for the following spring's surge of growth. Although the winters are cold enough to bring on dormancy, Florida also experiences sudden warm spells when the plants will break dormancy. Small shoots appear, which are then killed as the temperature drops to freezing again. This continual shoot production wastes carbohydrates that might have gone into lush spring spear growth.

Bugged by Asparagus Beetles

Q. **Last spring, whenever I went out to pick my asparagus, the tips were covered with asparagus beetles. What can I do to keep them from destroying the spears this year?**

A. If your planting is recent, take heart: Beetle damage is usually less serious in older beds. Both the common and the spotted asparagus beetles overwinter as adults in the stems of asparagus plants, under tree bark, and in garden debris. The most important way to control them is to scrupulously remove all the mulch and dead plant material from the garden in the fall.

Common asparagus beetles are found east of the Mississippi and north of North Carolina. Eggs are laid in April or May, soon after the adults emerge. Young asparagus shoots are sometimes blackened with tiny eggs standing on end. Within a week, the grayish, sluglike larvae hatch and begin feeding on the asparagus tips. They eat for two weeks, pupate, and emerge as adults a week or two later. There are two to five generations per season.

Handpicking is not effective for these beetles, since the adults fall to the ground when disturbed, and the young have usually done their damage by the time you notice them. You should pull out all volunteer plants and cut the shoots close to the ground every day to remove the eggs before the larvae can establish themselves. If you cleaned up the beds the previous autumn, gauze netting supported on a framework or spunbonded row covers will also give good control; however, you must put it up before egg laying begins. Rotenone controls the beetles, but we recommend it only as a last resort because it also kills ladybug larvae and chalcid wasps, important predators of the asparagus beetle.

The spotted asparagus beetle's range and life history are similar, but the greenish eggs hatch a little later and the orange larvae bore into and feed strictly on the berries. Only the adults, which are tan with 12 prominent spots, damage the spears. The insect can be controlled by removing and destroying the berries that form on the fernlike fronds of the female asparagus plants. The berries are green, later turning red.

Bedridden Asparagus

Q. **My first asparagus bed died out after ten years. The new one is four years old, but the spears are pencil-thin and the plants grow only 18 inches tall. The crowns are brownish. Could this be the problem?**

A. Fusarium crown rot is the most common reason for poor results in asparagus that is given proper care. "Almost all asparagus gets it eventually," says Dr. Stephen Garrison, an asparagus specialist at Rutgers University. Plants that are otherwise healthy can stay ahead of the disease for several years, then decline slowly. This is probably what happened to your first, and now your second, planting. Brown or yellow tissue on the crown (it should be white) indicates crown rot. Buy only certified disease-free crowns. The main home-garden varieties, 'Mary Washington' and 'Martha Washington', are very susceptible to fusarium, but two new hybrids, 'Jersey Giant' and 'Greenwich', are resistant.

Asparagus Wilt

Q. **Our asparagus spears came up this year looking strong and healthy—at first. Then they started to get limp and wilted. It was just a matter of days until this wilt progressively hit each stalk after it reached about 3 inches tall. This has been happening for three years now. What's going on?**

A. Stunting and yellowing or wilting are symptoms of asparagus wilt or root rot caused by fungi like *Fusarium* and *Verticillium*. These fungi invade the roots and stems of plants, interfering with the upward movement of water. In effect, the plant is dying of clogged arteries.

These fungi build up in infested soil where asparagus is established or where an old asparagus bed has been plowed under in recent years. After the asparagus dies, the fungi produce masses of spores that may live on humus in the soil for several years. As a result, seedlings that are grown nearby may be killed in great numbers.

The only way to "cure" the diseased section of your garden is to remove and destroy your asparagus planting. For your next asparagus bed, start with certified disease-free plants and put them as far from the old bed as possible. Choose a site with soil that's rich, deep, and well drained.

Rhubarb Right and Wrong

Your First Rhubarb

Q. A friend with a huge rhubarb patch has offered me some plants. How do I transplant them?

A. Dig rhubarb crowns as early as possible in the spring, before they break dormancy, or in the fall before the ground freezes. Divide the crowns, including as much root as possible. Each piece should have at least two large buds. Four to six pieces can usually be split from each crown. Don't allow the divisions to dry out before planting them 2 to 3 inches deep in a well-drained location.

Rhubarbering

Q. Should I cut the leaves off rhubarb in the fall?

A. Don't be too anxious to cut them. Rhubarb plants manufacture carbohydrates all summer, taking in sunlight and carbon dioxide through their leaves. These nutrients are stored in the root system, providing energy for next year's stalks. When the leaves turn completely brown in fall, you may cut them if they look ugly to you. However, because rhubarb leaves don't harbor diseases, it's not necessary to remove them after they've been killed by frost.

Bolting Rhubarb

Q. What causes rhubarb to bolt?

A. Bolting, or flowering, is a normal part of the rhubarb plant's life cycle, although it may not happen every summer. It is often triggered by stressful conditions, such as hot, dry weather. If a flower stalk appears, pinch or prune it off so the plant's energy will be concentrated on vegetative growth.

Worn-Out Rhubarb

Q. My red rhubarb stalks are small, porous, and tough, and they appear to have sting spots on them. What can be wrong?

A. Your plants may simply be worn out and need dividing, especially if they've been growing in the same location for five years or more. In early spring, dig them up and split the crowns into well-rooted pieces having two or more eyes or buds on each. Cut out any diseased or dead roots. If you replant in a new location, choose a very well drained site where tomatoes, peppers, and strawberries have not been grown for several years. (All these plants can harbor verticillium wilt, which rhubarb might contract if it follows them.) Dig in a few inches of compost, and apply rock fertilizers or bonemeal if necessary. Plant the crowns 2 or 3 inches deep and 3 feet apart, and keep the bed weeded and watered. Begin pulling stalks in the second year.

If the sting spots on the stalks are small, black blotches with holes, they may be egg-laying punctures of the rhubarb curculio—a slow-moving, ½- to ¾-inch-long, snouted black beetle that looks as though it's been dusted with yellow powder. Look for similar spots on the roots and crown. The curculio uses rhubarb only for egg laying. It feeds on a weed, curly dock, to which the larvae also migrate after hatching. Control the insects by handpicking and by eliminating curly dock near the garden.

Brassica Basics

Direct-Seeded Brassicas

Q. Most gardening books suggest starting seeds for plants like broccoli and cauliflower indoors six weeks before the last frost. When should they be planted if I want to sow the seeds outdoors?

A. Broccoli and cauliflower seeds take about 2½ weeks to sprout when the soil temperature an inch deep averages about 50°F, ten days when it is 59°F, and six days when it is 68°F. If you plant them outdoors 2 weeks before the last frost date (about the same time you would set out transplants), the seeds will sprout in about a week. You can plant the seeds outdoors earlier, but they will take longer to germinate. Though outdoor-sown seedlings will grow faster than transplants, they won't catch up with them, so your harvest will mature 2 to 3 weeks later.

Clubroot Clobbers Brassicas

Q. Last year my broccoli, brussels sprouts, cabbage, and cauliflower had clubroot. Can you tell me more about the disease and how to control it?

A. Clubroot is caused by a soilborne fungus that attacks the roots of crucifers, including radishes, turnips, mustard, and the brassicas. Severely infected plants develop large, clublike swellings on the roots, and the stunted, yellowed topgrowth wilts on sunny days. The fungus produces spores inside the clubs, and these are released into the soil when the roots decay. The spores can remain viable for ten years or more.

Because of its persistence and ability to infect plants under a wide range of conditions, clubroot is very difficult to control. There are no resistant brassicas yet available. Raising the soil pH with lime to 7.0 or above can reduce or prevent infection where spore counts are low. (To help keep spore counts low, pull and burn clubbed roots.) Since the lime must be mixed uniformly throughout the root zone to suppress the fungus, this technique works best with sandy or loam soils. Clay and muck soils are well buffered against chemical change, so it takes more lime and often more than one year to raise their pH significantly. Depending on soil type, you may need to add lime every year to maintain a high pH. Your county agent will be able to recommend application rates based on soil test results.

Headless Broccoli

Q. My early broccoli didn't produce heads this spring. Why?

A. Head formation in broccoli (and cauliflower) depends on three factors—cool weather, plenty of water, and adequate calcium. Hot weather, drought, and/or a soil calcium deficiency can all produce nonheading broccoli plants. Broccoli prefers cool temperatures, particularly at night. A sudden hot spell can result in no heads at all or cause the plant to bolt to seed within a few days. Early in the season, broccoli needs at least an inch of rain per week. Broccoli planted for fall harvest needs slightly less water, but the supply must be just as steady. To correct a calcium deficiency, spread crushed limestone over your future broccoli patch in the fall, then till it in.

Buttoned-Up Broccoli

Q. Last year I started seeds of 'Green Comet' broccoli at the end of March and set vigorous transplants into my garden in May. They grew into lush 3-foot specimens, but not one of them produced anything more impressive than a button head. What went wrong?

A. If broccoli plants are exposed to cold weather when very young, they may make small "buttons" (or miniature flower heads) instead of heading up. "Buttoning" can be induced by chronic temperatures of 50° to 55°F or by a few days at 40°F. Seedlings in a cool greenhouse or coldframe are especially susceptible. The ideal range for broccoli transplants is 70°F during the day and 60° to 65°F at night. Once a plant has buttoned, it won't produce a primary head, but it will form an abundance of smaller lateral heads if given good care throughout the summer.

Bugs in Broccoli

Q. My harvested broccoli was full of aphids and worms last fall. How can I keep these pests out of the edible parts of broccoli?

A. Broccoli, like other cole crops, attracts aphids and a variety of worms. The aphids cling to the undersides of leaves and flower heads, stunting plants and killing seedlings. A fine, forceful spray of water from the hose, companion plantings of mint, and finely ground limestone sprinkled over the heads and foliage of broccoli all discourage aphids. For worms, protective netting or spunbonded row covers can keep moths away from plants during their egg-laying cycle, and tilling the soil several times in fall and spring should expose and kill any remaining eggs. *Bacillus thuringiensis* (Bt) also stops cabbageworms ("A Cure for Cabbageworms" on page 123). But no matter how you try, some insects *will* find their way into the kitchen after harvest. Plunging broccoli into warm water with a little white vinegar should float the bugs to the top. Never soak more than 15 minutes. We suggest warm water because hot water will destroy nutrients, and cold water, from experience, doesn't clean as well.

Blowup in Brussels

Q. **Shortly after I topped my brussels sprouts last fall, several of the topmost sprouts on each plant opened and elongated to form new leaders. What caused this?**

A. Topping too early can cause the upper sprouts to "blow up," as commercial growers call the response. To produce a stalk of fairly uniform sprouts for once-over harvest, J. A. Cutcliffe of Agriculture Canada advises eastern Canadian growers to top their plants when the sprouts in the seventh to ninth whorl of leaves from the bottom are about the size of a small pea. At that time, the sprouts at the bottom of the stalk are ½ to ¼ inch in diameter. California growers also top when the lower sprouts are about ¼ inch in diameter. In both cases, the crop is harvested about a month later, yielding sprouts ½ to 1 inch in diameter, the preferred size for freezing.

Cabbages Hate Maples

Q. **Each fall I cover my garden with 10 to 20 inches of leaves, mostly maple. I've had very disappointing yields from all of the cabbage family. Can leaves stunt cabbage?**

A. Yes. Maple leaves contain phenols, which reduce the growth and yields of brassicas and other vegetables by inhibiting root elongation, says Dr. David Hill of the Connecticut Agricultural Experiment Station. Early crops are most vulnerable because the phenols are quickly released when the leaves begin to degrade in spring. Fall crops are usually not affected because most of the phenols have leached by midseason, says Hill. Large quantities of raw leaves can also inhibit growth by tying up nitrogen as they decompose and by keeping the soil too wet, especially if the season is cool and rainy.

You can solve all three problems by composting the leaves for at least nine months before putting them on the garden. In that time the phenols will leach, nitrogen levels will stabilize, and the leaves will degrade into drainage-enhancing humus. Shred the leaves if possible and turn the pile occasionally to keep it hot. A cold, compacted pile may take a year or more to decompose sufficiently.

Saving Cabbage Seed

Q. How do I go about saving seed from cabbage?

A. Cabbages are biennial, flowering the second season, and must be overwintered to set seed. No protection is needed where winter temperatures stay above freezing (32°F). In severe climates, store the plants in pots in a root cellar or in a pit in the garden. When you replant in early spring, cut an inch-deep cross in the top of the head to let the seed stalk come through.

Since some cabbages are self-sterile, plant at least two. If other brassicas (wild mustard, broccoli, cauliflower) are blossoming nearby, you'll need to keep insects off your cabbage flowers. Shield the flower heads with gauze or other fine mesh, and cross-pollinate the plants by hand, using an artist's camel's hair brush. After the flowers have faded, remove the mesh. In 30 to 40 days, the seed-pods will yellow and turn brown, then split and scatter the seed. Since the pods ripen at varying rates, it's best to remove them as they darken. After they've dried, separate seed from the hulls by rubbing the pods over a screen. To prevent seed-transmitted diseases like black rot and blackleg, put the seed in a loosely tied cloth and soak in 112°F water for 30 minutes. Dry the seed thoroughly right away and store in a cool, dry place.

Cabbage Maggot Control

Q. In my Illinois garden, the roots of my cabbage and broccoli are severely attacked by cabbage maggots. Is there some way to rid the soil of them?

A. You can protect brassicas from the egg-laying parent flies by tenting them with fine gauze (at least 20 threads to the inch) tacked to a wooden frame around the bed and supported by wires across the beds at 5-foot intervals. Rodale Research Center tests showed that Reemay, a spunbonded polyester material, is a very effective barrier. Plant crops where brassicas (or their wild relatives like wild mustard) were not grown the previous season, since the insects overwinter in the soil.

About mid-May in your area, the ¼-inch-long adults emerge and fly close to the ground, then lay small white eggs in the soil near the brassica stems. Four-inch tarpaper disks can reduce egg laying in the immediate root zone. Eggs hatch in three to seven days, and the larvae seek out the roots, feeding on them for three to four weeks. Of the three generations per season, the first is the most destructive, since the maggots thrive in cool, moist soil.

A promising new control is Seek, a beneficial nematode that destroys cabbage maggots and other soilborne larvae and remains active in the soil from six months to two years. The nematode comes mixed with cedar shavings. It can be applied as a mulch or by adding water and spraying the strained mixture on the infested soil. The nematodes enter the maggots, killing them within a day or two.

A Cure for Cabbageworms

Q. Is there a cure for cabbageworms?

A. For cabbageworms, the most effective treatment is to spray plants with *Bacillus thuringiensis* (Bt). This biocontrol is commercially available in garden stores and from many mail-order sources under a variety of names, including Dipel, Biotrol, and Thuricide. The spray is completely harmless to all life forms except caterpillars and will not upset the natural insect balance in your garden.

Trichogramma in Your Garden

Q. I've read about the trichogramma wasp controlling cabbage loopers on a large scale in Texas. Are they effective in the home garden? Do they survive colder climates?

A. The tiny trichogramma wasp, which destroys a variety of worms by laying its own eggs in theirs, can be effective in home gardens. The gardens should be large (or in a more rural setting) to attract enough cabbage loopers and cabbageworms for the wasp to establish itself. If you're raising a dozen or so cabbage plants in a suburban backyard, the wasp may not have enough insects to feed on all season. Also, you must know the life cycles of the insects you want destroyed and release the wasps during the pests' egg-laying period. Your county extension agent can help you determine the time for optimum wasp releases in your area. As far as survival in cooler climates goes, the trichogramma wasp survives wherever the cabbage looper does. If you have a small cabbage crop, it may be more effective to handpick the worms. *Bacillus thuringiensis* (Bt) is an effective control.

Burned-Out Cabbage

Q. **What is causing the edges of my cabbage leaves to turn brown? When I cut the cabbage in half, the inner leaves are brown-edged, and I have to compost them.**

A. It sounds like your cabbage is a victim of a cabbage disorder called tipburn. The discolored leaves are caused by using too much nitrogen or general-purpose fertilizers, which produce large plants with big outer leaves. That creates a condition where insufficient calcium is transported to the leaf tips in the head, resulting in tipburn. Tipburn usually develops only when a period of heavy rain is followed by warm and relatively dry days. Such conditions stimulate the movement of calcium to the outer leaves but not to the rapidly growing leaves within the head. Use slow-release organic fertilizers like compost and aged manure to keep from overdosing your plants with nitrogen, and mulch your patch to keep soil moisture even.

Color My
Cauliflower Purple

Q. **My white cauliflower picks up the color from my purple cauliflower. Should I plant them farther away from each other?**

A. The neighboring purple variety isn't the problem. Sunlight on the cauliflower head (called the "curd") causes it to turn from white to purple, yellow, or green, depending on the variety. Blanching will prevent it from coloring. To produce the best-looking white curd, start blanching as soon as the developing head begins to push back the inner leaves. Make sure the head is dry, then blanch by gathering up the longest leaves around the head and holding them in place with a strip of cloth, soft twine, or clothespins. You can also rip off a large bottom leaf and place it over the head. Many newer cauliflower varieties are self-blanching. They have longer leaves that protect the curd.

Keeping Cauliflower Cool

Q. In my growing season, days are hot (80° to 85°F), and nights are cool (40° to 60°F). My cauliflower grows only 4 to 5 inches high, then develops tiny florets that turn brown. How can I get them to produce larger heads?

A. Good-quality cauliflower is difficult to produce where night temperatures are so cool. At 50°F or below, the plants become susceptible to a physiological reaction known as "buttoning." Transplant seedlings no more than 30 days after germination, as older plants seem to be more prone to buttoning, says extension horticulturist Orville McCarver of Montana State University. He also recommends a black plastic mulch, which raises the soil temperature about 7 degrees. Clear plastic or polyester row covers raise air temperatures 10 to 15 degrees during the day and 3 to 4 degrees at night in spring. Plant in full sun and use both plastic mulch and row covers to get the plants off to a fast start. Check plants daily and don't allow the temperature inside to exceed 75°F. Even if button heads form, says McCarver, leave the plants alone, because they may produce normal-size heads later.

Wait for Kale

Q. When should I plant kale, and how much should I plant?

A. Kale is very frost-hardy, and seedlings can be set out unprotected as early as four weeks before the last frost date. But for the best eating, you should plan for the crop to mature in the cool season. A light frost greatly improves the flavor of the leaves, and kale retains its good eating qualities through intense cold. People often report brushing the snow from plants to harvest leaves in midwinter.

You should plant seedlings *no later* than eight weeks before your first autumn frost date. But if you've got the space, you can plant them earlier and let the plants get much larger before the harvest begins. Start seeds in flats in late spring and transplant them four weeks later. An earlier planting gives you a much longer harvest. Cook the large leaves. Small leaves are tender enough to include in salads. Kale should be eaten immediately after picking, like sweet corn, because the sugars convert rapidly and the leaves become bitter. Plant 6 to 12 plants per person.

Spotting Kale

Q. My kale gets alternaria leaf spot. Can you tell me what spreads the disease and how to prevent it?

A. Alternaria is caused by a fungus that attacks almost all the crucifers, including the brassicas, oriental cabbages, radishes, turnips, and horseradish. Leaf spots start as round yellow pinpricks and enlarge in concentric circles to 2 or 3 inches in diameter. These circles gradually become sooty with fungal spores. The disease can also cause cankers on cabbage stems and browning of broccoli and cauliflower heads.

Seeds from infected plants carry the fungus, which kills seedlings or causes them to develop wire stem, a lesion near the soilline. Discard infected survivors—they never grow to full size and don't yield well. Seeds can be cleansed of the fungus by immersing them in water held at a constant 120°F for not more than 30 minutes. In the garden, alternaria is spread by wind, splashing water, and gardeners working among their plants. Space plants generously and avoid overhead watering to keep the leaves as dry as possible, since the spores need moist conditions to germinate. Because older leaves are usually infected first, you may be able to limit the disease by picking them as soon as spots appear. If the disease has been severe, dust with sulfur. Grow kale and other susceptible plants in a two-year rotation with noncruciferous crops.

Leads on Lettuce and Chard

Too Late for Lettuce

Q. I can't get head lettuce to form heads. What could be the problem?

A. You may be planting it too late. If hot weather sets in before head lettuce matures, it won't develop firm heads before bolting to seed. One week can make the difference. In field trials conducted at Cornell University, lettuce plants set out on May 12 produced a larger number of firm heads than plants of the same cultivars set out on May 17.

Plant during the first week of May if the ground isn't too wet, Cornell extension agent Roger Kline recommends. Space vigorous, hardened transplants 12 inches apart in rich, porous soil and protect them from frost. Make sure the soil stays moist until the heads mature. You can improve your chances of success by planting relatively heat-tolerant cultivars like 'Ithaca', 'Minetto', and 'Montello'.

Head Start on Lettuce

Q. **For the past two years I have tried to grow head lettuce, but it rots just as it is starting to head. What causes this?**

A. Dr. Jim Utzinger, extension horticulturist at Ohio State University, says it's likely that your plants succumbed to bacterial soft rot. Since this disease is enhanced by constant moisture and warm weather, the solution is to set out transplants six to eight weeks before the average last frost date. Head lettuce is fairly frost-tolerant and will survive night temperatures as low as 29°F. Grow the plants under row covers or hot caps to protect them from frosts.

A Miner Disaster

Q. **Leafminers attack my beets and Swiss chard. I've tried everything to stop them, but nothing is working. Please help!**

A. The best way to protect your plants from miners is to screen the pests out. Spunbonded row covers like Reemay, anchored around your bed with soil, work well to stop miner attacks. Since leafminers usually pupate in the soil, you should plan to grow beets and chard in a different area for the screening to be successful.

If leafminers have already gotten to your crops, burn or compost any miner-infested leaves. (You can recognize these by the pale tunnels winding across the upper surface.) Also keep weed hosts cut down, especially lamb's-quarters, one of the miner's favorite snacks. Because the miners are leaf chewers, you could try dusting the leaves with sabadilla dust, an insecticide made from the seeds of a tropical plant in the lily family.

Chapter 9

Storage Staples
Potatoes, Onions,
and Other Root Vegetables

Potato Problems

**Use Seed,
Not Feed, Potatoes**

Q. What is the difference between seed potatoes and potatoes from the grocery? Can't I just use grocery-bought potatoes for planting?

A. When you buy certified seed potatoes, you're buying a known variety of potato, guaranteed to carry minimum risk of disease. Plain seed potatoes, by comparison, are not classified or certified, so you know the variety, but not if it's disease-free. Potatoes from the grocery store are the poorest risk for planting. You don't know the variety, whether the potatoes are diseased, or if a sprout inhibitor, which prevents normal sprouting in the bag (and in your garden), has been applied. A viral disease in a potato is not harmful to you when you eat it, but if you plant a virus-infected potato, the disease will appear when the plant is growing. It will be transmitted to other plants by insects, usually aphids, and can ruin the crop. So rely on good seed potatoes—not the grocery store—when planting.

When to Spade Spuds

Q. How do I know when my potatoes are ready to be harvested?

A. For storage, potatoes are ready to harvest when the tops of the plants have died back completely. In the northern part of the country, harvest time usually starts in September, when the days are getting cool and frost is not far off. Wait for a warm, dry day to start digging them up. In damp weather, bruised tubers have a greater susceptibility to rot. Cloudy days are ideal, since too much light will green newly dug potatoes and alter their flavor after a few hours. If you're using potatoes for storage, their skins should be tough enough so that they cannot be rubbed off with your finger. Use a potato fork or pointed shovel. Be gentle as you dig. Each bruise decreases storage life. "New" potatoes—the earliest crop of the season—may be dug anytime after the blossoms form. Although these potatoes are no more than an inch in diameter and don't store well, they are delicious and go well with many midsummer garden vegetables.

Fall Potatoes

Q. Seed potatoes are hard to find in fall, and I can get very few of them to sprout. How can I turn part of my spring crop into seed potatoes for fall planting and harvest?

A. Failure of spring-crop potatoes to sprout in fall is a common problem, says Malcolm Beck, commercial composter and organic farmer in San Antonio, Texas. The tubers' natural dormancy is reinforced by the high soil temperatures that prevail at fall planting time. You can help the tubers break dormancy by placing them in the refrigerator 30 days before the fall planting date, says Beck. After two weeks, remove the potatoes from the refrigerator and expose them to light in a cool place to induce sprouting, then plant. You may not get full rows, but you'll get a crop. Use golf-ball-size potatoes for planting; smaller ones don't yield as well, and larger potatoes cut into pieces are more susceptible to dehydration and rot.

Explorers in Mulch

Q. **I'd like to try the new 'Explorer' potato that is grown from seed. Usually I plant my tuber pieces on top of the ground and then cover them with mulch. Can 'Explorer' be grown this way, too?**

A. No one we know has tried it yet, but we don't see why mulching 'Explorer' potatoes shouldn't work. Either plant the root ball of your potato seedling right in the soil as you would a tomato seedling or simply set the root ball on top of the soil and, to prevent drying out, surround it with compost. Then add layers of mulch as the plants push out their leaves. The mulch should be deep enough to prevent light from reaching the newly formed potatoes. Mulch will keep weeds down and preserve the moist and cool soil temperatures potatoes like. The developing tubers won't have to fight heavy soil, and they should be right where you need them for an easy harvest.

Heartless Potatoes

Q. **The white potatoes I raised last season were very large, but most of them were hollow. Can you tell me why?**

A. Hollow heart—a star-shaped cavity at the center of the tuber—results when conditions such as high rainfall (especially after drought), excessive fertilization, and wide spacing overstimulate growth. Varieties that produce large tubers, such as 'Katahdin' and 'Kennebec', are most susceptible. Early varieties like 'Norland' and midseason varieties like 'Superior' and 'Chieftain' produce smaller tubers and are much less prone to the disorder. The best control is to space plants 7 to 10 inches apart, depending on the variety. Close spacing increases competition, encouraging slower, more uniform growth and smaller tuber size. Don't overdose the plants with nitrogen, but maintain high potassium levels and keep the soil evenly moist.

Slushy Spuds

Q. **My 'Nooksack' potatoes were a healthy crop, but they became a slushy mess when I boiled them. Why?**

A. 'Nooksack', a russet, was developed primarily for french fries. Slushiness is due to the potato's high proportion of dry matter, explains Joseph Pavek, U.S. Department of Agriculture (USDA) potato breeder at the University of Idaho. 'Nooksack' potatoes will taste all right when boiled if you cook them in the minimum amount of water, watch them carefully, and remove them from heat and then drain them as soon as they are cooked. "I've found that potatoes with high dry matter tend to cook faster than the ones with low dry matter," says Pavek. Try harvesting 'Nooksack' earlier to limit the amount of dry matter.

Spotty Potatoes

Q. Although my homegrown potatoes seem healthy, they have a little circle of dark specks around the edge when cut in half. Are they safe? What can I do to prevent this?

A. The dark ring is probably caused by the quick death of the potato plant itself. Rings can occur if the immature plant dies rapidly from disease, air pollutants, or cutting off the foliage. Killing the plant cuts off the nutrients that the developing tubers received from the vines. In the North and East, an early frost will quickly kill the plants. Another possibility is too little water—once the potatoes are fully grown, we tend to forget that they still need plenty of water. As for safety, though their appearance may not be perfect, the potatoes are fine to eat.

Green Potatoes

Q. We decided to follow mulch maven Ruth Stout's advice last year to use unworked ground for potatoes. We placed our seed potatoes on the weeds and covered them with a thick layer of dry grass from a recently thatched football field. The potatoes grew beautifully, but under the red skins some of the potatoes were bright green. What do you think caused this?

A. Sunlight is the culprit. Potatoes exposed to light begin to photosynthesize, and like the leaves of the plant, they'll turn green. The green on both the leaves and tubers of potatoes is solanine, a substance that can be toxic. You can eat these potatoes if you peel away the green parts before preparing them. This year, increase the amount of mulch you use to prevent light from filtering through to the tubers.

Wiry Worms

Q. In our Washington State garden, our potato crop is regularly decimated by wireworms. What can we do to control this pest?

A. Wireworms are the larvae of the click beetle. These tough grubs live in the soil for a number of years and feed on a variety of plant roots. They are generally at their worst in sod ground and land recently plowed out from sod crops. Their numbers decline under row crop and small grain cultivation and can sometimes be substantially reduced by frequent tilling. Wireworms frequently appear to be more damaging to root crops such as carrots and potatoes when these crops are left in the ground after the harvest is mature. Prompt harvest, thorough cultivation, and rotations relying on green-manure crops of annual plants like winter rye rather than sod crops can effectively if gradually lessen losses caused by this beetle grub.

Colorado Potato Beetle

Beetlemania

Q. Where does the striped potato beetle come from? We planted two patches of potatoes this year, about 200 yards apart. Neither place was used for potatoes in the past, as far as we know. One patch had no beetles, the other was covered with them. Why?

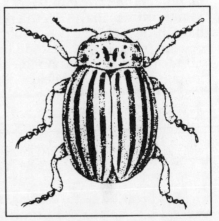

A. Though it may seem that the potato beetles just descend in great numbers out of the sky, they actually build up populations gradually for the first couple of years, then stage a population explosion. You may have had a few potato beetles the year before last and not noticed them. You don't have to raise potatoes to have potato beetles—they also eat ground-cherry, horse nettle, and other weedy members of the nightshade family, as well as potatoes, tomatoes, peppers, and eggplant.

Fortunately, on a smaller patch, potato beetles are not hard to control by hand if you *scrupulously* kill all egg clusters of the first generation, or at least kill all the red grubs that hatch in May or

June from those first clusters of orange-yellow eggs. If this first invasion force is not exterminated, each grub will pupate in three weeks and become an adult. And these adults will lay the eggs that give you a beetle baby boom. In the South, the situation is worse, since a third generation is possible. For the squeamish or those with larger plots, rotenone provides effective control.

Unknown to you, a few of this year's beetles probably did move over to the other patch in the fall, ate a little, and hibernated. They'll be out in force next year. Should you continue to have beetle problems in one garden and not in another 200 feet away, then you may have a potential breakthrough in bug control. First, check such things as: Are you growing the same variety in both plots? Is there more groundcover to harbor predators around one patch? Are there different weed species around one garden and not the other? Did you use the same fertilizers? And most important, are the soil types the same? If you have differing soil types, you may find that a deficiency in one soil is weakening the plants and encouraging the beetles, while the other soil has no such detrimental effect on the plants. Last, check to see how many flea beetles were active in the two gardens. Some gardeners have found that where flea beetle populations feed on potatoes, the potato beetles don't feed. If the leaves of your potatoes are all peppery with little holes, that's flea beetle injury.

Picking at Potato Scab

Q. **I have a problem with potato scab that seems to get worse every year. How can it be controlled?**

A. Common potato scab (*Actinomyces scabies*) is a disease that occurs everywhere potatoes are grown. The disease has no aboveground symptoms, but affected tubers have sunken or raised corky areas. You can eat the potatoes if you cut away the diseased parts. The disease organism thrives when the soil's pH is between 6.0 and 7.5. It is not active below pH 5.2. But like most vegetables, potatoes do best at pH 6.0 to 7.5, so lowering your soil's pH isn't the solution.

The best steps you can take to control potato scab are to plant scab-free seed potatoes and rotate your crop. In the rotation, avoid other root crops like turnips, beets, and carrots, which are also susceptible to scab. Also, research has shown that potatoes grown in dry soil are more susceptible to the disease. Dr. Richard Cole of the Department of Horticulture at Penn State University says that you can foil the disease by maintaining adequate soil moisture at the time of tuber set (one or two months after planting). Don't use fresh manure if you think the livestock may have eaten scabby potatoes. No variety is truly resistant to scab, but tolerant varieties include 'Cayuga', 'Cherokee', 'Chieftain', 'Early Gem', 'Menominee', 'Norland', 'Onaway', 'Ontario', 'Russet Burbank', 'Sebago', 'Seneca', and 'Superior'.

Late Potato Blight

Q. Our potato plants start out vigorous, then develop brown spots on the leaves, shrivel, and die. Do you have any suggestions for this year's crop?

A. Your potatoes are being infected by the late-blight fungus (*Phytophthora infestans*). This blight can kill plants within a week or two under ideal conditions (100 percent humidity and temperatures between 61° and 72°F). First, plant only resistant varieties like 'Kennebec', 'Cherokee', 'Essex', and 'Pungo'. To reduce the humidity, don't use overhead watering on your plants. Clean up thoroughly after harvesting, and burn or cull infected potatoes to help control the disease, since the fungus overwinters in infected tubers and is spread when they sprout. Don't dig the crop until two weeks after the tops die to prevent harvested potatoes from developing blight and rotting in storage.

Asking about Onions and Garlic

Storing "Splits"

Q. When I try to dry onions that have twin bulbs in one outer casing, they seem to retain moisture between the bulbs and go bad. The only way that I've found to save them is to take off the outer casing, separate, and clean each bulb, then freeze them. Is there a sure way to dry twin-bulb onions?

A. The best thing you can do is correct your growing habits so you don't have to fool around with split onions. Splits are formed when the soil is allowed to dry out during bulb formation. This year, when the tops get about 10 inches tall, put a thick mulch around them, and periodically check to see that the area doesn't go completely dry. That way, you shouldn't have any problems.

Flowering Onions

Q. Why do my onions, planted in our Santa Rosa, California, garden, want to make flower heads instead of nice, plump bulbs?

A. Your onions have been fooled. Fall-planted onions can grow too much before winter, especially in your mild climate. When spring comes, they act as if a season has passed and go to seed. The same false maturity will show up in spring-planted onions if a late cold spell persuades them that winter is coming. Plant your onions later in the fall and spring or space your plantings over several months so part of your crop escapes bolting. If you grow your onions from sets, perhaps they are too large or were stored in too warm or too cold a place by the seedsman. If so, many will go to seed no matter when you plant them. In general, sets less than ½ inch in diameter resist bolting, so you should resist the temptation to buy the biggest sets.

Onions Won't Keep There

Q. Can I leave mature onions in the ground through the winter if I mulch them like carrots?

A. No. Carrots need cold (32° to 40°F) and very moist conditions (90 to 95 percent relative humidity), but onions keep only when it's cold and dry (60 to 70 percent humidity). The earth is too damp for onion storage—they'll rot. It's especially important that the necks of onions be kept thoroughly dry to keep out decay-causing organisms. If onions freeze, they'll deteriorate rapidly soon after thawing. Onions will keep well in a dry root cellar, a basement, or a cool attic. If you harvest in summer, you may have to move the onions around the house to provide good storage conditions through several months.

Off with Their Heads!

Q. Some of my onion sets produced big onions, but others sent up a fat flower stalk and produced very small bulbs. Will I get larger onions if I cut off the stalks?

A. Yes. The plant uses the food stored in the bulb to produce flower stalks and seeds. Onions that flower are also likely to have woody centers and keep poorly. Cool weather stimulates flower-stalk production, so avoid planting in the fall or early spring. Snip off flower stalks as they appear. Cutting the stalks promptly will give you larger bulbs, but you should still use them before onions that didn't produce stalks.

Pick a Peck of Pickling Onions

Q. Can you tell me how to grow the little white onions used for pickling?

A. You can grow pickling onions the same way you would grow onions for sets—by seeding directly into the garden at close spacing to keep the bulbs small. Buy seed of an early white onion and sow thickly in a bed or 4-inch-wide band so the seedlings stand ¼ to ½ inch apart. Go easy on the fertilizer to avoid lush growth. Choose a weed-free area if possible—weeding crowded onion seedlings is tedious work. Plant 4 weeks before the last spring frost if you want pearl onions by the time the peas come in. The rest of the crop will mature at pickling size about 12 weeks after sowing.

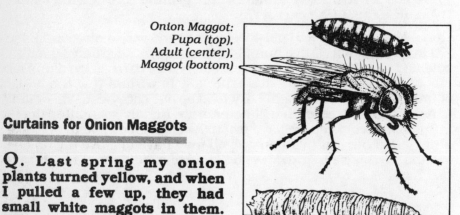

Onion Maggot:
Pupa (top),
Adult (center),
Maggot (bottom)

Curtains for Onion Maggots

Q. Last spring my onion plants turned yellow, and when I pulled a few up, they had small white maggots in them. How can I prevent this?

A. Rotate plantings and cover emerging crops with fine mesh netting or a spunbonded polyester row cover such as Reemay. Seal the material securely by mounding soil around the edges. This prevents most emerging adult onion maggots from laying eggs at the base of the plants. Since the insects thrive on decaying organic matter, don't mulch, but do keep down weeds and harvest the crop completely. Onion maggot populations tend to be higher during very rainy periods, so row covers may be unnecessary in a dry year.

Onions Neck and Neck

Q. Last year I had a beautiful crop of 100 red and white onions, but half of them rotted at the neck in storage. How can I store my onions successfully?

A. Neck rot is the most common cause of onions spoiling in storage. The botrytis fungus that causes neck rot can infect an onion through any wound but most often enters through the wound left when the top is cut off. The fungus grows down into the onion, causing the inner scales to soften and turn brown, as though they had been cooked. The onions may look normal on the outside until decay is well advanced. The foul odor characteristic of spoiled onions is produced by bacterial soft rot that often follows the fungus.

Spores of the neck-rot fungus won't germinate under dry conditions, so the best way to protect your onions is to cure and store them properly. Avoid bruising the onions during harvest, and cure them in a single layer on slats or screens in a dry, well-ventilated place. Make sure the necks are completely dry before clipping or bunching and tying the dried tops. Store the onions in a cold, dry place where air can circulate around them. Temperatures close to freezing coupled with low humidity (60 to 70 percent) help to inhibit the fungus. If you've consistently had problems with neck rot, grow thin-necked rather than thick-necked onion varieties for storage. Thick-necked onions are more vulnerable to infection because they dry more slowly (and sometimes less completely) than thin-necked types. And hold off on nitrogen-rich fertilizers, which can produce soft, lush topgrowth.

Chilled-Out Garlic

Q. My summer-planted garlic won't come up. What's wrong?

A. Garlic won't sprout unless it's given a cold period of several weeks at no warmer than 50°F. It doesn't matter when the cloves are treated. For a strong stand of summer-planted garlic, store the cloves in the refrigerator for a few weeks before planting. Fall-planted garlic sprouts readily in the spring because it has been well chilled by winter temperatures.

Green Elephants

Q. When I dig my elephant garlic bulbs, the skins are split and the cloves inside are green. Why does this happen?

A. You may be feeding the garlic too much nitrogen and not enough phosphorus and potassium. To get strong skins and large cloves, work in bonemeal for phosphorus and greensand or kelp meal for potassium before planting. Exposure to sunlight due to shallow planting turns garlic cloves green. Green cloves are usually too bitter to eat but can be used for planting. Set cloves 4 inches deep, harvest as soon as the tops wither, and dry the garlic in a shady place before storing.

Invisible Garlic

Q. Last fall I planted garlic, but it never came up. Do you think it rotted? How can I prevent this?

A. It probably did rot. For the best results, select grocery- or nursery-bought cloves that are fresh, firm, and show no sign of any kind of rot, says garlic specialist Dr. R. E. Voss of the University of California at Davis. The bigger the cloves, the larger the bulbs will be. Fluctuating winter temperatures can heave the plants right out of the ground, so set cloves 2 to 3 inches deep. They usually sprout within two weeks. Plant about a month before you expect heavy frosts, at which time you should cover the garlic with a winter mulch. The bulbs will be ready to harvest in early July.

Moldy Bulbs

Q. I plant garlic in the fall, but in mid-May the tops dry up and the bulbs begin to mold. Can you help me solve this problem?

A. Because garlic requires good drainage, your soil may be too wet, according to Betty Walker, manager of Nichols Garden Nursery in Oregon. She suggests that you make a raised bed in another location, incorporating lots of compost to improve drainage. And don't leave the garlic in the ground too long: Harvest the bulbs as soon as the tops die.

Water-Soaked Cloves

Q. **The skin between the cloves of my garlic bulbs rots. What is the problem?**

A. The most common reason for rot between the garlic cloves is too much water just before harvest. Garlic needs ample water while the bulbs are developing, but when the tops start to die, stop watering. If it rains, pull the bulbs. If the rotting occurs after harvest, high humidity, such as in a refrigerator, could be the problem. Garlic keeps best in a cool (40° to 60°F), dry place.

Carrot Quandaries

Speeding Carrot Sprouting

Q. **The weeds always get ahead of my carrots. Is there some way to get the seed to sprout faster?**

A. Try soaking the seed overnight. When sowing carrot seed, cover it with vermiculite, sawdust, or peat. Many soils tend to crust over, preventing the delicate seedlings from emerging. Radishes planted at the same time will sprout ahead of the carrots and break the crust. If you plant in furrows, the quick-sprouting radish seedlings will mark the carrot row. Hoe between the rows until the radishes emerge, then apply mulch. Just be sure to pull them up before they start to crowd the carrots. The bed-planting technique requires more diligent weeding at first than row-planting, but within about six weeks, most weeds will be shaded out by the carrots' ferny foliage.

How to Harvest Carrots

Q. **I want to grow carrots this year. How do I harvest and store them?**

A. Don't harvest carrots until the ground has had a good frost or two. Cut the tops anywhere from ½ to 2 inches from the top, and don't wash the carrots. Store in dry sawdust or straw, or in moist sand, peat, or moss. The carrots should be stored at a temperature of 32° to 40°F and a relative humidity of 90 to 95 percent. They should last six months or more when stored this way.

Embittered Carrots

Q. **I have grown carrots for a good many years, but they are always bitter. I would be grateful for a solution to this problem.**

A. Carrots with an uneven supply of moisture or nutrients will become bitter. Under these stressful conditions, the plants produce a bitter substance called isocoumarin. Besides providing water at the first signs of drought, prepare your seedbed by digging in rotted manure. That will supply both nutrients and moisture-holding organic matter. Check regularly for signs of insects and disease, which can also stress the carrots and cause bitterness, and control them promptly.

Avoiding Split Ends

Q. **Almost all my carrots split open last year. What was the problem?**

A. Deep drying of the soil followed by heavy rain or watering causes carrots to split. To prevent drying, mix completely rotted manure or compost into the soil at planting time, mulch the plants, and water regularly and generously during drought.

Undercover Carrots

Q. **This season my carrots and parsnips were destroyed by maggots tunneling into them. What can I do to keep this from happening again next year?**

A. The best way to protect your root crops is to cover them with a spunbonded row cover such as Reemay, cheesecloth, or wire mesh screen. The damage is caused by the larvae of the shiny green, yellow-headed carrot rust fly. Adults emerge from the soil in May and lay eggs, which hatch in 3 to 17 days, around the base of the plants. The maggots work their way into the soil, attacking tender root tips and leaving rust-colored burrows. Second and third generations emerge in August and September. The flies also attack celery, parsley, dill, and fennel. Grow carrots and parsnips in an area where host plants were not grown the previous season. Some gardeners also report success with spraying a solution of ground wormwood on the soil around the plants before eggs are laid.

A Blight on Carrots

Q. The foliage on our last three crops of carrots died back just as the roots were sizing up. After a while, the tops grew back. Can you explain this?

A. Leaf blight is the problem. It can be caused by two different fungi (*Alternaria dauci* and *Cercospora carotae*) or a bacterium (*Xanthomonas carotae*). All three diseases overwinter in carrot residues and in soil. Clean up infected tops and roots and compost them in a hot pile or bury them outside the garden. If possible, grow carrots in three- or four-year rotations with other crops. Plant in rows instead of beds to improve air circulation around the plants. Water early in the day so the foliage is dry by nightfall, and don't work among the plants while they're wet. Though there is no blight-resistant cultivar, 'Orlando Gold' is tolerant of the blight fungi, according to USDA carrot breeder Dr. Clinton E. Peterson.

Catty Carrots

Q. Cats have used my carrot bed as a litter box, and I'm afraid they might carry *Toxoplasma gondii*. Are the carrots safe to eat?

A. Carrots and other root vegetables from infected soil are safe to eat if you scrub and peel them first, says Dr. J. P. Dubey, the USDA animal parasitologist who discovered the disease cycle of *T. gondii* in cats. Boiling or steaming for a few minutes removes all risk by killing the one-celled protozoan parasites. *T. gondii* is carried by as many as 40 percent of all cats in the United States. The protozoan is excreted in their feces, through which it can infect humans and other warm-blooded animals. If contracted by pregnant women, the parasite can cause brain disease and impaired vision or blindness in the unborn child. Young children and adults with damaged immune systems are also at risk, but healthy adults are resistant. The parasite can remain infective in cat feces outdoors for 12 to 18 months, says Dubey.

Gardeners are more likely to pick up the parasite on their hands directly from the soil than from eating vegetables, says Dubey. Wear gloves when gardening and wash carefully afterward, especially under fingernails. Try to keep cats out of the vegetable and flower beds by using fences, repellents, or mulches (such as cardboard or plastic) that they can't dig through. If they get through your defenses, removing the feces along with the soil immediately surrounding them will remove most of the parasites.

Sweet Potato Sagas

Skimpy Sweet Potatoes

Q. **My sweet potato plants produce mostly vines and very few potatoes. Why?**

A. Too much nitrogen in the soil promotes vine rather than root growth. Prepare the soil for sweet potatoes with moderate amounts of compost and some wood ashes or other potassium-rich material, but don't add high-nitrogen sources like manure, cottonseed meal, and bloodmeal.

Sweet Potato Primer

Q. **What nutrients do sweet potatoes need, and what pH is best for them?**

A. Although they aren't known as a poor-soil crop, sweet potatoes do not like too much nitrogen. The soil should have adequate amounts of phosphorus and potash, but heavy potash fertilizing makes the roots short and chunky. Sweet potatoes prefer a slightly acid soil, growing best when the pH is between 5.2 and 6.7. Sweet potatoes do best in a light, sandy soil and require a long, hot growing season. They need 140 to 150 warm days and nights from the time transplants are set out. Too much water during the last few weeks before harvest will cause the roots to crack.

Shot-Holed Sweet Potatoes

Q. **Some of my 'Allgold' and 'Centennial' sweet potatoes have dark brown skin, and some have small holes about the size of a common nailhead. What's the problem? Also, how long does it take these varieties to mature?**

A. Brown or tan skin can be caused by high organic content in the soil, according to Dr. Ron Robbins, director of the Sweet Potato Research Station in Chase, Louisiana. Small holes are often the work of grubs. However, both problems are cosmetic, and neither should affect the eating or storage quality. Because sweet potatoes are swollen underground stems rather than fruits, they do not mature or ripen but can be harvested as soon as they are large enough. Most popular varieties, including 'Allgold' and 'Centennial', reach harvestable size in about 120 days. 'Travis', a relatively new variety, is ready to eat in only 90 days.

The Evils of Weevils

Q. **How can I keep weevils out of my sweet potatoes?**

A. The best control is to plant a resistant variety like 'Regal', advises J. M. Schalk, a research entomologist at the USDA Sweet Potato Laboratory in Charleston, South Carolina. Though the roots of 'Regal' are about 80 percent resistant, you'll still find weevils in the vines, says Schalk. Sweet potato weevils are ¼-inch-long, antlike beetles with long snouts, blue-black heads and backs, and reddish legs. Adults lay eggs in sweet potato stems and tubers, and the larvae spoil the potatoes by tunneling through them in the ground and in storage. There may be up to eight generations a year. Inspect your plants regularly and begin spraying weekly with pyrethrum as soon as weevils appear, making sure to cover all leaf surfaces. When you dig the sweet potatoes, store only those that show no sign of weevil damage. Clean up and destroy dead vines and potato pieces. Control weeds, especially wild morning glory, in and around the garden to deprive the weevils of wild hosts.

Soft Touch with Sweet Potatoes

Q. **Though I try to avoid bruising my sweet potatoes when I dig and store them, most of them develop hard, dry, black sunken spots that may go deep into the root. How can I get them to keep better?**

A. The black spots are a sign of fusarium surface rots. Careful digging, curing, and storage are the best defenses against these rots. These diseases are soilborne and usually infect sweet potatoes through wounds at harvest time. They can enter through an injury as small as that left by a broken hair root. After infection, the diseases grow slowly in storage. No commercial variety is resistant. Dig your crop when the roots have reached an acceptable size in September or October. Don't wait to dig until cold weather sets in— that only makes the potatoes more likely to rot. Handle them carefully to avoid injury. For a week after digging, cure the potatoes under conditions as close to 85°F and 100 percent humidity as you can manage. One way is to seal a basket of sweet potatoes in a plastic trash bag and keep it in a warm room or shed. Curing helps the potatoes seal off wounds and resist decay. After curing, store the potatoes at 55°F. Cooler temperatures may cause chilling injury, while warmer temperatures encourage soil diseases. Try to keep the humidity high. If you store the potatoes in a dry basement, keep them in an unsealed plastic bag.

Radishes, Rutabagas, and Other Robust Roots

Bearded Radishes

Q. Why do my radishes sometimes develop many fine roots that look like beards?

A. Soil compaction and crowding are the most likely causes, according to Dr. Hasib Humaydan, a vegetable breeder and the vice president of research at Harris Moran Seed Company. Plant radish seeds 1 inch apart in soil loosened to spade depth. Work in compost, but keep out large chunks of undecayed organic matter that could check taproot growth. If the radishes are undersize and the edges of the older leaves are dead, your soil could be low in potassium. Have a soil test performed and add wood ashes, greensand, manure, or compost if necessary.

Mild-Mannered Radishes

Q. My radishes are too hot to eat, no matter what variety I plant, when I plant them, or how I prepare the soil. Can you tell me how to grow a mild radish?

A. The "heat" or pungency in radishes is controlled primarily by genetics, so you should continue your search for a variety you like. Contrary to popular belief, soil preparation and planting time don't have much effect on how hot your radishes are. Young radishes are actually hotter than those left in the ground longer. But while mature radishes are milder, their texture becomes woody and pithy. A new variety called 'Fancy Red' is reportedly milder than many others. 'Faribo White Snoball', a white-fleshed variety, is also said to be extremely mild. If these are still too hot, prepare radishes for eating by slicing them, setting them in a bowl of cold water, and putting them in the refrigerator for 30 minutes. In addition to making the radishes crisper, the water will draw out the compound responsible for the pungency, resulting in an even milder radish.

Rootless Root Crops

Q. I got plenty of greens but no roots on my radishes and turnips. What am I doing wrong?

A. You're probably crowding the plants or giving them too much nitrogen. Space the seeds or thin the plants so radishes grow 1 to 1½ inches apart and turnips 3 to 6 inches apart, depending on the cultivar. Use high-nitrogen fertilizers sparingly, or skip them if the previous crop was heavily fertilized.

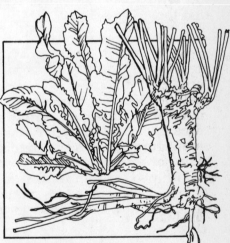

Horseradish

Homemade Horseradish

Q. What is the best way to grow, harvest, and prepare horseradish?

A. Horseradish, a perennial herb of the mustard family, must be started from a root cutting. Plant the cutting early in the growing season (as early as February) in deep, moist loam with a high organic content that will allow roots to grow long and straight. Poor soil can cause gnarled roots, which are harder to prepare. For best results, horseradish needs the cool weather of autumn, so don't plan to start the harvest until after September. Some gardeners gather a few roots at a time, leaving the other hardy roots stored in the soil. Others harvest all the roots they'll need, storing them in sawdust or damp sand in the root cellar or refrigerator. Horseradish tastes best freshly grated in a blender and mixed with vinegar to the consistency of a sauce. It can also be mixed with oil, lemon juice, and chopped hard-boiled eggs as a sauc, or served with grated beets. Try adding other spices, including dill and mustard.

Tried-and-True Turnips

Q. Do you have a "tried-and-true" method for storing turnips in the ground during the winter to keep them fresh for the table?

A. We don't recommend in-ground storage for turnips because the succulent roots are prone to rot and frost damage. The protruding shoulders of turnips are also an easy meal for hungry mice. Turnips are best stored in a cool basement or root cellar. Roger Kline of Cornell University has found a container of moist vermiculite ideal for storing his turnips. Moist sawdust or dry leaves also work well.

Rude Rutabagas

Q. My 'Purple Top' rutabagas are bitter and strong-tasting. Can you help?

A. You may be harvesting the rutabagas too early, says Rob Johnston, president of Johnny's Selected Seeds in Albion, Maine. It's best to dig them after several hard frosts, because the cold temperature changes starch to sugar and gives the roots a sweeter flavor. Johnston suggests delaying planting until the end of June or early July so the rutabagas won't reach harvestable size until fall. For best flavor, rutabagas require a fairly fertile soil, he says. You might also want to try some varieties with improved flavor, such as 'Laurentian' or 'Pike'.

No-Wax Finish
for Rutabagas

Q. When I harvested my rutabagas, I cut the leaves off close to the body, washed the dirt off, and let them dry for half a day. I dipped them in hot wax, but within a week they began to spoil. What did I do wrong?

A. Perhaps the cut surfaces did not have a chance to form their natural seal before you waxed them, says Vince Rubatzky, extension vegetable specialist at the University of California at Davis.

Wait a day or so before waxing, until newly exposed areas no longer look wet but are milky and scalelike. Your wax may also have been too hot, suggests James Hicks, post-harvest physiologist at Cornell University. The wax should be no hotter than 270°F. If your storage area stays at 32°F and has high relative humidity (98 to 100 percent), you may not have to wax the rutabagas at all, says Hicks. In fact, USDA research shows that they keep best when left unwaxed in the proper atmosphere. If you have an area with cold, humid conditions, just slice off the leafy tops, being careful not to cut into the root, and store. Don't trim the lateral roots or wash the rutabagas until you're ready to eat them.

Ice-Bound Parsnips

Q. The ground froze solid before we finished eating all our parsnips. Is there a way for us to harvest them?

A. If the frost has penetrated only a few inches, try freeing your parsnips by using a heat-trapping black plastic mulch to thaw the soil. If that fails, forget them until spring. Trying to break the roots out of frozen ground is futile and is almost certain to ruin them. But when the ground thaws, dig them all promptly and store them in the refrigerator. Overwintered parsnips are one of the first plants to sprout in spring, and the sprouting will ruin their eating quality.

Chapter 10

The Staff of Life
Corn, Grains,
and Other Crops

Corny Concerns

Skimpy Corn

Q. My corn grows well, but 90 percent of the ears are short and poorly filled. How can I correct this problem?

A. Short, poorly filled ears are caused by spacing plants too closely, poor pollination, insufficient water, and low fertility. For best pollination, plant corn in blocks of four or five short rows rather than in long double rows. Work in plenty of manure or compost and space plants 15 to 18 inches apart in all directions. Control weeds while the corn is young and make sure the root zone stays moist. To be sure you're planting the best variety for your area, ask your county extension agent for a list of locally recommended corn varieties.

The Indians Got It Right

Q. I want to use fish as a fertilizer for corn. How do I do it?

A. Plant one fish in each corn hill or lay the fish in a trench between rows and cover with soil. Put fish at least 6 inches under the surface, well away from young plants' roots but close enough for mature plants' roots to penetrate. Fish are a good source of nitrogen and phosphorus. Their wastes on the ground can attract animals, so keep the fish in a bucket while digging the holes. If you have problems with animals, put screening over the seedbed and weight it with stones.

The Supersweet Corn That Wasn't

Q. Last year, I planted 71-day supersweet 'Crusader' corn alongside 110-day 'Rainbow' ornamental corn. Both varieties tasseled at the same time, and the 'Crusader' corn didn't taste sweet at all. Any suggestions?

A. Most supersweet corn, including 'Crusader', loses much of its sweetness if allowed to cross-pollinate with other corn varieties. Isolating the planting usually isn't practical (varieties tasseling at the same time need 400 yards between them), but planting the 'Crusader' corn a month later than 'Rainbow' is one solution. You could also substitute a different type of supersweet corn, one with a sugar-extender gene, such as 'Miracle', 'Incredible', and 'Silverado' (a white variety). These don't require isolation to develop maximum sweetness.

Pooped Popcorn

Q. I'm going to plant popcorn again this year, and I'd like to know how to dry it properly for popping. Last year, half popped and half didn't.

A. Moisture content is important to popcorn. Even if you let the ears dry on the stalk, they might need extra drying. Remember, too, that popcorn takes longer than sweet corn to mature. Seed catalogs usually feature varieties that take a minimum of 90 and up to 120 days. Growers are usually cautioned to dry popcorn without artificial heat, but one reader claimed success by drying the kernels (removed from the cob after a period of natural drying) in an oven, at the lowest setting, for two hours. Store popcorn in glass jars.

Prepopped Corn

Q. **When we harvested our popcorn last fall, we found that some of the kernels had split and the starch had pushed out and hardened. What caused this?**

A. Too much water during kernel enlargement is the most likely cause of splitting, but the disorder seldom reduces yields significantly, according to Dr. Bruce Ashman, a popcorn breeder at Purdue University. The older, thick-hulled cultivars resist splitting, but they make tougher popcorn than modern selections.

Maggots Maul Corn

Q. **Maggots destroy my corn before it even comes up. What can I do about them?**

A. Keep planting. Seed-corn maggots, the larvae of a small grayish-brown fly, tunnel into the seeds of corn, peas, and other large-seeded vegetables. If infested seeds sprout, the seedlings are weak and soon die. Usually, injury is worst early in the season in cold, wet soil high in manure or other organic matter. The flies, which emerge in spring, are attracted to organic matter for egg laying. After feeding for one or two weeks, the maggots pupate in the soil and emerge as adults about two weeks later. There can be several generations a year. To make the soil less attractive to the adults, turn under manure, compost, or cover crops in fall so they can decay by spring. Delay planting until the soil has warmed up, and plant seeds in shallow furrows to speed emergence. Monitor germination closely. If there is heavy maggot damage, replant immediately so the seeds germinate before the next generation of adults emerges.

My Corn Has Fleas

Q. **Last summer, tiny black beetles damaged my corn, especially the ears at the silk end. What can be done to control them?**

A. If the beetles jumped away at your approach and some of the corn leaves were riddled with shotholes, the pests were flea beetles. Since their numbers can vary greatly from year to year, the population may not reach damaging levels in the coming season. Research has shown that mulching crops with chopped clover and companion planting with other vegetables, herbs, or cover crops such as clover or annual ryegrass can reduce flea beetle numbers. Flea beetles stop feeding and hide in wet weather, so you may be able to discourage them from feeding by giving your corn frequent light waterings with a hose or overhead sprinkler. Dusting the plants lightly with wood ashes or lime or spraying them with a garlic/hot pepper solution may also help repel the pests. If these methods fail, dust or spray with rotenone to kill them.

Derailing a Double Pest

Q. **How do I control corn earworms, which I understand are the same pests as tomato fruitworms?**

A. They are one and the same. On corn, the worms feed on tassels first, disrupting pollination. But most of the damage is to the ear. Late-season corn is particularly susceptible. Keep them out of your ears by applying a few drops of mineral oil into the silk just inside the tip of each ear, after the silk has wilted. The oil, which is completely tasteless and will not affect the flavor of the corn, suffocates the worms. You can also handpick the worms after the silk begins to turn brown and pollination is complete. Corn varieties like 'Country Gentleman' and 'Silver Cross Bantam' have long, tight husks that prevent earworms from penetrating. *Bacillus thuringiensis* (Bt), the bacterial disease that kills many caterpillars, works well as long as you apply the powder or spray while the insects are feeding. You can also plant a row of earworm-repellent cosmos flowers near your corn and tomatoes. If the infestation gets more severe, use a garlic spray before spraying or dusting with rotenone.

Ban Backyard Smut

Q. **What can I do to prevent smut in my sweet corn?**

A. Remove and destroy all affected corn plants before the gray boils burst and release thousands of fungus spores throughout your garden. You can recognize ripened spore masses because they have an oily appearance. Corn smut is a common fungus that causes kernels, tassels, husks, and ears to grow monstrous galls or boils. The disease spores spread to other cornstalks by the wind when the membranes break (spores germinate best at between 80° and 92°F). Wherever a spore lands, a new boil forms. A dry spring followed by a wet spell when corn reaches a height of 1 to 3 feet creates the perfect conditions for the fungus.

Although smut spores can remain viable in corn debris, soil, or even manure for five years, they are destroyed by the high internal temperatures of a compost pile that reaches 150°F. You can also burn infected crop residues. Do not till contaminated residues into the soil. Make sure that you thoroughly clean up and properly dispose of all crop debris in the fall, too. If your corn was hit by the disease last year, smut spores are probably dormant in your garden. Never grow corn in the same place year after year. A three-year rotation plan will cut down the chances of reinfection.

Growing Tips for Grains

Swatting Small Grains

Q. My father planted a small plot of wheat and triticale last spring that gave us a very nice harvest. The problems came, however, when we tried threshing it with everything from baseball bats to tennis shoes. Nothing seemed to produce much for the time and labor involved. Isn't there a more effective way to thresh and clean small quantities of grain?

A. We usually recommend threshing (breaking grain away from the husks) small amounts of grain by some kind of a beating action, which you've tried. There's no doubt about it—while this action is the least complicated, it seems clumsy and time-consuming. But small-scale threshers aren't made in this country anymore except for precise experimental work. That kind of engineering puts them way out of the gardener's price range. Old models can be found at farm auctions, in the back corners of some old barns, and sometimes in farm swap listings.

Amaranth Mixup

Q. I'm confused about amaranth. I received some seed that I planned to experiment with as a supplemental sheep feed. An agricultural extension agent here in Mendocino County, California, convinced me not to, because of what he called "toxicity and nonacceptance." What is the story on amaranth?

A. The botanical genus *Amaranthus* has several different species. Most of us know the native pigweed (*A. retroflexus*). It is quite different in plant type from grain (*A. hypochondriacus*) or vegetable amaranths (*A. caudatus* and *A. cruentus*). Pigweed tastes very bitter and is well known for deleterious effects on animals, particularly swine, if eaten in large amounts. Cultivated amaranths—both grain and vegetable—are safe for people and animals.

Amaranth Bash

Q. I'm growing grain amaranth in my garden this year. How can I tell when the seeds are mature, so I'll know when to harvest? Also, how can I separate the seeds from the seed head?

A. Seed heads should be harvested at the early stages of maturity. Pull off a small portion of a head and rub it lightly between your fingers. If the seeds come off easily, it could be time to harvest. To make sure, try the "dough stage" test. Chew on a seed. If it's doughy, it's not quite ready to be harvested. Mature seed should be firm. But don't wait too long—if the plants become too dry in the field, too much seed will fall to the ground. When harvesting, collect the seed heads with as few stems and leaves as possible. Hang the heads in clusters or put them in a burlap bag. Store in a dry place. A simple method of threshing is to put the heads in a cloth bag and beat it against a concrete floor. Seed can be separated from the chaff by sifting through a common 16-mesh household screen.

Questioning Quinoa

Q. Can you tell me more about a cereal grain commonly grown in the South American Andes that scientists are experimenting with as a high-altitude crop?

A. The plant you are referring to is no doubt quinoa (pronounced kee-no-ah), a crop that has been cultivated by the Peruvians for thousands of years in high altitudes where amaranth (traditionally the staple grain) doesn't grow well. Though more closely related to lamb's-quarters, quinoa is grown and used in much the same manner as amaranth. The seed heads are smaller than amaranth's, but the seeds themselves are larger—about the size of a grain of millet. They can be ground into a flour or cooked like rice. (Quinoa is being test-marketed in Denver under the name "Incan Rice.") It has a nutty flavor and a texture like wild rice, according to agronomist Duane Johnson of Colorado State University, who is working with the plant. If you live in the mountains, give quinoa a try, but if you're a flatlander, don't bother. The plant grows poorly below 6,000 feet.

Grow Your Own Broom

Q. I want to make my own brooms. Is broomcorn difficult to grow?

A. No, growing broomcorn is as easy as growing sweet corn. After the soil has warmed up, plant the seed in hills 12 inches apart or sow 4 or 5 inches apart in rows. Cut the heads about three months later when they begin to fill out but the seeds and sweeps are still green. Fully mature broomcorn will have red heads, which make an attractive broom, but the fibers are not as strong as green ones. Cut the stalks about 3 feet from the top. Hang the heads or lay them flat to cure. Cured outdoors, the heads will bleach. Broomcorn mildews easily, so if you let it dry outside, take it in at night and during rainy weather. To make a broom, you'll need about 30 stalks.

Peanut Problems
and Sunflower Solutions

Peanut Roast

Q. How can we roast our homegrown peanuts?

A. After you dig the peanuts, let them dry in the shell on the vine for three to seven days in a sheltered but airy spot, says Melanie Miller, home economist for the National Peanut Council. The moisture content will drop from about 30 percent when freshly dug to 12 or 15 percent after three or four days. It's best to store peanuts in the freezer until you want to roast and eat them, says Miller. To roast, spread one layer of dry peanuts on a cookie sheet and place in a 350°F oven. Roast unshelled peanuts for 20 to 25 minutes and shelled peanuts for 15 to 20 minutes. Once roasted, peanuts become stale in about six weeks. Don't eat moldy or damaged peanuts. They may contain aflatoxin, a carcinogen.

Not a Nut in Sight

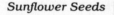

Q. When I dug peanuts in my New York State garden, I found that the shells were watery and soft. Many had no nuts inside, while others had small nuts that shriveled when dry. What went wrong?

A. Your peanuts were immature. You may have planted them too late for your area, chosen a long-season variety, or dug them too soon. Try growing Spanish peanuts this year. They usually give good results in northern climates, since some varieties mature in as few as 100 days. Plant the seed as soon as possible after the last frost date in your area. Then, when the plants are a foot high, hill the soil up around them. That will enable the fruiting pegs to start forming peanuts earlier in the season. Don't dig them until after the leaves have been killed by frost. Mature peanuts have a well-defined shell that is dry and hard. The nuts inside should fill the shell, and their papery hulls (the red "skin" on dry peanuts) should be brownish.

Sunflower Seeds

Shelling Sunflowers

Q. I have a large crop of sunflowers this year. I'd like to shell them mechanically but can't locate any shellers. Can you help?

A. As far as we know, there aren't any sunflower shellers for small-scale use available, but a grain mill will work. You can use any mill, as long as the stones open wide enough to accommodate the largest seeds. Because seed size varies, smaller seeds tend to slip through the mill, so it's necessary to grade them first and process different sizes separately. Three sizing boxes should do it. Make a wooden frame and staple ¼-inch hardware cloth to the bottom. The second and third boxes should have two layers, moved slightly to narrow the mesh openings. After shelling, winnow seeds outdoors or in front of a fan.

Weevil Woes

Q. When I was shelling my sunflower seeds, I found that they were infested with small white larvae. How can I control them? I shell my seeds mechanically, so even a few would ruin the whole crop.

A. Your sunflower seeds are probably infested with seed-weevil larvae. You should be able to obtain close to complete control through a combination of fall plowing and early planting. Since the larvae overwinter in the soil after dropping from dry sunflower heads, plowing or tilling 6 to 8 inches deep will kill up to 40 percent of them. Adult weevils emerge in early summer and will fly in from more than a mile away to lay eggs on your developing sunflower heads during July and August. They won't lay eggs on seeds that have begun to form, however, so the other key to control is early planting. Sunflowers are surprisingly frost-tolerant and will grow when the temperature is as low as 50°F. If you sow them by late March or early April, your sunflowers should already be setting seed by the time seed weevils are ready to lay eggs.

Chapter 11

Special Vegetables
Celery to Salsify

Celery Queries

Lime Your Celery

Q. What caused the center stalks of my celery plants to turn brown and rot all the way to the ground last summer?

A. Blackheart. This disorder is caused by a calcium deficiency in the young, rapidly growing leaves at the center of the plant. It is most likely to occur if the soil pH is 6.0 or lower. Add lime to raise the pH to between 6.5 and 6.8, so plenty of calcium will be available. Stressful growing conditions like hot weather, alternately wet and dry soil, and high salt (especially potassium) levels can cause the disease by preventing celery from taking up calcium even when it is available. Try planting your next crop so it will mature late in the season when the hottest days are past. Dig in plenty of finished compost, mulch the plants, and water regularly to maintain the high moisture levels celery demands, especially during the last month before harvest. If your soil tests high in potassium, avoid fertilizers like wood ashes and manure.

Sickly Celery

Q. What's wrong with my celery plants? The leaves become mottled, then develop brown spots, turn yellow, and shrivel. Three varieties in different places have all had the same problem.

A. Your celery probably has late blight (*Septoria apiicola*). Cool, moist conditions promote this disease. The blight is caused by two types of fungus, which can appear alone or together. The large-spot fungus starts as small, yellowish specks that turn pale brown as the leaf dies. The spots may reach ½-inch in diameter before producing small, black dots that are fruiting bodies. When these become wet, they release spores that cling to tools and clothing and are spread to other plants or are splashed onto plants from rain or irrigation. The small-spot fungus is similar but spreads faster, and the fruiting bodies appear before the yellow spots.

The best way to control the blight is to use seed that has been aged two years. By then, any spores that were on the fresh seed will have died. Seed companies don't routinely age celery seed, so store your seed for a season under cool, dry conditions or soak it in hot water (122°F) for 25 minutes before planting. Seeds remain viable for five years. When you water your plants, make sure you don't get any water on the leaves. Wet foliage is more susceptible to the growth of celery late blight. If you find the fungus in your garden, burn infected vegetation and rotate your crop. The disease can overwinter in garden refuse and soil.

All about Okra

Cracking the Okra Germination Code

Q. I have heard that you can speed up okra germination by using freezing and hot-water treatments. How do I do it?

A. Put okra seed in the freezer overnight, then soak it in hot tap water for ½ to 1 hour. The point, says Elizabeth Whittle of Hastings Nursery, is to crack the hard seed coat. It's this outer covering that inhibits germination. Just soaking the seed at room temperature for 24 hours will also improve germination. And you can rub the seed lightly between two pieces of sandpaper, or nick the seed coats with a sharp knife before planting.

Picking Okra Pods

Q. This is the first year I've grown okra. Could you tell me how it should be harvested?

A. Okra pods are ready to pick a few days after their flowers fall. Harvest them promptly while they're young, and pick them daily to ensure the best quality and keep the plants producing until frost. The pods should be soft and the seed no more than half-grown if you're going to serve the pods whole. Once the pods have reached their prime—on or off the plants—they quickly become woody. Use them at once or freeze, can, or dry them promptly. To dry okra, slice the pods or leave small pods whole and string them. Hang the strings in a well-ventilated place, out of the sun, until the okra is dry.

Okra

Too Cold for Okra

Q. I planted 'Lee' okra in March. It began blooming when it reached about 30 to 35 inches tall, but the pods fell off when they were only ½ inch long. What was wrong?

A. You probably planted too early. Though okra grows in cool weather, it doesn't produce enough pollen to set seed at soil temperatures below 70°F and air temperatures below 75°F. The unpollinated pods just drop off. Since early planting does not increase production, time your next crop so the first bloom coincides with summer temperatures.

Okra Mummies

Q. We waited for warm weather to plant our 'Clemson Spineless' okra. It grew to treelike proportions but produced a lot of mummies—small, undeveloped pods that fell from the plants. Why did this happen, and what can I do about it?

A. First, since okra pods are almost 90 percent water, make sure your plants are watered regularly and deeply. Second, you mentioned that your okra grows to near tree size. If you are putting on too much manure, there will be too much nitrogen available, and the growth will go into the plant, not the pods. You also may not be harvesting the pods promptly. If you allow some to overripen on the plant, new production will stop. Last, if your area had a lot of rain over a long period during the growing season, the problem could be inhibited pollination, in which case pods would not develop properly.

Bottoms Up for Okra

Q. When my okra gets about knee-high and begins producing, the leaves start dying from the bottom up and the stalk turns brown inside. Can you help?

A. Your okra plants are probably suffering from the soilborne disease fusarium wilt. Wilting, curling, and the slow death of the plant are symptoms of fusarium. The fungal disease invades the host's vascular system, showing up as dark streaks if the stem is split lengthwise. No resistant okra variety is available. Plant pathologist Dr. Donald Sumner of the University of Georgia recommends controlling fusarium wilt with a two-part program. First, add as much compost to the soil as you can. Compost contains beneficial fungi and nematodes that will kill fusarium organisms. Second, try crop rotations. This year, plant okra in an area where corn, mustard, or collards grew last year. These crops aren't hosts to fusarium wilt fungus, so the population in the soil should be relatively low. But since the fungus can live in soil for ten years or more and is easily spread by cultivation, controlling it by crop rotation may not be possible in a home vegetable garden. Okra is an attractive plant—try growing it along the back of a flowerbed that is not infested with fusarium.

Fun with Fennel
and Other Gourmet Treats

Fennel

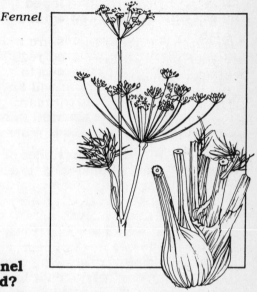

Flummoxed by Fennels

**Q. How many kinds of fennel
are there? How are they used?**

A. There are three edible fennels—common fennel, Sicilian
fennel (*Carosella*), and Florence fennel (*Finocchio*). Sweet fennel,
the common garden fennel grown as an herb, is prized for its seeds
and leaves. Its uses are varied, but it primarily serves as a flavoring
in soups, tea, breads, cookies, candies, and even liqueurs. Its feathery foliage also makes a lovely garnish. Sicilian fennel, cultivated
in Italy and usually eaten raw, produces tender young stalks similar to those of celery or asparagus. Florence fennel, with its thick
stalks and bulbous, celerylike base, can be chopped for salads,
braised, stir-fried, or steamed. All fennel has a sweet, slightly anise
flavor.

Fall-Ripened Fennel

**Q. My Florence fennel went to seed in late August without
forming bulbs. What went wrong?**

A. Hot weather causes fennel to bolt without bulbing. Since
Florence fennel needs a 90- to 100-day season, it may not be possible to plant early enough to harvest a spring crop before the heat
sets in. Time your next crop to mature in fall. Start seeds in a flat in

June and set out the plants in July. Fertilize heavily with compost or manure, mulch the plants to cool the soil, and water regularly to stimulate fast growth.

Blanched Endive

Q. Every time I try to blanch endive, the outer leaves rot by the time the center is blanched. What am I doing wrong?

A. You can reduce the chance of rot by keeping the leaves dry. Pull off any injured or decaying leaves, and cover the plants to exclude light and rain. Roomy containers like boxes, buckets, or trash cans work better than small ones because the air underneath is less humid. Cover a few plants at a time, and don't wait too long before picking—endive spoils quickly once it's blanched. Blanching takes one to two weeks in summer.

You should also try growing some endive to mature in late fall in a coldframe or cloche. You'll find it a little less bitter than the summer crop, and it may suit your taste without blanching. Broad-leaved cultivars do well under cool fall conditions, and their tightly packed inner leaves blanch naturally by the time the head matures. If they're still too bitter, blanch them by covering the cloche or coldframe with any material that keeps out light.

Witloof Woes

Q. What is the secret of growing tight chicons? I forced witloof chicory roots in my cellar this past winter, but their leaves were loose.

A. To form compact heads, chicory roots must be planted 6 to 8 inches deep in sand, fine soil, or sawdust. Keep the box or container covered to exclude light. The heads will reach a height of 6 inches in three or four weeks. Harvest the chicons by cutting them from the root. 'Zoom F-1' is the only cultivar that doesn't need to be planted deeply or covered.

Where to Grow Jicama

Q. My neighbor invited me to try an unusual vegetable called jicama. It was fairly large and crisp, and it seemed to be a somewhat sweet, watery tuber. He said it is grown in Mexico. What is jicama, and what is its nutritional value? Can it be grown in Michigan?

A. The jicama (pronounced hee-kah-mah) is a tropical plant that is grown primarily in Mexico, the Philippines, Hawaii, and Formosa. Since it requires a frost-free, nine-month growing season to produce large tubers, that leaves Michigan out of the market—unless, of course, you have a greenhouse. If you're willing to settle for smaller-size tubers, jicama can be grown as far north as Massachusetts if you start the seeds inside and harvest them before the first frost. This vegetable is virtually unknown to cooks and gardeners in the East, and it's still relatively new to California markets. A brownish root shaped like an irregular turnip, jicama has a very tough, thick skin that peels off easily, leaving the sweet, white flesh beneath. Roots range in weight from 1 to 6 pounds and in diameter from 3 to 6 inches. Fresh jicama tastes a lot like water chestnuts. In fact, many economy-minded cooks use it as a substitute for water chestnuts in oriental stir-fried dishes. Primarily eaten raw, jicama is rich in vitamins A, B, and C, as well as in calcium and phosphorus.

Chayote— by Every Other Name

Q. I cannot find information on raising mirlitons, also referred to as vegetable pear.

A. You might have better luck if you look for information on chayote, a more common name. But besides the two names you mentioned, it's also known as mango squash, christophine, and chocho—not to mention its other names outside North America.

Chayote is a tender plant requiring full sun, warmth, moisture, well-drained soil, and lots of space. It's best propagated from shoots taken from a crown division. Plant in hills and give it climbing space. It will reward you with shoots, fruits, and tubers that have many uses in the kitchen. Gardeners in Louisiana, Mississippi, and the southern areas of Florida, California, and Oklahoma have the right climate for chayote, and greenhouse growers farther north can consider giving it a try.

Starting Salsify

Q. **I can't get salsify to germinate. Covering the seed with compost and potting soil hasn't helped. How can I get it to come up?**

A. Start with fresh seed; salsify seed loses viability after one year. Salsify germinates best under fairly cool conditions. (The optimum germinating temperature is 65° to 70°F, the same as for peas.) Hot weather inhibits germination. Sow seed ½ inch deep any time from six weeks before until two weeks after the last frost. Even under ideal conditions, the seed may take from 7 to 20 days to sprout. Be careful when cultivating—young salsify looks grasslike and can easily be mistaken for weeds, especially if the row germinates unevenly.

If outdoor planting fails, try germinating the seed indoors using the following method: Soak the seeds in cold water for 48 hours, changing the water once. Drain the seeds, then layer them between wet paper towels in a saucer or a plastic bag. Keep the seeds at room temperature during the day and in the refrigerator at night. Check them daily. The alternating temperatures should induce germination in four to five days. Be careful not to break the roots when planting.

Humbug?
No, Hamburg Parsley

Q. **I saw a plant in my seed catalog listed as "Hamburg parsley." Is this an herb or a vegetable?**

A. Hamburg parsley is a variety of parsley, *Petroselinum crispum*, which is considered a vegetable and is grown for its parsniplike root (thus its varietal name, *tuberosum*). Known also as turnip-rooted parsley, the plant has a smooth-skinned, fleshy white root and flat, parsleylike leaves, which are also edible. As soon as the ground can be worked in spring, plant Hamburg parsley in soil that has been manured and deeply cultivated the fall before. Sow seeds ¼ inch deep in rows 12 to 18 inches apart, and thin the seedlings to stand 6 to 9 inches apart. Germination is slow, so you may want to mix the parsley seeds with radish seeds to mark the rows. To speed germination, soak the parsley seeds overnight before planting. The roots will be ready to harvest in the fall. A frost makes Hamburg parsley sweeter. Five- to seven-inch-long roots are most tender. The roots can be cooked and mashed, sliced and fried, grated in a salad, added to soups and stews, or roasted with meat. They taste like a mild parsnip or like parsley-flavored celeriac.

A Second Salsify

Q. **A stand at a farmers' market here recently offered a plant called "black salsify." It looked intriguing. Is it a kind of salsify? What do I do with it?**

A. Black salsify, more properly called scorzonera (*Scorzonera hispanica*), is not a kind of salsify (*Tragopogon porrifolius*), although it is also a root and has a similar oyster flavor. To use the roots, steam or boil them until tender—about 45 minutes—and drain. Then, rub off the black or charcoal-gray skin. Serve the roots hot with melted butter or a mushroom or cream sauce. You can also bake or fry them or use them in soup. If you must wait before using cooked roots, put them in water with lemon juice or vinegar to prevent discoloration.

Scorzonera is easy to grow from seed. It does best in a loose, sandy loam that has been cultivated 12 to 18 inches deep. Add compost or well-rotted manure to the soil for larger, straighter roots, but avoid high-nitrogen materials, which encourage the roots to fork and become hairy. Harvest at the end of the growing season. Dig carefully and handle gently: The roots can be brittle and may break easily.

You *Can* Grow Great Fruit

Chapter 12

Garden-Fresh Fruit
Strawberries,
Grapes, and Bush Fruits

Strawberry Worries

A Berry Poor Crop

Q. My strawberry plants are a beautiful dark green, but the few berries I get are small and puckered. What's wrong?

A. The problem could be excess nitrogen, which stimulates lush leaf growth and inhibits flower production. Fruits that form inside the overfed canopy may be misshapen because the dense leaves interfere with wind pollination. Heavy foliage also stays wet, favoring the development of diseases such as botrytis, which can infect flowers and deform fruits.

If your plants bloom normally, the problem could be late frosts. Open flowers exposed to temperatures below 30°F become blackened and die. Closed flowers may be partly damaged and later produce malformed berries. Cover your plants if frost is predicted during bloom, or grow them under polyester row covers until frost danger is past. Even if temperatures stay above freezing, cold, rainy weather at bloom time can inhibit pollination, producing small, knobby fruits.

A third possibility is insect damage. When they're abundant, mites and sucking insects such as tarnished plant bugs and thrips can damage flowers and fruits. You'll have to examine the plants closely to find these small pests. Flat, seedy brown tips on berries are a symptom of tarnished plant bug damage. If necessary, apply insecticidal soap or a botanical insecticide such as pyrethrum, rotenone, or sabadilla.

Sloping Strawberries

Q. I grow strawberries in a 35-by-6-foot plot on a fairly steep slope behind my garden. I can't work nutrients into the soil because of severe erosion. Will this keep me from gardening organically?

A. Because strawberries like sun, moisture, good drainage, and soil loaded with organic matter, we suggest that you terrace your slope to make adding that organic matter easier. Try creating a semipermanent bed by alternating rows each year. Let runners get established in rows next to the mother plants, then remove these. Work organic matter into empty rows and mulch to prevent erosion. By rotating your strawberry plants this way, you'll prevent the weeds and diseases that plague plots used for the same crops year after year.

Wedge-Shaped Strawberries

Q. This is the second year for my 'Sure Crop' and 'Ozark Beauty' strawberries. The problem is that they are not shaped like strawberries; they are flat on the opposite end of the stem instead of pointed. Can you tell me what the problem is?

A. Most bigger strawberries are "flat" rather than pointed. Wedge-shaped would be a better description. As long as the berries taste good, ripen well, and size up decently, don't worry about how they look. If all your berries are wedge-shaped, even the little ones, then possibly a mild freeze at blossom time may have injured the fruit so that it did not form correctly.

*Training
Strawberry
Runners*

Outrunning Strawberry Runners

Q. **Keeping strawberry runners under control is a lot of work. Can I keep the plants from forming runners, or must I cut each one off?**

A. There are a few strawberry cultivars like 'Tioga' and 'Redglow' that don't set many runners. These, however, aren't necessarily desirable, since runners produce next year's berries, increasing the yield for your planting. Everbearing strawberries also tend to produce few runners.

To control varieties that *do* form runners, try the hill system, which allows easy removal. Set the plants 1 foot apart each way in twin or triple rows. Remove *all* runners from the mother plants with a tiller or hoe. (Space the rows according to the tool you'll use.) Plants grown in the hill system become quite large and produce more berries than those grown in the matted-row system.

Thinning Everbearers

Q. **When is the best time to thin everbearing strawberries?**

A. Thin everbearers in late fall after the last harvest or in early spring before growth begins. Since the plants you remove will have initiated flower buds, you will lose some fruit, but the remaining plants will make up for the loss by bearing more and larger berries. When you thin, take out old and diseased plants first.

Everbearers Don't

Q. **My everbearing strawberries produce a strong June crop but nothing in August or September. How can I get them to live up to their name?**

A. Try a different variety, suggests Dr. Gene Galletta, director of the U.S. Department of Agriculture (USDA) Fruit Laboratory in Beltsville, Maryland. Many older everbearing varieties won't flower during the summer heat. However, newer, day-neutral strawberries such as 'Tribute', 'Tristar', 'Hecker', 'Brighton', 'Aptos', and 'Fern' produce a spring crop followed by lighter but steady production during the summer and a second heavy crop in fall. To fruit well in hot weather, strawberries need large amounts of water and a steady supply of nutrients within easy reach of their shallow roots. Lay soaker hoses in the beds and mulch the plants to keep the soil moist. Apply a balanced organic fertilizer such as fish emulsion lightly and often, rather than in one or two heavy feedings, and maintain a soil pH of about 6.0.

Strawberry Barrel Blues

Q. Last year we started a strawberry barrel. We used a wooden whiskey barrel, drilled 3-inch holes 10 inches apart, and planted a tube with holes in the middle for watering. Only 3 plants out of 50 lived. Why?

A. We can't find fault with your construction. Maybe your growing techniques were to blame. Here's a checklist of best techniques for barrel planting: Make drainage holes and place broken crockery, gravel, or brick on the bottom. Be sure all plants get plenty of sunshine. A rich mix of loam and compost or rotted manure—slightly acid, fertile, and loose—is the best soil for strawberries. Keep the soil wet but not waterlogged. Runnerless everbearing varieties are best for barrels. Choose varieties that are recommended for your area. Finally, strawberries are very particular about planting depth. Cover all of the roots right up to the shoulder, with the crown neither completely under nor completely above the soil level.

Beetled Berries

Q. What can be done about the little black beetles that eat holes in our strawberries?

A. The pests are sap beetles, which feed and lay eggs on ripe and fermenting fruit. You can reduce their numbers by keeping the berries picked and promptly composting overripe fruit in a hot pile or burying it at a spade's depth. Thin your plants, if necessary, so you don't overlook berries that could become breeding sites for the beetles.

Strawberry High Rollers

Q. Strawberry leaf rollers attacked my strawberries last spring and fall. Can you suggest a control?

A. *Bacillus thuringiensis* (Bt) sprays will control strawberry leaf rollers, but timing is critical. First-generation caterpillars hatch in May, usually on the underside of leaves. They soon move to the upper leaf surface, where each caterpillar bends a leaflet at the midrib and ties it with silk, forming a protective fold in which to feed and pupate. The caterpillars eat only the outer leaf surface, not the entire leaf, but their feeding causes leaves to turn brown and die. Reddish-brown moths with a ¼-inch wingspan emerge from pupae about 54 days after eggs are laid. These moths produce a second generation, which appears in late August and September. The caterpillars are most vulnerable to Bt between hatching and the time they fold the leaves. Young leaf roller caterpillars are hard to see because they are pale green and less than ½ inch long. Ask your county agent or state university entomology department when hatching occurs in your area, and then apply Bt two or three times at weekly intervals. Bt has the advantage of being harmless to the parasitic wasps and flies that normally keep strawberry leaf rollers in check.

Sudden Strawberry Death

Q. I have grown strawberries for several years with very good luck, but last year the leaves turned yellow, then brown, and most of the plants died. What can I do?

A. Move your patch. Verticillium wilt (*Verticillium* spp.), rhizoctonia root rot (*Rhizoctonia* spp.), and anthracnose (*Colletotrichum* spp.) are diseases that can cause strawberry plants to die suddenly. Dr. John Maas, a pathologist at the USDA Fruit Laboratory in Beltsville, Maryland, suggests that you have the disease identified through your county or state Extension Service. Some strawberry cultivars, such as 'Illinois', are resistant to verticillium wilt, and the Extension Service can recommend the best ones for your area. If it's found to be rhizoctonia root rot, rotation is the only control. If the disease is diagnosed as anthracnose, a common problem on strawberries grown in California and the Southeast, try purchasing berry plants from another region of the country. But no matter what the disease, Maas recommends moving the strawberry bed to another area, preferably one that has not been used to grow strawberries or vegetables recently.

Strawberry Mold

Q. Last year, quite a few of my strawberries were covered with a fuzzy gray mold. What can I do to reduce or eliminate this problem?

A. Your strawberries are infected with gray mold (*Botrytis cinerea*). It is usually worst during a cool, wet spring. You may not be able to eliminate the disease, but you can curb its damage and get a good crop. The most important control is site selection. Choose a location that gets full sun all day. Make sure it isn't in a low spot where cold air tends to collect. A raised bed helps ensure good air drainage. Space the mother plants and their runners no closer than 12 inches apart. Don't use the matted-row system, which crowds the foliage and prevents good air circulation. Too much nitrogen can lead to gray mold by creating a thick leaf canopy and a cool, moist microclimate. Mulch the plants and water early enough in the day so the fruit and foliage can dry before dusk. Pick off and destroy all infected fruit and leaves to reduce the amount of fungus that will overwinter. Cultivars that are resistant to gray mold are 'Catskill', 'Fletcher', and 'Tioga'; 'Dixieland', 'Midway', and 'Sparkle' have intermediate resistance.

Grape Expectations

Concord Cuttings

Q. How can I root 'Concord' grape cuttings?

A. In late winter, take cuttings from healthy one-year-old canes that have fairly short internodes (the distance between buds). Each cutting should be ¼ to ½ inch thick and 12 to 18 inches long, with four to six buds. If you can't plant them immediately, store the cuttings in the refrigerator in a plastic bag filled with damp peat moss. As soon as the soil is workable, plant the cuttings in a trench in the garden, covering all but one or two buds. Be sure the buds are not at or just below ground level—they will produce suckers later. Keep the cuttings moist and weed-free. Transplant them the following spring. You can also root cuttings indoors in individual half-gallon milk cartons or cans with drainage holes. Use a fast-draining potting mix. Cover the containers with plastic and place them in a warm room or on a heating cable. When the cuttings sprout, remove the plastic and grow them in a sunny window or a coldframe. Plant them outside when they're well-rooted and danger of frost is past.

Name Brands Are Best

Q. I have a 20-year-old grapevine that I sprouted from a store-bought blue-black grape. It has never produced fruit, even though it is covered with blossoms in the spring. My other vines give good yields. Is there any way to make it produce grapes?

A. While cultivated grape varieties are monoecious, with both sexes on the same plant, many wild grapes and some seedlings are dioecious, each having only male or female flowers. Since yours produces flowers and no fruit, even though there are other grapes flowering nearby, it is undoubtedly a male plant, and there is no way to make it produce fruit. But even if the plant were a female, the chances of it producing good-quality grapes are extremely slim compared with other fruits started from seed, according to University of California extension viticulturist Fred Jensen. Unless you want vines for ornamental purposes, you're better off sticking with named varieties.

Concord Discord

Q. Could you tell me why my 'Concord' grapes don't ripen all at the same time? There will be a few ripe grapes in a bunch, but most will be half-ripe and some still green.

A. Although uneven ripening of grapes is a somewhat mysterious disorder, it is usually caused by inadequate sunlight, too heavy a crop load on the vine, or in some cases, a potassium deficiency in the soil. Proper pruning will solve the problem of inadequate sunlight. Prune to distribute the foliage evenly along the trellis, spacing the buds out so that all the new growth gets plenty of sunlight. Most growers either prune too severely or don't prune their vines enough, which produces too many clusters. Next, thin the remaining grape clusters by 15 to 20 percent. It's best to do that just before or after the clusters have flowered. If you're still getting small clusters with small berries that don't ripen at the same time, your soil may lack potassium. A soil test will tell you for certain. To correct the problem, spread as much as 1 pound of wood ashes or ½ cup of kelp meal at the base of each vine. Grape roots are shallow, so just sprinkle it over the top of the soil, then water the ground heavily and mulch.

Thompson Grapeless

Q. Last year my 'Thompson Seedless' grapes didn't produce even one bunch, while a 'Concord' vine a few feet away was loaded. Can you tell me how to remedy this problem for this year's crop?

A. Proper pruning should solve the problem. Most grape varieties (including 'Concord') form fruit on the buds nearest the main stem. A popular pruning technique for these grapes is spur-pruning—pruning all canes back to 2 buds. Spur-pruning gives good production with these varieties but removes all fruiting buds on 'Thompson Seedless'. 'Thompson Seedless' forms fruit only on canes arising from the middle 4 or 5 buds on each one-year-old cane. The buds nearest the main stem and those near the tip of the cane produce fruitless canes. So for this variety, try cane-pruning instead. Select two long shoots on the vine, each with 10 to 15 buds. Before the plant leafs out in the spring, prune all other shoots close to the main stem, leaving only short spurs with 2 buds each. Those two canes will bear grapes. Next winter, cut the two canes flush with the trunk. Then select two new canes with 10 to 15 buds and cut all the other shoots back to short spurs, just as you did this year. Cane-pruning can be used for all grape varieties and often yields larger crops than spur-pruning.

Raising Raisins

Q. How can we dry grapes at home to make raisins? Are there any special problems we should watch out for?

A. Dry grapes for raisins in a food dehydrator or an oven for about 14 to 20 hours at 95° to 120°F. The raisins will be lighter in color and slightly plumper than those you find in the store. Grapes usually can't be sun-dried because that technique requires two weeks of dry, bright weather. Choose sweet, fully ripe grapes that still have stems attached, advises Linda Wood of the California Raisin Advisory Board. Discard bruised or moldy grapes. Split the grapes before drying either by blanching for one minute in boiling water or by slicing the skin with a knife. Otherwise drying can take longer than the normal time. After the grapes have dried, remove their stems by rolling a handful of raisins between your palms. Four and one-half pounds of grapes will yield 1 pound of raisins. To retain the color and nutrients for up to 15 months, store at 40° to 50°F. Raisins freeze well, too. Seedless varieties are best, but seeded varieties of table (not wine) grapes are fine if you cut out the seeds afterward.

Routing Elm Sprouts

Q. **We've recently purchased an old farm with a nice row of grapevines along the garden plot. Our problem is that there are elm sprouts growing from old stumps in the grapevines. Is there any way we can stop these from growing without hurting the grapes?**

A. Short of pulling up the stumps, there's no easy way to stop the sprouts. Just plan to spend a little time cutting the new sprouts off each year in early spring.

Sparrows Are Pests of Grapes

Fowl Play

Q. **Last season my five vines were loaded with grapes. The sparrows had a feast, but I didn't get any. What can I do?**

A. Since you have only a few vines, you can cover individual grape clusters with pieces of netting or paper bags. Don't use plastic—it heats up too much. Early in the season, thin the clusters to encourage fewer but larger bunches rather than many small ones. Then cut out the end of each bag to provide ventilation, slip it over the grapes, and tie around the base of the cluster. The opening isn't a problem because "birds don't bother anything they can't see," according to A. N. Kasimatis, grape specialist at the University of California at Davis. You may, however, find it simpler to cover the vines with bird netting. Be sure the netting contains an ultraviolet absorber, which will slow down the sun's deteriorating action. You can get up to 11 years of life out of treated netting, compared with about two if it's untreated. A 14-foot width is adequate for most vines, but if you have *vinifera* grapes or use the Geneva double curtain training method, you'll need a width of 17 feet. Don't skimp on the size—pulling the netting too tightly will reduce photosynthesis. And if the net doesn't reach the ground, birds will get caught underneath. Secure the edges to the ground with U-shaped pieces of wire, or weigh it down with boards or rocks. Clip ends together or staple them to the posts.

Wormy Grapes

Q. My grapes have little worms in them. What are they, and how can I keep them from ruining future crops?

A. The worms are probably larvae of the grape-berry moth. Adult moths are brown and gray and have a ½-inch wingspan. They're native to the northeastern United States and usually have two generations a year. First-generation caterpillars hatch on grape flower stems and young fruits in spring and spin webs in the fruit clusters as they move from grape to grape. After about a month, they form a cocoon on a leaf and pupate. Moths begin to emerge and lay eggs in late July. This second group hatches in August and bores into ripening grapes. When mature, they drop to the ground and overwinter as pupae on fallen grape leaves.

The key to control is good timing. Insecticides are effective only before the larvae enter the grapes. Starting immediately after bloom, spray the clusters every seven days with rotenone or every three days with *Bacillus thuringiensis* (Bt), continuing for two weeks. You may have to spray again in summer if the second generation is large. Contact your state agricultural experiment station for second-generation emergence dates to time sprays effectively. In summer, handpick and bury or burn webbed bunches and leaves bearing cocoons. Rake and burn all fallen leaves in autumn or bury them by cultivating in early spring. Be on the lookout for reinfestation from nearby wild and cultivated grapes.

Powdered Grapes

Q. The blossoms of my seedless grapes growing in Iowa turned brown and dried up. Are they diseased?

A. Yes. Several diseases produce these symptoms, but by far the most common one in your area is grape powdery mildew (*Uncinula necator*), according to Dr. Robert Pool, a viticulturist at the New York State Agricultural Experiment Station in Geneva. Powdery mildew also covers leaves, canes, and young fruit with white patches. You can control the fungus with a sulfur dust or spray. Make the first application when new shoots are 6 to 8 inches long, the second about two weeks later when shoots are 12 to 16 inches long, and the third at early bloom stage. If mildew symptoms continue to appear, spray or dust when the fruit is half-grown and again when it begins to ripen.

Blueberry Blues and Currant Problems

Making More Blueberries

Q. How can I propagate blueberries?

A. The most common method is by rooting cuttings. Take softwood cuttings from new shoots in the spring after the leaves have fully expanded. Prune the shoots to 3½ inches long, avoiding those with flower buds, which are fat and round. Pinch off all the leaves except the two at the top. Fill a flat with equal parts of peat and perlite. Stick the cuttings into the rooting medium, 2 inches apart each way, allowing only the growing tip to protrude. Place the flat in a partially shaded area and keep the medium well watered. Cover with a tent of plastic for humidity and water-retention, but remove it for at least an hour every other day to allow air to circulate. Roots will form in a few weeks. Then pot up the newly rooted plants in a soil mix containing some leaf mold or other acidic material. Pinch off all flower buds and the following spring, transplant to a permanent location. Remove flowers then, too, and the next year you may get a small harvest.

Mounding is another way to start new plants. Build a wooden frame about 1 foot high and 3 feet square around the blueberry bush. Fill this structure with a mixture of moist peat moss and rotted sawdust, mounding the medium around the canes of the bush. They will form roots beneath the surface of the medium. The canes can then be cut off below the roots and planted. Both cuttings and mounding will reproduce the parent plant exactly, so you'll get more plants of a specific cultivar.

Blueberry Blues

Q. Though they're planted in some of Minnesota's finest acid soil and mulched with oak leaves, pine needles, and manure, our blueberries haven't fruited in six years. Why?

A. If you planted highbush varieties, and if winter temperatures in your area drop to −31°F, the problem may be lack of hardiness, says Dr. Jim Luby, a fruit breeder at the University of Minnesota. Though the bushes survive these low temperatures, the flower buds and often the branch tips are killed. Three blueberry varieties hardy to between −30° and −35°F are 'Northblue',

'Northsky', and 'Northcountry', developed by Luby and his colleagues at the Minnesota Agricultural Experiment Station. Though these varieties may sustain some injury in the coldest winters, they will produce reliable crops, says Luby. The bushes are lower-growing than highbush varieties, so they're better protected by snow cover.

Slow Down for Sweetness

Q. **I have several varieties of blueberry and they bear large, plentiful fruit, but the berries are very tart. How can I grow sweeter blueberries?**

A. You may be picking the berries too soon. Blueberries need about five days after they turn blue to reach maximum sugar content, says Dr. P. Eck, a pomologist at Rutgers University. Timing the harvest properly is important because blueberries don't ripen off the bush—if you pick them sour, they stay sour. Cover the bushes with netting when the fruit colors up, advises Eck, or birds may beat you to the ripe berries. If your berries are sweeter in some years than in others, the weather may be partly to blame. A long period of rainy or cloudy weather during the ripening period can cut down sugar production by the leaves, resulting in sour, watery fruit.

A Web of Trouble

Q. **My blueberries attract a pest that spins webs around the fruit clusters and shrivels the berries. What is it?**

A. Webbed berries are a sign of the cranberry fruitworm, a green caterpillar. The adult is a moth that lays its eggs on the fruit when the largest berries on early varieties have reached about one-quarter of their maturity. After hatching, the caterpillars bore into and hollow out the berries, leaving them shrivelled and filled with sawdust-like frass. They move into adjoining berries as they grow, each caterpillar eating as many as four fruits. After about 24 days, the caterpillars crawl to the ground and pupate in mulch or beneath about ½ inch of soil, emerging as adults the following spring. Handpick and destroy fruit clusters as soon as you notice webbing. In early spring, rake up and burn the old mulch and shallowly cultivate the soil under the bushes to destroy overwintering pupae. Fertilize if necessary and put down a fresh layer of mulch.

Mummified Blueberries

Q. Could you tell me what's wrong with our blueberries? We mulch and fertilize them. The bushes look healthy, but the berries turn hard and red instead of blue. Even the birds reject them, so we know they are inedible.

A. Your blueberries have "mummy berry," a disease caused by the fungus *Monilinia vaccinii-corymbosi.* It is quite common in the North. Spores of the fungus infect the developing berries at flowering time. The diseased berries appear to grow normally at first, but instead of ripening, they first turn a reddish-tan color and then become the gray, hard, shriveled mummies that give the disease its name. The fungus overwinters in the mummies, most of which fall to the ground. Spores released by the mummies the following spring are blown to the newly opened buds and perpetuate the cycle.

You can break this cycle and control the fungus by removing the mummified berries. Clean up and discard all the mummies you can find in fall. Before the bushes break dormancy next spring, rake up and discard mulch residues and cultivate shallowly around the bushes to bury any mummies you might have missed. Fertilize if necessary and apply a fresh layer of mulch 2 to 4 inches deep. If there are no other diseased blueberries nearby to reinfect your bushes, you should be able to eradicate the fungus in one or two seasons.

Currant Affairs

Q. Our currant bushes no longer bear well. How should they be pruned and fertilized?

A. Currants fruit best on one- to three-year-old wood. Remove older canes and all weak, diseased, and broken shoots. Thin the remaining growth so that every bush has three or four each of one-, two-, and three-year-old canes. Prune the oldest canes every year and leave just enough young shoots to replace them. For maximum yield, currants need cool, moist soil rich in nitrogen. Top-dress annually with an inch of manure or compost or scratch in about ½ pound of cottonseed meal around each bush in early spring. Apply about 2 inches of mulch, and water during drought.

Cutting Down
on Currantworms

Q. Inch-long green worms with black spots stripped most of the leaves off my currant bushes last year. What were they, and how can I prevent injury next year?

A. Imported currantworms, larvae of the currant sawfly, defoliated your bushes. They hatch about the time the leaves reach full size and usually start feeding near the center of the bush. The ⅓-inch-long, wasplike adults are black with yellow markings on the abdomen. Females lay shiny white eggs in rows on the underside of the leaf veins in late spring. After feeding for two to three weeks, the larvae crawl to the ground and pupate. A smaller second generation emerges in June or July. These overwinter as pupae. Handpick the worms or treat with rotenone or pyrethrum as soon as they appear.

Puny Gooseberries

Q. My gooseberries bear well, but the berries are very small. How can I get bigger fruit?

A. Watering, feeding, and pruning should help increase fruit size. Gooseberries need cool, moist soil, especially in a warm climate such as yours. Maintain at least 2 inches of mulch under the plants, and make sure they get an inch of water a week during the growing season. In early spring, feed with a complete granular organic fertilizer or top-dress with about an inch of rotted manure or compost. Bushes crowded with canes more than three years old often bear poor-quality fruit. Cut out older canes and weak or diseased younger growth, leaving the bushes with three or four canes each of one-, two-, and three-year-old wood. Remove the oldest canes each year and leave enough new shoots to replace them.

Getting the Worms
Out of Gooseberries

Q. Some of my gooseberries had a brown spot on the skin and a small white worm inside. Can you identify the insect and suggest a control?

A. Maggots of the currant fruit fly were feeding on your gooseberries. Infested berries ripen prematurely, and many fall to the ground. When full grown, the maggots leave the fruits and crawl 1 to 2 inches underground, where they overwinter as pupae. The housefly-size adults, yellow-bodied with dark bars on the wings, emerge during bloom. Within a week, the females begin laying eggs in the developing fruits. To kill the flies before they can lay eggs, apply rotenone two or three times at weekly intervals, starting as soon as the flowers fade. Destroy infested fruit.

Thorny Problems
with Blackberries and Raspberries

Polar Berries

Q. **I raise bush fruits in Wisconsin. Every year my blackberries have a profusion of blossoms, but once the developing fruits reach the size of peas, they just dry up. Why do I have this problem when I've had such healthy bushes and blossoms?**

A. Blackberries aren't reliably hardy in Wisconsin. Thornless varieties are only hardy to about 0°F, and the thorny types will be injured below −5° to −10°F. If the canes have been damaged by very cold temperatures, plants may look normal and will flower as usual; however, once the berries begin to form, the damaged canes can't supply enough water to the fruits, and they dry up. To check for winter injury, scrape the outer skin off part of a cane. Damaged canes will be brown on the inside rather than green. You may be able to prevent winter injury if you lay down the canes and cover them with a thick layer of mulch in late fall. The plants will also overwinter better with a continuous snow cover.

If you can't find any evidence of winter injury, look near the base of the stems for brown or white lesions 1 to 6 inches long. These lesions are caused by a fungus, and canes should be pruned off and burned. Dust sulfur on the crowns before plants emerge in spring and again after the canes come up. Sterility, or sterile-plant virus, is also a common problem in northern blackberry areas, according to Dr. Robert Skirvin of the University of Illinois. Afflicted plants look deceptively healthy and bloom profusely, but the berries never develop beyond nubbins (a common name for this disorder). There is no cure for sterility, so the plants should be dug up and destroyed. Dig out any suckers that might appear later in the season from pieces of root left in the ground. Grow a different crop there for at least one year before planting blackberries again. Buy only plants that the nursery can assure you have been propagated from proven bearing stock that is virus-free.

Second Spring
for Blackberries

Q. This fall my blackberries are greening and putting out buds. So far they haven't bloomed, but I'm afraid they'll be damaged by cold. Will they bloom next year?

A. The phenomenon you've described is fairly common and has been nicknamed "November bloom," according to Dr. Owen Rogers, ornamentals specialist at the University of New Hampshire. It's nothing to worry about, Rogers says, because usually no more than 1 percent of the flower buds open, leaving plenty for spring.

Cutting Off
the Raspberry Crop

Q. Three years ago I planted 'Blackhawk' black raspberries that still have not produced any flowers or fruit. I fertilize the plants well and prune the canes to 6 inches high each fall. What can I do?

A. Don't prune black raspberries until after they have fruited for the first time. Like red raspberries, they produce fruit on two-year-old wood—that is, canes that grew for a full season the previous year. As soon as you've harvested the crop, cut all canes that bore fruit to the ground, and thin the remaining canes to stand 8 to 10 inches apart.

Relocating Raspberries

Q. When is the best time of the year to transplant raspberries? Mine have gotten so thick that my neat rows have all but disappeared.

A. You have a choice: Transplant in the fall, after a killing frost when all the leaves have fallen from your plants, or in the early spring, when you can get a shovel in the ground but before the beds have leafed out. Pick a new cane (the bark on old canes hangs in tatters) and spade around it until you can lift out the soil and roots in a large shovelful. After you set it in a predug hole, cut back the cane to 6 inches or so. If you have black raspberries, it's safer to transplant them in the spring—they are not as cold-hardy and vigorous as the reds.

Netting a Good Crop

Q. How can I keep the birds out of my black raspberries? I've tried nets, pie pans, and so forth, but nothing seems to stop them.

A. Netting is the only way to keep them out, but it must be held away from the bushes so the birds can't reach through. The quickest solution is a frame made from arched PVC pipes or poles lashed to form a teepee. Cover the supports with netting. For a more permanent screen, we recommend that you set 8-foot-tall posts (or higher than your bushes and with enough room to work in) 8 feet apart around the edge of your patch and in rows through the patch 8 feet apart. Nail framing along the top of the posts, connecting one post to the other. Some good framing materials are 2-by-4s or even 2-by-3s. Next, nail wire screening (of a mesh small enough to keep out birds) all around the outside posts as if you were putting up a fence. Be sure to allow space for a gate of some kind. Then fasten screening over the top of the framing to form a "roof" over the bushes. Planting elderberries and mulberries may also protect your fruit. Given the choice, birds prefer these berries over raspberries and blackberries.

Bugged by Black Raspberries

Q. This year many of my black raspberries had dry, red to brown spots on them. What was the problem?

A. The problem may have been feeding injury caused by wasps, hornets, stinkbugs, or other plant bugs. These insects pierce individual drupelets and suck out the juice, leaving dry spots on the berries. If damage is intolerable, protect the fruit with fine netting. Reduce stinkbug numbers by cleaning up weeds and plant debris to deprive the pests of alternate hosts and overwintering sites.

Raspberry Beetles

Q. I found worms in my red raspberries this year and couldn't use the fruit. What are they, and how can I keep them out of the berries?

A. The pests are raspberry fruitworms, the larvae of ⅛-inch-long, light brown beetles that emerge from the soil in early spring to feed on unfolding leaves and flower buds. The females lay eggs on

early spring when the tree is still dormant. To keep the budstick in storage, place it inside a plastic bag that is not completely airtight but is kept moist, and store in the refrigerator.

Frosted Fruit

Q. **Here in Cornville, Arizona, folks say, "five peach trees, five peaches." We live at the bottom of the few miles of geographical declivity that separates Arizona's northern forest from its southern deserts. The desert spring in February and March is followed by forest-country freezes in April and May. How can we retard our trees' early blossoming or ward off the subsequent frost kill?**

A. We contacted Robert Kurle of the North American Fruit Explorers for advice concerning your area. He answers: "We certainly would not recommend your area for fruit growing, but since you are so determined, here are some recommendations. For apples, try grafting on the 'Court Pendu Plat' variety, known as the 'wise old apple' because it blooms several weeks later than other late apples. Another solution is to grow dwarf trees that can be covered if it freezes. Good candidates for your specialized conditions are apples on Malling IX stock, pears on quince C stock, genetic dwarf peaches and nectarines that bear when 15 inches tall, apricot on *Prunus besseyi* rootstock, and the compact 'Lambert' cherry that grows to one-fifth the size of a normal sweet cherry. Overhead sprinkling systems and heaters can also be of value. Try other late-blooming tree and fruit crops like Chinese chestnuts, persimmons, beach plums, suda cherries, and fall-bearing raspberries. Another approach is to grow fruit trees in pots that can be moved under shelter or easily covered in case of frost."

Oiling Up the Orchard

Q. **When is the best time to spray dormant oil on fruit trees?**

A. Spray in late winter, before any leaf buds begin to open. A light film of dormant oil sprayed on fruit trees will cover aphids, thrips, mealybugs, whitefly, pear psylla, scale, and spider mites that are clinging to the bark. It suffocates them. The treatment will also destroy the eggs of codling moths, oriental fruit moths, and assorted leaf rollers and cankerworms. But if the buds have burst, the coating of oil will also smother the emerging plant tissue. Don't spray before late winter for two reasons. First, it's the time when insects and their eggs are coming out of dormancy; their shells and protective coverings are softer and more porous then, so they're vulnerable to the effects of the oil. Second, the oil/water mixture should not freeze on the tree; when you spray, the temperature should be above 40°F. Delay spraying if freezing night temperatures are predicted. Choose a calm day. Spray the whole tree at one time, concentrating on the trunk, large branches, and crotches, rather than spraying down a whole row of trees at one pass. If you've experienced extremely bad infestations of these insects, you might treat your orchard a second time. Dormant oil can also be used after the leaves have dropped in the fall. Never spray when any foliage or fruit is on the trees.

No Browsing, Please

Q. What's the best way to keep deer out of my orchard, short of shooting them?

A. The only method known to be 100 percent effective in keeping hungry deer out of orchards and fields is an 8-foot-tall woven wire fence. Electrified fences also seem to work well but are quite expensive. Scare devices and repellents have produced mixed results. Foxglove and castor beans have been reported to repel deer. Trap crops such as soybeans and corn planted around the perimeter of the orchard or garden often keep deer from venturing farther onto your land for food. Of the repellents, human hair wrapped in cheesecloth and hung from the lowest branches of trees and bloodmeal or human urine sprinkled around the base of trees are the most popular. But famished deer will often gnaw the bark off fruit trees despite these repellents. To discourage deer from "tip-pruning," wrap wire around the shoots in a spiral and extend the straight tip of the wire just beyond the end of the shoots. Thin iron-based wire will rust off in about a year, so you don't have to remove it before it interferes with the next season's growth.

About Apples and Pears

Apple branches:
Standard (top),
Spur-Type (bottom)

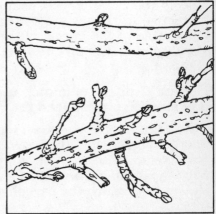

Winning Your Spurs

Q. **How are spur-type apple trees produced? How do nurseries propagate these trees, and how big can I expect them to grow?**

A. All spur-type fruit trees are developed from natural mutations with more than the average number of spurs—the short growths on the stems. These unusual trees were first grown in the late 1950s in Washington State from sprouts of trees that had died back to the roots after an exceptionally cold winter. The spur types on the market usually have a compact growth habit roughly equivalent to that of trees on semidwarfing rootstocks. A spur-type cultivar is grafted onto a standard rootstock, which is more vigorous and more extensive than a dwarfing rootstock, creating a stronger tree. Yields are high, since each spur is capable of producing an apple. (Production begins two to three years after planting, about the same as with dwarf apples.) Fruit thinning is especially important with spur-type trees, as overloaded branches can easily break.

Restoring Old Apple Trees

Q. **We bought a small farm recently with about a dozen neglected mature apple trees. We plan to prune them and apply a dormant oil spray. Is it safe to scrape the outer layer of bark to dislodge insect breeding grounds and diseased patches?**

A. Scraping the outer bark of your apple trees and using a dormant oil spray are excellent techniques. Pruning is usually best if done over a period of several years. Too much hard pruning in one year can cause excessive sucker growth and delay fruiting. Rotten knotholes in the trunk can be chiseled or trimmed to solid wood. But if they are deep enough to weaken the tree, it might be better to replace the tree with a dwarf interstem tree from a reliable nursery.

Tiny Apples

Q. **Our 'Golden Delicious' and 'Red Delicious' apple trees bear very small fruit. We feed the trees. What is wrong?**

A. Many apple varieties, including the ones you grow, tend to set more apples than the trees can handle. Several weeks after the trees bloom, thin the young apples until they are about 6 to 8 inches apart on the branches. This allows about 50 leaves per fruit, enough to produce the carbohydrates needed to mature a crop of full-size apples.

Drop Everything

Q. **I know trees are supposed to have some fruit drop, but last year my 'Rome' apple tree had June drop, July drop, August drop, and so on until there was no harvest. Can I do something now to prevent this next year?**

A. Several conditions can contribute to premature fruit drop just before harvest time. A tree often drops fruit because it is unable to support a large load. Many trees bear a heavy crop every other year rather than a crop of moderate size every year. To promote the annual bearing of a moderate crop, prune carefully and thin the fruit each year. Good soil fertility is essential, because a tree is prone to dump fruit if it runs out of fertilizer in late summer. Compost is an excellent source of nutrients. Sometimes too much or too little lime in the soil can cut off the nourishment just when the tree needs it badly, so check your pH and adjust it if it's very far off neutral (7.0). Lack of adequate rain during the summer and early fall can also keep vital nutrients from reaching your tree. Keep a thick organic mulch over the roots to retain moisture.

Unfortunately, some of the best late-maturing apples are prone to drop before they are ripe. 'Macintosh' apples are especially likely to drop early, as are many other members of its large family, including 'Early Mac', 'Macoun', 'Milton', 'Puritan', and 'Spartan'. Other apple favorites that are often early droppers are 'Earlyblaze', 'Niagra', 'Northern Spy', 'Red Astrachan', 'Rhode Island Greening', 'Rome', and 'Twenty Ounce'. Varieties more likely to stick to the tree until maturity are 'Cortland', 'Delicious', 'Empire', 'Holly', 'Honeygold', 'Idared', 'Lobo', 'Monroe', 'Mutsu', 'Spijon', and 'Stayman'.

Slow Summer Pruning

Q. **I summer-pruned my apple trees last July. In September the 'Cortland' bloomed heavily but later produced a very light crop. None of the other trees had this problem. What went wrong?**

A. July is a little early to prune, according to Dr. Alan Lakso, a plant physiologist at Cornell University, but it depends on the variety and climatic conditions. The rule of thumb is to wait until the shoots have stopped growing and terminal buds have formed (they'll look plump and dormant). 'Cortland' is a fairly vigorous variety and may have been induced to bloom if it was still actively growing when pruned.

Potato/Apple Problems

Q. **Some people say that as apples ripen, they release ethylene gas, which causes potatoes to sprout. To avoid this, you shouldn't store them together. But other people claim that the ethylene gas released by apples acts as a natural sprout inhibitor. Who's right?**

A. Both are right. Ethylene, a plant hormone given off by apples as they mature, can stimulate potato sprouting *and* inhibit it. Under warm conditions, the gas may encourage sprouting. However, if the area in which they are stored does not have good ventilation, enough ethylene gas may accumulate to inhibit sprouting. To prevent sprouting when apples and potatoes are stored together, make sure that temperatures never go above 45°F. Above that point, ethylene is released more rapidly. But the best advice is to store potatoes and apples apart.

Blistering Trees

Q. What causes the blisters on the trunk of my apple trees? Recently, they burst and secreted a brownish liquid. What's wrong?

A. Water blisters on the outer bark of the trunk are caused by the uptake of excess manganese from very acid soils. It's normal for them to burst, releasing a brown liquid that streaks down the bark. The blisters do not penetrate to the cambium. Manganese itself won't hurt the tree, but the low pH it indicates leads to reduced growth and yield. To control the problem, raise the soil pH by adding crushed limestone to the soil. Wood ashes, marl, and ground oyster shells are also very helpful and may be added to the compost pile.

The Tender Trap

Q. I would like to make moth traps for our apple trees. Can you tell me how?

A. Traps can take any form as long as they catch the pest in either the moth or larval stage. For flying insects, the easiest trap is to coat any type of surface with a sticky medium (Tanglefoot, pine tar, or anything similar) and hang it in the tree. Research indicates that moths are attracted to circles as opposed to squares, and the color orange seems to be an especially effective attractant—as are red and blue—while yellow is not very effective. Because insects follow a scent upward, traps do best when positioned on the windward side of a tree. Hang these traps at blossom time to catch the emerging moths at a young stage. Another effective form of hanging traps is nothing more than an attractive mixture placed in small containers of water. The moths are drawn to it and drown. You can successfully trap codling moths (the "worm in the apple") by pouring a mixture of molasses, water, and a little sugar into buckets. Codling moths are also sometimes attracted to sassafras oil. Try making a solid bait for codling moths by filling a small ice-cream cup two-thirds full of sawdust, stirring in a teaspoon of sassafras oil and a tablespoon of glacial acetic acid, and then adding enough liquid glue to saturate the sawdust thoroughly. When the cup is dry, suspend it in a mason jar partly filled with water.

To trap gypsy moth larvae, wrap several layers of burlap around the trunk and fold the top over to form a good shelter. Worms will be attracted to the burlap when they feel it is time to pupate. You can then crush the caterpillars inside the band or remove the band and shake them into a pail of water and kerosene. You can also apply bands of sticky material around the trees to foul up the pests as they travel up and down the tree. Inspect the bands every few days to kill any insects and reapply the sticky material.

Tanglefoot Tangles

Q. **We have several dwarf fruit trees. For the past five years, we've applied tree Tanglefoot to control gypsy moths. This week, we noticed the bands were dry and cracked. As we scraped, we found small white worms under the Tanglefoot, and the bark appeared to be rotted away. Will we lose the trees?**

A. Tanglefoot is used to control ants, gypsy moth caterpillars, cutworms, and other insects that tend to crawl up a tree. Heavy or careless applications can damage the bark. If you use a narrow band on a bearing tree for a season, you shouldn't have any problem, but avoid continuous applications. For extra protection on smooth-barked trees, put the Tanglefoot over a paper wrap. On rough-barked trees, cotton batting can be placed under the paper wrap to prevent bugs from climbing through crevices. On young fruit trees, always apply Tanglefoot over paper. The small white worms you noticed were probably feeding on the dead bark under the Tanglefoot. Carefully scrape the dead bark and old Tanglefoot from the area and determine the degree of damage. If your trees are seriously injured, a plastic wrap may prevent dehydration and help heal the damage.

Scabby Apples

Q. **I planted two 'Haralson' apple trees five years ago, and I manure them each fall in an area equal to the spread of their branches. Why are they producing only a few flowers and fewer scabby apples?**

A. "Your five-year-old apple trees should be producing abundant yields, especially with the manure applications. They may have poor drainage or be too close to large trees that shade them or rob their roots of nutrients, or they may have scab," explains Robert Kurle of the North American Fruit Explorers. "For scab control, use a spray of a handful of wood ashes and ground limestone to 2 gallons of water. We recommend that scab-resistant apple varieties like 'Prima' and 'Priscilla' be planted. Using dormant oil spray in early spring and giving your trees a mild pruning to let the sun through should also help.''

Blotched-Up Apples

Q. My 'Yellow Delicious' apples were covered with black mildew. It scrubbed off in a bleach/detergent solution, but could you tell me what caused it and how to prevent it without spraying?

A. If the apples felt sticky, the discoloration may have been caused by sooty mold. The mold colonizes honeydew that drips onto fruit from colonies of aphids feeding on nearby leaves and shoots. Aphids can be washed off with a high-pressure spray from the garden hose or killed with insecticidal soap. Apples can also be discolored by sooty blotch, a minor fungal disease that leaves an olive-green to brown or blackish stain on the skins. Sooty blotch often occurs with another minor fungal disease called flyspeck. Flyspeck creates circular patches of raised, shiny black dots on the fruit. These fungi infect apples during cool, wet weather in spring and fall. Since these diseases are skin-deep and don't spoil the flavor of the fruit, scrubbing or peeling the apples is probably the best way of dealing with them. If you can't stand the appearance, the sulfur sprays used to control apple scab should also control these fungi.

Cedar-Apple Rust

Q. We have cedar galls on our cedar and arborvitae trees, and we're wondering whether our nearby apple trees will be harmed. Is there anything that can be done about the galls?

A. Your apple trees will certainly be harmed! What your trees have is a curious disease called cedar-apple rust. It starts when spores are blown from infected cedars to apple trees, where they cause bright orange spots on the foliage and to a lesser degree on the fruit. The infections on apple foliage produce another spore stage that reinfects the cedar and keeps the vicious cycle going. The best control is to remove all red cedars, wild apples, and crabapples within a radius of one to two miles of the orchard. If this is impractical, you may want to cut down your apple trees and plant resistant varieties to break the destructive cedar-apple cycle.

Resistant varieties recommended by the USDA include 'Baldwin', 'Delicious', 'Rhode Island', 'Northwestern Greening', 'Franklin', 'Melrose', 'Red Astrachan', 'Stayman', 'Transparent', 'Golden Delicious', 'Winesap', 'Grimes Golden', and 'Duchess'.

Quince Rust Carryover

Q. I have a small quince bush in my yard, and I recently read that it can carry quince rust disease. Are my apples in danger?

A. Not unless there are junipers in the area. Like cedar-apple rust, quince rust requires red cedars or junipers to complete its life cycle, and it can't spread directly from quince to apple. The disease is relatively uncommon, so even if you have both junipers and an alternate host like quince, apple, pear, or hawthorn, you won't necessarily have a problem. Quince rust usually causes distorted fruit and sometimes affects twigs and buds, but it seldom spreads to the leaves. 'Red Delicious' apples are quite susceptible; varieties such as 'Rome' and 'Jonathan' are resistant. Control the fungus by pruning and burning diseased parts or by spraying with wettable sulfur.

Attack of the Pear Killers

Q. My pear trees are being injured by an insect or parasite that seems to enter the tree at or below ground level. I've never seen it. The bark splits and dries out. The wood under the bark is hard and dry, and the cambium layer is gone. The condition creeps up the trunk to the limbs. What is this?

A. From the brief description of the situation, it's hard to diagnose the problem. It could be damage from lawnmowers. It might be a bacterial root canker or type of root injury. If it is a canker, we suggest you remove any dirt from the infected area, trim away dead bark and limbs, and paint the infection with a brown creosote made from wood. Recovery is usually slow. If the trees have to be completely removed, don't plant other pear trees in the same location. Trim back the entire tree to compensate for root damage and fertilize the tree well. You might stake the tree to prevent wobbling until new roots grow. Contact your county extension agent if several trees have the same symptoms.

Cracked-Up Pears

Q. Why do my pears develop deep cracks that make them inedible?

A. Deep cracks, unnaturally rough, russeted skin, or deep, corky pits are all signs of a boron deficiency. Contact your county extension agent to have your soil or a sample of fruit tested to confirm this diagnosis. One way to correct the problem is to add unprocessed borax, a natural source of very slowly available boron, to your soil. Be sure to use *unprocessed* borax. (*Processed* borax, the kind found in grocery stores, can injure or kill plants.) Use borax sparingly. An excess of boron is harmful to soil and plants.

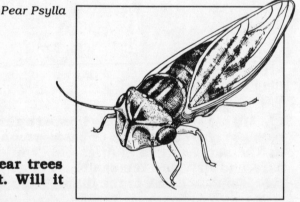

Pear Psylla

Sooty Pears

Q. My three dwarf pear trees are covered with soot. Will it harm them?

A. The "soot" on your trees, called sooty mold, won't hurt them, because it's not a disease. It's a saprophytic fungus that lives on the sticky honeydew secreted by small (1/10-inch-long) insect pests called pear psyllas. They rarely do serious damage, but if you find the sooty mold unsightly, spray the trees with a dormant oil in early to mid-April, before the psyllas lay their eggs on spurs and branches. Repeat seven to ten days later. If psyllas and sooty mold are a problem later in the season, dust trees with diatomaceous earth or ground limestone.

Stone Fruits: Peaches, Plums, Apricots, and Cherries

Plucky Peach Tree

Q. A year ago, my parents planted a peach tree in their back-yard. The snow that winter broke off the main trunk. This year, the tree developed leaves, but it's getting wider, not higher. Can it be saved?

A. There's a good chance the tree will grow. Prune to one vigorous central leader. Cut off low side branches to force growth into this upward-growing leader, which will become the new trunk. One caution: Make sure the growing shoots have not come from below the graft (the swollen part that is usually right above the ground); if shoots are that low, you've lost the variety you started with and should buy a new tree.

Frost Fighters

Q. I live in a mountain valley of Kentucky. Every year we have about three weeks of warm weather, which puts every peach tree in bloom. This is followed by several nights of frost, leaving us without any peaches. I have considered using smudge pots but cannot find them anywhere. What do you advise?

A. Smudge pots are actually outlawed in some states. If yours is not one of them, you can use an empty tar barrel with one end cut out to burn charcoal on frosty nights. Place a barrel near enough to a tree that the heat can help it but far enough away that it won't burn the blossoms. If only one or two trees are involved, covering them with sheets or blankets takes only a few seconds and will save the buds. Another trick for the home gardener is to put an electric fan under the tree so that it forces air up and into the branches or to the side of the tree. The fan creates air currents that prevent frost from settling long enough to injure buds or blooms.

*Protecting Fruit
Tree Trunks*

Winter in the Southwest

Q. **Last spring I noticed a deep vertical split in the trunk of one of my peach trees. What caused it? Is there a way to protect my other trees?**

A. The problem may be southwest injury, which occurs in midwinter when the temperature drops rapidly on clear nights following sunny days. The low winter sun shines directly on the trunk all day and can raise the bark temperature on the southwest side more than 60 degrees higher than the air temperature by midafternoon. Snow aggravates the problem by reflecting more light onto the trunk. When temperatures plummet after sundown, rapid freezing of water in the trunk causes the bark to split. Tissue around the split dries out and dies, weakening the tree. Research on winter injury to peach trees conducted at the Georgia Experiment Station by Dr. R. A. Hayden showed that three- to seven-year-old trees are most vulnerable to southwest injury. The trunks of younger trees are too thin to absorb much heat, and the older trees are insulated by corky bark. To prevent this injury, keep the sun from warming the trunk. You can do this by leaning boards against the trees for shade, but the standard practice is to coat the trunks up to the scaffold limbs with white latex paint. The paint reflects sunlight and keeps the cambium temperature from rising more than about 10 degrees above air temperature. Use paint that doesn't contain mildew-killing compounds and apply it in late autumn after leaf fall.

Bitter Split Pits

Q. **Our 'Elberta' peaches develop split pits, gumming, and a bitter aftertaste, and often one side of the fruit ripens while the other side remains green. Is this a blight?**

A. Split pit and lopsidedness are physiological disorders, not diseases. Split pits occur under conditions that stimulate rapid growth of the fruit while the pit is hardening, such as warm weather, high rainfall or heavy irrigation (especially after a drought), or heavy feeding with nitrogen. This disorder is most common in years when fruits are large and the crop is light. Split pits, like other wounds in peaches, often exude bubbles of gum. The bitterness is thought to be caused by ethylene released by the pit. Lopsidedness is fairly common in peaches, plums, and cherries. Their flowers have two ovules, but one usually withers before bloom. The other ovule goes on to produce a seed, and that side of the fruit is often larger, sweeter, more colorful, and sometimes earlier-ripening than the other side. This is caused by uneven concentration of growth hormones. To help control these disorders, keep the soil evenly moist, especially during the early stages of fruit development. Don't overfeed with nitrogen and try not to overthin the fruit.

Rotten Luck

Q. **How is peach brown rot transmitted from year to year, and how can I control it? My early peach is not affected, while a nearby late peach is hit badly every year.**

A. Peach brown rot is a fungal disease that overwinters as cankers on twigs and infected shrunken fruit (mummies) on the tree and ground. In spring, the spores germinate during moist, warm weather above 70°F. They infect the blossoms, which turn brown and rot. The resulting fungus spreads to the fruit, and the peach develops a brown, mushy spot that may become covered with a gray powder of spores. Your early peach tree may escape because warm, moist weather occurs after the tree blossoms, or that variety may be less susceptible to brown rot. 'Baby Gold', 'Goldhaven', and 'Elberta' are among the most resistant peaches; 'Mayflower', 'Red Bird', 'Hale Haven', 'Summer Crest', and 'South Haven' are among the most susceptible.

Your best bet against peach brown rot is sanitation. In the fall, pick up and burn or bury all fallen mummies. Prune out any badly cankered twigs before leaf fall. During early spring pruning, thin the trees to encourage rapid drying after rains. Peaches are more likely to become infected if they're punctured by insects, so control of pests like plum curculio is important. If the problem persists, spray with a wettable sulfur powder at blossoming and after rains.

Consult your county agent for the best timing of the spray in your region. Dip freshly picked peaches into 120°F water for approximately seven minutes. This won't harm the peaches, but the heat will kill the fungi.

Plum Disappointed

Q. I have a prune-type plum that was loaded with fruit last year. However, as they started to ripen, brown spots appeared on all the plums, and they either rotted or shriveled up. How can I control this problem organically?

A. What you describe is undoubtedly brown rot (*Monilinia fructicola*), one of the most common and serious fungal diseases of stone fruits. The first symptoms usually appear on the flowers as brown spots, followed by a gray fuzz in humid weather. The rotten flowers may cling to the twigs for some time. Frequently, the infection travels to the twigs, where a depressed, reddish-brown, shield-shaped canker forms. Because the fruits' main source of infection comes from these flowers and twigs, the best time to control brown rot is when your plum tree is in bloom. Dust or spray with sulfur two to four times after the blossom buds show pink until the petals fall. Sanitation is also very important. Twig cankers and rotted, shriveled fruit are the primary overwintering sites for spores, which infect the flowers the following spring. Remove and burn all infected fruit and twigs.

A Knotty Problem

Q. Many branches on our plum tree have developed rough, woody swellings, but the tree is still growing and bearing well. What causes this disease, and will it eventually kill the tree?

A. Your tree has black knot, a fungal disease that also attacks cherries. The fungus elongates the knots from year to year, stunting and gradually killing the branches by reducing the flow of water and nutrients. Black knot is spread by spores released during wet, warm spring weather. The spores infect new growth, producing olive-green swellings by late summer or the following spring. The swellings become black and warty and usually begin producing spores of their own the second spring after they appear. Cut down badly infected trees with many dead branches and remove knotted wild plums and cherries within 500 feet of trees under cultivation. If you feel you must keep infected trees, cut off all infected twigs and branches at least 4 inches below the knots and burn them. Do this in early spring while the trees are still dormant. Cut out knots on the trunk or scaffold limbs along with an inch of surrounding healthy wood. Coat the wounds with tree-wound dressing. The plum cultivars 'Formosa', 'Santa Rosa', and 'Shiro' are only slightly susceptible to black knot, and 'President' is resistant.

Spurring On Apricots

Q. **Our three-year-old apricot trees are producing numerous short spurs on the branches. How do we prune the trees? Should we cut these spurs off?**

A. Prune young apricot trees lightly, just enough to shape them. You can either train apricots like peaches, which have three main limbs, or like apple trees, which have scaffold branches on a single trunk. (This method is called the modified leader system.) Since the fruit buds are produced on one-year-old shoot tips and spurs, don't remove them this year unless the trees have set such a heavy crop that branches might break. After about three years, these spurs and shoots will stop producing. When the trees are dormant, cut back the nonproductive branches to stimulate new growth.

Birds and Bees and Cherry Trees

Q. **I have one tart and one sweet cherry tree, both self-fertile. For the past three years, most of the cherries have fallen off both trees when only ⅛ to ¼ inch long. The trees aren't bothered by insects or diseases, but sometimes we get bad weather when they bloom. Why don't the cherries ripen, and is there anything we can do about it?**

A. Young, vigorously growing trees sometimes invest their energy in vegetative growth at the expense of fruit production. If this is the problem, your trees will outgrow it and ripen their fruit when they become more mature. Bad weather at flowering time can prevent pollination, causing a crop loss. Cherry flowers are most receptive to pollen the first two days they're open. If cold, damp weather keeps bees away, most of the flowers won't be pollinated. If you consistently get unfavorable weather when your cherries bloom, you might have to pollinate them by hand or keep a beehive near the trees. Bees will be more likely to visit the flowers if they don't have far to fly. Beekeepers will usually rent you a hive during bloom season.

Cherry Fruit Fly:
Pupa (left),
Adult (center),
Maggot (right)

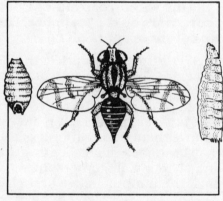

Cherry Fly Traps

Q. Every year there are little white worms in my cherries. How can I keep them out?

A. The worms are cherry fruit fly maggots. The only way to keep them out is to trap or spray the flies before they can lay eggs in the cherries. Adult cherry fruit flies are two-thirds the size of houseflies and have yellow marks on the thorax, four narrow, white bands on the abdomen, and black bars on their clear wings. To trap them, coat two or three bright yellow 10-by-10-inch boards with Tack Trap or Tanglefoot. Hang these boards in the tree about three weeks after bloom, just after the flies emerge from the ground. The boards will be even more attractive if you attach a small jar containing a solution of equal parts household ammonia and water. When the female flies are ready to lay eggs, they can be attracted to sticky, red, apple-size plastic (or wooden) balls. Hang six balls in the tree when you begin to catch flies on the yellow boards. The traps alone might catch enough flies so that you get an acceptable cherry crop. If you find that they don't, spray with rotenone as soon as you see flies on the red balls, and repeat at weekly intervals if trap counts warrant it. Two or three applications should be enough.

Citrus and Other Tropical Treats

Grappling with Grapefruit

Q. **We have a 20-year-old grapefruit tree that's taking over the yard. When and how can we prune it?**

A. In citrus trees, flushes of growth alternate with periods of rest throughout the year. Prune during any of the rest periods, but preferably in winter. Pick a time when most of the fruit has been harvested. Unless you need to remove diseased, competing, or crossed and rubbing branches, try to avoid opening the canopy of the tree. Letting sunlight in can stimulate a jungle of water sprouts and cause burning of the exposed bark. Instead, head back branches to strong lateral shoots, trying to maintain the natural shape of the tree. If you need to remove lower branches, paint the exposed trunk and bases of scaffold limbs with whitewash or a half-and-half solution of water and white latex paint (without fungicide) to protect against sunscald. Citrus trees can also be sheared into formal or semiformal shapes, but this reduces fruit production. Your county extension agent will have more information on pruning citrus.

Whitefly Attack

Q. **There has been an outbreak of citrus whitefly in this area, and garden centers prescribe malathion. Is there an organic alternative?**

A. Like greenhouse whiteflies, citrus whiteflies feed on the undersides of leaves, scattering like flying dandruff when disturbed. The adults and their scalelike nymphs suck sap and excrete honeydew, which becomes covered with sooty mold. Horticultural oil sprays used against scale insects will also control citrus whitefly. Follow dilution directions on the label. Oil sprays may cause some cosmetic damage to fruits and can make the trees more susceptible to winter injury if applied in late fall. If you must spray in late fall, use commercial insecticidal soap, which is known to control greenhouse whitefly and related insects.

Bringing Up Kiwi

Q. I tried to start kiwifruit from seed but it didn't germinate. What went wrong? Also, will the vine be hardy in my area— Oregon?

A. Kiwi seed germinates best when sown immediately after removing it from the fruit. It takes three weeks at 65° to 75°F for it to sprout. When the seedlings are 3 inches high, transfer them to 3- or 4-inch pots. Plant outside after the danger of frost is past. The vines will flower within several years, but since they are dioecious (sexes on separate plants), you'll need a male and a female plant (or at least one male for every eight females) for fruit to be produced. You can also graft a male branch on a female vine. Fruit quality will be unpredictable because you started with seed. For more certain results, grow the named varieties available from nurseries. The vines of *Actinida chinensis* are hardy to 10°F (0°F if well mulched) and should survive in your area. As a rule, they can be grown wherever wine grapes are found. Hardy kiwis (*A. arguta*) are hardy to −25°F.

Fruitless Figs

Q. My fig tree is loaded with fruit every year in late summer, but only a handful ripen. I don't feed the tree, but I do keep it watered. What else should I do?

A. Figs need warm weather to ripen. If the fruit is almost ripe when cool fall weather comes, try covering the tree with a clear plastic tarp to raise temperatures and extend the season. If that doesn't work, transplant the tree to a warmer microclimate, such as against the south wall of a house. Even if they're not fertilized, figs growing in rich soils can produce lush new growth that doesn't set fruit until late in the season. To induce earlier fruit set, limit new growth to a few well-spaced stems so sunlight can reach the center of the tree. Root pruning in spring or early summer can also control topgrowth and stimulate fruiting. Cut roots by repeatedly driving a spade into the soil all around the dripline. A good way both to control growth and protect the plant in winter is to grow it in a 30-gallon container that can be moved indoors. If none of these techniques works, try planting a shorter-season variety, such as 'Osborne Prolific' or 'Hardy Chicago'.

The Wild Bunch: Mulberries, Pawpaws, and Persimmons

Mulberry Flowers:
Male (top),
Female (bottom)

Mum Mulberries

Q. I planted eight seedling mulberry trees. All are doing well, but half of them don't produce any fruit. Can you tell me why?

A. Mulberry trees are usually either exclusively male or female. Occasionally a tree will grow that has both male and female flowers. Trees that produce only male flowers will never have berries. However, female trees will often set fruit without the benefit of pollen. Mulberry flowers, both male and female, are catkins. The male catkins are longer. Viewed through a magnifying glass, male florets will show four stamens. If your nonproductive trees have female flowers, chances are the plants haven't yet come of age. Mulberry seedlings tend to be quite variable, and bearing age can differ widely from tree to tree.

Pawpawless Westerners

Q. I'm curious about pawpaw trees. Can I grow the fruit in my La Mesa, California, climate?

A. Probably not. Pawpaws need a winter chill to break dormancy in the spring. They do best in areas with cold winters, humid summers, and 30 inches or more of rain a year, most of it falling during the growing season. Pawpaws are hardy to −30°F and thrive in USDA Hardiness Zones 5 through 9.

Persistent Persimmons

Q. I have two American persimmon trees that I raised from seed. One tree never bears fruit; the other bears heavily, but the fruit never falls and can't be shaken off the tree, even in winter. The parent tree produces excellent fruit. Is there anything I can do besides cut them down?

A. Yes, you can improve your trees by grafting scionwood of a named variety or of a good wild type onto the branches. Use the same techniques you would use to topwork an apple tree. As is true of most fruits, persimmons grown from seed rarely produce fruit of the same quality as the parent. In addition, persimmons are usually dioecious—they produce male and female flowers on separate trees. Your nonbearing tree is probably male. Leave some of the branches on the male tree intact to be sure pollination occurs.

All Puckered Up

Q. We picked our oriental persimmons a little early and they're puckery. How can we make them edible?

A. A time-tested way to remove astringency is to tightly seal firm-ripe persimmons in a plastic bag with a few ripe apples. Leave them alone for a few days at room temperature. Ethylene gas given off by the apples ripens the persimmons, which are ready to eat when soft. Researchers in Israel recently found that bagged persimmons ripened just as well without the apples. They attributed ripening, which occurred in three or four days, to low oxygen levels in the tightly sealed bags. Persimmons will keep in the bags for about ten days at room temperature.

Mixed Nuts and Maple Syrup

Unripe Almonds

Q. Last year, my 'Hall's Hardy' almond trees finally bore a crop, but half the kernels were nothing more than dry husks. The trees weren't affected by insects or disease. Can you suggest a reason?

A. The withered nut meats indicate that the trees didn't receive enough heat units to mature. (Heat units, or growing degree-days, are a measurement of temperatures accumulated over the growing season.) Just prior to ripening, the kernels resemble a milky liquid. If the nuts fall from the tree too soon, the liquid just dries up instead of solidifying. There's really nothing you can do except hope for a longer stretch of warm weather. Planting on the south side of a building or wall isn't recommended, as it increases the risk of frost damage to the blossoms.

Grubby Chestnuts

Q. Last fall two-thirds of my Chinese chestnuts had worms. Is there a way to control them?

A. You can control chestnut-weevil grubs by picking up all nuts that fall to the ground every day, according to Dr. Warren Johnson, an entomologist at Cornell University. Store the nuts in tightly sealed containers and destroy any grubs that emerge. Since the weevils overwinter in the ground, in three to four years you will greatly reduce the number of infested nuts if you follow this practice every season.

Pruning for Plenty

Q. I planted two American filberts this spring. How should I prune them for best nut production?

A. American filberts grow naturally as freely suckering shrubs. Prune them to five or six main stems, and if necessary, thin the tops so that light can reach all the branches. Cut out the older stems when they become unproductive and train some of the suckers as replacements. Vigorous suckers with strong roots make good transplants if you want to start new bushes. For better pollination, many experts recommend growing three different varieties, so consider planting one more.

Jet-Setting Filberts

Q. Eight years ago we planted one European and one American filbert, but so far only the American bush has produced a few small nuts. Aren't they supposed to pollinate each other?

A. The European filbert will pollinate the American but not vice versa, says Douglas Campbell, filbert grower and member of the Northern Nut Growers Association. However, bloom times must overlap for pollination to be successful, and this rarely happens when only two plants are grown. To ensure a bountiful supply of nuts, you should have at least three—preferably four or five—different varieties of each species. Most American filberts offered for sale are close to the wild state and are not very productive. Campbell recommends planting European filberts or Euro-American hybrids instead, since Europeans and hybrids pollinate each other if enough varieties are planted. The hybrids combine the hardiness and filbert-blight resistance of the American filbert with the large, thin-shelled, flavorful nuts of the European species and are three to four times more productive than ordinary strains.

Stratified Seed

Q. I want to plant hickory nuts for rootstocks. I've been told that the seed should be stratified. What does this mean?

A. Stratification (also called moist-chilling) is a technique to break seed dormancy by reproducing winter conditions. Trees and shrubs with a hard seed coat must be soaked two to four days before chilling. Then put the seeds in a moist medium such as sphagnum moss, vermiculite, or old sawdust. Mix the seeds with one to three times their volume of medium, or alternate layers of seeds and medium. Put the mixture or layers in a container that will allow aeration, such as a polyethylene bag, tin, or jar with a perforated lid. Store at temperatures just above freezing (35° to 45°F) for one to six months, depending on the species. Hickories should be stored for three to four months before planting. Storage time and temperature recommendations for most trees and shrubs can be found in *Seeds of Woody Plants in the United States* (USDA Forest Service, Agriculture Handbook #450). Check with your local public or university library.

Hickory Headaches

Q. My hickory nuts, especially those still in the green shucks, often contain small, brown-headed worms. How can I get rid of them?

A. The pests could be pecan weevils or hickory shuckworms. Adult pecan weevils are ¾-inch-long, brown, long-snouted beetles that emerge from the ground in August or September and crawl up hickory or pecan trees. They feed on the shucks and nuts before the shells harden (often causing the nuts to drop prematurely) and lay eggs in nearly mature nuts. The creamy white, brown-headed grubs feed on the kernels till they mature, then cut round ⅛-inch exit holes and enter the soil to pupate for two or three years. Pecan weevils usually don't move far from the tree where they hatched, so if your trees are isolated, you should be able to reduce the population without spraying. You can monitor weevil emergence and intercept many of the adults by tying skirts of burlap around the trunks by August 1. Those that avoid the burlap can be caught by spreading sheets under the trees and jarring the limbs with a padded pole. Pecan weevils drop to the ground when disturbed. If you still get too many wormy nuts, try a botanical spray such as rotenone.

The hickory shuckworm, a brown-headed, off-white caterpillar under an inch long, is the larva of a moth that may produce up to four generations a year. The caterpillars bore into pecans and hickory nuts before the shells harden (causing premature drop) or feed in the shucks of older nuts, which fail to fill out properly and develop stained shells. Because it is highly mobile and can produce several generations each year, this pest is hard to control. The caterpillars overwinter in shucks both on the ground and in the trees. You can reduce the population by cleaning up and burning all the old shucks in fall. If you need to spray, apply a botanical insecticide three times at two-week intervals, starting in August when the shells begin to harden.

Twig Girdler

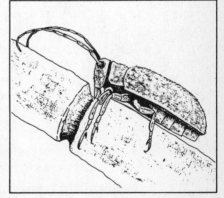

That's Some Girdle

Q. A bug girdles the small branches of my hickories and pecans, causing them to break off. What control do you suggest?

A. Your trees are host to the twig girdler, which lays eggs in the girdled twigs in late summer and fall. The grubs feed in the wood until the following August, when they change into adults. Gather and burn girdled twigs of domestic and nearby wild trees in late fall and winter to kill the eggs and young grubs.

No Better Nutcracker

Q. I hate to crack hickory nuts one by one. Is there an easier way? I tried a pressure cooker method, but it did not work.

A. Sorry—as far as we know, hickory nuts need to be cracked one by one. The task is easier if you use a nutcracker designed specifically for tough nuts like black walnuts, hickory nuts, and butternuts, but the 16-ounce hammer is still the preferred tool of many nut enthusiasts. To make cracking easier with whatever tool you use, don't let the nuts dry out and plant varieties known to be good crackers, such as 'Porter', 'Walters', 'Weschcke', 'Fayette', or 'Henry'.

Stop Those Stinkbugs!

Q. My pecans become partly black and bitter. I was told this is caused by a virus transmitted by a bug. Can you give me more details and a remedy?

A. Your pecans have kernel spot, which isn't a virus but a feeding injury caused by stinkbugs, leaf-footed bugs, or related species. The bugs pierce the shells of the maturing nuts and inject saliva that partly dissolves and discolors the kernel. The adults are ½-inch-long, green or brown, shield-shaped insects. They winter in plant debris, emerging to lay eggs in early spring. The young bugs feed on weeds, vegetables, and field and cover crops, then fly to trees when full grown. There may be up to four generations a year. Control these pests by reducing their breeding areas, says Dr. Jerry Payne, pecan specialist at the University of Georgia. Keep weeds mowed and avoid planting summer cover crops. (Winter cover crops like hairy vetch and crimson clover don't harbor the pests.) Watch for the bugs on your vegetables and handpick or spray with soap, pyrethrum, rotenone, or sabadilla if they become numerous. Clean up dead plants—the pests' winter quarters—in fall.

Walnutless

Q. My English walnut trees refuse to set fruit. One set two nuts three years after I transplanted it, but it hasn't set a crop since. What can I do?

A. Walnut trees take from 4 to 12 years after transplanting to begin producing nuts. Your trees may simply be too young. A problem with pollination could also be contributing to lack of nut set.

This often happens when only one walnut cultivar is planted. Many times, the pollen and the pistils on a tree mature at different times, so pollination does not occur. Planting another variety usually solves this problem. Contact a local nut tree association for suggested varieties.

To Prune or Not to Prune?

Q. Should the leaders of newly planted Carpathian walnuts be cut back or left unpruned?

A. Cut them back to 24 to 30 inches above the bud union, advise nut researchers Bill Reid of Kansas State University and Loy Shreve of Texas A&M. Taprooted trees such as Carpathian walnuts and other nuts suffer massive root loss with even the most careful transplanting. If the top isn't pruned, more buds will sprout than the reduced root system can support, resulting in weak growth that may not survive such stresses as drought, disease, and winter temperatures. Pruning channels the tree's limited resources into fewer buds, which should produce a strong new leader.

Tents in Walnut Trees

Q. Every year, fuzzy, yellow-brown caterpillars about an inch long make webs in our English walnut tree. How can we stop them?

A. The caterpillars are fall webworms, which spin loose tents on the ends of branches and skeletonize the foliage inside. The dirty white tents are unsightly, but there are seldom enough caterpillars to injure the tree. When the tents begin to appear in early summer, prune infested branches or spray with *Bacillus thuringiensis* (Bt).

A Boring Subject

Q. I was disappointed when I found worms in my walnut harvest this year. Is there any way to avoid an infestation of them in the future? What are they?

A. Most likely, they are filbert worms. Filbert worms bore into nuts, including acorns, filberts (hazelnuts), chestnuts, and walnuts. They look like small, pinkish caterpillars about ¾ inch long while they're feeding in the nuts. In their adult stage, they turn into moths with a wingspread of about ½ inch and two golden bands across each forewing. They lay their eggs singly on top of leaves. Filbert worms overwinter in silken cocoons found in the soil, leaves, and debris on the ground, so fall cleanup and mulches are useful. Adult moths usually begin to emerge in early July, and may continue to appear through late August and early September, at which time their egg laying begins. The eggs hatch in about eight or nine days, and the new larvae go hunting for nuts. In the future, avoid this pest by practicing good sanitation under the trees. Harvest nuts as early as possible and dry them immediately.

Rotten Walnuts

Q. Last year a disease rotted the hulls of all my Carpathian walnuts and turned the kernels black. How can I combat this problem?

A. Your nuts were spoiled by walnut anthracnose, a fungal disease that also causes spotting and yellowing of leaves. Anthracnose can defoliate trees by midsummer, which saps the energy of a tree so it can't fill out its nuts properly. Infected nuts often drop prematurely and have dark, shriveled kernels. The fungus spreads fastest in wet summer weather, when the brown spots characteristic of the disease become a common sight on leaves of wild trees. You may be able to reduce infection by raking and burning all leaves and diseased nuts in fall. However, the most effective control is to replace or topwork susceptible trees with resistant varieties like 'Reda', which is hardy to central Kansas.

Sweet Trees

Q. I just moved to Vermont and would like to experiment with making my own maple syrup this winter. Although I have my pick of trees, I don't know which ones are best for tapping. Any suggestions?

A. You're in prime territory for making your own maple syrup! But don't attempt to tap your trees until the sap rises—when daytime temperatures reach above freezing but nights are still below freezing. Try any or all maple species that are available. The sugar maple, *Acer saccharum*, and the very closely related black maple, *A. nigrum*, are best for sugar content and taste. Coming in a close third is the Norway maple, *A. platanoides*, followed by the common box elder, *A. negundo*. Next in quality is the red or swamp maple, *A. rubrum,* and the silver maple, *A. saccharinum.* Bear in mind that the sugar content of maple sap also differs widely from tree to tree, even in the same species.

Spigots for Sugaring

Q. After tapping trees for maple sugaring, what do I do with the spigots? Should the holes be plugged after they are removed?

A. Robert Foulds, an extension forester in Vermont, tells us the tapholes should not necessarily be plugged when the spout is removed. He knows people who tap maples and have fitted dowels in the holes, but it does not seem to make a difference. The wood in the immediate area of the taphole is dead, and the bark around the hole might be stained. However, a hardy tree will heal in two years, so the emphasis is on keeping your trees as healthy as possible. The following year, tap no closer than 16 inches above or below the old taphole and ½ inch to either side. It's also important to wash the spouts, then sanitize (in a solution of 1 part liquid bleach to 20 parts water), drain, and store them in a covered container for the winter.

time as cold-hardy vegetables like cabbage and leaf lettuce. Acclimate the seedlings for a week before transplanting by keeping them in a coldframe that's vented on mild days or by setting them outside in a sheltered place on days when the temperature stays above freezing. Like the vegetables, these flowers will tolerate light frosts but not hard freezes. Hardy annuals are even more frost-tolerant if sown directly outdoors in fall or as soon as the ground can be worked in spring. Some, like bachelor's button and larkspur, will germinate in fall and survive the winter as seedling rosettes if protected by snow cover or a light mulch. Many hardy annuals will self-sow prolifically; watch for their seedlings when you clean up in fall or begin cultivating in early spring.

Sprouting Small Seeds

Q. I have tried unsuccessfully to germinate the fine seeds of browallia, begonia, calceolaria, and other flowers. Do you have any suggestions?

A. The seeds of all three require light to germinate, so don't cover them after sowing. Use a light medium, such as a 3:1 mixture of peat and vermiculite. Was the soil warm enough? Ideally, the temperature should be 75°F, although tuberous begonia seed will germinate at 65°F. Begonia and browallia seed will sprout in two to three weeks; calceolaria takes five to ten days.

Generating Geraniums

Q. I haven't had any luck starting geraniums from old plants. What's the best technique?

A. Geraniums root best in the spring and summer when they are putting out new growth. If you take cuttings in the late fall or winter, they are more likely to rot than root. For success, take the cuttings from succulent young growth rather than larger, woody stems. Cut 2- to 3-inch pieces from the tips of the stems. Include several nodes (the point where the leaf meets the stem) in each cutting. Take off the lower leaves and stick the bottom part of the stem into a sterile medium of vermiculite and sand. Put in a sunny place and keep the medium evenly moist. In two to three weeks, dig up a cutting to check on its progress. When ¾-inch roots have formed, pot the young plant.

Perpetual Geraniums

Q. I grew over 40 geraniums this summer and hated to let them freeze, but I would have had no place to put them if I had potted them all up. Is there some other way to overwinter the plants?

A. Geraniums, which are treated as annuals but are really tender perennials, can be carried through even northern winters. Choose your nicest plants, cut them back severely, and pot them up to add color to your home in the gray season. Dig up the remaining geraniums and store them without soil in a cool, humid storage area such as an unheated, earth-floored basement or a root cellar. In the spring, prune back to the main stem and replant.

Blackleg Kicks Geraniums

Q. About a week after we transplanted our geranium seedlings into unsterilized soil, the leaves on many of the plants turned red; the stems darkened and the plants died. What killed them, and how can we prevent a recurrence?

A. Your plants had blackleg, a common disease of geranium seedlings and cuttings that is caused by the soilborne fungus pythium. It can be prevented by practicing good sanitation. Pasteurize potting soil by heating it to 160° to 180°F and holding that temperature for 30 minutes. Disinfect pots, flats, and tools by soaking them in a solution of 1 part chlorine bleach to 9 parts water for 10 minutes. Space potted plants so the leaves don't touch, and avoid overwatering.

Doubt about
Double Impatiens

Q. I grew double impatiens from seed but was disappointed when many turned out to be single or only semidouble. Did I get ripped off?

A. No. Right now, the best you can expect from double impatiens seed is 40 to 50 percent fully double flowers. Reputable seed dealers indicate this on the package. When double-flowered impatiens first appeared in 1968 as a mutant, propagation was a problem because the plant didn't produce viable pollen. Renowned breeder Claude Hope solved the dilemma by crossing doubles with semidoubles and singles, and seed was made available in 1983. But because of the mixed parentage, the progeny are not all double. New varieties like 'Rosette', 'Duet', and 'Double-Up' are much improved over early strains, with more compact foliage and large, roselike flowers.

Impotent Impatiens

Q. **Three years ago we were given a red-flowered impatiens with variegated leaves. It grows well from stem cuttings, but its seeds won't germinate. Do they need special treatment?**

A. Your impatiens is almost certainly one of the New Guinea hybrids, which generally produce very few, mostly sterile seeds. The only New Guinea hybrid that can be grown from seed is 'Sweet Sue', an orange-flowered variety with bronzy green leaves. Continue to propagate your plant from cuttings—it's the only way to reproduce the other New Guinea varieties.

Statice Symbols

Q. **Can you tell me how to grow annual statice and the best time to pick it for drying?**

A. Statice (*Limonium sinuatum*) needs a long season for profuse bloom. Buy hulled seeds for high germination rates. Sow it in flats indoors at 70°F six to eight weeks before the last frost. Transplant to small pots or other flats when the first true leaves appear. After the last frost, set out the plants about 12 inches apart in fertile, well-drained soil in full sun. Statice tolerates drought but will produce many more flowers if watered in dry weather. Statice produces a flower head crowded with many small, papery, funnel-shaped blooms, not all of which open at the same time. For maximum color, cut the stems when most of the funnels are fully open. If you wait too long, the oldest flowers will begin to brown or fade. Yellow and white varieties sometimes fade faster and may need to be picked sooner than darker colors. Cut the flowers on a clear day and hang them to dry in a well-ventilated place out of direct sunlight.

Strange Sunflower

Q. One of the 'Mammoth' sunflower seeds I planted grew 11 feet tall and produced 32 flower heads, none more than 6 inches across. Is this rare? What caused it?

A. It *is* unusual. Sunflower expert Dr. Charles B. Heiser, Jr., of Indiana University explains why: Giant cultivated sunflowers are descended from the common or wild sunflower *Helianthus annuus*, which is a tall, branching plant that produces many small flower heads. Native Americans domesticated this species, selecting and propagating mutants that produced unbranched plants with single heads. Modern plant breeders have reinforced this characteristic in varieties like 'Mammoth', but occasionally the ancestral branching habit comes through, producing a plant like yours.

Less-Sweet Peas

Q. I saved my own sweet pea seed for many years but last year was unable to do so. None of the varieties I've grown this year have that good old-fashioned fragrance. Can you help?

A. The original strains of sweet pea were extremely fragrant— they were said to have one of the most delicious scents in the plant kingdom. Their sweet odor and masses of colorful blossoms made them the most popular flowers at the turn of the century. But because these older types languished in the heat, which shortened their bloom time, breeders worked to replace them with more heat-tolerant varieties. Unfortunately, much of the distinctive fragrance was sacrificed in the process. More recently, breeding efforts have been made to regain the scent. Some recent cultivars to try are 'Snoopea', 'Rosy Frills', 'Leamington', and 'Royal Wedding'. Old-fashioned varieties once again available are 'Antique Fantasy' and 'Painted Lady'.

Mildewproof Zinnias

Q. My zinnias produce only one flush of bloom before mildew spoils the leaves and flowers, even though I grow them in full sun with wide spacing. Can you recommend disease-resistant varieties?

A. Yes. Of more than 40 zinnia cultivars grown in ten years at the Rodale Research Center, Kutztown, Pennsylvania, the 'Ruffles' series (especially 'Scarlet Ruffles') has been outstanding for disease resistance and flower production, even under crowded conditions in less than full sun. 'Chippendale', 'State Fair', 'Yellow Marvel', 'Small World Cherry', and the 'Border Beauty' series are tolerant of powdery mildew.

Puzzling Perennials and Biennials

Divide and Multiply

Q. When is the best time to divide my perennials?

A. Many perennials die down by themselves in the fall, making this a good season to dig up the plants (very carefully!) to divide them. The advantage of dividing perennials in the fall is that they can get established before the next season. Established plants will be less likely than spring-divided plants to have a setback, which can cause reduction or loss of bloom for a year. The disadvantage is that the looseness of the soil around the transplanted perennial may cause heaving during the soil's alternating freezing and thawing in winter and spring. A thick mulch will help keep the division's roots underground.

Feeding Perennials

Q. I recently moved to a house that has a perennial flower border. What's the best way to fertilize it?

A. In general, perennials don't need heavy doses of fertilizer, since they produce only flowers and not fruit. (The practice of dead-heading—removing faded flowers—prevents seed-head formation.) Most herbaceous perennials can be maintained from year to year by mulching with compost, grass clippings, leaves, pine needles, or straw. You can top this with wood chips or pine bark if you prefer their textures, but they decompose too slowly to be of nutritional value. Perennials like astilbe, bleeding-heart, delphinium, and Shasta daisy, which are heavy feeders, should receive several summer applications of manure tea or fish emulsion. On the other hand, keep high-nutrient mulches away from species such as yarrow and butterfly weed, which grow best in a relatively infertile soil.

Bringing Up Baby

Q. I've been unable to grow baby's breath—either perennial or annual—from seed. Can you suggest a successful technique?

A. Sow seed of perennial baby's breath (*Gypsophila paniculata*) indoors in flats of light, porous potting mix in late winter or early spring. Barely cover the seed. At 70°F, the seeds will germinate in one to two weeks. The seedlings quickly develop heavy roots. Transplant them into 2¼- or 3-inch peat pots as soon as the first true leaves appear, and grow them in a cool, bright window or a frost-free coldframe. After frost, set the plants in well-drained, deeply dug flowerbeds in full sun. Baby's breath is a lime-lover: Add ground limestone as needed to maintain a pH of 7.0 to 7.5. Annual baby's breath (*G. elegans*) doesn't transplant well and blooms for only about six weeks even if faded flowers are removed. Direct-seed in spring (pH requirement is the same as for the perennial type), and make successive sowings every two weeks until hot weather if you want to prolong its season. Alternatively, sow pinches of seed in 3-inch peat pots two or three weeks before the last frost. Set these out about 8 inches apart before the pots check growth and stimulate premature flowering.

Crown Rot in Canterbury

Q. My Canterbury bells (*Campanula medium*) develop a type of rot that turns the base of the plant to mush. How can I prevent it?

A. Canterbury bells are very susceptible to crown rot, which is caused by two soilborne fungi, *Sclerotium rolfsi* (Southern blight) and *Sclerotinia sclerotiorum* (stem rot). These diseases are most destructive during warm, humid weather when the soil is moist. To prevent the disease, make sure the soil drains well and avoid overwatering. Keep the crowns as dry as possible by setting them at or slightly above soil level when planting. A traditional rot preventive is to fill in around the crowns with coarse sand instead of soil. Space plants so air circulates freely. Feed moderately; too much fertilizer produces lush, succulent leaves that mat over the crown and keep it wet. Well-timed planting of these biennials also helps prevent crown rot. Sow seeds in flats in late June or July, then line out the seedlings about 10 inches apart in a coldframe. Early the next spring, move the mature plants with a ball of earth into your flower beds. Pull and discard after bloom in June, since the fungi overwinter in dead plants and in the soil. If you have infected plants, dig out 6 inches of surrounding soil along with the plants.

Daylilies Get Spring Fever

Q. **Several leaves of my daylily (hemerocallis) plants have spots or brown blotches on them, and some plants die from the top down. They don't bloom as heavily as they should. What's wrong?**

A. The symptoms you describe are collectively called spring sickness. This is actually cold injury caused by late spring frosts, explains Ned Irish, publicity director of the American Hemerocallis Society. The leaves and flower buds can be damaged before they emerge from the crown of the plant, and symptoms may not show up until weeks later. There's not much you can do to prevent injury, although a heavy mulch of wood chips or pine needles sometimes helps, says Irish. Trim off browning leaves at the base. Some purple and lavender varieties seem to be especially susceptible, he notes, so you may want to try other colors as well as varieties reported to be hardy in colder climates.

Curbing Clematis Wilt

Q. **My clematis vine was green as grass and blooming beautifully when suddenly the leaves started dying. What made this happen?**

A. Any serious injury to the base of the vine, such as from a lawnmower or rodents, can cause the top to die back. If there is no evidence of such injury, the vine may have clematis wilt, a fungal disease that produces reddish lesions that girdle the stems, causing the foliage above the lesion to suddenly wither. On established plants, the older, woody stems in the upper part of the vine are usually attacked first, says Jim DeRue of D. S. George Nurseries in Fairport, New York, a nursery that specializes in clematis. On young plants, stems may be girdled just above the ground. If unchecked, the fungus moves up and down the stems, eventually killing the plant. Rainy weather and thick, tangled topgrowth that doesn't dry out favor the spread of the disease.

You can save a wilt-infected plant by radical pruning, says DeRue. As soon as you notice topgrowth withering, cut the vine back to 6 inches above the ground, or lower if there are lesions below this point. The vine will usually send up new shoots from the base, though clematis can be slow to resprout. To help prevent reinfection, immediately burn the prunings or dispose of them in a trash bag. Clematis hybrids in the *jackmanii* group are most susceptible to wilt, but no clematis is immune. The best way to keep from losing a plant is to take special steps at planting time, says DeRue. Clematis are fussy about their roots, which need both good drainage and moist soil. Choose a well-drained site and dig the planting hole 12 inches wide and deep. Put 6 inches of gravel in the bottom, then fill the hole with topsoil. Set new plants deeply enough so the lowest pair of buds (they're opposite each other on the stem) is below the soil surface. If the top dies for any reason, these buds will sprout and renew the vine. To help keep the soil moist, mulch the plants or shade the root zone by planting a ground cover.

Boredom Strikes Iris

Q. **I discovered borers in my bearded irises last summer, so I dug them, discarded the infested rhizomes, and reset the healthy ones. How can I keep the plants borer-free?**

A. After frost in fall, remove and compost or burn leaves, stems, and debris of irises and nearby plants to destroy overwintering eggs. In early spring, look for small holes and irregular, water-soaked streaks in the leaves; these are tunnels made by surviving larvae as they bore down toward the rhizome. Squeeze the leaves to crush the pests. Borer damage is easier to detect when the plants aren't overcrowded. Divide the clumps every three to four years in July so that you can find the borers in the rhizomes before they pupate.

Keeping Lily-of-the-Valley Cool

Q. **My lilies-of-the-valley flower well, but by August the leaves develop brown targetlike spots, then yellow and die. Why do they die back so early?**

A. Leaf-spotting fungi and hot, dry weather can cause lily-of-the-valley to die back early. Control the fungal diseases by raking off and burning all the dead foliage every fall or composting it in a hot pile. Lily-of-the-valley is a woodland plant that grows best under cool, moist conditions. To help keep it green all summer, top-dress with leaf mold or compost in fall or early spring and water during hot, dry spells.

No Luck with Lupines

Q. **I've had no luck getting lupine seeds to germinate. Can you help?**

A. Use fresh seeds to ensure viability. Before sowing, nick the hard seed coats or soak the seeds in warm water overnight. Plant them outdoors in early spring or germinate them indoors at 55° to 70°F. Using another method, place the seed packet in the freezer for 48 hours, then wrap the seeds in a wet paper towel for 24 hours before sowing indoors at about 55°F. With either method, germination may occur irregularly over two to three weeks. To avoid breaking their taproots, transplant seedlings while they're young or avoid transplanting by sowing in peat pots at two seeds per pot, later thinning to the stronger plant.

Patience with Peonies

Q. **The peonies I planted last year grew only about a foot tall and produced no blossoms. Why are they so small?**

A. The plants need more time to become established. Depending on growing conditions and the size of the divisions, peonies can take three to five years to reach full size after transplanting, and there may be few or no blooms for the first two years. If the plants still fail to grow and flower well after that time, they may be planted too deep. The roots should be set so the buds (called eyes) are no more than 2 inches under the soil surface (1 inch in heavy clay). You can make peonies grow faster by feeding once a year with compost or any complete, granular, organic fertilizer, keeping grass and weeds away from the crowns and watering during summer droughts.

Peonies Nipped in the Bud

Q. **For the last three years my peonies have had small, aborted brown buds. How can I correct this condition?**

A. First, determine what's causing your problems. Both botrytis blight and bud blast can wither peony buds. Botrytis blight, a fungal disease, also rots the bases of young stems in early spring, causing them to fall over. Wind-borne spores infect buds, flowers, and leaves later in the season. Infected tissue turns soft and brown, then becomes covered with gray mold. Snip off and burn diseased plant parts during the growing season. In fall, cut off the stalks slightly below ground level and burn them along with the old mulch. Avoid mounding moisture-retentive compost or manure around stem bases. If only young buds are affected and there is no sign of disease, your peonies may have had bud blast, a physiological disorder. While its cause is uncertain, it has been attributed to potassium deficiency, poor soil, low spring temperatures, drought, shade, and root-knot nematodes.

Bewildering Bulbs

Forcing the Issue

Crocus Corm (left), Hyacinth Bulb (right)

Q. I first tried forcing crocuses and hyacinths last winter. After potting, I refrigerated them for six weeks, watering occasionally. I brought them to room temperature and gradually exposed them to light. The crocuses produced leaves but no flowers, and the hyacinth blooms were only a few inches tall. What did I do wrong?

A. You didn't chill them long enough, says Dr. August De Hertogh, bulb specialist and head of the department of horticulture at North Carolina State University. Crocuses and hyacinths need a minimum of 13 weeks at 40° to 50°F to force successfully. Large-flowered Dutch crocuses, such as 'Remembrance', 'Flower Record', 'Peter Pan', 'Jeanne d'Arc', and 'Pickwick', are much easier to force than species crocuses. Most hyacinth cultivars are suitable for forcing.

It's Transplanting Time

Q. When and how do I transplant hardy bulbs?

A. Dig them up when the foliage is about half yellowed. By then, the bulbs will have ripened but will still be easy to find, and the dying leaves will give you a convenient handle by which to lift the clumps out of the ground. Separate the bulbs and replant them immediately in well-drained soil enriched with compost and a sprinkling of any complete, granular, organic fertilizer. Be careful to set each species at the proper depth and spacing. Small offset bulbs can be planted at the same depth and location as mature ones, but they might reach flowering size sooner if you grow them in a nursery bed or garden row.

Bulbs

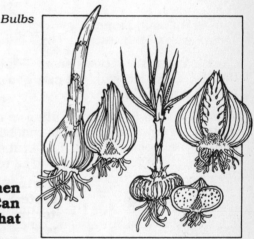

Menu for Bulbs

Q. I didn't add fertilizer when I planted my bulbs last fall. Can I apply it in spring? If so, what should I use?

A. Your bulbs will perform well if you apply a complete fertilizer this spring and a nitrogen supplement in the fall. Bulbs produce new roots in fall and actively absorb nutrients throughout the winter and spring. In a field study of the nutritional needs of bulbs conducted at North Carolina State University, Dr. Paul Nelson found that bulbs need more nitrogen than was previously thought. Based on his study, Nelson recommends an annual application of a slow-release fertilizer that will supply 5 ounces of nitrogen, 5 ounces of phosphoric acid (P_2O_5), and 3½ ounces of potassium (K_2O) per 100 square feet. Since nitrogen leaches readily, he recommends applying an additional 5 ounces of nitrogen per 100 square feet the following spring or fall.

Here are three organic fertilizers you can use to satisfy these requirements: (1) Apply 2 pounds of dried blood, 2 pounds of bonemeal, and 3 pounds of greensand or wood ashes per 100 square feet this spring, followed by 2 more pounds of dried blood in early fall. If your soil is acid, wood ashes will help raise the pH, but if the pH is already near neutral, use greensand. (2) Top-dress with ¼ inch of dried manure per 100 square feet (about 2 bushels) in spring and fall. (3) If you apply compost generously in fall, says Nelson, you might get away with just adding nitrogen in spring. Put down 2 bushels of compost in fall and 2 pounds of dried blood in spring.

The best time to apply fertilizer in spring is when the foliage spears have just emerged from the ground. If you apply it after the leaves unfold, be careful not to get any on the plants, or you may burn them. Don't scratch the fertilizer into the soil surface—you might damage the bulbs, and spring rains will wash in the nutrients.

Burned Bulbs in Florida

Q. We recently moved from Wisconsin to central Florida and would like to know if we can grow tulips, hyacinths, and other "northern" bulbs here.

A. You can if you are willing to take some time and trouble. In September or October, chill the bulbs in the refrigerator for 12 weeks, then plant them. The bulbs will bloom in midwinter. Because daytime temperatures often reach 80°F even in winter, each flower will last only two to three days, according to Dr. Benny Tjia, an ornamentals specialist at the University of Florida. The bulbs also deteriorate during the summer in the hot, dry soil, so it's best to treat them as annuals and discard them after flowering. If this is more than you want to take on, try some of the many beautiful and exotic tropical bulbs that will thrive in your area. Agapanthus, amaryllis, calla lilies, cannas, and clivias are just a few that are well suited to central Florida's climate.

Cannas from Seeds

Q. How can I sprout canna seed? Are any compact varieties available from seed?

A. Because canna seeds have a very hard seed coat, germination is usually poor unless they are nicked first. Dr. Jim Alston, director of research for Park Seed Company, recommends rubbing each seed on a piece of medium-coarse sandpaper until a small section of the black seed coat has worn away, revealing the white interior. Then germination is easy, he says. Plant the seed vertically ⅜ to ¾ inch deep in a seed-starting medium. At room temperature (70° to 75°F), the seed should germinate within 15 to 25 days. 'Seven Dwarfs Mixed', a relatively new dwarf canna from seed, grows only 18 inches tall. It comes in shades of red, rose, orange, yellow, and salmon.

Dahlia

Dahlia Dilemma

Q. The garden center where I bought my dahlias last year told me to dig them up after frost and hang them in the basement. I did this, but the roots died. How can I store the roots successfully?

A. Dahlia tubers need to be kept cold and protected from drying out. Here are some storage techniques recommended by Mark Algers, president of the American Dahlia Society. After frost, cut the tops back to about 5 inches, then lift the clumps gently so that you don't crack the necks of the tubers. Wash the soil off and look for signs of disease or injury. Let the tubers dry under cover for about a week. You can divide the clumps once they've dried or wait until spring. Make sure that each division has a piece of the stem attached; new shoots sprout only from that part of the tuber. Thin or immature tubers will shrivel in storage and should be discarded. Layer the tubers in dry vermiculite, perlite, sphagnum peat, or sawdust in containers that admit air. (Algers has found that tubers kept in plastic tend to rot.) Store the containers in a dark, frostproof place that doesn't get warmer than 45°F. Your dahlias should stay in good condition until spring.

Groundcovers for Daffodils

Q. Last fall I put in a large daffodil planting. Can you suggest a perennial groundcover that will look good, need very little care, and won't compete with the bulbs?

A. Periwinkle or vinca, Baltic ivy, and ajuga (carpet bugle) are evergreen in light shade or sun if sheltered from winter winds. Ivy will need an annual trimming once established. Several species of violet self-sow to form dense colonies in sun or shade. Sweet woodruff and many ferns are fine-textured groundcovers for humus-rich soil in light shade, where lily-of-the-valley also thrives. Strawberries (cultivated, wild, and alpine) are an edible-fruited but higher-maintenance alternative for full sun. Any groundcover will need routine weeding and watering until the plants grow together. After that, an annual application of screened compost, leaf mold, or a complete granular fertilizer and watering in dry spells will help keep both groundcover and daffodils vigorous.

Gladiolus Corms

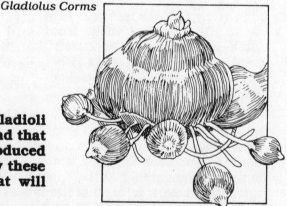

Glad for More Glads

Q. When I dug up my gladioli for winter storage, I found that most of the bulbs had produced bulblets. How can I grow these into good-size bulbs that will produce flowers?

A. Technically, gladioli grow from corms rather than bulbs. The small cormels can be grown into flowering-size (1- to 1¼-inch) corms in two to three years. Once you've dug the corms, cure them by keeping them at 85° to 90°F for 10 to 14 days. After curing, you can separate and grade them. Then store the corms and cormels in a cool, dry place until spring. Plant the cormels in an out-of-the-way spot or the end of a row at the same time you plant the rest of your glads.

harvest the umbels before the heads shatter. You can also plant garlic in early spring. Set cloves 2 inches deep in moist, sandy soil. And coriander, also known as Chinese or Mexican parsley, can be sown directly in late spring. Plant seeds 1 inch deep and thin to 8 inches in rows. You can enjoy these herbs in most of your pickling recipes, as well as with meats, salads, soups, and stews.

Herbs Make Great Mothballs

Q. **I've read about an herb that can be stored with woolens to protect them from moths. Can you help me?**

A. There are several combinations of herbs that can help prevent moths from feasting on your woolens. And it's easy to sew the dried herbs in small cloth pouches to place among your clothes. Dried rosemary leaves should keep the moths at bay. Other combinations of repellents include equal parts of ground camphor wood and wormwood; southernwood, wormwood, and lavender; or cedar wood shavings and ground sassafras root.

Herbs Up Close

Buggy Basil

Q. **Harlequin bugs appeared in my garden around the first of August and ate up my broccoli, then moved on to the basil. What can I do to stop them?**

A. Harlequin bugs, which occur in the southern half of the United States, overwinter as adults in garden debris and litter. You can cut down their numbers by thoroughly cleaning your garden every fall. In the spring, check the undersides of plants (especially brassicas) for their distinctive eggs. Look for small white "pegs" attached to black loops, standing on end and lined in double rows. Destroy any you find. Sometimes a trap crop of mustard or turnips will successfully lure the beautiful harlequin bugs away from your other crops. Handpick the bugs from the trap plants, dropping them into a can of water and detergent. Two botanical poisons, pyrethrum and sabadilla, will also control them.

Recharging Chives

Q. I've been told you can dig up and pot garden chives for winter use, but I've never had any success. Is there some trick to it?

A. Chives must have a cold rest period. For chives in winter, plant seeds in pots during late summer. Two to three months later you'll have sturdy young plants for winter use. You can also force garden-grown chives for late winter or early spring cutting. Pot some up before the ground freezes in the fall, but leave the pot in the ground for three to four months. Bring the plants inside during a thaw in January or February. The warmth will stimulate new growth.

Lavender Has No Thyme for Mulch

Q. Should I mulch my lavender and thyme plants this fall for winter protection?

A. English lavender and thyme are hardy perennials. They don't need to be winter-mulched (completely covered with straw) and should do well in most of the United States, provided they are in a sheltered, well-drained location. You need to take special precautions only where the temperature can go below −30°F. French lavender, however, is not as hardy and should be brought in during the winter where temperatures go below 0°F (north of U.S. Department of Agriculture Plant Hardiness Zone 7). We talked to professional herb growers from Washington, D.C., to southern Michigan, and they all confirmed that their English lavender and thyme do fine without winter mulch. (Most professionals do mulch the plants during the growing season.) M. J. Hampstead of Fox Hill Farm in Parma, Michigan, feels that winter mulch can hold moisture against the plants and cause them to rot.

Oregano's Lost It

Q. Our seven-year-old oregano plants have lost their pungency. Is this unusual? Can you recommend a flavorful variety to replace them?

A. Seedlings of a highly flavored plant of common oregano (*Origanum vulgare*) often fail to inherit their parent's pungency. Over the years, your original plants may have died and been replaced by flavorless, self-sown seedlings. To be sure of getting kitchen-worthy replacements, buy seeds of *O. vulgare* subsp. *hirtum* (also called *O. heracleoticum* and simply *O. hirtum*) or *O. vulgare* 'Viride'. If you start plants from seed, grow more than you'll need, then propagate the best-flavored plants from cuttings.

Roots for Soup

Q. I recently bought parsley root at my farmers' market, and it made great soup. How can I grow it?

A. Hamburg or root parsley is grown like common parsley. Harvest the greens as they are ready. But remove only a few sprigs at a time from each plant, so root growth isn't set back. Herbalist Bertha Reppert feels the leaves are much more flavorful than those of common curly-leaf parsley. She grows Hamburg parsley both for the pungent, broad leaves and for the parsniplike roots, which have a strong parsley flavor. The roots can be harvested about three months after planting, though they will continue to grow throughout the season and are sweeter after a frost. Since parsley is a biennial, the plant will sprout back the second spring and the roots will continue to grow. Be sure to harvest the roots before the plant flowers or they will be tough. Hamburg parsley is available from most seed companies.

Sage

Sage Propagating Advice

Q. When I divide old sage plants, the divisions die. How can I divide sage successfully?

A. The woody crowns of old sage plants can seldom be divided successfully. This herb is best propagated from seed or cuttings. Sow seed indoors at 60° to 70°F in late winter or early spring and set out the plants after the last frost. Alternatively, root 3-inch tip cuttings from established plants in late summer, winter them in a sunny window or a protected coldframe, and plant them in the garden by spring.

The Truth about Tarragon

Q. I bought a plant labeled tarragon at a nursery. How can I be sure that it's French and not Russian tarragon?

A. The crush-and-sniff test is the best way to determine if you have the valued culinary herb, French tarragon, or its weedy Russian relative. The leaves of French tarragon have a distinct anise (licorice) scent. The Russian smells more like lawn grass. The plants also look slightly different. French tarragon has long, narrow, glossy leaves and is rarely taller than 2 feet. Russian tarragon is much taller (up to 5 feet) and has lighter green, rough leaves.

Chapter 16

Advice on Lawns, Trees, and Shrubs

Help for Unhappy Lawns

Oaks over Grass

Q. What kind of lawn grass will grow on a dry hilltop shaded by oaks?

A. Improved tall fescue grasses such as 'Rebel', fine-textured ryegrasses like 'Manhattan 2', 'Yorktown 2', and 'Prelude', and fine fescues, including Chewings fescue, creeping red fescue, and hard fescue, should all do well in dry shade, says Dr. H. W. Indyk, extension turf-management specialist at Rutgers University. If you don't mind a coarse-textured lawn, plant a mix containing 60 percent improved tall fescue, 20 percent fine fescue, and 20 percent perennial ryegrass, he advises. Before planting, have the soil tested; if it's acid, add enough lime to raise the pH to 6.5. Sow the grass in spring or fall, when cooler, more moist conditions prevail. Keep the soil moist by watering lightly two or three times a day, if necessary, until the grass is established. Feed the new lawn with organic fertilizer high in nitrogen.

Lone Star Lawn

Q. **Can you recommend one of the newer varieties of grass for my sparse St. Augustine, Texas, lawn? The lawn is shaded by pine and sweet gum trees.**

A. "You need a turf-type, tall fescue, such as 'Falcon', 'Rebel', 'Mustang', or 'Olympic', for your shady southern lawn," says Eliot Roberts of the Lawn Institute. Because of the deep shade cast by the pine and sweet gum trees, he recommends overseeding each spring to keep your lawn thick and healthy.

Buffalo Grass, Won't You Come Out Tonight?

Q. **For our Flagstaff, Arizona, yard, we want a lawn that requires minimal irrigation but still looks nice. We've heard that buffalo grass is drought-tolerant and does well at our altitude of 7,000 feet. Can you tell us more about this grass and how to grow it?**

A. Buffalo grass, native to the Great Plains, is a gray-green, fine-textured grass that spreads by stolons to form a dense turf. Its adaptability to poor, alkaline soil and resistance to cold, heat, and drought make it a good lawn grass for semiarid regions. Once established, it needs only 1 inch of water a month (in areas with a minimum annual rainfall of 15 inches), versus 4 inches for bluegrass. Buffalo grass does have some drawbacks, however: It turns brown with the first frost and stays that way till spring; and in high-rainfall areas, cool-season grasses and weeds can crowd it out.

Depending on competition, buffalo grass takes two to three years to form a dense turf. Till the lawn to get a clean seedbed. Sow after the soil temperature reaches 60°F—about May 15 to June 1 in your area—at the rate of 1 pound of pure, live seed per 1,000 square feet, recommends Dr. E. J. Kinbacher, horticulturist at the University of Nebraska. Cover the seed 1.4 inches deep and keep the area moist. Germination occurs in 14 days. Buffalo grass does well without fertilizer, but an annual application in early to mid-June of 1 pound of nitrogen per 1,000 square feet (about 14 pounds of cottonseed meal or 100 pounds of dried manure at 1 percent nitrogen) makes the turf denser and greener, says Kinbacher. Mow once a month to 2½ inches for a manicured look or let the grass grow to its natural height of 6 to 8 inches.

Zoysia: Everything but Evergreen

Q. **The manager of my local garden center advised me to plant a zoysia lawn this spring. What are the advantages of planting zoysia?**

A. The big advantage of a zoysia lawn is that it grows slowly, so it needs mowing only every ten days to two weeks. Zoysia makes a tough, cushiony turf. It grows on a wide range of soils, from sandy to heavy loams, if there is good subsoil drainage. It thrives in high summer temperatures as well as in moderate shade. Since zoysias grow densely, a mature turf will crowd out weeds and requires little fertilizer. In addition, these grasses are practically free of diseases and insect pests. It's also a great grass to plant around a swimming pool, because it's salt- and chlorine-tolerant. Now for the drawback: It turns brown with the first frost and is late to green up in the spring.

Zoysia's Not Made for the Shade

Q. **Will zoysia grass grow well on a shaded lawn?**

A. No, says Dr. Martin Petrovic, a turf specialist at Cornell University, who instead recommends using a fine-leaved fescue mixture if the site is relatively dry. For every 1,000 square feet, sow a mixture of about 3¾ pounds fescue seed with ¾ pound of improved perennial ryegrass and ½ pound of a shade-tolerant cultivar of Kentucky bluegrass, such as 'A-34' or 'Glade'. You can sow a pure stand of Kentucky bluegrass if the area is moist, and if it's very moist, Petrovic recommends 'Sabre' rough bluegrass.

Doggone Dead Spots

Q. **My dog's "outings" have resulted in dead spots in my lawn. What can I do?**

A. To repair brown spots, dig out the dead grass and roots with a spade, fill the holes with topsoil, and rake smooth. Broadcast seed over the topsoil at the recommended rate, rake it in lightly, and mulch with a thin layer of straw or salt hay. Keep the seeded areas well watered until the turf is thoroughly established (four to six weeks). Because dog wastes are high in salts and urea, occasional spot reseeding will be an ongoing maintenance chore as long as your dog continues to use the lawn. One way to prevent dead spots, suggests Beverly Roberts of the Lawn Institute, is to train your dog to use a specific area of the yard that you have covered with bark mulch, cat litter, or other absorbent material. Change the material as needed. However, since dog manure can contain several internal parasites hazardous to human health, we recommend disposing of it—as well as the clumps of dead grass from lawn repair—rather than composting it (see "Dog Wastes" on page 57).

Choking Out Chinch Bugs

Q. We have chinch bugs in our lawn. What is the least toxic way to eliminate them?

A. You have several nontoxic options. Chinch bugs are ⅛- to ¼-inch, blackish-brown insects with white wing patches. The adults and their reddish nymphs kill grass by sucking out its juices, and they're most likely to damage lawns in hot, dry weather. They rarely feed in shady areas, so one long-term defense is to plant shrubs and shade trees. According to Eliot Roberts, director of the Lawn Institute, the best way to deal with chinch bugs is to let them run their course, rake out any dead turf, and overseed with a resistant perennial ryegrass like 'Repell', 'Pennant', 'Regal', or 'All-Star'. These new ryegrasses are protected by a seed-transmitted symbiotic fungus that makes them repellent to chinch bugs and other insects. The fungus remains viable in the seed for about one year, so check the date on the package before buying. You can also discourage their growth by keeping your soil rich with nitrogen. Tests show that chinch bugs not only live longer but produce more eggs when they eat plants grown in nitrogen-poor soil. Some natural sources of nitrogen are bloodmeal, manure, and sludge. Should the chinch bug infestation get severe, send out their natural predator, the big-eyed bug (*Geocoris pallens*). It won't repair the bare spots in lawns damaged by chinch bugs, but it will control the pests so you can reseed in late summer.

Grub Grabber

Q. Our lawn is crawling with grubs. What can we do to control them?

A. Grubs are beetle larvae that feed on grass roots. The Japanese beetle is the best known, but several other species might also be found in lawns. The best control is milky spore, commercially available as Doom and Japidemic. It's a bacterial disease (*Bacillus popilliae*) that kills only beetle grubs. You can spread the powder anytime the ground isn't frozen. It takes one to three years for the disease to give full control, but it remains effective indefinitely (see "Once and Done" on page 286).

No More Mole Holes

Q. Moles have made unsightly tunnels throughout my lawn. Traps haven't worked. Can you help?

A. The common or eastern mole spends most of its life underground, eating earthworms and the larvae and adults of many kinds of insects. Moles don't feed on plant material, but in making their tunnels they inadvertently sever grass roots, which are concentrated in the top few inches of the soil. The problem is worse in dry weather, when the raised areas of lawn are more likely to turn brown. Field research has shown that after a lawn has been treated for grubs, the mole population usually goes down. Apply milky spore "Grub Grabber," a bacterium that will control grubs permanently (see above). It takes several years to become established in the lawn, so in the meantime you might want to give traps another try.

Traps can be effective, but you have to be persistent. Moles are solitary animals, and it's likely that only one or two are responsible for the damage to your lawn. In its search for food, the mole makes an extensive network of tunnels, many of which are used only once. To find out which runs are used as "travel lanes," Dr. Bob Mormon, an extension wildlife conservationist at the University of Iowa, suggests stepping lightly on small sections of several tunnels so that you disturb them but don't completely collapse them. Mark these sections with stones or garden stakes. After two days, note which ones are raised—those are active runs and are good locations for setting a trap. Moles do not see but are guided by their highly sensitive nose, which leads them to their prey. So to set out traps successfully, sterilize them first to eliminate all human odor. To do this, scorch the trap over a burning newspaper, then use gloves when handling it. You can restore turf over unused tunnels with a lawn roller or by treading on it.

Top Tips for Trees

Planting a Christmas Tree

Keeping the Christmas Spirit Alive

Q. I'd like to have a live Christmas tree this year. How can I make sure it will survive after the holidays?

A. Consult with your county extension agent to select a species that's suited to your region. Although container-grown trees are more expensive than field-grown ones, they have a better chance of survival. If you live in an area where the ground freezes, be sure to dig a hole *before* the holidays so you can plant the tree. Fill the hole with leaves or mulch so it doesn't freeze, then cover it with a board. Store the soil you've removed from the hole where it won't freeze. After you buy the tree, acclimate it to the house by placing it in a protected place such as an unheated garage or shed for a week. The tree will dry out quickly, so keep the roots moist and the branches well misted. Wrap the roots of a balled-and-burlapped tree in plastic before setting it in a container.

Indoors, keep the tree away from heat. In fact, the cooler the temperatures and the shorter the time indoors, the better. Don't let the room get warmer than 68°F or keep the tree indoors longer than a week. After the holidays, harden-off the tree by returning it to the protected place for a week, then plant it. Fill the hole with the stored soil and tamp it down lightly. Water generously and mulch with 3 to 4 inches of hay out to the dripline. Stake the tree until spring. If the temperature rises above freezing during the winter, check to see if the tree needs water. If you can't dig a hole before the ground freezes, overwinter the tree in a cool place that gets some light. The temperature should be above freezing but below 50°F. (Growth will resume if the temperature climbs over 50°F.) Keep the tree well watered, and plant it as early in the spring as possible.

Getting the Jump on Gypsy Moths

Q. **Last year many of our alder and oak trees were completely defoliated by gypsy moths. What can we do to stop them this year?**

A. To protect your trees and shrubs, spray *Bacillus thuringiensis* (Bt) as the gypsy moth larvae emerge from their egg clusters in late April and early May. When the caterpillars eat the Bt, its spores paralyze their guts, and the insects starve to death within a few days. Safe for humans, Bt affects only caterpillars like gypsy moths, cabbage loopers, and tomato hornworms. Because it is difficult to cover the leaves of large trees, you might contract with a local landscaper or tree surgeon to spray Bt with a commercial spraying rig. When the caterpillars are active in late May and June, you can trap them. Tie burlap in a skirt around the trunk of each tree. The caterpillars will crawl under the burlap during the day to escape the heat of the sun. After they do, simply remove the skirts and shake them over a bucket of soapy water, where the larvae will drown.

Trying to reduce this year's outbreak by destroying the egg clusters in March and early April—before the hungry larvae start to hatch—is futile and can actually create more problems than it solves. Locating the 1- to 2-inch-long, tan oval egg masses is difficult because they are laid high in tree crotches, under rocks and roof eaves, and in woodpiles and other protected spots. Destroying the egg masses on your property often *helps* the gypsy moth by preventing a starvation-introduced population collapse later in the season. In fact, some biologists say the best thing to do about gypsy moths is nothing at all. The damage they do is unsightly, but few trees are killed. Gypsy moth populations usually diminish naturally after a few years.

Bouncing Birch Aphids

Q. **For the past three years, I've had aphids on my white birch trees. Their honeydew drips on everything below. How can I deal with them?**

A. In late winter, spray with dormant oil to kill overwintering eggs in bark crevices and twig crotches. If aphids reappear in summer, spray with insecticidal soap, pyrethrum, rotenone, or summer oil—the same oil used in the dormant season but applied at a higher dilution. To prevent foliar damage from summer oil sprays, carefully follow dilution recommendations on the label. Don't spray when shoots are elongating (very young leaves are highly sensitive to oil), when the relative humidity is over 90 percent (high humidity retards oil evaporation), or when the trees are suffering from drought.

Leafminers Lose Out

Q. Every spring, and again in late June or early July, our white birches are disfigured by the blotchy mines of birch leafminers. How can I control this pest?

A. There's a new product ready to come to your rescue—neem extract. The birch leafminer is a tiny sawfly whose larvae tunnel into the young leaves of birches, often causing most of the new foliage to turn brown. White-barked birch species are most susceptible. There are two or three generations a year, but the first is the most destructive. Later generations attack only the new leaves at the tips of branches.

In research conducted in New York State, U.S. Department of Agriculture (USDA) entomologist Dr. Hiram G. Larew and two colleagues controlled this pest with an extract of seeds of the neem tree (*Azadirachta indica*). The new commercial neem-derived insecticide Margosan-O will give virtually the same results as the extract, says Larew. Spray the trees when the leaves are half-grown; by then, the adult leafminers will have laid their eggs. Spraying when mines first become visible is equally effective, says Larew, but if the mines are fully developed, it's too late. If you notice some leaf damage developing after you spray, be patient. Though neem is best applied before mines are evident, it doesn't kill the larvae until they're almost grown or have already pupated, according to Larew. He thinks a higher concentration of neem extract might kill the miners more quickly, but he has not tested this hypothesis. Sprays for the second generation, which usually appears in June, are harder to time, but if you knock out the first generation, the second should be much less of a problem, says Larew. If there are infested birches near your treated ones, you'll probably have to spray every year. You can help injured birches recover by mulching them out to the dripline, feeding them in spring with a high-nitrogen fertilizer, and watering deeply during hot weather.

Curbing Dogwood Decline

Q. The lower branches on my dogwoods are dying. A friend told me the disease is dogwood decline and that it will kill the trees. Is there anything I can do?

A. Dogwood decline is a catchall term used to describe several problems. Drought and winter injury also cause branches to die, usually from the top down. According to Margery Daughtrey, a specialist in ornamental diseases at the research laboratory of Cornell University, your trees probably have a fungal disease called anthracnose, which is characterized by lower branch dieback. It affects flowering dogwoods (*Cornus florida*) from Connecticut south to West Virginia and Maryland. You may be able to keep the trees going by preventing other stresses, Daughtrey says. Prune the dead wood and water sprouts, and water during dry spells. Provide full sun if possible, even if it means pruning adjacent trees or shrubbery. Avoid wounding the trunk with a lawnmower or a weed trimmer. Another option is to replace the flowering dogwoods with kousa dogwoods (*Cornus kousa*), which are resistant to anthracnose.

Soaping Down
Hawthorn Lace Bugs

Q. By late summer, the leaves on my Lavalle hawthorn look more yellowish-tan than green, and I've noticed many small black spots on the undersides. If bugs are the problem, what is a safe way to get rid of them?

A. The tree probably has hawthorn lace bugs, which are only about ⅛ inch long and hard to see. The clear wings of the adults are marked with a dark pattern, giving them a lacy look. The bugs feed by sucking sap from the lower leaf surfaces and characteristically leave many small, shiny spots. As their population builds through the summer, the foliage looks more and more stippled and bleached. Adult lace bugs overwinter in bark crevices on their host plants, which include cotoneaster, pyracantha, and quince as well as hawthorn. Control the pests by spraying with insecticidal soap or pyrethrum in late spring when the first signs of damage appear. Aim the spray at the lower leaf surface where the lace bugs feed. Examine the tree each week through the summer and spray again if the pests reappear.

A Honey of a Pest

Q. I planted a honey locust thinking it would be pest-free, but last summer dark, 1-inch-long caterpillars with light stripes spun webs on the leaves and ate them. How can I control them?

A. The caterpillars were mimosa webworms, which feed only on mimosa and honey locust trees. This pest has become more widespread as honey locusts have become more popular. The first generation hatches in June. Remove the webs as soon as they appear or spray at high pressure with *Bacillus thuringiensis* (Bt), repeating at weekly intervals until feeding stops. Watch for the larger second generation, which usually appears in August. When it appears, apply the same treatment. In the Southeast and parts of the Southwest, there may be a third generation in September.

Tilting the Scales

Q. We have a magnolia that is infested with scales, which are tended by ants. How can we get rid of the pests?

A. The best way to eliminate scale is by spraying with dormant oil in late winter before the buds begin to open. Wait for a calm day when the temperature is 40°F or warmer and no overnight freeze is predicted. A band of Tanglefoot applied near the base of the trunk will keep ants from climbing the tree. Prune any nearby shrub or tree branches that could provide bridges for the ants.

Maple Splits

Q. What makes the bark on maple trees split, and what can I do to prevent it?

A. Bark splitting, a vertical crack in a limb or trunk that may extend into the heartwood, is caused by wide temperature fluctuations in winter. Fruit-tree growers know it as sunscald or southwest injury, since the cracks usually appear on the south or west side of the trunk when there is a sudden, extreme drop in temperature after the wood has been warmed by a sunny winter day. Ash, beech, horse chestnut, linden, London plane, and several other common shade trees are also susceptible. Trees standing alone without the shade of the woods and those with trunks 6 to 18 inches in diameter are more likely to crack. Though the tree seals the surface with callus tissue, deep cracks never knit and may reopen in subsequent winters. Besides weakening the tree structurally, they provide an entrance for bacteria and fungi.

Prevent cracking by shading the trunk in winter. Orchardists coat their trees with whitewash or white latex paint that doesn't contain a fungicide. Commercial tree-wrapping paper, plastic tree guards, and burlap are equally effective, as is tying a board to the south side of the trunk. To keep injured trees vigorous, water them deeply during summer dry spells, keep them mulched out to the dripline, and feed them with a high-nitrogen fertilizer in early spring.

Don't Spit on My Pines

Q. I recently discovered spittlebugs on my pine trees. Can you suggest a nonchemical way to control them?

A. Peter Rush, an entomologist for the USDA's Forest Service, recommends that as soon as you see the white masses of spittlebug foam on branches in the spring, spray the trees with a high-pressure jet of water, and repeat spraying a week or so later. Spittlebug foam, formed from plant sap, protects the nymph-stage spittlebugs within, but the insects won't survive once they fall to the ground. Rush says most trees can tolerate some feeding, so it isn't necessary to annihilate the insects. He adds that healthy trees planted in well-drained, fertile soil and watered regularly are less subject to attack.

Spruces from Seed

Q. I've tried growing white spruce and Colorado blue spruce from seed and cuttings with no success. How can I get them to sprout or root?

A. It's much easier to grow spruces from seed than from cuttings. Even so, the seed will need a period of cold temperatures to break dormancy. If you sow seeds in a bed outdoors after you collect them in fall, winter will provide the necessary chilling. Plant the seed ¼ inch deep in soil lightened with peat moss and sand to ensure fast drainage. Cover the bed with wire to keep out rodents, and mulch after the ground freezes. If you have only a few seeds, mix or layer them in a plastic bag with damp peat moss or vermiculite. Store the bag in the refrigerator for at least three months. At the end of the cold period, sow the seeds in containers of your usual seed-starting mix. Spruce seedlings are very susceptible to damping-off, so be sure to pasteurize the soil mix if it's homemade. Transplant the seedlings when they begin to crowd each other.

Colorado blue spruces produce more seedlings that are greenish-blue than bright blue. If you prefer the bluest ones, sow extra seed to be sure of getting some.

Bagging Bagworms

Q. On our Pennsylvania property, we have a Colorado blue spruce that is infested with bagworms. How can we get rid of them?

A. Burn their bags. Bagworms feed on many species of evergreen and deciduous trees and shrubs in the eastern United States. As they feed, the caterpillars spin silken, spindle-shaped bags and disguise them with bits of leaves from the host plant. They feed until late summer, then pupate in their bags. The black male moth, with a wingspread of about 1 inch, emerges and flies to the wingless female, mating with her through an opening in the bottom of her bag. She lays 500 to 1,000 eggs inside her bag, then crawls out and dies. The eggs overwinter in the bags and hatch in late spring when trees are in full leaf—early June in your area. You can effectively control this pest by picking and burning the bags before the eggs hatch in spring. (You may have to cut the bag off the twigs; the silk is strong and resists pulling.) If you can't reach the bags, spray with *Bacillus thuringiensis* (Bt) at seven- to ten-day intervals from shortly after hatching until you see no further evidence of feeding.

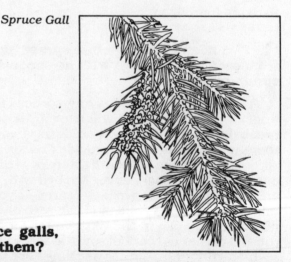

Spruce Gall

A Galling Problem

Q. What causes spruce galls, and how can I prevent them?

A. Spruce galls, conelike swellings of new growth, are caused by the eastern spruce gall aphid, whose galls appear at the base of Norway and white spruce shoots, and the Cooley spruce gall aphid, whose galls kill twig tips on white, Colorado blue, Sitka, and Engelmann spruces. Cooley spruce gall aphids also cause spotted, distorted needles (but no galls) on Douglas fir. Female aphids overwinter at the base of spruce buds and emerge in early spring to lay eggs near branch tips. The eggs hatch in about two weeks, and the nymphs crawl to expanding buds and begin to feed. Saliva injected during feeding causes the galls, which gradually cover the aphids, protecting them from pesticides, predators, and bad weather. In mid- to late summer, the nymphs leave the drying galls and transform into winged adults, which disperse to lay eggs on spruce branches, then die. The eggs hatch about 16 days later, and the young aphids immediately move to bud bases to overwinter.

Correct timing is essential to control these pests. While the galls are green and growing in spring and early summer, cut off and destroy as many as you can reach to kill the nymphs inside. Before buds open in spring, spray with dormant oil to kill overwintering aphids. If trees are heavily infested, spray with pyrethrum, rotenone, or insecticidal soap at bud break to kill nymphs before galls form.

Shrubby Solutions

Superhardy Shrubs

Q. Can you recommend some shrubs that can take our North Dakota winters?

A. There are quite a few superhardy shrubs for your area. Dr. Dale E. Herman, professor of ornamentals at North Dakota State University, has tested many species at sites throughout the state. He recommends the following shrubs. Russian pea shrub (*Caragana frutex* 'Globosa') grows round and compact, to 4 feet wide, without pruning; 'Miniglobe' shrub honeysuckle (*Lonicera* 'Miniglobe') is very hardy; and shrubby cinquefoil (*Potentilla fruticosa* 'Hurstbourne') has golden yellow blooms all season. You might also try some native plants, such as viburnums (*Viburnum trilobum, V. lentago*) and sumacs. 'Gro-Low' fragrant sumac (*Rhus aromatica*) forms an 18-inch-tall groundcover, and cut-leaved smooth sumac (*Rhus glabra* 'Laciniata') is a taller form with finely divided foliage.

Keeping Shrubs Evergreen

Q. **What can I do to protect my evergreen shrubs from winter damage?**

A. In winter, evergreens are damaged by wind and sun drying their foliage. To shield them, staple burlap around stakes set about 6 inches away from the shrubs. Put the stakes on the windward side if wind protection is needed and on the southwest side to keep the sun from burning the foliage. Evergreens planted where snow or ice may fall on them need a wooden A-frame or tepee structure for protection. You can prevent sheared yews or hemlocks from spreading under the weight of snow by tying string around them.

The Gall of Those Azaleas!

Q. **Last year my azaleas had ugly, greenish-white galls on some of the leaves. What caused them, and what can I do if they recur?**

A. Azalea leaf gall, also called pinkster apple and honeysuckle apple, is caused by a fungus that overwinters as spores in bud scales of azaleas and rhododendrons. Under moist conditions in early spring, it infects expanding leaves, shoots, and flowers, causing them to form irregular light green or pink galls that later become coated with powdery, white, spore-producing tissue. Infected rhododendron leaves may be yellowed or bleached and slightly thickened, with white fungal tissue underneath. This disease is more conspicuous than serious. Control it by handpicking the galls before they turn white and by pruning low, overhanging tree branches and nearby plants to increase air circulation around azaleas and rhododendrons.

Forsythia Bottom Bloom

Q. **Some years my forsythia blooms only near the bottom, and other years it doesn't bloom at all. Why?**

A. The flower buds are being killed by cold winters or spring frosts. Even though forsythia (*Forsythia intermedia*) is hardy to USDA Hardiness Zone 4, its flower buds are more tender, hardy only to Zone 5 or 6 (about −10° to −15°F). Forsythia planted in northern areas often blooms only near the base of the plant, where snow has covered and protected the tender buds. For more reliable flowering, you might want to try *Forsythia ovata*, a similar species with buds that are hardy to −29°F.

Fall-Blooming Forsythia

Q. **This fall my forsythia is greening and putting out buds. So far it hasn't bloomed, but I'm afraid it will be damaged by cold. Will it bloom next year?**

A. Yes. The phenomenon you've described is fairly common, and has been nicknamed "November bloom," although it can happen from August on, according to Dr. Owen Rogers, ornamentals specialist at the University of New Hampshire. It's nothing to worry about, Rogers says, because usually no more than 1 percent of the flower buds open, leaving plenty for spring.

Forsythia Pruning Primer

Q. **When and how should I prune my forsythia bush?**

A. The forsythia, like all spring-flowering shrubs, should be pruned after blooming. Next year's flowers will form on this year's new wood, so summer pruning allows plenty of time for the new wood to grow. Always cut out any dead wood. Then thin your shrub by cutting a third of the older, woodier stems to ground level. Cut back long stems to encourage branching and flower production. If the plant is unsightly, you can rejuvenate the entire shrub by cutting all stems to within 2 inches of the ground. Don't shear your forsythia like a hedge; the result will be compact, top-heavy growth with all the flowers at the top.

Help for Heather

Q. **Will heather grow in Maryland, where I live? If so, what special care does it need?**

A. As long as you have the right conditions or can create them, heather will grow in your area. Scotch heather (*Calluna vulgaris*) is hardy to USDA Hardiness Zone 4, and heath (*Erica carnea*), also occasionally called heather, is hardy to Zone 5. Plant heathers in full sun on an eastern or northeastern slope, away from direct winter winds. They grow best in very well drained, infertile, acid soil (pH 4.5 to 5.0). Double-dig the soil, adding plenty of compost and peat moss, but avoid manure or other nutrient-rich materials. If your soil is heavy clay, fill a raised bed with compost and peat. Space the plants about 3 feet apart and mulch with leaves, pine bark, or pine needles. Although heathers are fairly drought-tolerant once established, water frequently the first season. In early spring, shear the callunas to encourage new growth. Ericas do not need pruning.

Hibiscus No-Show

Q. Our hibiscus plant won't bloom. Any suggestions?

A. Erik Neumann, curator of education at the U.S. National Arboretum, offers two possibilities. You could be fertilizing the hibiscus with too much nitrogen, which causes lush, leafy growth at the expense of flowers. Try a more balanced fertilizer, such as fish emulsion. Or the plant may be growing in too much shade; transplant in spring or fall to an area in full sun.

Hollies Need Food

Q. My Chinese hollies and yaupons are loaded with red berries, but the leaves look yellowish instead of their usual dark green. We have sandy soil and I mulch with pine needles. How can I get the bushes to look healthier?

A. An unusually heavy fruit crop puts a great deal of stress on a plant, especially when the soil is low in nutrients, as sandy soils often are. Your hollies need a balanced fertilizer rich in nitrogen to restore good leaf color and healthy growth. A 1-inch topdressing of compost or rotted manure will feed the plants and provide humus to improve your soil's structure. Cottonseed meal is a good alternative. It won't add much organic matter, but its 7 percent nitrogen content will turn your plants green again. Broadcast it over the mulch at the rate of 4 to 5 pounds per 100 square feet before growth starts in spring.

Hydrangea Blues

Q. **I have several hydrangea bushes in my yard. They all have blue flowers, except the two in the front of the house, which have some blue and some pink flowers. Can I do something to get all blue flowers?**

A. You can change the color of your hydrangea flowers by altering the soil pH. They will bloom blue or pink depending on the availability of aluminum in the soil, which is determined by pH. (There also white-blooming varieties, which will never bloom blue *or* pink regardless of soil conditions.) The blooms in front of your house are being affected by the cement in the foundation. Cement is composed mostly of lime, and some leaches into the ground around the foundation, turning the soil alkaline and the flowers pink. Flowers farther away from the house aren't affected by the lime and remain blue. To get the whole plant to bloom blue, you'll need to lower the pH to between 4.5 and 5.5 near the foundation. Elemental sulfur (also known as flowers of sulfur) will acidify the soil. If, on the other hand, you decide you want pink flowers, raise the pH to between 7.0 and 7.5 by liming the soil. Alkalinity above 7.5 is likely to bring about yellowing and poor growth. The exact amount of sulfur or lime will depend on your soil type, but in general, for every 25 square feet of soil, use ⅓ pound of sulfur to lower the pH one unit or 1 pound of lime to raise it one unit.

Bungled Blooms

Q. **I have three blue-flowered hydrangeas, two on the north and one on the east side of my house. Though I prune them to 2 feet each fall and protect them in winter, only the one on the east side produces a few blooms. How can I get more flowers?**

A. In this species of hydrangea, the bigleaf hydrangea (*Hydrangea macrophylla*), blooms sprout from terminal buds on the previous season's growth. By pruning in fall, you've been removing most of the following summer's flower buds. The best time to prune these hydrangeas is right after bloom. Continue to protect the plants in winter—low temperatures can nip flower buds as effectively as pruning shears. If the bushes on the north side of the house still fail to bloom, try moving them to a sunnier, warmer location.

Summer Snowberry Cuttings

Q. Can I root cuttings from a snowberry bush in summer? If so, how?

A. Yes. Just remember that, as with any leafy cutting, it's most important to keep them from drying out. Take 3- to 5-inch-long tip cuttings in June or July. Pinch off developing fruit and remove the leaves from the bottom half of each cutting. Root the cuttings in pots of moistened, homemade seed-starting mix or use a soilless medium such as one consisting of equal parts of peat and perlite. Insert the cuttings to the level of the lowest leaves, spacing them so the leaves of adjoining cuttings don't touch. To maintain high humidity, place the pot inside a plastic bag, using soda straws or wooden sticks to hold the plastic above the cuttings. Keep the bag in bright light but away from direct sun; open it occasionally to check for drying. Rooting should occur in two to six weeks. Bottom heat of about 70°F speeds the process. When the cuttings are strongly rooted, transplant them to a nursery bed and mulch heavily the first winter.

Scentless Sweet-Shrub

Q. I have a beautiful sweet-shrub bush, and every year it is full of blooms. Why are the blossoms not fragrant?

A. There could be two causes. If the shrub was once fragrant, you can try really aerating the soil and working in a good amount of rotted manure. Occasionally revitalizing the bush in this manner will increase the fragrance of the flowers. However, more than likely you have a species of the genus *Calycanthus* that has nonaromatic flowers—*C. fertilis*. If this is the case, there is nothing you can do. You can recognize this type of sweet-shrub by its oblong leaves that are thin and either blunt or tapered. Its leaves are bright green and shiny on both sides or pale underneath. The leaves may be as long as 6 inches and the brown flowers up to 2 inches across. Look for nurseries that carry the fragrant Carolina allspice, *C. floridus*.

What about Weigela?

Q. How and when should I prune my weigela bushes? They're still young and vigorous.

A. In northern states, branch tips of weigela often die back in winter; remove this dead wood when the bushes leaf out in spring. It's best to do all other pruning shortly after bloom in June or July. As the plants mature, thin crowded stems to let in light and stimulate vigorous new growth from the base. Cut out spindly stems and old branches that no longer flower well, making the cuts at or near the ground. If the plants grow too tall and leggy, cut back the longest stems to a strong lateral branch, being careful to retain the shrubs' natural shape. By pruning moderately every year, you'll maintain a balance of old and new stems that should keep the bushes growing and flowering well for many years.

Chapter 17

Help for Houseplants

Super Houseplant Hints

Potting Soil Particulars

Q. What's the difference between potting soil and garden soil? Is there any reason why I can't use soil directly from my garden for my houseplants?

A. Yes, there are two reasons. First, garden soil can become waterlogged or dried out in a container. Second, garden soil may contain pathogens that will cause plant diseases. Potting soil includes ingredients such as peat, bark, vermiculite, and perlite. These are blended to hold the right amount of moisture yet also provide good drainage. Also, potting soil should be pasteurized to kill pathogens. Commercial potting soils have a wide range of pH, texture, and fertility. But there are really few differences between general potting soils and those labeled for African violets or cacti. You can have more control over quality and can save money by making your own potting soil mix. Use two parts garden soil, one part compost or leaf mold, and one part sand or perlite. Add 1 tablespoon of bonemeal per quart of mix. Pasteurize the mix before using (see "Pasteurizing Potting Soil" on page 259).

Pasteurizing Potting Soil

Q. Should I sterilize my homemade potting soil for house-plants?

A. A lot of people think you should sterilize potting soils, but they're wrong. Sterilizing kills *all* living organisms in the soil, be they good or bad. The way to get around destroying the good guys is to pasteurize the soil. Place the soil in a tray, and water it until it's thoroughly wet for uniform heat conduction. Preheat your oven to the desired temperature. A temperature of 130°F for 25 minutes will kill soil insects, while a temperature of 180°F for 30 minutes will kill plant disease pathogens.

Salty Mushroom Soil

Q. Is it a good idea to use mushroom soil for houseplants or in the home greenhouse?

A. No. Spent mushroom soil, a by-product of commercial mushroom cultivation, is very high in soluble salts. High salt levels injure plant roots and interfere with water uptake, causing wilting when the soil is moist, stunted or distorted growth, yellowed leaves, and scorched leaf margins. Leaching—watering heavily enough each time so a significant volume of water runs out of the bottom of the pot—reduces soluble salts to harmless levels, but this can take several weeks. By then, much damage may already have been done to salt-sensitive plants, especially seedlings. Carrying houseplants to a sink or bathtub for a weekly leaching can also be very awkward. Because mushroom soil contains a lot of limestone, it can have a pH well above neutral (7.0), which is high enough to cause nutrient imbalances in plants. Fresh mushroom soil shrinks greatly in volume as it breaks down, which can lead to compaction of the potting mix unless it contains equal volumes of more stable materials such as peat and perlite. Aging mushroom soil outdoors helps leach salts and stabilize structure, but the pH usually remains high and the piles quickly become weedy. You're better off with soil intended for houseplants.

Old Salts

Q. **All my clay pots have developed a thick white growth on their outer surfaces. I scrub it off, but it grows back. Any suggestions?**

A. The white "growth" is actually accumulated salts, usually caused by improper watering, a saline water supply, or overfertilization. If you have saucers or trays beneath the pots, they are probably holding excess water that drips through the drainage holes. As the water evaporates, some of it is reabsorbed into the pots, and salts of potassium, calcium, magnesium, and nitrates are deposited on the outside of the pots and on the soil surface. Either pour off the overflow water each time or raise the pots on a layer of pebbles to keep them from sitting in water. If salt buildup continues to occur, reduce the amount of fertilizer you use, and flush out the excess salts in the soil.

Beyond Fish Emulsion

Q. **I've been using fish emulsion on my houseplants. I know it is high in nitrogen but low in phosphorus and potassium. Is there a more balanced liquid organic fertilizer I could use?**

A. Fish emulsion has an NPK (nitrogen:phosphorus:potassium) formula of 5:1:1. It's a good fertilizer for foliage plants, which require nitrogen for leaf formation. Flowering houseplants, such as African violets, have a higher potassium requirement. However, the bulk of the nutritional needs for both types can be taken care of by adding amendments to the potting soil when it is prepared, then supplementing with a liquid fertilizer. Veteran greenhouse gardeners Doc and Katy Abraham of Naples, New York, make a soil mix from equal parts of manure-based compost, loam, and sand. They add 1 cup of bloodmeal for nitrogen, 1 cup of bonemeal for phosphorus, and 2 cups of wood ashes for potassium per bushel of soil. "Compost is the backbone of any soil mix," says Doc. The breakdown of organic matter releases humic acids, which make nutrients available to plants. They recommend feeding houseplants once every two to three months with fish emulsion or manure tea (cow manure is 2:0.5:2). Several liquid manure products are also available. Most houseplants aren't heavy feeders, so unless leaves begin to yellow, fertilizing more often isn't necessary.

Nautical Fertilizer

Q. **Is there an effective organic fertilizer that can be used on houseplants growing in water? Most result in immediate stagnation.**

A. Use the newer deodorized fish emulsions as a source of nitrogen. Pieces of aquarium charcoal (don't use briquettes designed for outdoor barbecuing) can be added to ensure sweetness and prevent stagnation. From time to time, add a little manure tea or liquefied seaweed—the charcoal will help conserve it for plant use. If water becomes covered with algae, change it from time to time.

Houseplant Hunger Signs

Q. **The new leaves on our houseplants sometimes stay small and turn light green. What can we do to prevent this?**

A. If new leaves are progressively smaller and paler than older foliage, it's a sure sign that fertilizer is needed or that you are overwatering. If you are giving proper amounts of water, try using some fish emulsion, compost, or manure tea. Potted plants should receive only as much fertilizer as they can incorporate into the food manufactured in their leaves—usually no more than three or four feedings a year. During the winter when they get little light, less fertilizer is needed. In the long days of summer, they use more. Young, actively growing houseplants take more feeding than mature plants.

Soap Your Plants

Q. **My friend told me that she uses soap flakes to keep the bugs off her houseplants. I would like to use the solution on my own plants. Are soap flakes organic?**

A. A solution of detergent-free soap flakes (such as Ivory or Octagon) acts as a mild insecticide against aphids and scale. Because it is mild and will probably not kill all insects on the plant, it can leave just enough pests to feed any beneficial predators and parasites. Soap solutions also wash off dirt, dust, and insect eggs. To make the solution, add 1 or 2 tablespoons of flakes to 1 gallon of tepid (70° to 90°F) water. Apply it to the plants by sponging thoroughly, dipping them into it, or by spraying. Leave the mixture on for one or two hours, and then rinse it off thoroughly with lukewarm water. Don't use soap solution on hairy plants such as African violets and begonias.

A Medley of Houseplants

Leave It to African Violets

Q. What is the best way to root African violet leaves?

A. Choose medium-size, healthy leaves. Prepare them by cutting the stems diagonally with a clean razor blade 1½ inches from the leaf base, according to Ronn Nadeau, a commercial grower. Fill a 3½- to 4-inch pot with a soilless mix, such as two parts shredded sphagnum peat moss, one part vermiculite, and one part perlite, and moisten it well. Using a pencil or a wooden stick, make three holes in the mix. Insert the leaf stems to a depth of 1 inch and firm the mix around them. Correctly planted leaves may soften and discolor for a few days, but they usually recover within a week. New shoots should sprout in about two months. When they grow 2 to 3 inches tall, transplant them into 2½- to 3-inch pots. Within five to seven months, you'll have new blooming plants.

Gnats Nab African Violets

Q. Lately I've seen fungus gnats around my African violets. I've been told they eat organic matter in soil and are harmless to plants. Is that true?

A. No. When numerous, the larvae of these tiny, highly active black flies feed on plant roots and crowns as well as organic matter. They're especially damaging to young plants, cuttings, and seedlings. To kill the larvae, repot your violets frequently into clean pots and fresh potting soil, and use one of the following three solutions. They're recommended by Bob L. Green, author of "Beginner's Column" in *African Violet Magazine*. To 1 quart of warm water, add 2 drops of dishwashing detergent or 2 tablespoons of Safer's Insecticidal Soap or 1 tablespoon of household bleach. Drench the soil with the solution, discard the runoff, and drench again. Use the bleach solution once a month or one of the other solutions every two months until you no longer see adult gnats.

Violets Fight Fungus

Q. My African violets have a very contagious soil fungus that has spread to my other houseplants. A white mold forms on the top of the soil, which has a very vinegary odor. What can I do to control this disease? It is stunting my plants.

A. Fungus likes a damp, dark area to grow in. To control it, move your plants into good light and fresh air, and give them proper drainage. Wash the infected plants and change the soil mixture to a light, airy soil with sufficient nutrients. If the plant itself looks like it has been afflicted with disease, destroy it. Otherwise, the disease spores will be blown all through the house, and you'll be fighting a losing battle. Use sterile media like perlite, vermiculite, washed sand, and peat moss to start seeds. When you water, don't wet the foliage. Water early in the day so leaves can dry in the sun, and never crowd the plants.

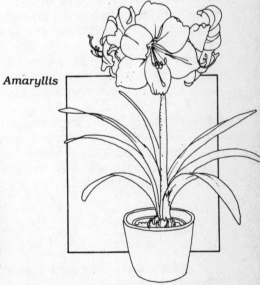

Amaryllis

Amaryllis Again

Q. Last Christmas I received an amaryllis that bloomed beautifully. It was outside for the summer, rested in the garage, and was repotted in late fall. How can I get it to rebloom?

A. Amaryllis bulbs often don't bloom the year after purchase while they produce new roots and rebuild their nutrient reserves. To ensure bloom in future years, grow your bulb in bright light and a rich, porous potting mix, such as equal parts of topsoil, compost, and sand or perlite. Move the plant to a sunny spot outdoors for the summer, and feed twice a month with fish emulsion (1 tablespoon per gallon) or compost tea. The roots will stay cooler and dry out less quickly if you sink the pot to its rim in well-drained soil or nestle it among the leaves of a groundcover. Taper off watering in September so the bulb will go dormant, then store it dry in a cool, frost-free place for 60 to 90 days. At the end of the dormant period, replace the top 1 to 2 inches of soil with compost. Water thoroughly and bring the pot to room temperature. Your amaryllis should bloom in six to eight weeks. Repot the bulb in fresh soil every two or three years. Use a clay pot that is 2 inches wider than the bulb. The weight of the pot will balance the top-heaviness of an amaryllis in full bloom, and its porosity will keep the soil from becoming water-logged.

Bloomless Birds

Q. My bird-of-paradise plants are thriving, but they haven't flowered in six years. How can I stimulate them to bloom?

A. Bird-of-paradise (*Strelitzia reginae*) is slow to reach blooming size when grown as a houseplant. Depending on conditions, seedlings may take five to ten years to flower, and divisions may take four years or more. Once they're mature, the plants need very bright light to set flower buds. Keep them in a south window in winter, and move them outdoors to a sunny spot in spring once night temperatures stay above 50°F. During active growth in summer, keep the soil moist but not soggy, and feed every two weeks with fish emulsion or compost tea. During the winter, don't feed the plants at all, and water only when the top ½ inch of soil is dry. Mature plants need large containers. Grow them in a rich potting mix, such as one containing equal parts soil, leaf mold or compost, and sand or perlite. In years between repottings, replace the top inch of soil with compost in spring, being careful not to injure the fleshy, rot-prone plants.

Cutting Up Cacti

Q. When and how can I root cuttings of Thanksgiving and Christmas cacti?

A. Cuttings can be taken anytime the plants aren't in flower, but if you root them in late winter or early spring, they may grow enough to bloom the first year. Take tip cuttings two or three segments in length; longer ones tend to fall over in the rooting medium. Two- or three-branched cuttings will produce fuller, more symmetrical plants than unbranched cuttings. Allow the cut ends to callous for a day or two before sticking them into the medium. You can start the cuttings in containers of moist vermiculite or a 50–50 mix of peat and perlite and repot them when rooted. Alternatively, you can root them directly in 3- or 4-inch pots of a pasteurized, coarse potting mix such as equal parts of garden soil or bagged houseplant soil, peat, and perlite. To get full plants fast, use three cuttings per pot. Place the containers of cuttings in sealed plastic bags propped up with wooden sticks or soda straws and set them in a warm, bright place shaded from direct sun. When the cuttings have rooted strongly enough to resist a gentle pull (usually in two or three weeks), remove the plants. After rooting, water only when the soil surface feels dry.

Christmas Chameleon Cactus

Q. **When I bought my Christmas cactus, it had white flowers. But every year since, the flowers have been pink. What happened?**

A. The flower color of a Christmas cactus can be affected by its environment. The environment in your home is probably different from that of the greenhouse where the cactus was grown. For white flowers, the night temperature should remain as close to 60°F as possible. If it's much lower or higher, the white variety sometimes blooms pink. An acid or alkaline soil can also cause pinkness, so test the pH of the potting mix and of the water you're using. Both should be near neutral (pH 7.0).

Rooting Out the Problem

Q. **After blooming profusely, my Christmas cacti changed from a healthy green to a sickly reddish shade. One of the plants died, and the other hasn't recovered its green color, though it continues to bloom. What went wrong?**

A. Most likely, your plants sustained root injury, which often does not become apparent until flowering or some other stress places a heavy demand for water on the reduced root system. When that happens, the topgrowth may wilt, discolor, or try to compensate by producing many aerial roots. The most common cause of root injury is overwatering, though fertilizer overdose and feeding by fungus gnat larvae can also result in severe root loss. Excess fertilizer (one sign is salt deposits on the pot or soil surface) can be removed by leaching. To help an overwatered or overfed plant recover, place it in a cool room out of direct sunlight and keep the soil barely moist. If you see adult fungus gnats—tiny, nervous black flies—flitting about the soil surface, drench the soil with insecticidal soap (see "Soap Your Plants" on page 261) until no more appear or take cuttings and discard the plant.

When repotting is necessary, use a sterile, acid mix of three parts porous, humus-rich soil and one part perlite, says Dolly Kolli, a member of the Epiphyllum Society of America and a Christmas cactus hobbyist and hybridizer from Mashpee, Massachusetts. Add 1 teaspoon of bonemeal per 6-inch pot, and feed every two weeks with compost tea from late winter until Labor Day. Keep the soil moist, especially when humidity is low, but don't let it get soggy.

Cymbidium Solutions

Q. I haven't had a bloom spike on my cymbidium orchids in more than five years. What am I doing wrong?

A. The most common causes of nonflowering in cymbidiums are low light, insufficient nutrients, and lack of a drop in night temperature, says American Orchid Society probationary judge C. Robert Phillips of Bethlehem, Pennsylvania. During the growing season (April to October), give the plants full sun with shading only at midday. Apply liquid fertilizer, such as fish emulsion, at every other watering. If you've had your plants for five years, they may need repotting. Use medium-grade Douglas fir bark and give the plants plenty of nitrogen. Cymbidiums need a 15-degree drop in night temperature to set buds. This should occur naturally if you grow your plants outdoors. "Cymbidiums will tolerate, and even enjoy, a degree or two of frost," says Phillips. If you follow this regimen for a couple of seasons and your plants still don't flower, you may have clones that are naturally reluctant bloomers. In that case, consider buying miniature cymbidiums, which are easier to flower than standards.

Boston Fern Basics

Q. What's the best care for my Boston fern?

A. Don't overwater or repot your Boston fern too frequently. Let the soil dry out slightly between thorough waterings. Mist the leaves twice a day, especially in winter when the air is dry. To clean the fronds, gently sponge with a solution of 1 tablespoon of white vinegar per cup of warm water. When fronds turn yellow, trim them close to the soil level. Pot up only when the roots occupy over three-fourths of the pot space. Boston ferns like to be potbound. Potting soils should be well drained. One composed of four parts sandy loam, one part sand, and one part manure will suit your fern. Side-dress with fish emulsion every third watering during its growing season. The plant grows best in indirect sunlight. It needs 68° to 75°F daytime temperatures, 50° to 60°F nighttime temperatures, and 50 to 80 percent humidity. Keep your Boston fern out of drafts. From fall through winter, the plant stops growing. Keep it at 50°F, reduce watering so the soil is barely moist, and stop fertilizing.

Rabbit's Foot Fern

Rabbit's Foot Replant

Q. **A friend gave me a large rabbit's foot fern in a wire hanging basket with the "feet" wrapped around it three deep. How can I repot it?**

A. A rabbit's foot fern with "feet" or rhizomes growing through the sides of the wire basket isn't necessarily rootbound. A plant that needs repotting will produce small fronds, grow slowly, and need frequent watering, and its lower leaves will turn yellow. If this fern needs repotting, there are two ways to replant it. Cut the rhizomes off the sides and bottom of the basket and transplant the fern to a new basket lined with 2 inches of unmilled sphagnum moss. Or cut away the old basket, removing the fern in pieces. Then replant the healthiest rhizomes in a new basket or several baskets, using standard potting mix. Small rhizomes can be poked through the sides and held in place with wire. Water thoroughly after planting. To revitalize a large fern without removing it from the basket, cut out the central portion, fill the space with potting soil, and cover with sphagnum moss. If the rhizomes surrounding the sides of the basket are growing too thickly and lack vigor, thin them by pruning some off.

Stressed-Out Gardenia

Q. **Most of the older leaves on my gardenia are yellowing and falling. I keep it 3 feet below a 75-watt plant light that burns eight hours a day. Why is it declining?**

A. Gardenias react to several kinds of stress by dropping their leaves. Your plant may not be getting enough light. Try moving it closer to the lamp, but be careful that it doesn't get too hot. Burning the light a few hours longer can help offset low light intensity. If your plant is potbound and hasn't been fed regularly, the yellowing leaves could indicate nitrogen deficiency. Feed every two weeks with fish emulsion. In early spring, repot if necessary into a well-drained, acidic, peaty soil. Cold or wet soil can also cause blotchy yellowing of leaves. Grow the plant at 60°F or higher and don't overwater.

No Goldfish

Q. **How can I get my goldfish plant (*Columnea*) to bloom again? The foliage is healthy, but blossoms never appear.**

A. Inadequate light can cause blossom failure. *Columnea* is a gesneriad and must be treated like its relative, the African violet. Try giving your plant indirect but bright light, 10 to 12 hours per day, perhaps by setting the plant in an east window. You may also be overfertilizing. Remove the plant from its pot and rinse the soil ball in water to flush out the excess nitrogen. Repot the plant in a soil mix to which you have added a sprinkling of bonemeal (use 1 tablespoon for a 5-inch pot). Phosphorus, the major nutrient in bonemeal, is required for strong, healthy blossoms and often stimulates the blooming of potted plants.

Never-Blooming Hoyas

Q. **I have some four-year-old variegated hoyas that are growing nicely but have never bloomed. Why don't they flower?**

A. Hoya, also called porcelain-flower or wax plant, is a genus of tropical vines, some of which are grown as houseplants on trellises or in hanging baskets. The thick leaves may be flecked with silver or variegated pink and white. The clusters of fragrant, waxy, white-and-pink flowers are carried on woody, leafless spurs that grow from the leaf axils; be careful not to prune the spurs when grooming the plants. Variegated cultivars are much slower to bloom than green types, says Jerry Williams of Rainbow Gardens Nursery, La Habra, California, which sells hoyas. To induce flowering in any hoya, grow it in very bright light and allow it to become potbound, advises Williams. Indoors, give hoyas full sun in an east or west window and light shade in a south window. If possible, summer the plants outdoors in bright shade. If they still don't bloom, hold back on nitrogen and substitute fertilizers rich in phosphorus (bonemeal) and potassium (seaweed extract or kelp meal), both of which stimulate flowering.

Punctual Poinsettia

Q. How can I get my poinsettia to bloom for the holiday season?

A. You can force the blossoms for Christmas by giving them 12 hours of darkness and keeping night temperatures between 60° and 68°F. Keep the plants under these conditions until the buds develop or the bracts ("petals") begin to color. When they bloom, take them into a sunny, draft-free room. Poinsettias' bracts will color up within six to ten weeks and can continue to bloom from December through Easter.

Chapter 18

Growing in Greenhouses

Good Houses Make Good Gardens

Glazing for a Grow-Frame

Q. I want to build a solar grow-frame and would like to know the best glazing material to use. Are glass panels better insulators than acrylic or fiberglass?

A. Glass, acrylic, and fiberglass are all good light transmitters. However, a single sheet of each has an R-value of about 1, meaning that none of these materials offers much insulation. To reduce heat loss, cover the inside of the glazing at night with some type of movable insulation such as rigid foam or an insulating window shade. For maximum efficiency, the cover material should fit as tightly as possible against the glazing.

A Black-and-White Issue

Q. I built a lean-to greenhouse that is attached to the south side of my house in Iowa. Should the back wall be painted white to reflect light to the plants, or black to absorb heat?

A. If you want healthy plants, you should paint the north wall of your greenhouse white, since light levels can be critical during

Iowa winters. If your plants lean toward the south, you may have to add fluorescent lights. Rather than using heat storage to moderate temperature extremes, we suggest that you install an exhaust fan with an automatic thermostat in the north wall. Put it 2 feet or less below the juncture of the greenhouse roof and the house wall. The fan will automatically draw excess heat into the house during the day and will return heat to the greenhouse at night. You will probably want to cover the glazing with an insulating curtain at night to prevent excessive heat loss. During the summer, block off the fan. Install vents on each endwall of the greenhouse, a louvered intake vent low on the east wall to draw in cool air, and a fan exhaust vent high on the west wall to draw hot air out.

A Lot of Hot Air

Q. **We plan to grow herbs in a solar greenhouse next year and have been exploring different ways of providing inexpensive supplemental heat. Would composting sawdust and chicken manure in 25-gallon plastic garbage cans increase the temperature in our greenhouse?**

A. Composting sawdust and chicken manure will add additional heat to the greenhouse, but don't use cans. By using closed containers for composting, you run the risk of encouraging the slow, cold decay produced by anaerobic bacteria. This will make your greenhouse smell more like a sewer than a warm, plant-growing place. For fast, hot, odorless compost, you need to encourage aerobic, oxygen-loving bacteria. Instead of cans, use open bins to store compost, and keep the piles supplied with plenty of air by turning their contents frequently. After a few days the steam will start to rise. Steam from the compost will condense on the glass or plastic and then drop down to the soil and plants, keeping things moist and green. When the sun comes up, the rapid heating of the inside air will accelerate the condensation, providing lots of moisture and heat, as well as extra carbon dioxide, to plants. After three weeks or so, the biological fire of the composting process will die down, and you'll have to start new piles with fresh sawdust and manure.

Cooling the Hothouse

Q. In our Florida summers, the temperature in my attached solar greenhouse is higher than outdoors. It often soars past 100°F, even though a ¼-horsepower exhaust fan high in the west wall draws in cooler air through a low vent in the east wall. The roof and walls are insulated to R-19. Any suggestions?

A. There are a number of options that will help lower summer temperatures in your greenhouse. First, the ventilation system should allow at least one air exchange to occur every two minutes. Check the cubic feet per minute (cfm) rating of the fan. Then calculate the area of the greenhouse to see if the fan is powerful enough to provide adequate ventilation. Second, frequent misting of walls, floors, and plants provides some evaporative cooling. Third, shadecloth, on either the inside or outside of the glazing, reduces heat transmission by 50 to 70 percent. Keep in mind that it reduces light by about the same amount, and plant growth may be affected. Another option, which depends on the kinds of plants you raise, is to move the plants to a lath house for the summer. Before returning these plants to the greenhouse, inspect them carefully to avoid introducing pest problems.

Polyethylene Policy

Q. We've been wondering about using polyethylene glazing for greenhouses. Isn't it harmful?

A. We don't feel there is any danger using polyethylene in greenhouses. It would take temperatures of 300° to 400°F to release potentially harmful factors in the plastic. In fact, we recommend polyethylene for the inner glazing of greenhouses. It is inexpensive and durable. However, ultraviolet light will degrade it within a year if it is used as outer glazing. We feel replacing it yearly would be wasteful.

Kerosene Kickback

Q. I have a 14-by-40-foot poly-covered greenhouse and wonder if it's safe to heat with a portable kerosene heater.

A. Although you can safely use an unvented kerosene heater for several hours in an emergency situation, it is generally not safe to use one as the main heat source for a greenhouse. Burning an unvented heater for several hours depletes oxygen from the air and also causes potentially harmful levels of combustion gases such as sulfur dioxide to build up. If your greenhouse is attached to the house, you can heat it by drawing in warm air from the house with fans. To heat a freestanding greenhouse, install a heater vented to the outside. Companies specializing in florist and nursery supplies offer several types of greenhouse systems, including hot air, hot water, and steam units. These are fueled by oil, kerosene, or natural or liquefied petroleum (LP) gas. These companies can help you design a heating system that suits your needs.

Not Just Hot Air

Q. **Would it be safe to vent the hot air from my gas-powered clothes dryer into my greenhouse?**

A. Yes, but there are drawbacks. The exhaust from your gas dryer will contain a lot of carbon dioxide and small amounts of polluting gases like carbon monoxide, nitrous oxide, and sulfur dioxide. However, in your greenhouse, the harmful gases should dissipate. The carbon dioxide will enhance growth. Gas flames, when ignited and extinguished or when improperly adjusted, can also give off ethylene. While it is a common plant hormone, it will cause some plants, especially tomatoes, to droop. The biggest problem with dryer exhaust is moisture. A load of wet clothes contains a gallon or more of water, all of which gets carried off in the exhaust as water vapor. The resulting high humidity in a greenhouse could cause excess condensation and outbreaks of disease.

Indoor Gardening Tips

Lethargic Ladybugs

Q. **Last December, I ordered 500 ladybugs to control aphids in my greenhouse. The greenhouse has a night temperature of 50°F and a day temperature of 75° to 80°F. When I released the bugs, they seemed lethargic, and almost all died within a week. Was my greenhouse too cold for them?**

A. No. The beetles should feed readily within a temperature range of 65° to 100°F. Ladybugs that seem lethargic upon release have probably suffered from cold in transit. (Temperatures below

30°F will injure them.) They could also have been weakened if they weren't given water while being stored at the insectary. The common ladybug (*Hippodamia convergens*) is often recommended as a biological control, but because of its fairly complex life cycle, even researchers have trouble getting consistent results. You'll have greater success controlling aphids with green lacewings. But order them in the fall, since they are more sensitive to the freezing temperatures they might experience during winter shipping.

Whitefly Woes

Q. **We have whiteflies in our greenhouse. So far we have tried a number of controls, including vacuuming them, dusting them with tobacco dust, spraying them with a solution of water and lime sulfate, and hanging sticky yellow cards to attract flying adults. Nothing has worked. What should we do now?**

A. In the greenhouse at the Rodale Research Center, whiteflies aren't a problem until late spring and summer. The greenhouse has no supplemental heat supply, and in winter it gets quite cool. This may be why the pest isn't much of a pest problem. We do have a whitefly population in our heated Quonset-type greenhouse, which we use for some winter research activities. We have had luck using potted tomatoes as "trap" plants for the whiteflies. We then periodically spray or remove leaves or entire plants. Occasionally on a mild day, we take the trap plants outside to prune them, removing many of the pests in the immature stages of growth. Shaking off the adults in the wind is also helpful. Also, many of the strong herb sprays that we've tried have killed adult whiteflies. Some of the herbs we've had luck with are eucalyptus (*Eucalyptus globulus*), rue (*Ruta graveolens*), and santolina (*Santolina chamaecyparissus*).

Hanging sticky flypaper around the infested plants works well to nab the adults. The flypaper must be replaced regularly, since the stickiness wears off. Hang it rather low around the pots for the low-flying whiteflies. We have also had success using the sticky yellow cards you mentioned. We use ¼-inch plywood sprayed with Rustoleum orange and topped with a mineral oil coating. When the trapped whiteflies cover the square too thickly, we wipe it clean and apply fresh oil. Also, proper air circulation helps to keep the populations from booming.

Greenhouse-Grown Problems

Spindly Sprouts

Q. I'm trying to grow tomatoes, lettuce, and Chinese cabbage in our solar greenhouse, but everything stays thin and spindly. Is there something I can add to the soil?

A. There's an easy way to learn if soil fertility is the problem. Feed your plants a nutrient tea, and if they respond with vigorous growth, you're on your way to successful crops. In wintertime gardening tests at the Rodale Research Center, we compared teas made with chicken and cow manures, bloodmeal, fish emulsion, and Fertrell. The chicken manure and fish emulsion teas promoted the best growth, although we don't recommend fish emulsion in greenhouses because of the possible salt buildup. The other organic materials are suitable if you can obtain them more readily than chicken manure. We use about 6 ounces of dried chicken manure per gallon of water. Don't expect tomatoes to grow as well in the cold months as lettuce and Chinese cabbage.

Cucurbit Flower: Unpollinated (top), Pollinated (bottom)

Hand Pollination

Q. We are about to add a solar greenhouse to our home so we can grow vegetables year-round. Can you tell me which vegetables need to be hand-pollinated and how to do it?

A. Cucumbers, melons, and squash (cucurbits), and tomatoes, eggplant, and peppers (nightshades) must be hand-pollinated. Pollinate the plants in the tomato family by gently flicking the blooms. That will jostle the pollen from the male part of the flower to the female. In the cucumber family, the male and female flowers are separate. You'll have to transfer the pollen from a male to a female flower with a small paintbrush. Pollinate in the early morning while temperatures are cool. At temperatures above 90°F, the pollen may dry out before pollination occurs.

Rotten Lettuce

Q. Last winter several large heads of my greenhouse lettuce rotted. How can I prevent this next year?

A. The spoiler of your lettuce was probably botrytis (gray mold), the same fungus that spoils lettuce in the refrigerator. Botrytis is mainly a disease of old, dying, or injured leaves and soft tissue such as flower petals. Infected areas first look soft, water-soaked, and discolored; the gray mold doesn't appear until decay is advanced. Botrytis spores need humidity levels close to 90 percent to germinate—conditions often found in a closed greenhouse on a cloudy day in winter. Botrytis usually attacks lettuce after it has passed its prime. To keep it from getting a foothold, make small plantings every two weeks so you can use the heads as soon as they mature. Improve air circulation by spacing plants so they won't touch at maturity or gradually thin them by harvesting alternate plants before they crowd each other. Vent the greenhouse on warm days, and run a fan to keep the air moving. Clean up dead leaves and fading flowers to help keep spore counts down. Don't splash water on the leaves.

Wilting Tomatoes

Q. I believe my greenhouse tomato plants have bacterial wilt. How can I control it?

A. To eliminate bacterial wilt (*Pseudomonas solanacearum*) from your greenhouse, remove all the soil and heat it to 120° to 125°F for ten minutes. That's a big job! An easier method is to compost the infested soil in a hot compost pile, which creates fresh, uncontaminated soil. An even easier method is to just replace the soil with new, clean soil. Clean all benches, growing beds, and pots with a mild bleach solution. The first symptoms of bacterial wilt are slight yellowing of the lower leaves or wilting of the younger leaves. If you pull a plant from the soil and cut open a root, it will be brown just inside the stem and look water-soaked.

Figs Indoors and Out

Q. **I plan to grow a fig tree in a container outdoors during the summer and bring it into my greenhouse each winter. Do you think the tree will continue to ripen its fruit?**

A. As long as it is given adequate drainage, a fig tree will do quite well in a container. Bringing it indoors in the fall should extend the ripening period. The main criterion for growing sweet figs in a greenhouse is lots of direct sunlight. In fact, depending on the variety, you may get a bonus second crop in early spring.

Part
FIVE

Keeping the
Garden Healthy

Chapter 19

Protecting Your Garden

Cautions on Chemicals

The Wrong "Organic"

Q. I've seen the following chemicals referred to as "organic" pesticides: carbaryl, diazinon, and malathion. Can I use these and still sell my produce as organically grown?

A. No! The word organic has more than one meaning. Organic gardening is based on working with nature, returning *organic* (from *living*) materials to the land, and enriching the organisms in the soil. Chemical fertilizers and pesticides only disrupt nature's cycles. The highly toxic pesticides you named are part of a branch of chemistry related to hydrocarbon compounds (organic chemistry) and are considered "organic" only because they contain carbon compounds.

Cleaning Out Chemicals

Q. When I first started gardening, I used the chemicals many books suggested. Now that I'm an organic gardener, my problem is disposing of these chemicals I've been holding for years. What do you suggest?

A. One solution is to return them to the manufacturer. They can be sent through the mail, but use great care to ensure that any container is padded and wrapped securely, with its contents clearly marked on the package. If you choose to dispose of chemicals locally, certain pesticide containers can be buried, burned, or chemically degraded. Check with your extension agent, an Environmental Protection Agency representative, or a specialist at your state college of agriculture for accepted disposal methods. Products containing mercury, lead, cadmium, arsenic, or inorganic pesticides must be specially handled and are usually disposed of by encapsulation. However, even this sealing of the pesticide and container in sturdy, waterproof cartons does not always prevent leakage, as we are now finding. Never dispose of pesticides or their "empty" containers in an open environment such as a landfill or dumping ground, or by burning.

Captan Kills Inoculants

Q. What is captan? Does it interfere with nitrogen-fixing inoculants?

A. Captan, a complex fungicide, is a chlorinated hydrocarbon compound that belongs to the same group of compounds as DDT. It's used to coat seeds to prevent rotting before germination. Because captan is antifungal and antibacterial by nature, it will kill the beneficial bacterial inoculants that encourage nitrogen-fixing nodule growth in peas, beans, and other legumes. And fungicides can harm many of the other beneficial organisms in your soil. Ask for untreated seed when you order seeds—many companies provide them (see "Giving Treated Seeds the Treatment" on page 92).

Organic Alternatives

Right On Ryania

Q. You've mentioned ryania as a control for codling moths. What is ryania, how does it work, and where can I get it?

A. Ryania is a botanical insecticide made from the ground stems of *Ryania speciosa*, a shrub native to Trinidad. It contains the alkaloid ryanodine, a stomach and contact poison that kills by causing muscle paralysis. Ryania is especially useful for controlling codling moths and certain other orchard pests because, unlike rotenone and pyrethrum, it kills target insects without eliminating beneficials. It is also effective against European corn borers, leaf rollers and other caterpillars, citrus thrips, sawfly larvae, and some beetles. It is ineffective against sweet-potato weevils, cabbage maggots, Japanese beetle larvae, plum curculios, and spider mites. Because of its fairly low toxicity to humans, ryania is cleared for use within one day of harvest. It retains its potency for several years if stored cool and dry and is highly stable when exposed to light.

Keep Your Powder Dry

Q. What is the storage life of powder made from dried pyrethrum flowers?

A. If the powder is fresh when you get it and you store it properly, it should last for at least ten years with little decline in potency, according to Dr. Cecil Still, a pyrethrum researcher at Rutgers University. "Oxygen and light are the major causes of pyrethrin breakdown," says Still. "Store the powder in tightly closed, lightproof containers in a cool, dry place. I have ground pyrethrum flowers dating back to the 1930s that have been stored this way in my lab, and they still show full insecticidal activity."

Marigold Mystery

Q. Are the new "scentless" varieties of marigold effective pest repellents?

A. Although marigolds are said to repel many types of garden pests, only their effectiveness against nematodes has been proven in tests. The new "scentless" marigolds are a type of African marigold (*Tagetes erecta*), which is *not* effective for nematode control. The kind that *will* control nematodes are French marigolds (*Tagetes patula*). However, scent has nothing to do with how well marigolds control root-knot nematodes, the most destructive garden nematode. Scientists really aren't sure how marigolds repel root-knot nematodes. One theory is that the plant's roots exude substances that kill the pests. But another theory gaining wide acceptance says that as long as there are no host plants in the area (a not-too-common circumstance, since nematodes will feed on almost any vegetable, weed, or grass), the nematodes eventually die. The French marigolds do not serve as a host. To control root-knot nematodes in your garden, plant the entire infested area with French marigolds for a full season. Spot plantings are not effective against them, although a heavy interplanting (four or five marigolds around one tomato plant) may provide some protection. Researchers at the University of Georgia found that the French marigold variety 'Tangerine' gave the best control, while 'Goldie', 'Petite Gold', and 'Petite Harmony' also showed good repellent qualities.

The Rundown on Rotenone

Q. Is it safe to spray rotenone in my garden?

A. Rotenone is a plant-derived insecticide that is considered organic because it is made from the roots of tropical plants, particularly derris. It poisons many kinds of insects and will suffocate fish, but it has proven to be harmless to warm-blooded animals. Rotenone has little residual effect, but its active period is rather short. When buying rotenone, read the labels carefully to be sure it hasn't been fortified with chemical toxins. Because rotenone is lethal to beneficial insects like bees, use it only as a last resort. A heavy dusting of rotenone will severely upset the natural insect balance of your garden. If you use it once, you may have to use it again that year, since the insect populations will be out of balance. If you must use rotenone, we recommend using the kind you can mix with water. The water aerosol seems to settle more quickly than the dry dust, and it sticks better. Wear a protective face mask to avoid inhaling the spray. Although the label warns against using rotenone within one day of harvest, two Canadian researchers found that residues are still present after a week. To avoid eating traces, pick a week's worth of vegetables before you spray. When you start picking again, wash everything carefully. If you spray your beans for beetles, remember that lettuce in an adjacent bed will catch some of the rotenone. And never spray near a body of water, since you kill the fish in it.

Giving Your Garden the Nicotine Habit

Q. What are the advantages and disadvantages of using tobacco dust as an insecticide?

A. Nicotine, the active ingredient in tobacco dust, is by far the most toxic of the botanical insecticides. Acting as a contact and stomach poison, it kills a very wide range of pests. Gardeners have used tobacco dust or an extract made by soaking tobacco in water mainly against piercing/sucking insects such as aphids, leafhoppers, and true bugs. The dust is effective against hard-to-combat ground-dwelling pests such as root aphids. It has also been used as a dog, cat, rabbit, and insect repellent. Tobacco dust is indiscriminate, killing beneficial insects and earthworms as well as pests. But the very high toxicity of nicotine to humans is its chief disadvantage. Smoking tobacco contains about 3 percent nicotine, and some samples of tobacco dust have been found to contain ½ percent—enough to be concerned about. But perhaps because of the casual way in which smoking tobacco is handled, people don't treat the dust with the respect it deserves, according to Bill Wolf of the Necessary Trading Company. "They dust it liberally around and inhale it," he says. The fine dust is very irritating to mucous membranes and eyes, and nicotine can be absorbed this way. If you use it, wear protective clothing and a mask. If applied heavily, tobacco dust can burn small seedlings and new leaves. It can also carry tobacco mosaic virus (TMV), a serious disease of tomatoes and other vegetables. Once introduced, TMV can survive in weeds and be carried back to crops by aphids and other insects.

Bee Wary

Q. Will the use of an organic insecticide (such as diatomaceous earth or rotenone) on my vegetables and fruits hamper pollination by bees?

A. It depends on the insecticide and how it's applied. Diatomaceous earth is lethal to bees—its sharp crystals pierce their bodies, causing them to dehydrate and die. If you must use an insecticide while bees are pollinating, bee specialist Dr. Philip Torchio of the U.S. Department of Agriculture recommends pyrethrum rather than rotenone. Even though it's more toxic to bees, pyrethrum breaks down faster—within six hours if the temperature is 55°F or higher. As a general rule, don't spray anything on your plants or trees while they are in flower. If you must spray, use a liquid formulation of pyrethrum or ryania—another botanical insecticide that is only slightly toxic to bees and other beneficials. *Bacillus thuringiensis* (Bt) is also safe, since it affects only caterpillars. Spray at dusk, when bees are least active. If the weather forecast predicts a heavy dew, don't use pyrethrum—it won't break down before the bees begin feeding in the morning.

All That Glitters

Q. **Is it true that aluminum foil is effective for insect control and as a mulching material? I can't understand how it would be beneficial.**

A. It seems unlikely, but it is true. This unusual mulching material serves three purposes—it retains moisture in the ground, reflects an extra dose of light onto the plants, and repels aphids. When aphids take off to fly, they head directly for the sky, and when they decide to land again, they reverse their direction. The reflection of the sky on the aluminum foil probably confuses the insects so that they are constantly reversing their direction. That means they never can land on plants. Tests also show that aluminum foil is most effective for only the first foot or so of space above the ground. Therefore, controlling pests on tall plants, like roses, may require structures to hold the foil aboveground. You can use all types of aluminum foil for insect control, but a special paper-backed kind, sold in many lumberyards as insulation material, will do the best job of mulching directly on the ground.

Bring Back Bt

Q. **I used *Bacillus thuringiensis* (Bt) last year. Will these bacteria, like milky spore, overwinter and be effective this year?**

A. No. Unlike milky spore disease (*B. popillae*), Bt doesn't reproduce or overwinter. Because it breaks down in sunlight, it remains viable for only seven days after application. You'll need to reapply as usual this year. If you stored your Bt in its container in a cool, dark place, it will remain stable for at least three years in wettable powder form and for one year in the liquid formulation. You can use it indefinitely when stored at 40° to 50°F. Don't keep Bt in a hot garage—at temperatures above 90°F, its shelf life drops to one month.

Once and Done

Q. Every summer we've had the same problem—Japanese beetles. Last year we treated our lawn with milky spore disease. Must we apply more powder this spring?

A. One application of milky spore normally is all you need. Although it may take 3 years for the disease spores to spread throughout your lawn, once established, the disease remains effective for 15 to 20 years because the spores stay in the soil. The disease is harmless to humans, warm-blooded animals, plants, and beneficial insects. Inoculating sod with milky spore disease halts the development of the overwintering Japanese beetle grub into an adult bug. As each infected grub dies off, its normally clear blood becomes creamy white with disease spores, which multiply and spread in the soil. That leads to a considerable reduction in the number of beetles emerging from the pupal stage—and fewer eggs laid, of course. This spring, you might try to convince your neighbors to treat their lawns with the disease, too. Community-wide application of milky spore is definitely the best defense against Japanese beetles.

Bring On the Beneficials

Bug Lights vs. Beneficials

Q. What is your opinion of bug-light traps? Don't they kill beneficial insects as well as pests?

A. These traps primarily attract moths and butterflies. While some of these moths are the adults of common garden pests such as cutworms, the traps won't provide effective control of garden insects. That's because many of them will have already laid their eggs, says Dr. Michael Peters, who has studied ultraviolet (UV) light traps for several years at the University of Massachusetts. Most beneficial insects like ladybugs and parasitic wasps are active only during the day, so black light traps don't affect them. Hover and tachinid flies aren't attracted to a light trap, either, says Peters: "For the most part, it's not knocking out a lot of beneficials." He adds that some helpful insects, such as the trichogramma wasp, are simply too small to be electrocuted by a bug zapper because of the spacing of the wires. On the other hand, Peters has observed significant numbers of a parasitic wasp called the ichneumon wasp, as well as the predatory rove beetle, that have been caught by UV traps. UV bug-killers do catch a fair number of night-flying mosquitoes, but many species of mosquitoes are day-fliers and aren't drawn to black light.

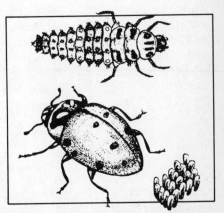

Ladybug:
Larva (top),
Adult (bottom left),
Eggs (bottom right)

Looking for Ladybugs

Q. What do the eggs, larvae, and adults of the ladybug look like? We handpick a lot of bugs and don't want to destroy this beneficial insect.

A. The ladybug usually lays its bright orange eggs in vertical clusters on leaves and stems. They're so similar to the eggs of the Colorado potato beetle and the Mexican bean beetle that you should wait until the larvae start emerging before you squash any eggs. Fully mature ladybug larvae are ½ inch long and black with orange spots. The ¼-inch-long, rounded adult beetle can be orange, red, pink, yellow, or even gray and may have black spots or be solidly colored. Don't confuse the adult ladybug with the Mexican bean beetle, which is the same size but has a golden lustre and brown spots.

Heave-Ho for Hoppers

Q. Will *Nosema lucustae* work against grasshoppers in my backyard?

A. If you are looking for a quick solution, *N. lucustae* will disappoint you. On the average, this protozoan disease of grasshoppers and Mormon crickets takes 21 days to establish itself in the guts of grasshoppers. On less than an acre of land, grasshoppers spread faster than the spores can kill them—and you'll feel as if you've wasted your money. If you want to use *N. lucustae*, the best bet is to get together with your neighbors and buy enough of the product for a large area. To control grasshoppers before they have the chance to become a problem, till the soil right after harvest. The most harmful grasshopper species spend six to eight months of the year as eggs in the surface layer of the soil. Tilling makes the soil unattractive to egg-laying females and helps destroy the eggs already laid.

Praying Mantis

Mantis Methods

Q. **We would like to get praying mantids, but last year we had terrible luck. Is it possible to raise mantids here in Indiana? How should we start them?**

A. Praying mantids can be raised anywhere in the United States if there is a sufficient supply of insects for food. The common large Chinese mantis is winter-hardy, and mantis eggs can survive freezing temperatures. Remember that birds and ants are natural enemies of the mantis and will take their toll of egg cases and newly hatched mantids. Keep egg cases collected in the fall or purchased commercially in cold storage through the winter for protection. One method to ensure undisturbed spring hatching is to suspend an egg case in a large jar. (Use a thin needle to attach a thread through the outer top edge of each case.) Secure the thread to the jar top, allowing the case to hang freely, and cover the jar with net or nylon. Place the jar in a warm spot, out of direct sun, and the mantids can hatch undisturbed. Once the shells of the baby mantids dry and harden, they are safe from ants, and you can release the hatchlings into your garden. It might take a few years to build up a concentration of praying mantids, especially if neighbors spray chemicals near your property. Collect cases each fall and release more mantids each spring to replenish your supply.

Mighty Mites

Q. Will predatory mites control spider mites on vegetables and ornamentals in my San Diego, California, garden? If so, when should I order them, and how many should I release?

A. A carefully timed release of predatory mites will provide control against spider mites, according to Jeff Hadden of Natural Pest Controls, Orangevale, California. As a rule of thumb, Hadden advises ordering predators six weeks before the date on which you first noticed pest infestation the previous year. Begin looking for mites with a hand lens early in the year. Look for them on the undersides of leaves of susceptible plants. If you wait to order predators until you see mite damage such as webbing, stippling, and graying or yellowing of the foliage, the pest population may be too large for the predators to control in time to save the plant. Weekly soap sprays will help keep pest numbers low until help arrives, but don't spray after you release the predatory mites—the soap will kill them as well as the pests. The best way to deal with plants that are heavily infested each year is to replace them with more tolerant species, says Hadden. Predatory mites are usually released at the rate of 25 mites per 2 feet of plant height. Of the several species available, the best for your situation is probably *Metaseiulus occidentalis*, sold as PMO, advises Hadden. PMO is the most general predator and is very tolerant of heat and dryness. If cover and prey are available, PMO should overwinter in your climate. To help PMO overwinter in the vegetable garden, plant a cover crop such as crimson clover, fava beans, or hairy vetch.

Trichogramma Turnaround

Q. Last year I purchased some trichogramma wasps and released them into my garden. They did an excellent job of protecting my crops from cabbage loopers. Are these wasps hardy enough to survive the winter, or should I purchase another supply this year?

A. To be safe, make a fresh release of the parasitic wasps each year. Although some trichogramma wasp species are capable of overwintering as eggs in their host's eggs, those effective against cabbage loopers are not. Cabbage loopers overwinter as pupae on leaves or on the soil rather than as eggs. It is possible that your trichogramma wasps could locate alternative hosts to parasitize and overwinter in, especially if you live near a wild area, but you shouldn't rely on that. Instead, make a new wasp release this coming summer.

Toad Tactics

Q. What can I do to entice the toads to stay in my garden? Since I don't have access to marshy areas, they're hard to come by.

A. Once you've acquired a few toads, cater to them by providing them with some moist, dark shelters located throughout the garden. Toads need to be kept moist because they're amphibians. During the day, they usually seek out cool hiding places beneath loose boards, under garden mulch, or in the shade of low-growing shrubbery. At night, they brave the darkness in search of cutworms, potato beetles, chinch bugs, ants, slugs, and other pests. Keep your toads happy by wetting down the shrubbery on a hot day. Make a little niche for them by cutting a small entrance in a box or by chipping out a small opening in the side of a flowerpot and burying it a few inches into the ground. Place the pot in the shade of a tree or shrub for added comfort. Since toads must have access to water, set out a shallow pan in the garden or in the box or flowerpot. The toad drinks through its skin, so the pan should be large enough for him to sit in. Look for a new supply of toads after a good rainfall, when they'll be hopping across roads, lawns, and pastures. It's worth the search when you consider that just one toad can eat up to 15,000 insects during one active season. If the weather is moderate, toads will watch out for your garden from March to mid-November.

Chapter 20

A Rogues' Gallery
of Garden Pests

About Insects and Diseases

Tracking the Enemy

Q. I always make a valiant effort to identify insects and diseases with the help of reference books and fellow gardeners. However, there are times when I just can't seem to pinpoint the culprits that are harming my plants. What can I do when I'm left in the dark?

A. When all else fails, contact your local county agricultural agent or the extension specialists who are located at your state's land-grant universities and colleges. If you want to send them specimens through the mail, follow this procedure: Wrap insect pests, including immature stages if possible, carefully in soft tissue paper. Preserve soft-bodied insects in a 70 percent alcohol solution. Package all insects in a small can, plastic box, or other strong container, and send them by first-class mail to the extension entomologist. Plant disease specimens should include entire plants, when possible, with the roots wrapped in moist soil, peat moss, or sawdust. Send these to the extension plant pathologist. Since it's not always easy for the specialist to identify problems, include a letter describing the crop, area, and pest- or disease-control history, as well as the location and type of damage.

Sunning Fungi

Q. I live in Miami, Florida. Because of the hot, humid climate here, I have found it extremely difficult to grow tomatoes and cucurbits. But it is an ideal climate for fungi. How can I grow these vegetables successfully without resorting to using a fungicide?

A. Growing tomatoes, squash, and cucumbers organically in South Florida depends primarily on meeting two conditions: The plants need full sunlight, and they require extremely fertile soil. Full sun is no problem if vegetables are field-grown or if your garden is not shaded. For shaded areas, we recommend "pot-planting." One Florida gardener has had great success using a few old plastic wastepaper baskets as containers. She fills the baskets with perlite and potting soil, then puts two or three plants in each. She reports that three wastepaper baskets supply her family with all the tomatoes and zucchini they can eat, with some to give away. She has no fungus problems.

Most organic gardeners in South Florida battle fungus with good soil. Compost, table scraps, and manure are all good for the garden. The plants that grow in many waterways and canals in Florida are a wonderful source of free enriching material. Seaweed, which is washed up on the beaches, is also a top-notch soil amendment. These plants concentrate nutrients and break down quickly in the garden. But be sure to wash salt from seaweed before using. Begin conditioning the soil in early summer, as soon as the previous year's garden is finished. Dig in table scraps, compost, waterweeds—whatever is available. Sheet-composting with any organic material helps keep heavy summer rains from washing away the nutrients you are adding to your garden. Although you can see improvement in your garden after a single summer of heavy mulching and fertilizing, it takes about three years to get the soil rich enough so diseases just can't keep up with the plants' growth. Don't try to get an early start by planting before the middle of September. It takes cool nights to set fruit, and during winter months the humidity isn't much of a problem.

Wilted Tomato Woes

Q. If my tomatoes were infected with fusarium wilt one year, will it affect anything else planted the next year in that spot?

A. No. Although *Fusarium oxysporum* affects certain other crops, including spinach, peas, radishes, cabbages, watermelons, and cantaloupes, and flowers such as dahlias and carnations, each is attacked by a different strain. (*F. oxysporum lycopersici,* for example, is specific to tomatoes.) To control fusarium, rotate susceptible plants on a three- to four-year schedule and grow resistant varieties.

Insects' Winter Wonders

Q. How do most insects manage to live through the winter in cold or freezing sections of the country?

A. There are few bugs that can migrate to warmer climates, so these cold-blooded creatures are forced to adjust to freezing temperatures. Chinch bugs are lucky; they produce an antifreeze chemical that keeps their insides from turning to ice. Others freeze without injury and await the spring thaw. Many species overwinter as eggs. The cecropia silkworm moth actually spins an insulating cocoon that traps air between double walls for maximum insulation. Some insects burrow their way down below the frost line and sleep away the winter.

Insects sense the approach of winter with a built-in clock that is geared to seasonal variations in darkness and light. This unique characteristic is known as photoperiodism. It serves as a vital early-warning system. For example, long before winter, the female grasshopper buries a mass of eggs wrapped in a gluelike jacket. Nature does not allow warmth to hatch the eggs unless they have been frozen *first.* In this way, it is impossible for a late warm spell in autumn to bring out baby grasshoppers to starve. In autumn, winged ants and ladybugs in California fly up into the mountains to spend the winter huddled by the tens of thousands. Many mosquitoes pass the winter as larvae frozen in ponds. When spring comes, they thaw out, metamorphose, and buzz off. Probably the most coddled of all wintering bugs is the corn-root aphid. Its eggs are carefully collected by a species of ant and carried to nests below the frost line. In spring the eggs are taken to the roots of early weeds to hatch.

Insects A to W

Aphid

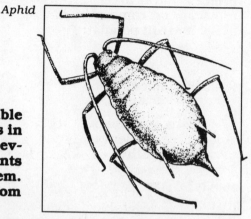

Action against Aphids

Q. Last year we had terrible trouble with aphids and ants in our garden. They were on everything, and my tomato plants developed mosaic from them. What can I do to keep this from happening again this year?

A. To control aphids, you must attack them on two fronts. First, develop a very fertile soil to produce healthy plants, which aphids have shown a tendency to dislike; and second, to battle peak populations, use one or more of the many controls available. Aphids, or plant lice, are small, soft-bodied insects distinguished by their pearlike shape, long antennae, and twin, tubelike appendages that project from the back end. There are dozens of species, many named for their favorite food preference. Aphids suck plant sap and cause withering of foliage and a loss of plant vigor. Excess sugars and sap are emitted from the insect's anus and are known as honeydew. Ants feed on honeydew and will tend aphids as men do cows. The ants distribute the aphids from plant to plant, quickly spreading any plant diseases with the aphids. In fall, ants carry aphid eggs into their nests to be carried back out in spring and set on plants, making control very difficult. There are two or three generations of aphids a season.

The simplest remedy is to gently rub leaves, crushing the aphids. Aphids can also be washed from plants with a forceful spray of water. A stronger control is an insecticidal soap spray (see "Soap Your Plants" on page 261). In some cases, aphids can be controlled by growing nasturtiums as a trap crop. Wait until the nasturtiums are infested, then pull them from the garden and destroy them, aphids and all. Repellent companion plants include garlic, chives and other alliums, coriander, anise, and petunias. The best-known predator of aphids is the ladybug. Other predators include soldier bugs, damsel bugs, big-eyed bugs, pirate bugs, spiders, assassin bugs, syrphid flies, and lacewings. Ladybugs and lacewings are commercially available. Since ants are often the major cause of aphid problems, you should also try to control them. Keep them away from your plants with barrier strips of small amounts of bonemeal or powdered charcoal. You can also wrap a band of cotton smeared with Tanglefoot or Stikem around the base of larger plants to catch the ants. Good garden sanitation and quick removal and composting of plant debris will help cut down both aphid and ant populations.

Rhubarb Remedy

Q. A few years ago, I took the advice of a friend and boiled some rhubarb leaves, saving the reddish-green water. Then I used the solution as a spray to control aphids. Surprisingly, it worked. But why?

A. Oxalic acid kills aphids. Found in spinach, rhubarb, and many leafy vegetables, oxalic acid is poisonous in high concentrations. Although rhubarb contains negligible amounts of oxalates in its edible stems, its leaves are rich in the soluble substances and should not be eaten. The oxalates in the leaves make aphids sick, too. You can mix a simple rhubarb spray by cutting up 1 pound of leaves and boiling them in 1 quart of water for 30 minutes. Then strain and bottle the liquid. To help it stick to leaves, squeeze in a dab of liquid soap when the solution has cooled.

Blister Beetle Blues

Q. My tomatoes and potatoes have what I think are blister beetles. They resemble potato beetles except they are long and slender, and they make my hands burn when I try to handpick them. How can I get rid of them?

A. You are right. They are blister beetles. Because these insects contain an oil that will blister your skin if you crush them between your fingers, be sure to wear gloves when handpicking. The beetles are ½ to 1 inch long and about four times as long as they are wide. They are black or grayish and may have yellow or gray stripes or a gray margin. The larvae overwinter in the soil. In the spring they burrow through the soil until they find a grasshopper egg mass to feed on. Although the larvae can be considered beneficial, even where there are a lot of them, they don't consume more than 25 percent of the grasshopper eggs. The best control, short of draping your plants with a protective cover such as spunbonded row cover or screen, is to handpick the adult blister beetles.

Cutworm Capers

Q. **I have been mulching my garden with grass clippings. Although they do a good job of keeping moisture in, the clippings make my cutworm problems worse. Should I give up mulching?**

A. No. Just change your mulch. A clean garden is your best defense against cutworms. Grass clippings, other organic mulches, and weeds provide them with food, shelter, and egg-laying sites. Switch to black plastic, the only mulch that doesn't encourage cutworms. Black plastic doesn't shelter cutworms, and it prevents young cutworms from entering the soil. Save your organic mulches for the compost pile.

Cutworms, the larvae of many species of moths, cut off young plants at ground level. There are also climbing cutworms that eat the leaves, buds, and fruits of vegetables, trees, and vines. Cutworms can be gray, brown, black, or mottled and are about 1½ inches long. They are active at night and hide in garden litter by day. Cultivate in the early spring to disturb and kill larvae that have overwintered in the soil and to remove weed seedlings before hatching larvae can eat them. Protect individual plants by putting a 3-inch collar made of stiff paper or plastic around them. Push the collar an inch or so into the ground. For serious infestations, you may want to try the nematode *Neoaplectana carpocapsae*, a microscopic wormlike organism that attacks cutworms and other insects that live in the soil. It won't harm beneficials or earthworms. Apply in the early spring around the base of your plants. You should see an effect within five days, but allow two months for maximum control. The nematodes will overwinter as far north as Minnesota.

Earwig

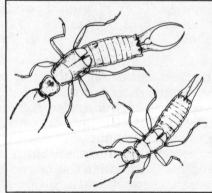

Earwig: The Garden Roach

Q. **In the middle of the night, something gnaws my seedlings down to stumps just as fast as I can set them out. What am I up against?**

A. Probably earwigs. At night, earwigs come out, often in hundreds, and skeletonize plants (rather than chewing neat holes). But the best time to stop them is in the daytime, when they hide in moist, dark places. They congregate under bark, stones, or mulch and between boards. You can control them by making traps that provide dark crevices and cracks. Rolled newspapers or bamboo tubes make effective traps. You can also use old garden hose sections or a piece of black plastic about 2 feet square and folded twice. Place these traps throughout the garden and in the yard beneath shrubbery, under groundcover plants, and against fences. Pick up the traps every day or two and knock out the insects into detergent and water or crush them. Most earwigs are beneficial because they feed on insect pests such as aphids, but a few species like the European earwig (*Forficula auricularia*) also feed on stems, foliage, and fruit. They're distinguished by a pair of sharp pincers at the tail end, and they look a lot like cockroaches—hence their nickname, "the garden roach."

Put Out the Fire Ants

Q. **Fire ants are all over my Fairhope, Alabama, yard and garden. Can you help me?**

A. Biologists at Florida State University recommend pouring 3 gallons of hot tap water on the ant mound to kill the colony. Eight of the 14 colonies they treated this way were completely wiped out. If you still see ants after a few days, repeat the treatment. Hot water is most effective when the ants are near the surface. Douse the mounds on a cool, sunny day after the sun has warmed it.

Another approach to fire-ant control was developed by the U.S. Department of Agriculture (USDA). Researchers isolated a growth hormone that prevents the larvae from developing into worker ants. With fewer and fewer workers to gather food and maintain the mound, the colony eventually dies of starvation. Stauffer Chemical Company produces and markets Pro-Drone, s synthetic version of the hormone. This product contains the synthetic hormone mixed with a bait of corn grits and soybean oil. This material breaks down quickly in the environment, and according to tests is harmless to mammals, fish, birds, and beneficial insects. It will remain active for months in the stomach of a fire ant. Check with your state department of agriculture and local garden stores for availability of Pro-Drone.

Hot Compost Kills Flies

Q. **I find a lot of fly larvae in my compost pile. What can I do to get rid of them?**

A. Your pile isn't heating up enough to kill the larvae. If you do not turn the contents frequently to aerate it, that may be your problem. Turn the pile every three to five days and it should stay hot. If you do turn the pile and it still doesn't heat up, your compost may not have enough nitrogen. Mix fresh manure or grass clippings into the heap, and it should heat up. If adding nitrogen doesn't work, the pile is probably too wet or too dry. A good compost heap is moist but not soaking wet. It should be as wet as a wrung-out sponge. To dry a waterlogged pile, turn it every day. When it dries enough, it will start heating if there is sufficient nitrogen. Cover the pile with discarded plastic bags to keep out rain.

Drat the Gnats

Q. **I sterilize garden soil in my oven to use for potting soil, but I still have a problem with fungus gnats. Is there a remedy?**

A. Fungus gnat adults, actually a type of fly, don't hurt plants. Their maggots, however, can damage roots. The maggots live in manure and decaying vegetable matter, so potting soil rich in humus can harbor them. Soil pasteurization (140° to 180°F for 30 minutes) should take care of the problem, except during the summer. Since the flies are only ¹⁄₁₀ to inch long, they can easily slip through screens and poorly sealed areas. If you see fungus gnats on your houseplants, kill the maggots by letting the soil dry out as much as possible without harming the plants. In a severe infestation, the plants won't grow well and the leaves will turn yellow. Give the soil a good soaking with a rotenone or pyrethrum solution.

Hunting for Hornworms

Q. **I'm surprised that I didn't see the tomato hornworms in my garden until they were 4 inches long, with cocoons on their backs! Can you tell me more about their life cycle?**

A. You can spot the well-camouflaged caterpillars earlier by looking for dark-colored droppings on the foliage. Some gardeners have found that spraying the plants with water causes the worms to thrash around and give away their locations. Adult hormworms are large, fast-flying, mottled gray or brown moths with five orange spots along each side of the body. Their long, narrow forewings span 4 to 5 inches, and they have two dark, diagonal zigzag lines on each hind wing. Watch for them at dusk, when they hover near tubular flowers like hummingbirds. The female moths lay round, greenish-yellow eggs singly on the undersides of leaves. The eggs hatch within a week, and the larvae grow to their full size—3 to 4 inches—in about a month. The caterpillars then burrow 3 to 4 inches underground and spend the winter as pupae in hard, brown, 2-inch-long spindle-shaped cases. These cases have a distinctive handlelike proboscis curving from the front. You may notice them when you work the soil in fall or spring.

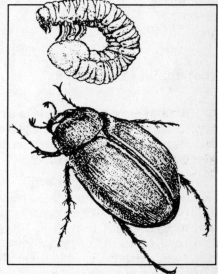

June Bug:
Grub (top),
Adult (bottom)

June Bug Jitters

Q. Are June bugs harmful? I understand milky spore disease infects June bug grubs and is a good method of control.

A. Full-grown June bug beetles can damage plants, including fruit trees and blackberries, by feeding on foliage and flowers. However, more damage is caused by grubs, the immature form of many common large beetles. Grubs harm corn by feeding on roots. They may also feed on the roots of bluegrass, timothy, and soybeans, as well as decaying vegetation. Milky spore disease is effective against 41 types of white grub, including those of the June bug.

Leaf-Cutter Lowdown

Q. Leaf-cutter ants are a terrible problem here in Athens, Texas. Every year they strip the leaves from my peach and plum trees and ornamentals. What can I do?

A. A single leaf-cutter ant nest can be anywhere from 10 square feet to ¼ acre and 15 feet below ground, housing hundreds of thousands of ants, according to Dr. James Robinson of Texas A&M University. It can have as many as 100 entrances. Because of the number of ants and the difficulty of access to their nests, these pests are hard to control. However, there are steps you can take to protect your trees: Wrap several layers of cheesecloth around the base of each tree trunk, cover with paper, and coat with Tanglefoot; replace the paper when it is covered with ants. Dr. William Whitcomb of the University of Florida has studied leaf-cutter ants in South America, where in some places they are an area's worst agricultural pest. In almost every backyard he visited, trees were protected by shallow concrete "moats," 4 to 6 inches wide, filled with water. You could try this, or a trench lined with plastic, if you have only a few trees. In the United States, leaf-cutter ants live only in Louisiana, Texas, and Arizona.

Rooting Out Root Weevils

Q. Strawberry root weevils are eating leaf margins of my rhododendrons and azaleas. My neighbor told me that they can kill the plants and that the only solution is to spray with Orthene. Is there an organic solution?

A. Yes. Adult root weevils—including the strawberry root weevil and black vine weevil—are brown to black, ¼- to ½-inch-long, flightless beetles. They crawl up plant stems at night and feed by notching the leaf margins. This is seldom fatal, according to Dr. Arthur Antonelli, entomologist at Washington State University. However, the larvae—white grubs that hatch in summer—can kill plants by eating the roots and girdling the crowns. To deter weevils, coat stems with a band of Tanglefoot or other sticky material. Antonelli recommends applying a strip of plastic first to avoid injuring the stem. Make sure that overhanging branches or walls don't serve as bridges for the pests. Introducing insect-eating nematodes is even more effective. The nematodes seek out and kill larvae in the soil. Researchers recorded 64.6 percent larval mortality within ten days of application on a California farm.

Slowing Sow Bugs

Q. **Sow bugs are taking over my garden. How can I keep them under control?**

A. Sanitation is the first step. Sow bugs have seven pairs of legs on gray, oval-shaped, segmented bodies about ½ inch long. They prefer damp, cool hiding places. You can find them under boards and stones and in mulch and manure. Any cool crevice can harbor a sow bug. As much as possible, clear your garden area of any materials that will appeal to the bugs. The drier the area, the better. Since the bugs favor young, succulent growth, seedlings need protection. One Southern California gardener has had success protecting his seedlings with paper collars. He cuts off the points of cone-shaped paper cups and slips a cup over each plant. You can also trap the bugs. Put rolled-up corrugated cardboard or newspaper in your garden. At night, the bugs will crawl into these "logs" for shelter. In the morning, collect and dispose of the bugs. But since an adult female hatches 25 to 75 young in a brood (she retains the eggs in a body pouch until after they hatch), you'll have to trap quite a few to make a dent in the population.

Mist Those Spider Mites

Q. **My beans and melons were infested with spider mites last summer. What can I do this year?**

A. Spider mites can be a big problem in hot, dry weather. The reddish-brown, yellow, or green bugs (the color seems to vary with the plant they are eating) are so tiny they are almost invisible without a magnifying glass. Look for pale splotches on the leaves, then check for mites with a hand lens. In a bad infestation, the whole leaf may turn a light color, sometimes pockmarked with reddish-brown patches, before dying. Spider mites don't like high humidity and moist soil, so keep your plants well mulched and mist regularly to maintain the humidity. Bursts of water will also break apart the webs of established mite colonies. If your plants are badly infected, you should be able to control the mites with an insecticidal soap spray. The trick to using the spray is to realize that only the adult mites, not the eggs, are killed by the insecticidal soap. So you must spray at least three times at one-week intervals to kill the mites as they emerge from the eggs.

Stalking Stalk Borers

Q. A 1-inch-long, grayish worm tunnels into the stems of my tomatoes, zinnias, and marigolds, causing them to wilt. I split the stems and remove the worms, but this is very hard on the plants. What is this pest, and is there a better way to control it?

A. The common stalk borer is the larva of a small, grayish-brown moth. It often becomes a pest in gardens near weedy fields and hedgerows where the female moths lay their eggs in late summer. The young borers are brown-and-white striped with a grayish-purple band around the body. They become a dirty gray as they grow. Borers attack many kinds of plants and are restless feeders, moving from one plant to another. For control, keep weedy areas near the garden mowed to discourage egg laying, and turn under, compost, or burn all garden residues that might harbor eggs. As an alternative to splitting stems, try injecting them with a *Bacillus thuringiensis* (Bt) solution. If you cut back injured stems on zinnias and marigolds, they'll produce sideshoots that will flower later in the summer.

Tripping Up Thrips

Q. Thrips have attacked my roses. What can I do?

A. The tiny, brownish-yellow, winged adult thrips are hard to spot (they're only 1/20 inch long), but their damage to rose blossoms is extensive. They are especially attracted to white flowers. The damaged rosebuds either turn brown or open to reveal distorted, brown petals. Thrips often lurk in the center of the open flower and feed on the pollen. Thrips are difficult to control. Keeping the weeds down and removing spent flowers will help reduce breeding grounds. One clover head can support 30 to 40 flower thrips, and a rose may contain as many as 200 thrips. Aluminum foil is one of the few materials that repels thrips because the reflected light confuses the pests. Protect prized roses with collars of aluminum foil. You can also use the foil as a mulch. According to USDA researchers, the mulch should extend 1½ to 2 feet beyond the outer edge of the plant. The foil mulch is not effective above 2 to 3 feet, so for taller plants you may want to hang or stake aluminum-covered boards. Researchers have found diatomaceous earth effective—especially if it's mixed with pyrethrum or rotenone—against greenhouse thrips on vegetables. It may also control the thrips on your roses. Sprinkle it on the blossoms and on the ground to control pupating thrips. The sharp particles will pierce the insects, dehydrating and killing them. Be careful not to inhale the dust, especially if it includes a botanical insecticide.

Pest Nests

Q. Last year we were plagued with wasps and yellow jackets in our yard. Can you tell me how to get rid of them?

A. Wasps and yellow jackets prey on garden pests. Unless they are a serious nuisance or a danger to hypersensitive people, you should probably leave them alone. To keep both types of wasps away from the house, make sure no food is left close by for them to eat. Cover trash cans with tight-fitting lids and clean up ripe fruit around the yard. Red or yellow clothing and some perfumes may attract the insects to you. Destroying nests hanging from trees or buildings can be dangerous. Wasps have barbless stingers, which permit them to repeatedly sting their victims. If you must approach a nest, warns Dr. Clarence Collison of Penn State University, do so only after dark and wear protective clothing. Spray aerial nests with a liquid or aerosol formulation of pyrethrum, rotenone, or a ready-mixed combination of the two.

Nests in the ground are slightly easier to deal with. Wear protective clothing and apply pyrethrum, rotenone, or both into the hole. Begin watching for wasp nests in spring. Because of their smaller size, the earlier you spot the nests, the less hazardous their removal will be. Wasps and yellow jackets die with the onset of winter, with the exception of the fertilized queens, which overwinter in bark and leaf litter. Each one killed eliminates one potential nest. You can lure the queens to a simple trap made from a mixture of sugar and soapy water in a pan. Commercial wasp traps are also available.

Control for Critters

Deterring Deer

Q. We had a terrible problem this year with deer eating fruit off our trees. Fencing is too expensive. Is there some way to repel them?

A. The only foolproof way to keep deer out of an orchard is fencing, but here are four repellents that in some situations have worked fairly well:

- Hang bars of deodorant soap in your trees; leave the wrappers on so they'll last longer.
- Mix 1 to 1½ dozen eggs in 5 gallons of water and spray on your trees. Reapply after each heavy rainfall.
- Hang a clump of human hair in a stocking from each tree. Cover with a plastic bag or weatherproof container, leaving an opening at the bottom. The hair should be replaced several times a season.
- Spray a solution of Tabasco sauce (2 tablespoons per gallon) on the foliage. Repeat every two weeks.

Shocking Treatment for 'Coons and 'Chucks

Q. There is nothing more discouraging than finding that raccoons and groundhogs have invaded my gardens again. Is there any way to keep them out for good?

A. Since both of these animals can either climb or burrow their way around obstacles and into your garden, take firm action by installing an electric fence. It may sound cruel, but it's the most effective way to stave off animal intruders. A little shock is just enough to frighten them without causing any physical harm. Some gardeners get by with one wire about 6 inches off the ground, but two wires, the second another 6 inches above the first, are better. Use steel or fiberglass posts if possible, since raccoons have been known to climb wooden posts over the fence to avoid coming in contact with the wire. Gardeners often assume that groundhogs (also called woodchucks) will burrow under a wire, but these rodents seldom do unless their dens are very close to the garden. Most of their digging is confined to den sites, and when they journey for a meal to your garden, they stay aboveground.

Gopher Grabber

Q. How does the gopher plant keep away gophers and moles?

A. Gopher plant or spurge (*Euphorbia lathyris*) has a poisonous milky juice in the roots and leaves. Gophers, notorious for eating anything, eat the roots and sicken or die. For best control, the plants, which grow to 4 feet tall, should be transplanted next to the gopher hole, spaced every 5 feet as a barrier. The gopher plant is an annual, but it seeds itself. If you save the seeds, sow in the fall for spring germination.

Serpentine Solution

Q. Last spring, we found that snakes liked to crawl into the piles of mulch we raked to the side of the garden until the ground warmed. It made the material a problem to handle. Is there an organic way to repel snakes?

A. Because snakes feast on garden problems like caterpillars and other slow-moving insects, you should not eliminate them completely from your area. We usually suggest removing all cover and hiding places and keeping grass and weedy areas trimmed. But snakes are known to enjoy the warmth of a compost pile or shelter of mulch. We're told snakes will hesitate to cross an area covered with ground limestone and that onions will drive them away temporarily. You could also whack the tip of the pile with a board or rake, chasing the snakes out before you handle the mulch materials.

Chapter 21

Rooting Out Weeds

Weed Worries

Chef's Best Weed Recipes

Q. My garden soil is very rich, so I use it in combination with other materials as a potting soil. How can I pasteurize my potting soil to get rid of weed and grass seeds?

A. There are two easy methods: Cook it in an oven or in a pressure cooker. For the oven method, fill a baking pan with 3 or 4 inches of soil and put a meat thermometer in the middle. Dampen the soil and put it in a preheated oven for 30 minutes, or until the temperature reaches 180°F. Don't let it get much hotter, or you will begin to destroy soil structure, organic matter, and all organisms in the soil. To prepare soil in a pressure cooker, cook for 20 or 30 minutes at 5 pounds pressure. Most weed seeds can be killed by a temperature of 175°F.

No to Herbicides

Q. I have crabgrass in my gladiolus patch. What herbicide do you consider safe? I can keep the weeds under control by hoeing until the glads get large, but then it is hard to work close to the plants.

A. The only two herbicides we can recommend are cultivation and mulching. Chemical herbicides have a detrimental effect on soil life and insect populations. By decreasing the number of soil microorganisms and insects, the chances for an insect imbalance or plant disease are greatly increased. You would be much better off to continue to hoe when the plants are young and then mulch heavily to restrict weed growth. If you don't have enough organic material for mulching, think about using something like newspapers to cover the ground. If your problem is severe, you may want to try a black plastic mulch with a small cut in it for each plant. Whatever you use as a mulch, don't use an herbicide. Any chemical combination designed to kill off plants will have an adverse effect on the biological systems of your garden.

Weedy Wildflowers

Q. We tried to grow a wildflower meadow on the five acres in front of our home, but so many weeds grew up that they hid the wildflowers. Is there a way of controlling weeds in meadows without using herbicides?

A. The best way to manage weeds in meadows is to try to keep them from sprouting in the first place. Some meadow gardeners have found that the most successful way to do this is to avoid disturbing the soil when preparing a seedbed for wildflowers. Tilling or digging turns up thousands of dormant weed seeds, which sprout faster than the wildflowers and choke them out. Instead, kill existing vegetation by covering the ground with black plastic for a month or more before planting. After you remove the plastic, mix wildflower seeds with damp sand, sawdust, or soil to get even distribution, then broadcast them on the bare ground and cover lightly with straw. Water regularly for good germination and growth. Since weeds are quick to colonize bare ground, some are bound to appear. Pull them before they go to seed. Adding a low-growing, fast-germinating bunch grass to the seed mix may help suppress weeds and hold the soil while the slower wildflowers become established. Suitable bunch grasses are sheep fescue, chewings fescue, red fescue, and annual rye. Using this method, a large site would have to be converted to meadow bit by bit over several years.

Variations on this method were successfully used to establish test plots for an ongoing observation of commercial wildflower seed mixes at the Rodale Research Center. The 4-by-20-foot plots were prepared either by tilling repeatedly, planting and turning under cover crops, covering the ground with black plastic, or covering with straw for the entire season before sowing the wildflowers. All plots were tilled shallowly before planting in spring. During the next summer, the plots that had been covered with plastic or straw had fewer weeds than the other plots. Eileen Weinsteiger, the gardener in charge of the project, thinks she could have obtained equally good results covering the plots for a much shorter time.

Weeds in Review

Besting Bermuda Grass

Q. How do I rid ¼ acre of Bermuda grass? I plan to start a strawberry patch and I want to do it organically.

A. Bermuda grass is an aggressive weed and one of the most difficult to control because it spreads by underground stems (rhizomes). Persistence is the key. Dr. James Miller, weed scientist at the University of Georgia, says that if you cultivate the infested area frequently for a full season, you should be able to reduce the amount of Bermuda grass by 90 percent or more. Winter tillage is especially effective in areas where temperatures fall to 25°F or below. Using a spring-tooth harrow or a metal rake, work the rhizomes to the surface after every freeze. (A rotary tiller isn't as effective because it tends to bury the grass.) Miller recommends continued cultivation throughout the summer, once a week and after every rain, as soon as the soil becomes workable. Chances are, you'll never eradicate the Bermuda grass, but if you plant strawberries in the fall and mulch heavily with straw or other suitable materials, you shouldn't have much of a problem.

Coming Up Clover

Q. If I plant clover as a cover crop and till it under in the spring, what's to keep the clover from coming up in all my spring and summer vegetables?

A. If you sow clover as a cover crop in fall, it will survive the winter as young plants. Though it begins growing in spring before the ground can be worked, it does not have time to seed before you turn it under. When thoroughly buried, it rots, roots and all, and helps loosen the soil. Two weeks after turning under a cover crop, you can prepare a seedbed. You'll find few traces of the clover in the soil, and it will not regrow.

Dandelion Day?

Q. I am the pastor of a church in Iowa whose building and grounds committee wants to spray the 1-acre-plus lawn for dandelions. Is there a practical nonchemical alternative?

A. Yes. Although you probably won't be able to eliminate every last dandelion, it is possible to reduce their numbers to a tolerable level. Eliot Roberts, director of the Lawn Institute in Pleasant Hill, Tennessee, suggests the following program: As soon as the blossoms begin to open in the spring, have the Sunday school class (or other willing volunteers) pick off the flowers. This will prevent seeds—and thousands of new dandelion plants—from forming. Have a group of older children or adults take a sharp knife or forked dandelion weeder and cut the long taproots as far down as possible. If the prospect of pulling weeds on such a large lawn seems a bit formidable, you may want to concentrate initially on the area around church buildings, where the visual impact of a healthy green lawn is most important. Since a lawn that is cut too short is weak and favors the growth of weeds, Roberts recommends mowing northern lawns at a height of 1½ to 2 inches. Also, applying a slow-release, organic fertilizer such as Erth-Rite or Fertrell, available at some garden centers, will make the lawn fill in with strong, vigorous grass, squeezing out weeds in the process.

Monitoring Mint

Q. **I would like to grow mint, but I've heard it will take over my garden. Is there any way it can be contained?**

A. Mint can be contained by sinking metal barriers, like lawn or garden edging, 12 to 18 inches into the ground around the plants. The rapid spread of the plant is due to underground stems, called stolons. The stems generally travel a few inches below the soil, but if they hit a barrier they will dig deeper. Cyrus Hyde of Well-Sweep Herb Farm recommends reworking your mint beds every three years to maintain their vitality. In the fall he digs and replants the beds with some of the younger plants saved before digging. Digging the beds will also reduce the likelihood of runners escaping into the garden.

Perpetual Poison Ivy

Q. **Is there a way to get rid of a patch of poison ivy without using weed killers?**

A. Poison ivy is a perennial, so it's hard to kill. The safest time to work among the vines is in winter when the leaves are gone. Keep your eye on the patch in fall and learn to identify the plant in its dormant stage. Be careful during any season. Bruised or broken stems and roots exude the same rash-causing oil as the leaves. And the oil can remain active for months on gloves, shoes, and clothing. The best approach is to clip vines and creepers to within 1 inch of the ground and never let them grow higher. Even though the plant is able to creep along by sending out long shoots, eventually the absence of aboveground foliage will affect the plant's reserves of strength. It also helps to cover the trimmed area with black plastic sheeting thoroughly anchored in place. On small patches, you can try pulling out the roots. It's best to do so in the early spring after the ground has thawed but while the plant is dormant. Never burn the vines, since the toxic oil that causes blisters will volatilize in the fire, and the smoke will contaminate you. Put on heavy clothes that cover as much of your body as possible, and wear cotton gloves that you can throw out when you're finished. Then put one hand inside a large trash bag so you can use the bag as an outer glove. As you gather roots and stems, fold the bag over them. You'll end up with a bagful of poison ivy without having to handle the mess twice, and very little will have touched your clothing.

Ducking Quack Grass

Q. **I have battled quack grass for the last two years. I've tried thick straw and leaf mulches, but the quack grass either goes right underneath or comes up through the mulch. What more can I do?**

A. Just keep pulling it. The trouble with quack grass is that its rhizomes—those long, ivory-white, spearlike stems underground—are so tenacious. Once established, this perennial grass spreads by both seeds and rhizomes. The seeds stay viable for four years or longer, and the rhizomes can shoot 2 feet underground (and through mulches) without surfacing. Quack grass is bad news for another reason—it excretes a toxin from its roots that inhibits the growth of some vegetables, especially corn. When you pull, try to get the main clump of roots beneath the leaves you're grabbing. Cutting the new topgrowth reduces the food reserves in the rhizomes, weakening them. Hoe or cultivate every week during the growing season. Spading late in the fall will kill many of the rhizomes by exposing them to drying and freezing. The thicker your mulch, the better. Heap on as many leaves, grass clippings, and straw as you can—at least a 6-inch layer. If that doesn't keep the rhizomes from branching out, spread a layer of black plastic over the mulch and anchor it securely. You can also sow an early-spring smother crop like buckwheat. Ths fast-growing, fibrous-rooted plant will establish itself in a month and shade out the quack grass. After two years of continuous cover-cropping, the quack grass should be gone.

Sedge Advice

Q. **Nutsedge is a very tough and troublesome plant in my garden. I have been told that the roots are edible and commonly used in Europe. Can you tell me how to cook it?**

A. There are a number of members of the sedge family that go under the name nutsedge. The member of this family most gardeners have come to know and loath is *Cyperus esculentus*, an edible perennial plant that reproduces by seeds and tubers. It inhabits cultivated fields and gardens. Like all sedges, it prefers wet soils and hates well-drained soil. Proper drainage is one way to control any member of the sedge family in your garden. The most practical way to control them in large areas is to allow the field to lie fallow for a year. Nutsedge's small tubers may be boiled, peeled, and seasoned, or even toasted and used as a substitute for coffee. In Europe, nutsedge tubers have been used for flour. Harvesting the tubers is also a good means of control.

Sumac Solution

Q. How can I stop my neighbor's sumac from invading my yard?

A. Although sumac plants are lovely to look at and are valued for their aromatic red autumn foliage and velvety red fruits, they tend to sprawl wherever they can. The shrubs multiply by sending out underground runners, which form a close mat beneath the soil. Although these shallow, spreading roots control erosion, they dominate other vegetation. To stop sumac from spreading, mow it every week during the summer months. Using a spade and pickaxe, dig out as many root runners as you can and compost them.

Thistle

Thistle Do It

Q. Can you tell me a way to get thistles out of my garden that really works? Years of chopping, tilling, and mulching have only made them worse. This summer I tried covering a 12-foot-square area with black plastic for three months, but shortly after I removed the plastic, the area was covered with thistle sprouts.

A. You're probably fighting the Canada thistle (*Cirsium arvense*). It's one of the most difficult perennial weeds to control because of its rhizomes (underground stems), which can travel 20 feet a season. That's why covering a small area with mulch won't work. However, a properly applied mulch is the best technique to use with thistles, according to Dr. Thomas Cordey of Delaware Valley College in Doylestown, Pennsylvania. Cordey, who has done extensive field studies on the performance of different materials, recommends a plastic mulch for warm-season crops and shredded paper for cool-season crops. Straw laid down at least 3 inches thick will also smother thistles. But he found that the weeds were able to come through a leaf mulch. Since Canada thistles are perennial, their rhizomes will lie dormant for three or four years, so your weed control program must be consistent. In addition to mulching, Cordey suggests plowing the garden deeply in fall to bring the rhizomes to the surface. Avoid rototilling the garden at any time. Tilling cuts the rhizomes, and each piece becomes a new plant. And any root pieces left on the tines can spread the weed problem to new areas of your garden. Cover-cropping isn't effective, either, says Cordey, because thistles can outcompete the cover.

Thistle vs. Lawn

Q. Is there any organic way to remove thistles from a lawn? I have tried digging them up with little success—there are far too many, and they seem to be too well established.

A. Unfortunately, short of large-scale mulching (see "Thistle Do It," above), or plowing the ground and starting over, digging thistles up is the best solution. The digging should be followed by repeated hoeings, for any piece of root left in the soil will produce new plants. Cut thistles whenever you can see them. Early in the season, this weed accumulates enormous food reserves in its roots. But as soon as the thistle matures and flowers, the reserves diminish. Weaken it by cutting at the base at the onset of flowering. If you can cut just before a rain, so much the better. The cut stem is hollow, and rainwater accumulates in it. If the temperature is sufficiently high, mold may result and hasten the destruction of the plant.

Index

Rodale Press, Inc., publishes RODALE'S ORGANIC GARDENING®, the all-time favorite gardening magazine.
For information on how to order your subscription, write to RODALE'S ORGANIC GARDENING®, Emmaus, PA 18098.

for Vincent's dad, too, "Vincenzo, *carissimo*! Grandma will come and see you in a minute."

Grandpa Angelo carried Vincent outside, set him down in one of the white iron chairs, and brought him a glass of orange juice. "In a little while, we'll have pasta, eh? But first, we give your daddy some time with Grandma."

"Daddy's crying," said Vincent.

"He's so sad, 'Cenzo," said Grandpa Angelo, sitting himself down heavily in the chair opposite. He started flicking through the tapes on his bench, next to his big tape player. "We must have some music now, eh?"

"Why?"

"Good for the soul!" said Grandpa.

"No — Daddy. Why's he sad?"

"He's sad because of your brother, dear one. He's missing Ben."

"And he hates my mommy. She said."

"No, Vincenzo, your daddy loves your mommy. He loves her since he was a little boy like you. She's his best buddy."

"I think Rob is his best buddy."

"Well, she's his best buddy and his true love. It's just . . . here!" said Grandpa, finding a tape. "It's just she's so sad and he's so sad, they forget their love."

"Mom forgot my school conference three times. The principal had to call. And then Dad went."

"Well, you see then. This is so hard a time for us. For me, too. I think of my Ben and it crushes my heart." He patted his leg and

236

"I won't."

"Okay, pal."

Vincent leaned against the arm rest; his father was singing with the Rolling Stones on the radio, using the heels of his palms like drums; Vincent thought he might fall asleep, if he wasn't afraid of the running-away dream, the dream which wasn't so scary in itself as the way his dream self kept wanting to look behind him. He knew that if he looked behind him, it would be the worst thing, worse than the flabby white monster with the big red mouth he saw by accident one time when he got up and his dad had *Shock Theater* on in the middle of the night.

It would be worse than that, Vincent thought; he wanted to tell his dad that, but his eyes were blurry.

"Wake up," said a voice, a voice that always sounded like it had a cough in it, or stones under it. Grandpa Angelo. "Wake up, *dormi*-head." That was the Italian word for 'sleepy', part of the song Grandpa Angelo sang when Ben was little. Vincent was sweaty and shivery, but he put his arms up and Grandpa Angelo lifted him out through the window of the car and held him against the rough wool of his blue suit. Grandpa Angelo wore blue suits all the time, even on Saturday morning in the house, even when he went to get a fireplace log or spray the tomatoes. Grandma Rosie said wearing the blue suit all day made Grandpa look like an immigrant, but he told her, "Rose, a businessman has a big car and a clean suit. Not just at business — all day long." Except

233

playing cards. When Grandpa Angelo used to play cards with his friends — Ross, Mario, and Stuey — he wore his stripey cotton T-shirt with straps over the shoulders. You could see the tufts of white hair stick up from Grandpa's shoulders over the straps, like feathers. If he saw Vincent, he would pull him down on his lap and rub his cigar cheek against Vincent's, and put red wine from his good glass on his finger and let Vincent lick it off. He would ask Vincent, "Now, Maestro, do I ask this most illustrious dealer for one card, or two?" And even back then Vincent was not so little he couldn't tell when the red or black numbers had a gap in them — and he would shake his head no, because Grandpa told him the time to draw to an inside straight was never, ever, never; it was madness and doom. Sometimes, when the weather was hot and the locusts were caroling loud, Vincent would even fall asleep under Grandpa Angelo's white iron patio chair, the chorus of locusts and the slap of the cards and the sound of Italian swears and the hot, almost too sweet smell of cigars all wound around and around him until they seemed like one thing. And he would wake up shivery and sweaty, the sky changed from sunny to sunsetty, or from fresh to shiny overhead, just like it was now.

"My little love," said Grandpa Angelo. "My best boy." He carried Vincent up onto the front stoop, under the cool shade of the big green awnings. Vincent was deeply fond of the awnings, the only ones on the block, and of the shiny green, absolutely square hedges that looked like plastic but smelled like vinegar.

"I love you, Grandpa," Vincent told him, nuzzling. And he did, too. He also loved his grandpa Bill, but his grandpa Bill always seemed to be a little nervous around Vincent. Like he would ask him, "Hey, Vince, you married yet?" Like a nine-year-old kid would be married and not even tell his own grandfather. Grandpa Angelo just gave you penne and red sauce, or white sauce if your tummy was upset, and wine from a spoon and Hershey's kisses from his pockets, and let you pick the grapes and tomatoes and only laughed if you dropped one — and not a phony, grown-up, really-mad-behind-it laugh, either. He really didn't care what a kid did as long as a kid said his pleases and thank-yous and didn't be a *diavolo* — Vincent didn't know exactly what that meant but knew it was a bad guy.

They were passing the kitchen, going outside to the backyard, when Vincent heard his dad say, " . . . what else to do, Ma. I can't take anymore."

"Patrick, *tesoro mio*," said Grandma Rosie, who was getting his dad coffee. "She's not herself. You must give her time."

"I have no more time, Ma!" Vincent realized, to his terror, that his dad was crying. "I want to have a life, Ma, not this . . . prison on Post Road that Beth never goes out of — I mean, not willingly, just up and down to her darkroom . . . Ma, I want out of this!"

Grandma Rosie swiveled her head around, fast, and then said in a big voice, meant

Vincent came to sit on his lap. "Do you ever get sad, 'Cenzo?"

"Sometimes."

"When?"

"Today was once. They were fighting and they . . . they scared Kerry. She yelled."

"I used to get sad when I was a little boy," said Grandpa. "I would get sad so many times because I missed my papa. I've showed you pictures of my papa, Vincent. He was such a big man . . . so big and loud . . . and he sang the Neapolitan love songs, with the voice of a Titian angel, my father. You know, that is why you are named Vincenzo, after him. And Paul, after your mama's brother Paulie."

"And what about my daddy?"

"What about him?"

"Is he named after somebody?"

"Yes," said Grandpa Angelo. "And this is another story about sadness. When your papa was born, I was on the road, selling cooking things. This was before we had our business, long before. I was far away, and I couldn't get home; and Grandma Rosie was just a young girl, having her first baby. The nurse who cared for her was from another country, like us — she was from Ireland. And when Grandma Rosie was frightened and sad, and crying out for me, this nurse — I think she was called Bridget, they're all called Bridget — prayed for Saint Patrick to ease her and bring forth a good baby. And Saint Patrick did do this. So, though this is an Irish name, this is the name Grandma Rosie gave your daddy."

"Where was he?"

"Who? Your daddy?"

"No, *your* daddy, when you were missing him?"

"He died, Vincent. He died in the first of the World Wars. He was a cook — all us Cappadoras, we cook, eh? But the bad guys attacked the camp, and your great-grandpa was shot, and he died right there, right where he was. He was buried there, too, not at home. I never saw his grave." Grandpa Angelo looked hard out at the grape arbor near the backyard fence. "And my mama, she had to clean houses, we were so tired and so poor. We missed my papa, and we were forbidden to say his name, because it would break my mama's heart. And that's when I discovered the opera. There was a teacher at the school in our village, and he had the record player, and he would play the operas and tell us to close our eyes and imagine what the places they were singing about looked like. The words sounded funny to me then, Vincenzo, because they were all so *sad*! So sad I thought they were silly; I was only a young boy, not even as old as you yet. In *La Bohème*, he was singing, 'Your tiny hand is frozen,' and I thought, How silly. And yet — and yet, the music was so magnificent! . . . The only true opera is Italian, Vincenzo. You know this. Like the only true food. We have to be nice to all the other people, and say, 'Oh yes, oh yes, this Mexican food is very good,' but we know better, eh?"

"Yup," said Vincent. "We know better."

"And so, when I was a grown man, and I, too, was a soldier, I was very afraid that I would die. This is in the second of the World Wars. I am an American soldier now, an American citizen, fighting against the evil of my own nationals, and the Japs — mostly for me the Japs, on the islands in the Pacific Ocean." Vincent leaned harder against his grandpa's chest, trying to picture his round, brown, white-haired grandpa thin and young like his dad, and scared, like his dad. "I was so afraid, I'd get this record player, which I bought, and I'd play the music. *La Traviata*. Not the Germans, not their pig music. The real opera. And it would make me happier and not so scared."

"How could it make you happier when it was so sad?"

"That's what I'm going to show you," said Grandpa Angelo, and he turned on the tape. There was a lady singing; she was singing pretty loud, but you could still tell she was about to start crying. The words were all jumbled up, like the singing on the tapes in Cappadora's.

"What's she saying, Grandpa? What's she talking in? Italian?"

"Yes, Italiano, Vincent. Just listen."

But Vincent proudly repeated the only words he knew in Italian besides *bambino* and some swears: "Non parlo Italiano."

"I know, but listen. I will tell you what she says. The singer is Mirella Freni, a great star. She's older now, but she was very young when this recording was made. She's talking to her little boy and she's saying, 'Tu, tu piccolo

239

iddio' — my little god. She loves her little boy and he's going away, and she's having a broken heart."

"Why's he running away?"

"He's not running away, Vincenzo," said Grandpa. Vincent could smell the gravy cooking in the house and he was meanly hungry, but he didn't want to be rude to Grandpa. Even though Grandpa was right about the opera, it did sound a little silly, to call a kid 'God'.

"Why's she calling him 'God'?"

"Because she loves him so much he's like a . . . like a saint to her. That's how parents love their children. That's how we love your papa. And how your papa loves you and Kerry and Ben. And your mama, too."

"So where's he going?"

"Who?" said Grandpa, who looked as if he was going to get up and jump around in his joy over the singing lady.

"The little boy."

"His papa is taking him to America. See, the mama, she's Japanese. Her name is Madama Butterfly. That's the name of the story. By Puccini. The papa, he's a bad guy. He fooled the mama and made her think she was his wife, but he got another wife. Very *malo, malo*. Bad. And now she's giving her baby to him."

"Why, if he's so bad?"

"I don't know, Vincenzo. Because she's poor, I guess. And because she's so sad that the papa doesn't love her that she wants to die. And if she loses her little boy, then she will want to die even more."

"My mommy didn't die," said Vincent, a throwing-up feeling creeping up. He held Grandpa Angelo tighter.

"No, no, of course not. If your mommy died, where would she be when Ben comes home? In heaven with the angels?" He kissed Vincent, his chin rough, smelling of his cologne, the heavy, fruity scent of his drawers and closets. "We pray for Ben to come home. And this mama, she's a Jap, you know, Vincent. The Japs are a crazy people. *Pazzi*. They think that if somebody does something bad to you, or if you screw up, you got to die over it. That's a crazy thing, Vincent. Regular people, like Italians and even Irish, like Grandpa Bill, they get up and kick somebody in the gool if he does bad to them. They get up and they have tenoots . . . "

"What's tenoots?"

"Nothing," said Grandpa. "They have *coraggio*, they have bravery. They try to fix something."

"Eat!" called Grandma Rosie from the back door.

"*Momento!*" Grandpa yelled back. "Now, listen to this part, Vincent. This is also sad, though it's supposed to be happy. This is why opera is so great. There's a whole story. If you like, I will copy this tape for you, so you can play it at home. In this part — this is the most famous song in the whole thing, it's called 'Un bel di.'"

"What's that?"

Grandpa spelled it out for him; it wasn't spelled like it sounded. "'One fine day,' Vincent. She's singing about how she thinks this jamoke

241

is going to come back to her and her baby and make her happy . . . "

The voice was really pretty, and the melody was so pretty. You could tell it was Japanese because of the tune, but it was even prettier than regular Japanese music, which Vincent had heard in school, and which sounded to him like skim milk tasted, like they didn't have enough instruments to go around. He lay back against Grandpa, and listened to the lady's heavenly voice, and tried to let his sadness float on it.

But all he could think of was that his hunger was all gone, and of the way the mama's voice sounded before, when she was talking to her little boy, who wasn't even lost yet, but it was as if he was already a million miles away from her, so far she could never hug him again.

13

May 1990

UNDER the mangy grape arbor in the backyard, which Vincent's dad never paid any attention to, though he always said he was going to and yelled if you goofed around with it, Vincent and Alex Shore were starting to set up this whole twig town for the little Playmobil guys to live in. They were big now, almost twelve, and they didn't really play with that kind of stuff much anymore; mostly, they rode bikes to Radio Shack or goofed around with the hoops at the park. Last night on the phone, they'd cooked up this big plan to use the spool of utility wire Vincent had found. They were going to string it from Vincent's window to Alex's, three houses down and across the street, and try to rig up a phone that really worked. But when Vincent's dad caught him taking out his bedroom screen and found the hammer and nails, he put a stop to the whole thing right away:

"Are you stupid?" he asked Vincent. "You want to clothesline some kid in a convertible?"

Which didn't sound so bad to Vincent, actually.

But the wire idea going bust kind of meant needing something to do. And it was hot, real hot for the last week of school. The pool

243

wasn't even open yet. Alex's mom wouldn't let them in the house because his brother Max had chicken pox.

At first they were just going to make some dirt barricades and stuff so the guys could have a war; but Vincent found some twine his father had cut off the tomatoes and showed Alex how Indians used to build wickiup — by tying a whole bunch of same-size sticks together at the top and then bending them out. Then you had a frame. Alex had the idea of using tissue to cover it; but Vincent said, "No, let's use that plastic wrap stuff, because then we can see what they're doing in there."

"They won't be doing anything," Alex said. "Unless we reach in there and move them around."

"No, you don't get what I mean. It'll be like we can set up little scenes, like one can be the deer-skinning hut or something. It'll be like a diorama at the Field Museum." Alex had never been at the Field Museum. "Well, it's where they have a lot of mummies and stuff, and they have all these dioramas of the hunter-gatherers and the Incas. Like models."

"I don't want to do it," Alex grumbled. "I just want to have a war is all."

"Well, that's boring and stupid," Vincent told him. "And anyhow, they're my guys." That didn't sound too good, Vincent thought, and he'd better be careful. Alex was his best friend — pretty much his only friend. On the other hand, he didn't want to do something really baby and boring like war. "Come on, Al. It'll

244

be cool," he said. As Alex thought it over, Kerry came out into the yard, wearing her velvet American Girl dress (she wore it all the time, and it cost like a hundred bucks; it drove Vincent nuts to see her, like, wear it to gymnastics under her jersey; but nobody ever stopped her). Kerry was lugging a big bucket, filled to the top. Vincent caught the high, hottish smell of it right away.

"Wait a minute," he told Alex. "Kerry, what's in that?"

"The stuff under the sink," she said, smiling. "I'm going to kill the bugs in the sandbox." Vincent went over and took the bucket away from her; she started to kick him right away — she was only four, so this really shouldn't have hurt too much. But she was a good kicker. Vincent had to stand on one of her feet to stop her.

"Kerry," he told her, "this is ammonia. It's poison. You can't play with it. Where's mom?"

"On the telephone."

"Did she let you have this?"

"Yes," Kerry said. Vincent thought, Well, maybe she did. Oh, well.

"You can kill box elder bugs better with just plain old dish soap and water in a squirter. And it's funner." He dumped the ammonia under Mr. Aberg's poplars, which Vincent's dad said were really about half trees of heaven and the other half eyesore. "Do you want me to get you some of that?"

"Uh-huh, uh-huh!" cried Kerry delightedly.

"I'm going to go get her something and get

some of that clear wrap, okay, Al?" Vincent went back to the grape arbor. "You want a Coke, too?"

"You're so damn bossy," Alex said.

"Cut it out," Vincent warned. His hands were balling up; they always did, he couldn't help it — even teachers knew it.

"My mom says you're so bossy because your mom never pays no attention to you."

"*Any* attention to me, Al. She never pays *any* attention to me."

"Well, that's what she says. And I think she's right. Your dad is at work all the time and your mom never pays no attention to you."

"You know, your mom is dumb, Al."

"Yeah," Alex said. "So?"

"Adults aren't supposed to say that stuff where kids can hear them. Your mom would kill you if she knew you told me that."

"So?"

"So, let's just get this game going, okay? We can have a war and a village of hunters, okay? We can do both." Alex shrugged. That was okay. He wouldn't leave if Vincent hurried up.

He went into the kitchen to snag two Cokes, and right away, even though he couldn't see her, he noticed how his mother was talking on the phone. Because she was really *talking*, saying, "Get out of here! How long have you known this? . . . But when did you really decide?" And then, "But will you even enjoy it? . . . You have? How many times?" She was laughing. His mother was laughing. He followed the telephone cord around the edge of the breakfast-room wall,

246

and there she was, all coiled up in a chair, twiddling her hair with one finger. When she saw him, she waved at him.

His mother waved and . . . grinned.

Vincent brought the Cokes back outside. Damn it. He had forgotten Kerry's bug spray. His mother was off the phone, but she was dialing it again. She called to Vincent, "Guess who's getting married?"

Vincent was so stunned he dropped the nearly full spritz bottle into the sink; it started to spill down the drain. His mother never spoke to him or anyone else first. He'd done, like, experiments, measuring how long it would take her to say anything if the phone didn't ring or Kerry didn't ask her for a cookie or something. And she could go hours, whole days probably. He had personally seen her go a whole day, once when his dad was out of town. She made beds and junk, like a regular person, except she never said one word, didn't even hum. It wasn't like she wasn't paying attention to him; she just didn't even see him.

Vincent didn't believe she was really thinking nothing; you couldn't. He and his cousin Moira had tried a whole bunch of times, once, to run around the house just one time without thinking of a pig. You couldn't do it. A person always thought; you couldn't drain your brain. In his humble opinion, it was really too much thinking — like static on the radio — getting in his mother's way. Aunt Tree had once said, when she thought Vincent was asleep, "The light's on but nobody's home," about his mother's head. But Vincent disagreed. Vincent pictured his mother's head more like a beehive, sometimes.

But now she was looking right at him.

"Candy," his mom said, and he thought, Does she want some? But then he realized she meant her friend the police lady, the one who sometimes came up for the weekend and let Vincent touch her unloaded gun for just a second, and let him play with her gold shield. "Candy's going to get married. Can you believe that?"

Vincent knew something was expected of him. "Well," he said. "She is pretty old."

"Oh, she's not so old, Vincent," said his mother. "She's what . . . forty, I guess maybe. She wants . . . she wants a baby before it's too late."

"Too late?" Vincent asked, feigning more interest than he felt, desperate to keep her looking at him this way.

"Well, women can only have babies for a while. Then they get too old and their bodies don't work that way anymore." You mean menopause, Vincent thought — they told them about it in school. He always thought, why was it a pause? Didn't it really just stop altogether?

"But that's when you're real old, right?" he asked, urgently, feeling his mother start to slip away.

"Well, but sometimes if you have a baby when you're old, the baby isn't right. It has birth defects." He saw then that she was gone. He could pop out one of his eyeballs right now and she'd say, 'Vincent, take that outside.' She turned back to the phone. "I want Laurie to take Kerry for me. Do you want to stay with Daddy? Are you big enough to stay alone till he gets home from work?" She frowned. "I wish Jilly was still around." Mom was always wishing Jill didn't get out of school and get married. But Vincent knew this wasn't one of those questions parents asked that they'd already worked out the answers to. His mother didn't do that. When she asked whether they had long division in fifth grade, she really had no idea whether he knew what long division was. She had no idea that he'd placed second out of the whole school in the spelling bee, and that the word he missed was 'withdrawal'.

"Take Kerry when?" he asked now.

"Next weekend, next weekend," said his mother. "Oh." She looked at him again then. "Candy wants me to take pictures. Of her wedding reception. In Chicago. And I said I would."

Vincent had to sit down. Alex was probably disgusted by now; he'd probably gone home. To tell the truth, Vincent should be outside, making sure Kerry didn't run into the street or something.

But he had to take this in. He could not believe this.

In the last few years, she'd gone on planes to New York for work, on planes to Florida. But she never, ever went to Chicago — not when Aunt Tree's babies were born, not when Grandpa Angelo had a heart rhythm, not even for Christmas or to look at bodies the cops thought were Ben.

"Are you going to go with Dad?" he asked.

"Well, maybe," said his mom. "No. I don't think so. I mean, Dad has to work. I guess . . . " She stared at Vincent as if they were both discovering secret buried doubloons. "I guess I'll just go by myself and stay at Aunt Ellen's. It's only one night. Right?"

"I guess. Will you be okay?"

"I think so. Will you be okay?"

"Sure." What would be different, thought Vincent; it wasn't like she told him when to go to bed or something. He scanned his mother's face as she stared off into the yard — he could see Kerry out there, gravely squirting the hose into the sandbox. It was almost as if his mother were trying to think about what she was doing; he could *see* her thoughts walk back and forth like puppets. Her hand fluttered toward the phone again. Dropped to her lap. "Do you think Dad will let you go?" he asked, worried.

She didn't answer for so long that Vincent thought she was purely gone. But then she said, "Uh, *let* me? Your father's not my boss, Vincent. I can go somewhere if I want."

But he was still astonished when, a week later, she actually did go, putting her duffel bag in the trunk with three of her cameras and her lights, even bringing up the black hood thing that made her look like one of those guys who took pictures in a big puff of smoke in silent movies. They stood around on the porch, waiting for Dad to get back from the hardware store.

"Do you want me to call you tonight, when Dad's at work?"

"I'm going with him," Vincent said.

"Oh. Good."

Dad backed the Toyota into the driveway and started lifting out the bags of turf builder he always bought, even though, as far as Vincent could tell, they never had anything but the worst, knottiest lawn on the block. His dad dropped the last bag, splitting it open slightly, and leaned his head against the open trunk.

"You okay?" Vincent asked him. His mom just stood there.

"Just getting ancient," said his dad, wiping off his face on the sleeve of the ratty flannel shirt he wore.

His mom leaned down to hug the air around him, and she squeezed his dad's arm. Vincent wondered, as he always did, whether his mom would kiss his dad; she didn't. Probably it was something you didn't like to do in front of a kid before puberty.

"Are you sure you don't need me to drive you?" his dad asked.

"I'm fine, Pat," said his mother. "I owe her. She never stopped."

"I think she's crazy. It's a crazy thing to do. This guy, he's crazy, too."

"Like she says, people have been fools for lesser things."

"I suppose." His dad smiled. "Kiss the bride for me. But not too hard." Dad always made these kinds of jokes about Candy, which Vincent had privately decided meant his dad thought

251

Candy was a lesbian, a girl who married girls. But she wasn't. He knew that for sure. She smelled too good. He personally thought Candy would be a great mother — just for all the equipment she had in her car alone. He would love to be Candy's kid.

That night during the rush, Uncle Augie was in a take-no-prisoners mood, yelling at everybody, right up to the chef, Enzo, who even Augie was normally scared of. "People are starving out there, Enzo!" he yelled. "People want to starve, they can go to Ethiopia, they don't have to sit in my dining room!"

Finally, Enzo pointed the end of his biggest knife at Uncle Augie and said, "You say one more thing and I'm going to stick this up your fat nose, Augusto. You crazy old sonofabitch. You ever hire anybody else who got the IQ of my mailbox and maybe somebody would get to eat after all!" Vincent's dad had to break them up. Vincent loved it when this happened, even though his dad didn't. He hated fights. Linda, the big red-haired waitress, took Vincent to one side of the kitchen, near the open back door where the Mexican kids were cowering in their white shirts with 'Cappadora's' embroidered on the pockets, and held his head right between her boobs.

"Shut up in front of the kid," she said, "Paddy, make them shut up."

Linda steered him out of the kitchen and gave him a plate of angel hair with white clam sauce, his favorite, which he had just started to eat at the bar, talking to Mickey, the carpet wholesaler, and Tory, the bartender, when Tory got a phone call for his dad.

"Go get Papa, sport," he told Vincent, and said into the phone, "Bethie, wait up, baby. I can't hear you. I'm getting him."

Uncle Augie was sitting on a wooden chair in the kitchen, mopping his face with a big handkerchief and drinking ice water. "Why would anyone ever drink anything but ice water, eh, Vincenzo?" he asked the boy.

"Where's Dad?"

"Outside. Smoking another coffin nail." Like Grandpa Angelo, Uncle Augie was a reformed smoker; he didn't even allow smoking in the bar. Their younger brother, Cosimo, had died from lung cancer.

"Dad," Vincent called out the door. "Mom is on the phone." His dad tossed the butt over the fence and picked up the phone. It was hot, so hot in the kitchen Enzo was working in his undershirt, which sort of made Vincent sick to his stomach to see. His dad pulled the cord out into the alley. He motioned for Vincent to come and stand next to him, and Vincent did, watching the pale ribbons of light he used to think, when he was little, were the aurora borealis, but which were really spots from Vanland across the beltline. He was so tired and sort of hypnotized by the lights he didn't notice how tight his dad's fingers were around the back of his neck; his dad was actually hurting him. When Vincent pulled away, the neck of his T-shirt was soaking.

"What else did they find?" his dad was saying.

253

And then, "Where the hell is that? Which Hyatt?
. . . Oh, Elmbrook, sure, sure . . . Candy what?
I thought she was getting married . . . " Vincent
watched the sweat drip like melting icicles off
his dad's upper lip. His dad looked funny; his
eyes looked too deep in. "I'm leaving now, sure
. . . Why? What are you going to do? Is Ellen
with you?" He covered the phone and said to
Vincent, "Get Daddy a glass of water, pal."
Vincent went inside to the ice machine. He filled
the glass three-quarters with ice, the way his dad
liked it, and then carried it slowly back, pushing
open the kitchen door with his behind. That's
when he saw his dad kneeling — he thought for
a minute, He's praying. Why is he praying? But
the phone was on the ground, and a squawky
little voice was coming out: "Pat? Pat? Are you
there?" His father's hands were pressed, one over
the other, against his chest, and his too-deep eyes
looked up at Vincent like one of those saints in
museums who've seen God. "I think I'm sick,
buddy," he said to Vincent. "I think there's an
elephant standing on me." He tried to smile.

Vincent reached over his father, picked up
the telephone, lowered the hook long enough
to make sure his mother's voice was gone and
he had a dial tone, and called 911.

14

BY the time his mom came tearing out of the night into the intensive-care waiting room, Vincent already knew his dad was going to live.

Though the doctors had tried for hours to talk right over him to Dad's friend Rob Maltese and Uncle Augie, he mostly heard everything — and he decided the doctor with the cowboy boots to be the guy he believed. Cowboy Boots talked in normal language, and he didn't act like Rob and Augie were stupid. Everybody else who came in did. From Linda to Laurie's husband, Rick, to Laurie, they all kept saying to each other, "He's in the best hands," "This is the court of last resort," "Thank God we have the university hospital."

And then, as if remembering he was there, someone would turn to Vincent and say, "Your daddy's going to be fine. He's in the best hands."

But Vincent knew that was just the kind of thing you said to a kid. He'd heard it a lot of times before.

So he didn't speak at all; he just listened, and whenever he saw the beige lizard-skin boots come through the swinging doors out of the intensive-care ward, he turned up his listening and used the kind of concentration he used when he built a model motor. It was only about ten o'clock when Boots told Rob and Augie, "Well, in the simplest possible terms, what we were able to do here, I hope, and I think, is stop a heart attack from happening. Until we do an angiogram, we aren't going to be one hundred percent about the condition of the arteries and so on; but thank goodness we were able to start a TPA right away . . . "

"What's that?" Uncle Augie asked.

"A blood thinner, to dissolve any clots, get things moving again," said Cowboy Boots. "What we always have to assume, when we have a guy this young with this kind of trouble, is that there's blockage . . . "

"But he just got this awful news from Chicago," Augie said. "His wife just called and said they found the baby's — "

Cowboy Boots waved a hand, but nicely. "It's true, you always hear that people drop over with an infarct from what we call stress. But you can scare the pants off a guy with normal arteries all day and that guy may sweat or get sick to his stomach and feel lousy, but he's not going to have a heart attack. All stress does is pop the balloon, essentially — it exposes an underlying condition, probably the result of hereditary . . . What did your father die from, Mr. Cappadora?"

"He died in the first war. He was a young man. In his twenties."

"Any other folks got heart disease in the family? Uncles?"

"Sure," said Augie. His voice seemed to say, Is this a big surprise or something? "Two of his

256

brothers died real young from heart attacks. One was just maybe forty-five or something. But the fourth brother, he's still alive. He's ninety. And we had a brother die from lung cancer. And my brother Ange, he had to get a pacemaker. He's fine now, though."

"So there you see. And — " Boots glanced at his clipboard — "Pat has a history of smoking, not quite a twenty-twenty history, but he started really young, he says. What, thirteen, fourteen?"

"He's talking then? He's conscious?" Rob pleaded. "He told you this himself? He's not brain-dead?"

"Oh, no, not at all. He's quite alert. He hasn't lost consciousness. He's very, very anxious, naturally. We had to give him something to quiet him down . . . "

"Are you going to operate?"

Boots pursed his lips. "Well, let's just take one world at a time here. Our job right now is to get Pat nice and stable, and then, as soon as we can, take a real good movie inside that chest. But I can tell you, his cardiogram doesn't look very bad at all. We aren't seeing Q waves, which often means we headed off the most serious — "

And then his mom burst in through the door, her eyes all smeary with makeup running down under them. She had on her ordinary jeans, and gym shoes unlaced, with no socks, but this really fancy satin blouse that looped way down in front, and one, just one, big dangly pearl earring.

"Where's Pat?" she asked Boots, grabbing his forearm. He didn't jerk it away — Vincent liked that — he just put his hand over hers and told her what he'd been saying all night, like, "The first thing you need to know is that your husband is out of immediate danger," that the prospects for recovery, cautiously, at least, were quite good . . . Mom didn't listen, of course. "I want to see Pat," she said.

That was Vincent's cue. He could say stuff now. So he spoke up: "I want to see my father. I want to see Dad, too."

Both Boots and his mother looked down at Vincent. "Have you had anything to eat?" Beth asked.

Eat? "Yes," Vincent said.

"We want to see Pat," his mom told the doctor.

"Well, I suppose, just for a minute or two . . . "

They were ushered into a lane of tile between curtained cubicles. Somebody — it sounded like an old man — was yelling about 'nigger nurses'. A baby was wailing out in the waiting room. The nurse, who reminded Vincent of the sisters at his school, Mount Mary, motioned to a cubicle right in the middle; the curtain was drawn back, and there was his dad. He looked a lot worse even than he had on his knees in the alley. His skin was blue around the mouth, and two tubes forked up his nose that ran to a metal plate in the wall. One of his dad's arms was tied down to a board and a bag of water hung above it, dripping,

dripping; Vincent timed it, exactly two seconds per drip.

"Pal," he said softly. "Come here." Vincent walked up to the bed, sideways. He wanted to hold his dad, and was afraid that his dad would touch him. "You saved my life, pally. I think you saved your old man's life. You're a brave kid."

Vincent felt tears pull at the bottom lids of his eyes, and he got busy trying to see his dad's chest, to see if his heart was beating under the flowered hospital dress. He barely noticed his mother get down on her knees next to the high bed and put her face down on his father's arm. But he started to pay more attention as the black makeup ran all over the gauze. What a mess, Vincent thought. That junk is probably not very sterile.

"Bethie," said Pat. "Oh baby. I feel like shit."

"Paddy, you look like shit. I'm so sorry, I'm so sorry I wasn't here. If I had known, anything, anything, my God, Paddy, I'd have been here . . . "

With an enormous tug, like he was lifting Vincent up to change the light bulb in the garage, Pat put his hand on Vincent's mother's hair, which was normal in front but all matted up in back, the way Kerry's was when she got out of bed in the morning — tangles and knots, like she hadn't brushed it in days. It gave him the creeps.

"You're my girl," said his father, and his mother started to cry, so hoarsely Vincent

259

first thought she was puking, but then it was embarrassing. The nurse looked in, sucked her lips in one of those sad smiles, and then drew the drape closed.

"Bethie, tell me," his dad said. "Tell me now."

She turned her big, dripping-black eyes on Vincent. "Not now."

"Listen, Beth, he called 911 tonight. He can hear."

And that's when she told them both about the shoe. About how she'd been having lunch or dinner or something at a hotel with Aunt Ellen, and all of a sudden Candy showed up in her beige silk wedding dress, and she had Ben's red baby tennis shoe. Vincent was puzzled; big deal, they had Ben's shoe a hundred years ago. But it wasn't that. It was, as far as the police could tell, Ben's *other* shoe, or one just like it, and it was left on a desk in the dining room of the hotel where Beth's class, that very day, that very weekend, was holding her twentieth high-school reunion. A big Hyatt out by the golf course where Grandpa Bill played. Not the Tremont. Not the hotel Vincent dreamed about sometimes when he had the running dream; he could picture those tiles, the color of meatballs, any time he wanted to, if he just closed his eyes. Sometimes, when he lay in bed at night, he tried to think about the tiles and the smell and standing on the luggage trolley first, so he wouldn't have the running dream. But it hardly ever worked. The dream came any time it wanted to.

"So this means," his dad gasped, "they're going to reopen the — "

"Shhhhh," said Vincent's mother. "Rest now. They never really closed the case, Pat."

"What do they think, that whoever — ?"

"Candy says maybe someone found it a long time ago, and it's a sick joke. Or maybe it was a different shoe, and some crazy just thought it would be a thrill, you know . . . "

"Did Ellen stay with you?"

His mother didn't answer right away. Didn't she know? Vincent wondered.

"Ellen didn't even tell me the reunion was that night. She told me, but not until I got there. I guess she thought I wouldn't come. And Candy didn't even get to go to her own wedding reception. I never took any pictures for her. Her husband seems very nice . . . "

"So what are they going to do now?"

"Candy?"

"No, Jesus, Bethie — the cops. Bender."

"We'll talk when you're better, baby."

"Beth."

"They're going to try to figure out if someone who came to the first reunion, or was there that day, brought the shoe back this time. Candy says they can get good prints off the rubber this time; they already did."

"And if they did, it could mean that Ben is — "

"It could mean anything, Paddy. It could mean that it's the person who took Ben and that they were trying to leave a message — "

Vincent jumped when the little beeper on the

261

TV screen over his dad's bed began to shrill; the nurse appeared instantly. "No problem," she said cheerfully. "No change. Doesn't mean a thing. Just a little malfunction." No one spoke as the nurse ran her hands over his dad's tubing and put a little probe in his ear that immediately beeped. "Everything's going just fine, Mr. Cappadora. But you have to rest soon."

"A minute. My wife just got here . . . Bethie, listen. 'A message'?"

"Maybe even like, to comfort us . . . "

"Beth! To comfort us?"

"We'll go now," his mom said. Where? thought Vincent. Where would they go? Would they leave his dad alone here? What if the machines all went off at once? What if there was a power failure?

"Where are we going, Mom?"

"Well, home, I guess. I mean, I guess I'll take you to Laurie's and then I'll come back here and sit with Daddy. You can't stay up all night . . . "

Vincent began to cry. "I want to stay here with Dad. I don't want to go to Laurie's. I have to take care of Dad . . . "

"Shhhh," said Beth, as the old person's voice began quavering. "What's that? What's the goddamned racket?"

"I'll take care of Dad," said Beth, pulling Vincent to her for an instant. He pulled back. His mother smelled, she really smelled like . . . he could almost remember the smell, like the kind of cologne Grandpa Angelo used to

262

use, maybe he still did, the kind that reminded Vincent of an old jewelry-box lining. She smelled as though she'd dipped her head in it, and it was weird, because his mother only ever smelled of Noxzema. She didn't even have any perfume that Vincent knew of. But before he could sniff her again, Laurie's husband, Rick, appeared and took him by the arm.

"Let's go with Laurie, okay, big buddy?" Rick said, winking over Vincent's shoulder at his dad. As Rick pulled him away toward the doors, Vincent saw his mother kneel down by the bed again and heard her whisper, "Paddy. I'll go anywhere. I'll do anything. The restaurant with your Dad. We can do that. I . . . want you to. Just get better, Paddy. Don't die on me. Don't die."

Now she's sorry, Vincent thought. She always wanted to kill him, and now she's sorry she almost killed him. Or maybe just pretending she's sorry. That's nuts, he thought. But what if she really had done it on purpose, like a curse? What if his dad had died right there in the alley, and Vincent had to go home alone with her, forever, and his dad was never going to come back, never be with him?

And what if one day she found out? About stuff? He felt the tap again in his tummy, the scratch, scratch of fear as he stared at the black back of his mother's matted curls, almost purple in the underwater hospital light. He had to tell himself that even when she squeezed him, or yanked on the back of his neck, she wasn't trying to hurt him, just her hands were. Her hands were rough. Sometimes she looked at him as if she wanted to lie on top of him, like a blanket. At those times, her hands were as gentle as a dental hygienist's, feather hands.

But if she knew . . . For a long instant, he had no doubt that if that ever happened, she would kill him, too. She would have no choice.

15

Beth

October 1990

IT was not possible.

The first time she'd walked into the derelict bindery that was to become Wedding in the Old Neighborhood, Beth had thought, This is a pit, this is a hole, so dank and forbidding it could drive Pollyanna to Prozac. Pat and his dad are going to undertake a slow double suicide to distract themselves from the reality of a family diminished by lost fathers and lost sons. It was nothing but a useless barn with graffiti-savaged tin walls in the middle of the west side's toughest frontier, a neighborhood in which only a few bold gay men had begun to stake claims on crumbling brownstones.

One of those men was the designer Beth had met that day months ago — a set designer of national reputation who also 'did' theme bars and restaurants.

Did he 'do' illusions, like David Copperfield? Beth had wanted to ask. She'd swallowed the remark; since Pat's heart attack, she'd swallowed so many unspeakables that one day they would probably rise up and choke her. Nevertheless, magic was what this transformation was going to require.

And there was no other word for it. Magic. In six weeks.

Beth had never seen anything quite like what had happened to the old warehouse. It was like a dream tour of the Italian imagination. Room opened upon room — one fashioned to resemble a wine cellar, with casks running wall to ceiling, labeled 'Ruffino', 'Conterno', 'Catello di Amma', cunning droplets of paint to represent spilled wine trailing down the walls. Elaborate plaster scrollwork framed the alcoves, with mottoes painted in colors of putty and sky blue. The tables in this room were rough cypress, spread with shawls and abutted by barrel-cask seats. In an alcove, a polished bar was nearly concealed, and a passage to the kitchen. It would be open for lunches, Pat explained, and for overflow on the three nights each week that the actual 'weddings' took place.

Pat led Beth next to the more formal bar, where a ceramic model of the Fontana di Trevi, coated in marbleized paint and more than five feet tall, took up the length of one whole wall. Each booth in the bar was made to look like a rose-trellised gazebo; each seated six. Behind the bar, bolts of satin in dove gray and rose were draped and caught with silk roses. Actual petals — Angelo got them for pennies from his buddy Armando, a funeral director — would be scattered like a carpet on the floor each night.

The real triumph was the banquet room itself. Vaulted beams of polished pine made the ceiling look like the Duomo in Florence, and the painting that would cover the whole thing (a

266

painter was up there now, Michelangelo-like, on his back on a suspended platform) would be on the theme of the seasons — marriage being, after all, the commencement of a wheel of birth and harvest.

"What are those for?" Beth asked, pointing to black wrought-iron balconies, six of them, tucked in at the corners of the beams.

"They're for people," Pat began, throwing up his hands at her look. "Don't ask me. It's my father's idea that there should be goddesses or something in them. This is what I really want you to see." He strode over to one wall and pulled a protective tarp. Beth literally jumped. She was looking at her own face.

"You're Mimì," Pat said, with the kind of uncorked delight she hadn't seen in him since he played Colt league. "And I'm Rodolfo." Slowly, he led her through the rest of the frescoes — some were not yet completed. Besides *La Bohème*, there were depictions of scenes from *Carmen*, *Madama Butterfly*, and more, each character a Cappadora family face. They were painted with a diaphanous technique that made not just the opera paintings but the walls themselves look hundreds of years old.

"How did he manage this, in so short a time? It looks like years of work. Oh, Paddy, it's gorgeous!"

Pat was shining. "It is, isn't it? We were so right to get Kip. This place is going to knock their socks off . . . And wait till you see the brides and the bandstand and this — and this, Beth . . . " He tugged up a corner of the

267

dropcloth that covered the floor. Beth gasped. The entire floor was parquet inlaid in a mosaic, deep burgundy around the edges radiating in to the twenty-four-foot face of a woman in profile. Her forehead and crown, above her olive cheek, was draped folds of cloth, created of varying shades of blond and yellow oak, so sinuous they seemed to move.

"Oh, Pat," Beth whispered. "The hood of gold."

"This is where we'll have the tables at first. And then, when it's time to dance, see, the tables just roll back . . . into this alcove thing. When Kip brought up putting the mosaic on here, I thought, This is too much. I thought it would be so garish it would be a joke."

"No, it's lovely. Lovely. But how will you ever let anyone walk on it?"

"No problem," Pat said with breezy delight. "We had a guy who does gym floors coat it. There's so much polyurethane on it you could drive a Zamboni over it."

"And will everything be ready for the opening?"

"It kind of depends on Dad." Pat hooked a finger at a table shrouded with plastic near the entrance, where Angelo sat in animated discussion with the designer. "They can't get together on the foyer. It's a big deal to Dad." In his baseball cap and cutoff shorts, Pat looked, Beth thought, maybe twenty. He looked not just rejuvenated but reborn, as if his life had a pure, unclouded focus, for once his very own, into which he could pour all his energy and creativity and tenderness. The idea for Wedding in the Old Neighborhood had been born the night of Jill's wedding, late at night, after most of the guests had left the back banquet room at Cappadora's in Madison.

Jill's wedding had been held not very many months after Beth had returned, after a fashion, to work. Returning to work had been so monumentally consuming for her that she could barely face Jill's moving out. Jill knew things Beth didn't know, like the names of Vincent's teachers and the parents of his friends; she was the one who made it possible for Beth to do what little she could with the children and still spend hours dabbling in the solitude of her darkroom, laboring to finish things she'd once been able to do with her mind on autopilot.

The whole family, in fact, had begged Jilly to hold off on marrying Mumit, a mahogany darling from Bangladesh she'd met only four months before. She was too young; they were too poor. Jill shrugged them all off; and that night at Cappadora's, truly radiant, she'd swept off with her groom to a brief honeymoon in Door County before Mumit started graduate studies in chemistry.

"You have to admit, they're happy," Tree had said a few moments later. "It was a beautiful wedding. Don't you wish you could go to a wedding like this every week? The dancing and the ice sculptures? The dresses? I wish I could have gotten married four times." She'd looked at Joey then. "To the same guy, of course."

That's when Angelo had begun to scribble

on the leftover napkins, scrolled with the young couple's names in gold leaf. He had been telling Pat for years that he was sick of the run-and-hustle of Golden Hat Gourmet. He wanted to preside over a place in his last years — to work beside his son and son-in-law in a crown jewel of a restaurant. Theme restaurants — part eatery, part theater — were springing up all over Chicago: fish joints with swimming mermaids behind glass built into the walls; rib houses housed in old filling stations, where the corn and garlic bread were delivered on trays fashioned from old hubcaps.

Why not an Italian wedding? he'd asked Pat, then Joey. Why not an Italian wedding, maybe three, four nights a week, with a bride and groom as the host and hostess? "With family style at each table, mostaccioli and meatballs, big loaves of bread — you'd save a ton on plating," Joey put in, excited.

"And a band — you'd have a band and a dance floor!" Pat cried. "The bride and groom, we could hire these kids who are trying to break into show business, you know, like kids who work at Steppenwolf or Second City, really beautiful kids. And they'd do the first dance . . . "

"*Bellissimo!*" cried Angelo. "Imagine it!"

"It'll never work," Augie grumped. "Too much overhead. What'll you do when she tears the dress the first night?"

"We could work out stuff," Pat shot back. "Arrangements with the tux and gown rental places. Free advertising. Stuff that's going out

270

anyhow. Who cares about the style? It might even be better if they were a little vintage. We could buy up the bridesmaids' dresses you see for cheap in the paper — Dad! All the wait staff could be the bridesmaids and the ushers . . . "

When Beth, limp with exhaustion, took Vincent and Kerry home at two a.m., the men and Tree were still talking, pounding the table, making fresh coffee and pouring shots of anisette. In the car, Rosie said, "There is no fool like an old fool." But she was smiling.

Even so, deep down Beth had never truly believed the battle to move back to Chicago would really be engaged. And once engaged, she'd never believed it could be won. As she saw it, Pat was lucky they had established a fragile ecosystem in Madison. The press hounding had died down; Beth was bringing in money with her portraiture and photo editing. From what she could observe, the children seemed healthy: Kerry had learned to talk and walk more or less on schedule; from the light that burned under the crack in his door late at night, Beth discerned that Vincent had learned to read chapter books to himself. She and Pat even had a semblance of a social life, occasional decorous dinners with Rob and Annie Maltese, and she still went to Compassionate Circle meetings with Laurie almost every other month.

Beth mentally dug in her heels. Pat would no more be able to convince her to move back to Chicago than he would be able to get her to dance topless in the Capitol rotunda. She would move to Chicago over her own dead body.

She had not counted on the prospect of refusing over Pat's.

She had not counted on what had happened the weekend of Candy's wedding. The weekend of her lunch with Ellen and Nick. The weekend of the second red shoe at the twentieth reunion. The weekend of Pat's heart attack. The weekend of Beth's sin.

Looking back, Beth could see that it had really all been decided, in the few seconds it took Candy when she had called to tell her that the alarm on her biological clock had sounded, and she and her old pal Chris had picked the first Saturday they could find open on their mutual calendars. There would be a blowout party afterward, and they wanted wonderful pictures. Imagine me a June bride, Candy hooted, and Beth, to her own surprise, caught the spirit, started razzing Candy about whether she and Chris had tried the bed voyage, and had it been rough sailing? No, Candy had screamed, laughing — she'd just closed her eyes and pretended he was Jessica Lange!

Beth drifted through raw-smelling piles of green wood and unassembled white-laminated slabs that would be tables in the soon-to-be-completed restaurant. Given everything that happened the weekend of Candy's wedding, moving had almost been an anticlimax. Really, not bad at all.

Even the house, which Tree had chosen for them (Beth refused to even go and look), was not so bad, though located not five minutes from the Tremont Hotel, smack in the middle of the neighborhood where all of them had grown up. Even the children were better than they should be. After Pat told him the 'good news', Vincent had disappeared for three hours. Pat had been sick with fear, but Beth was calm. She did not think anything serious would ever happen to Vincent. He had a tough hide. Once he'd thrown a bowling ball out a window and caved in the porch roof when Beth made him go to bed; he'd set off fireworks in the shell of a house under construction, and started more playground fights than Beth could count on both hands. And yet, she thought, if not thriving, Vincent was more or less okay. Maybe being around Angelo would help tame him. Joey had been a wild kid when he started working at Golden Hat; Angelo had turned him into a good kid.

Now with the men still deep in debate over the foyer, Beth drifted back outside and sat down on the ornate stone steps that had first caught Pat's eye. The rest of the battered brick exterior had been stuccoed in cream; wrought-iron grillwork and a sign were to go up next. She watched a gaggle of little black girls performing fast-footed double-dutch tricks on top of a carpet of shattered glass in the parking lot across the street.

Turning her face up to the hazy sunlight, she let herself drift back, five months — just five months — to the weekend of Candy's wedding, the weekend that had resulted in Beth's mortgaged vow to come back to Chicago forever.

Not half an hour after Beth had arrived, Ellen

had suggested the lunch. Her husband and Nick Palladino were working together on rehabbing an old women's college in Hyde Park, turning it into a sort of cluster mall and day spa; Ellen had been gabbing on the phone with Nick when Beth arrived.

"Three guesses who's here," she trilled into the telephone. And then Beth, all unprepared, was talking with Nick, asking about his children, laughing about his running into Wayne on a casino boat in Indiana. Ellen interrupted to ask why they didn't just talk in person; they could have lunch and then Beth could see the site at the college. It was gorgeous, what Nick was doing marbling the interiors. Beth found herself agreeing to plan a brochure.

Why not? Beth wasn't due to show up at Chris's South Shore penthouse for the wedding reception until eight that night, and she'd given herself so much time to get to Chicago — fearful that she could no longer read road signs and remember how to pay tolls — she'd arrived before ten in the morning.

"We'll goof around all afternoon and you'll still be a few minutes from the reception. You could even change in Dan's house trailer. Come on, let's make it a giggle, Bethie," Ellen had said. "It'll be fun. We'll go to Isabella on the Drive."

Beth had taken leave of her senses. She'd agreed.

But when she and Ellen pulled up in front of the cafe's discreet sign, Beth felt the thump and shift of the avalanche, heard its creak. "It's in a hotel," she'd whispered to Ellen. Ellen looked genuinely panicked.

"I didn't think . . . " she began. "Oh, Bethie, I didn't even think of it! Haven't you been in a hotel, ever? Ever since?"

"No," Beth breathed.

"Not even when you go to New York?"

"Bed-and-breakfast places," Beth said, measuring out her syllables. "Always."

"We'll just leave then," Ellen said reassuringly, starting the car. "I thought if it wasn't anywhere near where the reunion is . . . "

"The reunion," Beth said.

"You know, the twentieth reunion. It's this weekend. Didn't they mail you . . . oh shit, I guess they wouldn't."

"It's this weekend?"

"Yes, but Beth, that doesn't make any difference at all. I wouldn't go. Wayne, nobody would go. It just happened to be this weekend."

"Where?"

"In Elmbrook."

Beth put her hand over her mouth. "Oh God, Bethie," said Ellen. "Just forget it. I'll run in and see if Nick's there and we'll grab some deli and eat in a park. Okay? Will that be okay?"

But then, Nick appeared around the corner of the old hotel, his tightly curled black hair dusted with gray now, his suit as crisp as a silhouette cut from gray paper, and something in Beth's abdomen uncurled like a lazy cat.

"My God," she said to Ellen. "Look at him."

275

"He never gets old," Ellen agreed.

"What . . . what the hell." Beth suddenly got out of the car and ran into Nick's welcoming arms, kissing his mouth, which smelled of cloves, for just a millisecond too long.

Had she known, at that moment? Looked back upon, it all seemed choreographed, an elaborate series of steps and movements that all led into a single cul-de-sac, a loop with no exit.

Beth leaned her head against the pebbled ledge of stonework and prepared to let herself remember that day. She had to be alone, and she had to do it exactly the same way each time. She loathed herself when she did; but a hundred times over the months since that day, she had replayed that afternoon and evening, right up to the knock at the door, with filmic exactitude.

The three of them shared a bottle of wine at lunch — Ellen abstemiously denying herself more than one glass as designated chauffeur. They talked about . . . dumb stuff. The night they'd all piled into Nick's father's old Electra and crept up to the gates of the monastery once too often, and how the monks had let the Dobermans loose on them, costing Wayne the back of his leather jacket. The time some rogue from Cine Club had opened the wrong side of the treble curtains during the variety show, revealing Cecil Lockhart changing costumes between numbers, wearing nothing but a bra and tights, and how Cecil had simply struck a pose in the blue spot, while the audience sat frozen in horrified admiration. About smuggling

Beth back from her job as a camp counselor in Lake Geneva one summer night so she could attend the wedding of Cherry and Tony; Cherry was seventeen and pregnant, and Bill and Evie had forbidden Beth to go.

She remembered, then, Ellen's beeper going off. Ellen bitching that Dan wanted her to run over to some goddamned glazier's office a few miles away and roust the guy out to the site; all the glass was cut short and the carpenter was giving birth. Could Nick run Beth over to the site when they finished eating? Sure he could. Then Nick and Ellen going out to switch Beth's camera bags and duffel to Nick's car in case Ellen got stuck in traffic, while Beth snuggled back into the deep red leather banquette and drank and drank from a second bottle of Pinot Noir, wondering how she would manage to close one eye to shoot Candy's wedding photos.

Nick returning, a halo of sunlight around his dark head as he opened the door into the dark bar. Sitting down, not across but beside her. The talk shifting then to something smoky and late-night, in spite of the daylight burning outside the awnings. Talk about the covered bridge in Lake County, where they had lain, exposed to the summer night in Beth's convertible, Nick with nothing left on but one of those angelic-colored peach or pink Ban-Lon shirts that would've made any other guy look effeminate, but that only emphasized Nick's construction-crew tan, his Tuscan perfection. Beth, shorts and halter top rolled to a tangle around her thighs and neck, urging Nick to go ahead and do it. Nick

277

holding back, holding his bronzed hips just away from her, then swaying forward to let her grip him, crushing his mouth against her breast, then stopping, saying, No, we can't, we're going to be married, it's wrong. That no, all those rumors, even about Lisa Rizzo, were just that — rumors; he'd never done it before. He loved only Beth. He wanted only Beth.

She remembered Nick putting his arm along the back of the booth at Isabella, not quite touching her, and reminding Beth how he'd told her at his own wedding that he adored Trisha, he would be grateful for the rest of his life to her and Pat for introducing them, he couldn't be happier that she and Pat were getting married too, but the only regret he'd ever have was that he'd never made love to Beth.

And then — this was the part Beth hated herself for loving to remember the most — Nick bending forward and murmuring, "I still regret it, Bethie."

She hadn't said a word to him, only gone into the washroom to brush her hair, looking at her face in the gilded old mirror and seeing herself as Nick must have seen her, not as the gaunt scarecrow Beth who glared back at her from under fluorescent bulbs in Madison every morning, but as a slender, delicate woman worth desiring, the hollows under her eyes and cheekbones not pitiful but dramatic, her hair a tousled dark cloud, her lips puffed with arousal, knowing that when she came back, he would already have a key and would know the way to the elevator, to a room down a badly lit hall that hid the worn spots in the once-expensive wool carpeting — a room called the Violet Room, all done in antiques, with a marble washstand where Beth carefully hung her clothes, turning to Nick utterly without shame or even caution, knowing there was nothing to discuss or pledge or doubt, Nick telling her only, "Andante, Bethie. Andante. We waited a long time for this." Her nodding.

They had lain on top of the lavender coverlet for ninety minutes by the clock Beth glimpsed over Nick's head, touching and tasting each other slowly, until her every limb was shuddering, beyond her control, until the insides of her thighs were so slippery her leg slid off Nick's when she tried to roll onto him, until the moan at the back of her throat was constant, like a motor idling. Then Nick pulling back the sheets and — she thought of Pat once, when Nick entered her, not as long as Pat but thicker, more thoroughly filling her side to side, as she had always imagined him, beginning to move, slowly, slowly, shushing her when she began, frantically, to grab him and pull him closer, her mind emptied of everything but the feel of his golden, nearly hairless chest against her cheek, her treacherous body feeling pleasure for what seemed the first time since she had known such things were possible to feel, and then, when she could no more have stopped herself from coming than she could have stopped herself from exhaling, hearing the knock.

Hearing the knock and thinking, The hotel

is on fire. Thinking, Well, so the hotel is on fire, we'll still have five minutes. Five minutes is all I need, this five minutes, for the rest of my life. The knock again, sharper. Her name. Loud. A voice, a woman's, not Ellen's, a voice she knew.

Stumbling up, realizing she was still half-drunk, staggering as she dragged her jeans on over the bucking nerves between her legs. Buttoning her shirt. Her name again. Another, louder knock.

The rest Beth knew as if she'd read about it in a newspaper. The flower wreath in Candy's hair as Candy stood outside the door in her champagne-colored sheath.

The absurd exchange.

"I thought you were getting married," Beth had said.

Candy's reply: "I did get married." Candy glancing at her watch. "I've been married for an hour."

Candy had never asked Beth who was in the room with her. She had not apologized, except to explain that Ellen's housekeeper had told her where Ellen and Beth were having lunch. Nick had disappeared into the bathroom, Beth had gone back into the room only for her purse, leaving behind her underwear, getting into the squad car parked in front, next to its driver, the blond bride with the French braid, as the cafe manager stared in astonishment from under the portico. Some time later, at the Parkside station, Ellen had shown up with Beth's bags, and, in the first-floor bathroom, Beth had changed into the top of her evening outfit; her tie-dyed shirt had been drenched in layers of sweat, sex sweat and then panic sweat. For the first couple of hours, as Candy and Calvin Taylor popped in and out to brief her on the events at the Hyatt in Elmbrook, where state cops and Elmbrook cops and Parkside cops were questioning guests at the twentieth reunion of the 1970 class of Immaculata High School, Beth had not even thought to call Pat.

It was getting dark when Candy, extricating the elaborate little wreath of vines and gardenias from her hair, had asked Beth if Pat was on his way. Ellen had gotten up to call him; but Beth had run after her, a surge of guilt giving her legs power, and so it had been she who told her husband that when the doors to the ballroom were opened before the dinner, a tiny Red Parrot tennis shoe had been found on a speakers' podium. Told him that it had been, of all people, Barbara Kelliher who saw it, Barbara who nearly passed out and went running, screaming for Jimmy. That at first Jimmy and Karl Kelliher had thought it was somebody's sick idea of a joke, but that Jimmy had the presence of mind to make sure nobody touched it, and that he had overcome all his misgivings and called Candy, knowing she was probably clinking glasses with her groom at that very moment, knowing she would never forgive him if it turned out not to be a joke. It was Beth who told her husband that she had known from the minute she saw the shoe, in a sealed bag in Candy's hand, known from the tiny green plastic

281

'B' shoved on the laces to keep little fingers from untying them, that it was real — that it was Ben's.

It was Beth who had told Pat, heard him reply, then gasp, then heard the phone drop and finally disconnect. Beth who finally reached Augie and found out about Pat, and then rode with Calvin Taylor through the night, going over ninety, as he radioed the state squads they passed on the interstate. Who crouched at his bedside for three days, only vaguely aware of Rob's periodic relays of messages from Chicago. The shoe was authentically made in 1985. The shoe had prints. But the prints were somehow ruined. The interviewed alumni, fewer by many than five years before, were whistle-clean. The staff had seen no one even slightly odd or out of place.

The press were baying at the moon, Rob said. The way he'd heard it, some rookie cop or other started talking about the shoe as if it were common public knowledge that the first Red Parrot was the link to the kidnapping. Candy, who'd successfully suppressed that detail, was fulminating; overnight, Ben's face was again on the front of every Sunday edition in America. Since the media learned that Pat had been rushed to intensive care in Wisconsin, the hospital parking lot, Rob said, looked like the scene outside the prison when Gary Gilmore was executed.

All Beth wanted to do was watch Pat's face, watch its color slowly deepen from gray to a hint of rose. All she wanted to do was lean against his bed and pray for her husband, whom she thought of as her children's only surviving parent, to live. She sat, helplessly hearing Pat's goofy laughter when she'd told him that somehow, in spite of their best efforts, she was pregnant again, with Kerry — heard him singing the sleepy song to Kerry on the morning of her birth. Saw him drawing a heart with marker on her stomach when she was pregnant with Ben. Watched him playing shortstop in Colt League when they were kids, she licking Fudgsicles with a crowd of twelve-year-olds, Pat just enough older and more glamorous that the way he hiked his belt up over his palm-flat hips made the hair on her arms stand up. Beth sat there, stinking of infidelity, and she had promised Pat — God, fate — anything in those first few days.

And Pat, God, and fate had collected.

Beth had not spoken to Nick again. After he left repeated messages on her answering machine at home, about how was Pat doing and then about Ben, which Beth didn't return, she'd gotten a one-line note. 'I'm sorry,' it read, 'but I'm not sorry.'

Unsigned.

She'd wanted badly to call him then. She had fantasized about the sheer romantic rectitude of it — twenty-year journeys ending in lovers meeting. But not for her. Pat had lived. That was the end of it. She and Candy had never discussed Candy's wedding day. But since she and Pat had arrived in Chicago, Candy had been over to the new house twice. She'd brought bread and salt, knowing Pat would appreciate it, and news on the 'new' investigation. The trail was colder than a witch's heart. The Feebies were fucking around with the shoe prints; the reopened phone lines had sparked only a trickle of tips, most of frankly lunar quality. Barbara Kelliher had talked a handful of Immaculata volunteers into a small revival of the Find Ben center out of her house, but the turnout was feeble. Most of the old schoolmates were frankly aghast at the double curse on the reunions and shied away. Even Wayne only sent a check, for a thousand dollars.

There was, however, a new, computer-generated age-progression sketch of Ben being prepared. Something would pop, Candy said. Something. With the same certainty she knew that Rosie, riding in a car, would never forget to reach up to hold a button on her coat if they passed a funeral procession, Beth knew that nothing would pop, now or ever. But she thanked Candy anyway.

The second time Candy came over, the visit had just been social. They sat on the porch, Beth drinking coffee with brandy in it, Candy drinking seltzer because she thought she might be pregnant. ("I'm nauseated, but then I'm always nauseated," she'd sighed. "I probably have ulcers.") Beth nattered about Vincent. By September, Vincent had established a school record for missed homework assignments. The school counselor was evaluating him for an attention disorder, though Beth was sure he didn't have one: he spent long hours every night poring over the newspapers and watching TV, writing down game scores and filing them away in notebooks color-coded by sport. When Candy got up to leave, she'd half-turned and told Beth, "If you ever want to tell me what's wrong . . . "

Guiltily, Beth had broken in, "I hate being here is all . . . "

But Candy had shaken her head. "I factored that in, and I meant that if you ever want to tell me what's *really* wrong . . . "

But Beth would never tell. Not Ellen. Not Candy. It was part of the pact she'd made, to have to carry this final betrayal of Ben, of Pat, inside her, alone.

She was almost drowsing in the sun when Pat came out and sat down beside her. "Dad and Kip the designer are having a fight now. So they're happy. Everything's going to be okay, though this bitch is going to cost an arm, a leg, and a torso."

He was worried. Beth breathed in softly through her nose; he was worried, so he was fine.

"That's good, Paddy," Beth said. And they got up to drive back to their new home.

16

Reese

November 1991

"THEY keep the stuff in gallon containers, plastic, like it was milk or something,"
"But it's a solid."

"Yeah, it's like a cake, it's made of compressed crystals, and you just chip off as many of the granules as you need."

"How many did you need?"

"Well, we needed a lot. A hell — " Reese measured the shrink across the table; what would he think if a thirteen-year-old kid cussed? He'd probably think it was evidence of his mental illness. So that could work; Dad ought to get something for his money. "A hell of a lot. Almost a whole gallon."

"Where do you get . . . uh . . . ?"

"Calcium carbide."

"Where do you get this? Did you, like, have to lift it?"

"Lift it?"

"You know — steal it, Vincent."

This guy, thought Reese, was a very clue-free guy. "No," he said. "We did not steal it, partly because you can't steal it, they don't sell it anywhere anymore — except like a construction or a building place. Or a mining place."

286

"Mining?"

"Yeah, like copper mining or coal mining or something?" Reese glanced at the clock with the fat, red liquid-crystal numbers displayed behind the shrink. This had already taken twenty minutes. Reese immediately felt more hopeful. At this rate, he could spend the next forty minutes spinning out this yarn about the explosion; and, if Leadoff Man was on at one o'clock, and if he figured on Dad's customary twenty minutes to say goodbye to his pool buddy, Deuce — and the drive, the drive was, like, ten minutes on a Saturday — hey! he would be home by the bottom of the second, top of the third, no problem. Not only his favorite match (the Milwaukee Brewers, his old team, and the White Sox, his dad's team) but a game on which a lot was riding — quite a lot. He hated to miss a game he had money on, especially his own. If you had an operation the size of Reese's, you would miss some games. It figured. He wasn't, like, Tom Boswell or somebody. He didn't write about it for a living, being, basically, a kid. There were Stanley Cup playoffs on past his bedtime. And games during the day when he was at school. He kept up — with the papers and the radio and ESPN — you had to keep up — but it took a lot of organization, and he sometimes felt like he wasn't really watching the game for the fun of it. But this would be excellent. Quite precisely cold, it would be, if he could wrap up this little interview here and head on home.

"Coal mining?" said the clue-free one. He

287

looked about the age of Reese's cousin Jill, whom Reese could easily make cry.

"Yeah, they used to use what they would call carbon lanterns, this little light, and then there was a water tank thing, and you'd put a few grains of this stuff in there, and the reaction would, you know, power the light a really long time."

"Why didn't they just use batteries?" the guy asked, a long curl of his hair falling forward right between his eyes in a way Reese found disturbing.

"Well, duh, you should pardon the expression, they didn't *have* batteries at first, and then, you know, batteries are real expensive. If you have to have this helmet light burning, like, twelve hours, you go through them pretty fast. And if you got a whole bunch of guys, and every one of them has to have one of these helmets."

"Sure, I see, Vincent — economics." The shrink leaned back in his chair, comfortable-like.

"Right."

But the comfortable stuff was a wrong number, because right away the guy bored in again. "Okay, so, how did you get these chemicals?"

"They used to sell it in camping stores."

"But they don't now."

"No. They have Coleman gas and stuff."

"So, how did you get it?"

Reese looked at the clock. Very good, very, very good. Thirty minutes gone now.

"My friend Jordie's grandpa had it. He's an engineer."

288

"Did he know you took it?"

"No."

"And what did he do when he found out about . . . the incident? I mean, it's a pretty creative use of chemicals, but you can see how Jordie's grandfather might — "

"He was definitely unpleased. He was real unpleased."

"And your parents? Bet they were unpleased, too."

Reese gazed into the young man's eyes. He had practiced this, trained himself not to blink, lying awake in the dark until his eyes felt like they were coated with gum. It was worth it, though; it was a very excellent maneuver on teachers, for example, when they said, "Vincent. Can you explain this?"

"My parents were also unpleased. That's, uh, why I'm here."

"Your parents weren't satisfied with your explanation . . . "

"Uhhhh, no."

"And they wanted you to talk to someone?"

"Well, yes, they think I'm crazy. That is, my dad does. My mom . . . "

"Your mother?"

"Well, my mother didn't pay much attention to it."

"Why?"

"Well, she's pretty busy with my little sister and stuff."

"Well, sure. But I think, you know, it's possible that she was very concerned about this and simply didn't . . . "

"Anything's possible."

"So, you took the initial manhole cover off . . . How did you do that?"

"Well, you know, we lifted it."

"They're pretty heavy. You just lifted it up?"

"Yeah, but we had this long piece of pipe. I mean a very long piece, like five feet, and it was metal, not PVC. So we put it in the hole in there . . . "

"And you pried up the manhole cover?"

"Yeah."

"Wasn't that really difficult?"

"Well, you know what they say — 'Give me a lever and a place to stand and I can move the world.' Or something."

"They?"

"Well, he. Archimedes."

"Oh."

"Yeah." The guy looked a little concerned that a kid would know about Archimedes; adults had this idea of you and what you knew and the limits of it, and they got real hostile if you got outside it — they said you were showing off or being an asshole or whatever. So Reese said, "I saw that on TV."

"I see." The guy looked down at his file, and made a note, and pushed his glasses up on his hair. Now he looked even younger, like sixteen. Piece of cake, thought Reese. "So what do you think, Vincent? Is there any other reason, besides the explosion, that your parents wanted you to talk to me?"

Reese winced.

'Vincent.' It sounded like getting stung by a

290

wasp. 'Vincent.' It was just a wimpy, doofus name, a foot short of 'Vinnie'. He didn't care so much when his grandma Rosie called him ''Cenzo', that wasn't so bad. But 'Vincent' — hiss.

"Is something the matter?" Reese glanced at the clock . . . slowly now . . .

"Uh, just the name."

"Your name?"

"Its just that, it's not my name. Vincent."

"Oh. I see here, from your doctor — "

"Yeah, but see, what they call me is Reese."

"Oh. Why? Is that a nickname for Vincent?"

Utterly and completely clue-free, this guy. This guy didn't know whether he was in town or not.

"No," Reese said carefully, as if he were talking with one of the Wongs at school, the kids he tutored in math, who learned how to make clam chowder in biology instead of doing the regular stuff; they were all called Wong after the guy who wrote the biology book for simples. "My name is really Vincent Paul. But the guys . . . see, when I came to Chicago, this was last year, they heard them read my name off in the class, and somebody goes, 'Vincent Paul? Saint Vincent de Paul? He's named after the resale store!' And they all laughed, not real mean-like, but afterward, because I dress . . . I mean, I like my clothes real comfortable . . . they would call me 'Resale! Hey, Resale!' and then, 'Reese'.

"That's a pretty neat conversion. I mean, if you like it. But maybe you *didn't* like it. Was that painful for you? Did you feel they were making fun of your clothes?"

"Shit no!" said Reese, and then caught himself. The 'hell' was one thing. He could tell from the guy's face, which suddenly got very still, that 'shit' was another. "Pardon me. But no. It didn't bother me."

"Why not?"

"What's your name?"

"Dr. Kilgore."

"No, I mean your *name* name."

"Oh . . . Thomas. Tom."

"Well, Tom, imagine being named Vincent." Reese glanced at the fat red lighted letter. "Look, Dr. Kilgore, the time's up. I think my dad's waiting for me . . . "

"Oh, you're right, I guess. I was just thinking about those manhole covers. Sure. Well, next time we can talk more about . . . "

Absolutely, Reese thought. Totally. He figured his dad was paying this guy, like, fifty dollars an hour or something. The next time he saw this guy they'd be roller-skating on the el tracks.

"Sure," said Reese. And then he looked up, and goddamn his lousy luck and timing, there stood his dad, in the little kind of arched door to this guy's office, which didn't have a door — it didn't need one, because his office was the whole first floor, and people waited in a kind of porch thing. His dad had walked right in, which was very Dad-like.

"Mr. Cappadora," said the shrink, suddenly all smiles and hands. Reese had seen his dad have this effect on people before. His mom, with her big witch eyes and her skinny face — people backed off from his mom, not that she noticed (talk about people who didn't know whether they were in town or not). Point is, she creeped people out. But people wanted to give his dad a doughnut or something. Grandma Rosie's friends, they were all over him, like he was Reese's age, or Kerry's. And whenever he met Grandpa Angelo's friends, or even Grandpa Bills, for that matter, they were, like, "Paddy! Paddy, my boy!" and they were giving him stuff. Everybody knew before they even met him, like Dad was their long-lost brother or something.

"Mr. Cappadora, I wanted to go over a couple of things with you, a little background . . . I just didn't get a whole picture on the phone, because this was sort of in the nature of an emergency and all."

And Reese's dad was, like, smiling, sure, no problem, though Reese knew he had to be at the restaurant in, like, an hour to set up. Reese glanced at the clock. Bottom of the first now, for sure.

"Vincent," said his dad. "You can go sit in the car and turn the radio on." Vincent trotted out the door. Their big old boat of a Chevy was sitting at the curb, actually not right at the curb, about a foot off it, because his dad was not a very godly driver, though he always said, when they goofed around, "Italians are the best drivers, you know. Parnelli Jones. And Mario Andretti. All those guys are Italian."

"And the best singers," Reese would say. His dad was such a sap, but he was a good sap.

"Oh, absolutely. Frank. And Pavarotti."

"And Madonna. Trevor Ricci."

"Trevor Ricci?" his dad had asked, that once.

"From On the Rag," Reese told him.

"That's a band?"

"Yeah, dad, like Smashing Pumpkins. Or Nine Inch Nails. Or whatever."

And his dad would tell him this shit was not music — kids today didn't have any idea of what melody was — and Reese would say, yeah, for real, Dad, like those tapes in the restaurant, those two-thousand-year-old tenors singing 'Santa Lucia' over and over and over till you snapped. Now that was music!

The frigging car was locked. Reese took a long breath. He turned around and slumped back into the guy's office, and was about to throw himself down on this kind of swing thing outside the door, when he heard his dad say, " . . . that his brother was three years old?"

Oh, terrific, thought Reese, and edged closer.

"I knew . . . you'd said on the telephone that there had been another child." The shrink seemed to be apologizing now. He had heard that tone, that hushed, church tone, like someone was hugging you with his voice, whenever a teacher found out at the beginning of a term about Ben. It was the magic ticket, at first. They gave you soft looks, their heads tilted, and smiled at you no matter what you did, but it didn't last. By November, he was always riding the bench in the principal's office, and listening to extreme, rational lectures about how no matter how severe the grief we had to endure was, we needed to keep priorities straight, we needed to be strong, and try to accept responsibility, because the world wasn't going to cut you slack, you had to make the grade, and you know you have the ability, Vincent . . .

"So, Vincent was . . . seven when his brother died?"

Bastard, thought Reese. He could hear the collapse in his dad's voice. Dad couldn't handle much talk about Ben. The dumb bastard was going to drag Dad down a flight of stairs right now.

Vincent slid behind one end of a bookcase; it only stuck out about a foot from the wall, but he was small and thin for thirteen, so he could stand erect and eavesdrop without being seen. There was a fringe of soft dust along the back of the bookcase; Reese wiped it with his finger.

"He didn't die. That is, I guess, yes, he died. But we are not sure. Because Ben was . . . we believe Ben was kidnapped. In fact, the police are pretty much sure that happened, because of clues they found."

"Ahhh," said the bastard. Guaranteed shocker. "And you never found . . . ?"

"The case is still officially open, and the police still get leads sometimes. Last year, in fact, well . . . the thing is, there's not much hope, but I pray to God we'll at least find out someday."

"Oh, man. Oh, you must . . . it must . . . "

"And Vincent was right next to Ben when it happened. I'm amazed you never read about this."

"I don't read much. You say he saw the boy being abducted?"

"No . . . he — Ben — was just a baby, he was three that spring, and he wandered off . . . They were in a hotel lobby. We lived in Wisconsin then, and Beth had the children with her here for her high-school reunion."

"I see, I see . . . "

"Did he talk about Ben? About how he feels about what happened to Ben? Because I think, it makes sense, doesn't it, if a kid is like this, the way Vincent is, that there's a link?"

"Well, we have to presume that something that utterly traumatic . . . But no, Mr. Cappadora, he didn't bring it up. And that's not necessarily bad, especially at a first meeting. Kids aren't like us in a therapeutic setting. An adult will try to go straight for the problem. You know, 'I want to leave my wife' . . . 'I hate my boss.' We're aware that we need to consider issues, and we have the economics of the situation on our minds. But with a child . . . a child might not come out and say, 'I have a problem with this.' An adolescent child, particularly, and he's what? . . . nearly thirteen . . . will approach things in an oblique way, and the importance is establishing trust . . . "

"Yeah, that makes sense."

Frigging shit, though Reese. He's going for it.

And then his dad asked, "So, when he talked about the explosion? Did he tell you people were hurt?"

"No."

296

"Well, that's good, because nobody was hurt. Though this old lady fell off a chair in her kitchen and got an egg on her head the size of . . . fortunately, she knows Beth's dad. But I hope Vincent gave you some idea of the . . . scope of this."

"He told me about the calcium carbide."

"What they did, him and this Jordie Cassady kid, they poured a whole bunch of those crystals down the storm sewer. And they waited a long time. If they hadn't waited a long time, it might not have been so big . . . but see, Vincent knows about this stuff. It wasn't Jordie Cassady, though his father or his grandfather or whatever had the chemicals — in the garage, for Christ's sake. But Jordie's a good kid. I'm not saying my son is bad, I mean. But it was Vincent who knew how long to wait. He waited until the crystals were sufficiently mixed with the water in the main so that they could really . . . and then they lit this fatwood log — you know, the kind of thing you use to start a fire in a fireplace . . . "

"He told you all this?"

"The police told me all this. And he told the police. I guess. They had to look down at the paper for the name of the gas it creates. Acetylene gas.

When they lit it, you never heard anything like it. It was like . . . ten percussion grenades. Windows broke. Stuff fell off people's shelves. The goddamn ground shook. Beth and I are like . . . 'The furnace blew up!' And the manhole covers for three blocks — boom! Up in the air. It's one a.m. we're talking about."

Reese could hear his dad get up, and though he couldn't see him, he knew his dad was reaching for a bone, realizing he couldn't smoke in the guy's office, putting the pack back in his side pocket, and then pacing. He went on, "Thirty feet up, and these are big, heavy cast-iron mothers. We're lucky, somebody's cat didn't get flattened — and if it had been daytime, Jesus, somebody would've been killed." Reese's dad sighed, hard, like he did at the end of a Saturday night, when he came in the door, in the dark, smelling of smoke and garlic. Reese would hear him; no one else was ever awake. He would hear his dad sigh, loudly, and then start rummaging through the drawers, and he would want to run down to him and jump him from behind, like he did when he was a really little kid. Back then, his dad would never put him back to bed. He'd make him cinnamon toast.

"The thing is," Reese's dad was saying now, "Beth, his mother, and I . . . we've had a . . . it's been very, very hard. And the kid, the kid is this outlaw. He does, so far as I know, no homework. I mean, he'll write a twenty-page report on something like the Monty Hall problem . . . "

"The Monty Hall problem?"

"It's this probability deal. If you have three doors, and there's a big prize behind one, and you first choose number one, and it's not there, I think they ask, is there any greater statistical likelihood that the prize is behind number two or number three?"

"Is there?" said the shrink, sounding as dumb

298

as Kevin Flanner, whom Reese had once had to punch.

"Hell if I know. I run a restaurant. And these mathematicians all over the country, they write to each other on the computer and debate this thing . . . And anyway, once Vincent wrote a whole paper on this; he even called this guy in California in the middle of the night."

"That's very impressive. This is clearly a really bright kid."

"But the thing is, it wasn't assigned! It wasn't his homework; he had long division to do, and he totally blew that off, and didn't turn it in. So the school calls. They call ten times a week. They must have us on the speed dial by now, and I know, I know, we've all been through hell, but my God, the kid is going to go to the pen . . . "

"I don't think there's any danger of that, really. But the thing is, next time, we really need to get the rest of the family in here — your wife and — "

"Beth won't come."

"I'm sure she's as troubled as you are."

"Well, of course Beth cares about what's happening to Vincent. But since Ben's been . . . since this happened, she's not that willing to open up anymore. She went to a grief group, and we've gone to counseling, Beth and me, right after I was sick, last year. Once. There's been a lot of pressure. She's just . . . she won't deal with it anymore . . . "

"Why don't you let me talk to her? I'm sure

299

we can work something out. And . . . are your parents alive? And Beth's?"

"My folks are. And Beth's dad."

"Well, this is a whole family thing, Mr. Cappadora. There's been a lot of pain here, and maybe not enough of a chance for everyone to sort it out."

"I can't imagine my parents in a psychologist's office."

Kilgore laughed. "Nobody can ever imagine it. But it grows on you. So why don't we try to set something up?" Kilgore ruffled some papers. "You know, I can't stop thinking about this. Manhole covers went thirty feet in the air? Somebody saw it?"

"Yeah. Two people actually saw it. And Jordie and Vincent, of course."

"Cool."

"What?"

"I mean, I'm sorry, Mr. Cappadora. Pat. What I should be saying is that this is definitely dangerous, oppositional behavior, in a sense, risk-taking to the point of self-endangerment. Of course it is." Vincent strained to hear the shrink. He had gotten up, was moving away, out of earshot. Vincent leaned forward a fraction of an inch, and the guy said, "But thirty feet in the air? Boom?"

Reese heard his dad laugh, softly, very softly. "Did he tell you he's a bookie?"

"Get out of here!"

"Yeah, he's a bookie . . . football, baseball, hockey. Not the ponies. He just handicaps those for my buddies."

300

"This is some kid you have here." They laughed together, louder this time. They were laughing about a kid blowing up a neighborhood.

Jesus, thought Reese. I'm fucked.

17

THOUGH in his opinion Kilgore had missed his calling as a vet (he had more horse pictures on his wall than they had at Churchill Downs), Reese didn't entirely mind going back a second time.

It was partly the look on his dad's face when Reese agreed to try seeing the shrink again.

It was the same look Pat got when he'd finished raking the oak leaves for the third time in the fall. Like he could pretend that during the winter, some magic thing would change and it would never be fall again and he would never have to do the same job. It was a look that in Reese's mind was accompanied by the sound of someone dusting his hands together — there, that's done. On the whole, Reese would have preferred scraping paint off the Sears Tower to another little get-together with Clue-Free Kilgore ("Call me Tom, or even Doctor Tom, if you want" — Reese couldn't believe it). But he liked that it smoothed some of the wrinkles off his dad's forehead, made his dad's eyes open a little wider, like eyes that weren't always trying to read little print. He knew that his dad had been after his mom, and Rosie and Angelo and Bill, to go to a meeting with Kilgore, too. Rosie didn't care, but Bill wasn't too cool on the idea (or so Reese could gather from the one side of phone conversations he was usually able to get, because his dad had this, like, sixth sense about someone being on the extension, even if you put a handkerchief over it and held your breath).

The real reason Reese didn't mind going back to Kilgore had to do with Kilgore being a psychiatrist instead of a school social worker or something. Which Reese could easily tell, having spent a lot of time with school counselors when he was little over some goddamn school thing or other. Was he clinically depressed? Did he have (Reese's favorite; it made him sound like the reverse-vitamin-enriched kid) underachiever syndrome? Reese could tell Kilgore wasn't like the others because his office was decorated so cool, skinny white panels of handmade paper lined up with only one, the second to the last, violet, which went with some pillows Kilgore had on his couches. Now, if there had been two panels with purple, one on each end, it would not necessarily mean the guy had money. But the one, just the one, sort of thrown in there, was classy.

And sure enough, before he went back, Reese looked Kilgore up in the phone book and there he was, Thomas K. Kilgore, M.D.

So that meant Reese could tell him about the heart thing. Which he couldn't tell his dad. Since Dad had the heart attack, Reese didn't even feel like telling him when he had a sore throat. The heart thing — which had been going on for a while — would be a good way to use up time when he saw Kilgore again. It would distract Kilgore from Reese's eye — which he knew Kilgore would bring up; in fact, he knew his father had told Kilgore about it in advance. But not just that. Because it was getting concerning. The heart thing was happening almost every night now, not just once in a while, and sometimes in school, too. His heart would just take off, like a flapping seagull getting up steam to rise off the water, *bash*, *bash*, *bash*. The first time it happened, Reese thought, I'm fucking dying. And he tried to get up out of bed, but he was out of breath, so he lay back down. And gradually it slowed, until it felt like a regular heart again, which is to say it felt like nothing, like you didn't notice it. At first, because it didn't start happening until after the fight, he thought Asshole Kramer had broken a rib or something when he decked him. But it didn't hurt other times, like, at all.

So Reese figured it was inherited heart disease, getting started early. And when he went to the office, when Dad was talking to Kilgore in the sort of porch place outside, he got one of Kilgore's green books down — *Growing Up: Bio-Emotional Aspects of the Adolescent* — and tried looking up early-onset heart disease. He didn't get the book back in fast enough, though, because Kilgore had shoes like Mister Rogers (probably to keep from knocking up that lovely polished maple floor) and he was standing right there before Reese could do anything. Reese almost shed a skin.

"I'm sorry if I scared you," said Kilgore, all nice.

"It's okay." Reese was sweating. He took a deep breath. "Actually, I don't care, because there was this one thing I wanted to ask you about since I was going to be here anyway."

Kilgore sat down on the chair opposite Reese. "Ask away," he said.

"Where's my dad?"

"We're done."

"Okay, you're a doctor, right?"

"I'm a psychiatrist." Shit, thought Reese, okay. Let's make this as prissy as possible.

"But you have to be a regular doctor to be a psychiatrist? So you were a doctor once, right?"

"Yep, and I still am. I can prescribe antibiotics and everything." Kilgore smiled.

"What happened to your eye?"

"You already know. I heard my dad tell you I got jumped by some asshole."

"I just wanted to see if you got the license plate."

"The what?"

"Of the truck that hit you." Oh, what a riot, thought Reese.

"Well, actually, yeah, I know the guy. He's a sort of professional jerk."

"Jerk-about-town."

"Yeah," Reese said. He liked that phrase. Jerk-about-town. "But whatever. I'm having this problem at night . . . when I'm in bed . . . "

"Most guys your age have — "

Oh, Christ, thought Reese. "I don't mean *that*! I think I'm having a heart attack is what, and I don't want my dad to know, because he'll go totally crazy."

"Why do you think you're having a heart attack?"

Reese told him about the seagull in his chest. Kilgore got up for a minute and looked at a horse. Then he picked up a little spiral notebook and made a note, just like shrinks in the movies.

"Vincent, has this been a problem for a real long time?"

"Reese."

"Reese, of course. I'm sorry. It's just . . . you know, it's actually kind of weird. Not bad weird. Kind of neat. You don't meet that many kids who changed their own name. Just adults. Mostly ex-cons."

"I guess."

"But about your heart, Reese — how long have you been noticing this?"

"I figured you'd ask, so I actually thought about it. For months, off and on. But all the time since the fight."

"Was the fight a really bad experience? I mean, your eye looks like an undercooked Big Mac, but even so . . . "

"It wasn't any worse than any other fight."

"Been in a lot of fights?"

Reese sniffed, unconsciously. "My share."

"But this time you got hurt."

"I get hurt a lot."

Kilgore laughed. He fucking laughed! "Has anybody ever told you the meaning of the word 'counterintuitive'?"

"No." Reese bristled.

"I mean, if you get hurt a lot, are you the kind of guy who never makes the same mistake once?"

"Listen, Dr. Kilgore — "

"Tom."

"Tom — the reason I got beat is 'cause I wasn't ready for him, and also, the guy is like, five-ten, one eighty . . . "

"So why'd you piss him off?"

Why? thought Reese. Why is a good question. He knew why. He'd set out to find Kramer and piss him off, he knew that. Picked Jordie up on the way. They had to look two places: in the conservation park, where Kramer normally smoked like a big boy, and at the playground near the hoops, which was where they finally did find him. Kramer and his sensational friend, the rubber dick, Angotti. "I don't know," Reese said. "He annoys me."

"More that day than any other time?"

"No."

"So why that day?" Reese thought hard. And as he did, Kilgore said, "Did you have trouble with your mom? Your dad? Something going on at school?"

"No," Reese said. "Honestly. It was an ordinary Saturday morning. I didn't have to get back for any games or sports scores until like two or three. So I was just riding my bike."

"Riding your bike . . . "

"I was riding my bike around the neighborhood. I went down to where these younger kids play street hockey, at this one kid's house . . . "

"Do you play, too?"

"No," Reese laughed. "They're like nine."

"So why'd you go there?"

"I like to . . . " Reese looked up at Kilgore. He felt a single wing beat in his chest, subside. "I just like to watch this one kid play. He's really good."

"He a friend?"

"I told you, no, he's like eight. I don't even know him." Kilgore looked puzzled. "I just saw him in the neighborhood this one time and then I went past his house and he was playing street hockey. So I watched."

"How long ago was this?"

"Months. A few months."

"Months ago?"

"Yeah."

"So, when you go over there and watch, do you talk to this kid?"

"No, I just sit there on my bike and watch."

"Have you done this more than a couple of times?"

"What's the point?"

"Just curious."

"Well, like a dozen times. Maybe more. He's a really good street hockey player. And you know, I'm interested in sports."

"Does he remind you of somebody?"

What? thought Reese. "Like who?"

"Like maybe you, when you were younger."

Reese said, slowly, "No. He's really big for his age, for example. No, he doesn't look like me at all." The gulls, suddenly, gathered with determination. Reese leaned forward on the couch and hugged his arms to his chest.

"Reese? Reese?" Kilgore was on his feet.

"It's happening right now."

"The heart thing."

"Yeah."

"Reese." Kilgore sat down on the couch beside him. "I'm going to tell you exactly what's happening to you. You're not dying. You're not having a heart attack. You're having a panic attack, and though it feels very frightening and very real — and it *is* very real — it's not dangerous. It's not going to kill you."

"I didn't really think . . . " Reese gasped.

"But maybe you did. I know it feels like it's going to kill you because I had some once."

Kilgore put his hand on the middle of Reese's back. He pushed. Not like he was hugging Reese or anything. He just sort of pushed like Reese was a bicycle pump — press, release, press. "Blow gently and slowly out through your mouth, Reese. But keep it steady. Pretend you're blowing up a balloon." Reese did it, and as he did, he could sense the topping of the hill, the change that meant that, although the gulls kept beating, it was going to end, it was going to settle down. He gulped, waiting for the sensation of stopping. And as soon as it came, Kilgore didn't keep sitting there; he got right up and acted like nothing out of the ordinary had happened.

"So it was after the street hockey game?"

Reese still felt kind of sick, but he figured, if Kilgore was going to blow it off — actually, kind of a relief — he would play along. "Yeah. I went to get Jordie and we went to the playground."

"And you ran into . . . ?"

"I ran into Kevin Kramer."

"Jerk-about-town."

"Yeah."

"And what started the fight?"

"Well, they were playing basketball, and I sort of rode past."

"And that was it? Just right then, you were having at it?"

"No. Because I rode in between them."

"Ahhhhh."

"And this guy, his friend, Angotti, this guy with, like, gray hair, he's been held back so many times, had to jump out of the way."

"Oh."

"And they're like, 'Cappadora, you little freak' . . . "

"And you didn't want to put up with that."

"Would you?"

"No."

"It wasn't so much that they were making jokes about . . . my height . . . "

"No crime to be short. You know, Reese, it doesn't mean you're going to be short all your life, either."

"What they were saying was, I was, you know, stunted . . . all over."

"I see."

"This guy is like a sophomore. Kramer."

"I see."

"So I just said some thing, some ordinary thing, like . . . 'Don't talk about your old man like that,' and he goes out of his mind . . . "

"Is this the first fight you've had with Kramer?"

"Yeah. Well . . . " Reese considered it. "Not

310

really the first *verbal* fight."

"First physical fight."

"Well, he just moved here."

"I see."

"Right."

"But your other fights?"

"Look, people just can't keep their mouths shut."

Reese got up off the couch and went to stand in front of one of the horse pictures — he realized that the man holding the horse's bridle was Kilgore, and there was a little girl sitting on it, a little girl with blond hair like Kerry's. She had on this miniature-sized riding hat, a black thing with a big brim. You could hardly see her face. "Is that your kid?"

"My little sister."

"Your sister?"

"She's ten now. Big Irish family. There are eight kids. I'm the oldest and she's the youngest. I was already in medical school when she was born."

"What's her name?"

"Tess."

"They're not all T's, are they?"

"Yeah. Unfortunately, they are," said Kilgore. "Terrance. Tracey. Tara."

"You got pretty lucky."

"Don't I know it." He got up. "Reese, we're pretty much out of time. I want you to remember the balloon-blowing thing, because that kind of breathing helps bring a panic attack to a close sooner, if you can concentrate on it. Okay?"

311

"Okay."

"And next time we'll talk more about how you can stop having them. And why you're having them."

"Okay."

"And there's one other thing I want to show you." Kilgore reached out one hand and Reese cringed — Here comes the hug, he thought in disgust. But all of a sudden he was down on one knee; it was as if the guy had dug a piece out of his neck with the lit end of a sparkler.

"Jesus Christ!" Reese screamed. He was nearly crying.

"It won't hurt long," said Kilgore, and he was right. The place, the hollow just behind Reese's earlobe, which had felt electrified a minute before, was now simply limp. Reese pressed it gently. It felt pretty normal. "I'm sorry. But you had to understand how this depends on surprise."

"What'd you do?" asked Reese, rubbing his neck.

"We used to call them pressure points," said Kilgore, taking Reese's hand and putting his thumb against a place between two of his fingers? "See? You push . . . " And *bam!* Reese pulled his hand away.

"How'd you learn that?"

"Medical school. There are nerve bundles all over the human body. See?" Kilgore showed Reese a point behind the elbow, one near the small of his back. "You can look in an anatomy book and see where a lot of them are. Here — you can borrow mine . . . And you can tell when you find one, because you can make that place start to tingle if you press it just a little. And if you press hard, it will hurt like anything. You don't usually press that hard on yourself, of course."

"What're you . . . ?"

"It's just, Reese, you can bring down an ox if you know the pressure points, and if you're going to keep on getting in fights, I just thought you might . . ."

"Well," said Reese. "Thanks. I guess."

"I'm a short guy, too," Kilgore said. "See you next Saturday."

18

THE so-called family session lasted longer than double overtime, as far as Reese was concerned. It wasn't just that he was embarrassed by all of them (Grandpa Bill in aqua-and-green golf pants and Grandpa Angelo dressed like a pallbearer); he just had a feeling that getting them all together in one room was going to lead to ignition and liftoff. When his dad told his mom about the session — didn't ask her, just told her — she got that wild-horse look in her eyes that Reese recognized only too well.

Go slow, Dad, he thought. There be dragons here.

In those agonizing, dull minutes in the waiting room before it all started, Kerry (who also looked just great, because she'd insisted on wearing her purple net tutu) had really humiliated him. She'd had all five of her Red Riding Hood finger puppets on one hand. "Be the wolf, Vincent," she said all of a sudden. He took the wolf-head puppet and put it on his index finger and waggled it at Red Riding Hood. "I eat little girls like you for breakfast," he growled.

"You suck," Kerry said sweetly.

Great.

And then, of course, Grandma Rosie had clicked her tongue, once, so softly Reese knew it was an extra-special click just for him, like *he*

314

taught Kerry to swear, which he didn't; Kerry was able to cuss from birth. Just at that moment, Tom came out and herded them all in, and they spent another eternity getting all shifted around on Tom's couches and chairs.

Reese felt sorry for Tom. Talk about having your work cut out for you. Reese had never, not once in his life, heard Grandma Rosie say anything, a single sentence that began with the words 'I feel'. She just gave commands; she sized up stuff. He had never, on the other hand, heard Grandpa Bill say a single sentence that wasn't in the form of a question; Uncle Bick said talking to his dad was like being the host on *Jeopardy*.

And true to form, right away Grandpa Bill had said, "What can we do you for, Doctor?"

And old Tom didn't waste time then, he jumped right in. "I don't want all of you folks to think we're here only to help out the master criminal here," he gestured at Reese, like he was pointing a pistol and firing. "It's my hope that you'll all get something out of this, or I wouldn't have put you all through arranging your lives to get down here. But I also know none of you wants to see a kid you love in this much pain, and Vincent — our buddy Reese — is definitely in a lot of pain."

Everybody, even Kerry, nodded. "But what I've been hearing about, I'm just guessing, but I think it's that this is a whole family in a lot of pain, for a lot of years, and Reese can't get out in front of this until, basically, we open it

315

up and let a little fresh air get to it. You know what I'm saying?"

Grandma Rosie looked at Tom as if he had just told her she should shave her head, put on bells, and become a Buddhist nun.

"I do not see," she said softly, "how we can talk in this room and help Vincenzo be good."

"There's no guarantees we can, Mrs . . . uh, Mrs . . . " Tom was waiting for Reese's grandma to say, 'Call me Rose.' Wait on, Tom, wait on, Reese thought. "Mrs. Cappadora, there's no proof that in this situation, the healing is going to come from talk. But this kid you love is a real angry kid. And you are the people he loves. He might not act like that all the time, but that's the fact. And with a kid this angry, there's a whole world out there with its hands out, and the stuff in those hands is stuff you don't want for Reese. Next time it might not be sewer covers."

"You mean drugs," said Grandpa Bill.

"Bill," Tom said, not taking any chances on the old cozy first-name front this time. "Yes. There's certainly that, and other kinds of acting out. So what I want to know, while I've got you all here, is, is this new? I mean, was Reese always kind of the angry young man . . . ?" Tom smiled, right at Reese.

Nobody said anything.

"You've got a great kid here," Tom went on. "A kid with a mind that just doesn't quit. You all know it. And with a kid like this, the waste could be big."

"He came out angry," said his mom. A

316

hundred years of silence, and then *boom* — this. Good old reliably nuts Mom. Everybody, even Kerry again, turned to look at her. "He was always hard. I mean, since he was a baby, he had his own ideas of how he wanted to do things. Not all bad ones. I'm not saying Vincent is bad."

"Okay, Beth, okay. But when you say he was 'hard', was he difficult, like this?"

"No," she said. "He would only get mad at me when he was little. But after Ben died — "

Grandma Rosie gasped. "Beth," she said. "Benjamin is not dead."

"Oh, Rosie," said his mother. "He is dead. He's dead. If he wasn't dead, I would know it."

Here we go, thought Reese, let's talk about Ben for . . . like our whole lives.

"Beth," Grandpa Angelo said gently, "the children . . . "

"But I can't stand it! Everyone keeps pretending he's going to come back. I think that's half of what makes Vincent crazy. It makes me crazy. I don't care, Pat. I came here and why waste the money? I'm going to say this. I'm sick of it. 'Never give up hope.' 'Pray, pray, pray.' Well, why *don't* we give up hope? And just let whatever happens happen?"

"Because you can't just bury him, Beth." His dad spoke up. "You want to just bury him before we even know. I know why you feel that way, but . . . "

I'm here, thought Reese. I'm here.

317

"It sounds like there are a couple of camps in this," Tom put in, "and Reese is right in the middle of them. Reese, what do you think?"

Reese said, "Nothing, I don't think about it that much."

"Come on," Tom urged him. "Have you ever heard of the big purple elephant in the living room? There's this elephant right in the middle of the living room, and the whole family walks around it and pretends it isn't there . . . You've got to think about it, Reese. It's right in front of you."

"I don't, though."

"I don't, either," said his mother, and a warm pulse in Reese beat toward her. "I don't think about it ever. What does thinking about it do?"

"Well, in my experience, it sometimes, sometimes gives you some peace," Tom suggested, and then they were off, his mom pointing out that the family did not put Easter eggs on Ben's grave at Easter now or in the past. "He doesn't have a grave to begin with," she'd snapped — or hang a stocking for him, or buy him birthday clothes one size larger each year . . . and his grandmother putting in that she *did* pray for Ben every day, and so did her daughters . . .

Tom struggled to keep up, asking, "Does it bother you that Beth doesn't do that, Mrs. Cappadora? If you think she's given up, how does that make you feel?"

Grandma Rosie reached down and fingered her locket. "I am sorry for Beth. I have known Beth all her life. I love Beth like she is my own

318

child. I am sorry for her, because she . . . she has lost her heart. She has lost her faith . . . "

His mom snorted. Reese couldn't believe it; it was like she'd jumped up on the uneven parallel bars. But Grandma Rosie wasn't about to give up: "Bethie, dear one, you know you have gone away from God . . . "

"Oh, no, Rosie. No, Rosie. It was God who took the powder, Rosie. A long time ago. No offense, but . . . "

Gak and gak. Back and forth. Reese realized that, although he had never heard these words spoken, they were as familiar to him as the national anthem. He covered his ears. Finally, from the white throw pillow on the floor where he'd taken refuge, he could see the forest of their legs lengthen as Tom ushered them from the room. An instant later, Kerry's little purple twigs bounded out from behind the sofa. At last, Tom leaned down and said, "Hey, buddy, you got a minute to spare here?"

"I got five minutes, no more. In five minutes, I'm trying out for the White Sox."

"What position?"

"Center field."

"I don't want to interfere with a career in the show."

"They waited this long," Reese told him, "they can wait five more minutes."

"Actually, we've got maybe fifteen good minutes here."

Reese got up. "Maybe I should get down on the couch here, Tom, like in the movies. I never did that. You could say, 'So, Mister Cappadora, why do you think you look like a sheep?'"

"I think you'd fall asleep."

"Why?"

"You look like your candle burns at both ends, 'bro. Are you putting in enough sack time? Is it the business?"

Tom meant the betting. "No," Reese said. "That's just . . . I do that mostly on the weekends."

"It drives your father nuts, you know, Reese." Reese knew it didn't, not at all. His dad was as proud of his business as he was ashamed of it. It was the same way Grandpa Angelo felt about gangsters. "Most kids your age, they have a paper route."

"I can't have a paper route."

"Too strenuous, huh?"

"No." He hated to do this to Tom. "Kids . . . a kid once got kidnapped on his paper route. It was very famous. Johnny Gosch? They never found him. In my family, it's just not a thing . . . My father . . . my parents would freak . . ." Tom wasn't like other adults, though. His face didn't get all waxy and soft, like he didn't know where to put his cheek muscles, when Reese said it. He just shook himself a little — like, as Grandma Rosie said, when a goose walked over your grave — and plowed right on.

"And what about you? Would you freak?"

Stiffly, Reese told him, "It wouldn't scare me."

"Not even a little?"

"I don't know. Anyway, who wants to get up at goddamn three o'clock in the morning?"

320

"Not me," said Tom. "Or you. Especially if you get to bed pretty late. Do you go to bed at a reasonable hour? Ten?"

"Yeah, I go to bed." Reese shifted. "But then I have to wake up and change the tapes, and it takes me a while to settle down again."

"The tapes?"

"I sleep with music on."

"Must be very restful for your parents."

"I use earphones."

"What d'you listen to?"

"Mostly classical stuff at night. And opera. Italiano. You know. It's a birth defect, like you being a Red Sox fan."

"Pardon me, Reese, but getting up to change the tape deck all night doesn't exactly sound like healthy slumber to me."

"It works."

"So this is why you look like death on a cracker."

"Well, it's not the music . . . "

"What is it?"

Now. Reese thought. Now he was going to have to talk about it. He'd mentioned the running dream last session, just before they ran out of time. In fact, Tom had accused him of doing it on purpose, knowing perfectly well the time was up and the family was coming this time. Old Tom felt cheated; shrinks cranked up on dreams.

"Okay. It's the dream I started to tell you about."

"The running dream."

"Yeah."

"Where are you in it?"

"I'm in this big room, and the tiles on the floor are what I'm looking at. They're like . . . they look like meatballs. It's nutty. They're pretty ugly."

"Are you alone?"

"Shit, no!" Reese looked up. "I'm sorry. No. There's a zillion people there, and they're all talking."

"What are they saying?"

"Well, that's the thing. They're not saying anything."

"You said they're talking."

"I can tell they're talking because I can see their mouths move. But I can't hear anything. I'm just standing there, but I'm *not* just standing there." Reese frowned. "I'm running."

"But you can't move."

"Is that how everybody feels?"

"It's a common thing that happens in anxiety dreams. What matters is, who's chasing you? What are you running from?"

Reese strained. He tried to take himself back — the gulls flapped again, as if they were getting pissed, but it was okay, he knew how to breathe it down. He tried to look behind him. "There's nobody behind me. I'm running . . . *after* somebody."

"After who?"

"Uh . . . I don't know."

"You do know."

"I don't know. I mean, if I knew, why wouldn't I tell you?"

"You tell me why you wouldn't tell me."

Because I'll die, Reese thought. I'll die here on your couch if I tell you. Or maybe it'll be worse than that. Maybe I'll just shit all over your couch. Reese lay down on the couch, folding his elbows over his eyes. It wasn't the crying he minded, or even Tom seeing him; it was that he felt so damn worn out, so hauled down by anchors.

"I'm running after . . . somebody on the other side of the room."

"Who?"

"I don't know who."

"Listen, buddy," said Tom, getting up and tapping on the frame of one of the thousand horse pictures. "You know what I make an hour?"

"What?"

"A hundred and twenty bucks an hour is what I make."

"Well, congratulations," Reese said, sitting up. "Maybe you can buy some more horse pictures."

"And you know who pays me that hundred and twenty bucks?"

"Who?"

"Your dad."

BFD, thought Reese. It was, after all, his dad's idea, this whole head-shrinking party, in the first place. "So?"

"So, do you think your dad is a complete fool?"

"No, I don't think my dad is a complete fool."

"Well, you must. Because, if your dad wants

323

to pay a hundred and twenty bucks an hour for you to sit here and jerk around every Saturday, and sometimes during the week, if he's so rich that that doesn't even matter to him, that's jake with me. I'll take his money . . . "

"You would, too," Reese shot back. "You'd take it, even if you knew it wasn't going to do me any good . . . "

"Sure, for a while. Why shouldn't I? I make money; your dad feels like you're talking to someone, everybody's happy. Except there's this kid who's on the way to first-offender boot camp, which is you, but that's your choice, buddy. I'm not your mommy. I see plenty of tough guys come and go. They're all losers." Reese felt his fists begin to curl. Different from the rest, he thought. You preppy prick. "But pretty soon, at some point, ethics dictate that I'm going to have to say, 'Well, listen, your kid's got his head up his butt, and he isn't going to say jack to me — '"

"I'm going," Reese said.

"So go," said Kilgore. "I still get my hundred and twenty bucks."

Reese got up. His face was itching, crawling with ants. Air. He needed some air. Then he whirled around. "You know exactly who it is," Reese told him then, his voice snake-flat, the voice he knew scared the hell even out of the two Renaldo brothers, the twins who were juniors and had necks the size of Reese's waist. The voice Reese didn't even know where it came from, that sounded like some freaking Damien voice, even to him.

"Okay. Who is it? If you don't mind my asking."

"It's my brother."

"Oh. Your brother. Which brother?"

"Fuck you," said Reese. "Fuck you sincerely."

"Thank you very much, I'm sure. Which brother?"

"I only got one brother. Which is to say I have no brother. It's Ben. It's Ben."

"And what's he doing? Come on, Reese, what's he doing?"

"He's walking out the door."

"Where?"

Reese thought he might puke. His throat tasted like acute Slim Jim poisoning. He thought he didn't dare open his mouth. But he made it split, pried it like a hinge, and moved his tongue. Finally, he fetched a voice. "He's walking out the door of the hotel."

"Did you see him, Reese?"

Reese shouted, "I don't know! I don't know! I'm running, and I'm running. But I can't move . . . "

"Did you move, Reese, in real life?"

"I don't know! I was just a kid . . . "

"Look at him, Reese. Look at Ben."

"I can't even see him; his back is to me. And so is hers . . . "

"Hers? Your mother?"

"No . . . No." Reese struggled to breathe.

"Ellen? Your aunt Ellen?"

"No. No. The little old lady. The little skinny old lady."

"What's she doing?"

"She's walking behind Ben. She's following Ben. She's . . . opening the door for him."

"Reese," said Tom, gently, so soft, sitting down next to him on the edge of the sofa. "Do you think this really happened? Or is this part of the dream?"

"I think it's part of the dream," said Reese, "because it really happened." And in a moment he would remember with hot shame for years, even after it all came down, he reached out and took Tom's hand. And Tom, thank God, acted like he didn't even notice.

Part Two

19

Beth

May 1994

KERRY was screaming with such ear-splitting might that Beth barely heard the doorbell.

"Stop, Kerry!" she ordered, in the military voice she hardly ever used anymore.

But once Kerry stopped, Beth wanted to join her in a few righteous screams herself. The bell was ringing with the kind of persistence that told Beth she would not be able to pretend not to be home — it was ringing, in fact, as if someone outside were on fire.

"Wait!" she yelled. "Coming!" The bell fell silent. Then it rang again.

If she let go now, Beth could kiss all hope of untangling Kerry's hair goodbye; the child would not let her mother come near her again with a brush in hand for three days, minimum. But because Beth so rarely remembered to brush Kerry's fine reddish-blond hair — which Ellen insisted was an inheritance from her godmother — it was a welter of rats and snarls under a soft veneer. Kerry simply ran a wet brush over the top every morning before school. To Kerry, smooth on top was combed, just as under-the-bed was clean. "My teacher thinks my hair has

329

a lot of natural body, Mama," she told Beth. "She says it's like Rapunzel."

Christ, Beth thought, the teacher's a twit and she must think I clean toilets at a trailer park. "That was nice of her," she'd told Kerry. "But she really thinks that because your hair is so full of tangles it sticks out from your head three inches. If you don't brush it, Kerry, it's going to break off and you'll have little cowlicks all over. Real ugly." Beth had risen this morning with a small, unexpended premium of energy; she had learned to make use of these, because she knew the drill of her ordinary days — all the other days she had nothing but minimum motion to give. She intended to buy Vincent some cleats today as well. But first she wanted to set Kerry to rights.

"I do brush it. Every day," Kerry told Beth, her voice skating along the midline edge of whining and aggression. "It looks good."

"But once in a while *I* have to," Beth answered. And everything that came next was choreographed. All Beth had to do was wave the brush in any of the air space around Kerry's skull and Kerry, the most docile of children, would transform herself into a rabid wolverine, kicking and squirming and letting out yowls that made Beth want to bite her.

Distracted by the thought of some Jehovah's Witness standing on the porch, his eyes raised in a prayer for strength to minister to the occupants of a house from which such screams issued, Beth attacked one more particularly horrific clump. As she did, the hairbrush snapped, and Kerry tore off, out the door of Beth's bedroom and down the hall stairs for the front door, while Beth slowly picked up the shards of shattered plastic, and then followed her daughter, swearing softly.

"Are you in sixth?" she heard Kerry say as she rounded the last curve of the staircase. The door swung half-open between Kerry and the visitor.

" . . . in third? Were you the soybean?" She heard a child's voice, older, ungendered, say.

"Actually," said Kerry, "I was the feed corn." The spring festival, thought Beth. Had Pat gone?

"Who do you have?" the voice asked.

"Cook," said Kerry.

"I had Cook!" said the voice. "She's really nice!"

Beth jumped down the last two steps and put her arm around Kerry.

The bright noon sunlight, after the dark upstairs hall, had the effect of backlighting with a hard spot; Beth held up her hand to shield her eyes, but the kid was still a shape cut of black paper, a sun-shot halo around his head. He was big, though, big and heavyset, she thought, for a sixth-grader, but then Vincent was so small. She bumped her hip against the screen door to open it.

Years before, Ellen's mother had suffered a petit stroke. And long after, she would tell Beth it was possible for such brain events to happen in an instant, the time it took to speak a word; you could have them in your sleep and wake with nothing more than the sensation of having weathered a headache. But though the cadenza of sound Beth heard was as loud as a ripsaw and sent her staggering against the opening door, she did not lose an instant of consciousness. And she realized just as quickly that though the noise filled the street, the world, no one else could hear it. She reached up for her temple; the sound pounded, but now with a transparent quality; she could hear everything around it; the wind in the maples like water rushing from a pipe, crows clucking at each other like castanets. Bile sloshed over her tongue. But she gripped both sides of the door frame and bent nearly double, trying to measure her breathing and muster enough oxygen to fight the gathering pitchy dots that licked at the space in front of her eyes.

"Are you all right?" said the kid, backing off.

"Mommy!" cried Kerry in a tinny voice.

"I'm . . . all . . . right," Beth gasped.

"Mommy, are you going to puke? Should I get Georgia?"

The kid was backing down the three front steps. With real fear in his voice, he told Beth, "I mow lawns. I was just dropping off this thing with my phone number. I can do it later. I'll come back."

But Beth was now getting breaths she believed were restorative. How much time had passed? A minute? Ten? She couldn't stand upright, but she waved her hand at the kid, and at Kerry, in a gesture she meant to mean, No problem, right with ya. She did not want to terrify him. She tried to think of a plan, pitchforking options aside like sodden leaves. "Actually, I really need the lawn mowed," she said. "Could you do it today?"

The kid was astounded. "All right, sure! I just have to get . . . get my stuff. We live, like, two blocks."

"You don't need a mower. We have a mower," said Kerry helpfully. "And my big brother is supposed to do it. He's in high school. But he's lazy like a snake." The boy was already running down the walk, in high gear. Beth grabbed Kerry's arm, too roughly.

"Mommy, are you still sick?" Kerry said, looking up.

"No, I just . . . Do you know that boy?"

Kerry blushed; her skin was a video of emotional responses. Pat called her 'the Visible Woman'.

"Mom," she said seriously. "I was in my own house. That's not the same as stranger danger. He's a big kid in school."

"Oh," said Beth, her heart now beginning to slow. Okay, she said to herself, okay, okay. "What's his name?"

"Jason," said Kerry. "He's on patrol . . . No, Mom, no, I'm wrong. Jason is the kid with the Gameboy, and you know, Mom, he got reported, because he was standing there playing Mortal Kombat when he was supposed to be watching the little kids go — "

"So you don't know his name?"

"It's Sam. He's Sam Kero — Kero-something."

Kerry followed Beth through the back of the house. Beth ran for the basement stairs, shoving their sleeping dog, Beowulf, aside with one foot; he coughed irritably and moved into the family room. Down into the basement, throwing open the door of the darkroom, fumbling for the light switch — the bulb was out, she knew that, had meant to replace it, the safe light would have to do. Searching in the eerie redness for her biggest bag, Beth pulled out her work camera, her Nikon F-90, brand-new, and rummaged in the mini-fridge for film. She thought as she pulled out the film carton and ripped it open with shaking fingers, 200 should be okay, and the color is absolutely essential, and the yard has patches of light; it's only dark under the trees.

"Are you going to work, Mommy?" asked Kerry.

"Kerry!" Beth shouted. Her daughter jumped. "Kerry — yes, you know what? I forgot I have to take some leaf pictures. So, it's okay if you want to go play with Blythe, okay? Go ahead."

Beth snapped open the camera back and pulled the film leader, fitting it to the sprockets. She slapped the back closed and heard the whirr of the automatic winding. Her hands were slick with sweat. Line up, she thought, line up. I will use a telephoto; and I will switch to manual focus. So I can control . . . Kerry, as if from very far away, over mountains, was calling her. Kerry stood at the top of the basement steps.

"My hair is still a mess," she said, bored. "And you always say you have to watch me cross at rush hour."

Beth bounded up the stairs, cradling her camera against her breasts; sweat pasted her T-shirt to her sternum. "Just put your band on, okay, Kerry?" Kerry languidly pawed through her backpack, which lay on the hall floor, and found her rubberized band with glitter ladybugs on it. She wound her hair into an askew ponytail while Beth watched her, panting, with a hunger for her to be gone that Beth later realized must have horrified Kerry.

Georgia was pulling heads off her geraniums across the street. She waved to Beth, breezily, and pointed with exaggerated welcome to the door of her own house; that meant, Beth thought (line up, line up), that Blythe was home; Kerry could play. Line up, Beth thought, and made her own large gesture, pointing to her camera. Georgia made a big okay sign. They traded daughters back and forth all week.

Her fingers now actually slimy on the camera's surface, Beth slowly closed the door behind her. She let her eyes skim the line of family Christmas photos that marched along the walls, level with her chin. She leaned against the door. And then she was up, running for the second floor, pawing through Pat's drawers where he kept his cartons, hidden from her since his surgery, under his baseball programs and the collection of crayon drawings Vincent had once made, and the large paper cap he kept in a flat box, which he had worn during Kerry's Cesarean birth. Beth ripped the top of a package of Merits — tearing off not just the foil but an inch of the pack, so that the cigarettes tumbled and scattered on the carpet.

335

She pulled open the closet and stuck her free hand deep into one of Pat's coat pockets. He had matches. He always had matches, though he refused either to lie to her or admit he still smoked outside the house.

Beth lit the cigarette, pulling in deeply, unaccustomed, choking. And then she walked into Kerry's room and out onto the little porch that overlooked the backyard. She sat down against the wall, nudging aside the hell of Barbies that Kerry customarily left lying outside in desolate nudity under the dusting of September leaves.

She smoked.

The sweat dried on her shirt, stiffened. The sun burned on her face, but her body was icy, trembling. Adrenaline made her fingers needle and itch. She set the camera down gingerly, afraid she would drop it.

She heard the kid open the back gate. That was all right. She could tell him that the mower was . . . but then, no, she saw him trundling it around the side of the house, he'd already found it. He waved to her, looking straight up at her with round gray eyes, eyes that still looked almost lashless. Shielding the camera with her arms like a secret, Beth stood up and yelled to the kid, "I'm taking some pictures of the leaves. It's my job. I take pictures."

He nodded and leaned over, expertly starting the balky Toro on the first tug. And then he squared his shoulders and began to move, cleanly, starting from the back and making lines the length of the yard.

Beth leaned on the railing to steady her elbows and adjusted the zoom. No time for a tripod. She shot his face in profile as he moved out from the shade of the willow and worked his way past the swing set. When he rounded the patio, she shot him full on, as he lifted his head to wipe a sheen of sweat off with the arm of his flannel shirt. Letting the automatic advance roll, Beth shot at the rate of an exposure every few seconds. And in minutes, long before the kid had finished half of the backyard, she had shot the whole roll of thirty-six. She ran downstairs and searched for her dark bag. She couldn't find it. Line up, Beth thought, line up. You can do this. You've changed film by touch alone in a dozen dark places. She flipped off the lights, closed the door, and reached for her spool, winding the film to dry it.

And then she kneeled on the floor in the red light, her head pressed against the front of her handmade sink, which Vincent had painted with black marine paint, and said, "Domine Deus, Agnus Dei, Filius Patris; qui tollis peccata mundi, miserere nobis . . . miserere nobis." She heard Vincent open the door upstairs, heard it swing back and crash against the wall.

"Vincent," she whispered, imagining herself summoning him to find her purse, give the kid ten bucks. But her voice was less than a whisper. She dragged herself to her feet and went up the stairs on all fours. The yard was silent. Beth panicked, jerking open the front door.

He was gone, but there — a note. The kid had left a note, saying the mower had run out of gas. He would come back tomorrow. She ran to the garage. He had stowed the lawn mower neatly in the garage, in the space between the bikes.

Beth walked wearily up the stairs. Fifteen minutes more and she could print. "Vincent," she said, outside his door. She could feel the music from his boom box with her feet, throbbing. "Vincent." She tried to turn the knob. The door was locked. She tapped. No reply. The music wailed and thumped.

Beth stood back against the opposite wall, raised both feet, and kicked the door with all her force. The music collapsed into silence. Vincent opened the door. Beth saw, but did not analyze, the way his eyes streamed. He was crying.

"I want you to go downstairs and order a pizza," she told him. "I want you to do that first. Then, I want you to go get Kerry at Blythe's and put a tape on for her. Take the money for the pizza out of my purse." Vincent nodded dumbly. "I have to do some work in the darkroom, right now, and I have to do it all at once. So I want you to give Kerry some pizza, okay? Will you do that?"

He nodded again, furtively scrubbing at his eyes with the back of his hands. Then he slouched toward the stairs.

"Vincent," Beth said sharply. "Did you see the boy who was mowing the lawn?"

"*What* boy?" He scowled.

Checking her watch, Beth clattered down the stairs to the darkroom. Line up, she thought. They're only pictures. You make pictures twice a week. She made the motions mechanical, deciding to print each shot separately, eight by ten, though it would take forever. A contact sheet would be too small, too torturous. Enlarger. Stop bath. Fixer. Take your time.

She leaned over the bath. A drop of sweat fell from her chin, plinked on the mirror of the surface, and bloomed like the shape of an atom, widening, shimmying, finally disappearing.

And then, the edges of a face, growing more distinct, looking up at her, reaching up to her from darkness.

20

BETH left the prints strung on the line with clips.

Even from the open door of her darkroom, a distance of no more than four feet, many of them looked like copies, or a sequence in which the shutter had opened and closed, opened and closed, on the same subject in the same position. But when you came closer, you could see that each of the angles was subtly different, each a discrete variation of the boy's fair face with its sharp chin and raccoon's mask of light freckles beneath the eyes. Others, a few, captured his whole body. His legs were long — most of his length was right there — but grooved with the kind of effortless musculature he would have all his life.

The kind he had, indeed, had all his life.

By the time she came upstairs, Vincent was back in his room, and Kerry, red-eyed, has just completed her second straight hour of cartoon gluttony.

Beth flicked off the set, and Kerry prepared to launch herself into her bedtime routine.

But Beth caught her and pulled Kerry gently down with her on the deeply sunken end of the much-used pillow sofa. She held Kerry wordlessly, stroking the child's feathery globe of cheek with her own, rougher skin, and finally rocking her with a motion so small and slight it could have fooled a passing glance into calling it stillness. Kerry didn't object, but Beth could feel her arranging herself carefully on the brace of her mother's arms — Beth's hugs were not usually so indulgent.

But no matter what else happened during the rest of this day, what Beth had already seen gave her, for the first time in nine years, sufficient courage to let herself experience the yielding body of her youngest child. Kerry's fingers were spangled with marker dots; she smelled of fruit and dish soap, and something warmer beneath — down, innocence. Beth looked up over Kerry's tangled hair at the crest of the avalanche, the mountain of memory and half-memory, of rerun, regret, poignancy, and outrage, poised to hurtle down and paralyze her.

Nothing moved. Not a grumble. Not a single cold stone dislodged.

Beth led Kerry up to her room and listened while Kerry read from *Little House on the Prairie*. She was not a gifted reader, but she was a dogged plodder; her determination blazed from her like a scent. "I'm getting better every day, and I am nine now. Eighteen kids in class are still eight," sighed Kerry, and Beth wondered where Kerry found a child's confidence from the scraps of attention she had been fed while growing up.

"Night-night," Beth told Kerry, switching off the overhead light.

"You're not sick anymore, are you, Mommy?" Kerry asked.

"No, I'm peachy keen, peachy," Beth said.

She passed by Vincent's door and tapped it. "'Night," she called. "Thanks for watching Kerry." There was no answer but a vague growl under the pulse of the music; it was classical now — Perlman playing Mozart. Beth didn't try the door. She knew it would be locked.

She glanced at the clock. It was after nine. Pat would be home in an hour.

Ordinarily, Beth devoted this last hour of the day, the last interval before she could take refuge in a cold glass of water and three Trazodone, with reading English novels. The English didn't seem to have many children or care much about them when they did. What roused the English breast was a good water spaniel, a gentleman with a stick who'd come back from India to rejoin his ruddy-cheeked wife called Bea who gardened. The best books for Beth were those in which one day varied from the day before only in the variety of sandwiches at tea, in which vicars called on the sick, in which people went out for a drive to look at old button sets or used volumes of Thackeray.

But tonight, she could not release herself into a village just off the Montford road or a shop in Hastings Crossing.

She sat in the living room, the taste of cigarettes (she'd smoked three) acrid in her mouth. Pat was late. Then he came through the door humming, carrying an old double-sided cardboard that advertised the winter specials at Wedding in the Old Neighborhood. It would soon be time to put up a summer board, and Kerry liked to draw on the used ones.

Beth heard him put down his keys and turn on the kettle for his nightly cup of tea. She felt him check once, around the dark first floor, to see if he dared open a window and have a smoke before bed.

She said then, "Pat."

He jumped. "Bethie!" he said. "What are you doing up?"

Beth walked into the yellow glare of the kitchen and put her arms around Pat. Gratefully he rubbed her back. "What's up? Is Kerry sick?"

"No," she said, wanting to draw out this last stable moment, the last moment of snow bridge she had built and packed hard, so that it felt almost like concrete, you could walk on it. Their fragile suppositions were an ache, but at least they were used to them. Now, what would happen? What would give way?

Beth said, "I have to show you something."

Pat took off his sport coat and followed her down the stairs. Beth remembered the spent light. "Paddy," she said, "Get a light bulb for me, okay?" He turned and left the room. Beth could see the pictures in the faint wash of light from the upstairs hall — his hair now darker, almost maroon in the sun. He would call it brown, she supposed.

This boy.

Sam.

Pat came back with the light bulb and snatched out the old one, tossed it in Beth's huge rubber trash can. Replaced it in the dark. The light flickered, then shone steadily. Pat looked at the pictures. He stepped forward and tore one down, then two.

He said, "Beth."

She said, "It is, isn't it?"

They sat down side by side on the bench that ran along one wall in Beth's darkroom. Pat pulled down another fistful of pictures. They moved into her office. Beth sat at the desk, Pat on the overstuffed chair.

"Is this possible?" he said, his voice strangled in a way that made Beth wonder if he should have a tranquilizer or a nitroglycerin. She could almost feel the flutter of his toiling heart.

"He came to the door," Beth told Pat softly. "To mow lawns. I let him mow the lawn. He's coming back tomorrow. Because we ran out of gas for the mower."

Tears filled Pat's eyes and streamed down his jaw, dripping onto the front of his shirt. In every other respect except the tears, he did not seem to be crying; his breath was measured, even.

"Where does this boy live?"

"Two blocks, he said."

"Two blocks?" Pat cried. "Two blocks? Did they just move here?"

"Pat. I don't know how long they've lived here. But Kerry knew him, and she's been in school at Sandburg four years."

"Did she . . . ?"

"No, Pat, for God's sake. I would have never known unless . . . well, maybe I would have. But he looked just like the aging projection Morris made. And I shot in color so that we could see . . . His hair is so dark . . . It's possible, Pat, that it's just a kid who looks that way."

"Yeah," he breathed.

"And I wanted to show you, to ask you, before we called Candy or . . . or anyone."

"Let's call them now," said Pat. "Let's get up there and call, and get down to that house."

"No," Beth said. "It's late night, Pat. He's asleep. And we don't even know his last name."

"His last name? Christ, Beth, his last name?" He yanked off his tie, fumbled at his shirt pocket for the place he once kept his cigarettes, before the surgery, before he began hiding them from Beth. "But what if they're . . . doing things to him right now?"

"He didn't look or talk like an abused kid, Pat. And if he is, Pat, it's been nine years . . ."

"Oh, Bethie — oh, Bethie — two blocks. When he saw you, did he . . . ?"

"Nothing, Pat. Nothing. He had no idea. Pat, he was three."

"And he wouldn't know this house."

"No."

"Maybe he'd know me."

Beth felt a sudden, powerful splash of rage rise; she wanted to slap Pat hard, in the face. But she breathed in and out, slowly, taking her time.

Pat said, "I gotta have a cigarette, Bethie. I'm sorry." He grabbed a sheaf of the photos.

They sat on the porch, with the lights off. The sweat from Pat's hands had already smudged the prints.

"Two blocks," Pat said. "Two blocks. I never saw him."

345

"You're never around. And I never go anywhere walking. Just school. The drugstore. There are probably fifty kids in this neighborhood I've never seen in four years living here."

Beth leaned against her husband. Be a rock for me now, Patrick, she thought. I don't even want to see tomorrow, because even if it is Ben, we might have to know things that could bury us. Looked back upon, her nine years of quiet avoidance seemed . . . almost peaceful. Not like this clammy present fear.

But she felt Pat's fragility through his wet shirt, felt the slender rasp of his damaged breaths as he smoked.

Okay, Candy, she thought. Be my rock Candy.

"I think we should call Bliss now. Or Bender. Or Jimmy."

"Not tonight, Pat."

"Beth," he told her with desperate urgency. "What if he's not there tomorrow? What if whoever . . . And why would they still be here? What if they take him and get out of Dodge?"

"They live here."

"*They* live here?"

"He's not going anywhere, Pat. Like he told Kerry, he's in sixth."

And then, possessed with a lust to touch him, to praise his body for planting the seed in her that became Ben, for not dying yet, Beth took the prints from Pat's hands and kissed him, releasing her tongue deep into his mouth. He responded weakly, softly cupping one of her breasts, exploring the nipple with hands that

346

barely seemed robust enough to grasp. Beth pulled her shirt over her head and tossed it onto the porch. She unbuckled Pat's belt and lay back, wiggling out of her tattered jeans, centering him over her, drawing him inside her. She rocked to start him. "Please, Pat," she whispered. "It won't hurt anything." And finally Pat took hold, and gripped her arms and plunged into her hard on the hard step, hurting her, making her feel sore and open and new. In a minute he said, "Shouldn't we get . . . ?"

"I'm not going to get pregnant, Pat," she said. "Forget that. Just go ahead, go ahead, go ahead . . . "

Pat buried his tear-wet face against her breast and finished, in a shudder that came up his throat like a groan.

Just then they heard a voice, a neighbor calling in his cat. They lay still in the dark, cold as sculpture, as Beth felt Pat subside and shrink within her, and her own muscles contract, contract and relax.

"I'm going to call Dad," Pat said, when they heard the neighbor's door snap shut.

"Don't tell him. Not until we know."

"I won't. I just . . . I don't want to work tomorrow."

"Right."

Pat got up and arranged his clothing, using his thumbs to straighten his shirt collar as if he were headed for the bank, or for work. He buckled his belt carefully and put the change that had scattered on the porch back in his pockets. Last, he picked up the prints and held them to his chest. "I'm going in," he said.

Beth didn't answer. She drew on her jeans, retrieved her shirt, and lay curled with her hips on the mat, the pebbled cement under her pillowed arms, and strained to see the streetlight beyond the streetlight at their corner — the one two blocks down. She pretended that she knew she was looking at the right one. Call it the intersection of Menard and Downer, she thought. And she began to watch. I will have to make coffee, she thought, so I can be sure to watch until morning. And then she thought, No, I don't need coffee. The cold will keep me awake.

She drew up her legs and wrapped her arms around her knees, scanning her mind like a cookbook for a lovely antiseptic thought. Paint colors, tulip bulbs, low-cholesterol chicken Tetrazzini, tables of contents . . . yes. She would index the book of Sister Kathleen Noonan's oils for the exhibit catalog.

Page one, she thought, the bell at the Franciscan House in Saint Francis.

Page two, the doors of the Baptistery in Florence.

Page three, three angels above the door frame at a tea shop in the East Village in New York City.

Beth stared at the orb of radiant light, two blocks away.

348

21

THERE was no interval at all that Beth could later recognize as a period of sleep. She was awake, and looking at the light, her forearms prickled with the cold fall air, her eyes burning; and then she was awake, looking for the light, which was off.

It was morning. She scanned the street quickly for evidence of cars backing out of driveways to be at work by eight. There were none. It was early morning, before seven.

Beth rose and felt the cold wetness in the crotch of her jeans, looked up at her bedroom window, which faced the street. Was Pat awake?

Line up, thought Beth. I will wake Kerry; I will wake Vincent. I will measure coffee and put it in the drip. Then I will call Candy. While it's quiet, I'll call her. She pushed open the screen door, the moment when she could call Candy fluttering ahead of her like the tail of a kite.

Pat was at the table, reading to Kerry from the back of the Cheerios box. Vincent was eating toast, standing with his back to Beth. The lines in Pat's face looked carved in wax; he was ghastly, pouches larger than Angelo's, reddened bruises beneath his eyes.

"Kerry's having breakfast," he told Beth.

"I see, I see," Beth replied, catching a glimpse of her own stained and rumpled self in the bathroom mirror.

349

"What were you doing on the porch, Mommy?" asked Kerry.

"Watching the sun come up," said Beth, and then asked her son, "Vincent, do you need a ride?"

"Jordie's dad," he said quietly.

"Okay, that's good, that's fine." Beth walked into the kitchen and began to measure coffee into a filter. But Pat had already made coffee. Lots of coffee. She dumped the fresh grounds into the sink. She heard Pat tell Kerry to *mangia, mangia,* soon it would be time to walk to school.

"I'm going to ride my bike," Kerry told him. "I'm nine now. I'm older than eighteen of the kids in third."

"You can't ride your bike," Pat told her gently. "Kids in walking distance can't ride their bikes. And you don't have a bike lock."

"Will you get me a bike lock just in case, Daddy?"

"Yes, I will."

"Today."

"Yeah, sure," said Pat. "I'll get it right after you go to school, and you can put it on when you get home."

Beth listened, amazed. By the time Kerry got home from school, who among the people around this table — whatever happened, whatever the magnitude — would be able to think of bike locks and chains and combinations? Pat, she realized. Pat would. Pat would do it, beforehand, in penance, in petition. And so she wasn't surprised when he followed Kerry out the

350

door, kissing the child lightly and calling her "Chicòria," the name in Italian for a wildflower, Beth heard him start the car, heard him pull away . . .

Line up, she thought. Line up. Now what? She poured her coffee, raising it recklessly to her lips, burning the soft skin so badly that she felt a welt rise. Vincent was leaving. She caught up with him at the door and, suddenly, fearfully, laid her head against his shoulder, which was exactly at the level of her own shoulder. He stopped, shrugging his knapsack onto the other shoulder, looking out into the street with forceful intensity.

"Goodbye, Mom," he said, not looking. She saw his jaw jump and writhe, as though the muscles were being stimulated by jolts.

"Vincent," said Beth. "Wait." She needed urgently to tell him. She had to tell him, but what could she say?

'It's possible that a kid two blocks away is your brother, that Ben isn't dead anymore'? 'And we still don't know anything more about the way we lost him than we did that day you lay on the luggage trolley at the Tremont and slept with Ben's blanket across your chest'?

She said instead, "Vincent. I love you. I want you to know I love you."

He said, "Right. Thanks." Not a trace of surprise. He still didn't look at her.

Beth said, "Have a good time today."

"You too," he said.

Beth heard the crunch of gravel as Jordie's dad wheeled his immense cherry-colored Chevy van

351

into the apron of their drive. As the door closed behind Vincent, Beth saw something lying on the chair where he had stood, eating his toast. Half the chewed bit still lay on the edge of the table, next to Kerry's empty cereal bowl. There was a slip, no, a sheet of paper, in the chair. She picked it up.

It was one of the full-face shots of the boy mowing the lawn. It was not one that Beth had given Pat. This shot had been strung on the line last night. It was one of the best. Beth had meant to give it to Candy.

Beth ran to the door and yanked it open. The van was just turning the corner, lights winking. Still, she yelled, "Vincent, wait!" The brake lights seemed to come on for an instant, but then the van kept going. "No!" Beth cried. Fool. She should have kept him home. He was not a child of seven anymore. To send him off to school today was a mortal insult.

But it was past eight. She picked up the telephone and looked at it. She called Candy at home.

"Girlfriend!" Candy cried happily. "I'm running more than one thousand percent late. Can you eat lunch one of the weekdays?"

"Candy," Beth said. "There's something I need to tell you."

"What's wrong, Beth?" said Candy, instantly tensing. "Is Pat sick?"

"Candy, listen." She paused for breath. "I think I found Ben."

Because Beth had seen her do it so often, she could now watch the silence on the other end

of the line as if it were film, watch Candy Bliss
let her gargantuan bag slide down her arm like
a weary cat, see her raise one perfect finger to
the place just between her eyes and press, press,
press hard.

"Beth, do you mean that you got a letter or
a phone call?"

"I saw him, Candy. He came to my door."

"He came . . . he came to your door? Here?
He found you here? Ben would be . . . what
. . . he'd be twelve, Beth. You're saying he came
home?"

"No. He didn't know me. He lives here. They
. . . whoever it is that took him, lives in this
neighborhood, I guess."

"That's impossible."

"Well, he's here. Except I don't know it's
him. For sure."

"You do know."

"I don't know. He looks like the age
projection. His eyes were always a weird shade
of gray, without any blue, and they still are.
The shape of his lips and eyes — yes, I would
say with ninety-percent certainty that this is my
son. He has two cowlicks."

"The birthmark?"

"I didn't pull his pants down, Candy." As
she said it, a revulsive thing squirmed under her
heart. Who had . . . who had? Which scenario
was it? Come on, Mrs. Cappadora, choose door
one, two, or three? The con artist, the yearner,
the molester?

Was this *Ben*?

Nine years had telescoped into a day and a

353

night and a day. Was it over?

"I'll be right there," Candy was telling her.

Because it was one of her arts, Beth knew precisely how long it would take for Candy to drive from her own apartment to Beth's house, depending on the time of day. She glanced at the clock. She had twenty-five minutes.

Running upstairs, she stripped off her gummy jeans and shirt, which still stank of developing chemicals. She showered and carefully pulled on middle-level work clothes — cotton trousers, a tunic. She dried her hair instead of merely combing it with her fingers. She put on mascara. She sat down on the bed and forcibly tried to still herself. Dead legs, limp arms, hands that felt animate only around the edges of a camera, dead stomach that had learned to receive food as matter-of-factly as a supermarket scanner, dead heart with its battened receptors, all surged and tingled.

Could he be her Ben — her freckled babe, her rain-eyed darling, folded so long in death, silent as his baptismal gown lying in the cedar chest — come miraculously alive?

It was stupefying. Wonderful beyond imagining. It was terrifying.

And then, Beth thought, oh, God, my God, I will be able to touch Ben's hair. If she could do that, she would not care if her hand was then set on fire.

The doorbell rang; but before Beth could answer it, Candy walked in and took Beth into her arms without greeting. They stood in the fractured sunlight of the lower hall, where

354

Pat found them when he came home, dutifully carrying Kerry's bike lock and chain.

"Are you scared to death?" Candy asked.

"To death, to death," Beth told her.

"Scared?" asked Pat. "Scared of what? Let's go. I can't wait, Candy — we have to go there, right now."

"Go where?" Beth asked him irritably. "We don't know what house he's in, or if he's really in a house two blocks away. And anyway, he'd be in school."

"It's the short day," said Pat. School ended at 1:30 p.m. on Mondays.

All three of them looked at their watches. It was just after nine. Candy silently picked up the print Vincent had left behind and studied it, as Pat shifted the bike chain and lock from hand to hand.

"He said he'd come back," Beth said. "To finish the lawn. He ran out of gas."

"I didn't get gas!" Pat nearly screamed.

"He's not really going to mow the lawn, Pat," Beth told him, nearly laughing before she could stop herself.

"Of course, no one thinks we're going to sit here and wait for this kid to remember to show up and mow the lawn," Candy said softly. "You're just not thinking clearly. I can't imagine how you would. Or how I will. But I'm going to try, and the first thing we have to is — Beth, you said he goes to Kerry's school?"

"She says he's in sixth. At Sandburg."

"And they're two separate buildings, the elementary and the middle."

"Yep. Connected. There's one gym and all."

"Okay, so that's where we'll start. I'll call . . . well, I guess I'll call Jimmy Daugherty, though strictly speaking, this isn't what he does anymore, but I know how much he'll want to be involved if . . . if this is it. And we'll go down there and find out the kid's name and the identity of whoever's listed as his parent or guardian." She got up, pouring herself coffee no one had thought to offer her, and went on, as if dictating a list to an assistant. "Might need a subpoena. If the school isn't sufficiently impressed with the necessity of cooperating with the release of this information. Not a problem. Harry Brainard will help . . . "

Beth looked at Pat. "Circuit court judge," she said.

"But if we start with school pictures, yearbooks, this shouldn't be too much trouble. I would want to cooperate with helping solve one of the most intractable missing-persons cases in recent history, wouldn't you?" Candy tapped her teeth with her nail. "But first, I need to see the rest of the pictures."

Beth said, "On the hall table."

"Did Reese see them?" Candy asked rummaging in her bag for paper and a pen.

"I think he did," Beth told her. "One, at least." Pat looked up horrified.

"You showed Vincent?"

"I didn't show him. He looked."

Candy asked, "Can I see them now?"

Beth laid them all out, except the one Candy still held, end to end on the kitchen table,

356

in lines like the child's game called Memory. Candy put her glasses on and stood over them. As Beth watched her concentration, she realized Candy was crying — prettily, quietly, without either pretense or fuss, the way Candy did everything. "I'm sorry," she told Beth.

Beth said, "I can make more."

"This face . . . this face." And Beth thought of the side-by-side photos of Ben that Candy kept above her desk, tacked to her bulletin board, not dogeared, not wrinkled, carefully smoothed. All of them: his baseball-mitt picture; the first Missing poster; the second; the computer projection of Ben's face at six, at eight. "This face. When I went . . . Philadelphia, Santa Fe, Jersey. The child in Palo Alto. The little Grainger boy in Michigan. And then afterward, when we all presumed, even I presumed, that he had died, wherever I went — conferences, vacations, to see my mother in Tampa — I carried those copies. I still have them." She extracted a manila envelope from her purse and spilled the contents on the table. "And I realized, after the first few years, that I could no more stop looking for that face than I could stop breathing in and breathing out. It was like the fantasy of the perfect lover. 'Be there, Ben,' I would say. 'In this park. At this fair. Let me see you on the street. Let me bring you home to Beth.'"

Candy scrubbed at her eyes with the back of her hand. "And then there'd come a time, when I knew it was only a day or a few hours before I would have to leave, and I'd call and say I was in town. 'There was this kid . . . Right, you remember, the Cappadora kid . . . ' And I would ask about their unidentifieds. Their Baby Does. Autopsy pictures and graves. Potter's fields and beautiful plots. Wanting and hoping it would be Ben. Terrified it would be Ben. But mostly hoping. That Ben would be found. Done. Even if I had to tell you he was dead, that he'd been dead for years."

She reached out for Pat's hand. "I wanted to see this face. I wanted to have Ben back. For you. And me."

Then, shaking herself visibly, she stood up to find the phone. "I'm going to call my lieutenant and the chief and tell them, and we'll get things started."

"What should *we* do?" Pat asked. "Should we go down to the school?"

Candy paused. "Paddy, until we can ID this kid — I mean, prove for absolutely one-hundred-percent-beyond-the-remotest-shadow-of-a-doubt that this is Ben — you can't start calling the shots. And right now, this kid is the legal responsibility of whomever we learn are his parents . . . "

"His parents?" Pat cried.

"I mean, until we're sure it's Ben, we can't just go and grab some kid who might have gotten that red hair from his uncle Harold and take him to Wedding in the Old Neighborhood for braciole."

"So how are we going to find out for sure?"

"The whole routine. Blood tests. Identifying marks. The fingerprints, of course, of course. Dental charts . . . "

"He was three, Candy. He didn't have charts," Beth said. "We went through all that a million times when it happened. You remember."

"Well, right. I'm not all there. Could you folks excuse me for a few moments?"

'You folks'? It shocked Beth.

Wasn't Candy family? Or nearly? Hadn't she shared nights of too many beers, picnics in a humid field, Candy and Chris's second anniversary at Wedding in the Old Neighborhood, a barbecue at Rosie's, Candy taking Kerry horseback riding for the first time — all of these had telescoped on a dime, as had the span of Ben's absence. It was the day after the night of the day.

Candy was still a detective. They were civilians.

"Now I'm going to go down to the school with — " Candy scanned the table — "with this picture. And the others, of course. You guys stay here and listen for the phone. Jimmy will be calling as soon as they can find him. He knows to come here first. Sit tight now. Sit tight." She left, trailing her bag.

Beth left Pat in the kitchen and went upstairs, where she lay down on her neatly made bed. A few moments later, Pat came up and lay beside her. They did not speak or touch. The telephone startled both of them, but neither reached to pick it up. When the answering machine clicked on, they could hear Jimmy shouting, "Jesus Christ, Bethie! We're going crazy over here. Bethie? Pat? Are you there? Well, I don't know if you're there or not, but I'm on my way." He seemed to speak

359

for a moment to someone else: "I know. Can you believe this shit?" And then, "I'm on my way. Hang in there, Beth, Pat, Vincent."

How long they lay there, Beth would not later remember. Perhaps only minutes. Then the front door opened and closed, and she heard Candy pick up the kitchen phone. Beth raised herself and rolled off the bed; Pat had fallen, with automatic grace, asleep. She sat on the bottom step until Candy saw her. "They want a fucking subpoena," she said. "I'm on hold for Brainard." Beth said nothing

When Candy finally finished, she turned back to Beth and said tersely, "I have no patience for this. I'm sweating like a pig. They did let me look at the yearbooks. He's been there since kindergarten. His name is Sam Karras. We couldn't get the parents' names, but Beth . . . " Candy came and sat beside her on the step. "He's an only child."

22

AT Parkside, the longtime chief's last name was Bastokovitch. Over the years, Candy had often told Pat and Beth, the troops had created a whole dictionary of obscenities based on it. But Beth had never met him before his unmarked slid up the driveway next to Candy's.

He'd come, Candy warned, to counsel caution. "There was a belief," she said, flicking back the curtain and watching the big man's slow progress up the drive, "that if he ever got up, he'd learn his butt had got stuck to the chair. This is evidently a fallacy." She opened the door.

"Chief."

"Detective." Then, "Candace."

"I'm glad you came. It's time to proceed. I know you agree."

"Bliss, the kid is in protective custody; he's not going anywhere," Bastokovitch said softly, accepting Beth's offer of coffee with a sad smile.

"But that construction van is in the driveway, Ed," Candy pleaded. "That probably means the parents — forgive me, Pat — the suspects are there. You know me, Ed. I don't arrest first and talk later. But who can figure what the goddamn principal has done already? Called them? You have to know he's called them. They could be getting out the passports right now."

"There's an unmarked sitting right in front of the driveway, Candace," Bastokovitch sighed. "They'd have to tunnel out. We've looked up the people, Candace. They've lived in that house for seven years. Man, his wife, the kid. The wife's got . . . she's got cancer or something. Sick all the time. The husband works this business out of the house, every day. This case is big and long, Candace. We don't want to go off half-cocked. Every move we make is going to be scrutinized. You know it. So I say, let's go down there nice and quiet, one car of uniforms, maybe, and us, and we say, 'We need to ask you some questions. Sir. Madam.'"

Bender walked in the front door then, without even ringing the bell. "It's a house, Bender," Candy said, disrespectfully. "You know — knock, knock?"

He ignored her and nodded to Pat. "Is it true?"

"We don't know," Candy said. "How very solicitous of you to come."

"You are a very hostile woman, Detective Bliss."

"Yes, I am, Agent Bender. I have grown hostiler with age. By the time I'm sixty, I'll be spitting tobacco on your shoes."

Pat went out into the garage to get more chairs, the aquamarine folding chairs they used at the Wedding in the Old Neighborhood when there were real weddings or overflow Saturday nights.

"Where'd you get folding chairs that color?" asked Bender.

"There wouldn't be any harm in having a warrant," Bastokovitch mused then. "Can you get something?"

"I already talked to the DA's office. I talked to Kelly Clark. He's ready."

Bastokovitch looked long at Beth and Pat. "Good grief, you folks . . . you poor folks. Are you ready for this?"

Beth said, "You don't get to be ready for it." She sounded, to herself, coplike; she had a weakness for falling into Candy's rhythms whenever she spent more than fifteen minutes in her light.

"We're going to do this right." The chief sighed again. Beth heard Candy make a sound, hoped Bastokovitch hadn't. "We're going to take them," he said, again, this time holding out his hands, as if wishing for Pat or Beth to drop the flag and let the games begin. Then the front door banged open, and Vincent slouched into the hall.

"This is my son," Pat said quickly, jumping up. "This is Vincent. Vincent, you know Candy. This is Chief Bastokovitch."

Vincent looked straight at his mother. "Does Kerry have Girl Scouts?"

Beth thought a moment, ruffling a card file that had fallen all over the floor of her head, facedown. "Uh . . . I think."

"So she won't be home until after five."

"Right."

Vincent whipped his head once around the breakfast room, taking in the folding chairs, the stacks of photos still littered among the coffee

363

cups on the table, the murmurs and bursts of laughter from the kitchen where the uniforms were traipsing in and out the back door to smoke among the roses.

"The picture," Vincent said then.

Beth led her son out into the hall. "You saw the picture, and you know that I think it's Ben," she said softly.

"You think. Yeah. Well, it's Ben," Vincent said. "You know it is."

"Did you recognize him?"

"When?"

"When he came here to mow. You said you didn't see him." Vincent looked out the window, up the block; he could easily see over Beth's head, though he was no more than an inch taller than she.

"Is he the kid in the red house?"

Beth's hand flew up before she reckoned what she intended to do with it, which was slap Vincent's face. She had never — not in all the vicious fumblings, the hair pullings, the time she'd pushed him down on the lawn after he casually lobbed not one but two baseballs through two glass windows, or the times she'd locked the door and gone to bed, forgetting he was in the library or at a basketball game, all those manifest atrocities, significant and negligible, neglects and abuses — for all those, never had she slapped his face. She didn't now, but Vincent's head jerked sideways. It was just as if she had.

"You saw him? You *saw* Ben?"

"I didn't . . . know it was Ben." He dropped

364

his knapsack, anvil-heavy, in the middle of the floor, where it would lie unopened all night, as it did every night. "I just used to see this kid goofing around, and I thought he looked like Ben. I mean, I *guess* I thought he looked like Ben. I never really thought about it much." Beth watched his face reconfigure then, as if a front were passing over Lake Michigan, watching the restoration of his bored, cocky sneer, his Reese face.

"Why didn't you tell me?"

He started to turn, to go for the stairs. Beth asked again, "Why didn't you tell me? Or, for God's sake, your father?"

"I told Tom."

"You told Tom. Why didn't Tom tell us?"

"I don't think he got it. I don't know if *I* got it. He will now, I guess. I didn't make a big deal out of it."

"But why didn't you say something?"

"I don't know."

"Vincent, our whole life was . . . " He gave her a murderous look, and Beth tried to back-pedal. "You knew what was at stake! Why didn't you say something? Why didn't you tell me yourself?"

"Say something? Tell you? Tell you what, Mom?" he spat it out then. "That I'd found my long-lost brother down the street? Would you have believed me? Would you have even goddamn *heard* me?"

"I would have believed you. I would have listened."

He smirked.

"Vincent." Her voice stopped him, one foot on the bottom stair. "When did you first see him?"

"How long have we lived here?"

No, God, Beth thought, no. Her finger ends pounded, one, two, three, four years.

"It doesn't matter now, Vincent," she said, thinking, Of course it matters, nothing else but this matters, and why, what, how he could have been possessed to keep it a secret? Or was it possible, even remotely, that her son to whom computers sang and chemistry released its riddles had truly believed it wasn't worth mentioning? It was too un-Vincent. There was something else. There had to be.

But, struggling to breathe evenly, she said, "There isn't anything we can do about it. And . . . I should have told you this morning. It was stupid that I didn't." She stopped. "I'm sorry for it. But they took this boy out of school without knowing for sure. They think it's Ben. The boy you . . . saw in the picture. They think it's your brother. That he's alive." She added, fumbling, "That's why all the cops are here."

"Oh, thanks," Vincent said. "I thought it was, like, a fire drill or something." He shook his head. "Jesus. May I please go upstairs now and go to the bathroom? Mom?"

"Wait," Beth told him. She didn't know how to do it; she almost had, this morning, when she laid her head on his shoulder. "Vincent, I . . . it could be all right, Vincent." She took his hand, marveling at its clean warmth, its huge size — how long since she had really

366

held his hand? Not to scrub chocolate from it or snatch from it a hammer or an Exacto knife, not to grip it to cross a street, but really *felt* it, felt the supple palms, the emergent man's knuckles that had, outside her notice, replaced the indented dimples of childhood — long, tapered fingers exactly like her own, the 'piano hands' her mother had cherished such admiring hopes for, even when Beth bashed away at the keyboard with all the grace of a drill-press operator.

She raised his hand; he let her, neither yielding nor withdrawing, and laid it against her cheek. "Vincent, we've all been through so much. You've been through so much. Oh, Vincent, please forgive me."

She heard him say, "Don't," and imagined him looking up the hall, humiliated; they were not twenty feet away from the group in the breakfast room. She should have stopped, right then.

But she said, once more, "Can you ever forgive me?"

"Forgive you?" he asked. "What the hell did *you* do?"

She couldn't help it. A flute of anger.

She looked up and saw then, in her son's eyes, plain as the exquisitely backlit detail in a Karsh portrait, not anger, not affection. Pity. Unalloyed pity. No other thing.

"I'll call you . . . when . . . they . . . I'll tell you," she blurted.

"Fine," Vincent told her, slowly pulling away his hand.

Candy was calling her. Beth turned back into the kitchen.

"Is he all right?" Candy asked, and Beth, not trusting her mouth, nodded.

Pat spoke up: "I have to call my mom and dad," and it had the gratefully galvanic effect of restoring Beth's attention.

"No!" she and Candy nearly shouted at the same time — but, Beth would think later, for vastly different reasons.

"Pat, we need to go down there as quietly and unobtrusively as we can. This guy could have . . . anything in there. Another kid. An arsenal. We have no idea what's happening in that house," Candy said.

"She's right," said Bastokovitch.

A young officer bounded up the front steps and in the open door, placing a sheaf of papers, embedded with carbons, in Candy's hands. She thanked him.

"I'm going to go up with my buddy Bender here," Candy said. "Righto, Bob?" Bender got up, actually adjusting his muted paisley tie. Beth watched Candy take her gun out of her satchel and stick it carefully in the belt of her slacks, behind her back, just over her right hip. "You got?" she asked Bender, and he tapped his breast pocket. "Okay, then." Candy stopped, and briefly hugged Beth, hard. "Now we go."

Beth saw the brake lights of Candy's car blink to a full stop at the corner, and then she began to run. She didn't look back to see if Pat was following; she simply ate the blocks, forgetting to breathe, arriving at the turn to the red house just as Candy and Bender were crossing the parkway to the front stoop. Behind the van neatly stenciled with the words 'Karras Construction', two officers crouched with drawn guns.

Jimmy grabbed Beth's arms. "Don't," he hissed, surprised. She shook him off and bounded across the lawn after Candy, who shot her a look of unvarnished fury.

"I'm coming."

"Bullshit," said Candy. "I told you we don't know . . . shit, Beth, go back down there. He could be aiming a rifle at your head right now. Don't be an ass."

"Mrs. Cappadora — " Bender began.

"I want to see him."

"No."

"What are you going to do, arrest me?" Beth asked.

"Oh, fuck," Candy said. She turned her back, shoving Beth slightly behind her, and rang the doorbell.

He was little. A handsome, slender-hipped man with smooth Mediterranean skin, almost teen-looking except for two identical wings of white hair that framed his face. It was good hair, Beth thought; it was a vanity.

"Are you George Karras?" Candy asked.

"Yes," he said, smiling, opening the door wider. "What's wrong?"

"I am Detective Candace Bliss and this is Agent Robert Bender of the Federal Bureau of Investigation. Mr. Karras, do you have a twelve-year-old boy named Sam who lives in this house?"

"I . . . my son," he said, and then stumbled, sagging against the outer frame of the door. "What's happened to my boy? Is Sam hurt? Are you the police?"

"Mr. Karras, Sam is unhurt, and he is in custody of protective services of Cook County."

"He's at school," Karras said. "How did he get hurt?"

"Mr. Karras, you are under arrest for aggravated kidnapping in connection with the June 3, 1985, abduction of Benjamin Cappadora," Candy said evenly. "You have the right to remain silent. If you give up the right to remain silent, anything you say can and will be used against you in a court of law . . . "

"What?" Karras said, turning to Beth. "My son's at school. Who's Benjamin — ?"

"If you give up the right to remain silent, anything you say can and will be used against you in a court of law. You have the right to have an attorney present at any time you choose. If you cannot afford an attorney, one will be appointed to represent you. Do you understand these things, Mr. Karras?"

He said, then, "I get it. You got the wrong house. The people who lost the little boy, that kidnap case a long time ago, they live down over there. You can ask my neighbor lady — she knows the dad."

"Mr. Karras," Candy said, "may we please come inside?"

"Sure," said the man, smoothing his flannel shirt. "I was just doing the bills. But I don't think I can help you much. Because I don't know the family. You got the wrong house is all."

"They're not arresting us," Beth said.

"Huh?" Karras stared at her. "Are you a cop?"

"No," Beth said.

"We're his parents," Pat said then, puffing, dragging himself up the steps behind Beth. "We're Ben's parents, you sonofabitch."

"That's enough," Bender said.

"What?" Karras asked again. "Where is this kid? Is my boy hurt?"

Candy moved into the living room, where a large card table was set up next to a low corduroy-covered couch. There were stacks of invoices piled on one end next to an adding machine with a long tail of tape. "Mr. Karras," she said, "please slowly raise your hands — "

"What?"

"Raise your hands so that the officer can make sure — "

"I don't have a gun." The small man smiled, then, at Beth. "I was doing the bills. I don't have a computer." One of the younger patrolmen quickly patted Karras's sides, the inside and outside of his trouser legs. "Please, I don't know what's going on. This is my house. I didn't do anything."

Beth wanted to get down on her hands and knees and examine the fiber of the carpet, where a tiny pile of ground-in potato chips dotted a corner, to untie and explore the two huge pairs of boys' tennis shoes she saw neatly standing side by side just inside the door, put her fingers in the pockets of the Bulls jacket tossed on a hook. A well-oiled mitt snuggled deep into the cushion of a fat maroon chair, near the fireplace; on the television, a photo of a boy, crouched grinning in a green silk baseball uniform, was framed in wood and gold. There were a pair of ceramic candlesticks at each end of the mantel. Only one had a candle. There was a vase with silk gladioli, white. And above that, a painting — no, Beth thought, in quick correction, a retouched photograph. The woman looked straight into the camera with an antelope's shy grace and wide-eyed intensity; she wore a high-necked gray dress, a gown nearly, with a line of pearl buttons at the throat, and her pale hair haloed away from her forehead as if it were being lifted by invisible fingers. Blown, thought Beth; they had used a fan in the shoot. She reached for the edge of the couch, missed it, and sat down hard on the floor.

"Beth!" Candy turned, distracted, one eye still on Karras as he instinctively reached out a hand to help Beth.

"That's Cecil," Beth gasped. "That's Cecil Lockhart."

"Oh," Karras said, "Cecil. Sure. She's an actress. Did you see her on TV?"

Beth fought for a normal breath. She began to get up, settled for kneeling. "Why," she asked then, "do you have a picture of Cecil Lockhart?"

George Karras drew himself up, nearly proudly, then nodded, his lips pursed with a wistfulness, a sorry rue Beth would never forget.

He said, "That's my wife."

23

THEY could not make Candy stop apologizing.

When she thought about that first week, years later, it was Candy's utter despair that Beth remembered most, the coruscating blame she heaped on herself and Bender and even the devoted officers from her Parkside staff, blame in fistfuls, even after Beth begged her to stop, even after Rosie, for God's sake, put her hands on Candy's shoulders and said, "This is not right. You did everything. This family owes you its life."

It started the moment the three of them stepped out onto George Karras's porch and stood blinking in the late-afternoon sun — after Karras had told them, and Chief Bastokovitch had confirmed by phone, that his wife, Cecilia, had been a patient at Silvercrest in Elgin, a private hospital for the mentally ill, for the past four years. That he, George, was essentially a single parent of their only son — Sam, Cecil's child from her previous marriage, whom George had legally adopted not long after his own marriage to her, seven years ago.

Beth had tried, and to an extent had been successful, to make a blur of the moment George Karras said that, to blot out the remembrance of her nausea when the vein in Pat's forehead began to flutter, and sweat beaded at the neck of his shirt. "Legally adopted?" he'd said softly, dangerously, that I'll-break-anything-here Vincent-look in his eyes. "Legally adopted?"

Candy urging, "Pat, wait . . . "

And George continuing, fervently, anxiously, "No, no, it's fine, it's okay. You can check, I got the legal document right in my safe. With his birth certificate. Go ahead. Let's clear this up, okay?"

Jimmy showing up in the living room then, and he and Candy leading a rigid Pat outside, while Bastokovitch flipped open a steno pad and sat down heavily on George's couch, asking, in low tones, if Mr. Karras would like an attorney present before he answered some questions. Sighing, as he began, while even outside, Pat, Beth, and Candy could still hear George's voice piping up, "You just got to look at the papers. That's all. He's my son. He's my wife's child. It's a mixup. Just let me get them."

Outside the door, Candy had turned to Beth and Pat abruptly. "Please, please," she said, for the first time of what would turn out to be dozens, as it began to break over all of them, the thing that had somehow actually happened, and gone on happening, for long years, two blocks from the Cappadoras' front porch. "Please forgive me."

"What?" Beth cried. "Forgive you? What?"

"Please, please . . . No, don't forgive me. This is the worst fucking abortion in history. He was here all the time. I don't deserve you to forgive me."

And even Pat, ashen, raised his head and

374

told her, "Candy, no. You couldn't have known . . ."

But Candy would not be stopped. For the first time since Beth had known her, the ever-composed Candy indulged, those early days, in a virtual orgy of emotionalism — berating herself with curses even more fluent than her usual fare as fact after fact emerged.

It was Jimmy who told Beth how Candy slammed down her office phone and pulled a window shade off its cord when she heard that Cecil had cooperated fully with officers in an interview at her parents' house, just months after the kidnapping, even cracking a bedroom door so they could peek at her sleeping son, whom she described as four years old, not much older than Ben. "That," she had told Jimmy, "will make me wake up screaming the rest of my life." And after Candy learned that a clear set of Cecil's finger prints, taken during a mass arrest at a nuclear-weapons demonstration in Champaign-Urbana years before, existed in FBI files, she'd run up three flights to shout into the phone at Bender that she didn't care if the fucking bungling dirtbag lived in Budapest now, that Bender had better find him, because the Cappadoras were going to sue the government for millions; it was going to cost the government millions of bucks because some asshole FBI tech had been given prints on rubber, for Christ's sake, on the bottom of Ben's second tennis shoe, prints probably as clear as the dummy sets they gave you to study in the academy, and still managed to screw up lifting them.

"And you guys had a matched set!" Candy screamed. "Cecil Lockhart did everything but call you on a bullhorn on the night of the second reunion — 'I'm still here! I did it!' This could have been five fucking years ago! . . . Yeah, the kid is okay. Well, *maybe* he's okay. We don't know everything yet. . . . Does that justify it, Bob? All's well that ends well? And if I find out that this kid was touched, that a hair on his head was harmed, I'll personally get you then, Bob. Take it to the bank."

Beth had listened, terrified, then ventured helplessly, "You're taking too much on yourself, you're too close."

"Oh, really, Beth?" Candy snapped. "How about the fact that even I fucking spaced the Minneapolis connection? She only moved back and forth about fifty times." She stopped, then, and apologized for her sarcasm.

But even long afterward, when the whole sorry unraveling of nine years of near misses and sheer mishaps was pieced together as best it could be without the keystone information that only Cecil herself could have provided, Beth could not accept the intensity of Candy's guilt, the determination with which she turned away all of their comfort, their thanks. "*You* found him," she told Beth a dozen times. "Don't thank me. I didn't earn it." That the media, and almost every other official source connected with the case, seemed determined to laud her anyway (she was, if anything, even more elegant and glamorous than she'd been nine years before, even more irresistible as copy) — this only deepened Candy's frustrations. She told Beth, one night the following fall, that the only forgiving moment of the whole spring had been on the night of the 'arrest', which had, of course, quickly turned out to be nothing of the sort — the moment when she and Jimmy had the chance to see Pat see Ben.

Beth was able to summon that part herself, entire, play it back almost like a time-lapse film of a rose opening: All of them standing outside the emergency foster-care home in Wheaton, aware of two kids hanging out a second-story window to try to see them under the roof of the porch; George, his eyes and nose reddened, but his handkerchief neatly folded in his sport-coat pocket, arriving with Bastokovitch in the chief's car, passing the Cappadoras with a silent gesture, elbows in, palms up, something midway between a shrug and a plea, as he went inside. Then more waiting, Vincent plowing the soft dirt of a flowerbed with his toe, Kerry sitting on the ground, holding the whining, squirming Beowulf on his lead, Beth wondering why she'd given in when Kerry insisted on bringing the dog. Waiting for impossible minutes as the curtains on the inner door were drawn back, then dropped again; George finally emerging, blowing his nose, then the foster mother, gray and formidable even in a fuchsia sweat suit, already protective of her charge, flicking on the outside light in the gathering dusk. She'd come out onto the step and stood to one side, holding the screen door open behind her.

And then Ben.

It was Pat's gathered energy Beth could still feel when she thought of that instant — his coil; she thought he would leap up onto the step, leaving her behind, numbed, her arms hanging thick and useless. He had, instead, raked his hair, once, and then walked up to the step slowly, cautiously, the way a field biologist would approach a newborn antelope, and extended his palm, made as if to shake hands. And when the child only stared at him, as Beth held her breath, Pat had lifted his hand, run one thumb down the side of Ben's face, from his hairline to his chin, and asked, "How are you?"

"I'm good," the boy had answered automatically, and then, "Dad . . . ?" And when both George and Pat answered him, Beth began first to cry, then to breathe. Behind her, she could hear an enormous chorus of coughing and shuffling, as assembled masses of Parkside and state officers, who'd materialized from nowhere, let go. It was she who leapt onto the steps then, she and Kerry and Beowulf, Beth inhaling his smell as eagerly as the dog did, engulfing the child, nearly knocking him down as he stiffened and finally backed away, reaching for George.

"I know," the foster mother said then, freighting the two words with supreme kindness. "But he's just stunned."

Pat had told Ben, then, to get some sleep. George, calling Ben 'Spiro', which Beth learned later was George's Greek name for Sam, hugged him and propelled him back inside.

And that was when Candy said again, "I'm so sorry."

But Pat had turned to her, his face smoothed, flushed, the shortstop's face Beth had yearned for a hundred summers ago, and said, "Sorry? Candy, this is the best day of my life."

And to underline it, Pat, for whom working at Wedding was respiration, had barely gone in to work over the next few weeks. Between supervised hour-long visits, every other day, with the child they soon learned to call 'Sam', Pat and Beth consumed dozens of quarts of coffee and absorbed the information in reports Candy brought them, almost daily, of police interviews with Cecil at Silvercrest, interviews that hardly merited the name. Michele Perrault, the little lawyer George had hired, had almost gotten in trouble at the arraignment, Candy told them, when Judge Sakura asked whether the defendant had chosen to stand mute, and Perrault shot back, "Your Honor, that's the only way she can stand."

But it was dead accurate. The diagnosis, in lay terms, was catatonic depression. When she entered Silvercrest, years before, Cecil had, Candy said, showed some animation — spoken occasionally in the trained, spheric actor's voice that took the staff by surprise, especially when what she said was senseless. Now she was still as a well, making no noise even when she yawned or scraped her leg on a piece of furniture. At Silvercrest, in Cecil's room, in the dayroom, in her supervising physician's office, Candy and, after her, Robert Bender, Calvin Taylor, others,

379

had spent hours with Cecil.

They had shown Cecil pictures, pictures that George, in a fumbling open gesture that made Pat cry, had duplicated for the Cappadoras — pictures of Cecil on her mother's porch with Ben on a brand-new red bike with training wheels, pictures of George with Ben sitting on his shoulders on a mountain path. A picture of Ben on Santa's lap, with his hair still dyed Vincent-brown, no more than six months after . . . How had she dared? Beth thought, and then thought, Of course, what else would she have done — was Cecil, after all, stupid or just crazy? That picture, the one that attracted Beth most, had to have been taken the fall after the police interviewed Cecil, after she had moved back to Chicago from Minneapolis. Candy said Cecil's mother had confirmed the move, that Cecil had showed up with a grandson Mrs. Lockhart had never even met before. Beth pressed Candy: Why had Mrs. Lockhart believed Cecil? Didn't she connect the sudden grandson with Ben's much-publicized loss?

"If she did, she's not saying," Candy replied.

In the meantime, after the Ben pictures failed, the police, with the help of Cecil's psychiatrist, had tried evoking responses with other stimuli: hippie music from high-school times — Cream and Jimi Hendrix and Donovan. They had brought her mints, which her nurses said Cecil loved, and watched Cecil reach out and gobble them, the only movement she ever made voluntarily. They had brought in a videotape machine and showed Cecil long excerpts of herself in the *Hallmark Hall of Fame* production of *Major Barbara*. They had brought in a big poster of Cecil, her platinum hair upswept in a magnificent Gibson pouf, in her one-woman show *Jane Addams of Hull House*, the performance that had won her the Grace Dory Arts Achievement Award just the summer before the reunion. They brought out front pages, old headlines ('Mom Blasts Kidnapper: You Heartless Bastard!').

And, as her doctor predicted up front, they had elicited . . . nothing. Less than nothing. Cecil was more than vacant, Candy told Beth; she was bottomless. She ate her mints; she got up when her angel-faced nurse, Mary, put pressure on her elbow. Whatever she knew, if she any longer knew anything at all, walked in her alone.

George was pitifully eager to help fill in blanks. He came to the Cappadoras' house more than once, unbidden, and then chafed miserably at their kitchen table, his eyes drawn again and again to the baby pictures of Ben on the walls. He brought his son's growth charts from the pediatrician, his dental records; the description of the broken wrist Sam had suffered in a soccer match at age nine. Beth brought him coffee, with cloth napkins she had to go upstairs into a dresser to find, brought cream in a pitcher, things she never did, to soothe him.

And finally, one night, when Ben was still in transitional care, George had blurted, "You guys probably think I should feel more guilty. And I do feel guilty, I do. But how can I blame myself?

It's probably impossible for you to believe how little I knew about any of this. All I know is my boy — God forgive me, he's my boy, too. I mean, Beth, Pat, look at it from his point of view. He's already a kid whose mother's in the loony bin. God bless her. Poor Cecilia, she was the most gorgeous . . . You know, Beth, when I met her, I didn't think she was a day over twenty-five, and she was really in her mid-thirties by then. She was so delicate and so sweet, like a flower." George tapped his chest. "We were running this promotion deal; you got tickets to that theater out there by the airport. She had just moved back from Minneapolis, and she was in *My Fair Lady*. And here am I, this dummy who builds decks. That she would look at me . . . that woman, this girl, would look at me . . . I couldn't believe it."

He sipped his coffee, his pinkie delicately extended. "And then, you know all this, there was the boy. He was — well, Beth, he was just like . . . like he is still, even now. So happy and game. So smart and strong. I fell in love with him as much as Cecilia. It was Cecilia who wanted to get married, right away, almost like she could tell she was going to . . . oh, Jesus God. Before she was hospitalized the last time, she . . . she got his hair cut all short, in a buzz, not an eighth of an inch long. And it grew in all reddish. Brownish red. I noticed. God, I thought, kids change. I never knew the father. Irish, I thought. I build garages. Pat, I just build decks and garages. He's my boy. I adopted him as my own boy. But even before that, he was my boy."

George ran his hands though his perfect hair — Was it whiter, in only weeks? thought Beth. Was this just a myth, or did it actually happen to people? George said, "I figured, of course, Cecilia and me, we'd have more; but she got so sick, so fast, and then I found out she really wasn't so young. And Jesus, the shock treatments. Times I'd come there, they'd have her bound up in belts. She'd bite at the . . . And then, later, when she didn't even know me anymore. Didn't even know her mother or the boy. But I had Sam. My Spiro. I had my little all-star. See?"

Beth could feel the dampness at her neck; her shirt collar was soaking with unwiped tears. Her nose was running; she'd hadn't even been aware she'd cried. "George," she said. "You don't have to tell us."

Despite the ache of sympathy they felt, Pat and Beth agreed to stand firm. Whatever George would be to Sam, he was not going to be another father. And yet, they never turned him away — he was their only window into the cocoon from which Ben had emerged Sam.

Charges were issued. The state of Illinois had charged Cecilia Lockhart Karras with aggravated kidnapping and stood prepared, depending on what was learned about the conditions under which Ben had lived for nine years, to tack on everything except the abduction of Patty Hearst: false imprisonment, child abuse and endangerment, interference with custody, secreting a child, civil rights violations. Candy smiled when she read the complaint: "They left out forgery and possession with intent . . ."

But Candy knew, as everyone knew, as Beth knew, from the first moments of dawning comprehension in George's living room, that the whole legal process would turn out to be mostly theater, an elaborate pantomime intended for no purpose but completion, like binding up the newspapers, corner to corner, with twine, and setting them at the curb. All the hearing would accomplish, Candy predicted, would be to make a public witnessing of tying that knot, securing it, snipping the cord.

Cecil would be led down the steps of the courthouse at Twenty-seventh and California just as she would come up, with lights she probably didn't see panning her face, and words she didn't hear burbling in her ears, go back to Silvercrest as free a woman as she had been when she was taken to Cook County Jail in the hospital van. She would go back to the room no one knew for sure whether she recognized, to be ministered to by rough or gentle hands no one could tell whether she felt; to stare at television if it was turned on in front of her; to sit with her fingers interlaced until someone took her hand and raised her to her feet; to soil herself raw without any apparent discomfort. Sending Cecil to prison would be redundant; no one had any lust for it, Beth, even Pat, least of all.

24

Reese

June 1994

ALL five of them in the social worker's office felt like a crowd. Nobody knew where to go. Reese finally flopped on one end of the couch — one of those nubbly orange numbers that show up in places Reese had frequented, public-bucks places, like school social workers' offices. Tom, now, Reese thought, Tom wouldn't have put a couch like this one in his garage. He concentrated on watching a spider pick delicately in and out of the canyons of the acoustical tile. The murmur of his parents' voices blended with the social worker's drone, until, if he tried, Reese could pretend he could hear a fly buzzing, running from the spider through miles of tiles.

He swung his feet down and stood up.

The kid was staring out the window, with his back to Beth and Pat.

" . . . certain adjustments," said the social worker, looking up, startled, at Reese. His parents were staring at him, Dad looking particularly annoyed, but the social worker was prepared to go right on, apparently even if Reese stood on his head and peed on the floor. "We have a list of agencies, here, and you can choose to access — "

"Can I go outside?" Reese asked then, and thought, Damn, I sound like Mommy's little boy. "I'm going outside. It's getting hot in here."

"I can open a window," the social worker suggested thinly.

"It's all right," said Pat. "There's no real reason that . . . they . . . "

"Of course not," said the social worker.

"Wanta go?" Reese asked the kid, who blinked as if he wasn't sure he got the dialect. "Wanta go outside?"

The kid shrugged. Reese opened the door. There was a kind of playground outside, with a couple of basketball courts; some other disadvantaged deefs were swinging on the swings or kicking around an old tetherball, still on its string. Wonder what they're in for, Reese thought, holding the door open for the kid, who passed through quickly, head down, fists jammed in his jeans pockets.

"Vincent," said Beth, then. "You *will* keep an . . . " Reese saw the look his dad gave her then, as if even he couldn't believe she could be that stupid. But it was already almost out; Reese knew what she was going to say. He shrugged and let the door bang shut behind them.

It was colder outside than it looked. Especially for late spring. The kid was wearing just a flannel; Reese was glad he had his leather. He shrugged it up onto his shoulders, as always feeling the momentary surge of joy it gave him. It moved like another, tougher skin. He took out

386

a butt, examined the angle of the view from the window — he could see his dad, but his dad had his back to him. Not worth it.

"So," he said to the kid, carefully replacing his cigarette and folding the pack. "Was the guy here this morning?"

"The guy?" said the kid, not tracking.

"The guy, the guy — the guy who was your stepfather — George What's-His-Name," Reese said.

"He came to the foster-parent place real early," said the kid. "He didn't want to come here."

"So how does it feel to be a celebrity, Ben?" Reese asked. "Mug on the front page. Major miracle on Menard Street . . . " The kid gave Reese another measuring look. He thinks I really want to know, Reese thought. What a deef.

"Actually, it's kind of sickening," said the kid. "I mean, all these days, the past two weeks, the psychologist is saying, 'So, you must be having a lot of feelings about all this.' . . . How can you have feelings about something you didn't even know was going on?"

"Is this, like, your permanent counselor now?"

"Permanent?" They walked over onto the concrete and Reese propped his foot on one of the baby swings.

"Take a clue here, Ben," he said. "You have now entered the counseling zone. This is the champion mental-health consumer family you will be living with here. My mom and dad off and on go to marriage counseling, and she used to go to grief counseling, and Kerry goes to, like, drawing counseling, and I myself hold the world's record in my age cohort for consecutive visits to a shrink . . . "

"Why? What's wrong with you?"

Reese kicked the swing.

"Nothing. Nothing has to be wrong with you. It's just . . . school shit. And so forth. It's mainly my dad who thinks I'm this major fuckoff."

"And what about your mom?"

"You've met my mom."

"Well . . . " said the kid, turning away, which Reese didn't want.

"No, my mom isn't like this bad person or anything. She's just like . . . 'Ground control to Beth Cappadora,' you know? She doesn't get stuff half the time, or you think she doesn't." Reese sighed. "Anyhoo, I wish we had a car."

"You don't have a car?" said the kid.

"No, but a car is a thing you can always have if you want."

"What do you mean?" the kid asked him.

"I mean, a car is just there . . . for you . . . "

"You steal cars?"

"No, I don't *steal cars*. But you can borrow a car, no harm, not much foul, you know what I mean."

"That's just a kind of stealing."

"Well, I want to know that I flourished in my youth," said Reese. The kid looked around him, like he was trying to find a cop or something. Shit, thought Reese, next topic.

"So what do you do?" he asked the kid.

"Do? I don't do anything," said the kid.

"I mean, like, what do you *do*?" The kid's

gray eyes widened then, and Reese, staring at him, almost lost his train of thought, the kid looked —

"I play ball."

"B-ball?" The kid nodded, and walked over onto one of the scarred concrete courts where two black Bulls signature balls nodded together under a bush. The other deefs kept kicking the tetherball, shuffling away from Reese's approach like herd animals.

"You any good?" Reese called, going after one of the balls.

"I play city league," said the kid. "Traveling squad. First string."

"Traveling squad?" cooed Reese. "Oh, my goodness."

"Look, I'm in sixth grade. The other kids are in ninth, okay? It's the height."

"Though where you got that . . . "

"Whatever."

"Wanta shoot some. Play Horse?" The kid shrugged. His hands were big; Reese watched him spin and fondle the ball, like it was a pet, before he dribbled — then, release, drop, release, drop. The kid had seriously big hands, and — Reese looked down — feet to match.

They took positions, pretty far back — After all, Reese thought, he's first string *traveling squad*. He watched the kid shoot — looked like an old Olympic basketball video — squared up, with the follow-through down the wrists to a fingertip flip. Good little kiddie, thought Reese, plays by the book. Size didn't matter much here; the kid was as heavy as Reese was, and all but an inch as tall. Reese took a step back, one-armed it. "Nothing but net," he said.

The kid stepped back, took the ball, and matched it, no problem.

"Free-throw line," said Reese, and bricked one off the back of the iron. It went wide.

"My turn," said the kid happily. He stood up in that old-fashioned way, and Reese saw his face change: he had one of those faces that told you he was only doing what he was doing — not revising the names of people on his permanent shit list or anything else. He was right there. Reese could tell before the ball left the kid's fingertips that it was good.

And so Reese zipped his jacket to get rid of the flapping pockets, balanced the ball on one hand, and zeroed in. He missed again.

"That's *h*," yelled the kid, who stood beside Reese and drained one without seeming to even set it up.

Reese heard that fat bastard Teeter, the basketball coach at school, who also taught P.E., saying, "It's a mental thing with you, Cappadora. You're about one taco short of a combination plate about half the time. If you could just think about what you're doing . . . " He tried to look through the shot, but he could feel it go wrong the minute it took flight.

"That's *o*," the kid said again, with pure joy.

"I let you," said Reese, dribbling down the lane — he leapt and finger-rolled it in. "Net this, bozo."

"We're playing Horse."

"You did okay standing still, huh, First String?"

"I can take you," the kid said evenly.

Reese drove for the basket again, skipping onto the paint, looking for the sweet spot of his driveway nights — boom. "Okay, buddy, ready to go downtown?"

The kid was confused. "What are the rules?"

"I don't play in city rec, my man." Reese drove again, missed his lay-up, and spun as the ball flirted off the far side of the hoop.

"Is this Make It — Take It or what?"

"Your ball, rookie," said Reese. He didn't have to name the game, though clearly the game would have been Make It — Take It if he'd nailed the last shot.

"To what? To what?" said the kid, dribbling absently. "To eleven?"

"Just play," Reese told him. And the kid checked the ball, then made as if to dribble left, but instead dropped right three steps and set up for a shot off the board. "Count it!" he cried, and tossed the ball to Reese, murmuring, "Check."

Reese ignored him and lined up at the top of the key. The kid seemed to be measuring him, wondering how to slide, avoiding Reese's eyes. Then Reese cut right, leading with his dominant hand and bouncing the ball slightly too high. Reese thought he could anticipate the kid, so he kept on coming. He knocked the ball off the kid's thigh, recovered it at the top of the key, shot, and missed, with the ball bouncing off the rim. But Reese slipped for the board,

391

got his balance, and tipped it in easily over the kid's extended arm.

"Who are you?" Reese asked him then, dribbling, panting.

"I'm Grant Hill."

"I'm Pippen."

"Okay." They played in earnest then, with Reese holding on to the lead, the kid repeating the score after each basket. Then Reese aired one and the kid boxed out, grabbed the rebound, took it back, and drove for the lay-up. "That's evens up," said the kid. Reese lined up. When the kid came in, he turned, feinted, and raised an elbow. The kid stumbled.

"Sor-ree," Reese said, grabbing the ball.

"You fouled," said the kid.

"This ain't the YWCA, Ben," Reese said.

"It's not Ben."

"Okay . . . Ben," Reese mumbled, driving past the kid toward the baseline. But the kid shifted his position — he had a way of sliding more than running, it was hard to follow — stepping in to take the charge. Reese struggled for concentration; he was chasing the ball, not moving with it, damn it, so he drove hard right at the kid, leading with his left arm and whacking the kid across the bridge of his nose. The kid kept his head, but Reese could see his eyes water, and then, as Reese went up for the shot, his eyes still on the kid's face, this look, this look of fear . . . he looked like Ben, who would not even slide down the plastic slide into the six-inch-deep wading pool unless he, his brother, stood there with open arms. That same wide-open look, right across the bones of his cheeks. Scared. Game. Coming. Ben, Reese thought . . . and in the instant of lost concentration, the kid batted the ball away; and both of them ran for the corner where the ball bounced. If he went for it, Reese saw the kid would fall out of bounds. The kid had no options. He had to just dive. The ball hit Reese's leg hard and out of bounds.

"Christ!" Reese winced. It hadn't nicked him where it mattered, but groin was groin; it was close enough. "You dumb shit."

"You did it," said the kid. "And it's my ball."

He took it, went left, and laid it in with a reverse lay-up that put his body between Reese's arms and the ball. Two. "I'm up now," said the kid to Reese, who was bent over, sucking air, while the kid was breathing like he was asleep. "What's it to? Twenty-one now?" The kid was excited. He almost laughed.

"Just play," said Reese.

"Go to twenty-one . . . Vinnie?" said the kid. He said it way soft, but Reese heard it and drew back, gathering, the way he had in the moments before a dozen fights, a hundred. He took the ball and dribbled around the back court, giving himself some time, raising up for a long jump shot. Sweetness.

"You see that in rec league, Ben?"

"Yep," said the kid. "In girls'." And the kid took the ball, driving right, but Reese knew his moves now, and simply spun on his heel left and stiffed him with both arms. The kid was caught under the chin and went down, off the court and into the trampled dirt, his leg doubled under him, his lip bloody.

"Shit," Reese said. "I didn't mean — " But at that moment his father barreled into him like a snowplow, knocking Reese flat on his can on the concrete, with a pain that shot up his tailbone and would have made him scream if he hadn't bit down.

"You little shit!" said Pat. He reached up and yanked off his tie. "You bully!"

"Jesus Christ, Dad!" Reese said, struggling to stand.

"I'm all right," said the kid.

"Are you hurt . . . Sam?" Pat asked him, pulling out his handkerchief. The kid waved him away, staring over Pat's shoulder at Reese.

"I'm okay, I'm okay."

"Can you go a day — this one day — without trying to hurt something?" Reese saw his dad's eyes crinkle in pain. Oh, shit. Was that sad pain or heart pain? Oh, shit, Reese thought.

Beth came out of the growing shadows under the overhang of the county building. "What happened?" she asked. "What happened to him?"

"We were playing ball is all," Reese muttered.

"It's okay," Sam said desperately. But Beth gave Reese the look she gave him once a year, like she was really seeing him or something, before she reached out to touch Sam's arm. She ran her hands over him as if she was patting him down for weapons.

"Nothing broken?" she said in her little metal

394

voice, her I'm-just-so-fine voice, her school voice.

They put Reese in the front seat with Beth. Dad sat in back with the kid. Nobody even mentioned going to get Kerry from Grandma's place. At Benno's the pizza they ordered sat there, grease hardening in ridges like a relief map. The kid ate two pieces, carefully picking off the pepperoni, which Reese's father absently speared off the plate with a fork and ate himself. Reese watched his dad; Pat was sweating heavily, as if he'd been running. He hoovered the Coke in.

"Eat something, Vincent," said Beth. She should get a T-shirt that said this, Reese thought. So he made a game of seeing how long he could chew a single bite, watching Beth watch him, her own mouth moving in synchrony. If Reese made a monkey face, would his mother do it, too? The thought made him grin.

The kid looked up then, and asked, "Can I have some milk?"

As his father waved for the waiter, Reese asked, "You drink milk with pizza?"

They all stared at him, as if he'd told the kid to go fuck a tree. Reese got up and went into the john, where he messed with his hair and washed his face. He was drying off when Pat stuck his head in and said, "Let's go."

★ ★ ★

Dvořàk, thought Reese, lying back on his bed — his lumpy good bed; they'd bought a new

395

one for young Sam, didn't even attempt to take this one back. The Largo from the 'New World'. Excellent choice for a slight case of jits. He cranked it, wondering if he could levitate soundlessly simply from the vibrations out of the headphones. When he got up to get a glass of water and to change to his oldest Metallica CD, he heard Beth down the hall in the kid's room.

"Do you want a light?" she asked.

"No, I don't sleep with a light," said the kid.

"This must feel very strange to you." The kid didn't answer. "You want a blanket?" Wow, Mom, thought Reese, it's only frigging May. Right through the bathroom wall, when he went in, Reese could feel Beth touching the kid; she couldn't keep her hands off him, though he noticed, every time they saw Sam in the last week, she always drew back before she touched, as if the kid was hot.

"Saturday tomorrow," called his dad, coming up the hall. "You want to take in a game?"

"Okay," said the kid.

Father city, thought Reese. Yep. Going to take a lot of games, though, Dad. Lot of catch-up to play this season. He ran into Pat when he opened the bathroom door. His dad looked as if he were ready to have a talk; Reese tensed. But Pat only leaned against the frame of the door.

"Vincenzo," Dad said, and Reese felt his throat close. "Please, please . . . "

He heard their bedroom door shut. Mom would be in tranquo-land now; he could drive a front-loader up on the porch and she'd maybe turn over. His dad, he wasn't sure; his dad might stalk around some. And sure enough, Reese heard his parents' mattress sigh and the jingle of Pat's change as he put his pants back on. The Metallica was making Reese even more jumpy. He got up and rummaged around until he found the African sax guy whose name he could never remember. There, he thought, laying one hand exactly parallel with the other along the sides of his hips. Nothing strenuous. Drift . . .

Didn't work. Needed Puccini maybe. He rummaged again.

Reese woke up in the dark. His father must have turned out the light. Turning, he felt under his back the familiar lump. Over the years, Reese had occasionally tried to figure out what the constant body pressure was morphing Ben's red bunny into looking exactly like. He thought sometimes it looked like a tadpole now, except for the one remaining ear. Easing up, careful not to press his groaning bladder, Reese pulled it out from under the bottom sheet. One eye. A humped, fat shape, in places its red plush worn nearly transparent pink. Embryo, thought Reese now. That's it. Igor the Embryo.

Still carrying the formless thing, Reese got up to pee, and put the red bunny down on the sink. His father was snoring, the strangled choke that drove Reese nuts. The one that made him breathe along with Pat until sleep drove him under. It was after he shut off the water that he heard the sound.

Kerry? But Kerry was at Grandma Rosie's.

Reese walked down the hall, keeping close to the wall, and toed open the door where the kid, Sam, slept.

He was asleep, or at least his eyes were shut. Reese stepped closer. Sam was lying on his back with his arms thrown out, sleeping that kid-sleep where you go down so hard you drool. Reese looked for eye movements. The kid was zonked. Then, Reese opened his hand and let the chafed red shape of the bunny Igor fall next to the bed. But as he turned to walk out, he heard the kid groan. Sam's arm came up over his face and he said, "No. I just don't . . . no . . . "

Did he mean 'I don't know'? Or was he trying to stop something? The kid moaned again.

Reese sprinted for the door — what if the kid woke up? But Sam rolled over and again, this time softly, he said, "Oh, no."

There was a space between the door and the opening to the closet. Reese leaned against the wall and slid down soundlessly. He folded his arms over his raised knees and adjusted his eyes to the dark. If he strained, he could see the hands on the clock face above Sam's dresser.

It was three a.m. So. Maybe three hours. Reese had gone without blinking longer. Anyone with training could watch that long. It was just . . . Reese leaned forward, his chin on his arms. You couldn't tell . . . But then the kid tossed once again, the upper part of his body shifting into a shaft of light from the street lamp on the corner. There.

Reese relaxed. He could see his face.

25

Reese

June 1994

FOR a dime, Reese would have bagged the last couple of weeks of school. But he figured that all he needed to do was get his dad on edge, and his brand-new driver's license would be folded six ways and stuck where the sun didn't shine in about five minutes flat. Dad was still Dad — in fact, he was extra-jovial Dad now that the sainted Sam was actually living under his roof — but he wasn't going to tolerate anything that would kick back on 'the family'. Reese could picture the headlines: 'Miracle on Menard Street: Regaining a Son and Losing Another?'

Fuck that. He had two lousy weeks to keep his nose clean, and he was determined to do it. Though the strain was getting to him. He had two term papers due, and he'd been using the books he needed to write them to prop up the broken leg on the old bed that had been Ben's. Jordie had accused him of thinking he could absorb all the facts about multiple personalities (his chosen topic for psychology) by sleeping on them.

Reese figured he knew everything about multiple personalities by osmosis, from living with his mother. But he had to settle down, and with his house the Grand Central of the universe, that was pretty hard to do.

He couldn't get away from it. Everywhere he went in school, some teacher had a copy of the *People* magazine, the one with Sam dribbling in the driveway on the cover — the one with the headline that said, 'Back . . . But Not Ben', and underneath, 'The Incredible Odyssey of a Lost Boy.' Some dildo in fourth-hour study hall even asked Reese to fucking autograph it. He did. Taking pity on the kid, he wrote, 'Best Wishes, Daffy Dick', when he by rights should have written something much more blistering. His mom had had a veritable shit hemorrhage when she'd seen Sam's picture on the cover — even more than she'd had over the first *People* cover, which Reese still remembered vividly.

He'd heard her yelling downstairs, "What do these people think? That we have no life?"

And his father answering, "Beth, that's what you used to do for a living . . . "

Tom, being Mr. Detective Psychiatrist, had of course asked him, a couple of times, "Are you *sure* you didn't know it was Ben?" And Reese couldn't believe it — like, why wouldn't he have said something? If he had been really sure? Knowing the only thing his parents wanted on the entire earth was to find Ben?

And Tom had said, "Because maybe it wasn't the only thing you wanted on the entire earth."

Which was what was frustrating about Tom; he always thought he could trick you into revealing some deep subconscious longing by

400

bringing up something so far out of the ballpark it was on top of a bus heading up Waveland Avenue. Reese, in fact, had thought about it himself, and the only real reason he hadn't mentioned the red-haired kid to his mother was because it was just too damned ridiculous to think that his long-lost brother lived around the corner. The kid didn't even really look like he remembered Ben; in fact, he didn't even remember Ben, not that much.

"I was seven years old, for Christ's sake," he'd told Tom in disgust. "What do you remember from when you were seven?"

"I remember that I had a little brother who was three months old, who died of SIDS, and I was the one who found him, and it took me ten years to figure out why I was afraid of going to sleep," Tom told him.

Trust old Tom to have a big, dramatic answer. Well, that's why they said shrinks had to be crazy themselves.

And then Tom had started asking him a whole bunch of stuff about how he felt about Cecilia Lockhart, which Reese totally had nothing to say about — I mean, how could you be mad at a crazy lady for something she didn't even know was wrong?

And when that didn't get anywhere, Tom had gakked on about how was he feeling about Sam, was he mad at Sam? Reese couldn't figure why Tom would even ask. Mad? Mad for what?

"For getting all the attention," Tom said.

"I'm not a kid, Tom," Reese told him. "I mean, if you lost a kid and hadn't seen him for

401

nine years, wouldn't you sort of want to spend all your time with him, and be sort of obsessed with him? It's pretty natural. Especially if you had this other kid that was — "

Tom had really zeroed in on that. "Another kid who was what, Reese? What?" Reese had shrugged. "What, Reese? Another kid who wasn't worth being obsessed with?"

"Dr. Kilgore, this psycho crap can get really tedious."

Tom had laughed then, and asked Reese how he thought it would be if he had to listen to it forty hours a week, coming from his own mouth. And Reese had sort of loosened up then. He'd told Tom he was thinking of becoming a psychologist himself — you didn't have to get dirty, you didn't just bury your mistakes like other doctors. Plus, Reese figured that Tom could have paid for a strip mall just with what he'd made off the Cappadoras alone over the years.

They talked about sports, about this idea Reese had that maybe he'd try out for basketball in the fall, finally, junior year being his last chance and all. Tom thought it was a pretty good idea, but Reese wasn't sure. He wasn't much of a joiner, and though he did love the game, and had some pretty heavy fantasies about suiting up and actually showing he could do it, he just didn't know if he could take the boredom of drills and shit.

Nonetheless, he'd been doing a lot of stuff in the driveway, putting up folding chairs from Wedding and dribbling around them until he was sweating like a warthog. Sam would come out there and do it, too. Reese had to admit, the kid was fast in spite of how big he was, and he already knew things it had taken Reese years to learn, like never really letting your palm touch the ball: Sam could dribble so low a snake couldn't ease under, with those hard, long fingers, just the tips tapping, all control.

Dad would come out, in this suit, and try to play a few points with them — it was just like Grandma Rosie used to say about Grandpa: he looked like an immigrant, mowing the lawn in a sport coat. Dad always tried to get in on it when Sam and Reese were doing something; it never failed to stiffen Sam up, Reese noticed.

But Sam played baseball, too, and practice was starting, so most of the nights Reese dribbled and lobbed and dribbled on his own.

The last few days before school ended, Reese began taking a pumpkin into the deserted gym and trying some things in there. Mostly seeing if his fadeaway jump shot was really as good as it felt in the driveway and on the playground. He'd been lifting weights a little bit, to build up his arms. People didn't know it, but it took a lot more strength than a regular shot from midcourt, because you were rearing back from the guard, basically weakening your stance, instead of putting all your weight forward. But it could get a much bigger guy off you, and Reese knew that with his size, he was going to have to be able to be dead solid perfect with that and the free throws or he'd have no chance at all. Until he'd started trying to perfect the fadeaway, he'd never understood just how incredible Jordan's shot really was. And Jordan didn't have that much height, either. I mean, he had ten inches on Reese, but by NBA standards six feet six was no giant. Some nights, by the time Reese got home, his arms ached. He'd watch Sam and think, That kid's going to go right up and stuff 'em if he keeps growing like he is now. Was he jealous of Sam's size? He didn't think so. It just would have been a whole lot easier if he'd gotten a few more of Mom's big-Irish genes than Dad's scrawny wop ones. Look at Uncle Paul. You could float a cat in one of his shoes.

Jealousy. Nervousness. Half the time, Reese realized, he was hanging around after school trying to figure out what he was really feeling about Sam. If nothing else, his years with Tom had taught him that no matter how smart you were, when it came to how you felt about things, you were pretty much always the last to know. The first time he saw Sam, and knew it was Ben, in the counselor's office while Sam was still in foster care, Reese had almost started to cry, he was so glad. It was like Ben had this light all around him, and he couldn't believe that if he walked right up to the kid, Ben wouldn't just grab his arm and start talking about the time the squirrel got stuck in the car engine or the time Ben fell off the end of the long pier at Lake Delavan, or about the tree house in Madison. Even if he remembered the day in the lobby, fuck, he was just so glad Ben wasn't dead . . .

But Ben — that is, Sam — had looked Reese

right in the face. And he couldn't have been faking it. He looked like he'd never seen Reese before in his life. "This is your brother," said the social worker. "This is Vincent."

The kid had offered to shake hands. "Hi, Vincent," he'd said, and goddamn if his voice didn't sound like Ben, that funny, deep, hoarse voice that used to sound so weird out of a little kid. That was when Reese had wanted to run, to just get away from all of them, this fucked-up unlucky bunch of people who didn't even recognize each other, any of them. He could be like Horace Greeley or Thoreau or somebody and just head out, and work on the railroad or something. Did people still work on the railroad?

But he'd known, even then, he would never do it. He was too lazy and scared, and that was when he'd started getting irritated with the kid, with his 'Yes, ma'ams', and his table manners and his phobia about germs. It hadn't taken Reese — or Kerry, for that matter — long to realize that Sam had this psycho-thing that if you breathed on his food, he wouldn't eat it. And so Vincent got so he could just exhale a little at the dinner table, just as Mom passed Sam his plate, and then Sam would sit there, looking all sick, swallowing like the food was old socks that stuck in his throat. But then Kerry had started doing it, too, and Dad lowered the boom.

The kid was never anything but nice and polite to Reese. Nice and polite and just . . . in himself. It drove Reese nuts. He had no idea what to do to get to Sam. Sam just didn't talk.

One time, the kid had come down while Reese was watching *Hell Is for Heroes* about one o'clock in the morning. Sam sat down, and after about half an hour he had said, suddenly, "So, is that where you got it?"

"What?" Reese had asked.

"Your name." There was a guy in the movie called Reese. But that didn't have anything to do with *his* name, Reese told Sam, and explained the 'resale' thing, and the kid was like, well, Vincent's a good name, too — like Vincent van Gogh. Reese had been pretty shocked, a little kid knowing about Vincent van Gogh.

But what he had said, and he sort of regretted it, was, "Yeah, and he was nuts, too."

Sam, though, hadn't seemed to mind. All he'd said was, "But you didn't cut your ear off. At least not yet."

A pretty decent kid, in some ways. He never got in your way. It made Reese wonder what it would have been like, having a kid brother; Kerry had always been so little, he couldn't remember a time he didn't have to take care of her. Though Tom said that when they grew up, that would 'bond' them closer. Like they were covered with some kind of rubber cement.

Go out, reverse, imagine the big blocker, fade back, shoot. Reese did it over and over. Sometimes for an hour or more. He got so he was making it about ninety percent of the time; of course, there was no real defense there, so he was probably giving himself breaks. Between concentrating on the shot and thinking about Sam, he didn't notice Teeter the day the coach came up behind him, reached over his head, and slapped the ball away.

Reese's heart felt like he'd been filled with helium. "What . . . ?" he yelled, whirling around. Teeter was built like a mastodon; they said he'd guarded Pistol Pete Maravich back in college, but that was twenty years ago, and now he looked like he'd eaten Pistol Pete and his brother for breakfast. Coach Teeter had to go three hundred pounds dry.

"If it ain't Cappadora, the terror on the playground," Teeter said, in that weasly sort of southern voice Reese always associated with drill sergeants in movies. "I been watching you in here, Vince. Going to drop out junior year and try to make the draft?"

"No," Reese told him, recovering his ball. "I'm just goofing around."

"Pretty famous guy now," Teeter said. "Huh?"

"You got me confused with my brother," Reese told him. What the hell, why piss the guy off? He still hadn't formally decided not to try out next year.

"All you Cappadoras are famous, right? Maybe that's why you don't think you have to show up for school except on alternating Tuesdays during the full moon, eh, Vince?"

Reese said nothing.

"Oh, I forgot," Teeter went on. "It ain't Vince. It's Reeeese. That's right. Reeeese. Pardon me. So, Reese, you like basketball?"

"I like the game," Reese said evenly.

"They say you take 'em pretty well out there in the street."

"I do okay."

"Wanta try with me?"

"I don't care," Reese said. They played a little Make It — Take It. Teeter was still fast, in spite of the poundage, and Reese had to hustle him; the coach also had natural size, so the lay-up was easy for him. But he couldn't get around Reese's fadeaway.

Finally, puffing, Teeter said, "You got a pretty fake there."

Reese was caught off guard. He smiled. "I work hard at it," he said.

"You thinking of coming out for the team next year?"

"I've been thinking about it."

"You think you could make it?"

"I might try," Reese said evenly.

"Do you think that the other guys would be willing to put up with all your shit, just because you got one shot?"

Reese felt all the blood pound into his face. The fat fuck. He'd drawn him out, right into the water, and then let him go.

Teeter went on. "I been watching you, Cappadora. Not just in here. You got a chip on your shoulder the size of Mount Rushmore, and you ain't got the size or the heart to back it up."

Feeling the curling of his hands, the telltale signal Reese had come to fear, he answered, "I do okay."

408

"You do okay, huh?" Teeter stuck his pork face right up next to Reese's. "You do okay because everybody feels sorry for you. I knew your father growing up, Vince. Nicer guy never walked the earth. Everybody felt like hell, all the shit he went through, and then, what does he get? This runt who thinks his shit don't stink."

Teeter waved one broad finger under Reese's nose. "You got speed and moves. But you come out for my team, you gotta know right then you ain't no special case. You'll be the same as the rest of them, maybe a little lower on the scale because you been living your whole life on getting the breaks . . . "

"I've never — " Reese began.

"Come on, Cappadora! You think you're such a big man, how about acting like it? *Are* you a big man? Or just a bully?" He scooped up the ball, Reese's own ball, balancing it in his big ham hands, and bounced it once off Reese's forehead. Then again. The bridge of Reese's nose stung like a sonofabitch. His eyes began to run. But he didn't put up his hands to block Teeter's attack. Teeter did it again. And again. "Big man, Reese, huh? Wanta go? What're you going to do now? Can you take it, Cappadora? Or are you just a pussy, deep down?" And he drew back to give the ball a little more punch, but then Reese's fist came up and he snatched the ball down, almost pulling Teeter off balance.

The big man's face slackened. And he took a step back. Oh shit, Reese thought, that was

409

the way they all acted. When they saw the look. What did I ever do to you, you fuck? All I was doing was messing around. Maybe trying to do the ordinary thing, just once. And even that got him in the shitter. Reese felt again that ferocious urge to take off, to smash Teeter's meat nose into his brain and then run, forever, to a place where he didn't have to carry around every fucking thing he'd ever done or thought like a load of bricks on his back.

"Look," Reese said, then. "Look, I just — "

"Forget it," Teeter said, whirling and slouching away. "Your kind of attitude, nobody needs."

And Reese just stood there, both arms wrapped around his ball, holding it to his chest as tightly as he could, while Teeter flipped off the light switch to the overheads, leaving him in the dark.

26

Beth

WHAT it seemed like to Beth was watching a tiger in the zoo.

There were times when the animal's eyes locked on yours, but there was nothing in the contact. You could never be sure whether the tiger was aware of you, individually or at all, or whether you were simply scenery, an unremarkable figment of the landscape. Did a tiger recognize a human being as distant kin, even as alive?

As she watched Sam pace, from the front porch to the back window, followed ceaselessly by Beowulf, she wondered whether he recognized her even as a member of the same species. His motion was constant, from the moment he got home from school (it took him two weeks to walk in without ringing the doorbell) until he politely, promptly closed his door at night. Even when he sat doing his homework at the kitchen table, his legs bobbed and jittered. Beth wondered if he needed . . . something — vitamins, sedatives, more milk. In his laboriously printed eight-page dossier on Sam's traits, George had indicated that his son always displayed a surplus of energy. 'He's like a half-grown puppy,' George had written. 'He'll run and run and run and then he'll just fall down and sleep, wherever he

411

is.' Beth had seen no evidence of that, Sam's eyes were puffy, mornings; his sleep was not like that of an eager, healthy little hound.

The social worker called nearly daily, ("It's probably the first time in her life she ever did anything interesting that didn't involve five adults having sex with the kid," Candy had explained.) Sam's anxiety was natural, she explained. He was experiencing, on some level, the stages of mourning — shock, denial, anger, alienation.

"How do you know?" Beth asked her one afternoon.

"I . . . I don't," the case worker admitted. "I just . . . guess a kid in that situation would feel that way."

Beth remembered the kinds of questions the reporters used to ask the myriad experts whose headshots she took for Sunday specials. "What does the research say?" she asked.

"There isn't any."

"What do you mean?"

"I don't think this ever happened before," said the social worker. "Kids, if they're kidnapped, either are found right away or pretty much never found. Alive, I should say. I'm sorry, Beth."

The social worker described the case of a little girl mistakenly given to the wrong parents at the hospital, literally switched at birth. There had been a lot of publicity; hadn't Beth read about it? Beth made polite noises; she hadn't read anything about a missing child in more years than she could recall. This child, the social worker went on, was quite well-adjusted

412

in most ways. Good grades. Popular. The way the natural parents found out was that the daughter they believed to be their biological child died from a congenital heart ailment, and blood tests proved she could not have been their child. There was a big probe into hospital records, and it all came out.

"And did she ever see the father she thought was her real father again? The man she grew up with?" asked Beth. "Do they have contact?"

"Er . . . yes," said the social worker. "Actually, she still lives with him. She didn't want to return to the natural parents, and a judge ruled in her favor. But then she . . . "

"What?"

"Changed her mind."

"Oh."

"And went back to her real . . . er . . . first family."

"Oh," said Beth.

"But she was much older, a teenager, and the circumstances . . . " the social worker's voice trailed off.

The circumstances in their house were so different, Beth sometimes felt they were all strangers brought together to act in a play without rehearsal.

★ ★ ★

As vigorously as Beth resisted it on the first Saturday, the family began arriving before any of them were even awake. Angelo. How could she close the door on Angelo? And he could not have done better; he didn't leap on Sam and crush him, though Beth knew he must have wanted with every beat of his straining, mechanically charged old heart to do just that. He sat, tears streaming down his face, and told Sam about the frescoes at Wedding in the Old Neighborhood. "They look down on the *matrimonio*, the wedding. Each one of them is one of the operas, Ben," he said.

"It's Sam, Ange," Beth reminded him softly.

"Sam, of course. This is a good, strong name, Sam. I am an old man, Sam, and foolish," said Angelo. "But let me tell you. In the one, it is *La Bohème*, the face of Rodolfo, the artist made the face from a picture of your papa, of my son, Patrick. And do you know Menotti? *Amahl and the Night Visitors?*"

Sam, to Beth's astonishment, nodded. "I saw it at school, on the big TV," he said.

"The little boy? With the crutch?"

"Yes?"

"That is you, Ben . . . Sam. That is you. The little boy is you."

"Cool," said Sam. "Can I see it?" Angelo looked up at Beth, his faded eyes brimming.

"Soon," said Beth. "Let him settle down a little, Ange." She hadn't insisted for nothing that no one except her, Pat and the kids visit Sam at first. Now, on his first real full day home, she could feel Sam's fragile shell giving way, feel his confusion. She wanted to stand and motion for everyone to leave. But it would have been like trying to divert a river.

"Who's Reese?" Sam asked then.

"Reese," Angelo said. "Ah. Of course. He is Pinkerton, in *Madama Butterfly*. A bad man, unfortunately. I told Vincent, make another choice. So he chose Don Giovanni, a worse man! So, we left it be Pinkerton."

"Lot of walls," Sam commented.

"Lot of walls?" Angelo bellowed. "You should see it. This is a big place, Sam!" He turned his head as Tree came in. "And your auntie, she is the mama in *Amahl*. She is your mama on the walls."

"Ben," Tree said, kneeling, holding out her arms. Looking at Beth all the while, Sam walked into them, uncertainly, and Tree burst into tears. "Oh, Ben. Oh my God." Poor kid, thought Beth; she wanted to hang a sign around his neck that said 'The Name Is Sam.'

And so it went, the same scene, over and over, all weekend and into the week. By the simple sight of him, everyone, Paul, Bick, her father, seemed driven to attitudes of penance, of worship, as if he were a vision in a grotto instead of a twelve-year-old with badly scabbed knees.

After hugging him, holding him at arm's length and hugging him again, Bill thanked Sam for coming home while his grandfather was still alive to see it.

"You're welcome," Sam replied gently. "Are you sick?"

"No, no," Bill told him, heartily. "No, I'm not sick. Don't you worry. I'm just so happy, son."

"I'm your uncle," Bick told Sam eagerly.

415

"And you were named after me. They call me Bick, but my real name is Benjamin." And without waiting for Sam to open his mouth, Bick asked, "Do you remember me? Do you remember the time I pulled you out of Lake Delavan . . . ?"

If anything was accomplished by all of it, Beth thought later, it was the fact that Sam, hopelessly confused and exhausted, desperate to give appropriate responses to questions for which he had no answers, began to hang close to Beth's side or, if she was out of the room, to follow Reese wherever he went. As the living room filled with a teeming crowd of neighbors and family, police, and the occasional reporter who slipped in grinning brilliantly and continued to grin, protesting innocence, while being ejected, Beth watched Sam and Reese dig mitts out of the garage, lock the gate, and wordlessly begin fastball catch in the yard.

They would get to maybe three apiece and then another pilgrim would arrive. Another blessing, another profession of amazement, another pronunciation. Rachelle. Aunt Angela. Charley Two's daughter and his son. The Bonaventuras. The Rooneys and the Reillys. Recently retired Chief Bastokovitch from Parkside. Paul's best friend, Hank.

Barbara Kelliher and her two daughters.

Barbara, who for some reason was the only face that caused Beth to blubber like a fool — Barbara, her neat cheerleader's haircut still pert and suspiciously chestnut-brown against over-pink cheeks, her Chanel still preceding

416

her into a room, who had known Beth only slightly in high school but who had decided, on the basis of something Beth could only understand as the same quality of resolve that once made Barbara able to smile and raise a fist cheerfully while doing Chinese splits, to simply suspend her own life and rush chivalrously to the defense of Beth's. Beth caught her around the waist and would not let go; and after a moment of shocked resistance, Barbara returned Beth's embrace, and began to rock her, rocking her as a mother rocks a baby on her hip.

When Beth's sobs subsided to hiccoughs, Barbara asked to see Ben. Beth went to the window to call him.

"No," Barbara told her. "Just let him be. Just let me watch him a moment." She turned to Beth as Ben spun to grab a high fly. "It's you he looks like," she said.

Sam fell asleep on a lawn chair, still holding a rubbery slice of pizza about eight o'clock that night. Beth had to help him up to bed and at nine the next morning was still heavily, soddenly asleep. Beth hated to haul him out, but Rosie and Angelo had arranged and paid for a special mass at Immaculata. Pat insisted all of them go, and go humbly, and was already arguing with Vincent about the condition of his chinos before Beth had had her first cup of coffee.

Blocks from the church, Beth already noticed a kind of electricity in the streets, an extra stillness only enhanced by the presence of more than the usual number of cars, nose to tail, even blocking driveways. It felt like an Easter or Fourth of

July morning, a concealed and unaccustomed bustle belied by the absence of workday traffic. When they turned off Suffolk Avenue onto the boulevard, even Vincent gasped. The street in front of the church was blocked at both ends and clogged with satellite trucks and a welter of police squads — from a dozen villages and the city of Chicago, from the state — all with hood lights flashing, the concussion of rotating spots and floods creating a sort of artificial sunrise. On both sides of the plastic-tape cordon, whole families stood craning over the heads of reporters, knocking over sawhorses. "There must be a thousand people," Vincent breathed, his voice almost childish with awe.

As it turned out, the Cappadoras could park nowhere near the entrance; and they had to fight their way to the door of the church as the bells tolled for eleven o'clock mass. None of the assembled crowds seemed even to recognize them until they were on the threshold of the foyer door. Beth was almost disappointed on behalf of the press; something in the nature of this was making them expect to see a little red-haired boy, led by beatific young parents, instead of a bleary-eyed adolescent with his baseball cap ruefully turned backwards, flanked by short, dark, nearly identical men (one young, one middle-aged, neither beaming), a nondescript graying brunette in ill-fitting clothes, and a strawberry-blond girl in a miniskirt and tights. What truly stunned Beth was the fact that the church somehow was filled not with leakage from the curious throngs outside but

418

with faces she recognized. Every face was lifted entire from her past and Pat's. What kind of screening process could have accounted for the uniformity of it? You rarely knew every face even at a family wedding, Who had been the arbiter? Who had known enough to let only the insiders pass? Beth later learned that, in fact, there had been no gatekeeper; somehow, those who knew they should enter had done so, and, with the exception of reporters, those who knew they should only look on had not tried to do more.

As Beth and Pat walked up the aisle with the children to where Rosie, Angelo, Bill, and Bick stood, with Paul and Sheilah behind them, dressed in night-class finery and holding open seats in the first pew, they passed dozens of outstretched hands and lifted, tearful faces. Classmates and neighbors; Candy, of course, as well as cops Beth had never seen out of uniform, even many who'd long since transferred to other departments; a whole contingent of Madison friends: Laurie, of course, with her husband and children, and Rob and Annie Maltese, but others, too — the blind man on the corner who had given Ben and Vincent Life Savers when Beth strolled them around the block with their Big Wheels a generation ago, and Linda, the waitress from Cappadora's.

The opening hymn was 'Amazing Grace', and Father Cleary, who had known Beth and Pat all their lives, lost no time in forging the link. "We meet today in the midst of what the Church calendar refers to as 'ordinary time'," he said. "That is, we are not in the wake of or anticipating one of the great festivals of our liturgical tradition. But clearly, there are indications, including the fact that all the seats are filled" — self-conscious laughter — "that this is not an ordinary occasion; it is in fact a festival that celebrates not only the reaffirmation of our faith — and, as some of you may not recall, we do this every Sunday — " more laughter — "but of the power of faith and the mercy of God, which surpasses all our poor power to understand or estimate. Today, we celebrate, as we did in song, the mercy of God as symbolized by the homecoming of a child who was once lost, but now is found." Father Cleary coughed, once, nervously, and Beth forgave him for his obvious awareness of the cameras, and his ambivalence; she wondered if he'd set the VCR in the rectory to tape the noon news.

"We celebrate," Father Cleary continued, "the presence among us, in its wholeness, of the Cappadora and Kerry families, families with long roots in this Church, this school, this community, whose tragic loss nine years ago was a sorrow from afar for people all over the world, but a personal sorrow for those of us who have known Rose and Angelo and Bill and Evelyn, and Pat and Beth — children I baptized on a couple of fine Sundays some years ago. As you all know, their son Ben was taken from them nine years ago, when he was only three — and, by what can only be called a modern-day miracle, returned to them just weeks ago, not maimed, not torn, but healthy and whole.

"I will not ask the Cappadoras to stand, not only because you all know them well, but because they have already stood too much scrutiny, too much examination of their personal Calvary. But I will ask you to join with them today in their gratitude and their faith, faith that sustained them, which never wavered when the faith of those less strong would surely have collapsed, to welcome, with them, the return of Ben — " he stopped, glanced down, then looked up, straight into Beth's face — "of Sam Karras Cappadora" — Beth felt Sam, next to her, straighten his shoulders — "to his family and to our family of worship.

"Though not every celebration of the Eucharist at Immaculata is televised on worldwide TV," he continued, over yet another appreciative ripple, "we have made the decision to allow a certain level of media today in our sanctuary, because we wish to allow those who cannot be here to share today in this community of worship, in this festival that reaffirms the strength of a community, and its heart . . . And we are asked to remind all of you that Angelo and Patrick Cappadora and their families invite you to a luncheon at Wedding in the Old Neighborhood, 628 Diversey Street, Chicago, Illinois, immediately following the service, and that it is the hope of the family that each and all of you will attend. Maps are available on a table in the baptistery. And now we wish to begin this festival, in ordinary time, by saying,

421

The Lord is with you."

"And also with you," the crowd murmured as one.

"Lift up your hearts," Father Cleary commanded, in his old but still sonorous voice.

Beth did not know what made her look over her shoulder — a rustle of sound at the back of the church? Simple discomfort with the beginning of the liturgy, which she, lapsed and lacking, had to struggle to follow?

But she did look, and just to the left of the aisle, small in his pinstriped blue suit, stood George Karras. From a distance of thirty yards, Beth could feel his agonized unease, the effort it took for him to stand still, without straining at his tie or shooting his cuffs. She did not think about it very long. Had she stopped to think, she might have thought of a dozen things that would have stopped her from moving — the media possibilities, the imagined wrath of various Cappadoras, even the clutch of pity and dismay at her own stomach.

She got up, eyes turning speculatively to follow her, and walked quietly to the back of the church and extended her hand, which George, gulping in humiliation and relief, took. She led him back, toward the first pew, and it was only as she neared the family, the last few feet, that she dared to look up — and it was Sam's face she saw, turned on her and George, with a look she had never seen on it before.

It was, she later guessed, joy.

27

Reese

PLEADING a sudden urge to spend a few hours alone, loosening up and practicing, Reese gave it his best try, getting out of going to the restaurant for the big hooha lunch after church.

After all, he reasoned, his dad didn't know anything about what had happened at school with Teeter, that fat bastard; so in Dad's mind, Reese was still toying with the idea of going out for the basketball team next fall. And Reese was content to let Dad think that, as long as it lasted. Wherever the hell he was really going, Dad seemed to assume he was at the rec center or somewhere, doing drills. "Working on the free throws?" Dad would ask him every so often, just to prove that, even though no one else in North America knew there was a kid in the whole Cappadora family besides Sam, his dad at least still knew Reese existed.

"Sure, Dad," Reese would say. "Workin' on 'em."

"'Cause you know, the team that gets the free throws wins the game," his dad would say. "And height doesn't count for tick on the free-throw line."

"Right, Dad," Reese would agree. Dad would look all content then. Just the mention of Reese

423

doing anything 'constructive', as his dad put it, got everyone off Reese's case. Which was fine by him.

But he should have known better than to pull the old sports hole card today; it was actually fairly stupid, given that tryouts were a half-season away anyhow. There was no way he was going to get out of playing his part in the goddamned manger scene. When Reese brought it up, Dad gave him one look, and it wasn't a 'Please, Vincenzo,' look, either. It was a 'Don't screw with me' look, and there was no use arguing. Dad could be as stubborn as a pit bull when it came to some things, and it was for damn sure that one of them was the full-out 'Aren't we happy' treatment for the benefit of the masses.

In fact, Reese felt damned sorry for Sam, who looked like his underwear was about six sizes too small, and he only looked worse outside the church after that poor little guy George gave him a kiss on the forehead and told him he wouldn't 'bother the family' at the party. Dumb shit. Didn't he know the kid already felt like a piece of crap for leaving his father? George was an adult, and he could have managed to come down there and have a sausage sandwich if it would make Sam feel better.

On the other hand, Uncle Joey and a couple of the others had been standing around outside the church doing the Italian hand-jive, and that could only mean they were talking about the nerve of that guy showing up at the mass at all — they were the Cappadoras! Whatever else he was, George was that bitch's husband! Probably George had a good idea of what might happen if Joey got a few Seven and Sevens in him downtown. Uncle Joey was pretty decent, generally, but he was a hothead — as were, Reese realized, about sixty-five percent of all the adult men he knew.

As they all piled into the car, dodging yelling reporters, Reese reflected that some of it, to tell the truth, wasn't all bad. The media thing was ultra-boring, though some of the guys, even Jordie, had this totally kidlike idea that being in the newspaper would make you feel important or something. The good part was that Heather Bergman and about five of her equally foxticular friends had decided to become his mother hens over the past couple of weeks. The other girls were okay, but the way Heather's blunt-cut blond hair moved at the exact level of her lips when she turned her head could transform Reese into one giant bulge in about fifteen seconds. And before all this, she'd been like, "Cappadora, that little hood." Now it was, "I never knew you were so sensitive, I never knew you went through all this . . . " Where had she been living, Zaire? Last week, as they'd walked home from the library, after what had been for Reese a fairly agonizing two hours of trying to remember Civil War dates while inhaling the smell that seemed to come from the hollow directly below the scooped neck of Heather's jersey, he'd managed to back her (and she wasn't protesting) against the wall of the unfinished library addition, and in the course of making out for maybe twenty

425

minutes, he had not exactly felt her up, but his forearms had made definite contact when she'd thought he was just touching her cheek with his hands.

At least, he figured she just thought that. Or did girls know exactly what you were doing, too? And just pretend they had no idea? And she was like, "Reese, you're sweet," afterward, instead of looking like she wanted to belt him, which was okay, too, as long as it lasted.

But this. Shit. When they got there, the parking lot at Wedding and the street in front looked like the biggest concession for used Eldorados in Chicago.

They managed to get through another press gang, and went inside. It never failed; Reese was always surprised at the sheer goofy magnificence of Wedding, every time he walked in. This time, he got a kind of kick out of watching Sam, who'd never seen it before — watching him look up and take in the stained-glass rose windows and the replica women (even Reese thought they were beautiful, although nuts), Juliet and Santa Lucia and the one he always thought of as the Tuscan Goddess of Sexual Intercourse. He had no idea why there were women in balconies in the eaves of Wedding in the Old Neighborhood, and he always thought it made the place kind of look like the Pirates of the Caribbean ride at Disney World; but everyone seemed to either love them or get a chuckle out of them, or both. He followed the kid around the banks of linen-covered tables, as Sam goggled the frescoes, stopping particularly long in front of the Gian Carlo Menotti one — was it possible that he actually recognized his own face? And then Reese took Sam by the arm and brought him out to the bar area, where the model of the Fontana di Trevi gushed Champagne out of a jug in the arms of the sea god. They got Scottie to give them a glass and each had a sip. It was cheapie stuff — Angelo always insisted that he wasn't going to run Moët et Chandon through plastic pipes. But Sam seemed to like it.

And then, of course, Mom caught up and nabbed the glass, and then they sort of hung around the cloak room while ten thousand relatives streamed past. The place was all set up as if it were the 'big' night at Wedding, Saturday night, when people brought their out-of-town relatives to visit the restaurant. There was usually just one bride and groom, but today there were two: the sweet, pretty bride, who looked like his cousin Moira would look when she grew up, and the hot one, who looked like she belonged in the swimsuit issue of *Sports Illustrated*. He remembered that one's name, Claudia. There were two others, but he could never keep them straight. He was fairly certain that two of the three grooms were gay — one was a dancer, even — but they were all great-looking and big. The two here today, one was the one Grandpa Angelo called 'the Nazi' behind his back, because the guy looked like something out of *The Sound of Music*.

By the time Mom actually got herself calmed down enough to walk into the banquet room, the tables were all filled. People were eating.

"Vincent," she said, "come over here. I want us all to walk in together." Big production, Mom, Reese thought. Shit. Oh well. He looked behind him for Sam, who was goofing around running under the coat racks with Kerry. His size fooled you: he was only this little twelve-year-old. Reese's stomach felt another tug of pity.

When they came out of the bar area into the room, the band leader caught sight of them and struck up that old song about 'I'll be loving you always,' which Reese thought was intended for nothing except to get everyone chewing on their sausage to start bawling; even Father Cleary was in tears.

What it did, though, was make everyone stand up, and as soon as they stood up, they started to applaud. And once they started to applaud, it seemed like they would never stop.

Sam sort of hid his head against Mom's shoulder, and Reese tried unobtrusively to move over a little so that he was shielding Sam from most of the faces in the crowd. But everybody kept on applauding and yelling for about six hours, and the band kept playing cheesy songs, like 'Danny Boy', and everybody cried harder. Reese thought he was going to puke. Even he felt like he might start bawling.

But at last, the bandleader, Billy, got everybody to quiet down and said, just, "Welcome home." Not the name, thank God. Nobody really knew exactly what to call Sam. And Sam kind of waved, and everybody clapped a little more then, and finally they sat down to eat. Which was good, because Reese, who

428

normally didn't eat much of anything, was starving. And Sam was eating like they were going to outlaw ravioli tomorrow.

By the time they set up the table with tiramisu and cannoli, the busboys were moving the front tables back a little to clear the dance floor — boy, thought Reese, they're going to do the whole deal. The first bride, the one who looked like his cousin, had bustled the back of her dress and was getting ready to dance with the fag groom. What they did first, on a regular night at Wedding, was dim all the lights and have the bride and groom dance to 'Sunrise, Sunset', usually with Grandpa Angelo cutting in at some point to represent the father. Reese's dad even cut in sometimes, even though he didn't like to dance. So they did that now, and then the lights came up, and the bride picked up her skirts. The sweet bride just picked them up a little; but Claudia, Reese recalled, hiked them up way high, so you could see her garter on her thigh — tough luck it wasn't her. He knew then that they were going to do the tarantella, and sure enough, pretty soon half the joint was up dancing, too.

It always killed Reese to see people who weren't Italian do the tarantella; it was like watching people who weren't really Polish or married to Polish wives trying to polka. They thought all you had to do was stand there and kick your feet, one after the other — boomba boomba boomba boom — when in fact there were steps to it. Vincent knew them, had since he was a kid, but would rather have been burned at the stake than actually do them. To his surprise, though, his father got out there and put his hands palms-up on the back of his hips, the way you were supposed to, instead of just putting your hands on your waist, the way Grandma Rosie did when she was mad — which was the way people usually did it. Back when the place first started, in fact, Grandpa had to demote a really beautiful bride to waitress because she couldn't get the hang of doing the tarantella like what Grandpa called 'a real madonna.'

Today, though, the Cousin Moira bride was in top form, her satin shoes flying like little pistons, and when everybody was out of breath, the band started playing it faster, and Dad started motioning for Sam to get up and dance too. Reese thought he'd pee from shame for the kid. But Sam, affable the way he was, he got up, and he started talking to Dad, and Dad motioned to the bandleader. Billy stopped right away. "My son doesn't know the tarantella, but he knows the miserlu." He stopped and bent down to hear what Sam was saying. "The sertu — it means 'the tail'. Do you know that?"

"But of course," Billy smiled, and he started playing, real slow, 'Never on Sunday.' Grandpa Angelo came over and gave Sam one of his great big linen handkerchiefs with the A and the C embroidered on them in red. Reese figured this was part of the dance; he'd seen it once, at a Greek wedding on TV. Sam stood there, holding the handkerchief and looking around him, until — My God, Reese thought, no way — Mom got up and walked over and put out her hand. And Sam started to show her the steps, which were slow, right foot over left, then behind, then a little hop and a turn. Mom wasn't much of a dancer, but she looked dreamy, like she was drunk; she looked almost beautiful. And then Dad took Mom's hand, and Sam pointed out how you had to hold your arm up, in an arch, and Grandpa Bill got Grandma Rosie up . . . it was enough to gag you.

In a while, his mom had the hang of it. She was weaving and dipping gracefully, her shoulders swaying, smiling up at his dad, and there must have been fifty people in concentric rings, Sam right at the middle, still leading, still holding the handkerchief, kind of laughing even, his reddish hair a little plastered up with sweat. He caught Reese watching and rolled his eyes.

Oh, Ben, Reese thought. He looked away from the kid and up, away from the kid, at the frescoes on the walls. At Ben's face, the wise and wondering angel face of a little crippled boy seeing God, and then at himself, his face proud and probably better-looking then he actually was, but painted to represent some bastard whose biggest contribution to history was getting some pretty Japanese chick to off herself.

He went out to the bar to see if Scottie could be talked into letting him have another glass of Champagne.

28

Beth

EVEN after the nurse and the bailiff brought Cecilia in and settled her in the enclosure beside her attorneys, Beth forgot to sit down.

She felt Pat pulling on her arm and twitched her wrist away in irritation, only then recognizing that the press, the officers, and Judge Sakura were already seated. A young Asian man, the judge was regarding her with a waiting glance, an endless and mild dispassion. Beth sat down then with a thud, wincing as she knocked her tailbone on the edge of the bench, aware of the zipping sound of a seam in her skirt splitting.

If she craned her neck slightly, though, she could still see the angelic wide face of the nurse, and just beyond her, Cecil. Had she not had the foreknowledge of Cecil's identity, Beth would have picked her out only because she wore jail-orange cottons, like a doctor's scrub suit, the only person in the courtroom not dressed in Sunday-like finery.

Cecil was not only changed. She was buried.

Crammed into the pants and tunic, the swanlike girl Beth remembered now was frankly fat, packed with rolls of flesh, odd protuberances where the skin was simply pushed beyond containing. You could still spot, in the point

432

of her chin, in her wrists, the tiny, still-perfect bones. Cecil looked like a funhouse mirror image, a stuffed-toy Cecil, watching her nurse with rapt attention.

Beth had half-expected to feel a spurt of pity for Cecil, or rage, or something. She felt only a ravening curiosity. She wanted to crack Cecil open like a matrushka doll, opening shell after shell, searching for the woman who had stolen her baby, and beneath that the talented, patrician, disdainful teenage hotbox, and then the sharp-elbowed neighbor kid always glomming onto Ellen.

But Cecil's attorney, Michele Perrault, stood up now — small as a child, with feathers of short dark hair, dressed in jewelly colors like a medieval troubadour — and so did the D.A., both with words slung on their hips like six-guns. It was the chief deputy D.A., Candy pointed out, only because this was the Ben Cappadora case, and press from Boston to Brisbane were sardined into the courtroom, watching on closed circuit in two other rooms down the hall, and flowing down the steps outside, onto the curbs, onto the lawns, a human waterfall in the hazy summer sunlight.

"Your Honor," began Michele Perrault, "I have done this work for a very long time . . . "

Judge Sakura smiled. "We are all aware of your longevity as a litigator, Ms. Perrault," he said with immense sweetness.

Perrault softened then, too, and glanced around her almost girlishly, as if suddenly aware of all the cameras and poised pens, the

433

sketch artists busily drawing.

"I've done this work for a very long time, relatively speaking," Perrault began again. "And I have spent many hours with my client, Mrs. Karras, over many days."

"And?" asked Sakura, scribbling.

"And I have been able to get nothing, nothing out of her that gives me reason to believe that my client can understand the charges she faces. I have the gravest doubts about whether she can assist in her own defense. Usually I can get some kind of response from virtually anyone, no matter how impaired. But my client shows no indication she knows there is someone talking to her at all."

"While I can understand your conviction, Counsel," Sakura said, "I'd like to know if you have any documentation about Mrs. Karras's mental-health history that can support your opinion."

"I do, Your Honor," Perrault said quickly. "May I approach?" The judge nodded, and Perrault brought him a sheaf of papers. "These were obtained from the psychiatrists who have treated Mrs. Karras at Silvercrest."

"For the past four years?"

"And previously, Your Honor. Mrs. Karras has been hospitalized on eight occasions, for periods of several days to several months, and has undergone a wide range of drug treatments and other therapies intended to address her condition."

"Which is?"

The D.A. spoke up then, as if, Candy would

tell Beth later, he simply needed to pee on the tree and prove he'd been there. "With all due respect to Ms. Perrault, Your Honor, she is not a medical doctor, and not qualified to describe — "

"It's all in the documents, sir," Perrault told him. "In lay terms, Mrs. Karras is catatonic."

Perrault read from her copy. "Mrs. Karras has a long history of mood disorders, going back to her teens, and immobilizing depression that has persisted, off and on, for the past six years, becoming total four years ago. She has not" — Perrault waved at Cecil's blank presence — "been any better or worse than this since then."

"I need to study these records, of course," Sakura said. "I'm sorry if I interrupted you, Ms. Perrault. Did I? But I need to know if the attending physician is present today, and if he can explain to us Mrs. Karras's condition at the time the alleged abduction took place."

"He is," Perrault said. "But he was not treating Mrs. Karras at that time. Her physician at that time was a psychotherapist in Minneapolis, where Mrs. Karras lived on and off before her marriage to Mr. Karras, after her divorce from Mr. — " she sprinted back to her files and consulted a clipboard — "from Adam Samuel Hill, a theatrical writer, to whom Mrs. Karras was married for . . . well, a total of three years. That therapist was a woman in her sixties, and died two years ago, Your Honor. Mrs. Karras was not hospitalized during that period of her second marriage. And Mrs. Karras's former husband — "

"Is he here?"

"Mr. Hill is disabled, he suffers from multiple sclerosis, Your Honor. But I have a sworn affidavit from him about Cecilia's intransigent emotional problems during their marriage. He is extremely apologetic that his condition makes it very difficult for him to travel."

"Do we have other — ?"

"Mrs. Karras's mother, Sarah Lockhart, is here today. With your permission, I'd like to ask her to describe her daughter's emotional state at the time of the kidnapping."

Sakura nodded at the D.A. "Is this okay with you?"

"Again, sir," the D.A. said, "I have to point out that I am not aware that Cecilia Lockhart Karras's mother has any credentials that qualify her as an expert medical witness."

"You know that this court is not going to regard her as such."

"Thank you, sir. The state is appreciative."

"Not at all." The judge nodded to Perrault, who asked to call Sarah Lockhart. As the trim older woman walked rapidly and silently from the back rows of the huge room, the bailiff Beth had heard Candy call 'Elvis', though his bronze tag said something else, turned to the clerk for the swearing-in. They didn't use a Bible, Beth noticed. She supposed that was out of fashion.

She still recognized Mrs. Lockhart; she had not seen her in twenty years. Beth studied the older woman's face carefully as Perrault explained how cooperative Sarah had been, how shocked, how horrified she had been to learn that her grandson was another family's purloined child. How she had helped, as Cecil's legal guardian, to obtain medical histories from Cecil's hospitalization. How bitterly sorry she felt for the Cappadoras —

"We all understand," the D.A. put in, with a tick of annoyance, "how Mrs. Lockhart must feel."

Perrault then burrowed right in, asking Mrs. Lockhart how well she knew the little boy known as Sam Karras.

"Very well indeed," the old woman whispered. "He was my grandson." And she looked point-blank into Beth's eyes, Beth thinking, This is how Cecil would have looked one day — sweetly rounded and Yankee and just the least bit arty, like a matron who'd started the town's most active book group — had Cecil been spared the hot injection of madness. Sarah Lockhart's eyes begged Beth. "I never had any idea that he wasn't Cecilia's child. Cecilia's own child by birth."

"But you were not present for the birth of the child your daughter presented to you as your grandson."

"No. She and I . . . Cecilia had a great deal of difficulty in her relationships with her father and me. When she was little, we considered her high-strung . . . She had tantrums and then blackouts . . . we thought, an artistic temperament . . . "

It was not until Sarah Lockhart's recitation actually began — told Rosie-fashion, with whorls and wings of wee, irrelevant detail — that Beth realized it: There was to be no flash of illumination. Ever.

Over the long summer of the investigation, Beth had herself come to know Cecil as well as the family who had raised her.

That is to say . . . not at all.

So, half-lulled by the heat of the hundreds of bodies around her in the room, Beth listened to the scant facts of Cecil's life as her mother, the D.A., and Perrault understood them: her first three marriages, all to theater types, none of which lasted longer than two years. And the pitiful truth that, of all those husbands, the Lockharts had actually met only one: George.

Beth heard about the friends the police had tried to find from Cecil's flighty periods in Minneapolis, California, and New York. Friends? None of them had ever even shared a meal with Cecil, though a few apartment neighbors in Minneapolis thought they remembered seeing Cecil with a little boy. They seemed to remember that she referred to him as her 'nephew'. The one true hope, a designer Cecil had stayed in touch with since college, had died the previous year from AIDS, as had his lover.

Beth could barely rouse herself even when Mrs. Lockhart began to cry, as she described Cecil's reaction when Adam Hill — "a drama critic, quite well-respected, much older" — abruptly took up with a younger woman, a dancer.

"It was one of the few times that I felt Cecilia really opened up to me," said Sarah Lockhart.

"She was heartbroken. She said she felt used up. Adam never wanted her to grow old, or even to grow up, and she wasn't even thirty at the time. Of course everyone thought she was years younger." Mrs. Lockhart began to frankly sob. "And I tried to comfort her, assured her that there were compensations for getting older. She would find a good man and have a child . . . but of course, she couldn't." She looked suddenly at Beth and Pat and said slowly, "We were talking about it last night, her father and I. I'm the only one who can understand Charles very well since the stroke, and we realized that was why she did it, because of the miscarriage . . . "

Beth leaned forward in her seat, her arms stabbing with adrenaline prickles, aware only of Candy sitting up sharply, adjacent, reaching forward to curl her hand around the back of the bench in front of her.

"The miscarriage," said the D.A., looking up at Perrault, whose neck was flushed as deeply as her rosy scarf.

"I don't know this," Perrault said. "Your Honor, I . . . "

Sakura slipped his wire-rimmed glasses off and massaged his eyes. "Was Mrs. Karras given a routine physical exam in custody?" The lawyers scrabbled through their papers.

"A battery of neurological tests; we have the results right here, which counsel also has," the D.A. said quickly.

"A physical exam?" the judge asked again, patiently.

"We were concerned with the patient's mental

439

and emotional state . . . " the D.A. replied softly.

"Which can, of course, be affected by her physical afflictions," the judge said with a sigh. "Mrs. Lockhart, did you forget to tell the police that your daughter had suffered a miscarriage?"

"No."

"Then, why does Ms. Perrault seem shocked by this knowledge?"

"I didn't tell them."

"Why was that?" the judge asked softly.

"Because I wasn't sure. I still don't know. Perhaps Charles and I should have brought it up, but we thought better of it."

"Then, I'm sorry, Mrs. Lockhart, I'm not following you."

"I'm not following either, Your Honor," Perrault put in, but he silenced her with a measuring look.

"You have to understand," Sarah Lockhart pleaded. "We saw our daughter perhaps, oh, three times before she moved back to Chicago with Sam. She didn't even come home when her father had his first stroke, and was expected to die, though he did recover fully that time . . . " Sarah Lockhart breathed heavily, and Beth found herself straining to lend the old woman composure across the few feet of air that separated them. "Though I did try, I only spoke with her at any length one other time after the night she told me that Adam was leaving her."

"And then?"

"And then, she said that the reason he left her was because she was pregnant, and that she was going to get . . . old and fat."

"So you went to her?"

"No, because all at once she said the pregnancy was all over; she'd had a miscarriage! And then I didn't see her again until the authorities contacted us and told us she was in Bellevue; have you ever been there?" Mrs. Lockhart winced; it was long ago, Beth thought, but perhaps not long enough. "Cecilia was just about like she is now, except that she seemed to know me, she would squeeze my hand a little. And the nurses couldn't get anything out of her. They'd kept trying to find someone to help her, but she . . . she kept closing like a shell." Mrs. Lockhart's dainty hands made a small clam shell, slowly meeting. "It was the police who finally found us, found our address, because Cecilia had been fingerprinted when she was a young woman, arrested in some rally or something, not a crime."

Beth heard Candy's rapid snort, and saw, from the corner of her eye, FBI agent Bender stiffen.

"So when you talked with police and investigators from the district attorney's office, you didn't think to bring up this miscarriage . . . "

"I didn't know if she'd had a miscarriage! You didn't ever know whether what Cecilia said was true or a dream!" Sarah Lockhart burst out, for the first time angry. "I just knew that my child was slipping into this darkness, and I had to make all kinds of decisions with

441

my husband about whether they should attach electrodes to her head and put her in an icewater bath . . . "

"Mrs. Lockhart," the judge put in gently. "Do you need a moment?"

"No," she said firmly.

Perrault, dazed, seemed to recover herself and said, "Well. Then. Mrs. Lockhart, then, as you told police, you believed when Cecilia showed up in 1985 with . . . Sam, that he was her child. How is that possible if you thought she'd lost her baby?"

"Please!" Sarah Lockhart pleaded. "I loved her dearly, I love her still. Don't you understand? If I asked Cecilia a question she didn't like, she would threaten to kill herself, or never to speak to us again . . . and we knew that she meant it." She glanced down at her hands. "When she said she and Adam had actually gotten back together and had a child, but then split up, it seemed possible. When she said the court had given custody to Adam because she was too ill to care for him . . . well, what was I to believe? She seemed so ashamed."

"But if she was too ill to care for him?" Perrault ventured.

"Then, well, she got better! She seemed fine, and she seemed to be a good mother, even though the child was shy with her . . . well, I assumed that was because he was only getting to know her all over again after spending so much time with his father."

"And why didn't you confirm all this with Adam?"

442

Sarah Lockhart looked at the attorney with pure scorn. "Miss Perrault, I had never even met the man. He had left my daughter alone, and . . . and expecting, and then taken her child from her. Why would I have talked to him?"

"To know," Perrault fumbled helplessly. "To be sure . . . "

"Cecilia said Adam was ill, that he had multiple sclerosis. Which I now know is really true. He actually does. You don't understand. She could be very convincing. And . . . then, I just . . . I didn't dare."

"Why?"

"Because Cecilia said that if I called Adam, ever, she'd never let me see the boy again. And I . . . I wanted a grandchild. I wanted a healthy, loving child who loved me. I wanted to . . . believe her. And he was so big, I believed he was four, not three . . . " She turned her gaze on Beth, and Beth felt her own eyes tug and itch in response. "Beth, I swear to you on my honor, he was always such a big boy. And not red-haired. We all saw in the papers that Ben was red-haired. His hair got reddish when he got big, of course — and when Cecilia married George, of course, we saw Sam all the time."

Sarah Lockhart leaned forward, gripping the polished rail. "Beth, she never spanked him. She never hurt his feelings. When Cecilia was well, she was gentle and tender to Sam; she always read to him; she taught him songs. They played this little game where she taught Sam to pretend he was the echo from the well in the wishing

443

song from *Snow White*, and he knew all the words . . . "

Beth was nodding, nodding, transfixed, when she felt Pat bury his face roughly against her shoulder; she turned almost casually to cradle his head and felt, rather than heard, the whirr of cameras that would make the big color shot that would splash above the fold next morning. What Pat was thinking, of course Beth understood — his beloved baby in the arms of the serpent, Ben's lips forming words the witch pronounced for him. But what, Beth thought angrily, suddenly, was the difference? Would it have been better to hear that Cecil was a bad, absent, crazy mother, who smacked Sam or called him stupid, as she, Beth, had done to Vincent, and even Kerry — and more than once? Would Pat feel more righteous had he known that Cecil had forgotten to wipe Sam's nose or give him Triaminic when he coughed? If Sam were not strong, healthy, bonny, would that further authenticate their grief?

Then Beth noticed Candy, turned in her seat as if studying Beth's face for a lost coin or a dropped stitch. What, Candy, Beth thought, what? She glanced at her watch — wouldn't court break soon?

"Then George and Cecilia were divorced," Mrs. Lockhart murmured.

"Cecilia and Adam?" Perrault asked.

"No, Cecilia and George — George Karras. They are legally divorced."

"Right. Yes. Was this because George wished

444

to pursue other relationships?" asked Perrault, who knew better.

"No, oh my goodness, no," said Mrs. Lockhart. "He loved Cecilia with his whole heart. No one could have put up with . . . well . . . " George's small construction business did well, explained Mrs. Lockhart, but the insurance he had could not begin to cover the magnitude of costs associated with Cecilia's long hospitalization. And disability programs were limited if a woman had a healthy, working husband. "George was afraid her illness, if it went on forever, would eat up everything. That he'd have to sell the house and not be able to take care of Sam." She glanced again at Beth. "I'm sorry, Beth."

To her shock, Beth said, clearly, "That's all right."

When Sakura called a recess, reporters crouched all around Beth and Pat like elves, as they rose to leave the room — Pat was genially telling them, "I never really knew Cecilia but now, God, she's pitiful. You can't hate someone so absolutely pathetic." ('Ben's Father Forgives', Beth imagined the headline, inwardly smiling as she recalled the way Ellen had begun calling Pat 'the quotable saint'.)

Candy motioned to Beth then, and with that unearthly ability to part the press like the Red Sea, led her out the door into the corridor of the jail, where the bailiff stood sucking a Tootsie Pop just beyond the door.

"Elvis, baby," Candy said to him in her best flirty growl, "don't make me want you . . . "

Beth saw his name now, clearly: Elmer. He moved aside to let them pass.

"This is probably against some law," Candy explained in a whisper. "But I want to see her. You want to see her. Perrault is with her. You want to come in?"

Beth nodded. She could feel all her pulses, the backs of her knees, the underside of her chin. In a pen of what looked like chicken wire, Cecil was alone with her nurse and her lawyer.

"Cecilia," the nurse said, with the kind of respect Beth knew she could never summon over and over again, in the face of a clay figure, "Chief Bliss is here to see you. Is that okay?" Cecil didn't even blink. When a stray bottle fly lighted on her upper arm, the muscles didn't quiver. Candy knelt down in front of Cecil's beefy knees.

"Cecil," she said. "Listen. Cecil. Please tell me. Where is the baby's grave? Where is the baby buried?"

The baby? Beth's unease erupted in a flutter — another child? A murdered child?

"Have you checked?" Candy asked Michele Perrault. "Did you find a death certificate?"

Flustered, Perrault replied, "A death certificate? How could I check for something I didn't even . . . listen, Detective, you have to know that this came from left field for me. My client's mother never said one word about a pregnancy, though I can't imagine what she was thinking . . . I mean, in keeping it back."

Musingly, Candy said, "I don't think she needed a reason, Michele. Or at least, a reason

446

that would make sense to you and me."

"But to lie!" Perrault caught herself, with a guilty look, as if hearing how she sounded for the first time. "I mean, to forget such a seemingly important detail. Of course, Sarah Lockhart has been under enormous strain. It's not entirely unexpected."

"It's not at all unexpected," Candy replied, wryly. "I fully expect people to try to protect their children. They do it all the time. They do it in much more outrageous ways. In her mind, Mrs. Lockhart was clinging to the fact that with Cecil, she could never be sure."

"You know," Perrault said, "a miscarriage sometimes triggers an abduction. I mean, no one disputes the facts of what took place here. We're talking . . . what, four years after the fact, probably, but it still might have given us something to go after. Something in the way of a cause for Cecil's actions."

"Oh, Mrs. Lockhart probably understood that, somewhere deep down."

"So, are you saying then that she really did suspect Cecilia's child was Ben? Maybe without realizing it? Because I never got the impression she was being deliberately untruthful," Perrault said.

"Nor did I."

"Then why not talk about this miscarriage thing?"

"She probably told herself it was a long time ago. And that it didn't matter . . . " Candy paused, pressing her finger against the line between her eyes. "Or maybe . . . maybe, she

447

sensed something about the whole thing," she went on, more slowly. "The way I do."

"What?" Perrault asked.

"I mean, it isn't as though I've never heard of people who got knocked off their pins by a miscarriage — or even by thinking they had a miscarriage. And this isn't a normal woman. But something . . . maybe there really wasn't a miscarriage. Maybe there was actually a baby."

Beth broke in then, "What baby? Her baby?"

"Wouldn't that even be more of a reason to be absolutely forthcoming?" Perrault fumed. "Her having a grandchild out there somewhere? Dead or alive? Or is that what you're saying at all?"

"It's probably nothing," Candy said, kneeling, putting her hand on Cecil's leg. "I just . . . I don't know." Cecil's eyes began to dart down then, down and up, over and over. Her head began to follow the eye movements, as if a string were being jerked ever more vigorously.

"Don't think she really heard anything," the nurse said smoothly. "She's perseverating. She'll do the same movement over and over sometimes, unless you stop her. There, there, now, Cecilia . . . " She caught Cecil's bobbing chin in her hand. "That's good."

"Cecil. Help me find your baby's grave," Candy murmured again.

Beth was sure, later, that she imagined it. After all, Candy, utterly fastened on Cecil's face, said she never saw a thing. But Beth heard a tiny shushing sound and believed she saw Cecil's lips draw back and her teeth align the way an ordinary person's would before she

448

made the sibilant sound of an *s*.

Candy got up off her knees. "Bethie," she asked, "you want to take a ride with me?"

"Now?"

"Tomorrow. Maybe, you know, maybe even tonight if this all goes down as fast as I think it will. All Sakura's going to do is ask for another independent psychiatric evaluation and a physical, with periodic reviews of her condition . . . After all, this is a serious charge. But I think he'll basically dismiss, you know that, don't you?" Beth nodded. "Because even if she knew what she was doing nine years ago, she clearly doesn't know what she's doing now. And she probably never will. So, you want to take a ride?"

"Sure," said Beth. "Where?"

"Well, there are really two things I'm concerned with. You remember way back when I called Bender the first time, the coupon shopper who spotted Ben in the mall with the old lady?"

"In Minneapolis."

"Yeah," Candy said, her finger pressed against her forehead line, "I want to go see that little old lady. I think she wants to talk to me."

"I thought you wanted to find out about a baby."

"That, too," Candy replied, suddenly straightening up, and surprising Beth by smiling. "Try to keep up with me here."

Pat was only mildly miffed when Beth asked him, outside the courthouse, about going up north with Candy.

"What am I going to do with the kids?" he asked.

"Oh Pat, don't be tedious," Candy said. "Take them to the Six Flags of Italian restaurants — isn't that what *Bon Appetit* called it? We'll be back by tomorrow afternoon."

"Why don't you take your own husband instead of my wife if you want company?" Pat mock-whined, but smiling now.

"Chris is a babe," Candy admitted, "but would you want to drive nine hours in a car with a corporate lawyer?" She glanced at Beth. "Me and Beth, we'll sing the country Top Forty, okay?" Her voice dropped, suddenly directed, serious. "This is a thing that I just think I want Beth to see too. Okay?"

They drove in Candy's own car, a sleek new black Toyota Beth had never seen, not the chief's squad Beth could still not get used to seeing her drive. Chief Bliss. Crackerjacker cracker of the Cappadora case. Beth sighed. If those Florida bartenders could see her now. Candy swilled Coke and sang along with dirges about faithless men and woebegone women, doomed to meet when everything but the light of their love was extinguished by circumstance.

"No wonder they drink," Beth said after two hours of unrelieved longing in two-part harmony.

"Don't you like?" Candy asked, giving Beth a half-elbow to the ribs. "Aren't you a romantic?"

No, thought Beth, that I am assuredly not. "Are you?" she asked.

"Yes, I think I am. I think that all the bad

450

things in the world, including wars and religion, and all the good things in the world, including Shakespeare and country music, come from love. That's what I think."

"I'd have to agree, especially with the first bit. But I also think there'd be electric cars and a cure for AIDS and I don't know what all else if people didn't have to crack up over love about six times a lifetime or feel like they were missing out on something,"

"Not you," Candy said. "At least not you. Not over that."

Not me, thought Beth, oh my goodness no, not faithful little Elizabeth Kerry Cappadora. And Beth almost told her, then, about the day at the hotel, which had softened for Beth, become a kind of little romantic shrine she went to tenderly, without the scalding splash of guilt, now that Sam was home. Even when she woke wet from dreams of Nick, she was grateful for Pat's untainted presence beside her.

Sam, she thought, had raised them all up, and for all her anguishes and regrets, Beth liked to think that he might lead them all to a higher place where they could stand.

As if privy to her thoughts, Candy asked about Sam. "How's he fitting in?"

"Pat thinks he's going to be fine," Beth told her. "But he's still so . . . silent. We're going to Madison next week, for the Fourth. It'll be the first time he's been there since . . . well, since. He seems worried about it. I've asked him what's going on, but he just shrugs. I'm thinking of asking if Tom Kilgore will talk to him . . . "

"He's got a lot on his mind."

"Kerry thinks he's a celebrity, like someone whose face would be on a cereal box instead of a milk carton. And she's such a little chatterbox, asking him all the time how it feels to be kidnapped, asking him if he'll sign Blythe's soccer ball. But he doesn't get mad at her. I think maybe he's missed having brothers and sisters. He follows Vincent around all the time."

"And how does Reese treat Sam?"

"He ignores him."

Candy laughed. "Well, that's normal, right?"

Was it? Wearily, Beth decided to accept that it was. She sometimes felt as though she were studying Vincent like a tropical disease, trying to read the variations in his generally impassive expressions as if they were mutations in an exotic strain. But there had not been a school incident in months, and weren't all teenagers morose? At least the pierced-navel crew he'd started to hang with had been less in evidence of late, and Jordan had been showing up more often, probably drawn back by the sudden Cappadora celebrity.

Maybe, Beth thought, she was simply waiting for other shoes to drop that weren't even hanging in the balance. If she could spend some time with Sam, some time alone, Beth thought, growing sleepy. Maybe we can take a day together, he and I. I can explain Vincent to him. Or something.

When she woke, it was dark, Tammy Wynette was still warbling, and they were in front of the gates of a cemetery called Saint John of the Cross, in White Bear Lake, just outside Minneapolis.

"Why . . . what are we here for?"

"I have this hunch," Candy said. "Cecil was crazy, but she was a cradle Catholic, like you. And we know she lived less than two miles from here, in a rooming-house sort of place, after she left that guy Hill. I'm assuming she was still pregnant then." Stiffly, Beth unfolded herself from the bucket seat and followed Candy up to the gatehouse of the cemetery. A light burned in a window. "And if you had a baby who died, maybe who you killed . . . I'm not saying she did, but wouldn't you want that baby buried in consecrated ground? That would sort of be logical, wouldn't it?"

She isn't even talking to me, Beth thought. She'd doing what my grandmother Kerry used to call talking out loud. But it was Beth who spotted the sign on the gatehouse door, Will Return, and a clock face set at 9:00 a.m.

"It figures," Candy fumed. "Don't people visit their dead at night? So, what do we do, Beth? Wanta go get a room someplace and sleep? Wanta go to a disco and pick up guys?" She glanced sidelong at Beth. "Want to go to a show at the Guthrie? Want to go see Cecil's landlady? Maybe that tipster, our anonymous concerned lady citizen, maybe it was someone who recognized Cecil from before. And knew her kid. Knew Ben wasn't her kid. Huh? It's possible."

Candy started the car. "But that's ridiculous,"

453

she continued. "She said on the phone the kid was with an old lady, an old gray-haired lady in a big picture hat and sunglasses. Not Cecil. Well, maybe the landlady was a babysitter. Not Sarah Lockhart. Unless she was lying, she didn't even know Ben existed that summer."

"And she's not scrawny. She's plump. Not skinny like Cecil," Beth said.

Candy dug through her bag to root out the copy of the earliest timeline for Cecil's whereabouts during the first years after the kidnapping. The apartment complex in Minneapolis — the periodic long stints at her parents' house. "Here," she said finally. "The rooming house."

She scanned the one-way street they were driving on, looking for the address. "F. Scott Fitzgerald lived in this suburb with Zelda," Candy said suddenly.

Beth huffed, "I knew that."

"What I meant is, this must be a mecca for the wild at heart."

"Doesn't look like it."

Apple Orchard Court was only a half-step down from the manicured suburban middle-density expanses that surrounded it; the houses were older, wooden gingerbread in good repair. Twice in three blocks, Beth saw signs for bed-and-breakfast inns. "We could stay at one of those," she told Candy. "It's probably cheaper."

"I hate the locks on regular houses," Candy said. "Give me a Best Western anytime." She inched the car forward and glided into the drive of a white two-story frame number with tiny

454

topiary shrubs sculpted all along the massive front verandah. "This is it. This is where Cecil lived after she left Hubby Number Three."

The old man who came to the door had no idea who Cecilia Lockhart was. "My brother's the one you want. But he's playing gin at the church tonight. And he won't be home until after ten. They go late. But even then I don't know if he could really help because Rosie ran most of that show."

"Rosie?" Beth cried.

"Rosemary," said the old man. "My sister-in-law. She ran the rentals. And there were a score of young women and men who lived here — some of the men you couldn't tell if they were men or women, you take my meaning."

Candy flipped her shield out then, and the old comedian settled right down. "You're police," he said.

"I am, and all the way from Chicago, and though I hate to bother you at this time of night, I have to ask, is Rosie home now? Rosemary?"

"Oh my, no," the old man said earnestly. "That's even more difficult. She's ill. That's why we've been batching it, Herb and me. My Lydia died in eighty-nine, and now with Rosie so ill . . . "

"Too ill to talk to me?"

"Well, she's living up at the nursing home. Prairie View."

"Where's that?"

"Other side of town. By the new mall."

"Do you think I could use your telephone? Call her and see if I might visit her?"

"Well, you could," said the old man. "But that's the thing. Rosie's real sick."

"Is she dying?"

"No."

"Then?"

"She's not right. She's got this Alzheimer's disease. She don't remember anything except from the past."

"This was in the past," Candy said hopefully.

"I mean, real past, ma'am. From when she was a little girl in Sioux Falls."

Candy nodded sharply and reached out to grab one of the old man's gesticulating hands, to shove one of her business cards into it.

"Please tell your brother we'll be at the downtown Best Western," she said. "We'll be there tonight, if he'd give us a call. We'll come right over, no matter what time it is. This is extremely urgent business."

"Oh my," said the old man, glancing at Candy's card. "I will do that."

But at that moment, a huge, ornate old Lincoln Town Car pulled slowly up in front of the house, and an erect, smaller edition of the brother from Tampa, dapper in a seersucker sport coat, bounded out of the front seat and up the walk. Candy turned to face him. Yes, he said, he was Herbert Fox, and his wife, Rosemary, had indeed rented rooms to young people. Candy produced one of the glossy photos of Cecil in her heyday as an actor, and Herbert Fox studied it carefully.

"Well," he said. "This looks a lot like her. Like a girl I remember for one reason. But she

456

had red hair, you know."

"Did Cecil have red hair?" Candy asked Beth.

"She had every color," Beth said.

"A tiny little thing," Herbert Fox went on. "Sick in bed a great deal. My wife was very fond of her. Mother-henned her a bit. And of course, you know, we didn't realize when she moved in, but she was . . . expecting."

"That's the one, then," Candy said. "Mr. Fox, did Cecilia have the baby while she lived here?"

"Well, yes she did . . . that is, not right here in the house, but I know that my wife drove her to the doctor when her time came," said Herbert Fox. "And that was the funny part. She insisted Rosemary go back home and leave her there. And afterward, Rosemary went to Little Company of Mary, and they'd never heard of Cecilia . . . Hill. That was her name. Cecilia Hill. Apparently, it was a false alarm, and she didn't have the baby that time. But she didn't come back, either. Rosie was worried sick for a while. She was getting bad then, my Rosie, and every little thing really set her off. She'd go on about stuff for hours. Of course, we didn't know at the time how serious what Rosie had was . . . "

"Mr. Fox," Candy persisted. "Didn't Cecilia . . . Hill come back for her things?"

"No, she didn't."

"Are they still here?"

"No, no. There was no unpaid rent. So we just boxed up the clothes and things. The room

457

was furnished. A year later, after Rosie was real sick, a lovely woman, an older lady, came and got the girl's things. And this woman was very nice. She insisted on paying a month's rent, just for our keeping the things."

"And did she ask about Cecilia's baby? About the false alarm? Did she tell you about her grandchild?"

"Oh dear, no. She was a very quiet, polite lady."

"And did you tell her about what happened that night?"

"Well, she was the girl's mother, wasn't she? She'd know all about a girl's . . . delicate things, wouldn't she? I didn't think it was my business to meddle, and poor Rosie was way past understanding, so even if I'd found anything out, I couldn't have told her. Doesn't pay to be nosy just for the sake of it."

"And did you tell the police about this, when they interviewed you about Cecilia?"

The old man was honestly stunned.

"Police?" he whispered. "What? Did that little girl come to some harm?"

"No. No, she's . . . alive and well. But you haven't talked with police about Cecilia Hill? Cecilia Hill or Cecilia Karras?"

"Not before you."

Candy sighed. Gently, she took Herb Fox's limp hand and thanked him, and courteously began to explain the basic facts of Ben's abduction; but the old man suddenly looked drained of breath. "If you don't need anything else," he said, "I think I'll just turn in, officer."

458

"That's just fine, Mr. Fox. You've been more than helpful. Don't spend any more time worrying about this. It's all over."

In the car, she turned to Beth. Her face, already drawn, was further bleached by a shard of late moonlight through the front window. "You're thinking, aren't you, why didn't they ever talk with Herb Fox? And I'm thinking the same thing." Beth opened her mouth and Candy held up a warning hand. "But Bethie, wait. At the same time that I'm thinking why didn't they ever talk to Fox, I'm thinking, why should they have? There was no reason to think Cecilia had a child. We weren't trying to find a kidnapper, we already had her in custody. We already had good witnesses to her movements since the kidnapping. All this," she waved at the neat hedge around the rooming house, "happened before Ben was even born, years before the reunion."

Beth turned away, and Candy said, to her back, "You can call that sloppy work. I might even agree with you. But people don't know what they don't know."

"Police do," Beth said.

"Police especially don't," Candy murmured. "They've been in so many forests they sometimes don't see a tree unless it falls on them."

"What if," Beth asked, struggling with tears, "what if she did it before? What if she tried it before? And did she kill her baby?"

"Do you have an idea of how we could find that out, Beth? Because if you do, I'd like to hear it. We'll go to those cemeteries in the

459

morning. Or to the coroner and look for a death certificate, in case it wasn't a late-term miscarriage after all."

"The cemetery," Beth said abruptly.

Candy gave her a measuring look. "Okay," she said.

"And maybe I can think of someone else we might ask," Candy mused aloud. "But really, to say that your old pal Cecil wasn't much for enduring relationships is really an understatement, huh?"

"She wasn't my old pal," Beth shot back, thinking then, unbidden, just one enduring relationship. Just one.

"I'm sorry," Candy said then, "I'm just tired. I'm so tired I feel like I'm a hundred."

"Me, too," Beth sighed.

"And I, for one, could use several drinks."

Beth said meekly, "Me, too."

By the time they checked in at the hotel, there was only a double room left — "a first-floor corner," said the young man at the counter.

"Nothing on the third floor? I can't imagine every room — what do you have here, two hundred? — " Candy began.

"We'll take that," Beth told him exasperatedly.

"It's a very nice room," he huffed. "It's just that the twirlers are in town, and everything else . . . "

For the balance of the night, Beth and Candy, each lying gritty and fully clothed on her own queen-sized bed, listened to the stampede of high-school drum majorettes as they squealed and rampaged up and down the halls. At midnight, Candy sent down for cheeseburgers and pitcher Bloody Marys. She drank two, leaving most of her burger. Beth nibbled, but finally gave up and simply drank, too.

"I hate loose ends," she told Beth. "And I'm celebrating yet another month of perfectly planned sex with perfectly timed ovulation and perfectly awful results."

"I'm sorry," Beth said.

"Me, too." Candy flipped the card listing the pay-per-view attractions. "Most women spend most of their lives trying not to get pregnant. I never used any of the high-tech kinds of birth control in my life. Naturally, I thought I'd be an instant fertility goddess. I was thinking maybe we'd get two kids in before I ran out of steam." She slugged her Bloody Mary and turned her attention to the program card. "Want to watch Arnold? A sensitive Japanese flick about doomed love among serfs? At least now I can drink for the next week. Before my next appointment with Dr. Clomid. Now, here's a possibility. *Vixens After Dark* — how about that, Beth? See how the other half lives?"

"I'm afraid I've always been a failure as a vixen." Beth smiled.

"You are the original one-man woman," Candy agreed.

"No," Beth protested. "I had my adventure period." Candy made a face. "No, for real. Before Pat, when I was in college."

"I thought you got together in college."

"Not the minute I got to college. What I mostly did was try to pick out guys to sleep

461

with who looked like they understood the big mystery. And it took me a long time to figure out that they were probably thinking the same thing about me. I didn't really appreciate sex until I was probably thirty, you know?"

"All the wasted years," Candy said, leaning back on her elbows. Beth realized both of them were more than a little drunk.

"What about you?" Beth asked then, noticing the belligerent edge in her voice. "You say you're this big romantic, but the way you talk, you've spent most of your life trying to convince the boys that your pistol was as big as theirs."

"And don't think I don't regret it," Candy said. "I've had maybe two serious lovers in my life, not counting Chris."

"Which you don't exactly count."

"Beth, come on."

"I'm sorry about that, too."

"You are. You're a very sorry person." But Candy smiled. "Two serious lovers, and then the whole gamut of stuff you think you're supposed to do because you're a free-to-be-lesbian-feminist chick . . . which is mostly just boring."

"Is it?" Beth asked. "Is it boring?" She wondered if she was seriously drunk. "I mean, I've always wondered, and I've never asked you . . . I just assumed that it would be better between women, the sex part, because you would know what the person wanted . . . "

"And be really sensitive and tender, right?"

"Well, yeah."

"Actually, I hate to let you down, Bethie, but

there are just as many selfish and demanding gay women as there are straight men."

Candy smiled, a sort of private smile that made Beth feel, suddenly, very alone. "You know," Candy said. "It's not awful with Chris at all. It's nicer than I thought it would be, and I was determined to grit my teeth and bear it even if it wasn't nice."

"But you still . . . you've had other relationships anyway, right? I mean, you couldn't just . . . "

"I'm married, Beth," Candy said.

"I just meant . . . "

"Is it a marriage of convenience, a rather more goal-directed marriage than most? Sure it is. Or maybe it isn't. I mean, shit, don't half the people in the world marry people they're not exactly madly in love with because they want security, or children, or whatever? We just didn't pretend about it. And so why would I have cheated on him?"

"Well, Chris knows that you . . . "

"Do you cheat on Pat?"

Beth hesitated. "Of course not," she said.

Candy sighed. "I'm being hard on you, probably because I'm such a bitch today. I know exactly what you mean, and probably, Chris truly wouldn't even consider it a huge, huge deal. He's a man of the world, as he often reminds me. He's very proud of how PC he is about my past." She grinned. "It would be me that I was letting down, Beth. It's just a cheesy thing to do, in my opinion." She looked hard at Beth, who made a show of stirring the celery stalk in her tall glass. "Don't you think it is? Don't you think it's sort of the ultimate in dull, predictable behavior?"

She knows, thought Beth. I always knew she knew, but now I'm sure.

"I don't know," Beth stammered, trying to recover. "There could be reasons that people — not me, maybe, but . . . don't you ever think that maybe the great love of your life is still out there?" And maybe, she thought but didn't say, you met him once and gave him up, because while he was sweet and sexy and basic you were afraid you wouldn't be able to discuss Russian novels together?

Candy said then, sighing, "I guess. What do they call it? That 'lifelong passionate conversation.' But I'm never going to have that. Probably. Chris and I . . . it's not like that." She raised herself up on one elbow. "You know, Bethie, there were times, at the start, when I thought that you and Pat would split. What you went through . . . "

Eighty percent of us divorce, Beth thought, eighty percent. But Candy was continuing. "But later, I saw that you and Pat could weather anything. You can tell when people have . . . what you have."

★ ★ ★

In the morning, they drove to the cemetery against the early-morning traffic streaming into the city and Beth waited in the car while Candy went in to interview the caretaker. After about twenty minutes, Candy returned, a slip of paper

464

in one hand. She got into the car and sat for a moment, looking straight ahead, gripping the wheel. Beth thought she would burst.

"What?" she finally asked.

"It was a four-corner bingo, Bethie," Candy said. "Look here." She held up the paper. "Hill, Samuel Seth. A-14. Out of all the Catholic cemeteries in all the cities in all the world, she walked into this one."

Beth had not expected to feel so near tears. But neither she nor Candy spoke as they picked among the simple stones to the flat marker that read, after the name, 'April 6, 1983 – April 14, 1983.' And below it, 'Tomorrow and tomorrow and tomorrow.'

"That's weird," Candy said. Beth's voice wouldn't come. "So. He died in a week."

"But of what?"

"Of complications of prematurity," Candy said, and to Beth's look, added, "I saw the death certificate, Beth. They had it on file here. It was the county hospital. And remember, our old buddy Herb didn't even know she was pregnant when she moved in."

"Forget it," Beth said. "Let's just forget it."

"And what do you think the inscription means?"

"It's Shakespeare. *Macbeth*, where he talks about how life creeps in its petty pace from day to day. It's very famous."

"I guess I didn't go to that school," Candy sighed. "But it's not what you would imagine for a child. She was already probably not entirely there, Beth."

"It doesn't seem that strange to me," Beth said. "I guess because I wasn't entirely there, either, when I felt like that."

Beth drove on the way home, and Candy dozed restlessly. They were past Rockford when Beth suddenly sat erect and jammed the brakes.

"What?" Candy yelled. "What's wrong?"

"Her hair was white," Beth said.

"Whose hair was white?"

"Cecil's. I just remembered. The day of the reunion — I never think of it, I haven't thought about it in years. But Ellen said Cecil's hair was white. Dyed platinum. And Herb Fox said she was sick. She was always skinny. And even later, when she was well again and met George, he said she wore her hair up most of the time, in a bun. So she could have looked like a little old lady, even though she was young I mean, in a hat and everything."

"Detective Cappadora, that is very good work," Candy said. "That could be it. It very well could be. I thank you. Now, I'll just go home and relax, like Dr. Clomid says. I'll be pregnant by Friday."

29

BETH woke the next morning to the sounds of voices raised, arguing, below her window. She'd fallen into bed the night before, waving away Pat's urgent questions, not even bothering to brush her teeth, pausing only long enough to shuck her jeans.

Now, as she tried to bring herself to full consciousness — her head felt like a heavy flower on a stalk, likely to snap at a movement — she was shocked to realize that the angrier voice was Sam's.

"I already told you!" Sam was saying. "This is what I always do!"

And Pat's voice responded, "Look. Those kinds of fireworks are illegal. We'll go out on Rick and Laurie's boat and we'll see real fireworks. You can see them all over the whole city . . . "

"I'd rather stay with my dad, though," said Sam. "I don't remember Madison. And we have fireworks my uncle Pete brings from Missouri, and they're really cool, and only the grownups do the punks, so it's real safe . . . "

Beth sat up, settling her elbows on the windowsill to see the two of them. Vincent was down there, too, fiddling with stuff in the trunk of the car, but Pat and Sam were facing each other squarely in the middle of the driveway. The way they stood, Beth noticed with a pang, with their fists planted on their hips in confrontation, was exactly the same.

Beth had believed the hardest thing that she would have to face today would be to try to interpret for Pat not only the facts she and Candy had learned but their import. She had almost decided that the facts would have to be sufficient . . . at least until she'd had time to sort through all the empathy she couldn't help feeling about Cecil and her lonely, useless week of motherhood, followed by the later, even more lonely and ultimately useless years.

Beth jumped out of bed and into her jeans. She would sooner have tried to break up a three-dog fight than explain all that to Pat. He would call it Beth's crazy yen to ferret out the dark cloud behind every silver lining. It would enrage him, he would say her musings were the kind of stuff that filled up the second hour of made-for-TV movies. The tiff below was a welcome obstacle. Who knew, maybe Pat was right — that all they needed to do was give Sam time. There was no other alternative.

She bolted down the stairs and out the door. Sam and Pat were still bickering, and even Vincent was getting in on the act.

"Sam, it's actually pretty fun," he was saying. "All the other boats are out on Lake Mendota, and people are cheering and stuff. It's neat. You'll like it. And Rick and Laurie have this big pool in their backyard . . . "

"I'm not going," said Sam.

"Well," Pat told him gently, "you are going. You are going when the rest of us go, because that's what we planned. I'm going to go into the house and get the cooler, and when your mother is dressed and Kerry is ready, we're all going to get into the car and we're going to go."

"Maybe we can show you the house," Vincent suggested, then. Beth felt a spurt of pride surprise her; he sounded so reasonable, so nearly parental. "Don't you want to see the house where we lived?"

Still sulky, Sam said, "Why would I want to see where you lived? I don't remember being born."

"Aren't you a little curious? Lincoln didn't remember being born, either, but I bet he liked going back and looking at the little log cabin," Vincent said.

Sam said, "You're not curious about my life. You never came over to see my room or anything. You don't even like my dad."

Beth broke in, "Of course we like George, Sam." Sam looked at her, just noticing she was there. "It's not that we don't like him — "

"You don't even care about what he thinks."

"Not that much," Vincent agreed, cheerfully.

"Vincent," Beth warned.

"I don't think you like him, or you'd let me go and spend Fourth of July with him the way I want to."

"The fact is," Pat said, breathing harder. "You're our son. Not George's. We're doing our best, Sam, but some things we're goddamn well going to do as a family. That's how it is. There are some things that just aren't negotiable."

"You just want to show me off!" Sam cried

then, and turned to Beth, stricken. "I didn't mean that."

"I know," she told him. "Go get your mitt now, or whatever else you want to take, and let's go." Sam slumped into the house, Beowulf following him, chuffing hopefully.

Beth turned to Pat. "You know what?" she told him, suddenly inspired. "Let's take two cars. I want to run up to Peshtigo tomorrow and shoot some stock. And I was thinking I'd take him. Sam. Just him and me. Spend some time with him."

She noticed Vincent slowing down, suddenly concentrating on her, and felt like whispering under the force of his gaze.

Pat didn't notice. He griped, "Now? Why in the hell now?"

"Don't get all juiced, Paddy. I just thought, since I'd be halfway there . . . I've been wanting to do this anyhow, and I think it could help, if he just gets a chance to talk to one of us alone. It's okay, right? This is a good time, because he seems to be opening up, doesn't he?"

Pat stalked up onto the porch and hefted the cooler. "I don't care, Bethie," he said. "Though I can tell you, don't expect some big mother-and-child confession. I've spent a ton of time with him, between here and the ball field and the stadium and the restaurant and stuff, and the kid is completely cut off. He's so self-possessed I envy it."

"Maybe he's just scared to say things," Beth offered. "He didn't seem so in control this morning."

Pat smiled wearily. "Do what you want." Sam walked out onto the porch, Pat turned to him. "'Sgo, buddy. You can ride with your mom, okay?"

But Sam, with a last-ditch effort to save face, insisted on riding with Vincent, even though Kerry begged him to come with her in Beth's old Volvo and play Car Bingo.

He did cheer up at Laurie and Rick's, paddling amiably in their pool, eating not one but three burgers with everything, Rick's special recipe. Just before dark, they launched Rick's boat from the Robertson Pier, Rick deviling Laurie the whole time about all the years she'd teased him for taking the *Queen Mary* out on a lake the size of a postage stamp. "Bet you're glad it seats nine now, right?" Rick kept asking, while Laurie threw life jackets at his head.

They rocked gently on the dark water in the middle of the lake, and after a while the rockets began, to the north and east, washing the children's faces in green and blue and violet streaks of light. Covertly, Beth watched Sam and thought, once, she could see tears in his eyes. But when he caught her looking at him, he deliberately smiled, showing his big, even teeth, a smile that seemed intended to tell her that he was a good boy, after all, and not spoiled. She wanted to scoop him up then, and hold him bundled against her. Tomorrow, Beth thought then, tomorrow and tomorrow.

The next morning's start was held up until past noon by a long, late breakfast and a torrential flurry of goodbyes — of switching bags and bundles back and forth between the two cars four times to get it right, and the momentary loss of Vincent, who took off unannounced with his brand-new license to pay a surprise visit to old Alex Shore. After all that, Sam and Beth were content to sit spent in the front seat for the first hour, listening to Tom Petty sing about good girls who loved Elvis. Beth headed up Highway 51 toward Fond du Lac, where already a few trees were starting to turn, then onto 41, past Green Bay, near but not quite on the hip of Lake Michigan. She was feeling corky for some reason, renewed and released, and she laughed appreciatively when Sam suddenly started to sing along with her.

"How'd you learn how to harmonize?" she asked him.

"My mom could sing," Sam said happily, then slipped a glance at her. "I'm sorry."

"Honey," Beth told him. "I know she could sing. She had a beautiful voice. I think it's neat that you do, too."

"You knew my mother." It was not a question. "I mean, you knew Cecilia."

"Sure," Beth said, her heart quickening. It was the most he'd ever asked of her. "Everybody knew her. She was hot. Cute and talented. I was jealous of her, because she was friends with Aunt Ellen — with my best friend, Ellen."

"Why?"

"Because Cecil was so . . . grownup. And I thought Ellen would like her better. She didn't, though."

472

My God, thought Beth, why the hell would I say that?

"Was she nice?"

"She was . . . everybody was drawn to her. She was like a movie star, sort of."

"Not to me."

Beth's stomach fluttered. Slowly, she thought. Line up. "You mean, she wasn't nice to you?"

Sam laughed. He laughed! "No, I mean I didn't think she was like a movie star. She was just my mom. Even when I saw her on TV, when I was little, my dad says I would just go, 'Oh, there's Mom.'" Beth tried to laugh, and instead croaked. Oh, help, she thought — 'She was just my mom' — oh, help. But Sam went on, "Was my mom . . . mentally ill, back then?"

Beth winced. "No. She was different . . . " Beth felt Sam stiffen and tried to backtrack. "Not in a bad way. She was just . . . an actress."

"I think sometimes she got mental because of what she did."

Beth almost swerved, but then recovered the wheel. Was he trying to tell her that he'd been aware, when he was small, that Cecil had stolen him? "Because of what she did? What do you mean?"

"I mean, stealing a kid. I started thinking after I met you guys, maybe she didn't get mental because I was too . . . you know, hard for her to handle on her own. She got mental because she did this thing a long time ago."

"Sam," Beth said slowly, "you weren't hard to handle. You were the easiest kid in the world. Ask Dad. And Sarah . . . your grandma Lockhart said she was sick sometimes even when she was a little girl."

Sam nodded, and Beth thought, You wanted this, too, didn't you? Should I go on, risk spoiling what feels delicate and new? But I could lose the moment, too. I've lost more than my share.

"Sam, you make me wonder," Beth said, "if you knew that Cecil wasn't your . . . real mom."

"No. I thought she was."

"So you mean, you just started thinking about why she got sick since you came back, just this spring."

"Right. Do you have any other CDs?"

Beth was caught short. "What?"

"Any other ones. Because this one started over. Do you have any old Beatles or something?"

"All I want you to know, Sam, was that it wasn't . . . " But he was rummaging in the glove box, virtually holding up a semaphore that signaled 'End of Chat.' So Beth found him an Animals disc, and started nattering about Peshtigo, praying to draw him out, get him talking again.

"Do you know what the Great Chicago Fire is?" she asked.

Sam gave her a pitying look. "Uh, yes," he said.

"Well, did you know that there was an even worse fire, in Peshtigo, in this little town we're going to, and it was in the same year, in 1871, and on the same *day*?"

474

"Get out," said Sam.

And having snagged him, Beth pulled up next to the fire museum, in an old church just off 41. "We could go in here. It's cool. There's all this stuff that was found after the fire, like farm tools all twisted from the heat. They called it 'the great tornado of fire.' Want to?"

"Is that what you're going to take pictures of?"

"No. I was going to take some pictures in this little cemetery down the road, where a lot of people who died in it are buried."

"Why?"

"Well, I like cemeteries." Tomorrow, she thought. Tomorrow and tomorrow and tomorrow. "And, it's . . . you know . . . it was a great tragedy. Every single building in this whole town burned. Every one."

"And people . . . ?"

"Hundreds of people died. I mean, you know, lots more than died in the Chicago fire, Sam, but that was a big city, so that was what everybody paid attention to."

"We could go to the cemetery then."

"Okay."

Now, Beth thought, can I remember where it is? She turned the car around — the last time she'd been in Peshtigo had been . . . when? . . . in '91? She'd made pictures for *Midwest Living*, for a section on historical observances and ghost towns. But she barely recalled that shoot — it was like so many of the things she did the first years after the reunion, a gauzy dream. Today, she could look at whole contact sheets of pictures from those years and have no memory of ever having framed those images in her lens, or laid eyes on the people she must have spoken to and spent time with.

She remembered earlier times in Peshtigo, before Ben was lost, with much more clarity. The town had always been one of Beth's favorite photographic shrines. Once, newly pregnant with Kerry, she had photographed the graves of a family in the little cemetery outside the museum, where they lay under a huge tree that had long outlived them: Sarah, Beloved Wife; Alvey, Age One; Maria, Age Two; Arthur, Husband and Father. She had lain down on the grass above those bones, and thought — as she used to think, in her newspaper days, every time she made a picture of a stretcher burdened by a blanketed form so small it seemed to have no topography at all, if I feel this entire, if I let this wound me, my own will be spared. I will be absolved, by lent and prior pain, from destruction in the first person. The scythe will whicker blindly all around, but miss Vincent, miss Ben.

The memory of the self who actually believed such prevention possible touched Beth today with a kind of abashed pity, like a ten-year-old still believing in Santa Claus.

Wandering with that more innocent Beth, she missed the modest iron arch that marked Rock of Ages, and had to turn around in a farmer's stupendously green field. She remembered, then, that the incursion of road repairs had forced the moving of the cemetery's oldest graves up onto a hill more than a block away.

"That's where I want to go," she told Sam, "up on the hill. That's where the people from the fire are."

She pulled into the cemetery over a graveled rise, parked, and hurriedly began unpacking her equipment. The afternoon was getting old; and the late light, with its low color temperature, its orangeness, was what she wanted for compositions of the rectangular and rounded shapes of the headstones. She took out her little flash unit, for backup, the case with the Hasselblad, a fold-up reflector so new it still felt stiff and funny under her hand.

"What do you want me to take?" Ben asked, and Beth realized it still caught her off guard, how easily, naturally helpful he was — well raised, well-bred.

She gave Sam her bag and they began to hike up a narrow, stony path. Beth watched her son, only half-aware of the building drama of the late light. There was a crowned tomb with smaller headstones ringing it like pupils around a teacher's desk. "Let's take that," she told him; and Sam watched her as she squatted, shooting up from the base of the tallest monument.

"What do you see?" Sam asked her.

"What I'm looking at," Beth said, "is the way the big tombstone sits against the sky, almost like it's protecting the little ones. Here . . . " She unlooped the strap from around her neck and put the viewer in front of Sam's eyes. "See?"

He peered. "Yeah."

"Do you want to take it?"

"I never used this kind of camera."

"It's easy," Beth told him, putting her fingers on top of his, feeling the jolt that still accompanied her contact with his downy skin, showing him the buttons. "I'm going to stand up now, and you shoot it."

She stood up and, backing off a step, collided with something hard; she whirled, nearly topping an old man. Beth yipped in surprise, and to her relief, the stranger pushed his striped railroader's hat back on his sunburned forehead and began to laugh.

"Think I was a ghost?" he asked. Then, noticing Sam, who had continued to click the shutter, not even turning at his mother's shriek, he asked, "Who's the photographer?"

"My son," Beth said, adding, "Actually, I am. I take pictures for my job. But we're just playing around here." Sam stood up then, and extended his hand, carefully settling the camera on its strap around his neck first.

"Hello," he said, and the old man, taking the boy's hand, smiled at Beth, a conspiratorial smile of shared pride in Sam's almost antique politeness.

"I'm Will Holt," the old man said.

"I'm Beth. I'm from Chicago. This is Sam. Do you work here?"

"Work here, live here." He smiled, a farmer's face with permanent riverbeds along the margins of his jaw. "Not *here*, I mean. At least not yet, though I suspect the time will come. But live in Peshtigo. Always have."

"I'm looking for the graves of the fire survivors."

478

He laughed again, harder. "Got none of them, I'm afraid, young lady."

"The victims, I mean, of course." Beth blushed.

Beth noticed that behind him, Holt had a little wheeled cart, shaped like a wheelbarrow, but really more like a wagon. It was filled, as nearly as Beth could tell, with masses of red and blue flowers and piles of tiny American flags. Following her eyes, Holt told her, "Fourth of July. Wanted to get them cleaned off before it rains and they fade. That saddens people. The Christmas wreaths sat here until February. I felt bad about it. Had flu for a couple of weeks and was weak as a kitten most of the winter. Better start jogging, eh?"

"Better," said Beth. "Can I take a picture of that wagon?"

Holt gestured at the cart. "Well, sure, why not?" he said. Sam handed her the camera.

"Are all those from soldiers?" he asked Holt.

"No, not all, son," the old man said. "Some. But most are just from the graves of ordinary people. Their folks miss them, on the holidays." He turned to Beth, who'd finished her shooting, and continued, "Now, most of the fire graves are up there — not in the middle, over there, just under the aspens. Of course, that's not where they originally were; parts of this cemetery were moved a few years back."

"I know. I've been here before," Beth said.

"Ah," said Holt. "Live up here?"

"Chicago," Beth repeated. "I used to live in Madison."

"Madison," said Holt. "I went to college in Madison. Ag school. I was the Langlade County extension agent for more years than Ollie's cows have legs." He walked stiffly toward the cart and lifted its handle. "Then I retired and all. And now I do this, just whenever I want to. Little money. A little peace. I used to dig the graves with some boys, but now they have a backhoe for that."

Holt began to walk, and Sam followed him. Beth caught up. They walked along a wide, glimmering, flat swatch of green that led to the foot of the ridge. They passed a grave that looked too new for the rest of its companions. 'Caron Anne, Our Youngest,' it read. '1985 – 1988.'

"Now that's the Willards' youngest. The funniest thing — died of an ear infection. Seems that my grandkids get one of those a week, and it hasn't killed one of them yet. Her mother wanted her up here, though most people prefer all the landscaping in the new cemetery by the church. We all felt so bad, we wouldn't have suggested otherwise, and of course, there are generations of Willards up here, so she's among her people."

They walked on.

"That's a kid, too," Sam said, pointing.

"Right you are." Holt nodded, taking off his hat. "Places like this should be reserved for old folks like me, but it don't always run that way. Now, Grace Culver was the age of my older boy, Bill. Her brother told her on the school bus he was going to shoot her with his daddy's gun when they got home, and that's just what he did.

That was in '56. Yes, that's right — '56."

"My God in heaven," Beth breathed.

"Oh, ma'am, I'm sorry," Holt said, gesturing at Sam. "I never meant to scare him."

"I'm not scared," Sam said, his eyes level. "I was kidnapped once."

Holt shot a glance at Beth. She nodded. "He was," she said.

"Were you afraid?" Holt asked Sam.

"No," Sam replied. "I was little. And my mom, she . . . Well, I just got back before school let out."

"You were away for months?"

"Years. My whole life," Sam said.

Beth squirmed, adjusting her cameras. "It was . . . you probably read about him . . . we lived in Madison then. Benjamin Cappadora."

"Oh my yes, oh my yes," said Holt. "Goodness yes." He looked Sam up and down. "Still, you seem to have survived it." Then, to Beth, "And you, too. Things okay now?"

"Yes, mostly," Beth said, struggling with a sudden longing to tell this gentle ghost encountered in the graveyard, 'You should know better than to believe everything you think you see; our son was stolen, and we never really got him back, though you may have read otherwise in *People* magazine.' She wanted to ask, 'Now, Mr. Holt, you have long experience of human nature, does this polite and curious young fellow seem at home in the world to you? Like the prodigal son of one of the luckiest and happiest of families? And me? Do I seem like his mother? Or an actor? Actually, it was his other

481

mother who was the actor — '

Then Sam asked Holt if the graves nearest him were people from the fire. "They all have the same name," Sam said.

"Well, Sam, that's another one of those stories. Carrie Moss and her four children. Oldest was eleven, the youngest one three." Beth looked down at the neat gray stones, all exactly matched, then at Sam. Should she stop Holt? This was damned gruesome. Sam was transfixed. "Fellow was a railroad worker. Hailed from all over, you know the kind. But born here. The way he said, when they got hold of him in Madison, was that he was in love with Carrie Moss from when they were children. One day while her husband was out harvesting — oh, not a half-mile from the house — he came to their house."

"The guy . . . " Sam's voice was low, choked. "He killed them?"

"He did," Holt said evenly. "That house is still there right out on the road near Keller Creek. Nicely built. But nobody ever bought it. Frank Moss moved to Des Moines. No, I'm wrong there. It was Dubuque. This was just before the war — '43. Not all the crime happens in Milwaukee — no, not by a long shot. Not all of it happens in Chicago."

They walked up a small footpath to the knee of the ridge. A single stone stood just to the left of the path, and Beth stopped. No, she thought. Maybe Sam won't notice it.

David Taylor Holt. No dates, simply the etching of a water lily on the marbled rose of the surface. Sam squatted down, touching the stone.

"Is this a relative of yours?" Beth asked softly.

"Yep," said the caretaker. "I'm sorry to say that this is my son."

"Did he die in the war?" Sam asked. "Was he a soldier?"

"Sam, wait," Beth rebuked him.

"Oh, no, it's all right. I like to have him here — better than if we had to go down to Beloit, his mother and me. That's where he was living. He wasn't a soldier, son, just a college kid."

"Was he . . . was he sick?" Sam asked.

"No, no," said Holt. "Though in a sense I guess you could say he was. We thought it was what a boy goes through — some of the drinking, the bad grades, missing classes. But I guess you could say he was suffering a case of depression. He was in love with a girl — you might say she never returned that. And one night, well, he drove home, he'd been drinking, and he parked his car in the garage at the house where he rented a room. And he just left it on. He had a full tank of gas. The landlady, poor woman, she nearly died as well."

"He was mentally ill," Sam said. "That's too bad."

"Sam!" Beth didn't know how to react.

"You're right, Sam. He was ill. We just didn't know." Holt reached down and brushed a clump of clotted leaves from the face of the stone. "His mother, now, she thinks Donnie fell asleep. And I must say, I tell her that I do, too. But the truth is, I know better. I found this part of something, a poem he was writing. It was as sad as one of those country songs. He wrote, 'I may be weak and I may be strong, but I've been in this wicked world too long.' So I knew then he just couldn't wait. And he wrote this, probably at the Christmas before, when he was home for break. Months before. Well, well. It's been ten years now."

"You miss him," Sam said.

"I sure do," Holt said. He gave himself a shake. "Now, right up there, to the left, there are your graves. I'm sorry. I have to shake a leg here."

"Of course," Beth agreed. But she didn't want to leave him. She wanted to take him someplace fragrant and homely, like the Pepper Pot in town, and buy vanilla Cokes and steak sandwiches for him and for Sam. They could sit and talk in a warm ring of yellow light until all of them felt full and strong.

"Good luck to you, Beth," Holt said, jolting his wagon onto the small path. "Sam, you take care of your mother."

"You, too," Sam said, kneeling down again near the pink marble tombstone. "Why do you think it's a water lily?" he asked Beth.

"I don't know. Maybe he loved those flowers."

"They smell awful. But he was a nice old guy."

"He was," Beth said. "It's very sad."

"Yeah." Sam paused. "For him, you mean, or his son?"

"Both of them."

"I don't know about him." Sam pointed at the rosy stone, which glowed in the last blades of sun. "For him, it's probably better."

Beth froze, her camera dangling. "What do you mean?"

"I mean, he was so sad and all, it's probably better for him to just . . . sleep. There could be worse things than being dead."

Beth grasped, gasped. Her camera knocked against her chest. Suddenly she wanted to shake Sam, or slap him. "Sam, he's dead. His life is completely over. He's not asleep. He took his whole life away from himself, from his parents. And all for something he would have gotten over if he'd given himself the time."

Sam stirred the loose earth stubbornly with one toe. "Maybe not. Maybe he was just too sad."

I could just fall, Beth thought. The very ground under her feet seemed to drag at her, draw her down with the seepage of its accumulation of mourning. Worse and worse, the bones warned her through the sound of shivering aspens above her head, there is worse and worse.

The scythe had whickered and swung; and it had indeed missed Ben. Ben, as Sam, had endured a middling-hard childhood, and yet, as Sam, he had thrived. And now he wasn't thriving anymore. He was surviving, and only because of a base coat of basically healthy nature. Not because of having his family back. Not because of that at all. Their gain was his loss. Beth had been returned a child who was as remote from her as heaven.

And yet, and yet, wasn't she more fortunate and ungrateful than so many others she'd met at Compassionate Circle? She could see her child; she knew his favorite dinner was gyros and yogurt, that he was a fast, not altogether careful reader, that he could touch-type; she had seen how he transformed at bat from an oversized clown, pulling faces at his teammates, to a beautiful novice athlete with a clenched jaw and a level swing that made Pat's eyes tear up.

She knew where her son was, Beth thought, as the last of the sunlight drained from the band of sky over the ridge. And it was not here.

"Sam," she said then. "I want to ask you something."

"What?" he said, getting up, dusting off his hands.

"Do you ever wish you were dead?"

He said, quickly, "No."

"What do you wish?"

"I just said there might be things worse than being dead."

"Like what?"

"Like everybody always pulling at your life and making you stay at a place where everybody hates you."

"You think that . . . we hate you?"

"Not you."

"Who, then?"

"Well, Vincent." He picked up Beth's reflector, turning his head up toward the ridge. A light

486

winked up there, and for a moment Beth thought it could be a shooting star; then she saw it was a blinking light on a radio tower, warning planes that it was safe to come only so close, no closer. "When I was at the home, my dad and I talked, and he said we should make a list of what wouldn't be so bad about going back. And one of the things I put on the list was that it might be fun to have brothers and sisters."

"And?"

"And then . . . I mean, Kerry's great, but he looks at me like . . . Jesus, you see how he looks at me!"

"Sam, I don't think he looks at you any differently from the way he looks at all of us. He's . . . he's had a hard time."

"But it wasn't my fault! That's what I keep telling you guys!" She could not see him, just the outline of his bent shoulders, but Beth reached for him then, and folded him against her. He did not resist; perhaps she imagined it, but he seemed, momentarily, to cling.

"Oh, Ben . . . Sam," she said into his hair. "Do you know how many million years it was that I could never hug you? That you had to be without me to hug you, too?"

He patted her back then, like a fond colleague, as Angelo might have done. "They hugged me," he said. "They hugged me all the time."

She was barely able to summon the words that naturally followed. They would seal something, and her throat was paralyzed with pity and conscience.

"What do you wish, Sam?" she finally asked.

"I don't know," he said. "Just that . . . everything was like it was before. Except for that would hurt Pat and you. And I can't stand that, either. I just . . . don't know."

Beth thought back then to the early questions Sam had asked, and how hard she had to resist to keep from turning every answer into a forty-minute lecture. Had Beowulf liked him when he was a baby? Did he see Kerry right after she was born? Did Beth remember if he was allergic to cinnamon? He was sure he was now, though George said that was just because he once threw up after eating a whole pound bag of sticky buns. After weeks of the little questions, little answers, Beth had taken the plunge: she'd called Sam in one lazy Sunday afternoon and told him that she wanted to show him something. The apprehension in his eyes almost stopped her; but she pressed ahead, taking him upstairs to her and Pat's room, to where the large hooped cedar chest Rob Maltese had built for them as a wedding gift still sat, used mostly by Pat as a clothes rack for piles of shirts destined for the dry cleaner. She swept the shirts aside.

As a filer, Beth considered herself a failure. It was one of the sinkholes in her motherhood resume. Vincent's baby book was a virtual anthropological study, recording, in the margins when the spaces gave out, not just the date of the eruption of each tooth, but the development of moods, gestures, intellectual milestones that Beth considered evidence of genius. By contrast, Ben's and then Kerry's albums were basically repositories for cards and photos. Beth hadn't even been sure that the words she scribbled in as 'firsts' actually were, since the scribbling had so far postdated the actual events.

But she had done one thing carefully and well. Each of the children's christening gowns and 'coming home' outfits was sealed in a plastic envelope Beth bought from Sears, with photos and mementos of each of those momentous days and placed reverently, impervious to time and shift, in the cedar chest.

She'd lifted out first Vincent's package, letting Sam sift through its contents — he was curious, even avid — and then the one marked 'Benjamin Patrick Cappadora'.

"They're so little," Sam had said, laughing. "Was I really ever this small? They look like Kerry's doll clothes." Some of Ben's clothes, Beth thought then, in fact were now Kerry's doll clothes; and she'd almost said that.

But it happened then. Ben lifted the lacy gown Rosie had so lovingly embroidered up to his nose, inhaling its sweet, hamster-cage scent.

"What's that smell?" he asked.

"Cedar. It's supposed to preserve clothes and keep moths away. Lots of closets are lined with it. Didn't you ever smell it before?"

"No," Sam said firmly. "It could be . . . maybe it was that my yaya had a trunk like this. I think so. She brought it from Greece. Maybe I played with it when I was a kid." But his face didn't register confidence. "At least, I think so."

And then Beth had noticed, with growing excitement, that tears were welling in his eyes. She had never seen Sam cry, except for an instant at the intake center when he'd kissed George goodbye. Now, he was scrubbing at his eyes with twelve-year-old modesty, shaking his head.

"What? Sam?" she'd asked, daring to think, This is it. Something, some gear has engaged. He remembers. And then Sam had reached out and patted Beth on the shoulder. "I'm just so sorry," he said.

"For what, honey?"

"I'm sorry because this happened to you. I know you loved this . . . loved me so much when you did this. I'm so sorry."

"Sam, Sam . . . you don't have to feel that way."

He shook his head, more fiercely this time. "But I also think you believe that my mom and dad are bad people. And they're really not." He went on, Beth barely hearing him, her stomach gone icy. "Just because I'm really sorry that this happened doesn't mean I don't love my dad. And I love my mom, too, Beth. She doesn't mean to be sick." Numbly, Beth nodded, mechanically reaching for the christening gown, folding it against the creases so it wouldn't disintegrate. Sam was crying hard now, hiccuping. She wanted to hold him against her, stroke his broad back with its immature and jutting bones. "Beth," he finally gulped out, "can I see my dad today?"

When he'd gotten back, later, from George's, Sam was lighter, less antsy. He'd played a game of Sorry with Kerry. He'd come right out and asked Vincent to shoot some hoops. But Beth

490

had never forgotten the supplication in his face as he knelt by the chest, the confusion in his voice about the right way to talk to kindly strangers to convince them to help you find your way home.

She had tried to tell Pat about the cedar chest. He'd brushed it away. "Bethie, do you remember being six weeks old?" he'd laughed. "Don't stew over it. He'll come around."

Pat would listen now. He would have no choice.

As the shadows blanketed Rock of Ages cemetery, Beth and Sam locked the cameras in the trunk, and Sam asked if he could lie down in the backseat. "Sure, baby," she said. "Sleep."

There was worse and worse, Beth thought; they had given him life, Beth thought, tilting the rearview mirror to look at her sleeping son; that was a covenant. No one would ask them to give their boy back the life he mourned, at the cost of the life that had been restored to him. But wasn't that part of the covenant, too?

She needed to talk to Pat. She hadn't the heart to talk to Pat, or the courage. He would turn from her words with all his might and with all justification, and what would be left for her then?

A phone call, Beth thought then — almost stopping, almost forgetting that she would wake Sam, that it was late. No, she would look the number up tomorrow. She knew it was in the book. She'd looked it up half a dozen times over the past few years, noted when the office moved, when the number changed.

With the thought of the phone call secure above her mind, like a strap in a swaying subway car, Beth headed through the dusk, south toward home.

30

TO call first thing the next morning, Beth decided, would seem desperate. That it had taken four years to get to the point of making the call — and that no one but she knew that — was of no consequence.

She would work first. For . . . an hour. Decency demanded it.

She took out the last proofs of the photo essay that would appear two months from now in *Life* — the children-walking-away portraits. *Life* was going to run them as a six-page spread for no other reason than the fact of them. It was an arrival, big-league. But she had to admit that not one of the pictures was really anything that would merit a gold star beside her name in God's notebook. She still used the same tricks and conceits in her work that she'd developed as a novice. Venturing in new directions would have required thought and concentration, study, the willingness to expend emotional capital. She had not had it to give — and she often thought that she was lucky that a fairly good ability to make pictures had become second nature to her long before she'd taken up residence under the avalanche. Her 'new eyes' were as a kind of deformity born of that residence.

Beth recognized the truth that she could do most of her work with the eyes of her mind closed; that meant admiring that the real reason people paid her handsomely was the conjuring power of her last name, the little italicized credit that appeared under every picture of hers someone published, the explanation of who she was. The reason Wedding in the Old Neighborhood was being featured in *Bon Appetit* only now, when the food and the theme had been a spectacular draw for years. The reason a book publisher had offered Beth and Pat an actual million dollars (it still made Beth wince to think of the crumpling of Pat's jaw when she insisted they reject it) for rights to their family's story. The Cappadora name had been dredged from a stale estuary of tears and rumor not only unstained, but no longer just golden: now it was platinum.

This *Life* layout, for example. The editors naturally assumed that the subject had sprung from Beth's joust with fate. In fact, Beth had always taken pictures of children walking away, Their backsides appealed to her — a kid's personality showed in his walk. Before Ben disappeared, it had been, for her, a metaphor for growing up. None of the pictures she'd chosen for *Life* were of her own children, and lots of them were old: toddlers waddling away through the lilac bowers in the University of Wisconsin arboretum; a boy carrying his skates slung over one finger, crossing Lake Wingra on a winter morning.

There was one picture for which the editors would have paid an even handsomer bundle. But it was too late to include that one. And Beth had washed her hands of the notion, anyway.

Looking up at her tack board, Beth turned her full eye, both her real and her photographers' eye, on the one walking-away picture she had taken of her own children. It had been at Ellen's house, after a barbecue a few weeks ago. All three of them were heading up the driveway to the car. She had told herself then that she was intent on the rose-quartz quality of the twilight; but the photo — Vincent elbowing Sam just a little over Kerry's strawberry blond head as she skipped between them — was beautifully composed, the boys like a bridge over their smaller sister. Last spring, when she'd sold the layout, just after Sam was found, one of the editors had asked, ever so delicately, whether any of the photos depicted 'the boy'. Beth understood; the layout wasn't just poignancy, it was news. She'd almost given in. Just one backshot of Sam. Quickly, she'd told him no, there wasn't. And the temptation to give them this picture — was it to cash in? to confess? — was still strong. Even now, when she knew that the issue deadline would make changing the layout impossible.

Was she proud of her picture? Or, as she suspected Pat of being, proud of her wounds? Could she pick the two apart, ever? She did know that, whatever their origin, work and money provided satisfaction, however remote. She simply did not know how far that satisfaction went.

Would work sustain her? If everything else were gone?

Forty minutes had passed. She picked up

the phone. The company was called Palladin Reconstructions — the yellow pages ad, which Beth thought was clever, said, 'Have taste, will travel.' When he was a kid, Nick had always made much of his last name, which he thought linked him with his legendary Sienese ancestors. The underline read, 'Historical ruin in distress? We'll come to the rescue.' That was going too far. But then, as Dan, Ellen's husband, said, you couldn't argue with four million bucks a year, which was what Nick turned over, appealing to the lucky convergence of twin trends toward architectural recycling and nostalgia.

The phone burred, and Beth felt her stomach grip.

To her chagrin — she had been counting, secretly, on a secretary, even hoping for an answering machine — he picked up himself.

"Nick," she said.

"This is Nick," he replied.

"Nick, this is Beth. Beth . . . Kerry."

"Uh . . . Bethie!" He didn't sound the way she'd planned he would, overjoyed, hushed with gratitude. He sounded . . . just surprised. "Wait. I got to get rid of a guy." He was back in a moment, his voice lower, more particularly pitched for her. "Bethie, it's good to hear you. Is anything wrong?"

"Nothing," she said. And then, "Everything."

"What do you mean? Is Pat sick?"

"No, he's fine. I just . . . Nick, I know I never called after we . . . It just seemed — I couldn't."

"Bethie, I understood. And then everything

happened. I never got to tell you how happy I am. Your boy . . . I know Trisha called you. I wanted to."

"Thank you. It's a miracle. We're . . . it's almost too much to understand. But the reason I called was, I think of you, often. And I was wondering if we could have lunch. I know it's abrupt."

He paused. Oh no, Beth thought. He's thinking that I'm asking him to sleep with me. *Am* I asking him to sleep with me? "I mean," she said stupidly, before he could reply. "Really lunch. Not . . . that."

She could hear Nick smiling. "I must say, I'm struggling with disappointment," he offered gallantly. Beth sighed. "But really lunch is better than nothing. I can't wait. When? Today?"

They arranged to meet at some nowhere chain out by his office, near the airport, in two hours. Deliberately, Beth did not rush back to the shower to shave another layer off her legs; she didn't redo her hair. She simply put on slacks instead of the ripped jean shorts she was wearing, lipstick — and at the last minute, Rosie's mother's diamond studs in her ears.

Nick was slightly, ever so minutely, heavier, as if a child had drawn a crayon outline around him and shaded in a bit more. A prosperous man. When he put his arms around her, he still smelled better than anything human; it made Beth woozy.

It took a full hour just to fill Nick in on Sam's homecoming; he questioned her with the gentle patience of a good father, drawing out the painful liquor under the surface.

"And Pat? How's Pat handling this? How are you guys?"

"Pat's good," Beth said seriously, rearranging her lettuce under mounds of tuna salad. "He feels like . . . blessed. I mean, he already had the restaurant, and that was more or less a new beginning for him. He never guessed he'd have this, too. He's got, you know, all these plans. He says he wants to travel and all that. Though I don't believe him. I mean, Pat gets nervous after five hours with Kerry's class at Six Flags and starts calling the restaurant to see if the edges of the ravioli have been crimped . . . "

Nick laughed. "I can relate. I take a phone to the beach in Virgin Gorda. It's like you lose your eyes or something. You wait all year for the vacation and then you can't stand it."

She told Nick about the million dollars, and how Pat had argued when she refused to consider the offer. "He said that just because I won't talk about what happened to us doesn't mean it will go away. He kept reminding me of what I used to say when I took pictures of a guy who jumped off a building."

"And what was that?"

"I used to say, 'It happened.'"

"Well . . . "

"But I told him this was different. It happened, but it happened to *us*. We didn't jump off a building. We were pushed." Without really meaning to go so far, Beth suddenly found herself telling Nick that it was more than question of style — that she had suspected her husband of coming close to saying that it was an ill wind that blew nobody good. That he had all but said that lemonade could be made from lemons, that prosperity could erase the sour taste of the past nine years.

"Is that so outrageous, Beth? I mean, you can't say you're owed, but you are owed. Pat, he's right. It's college and retirement and . . . But it's not worth fighting over. Because you guys have to be doing okay, anyhow, moneywise. I see the restaurant all the time in the columns. And I see your stuff. So as long as Pat's health is good and stuff . . . "

"It's good. I mean, Pat's never going to be mellow. He's always going to be fretting about the staff . . . "

Nick sighed, a businessman's sigh. "Tell me about it. You can't get a decent worker for any money."

"Yeah," Beth said. She had not pictured them discussing the shortage of good help. "But he's happy, as much as he could ever be happy." Would they never stop talking about Pat? "It's . . . Nick, it's Sam I'm worried about. It's Sam and . . . the other kids, because of Sam." She explained the trip to Minneapolis, the trip to Peshtigo, how it confirmed what she'd feared even before then. As Beth talked, she kept asking herself whether it was their history, or that Nick was just spectacularly easy to confide in, or that she wanted him, or that he comprised a fresh and objective panel of opinion. Even with Candy she wasn't as open. She couldn't tell him enough.

"It's not as though Sam's ever bad," she said. "He does just what you tell him to. But he's . . . eroding. It's almost like you can see him being chipped away." Beth told Nick about the long afternoon with Sam at the cedar chest. About the way his grades had plummeted from stalwart B's to C's and D's. About the way his hustle on the practice field had deteriorated to a shamble. About the day Sam had gotten up from a sickbed, in the midst of a serious bout with strep throat, so as not to miss his weekly two hours with George.

"The social worker says he's in transition, but if he's in transition, shouldn't there be some sign of progress?" Beth asked Nick, who was cutting his remaining half of Reuben neatly into fourths. Sam, she went on, was in their house but not of it; he kept his room as neatly as a guest, carrying his own shampoo and toothbrush back and forth as if their home was a boarding school. When he was late coming home from school, she knew he'd ridden his bike to one of George's construction sites, or spent long minutes sitting in front of his old house. Beth could liken him to nothing else but the foreign-exchange students Ellen used to take in — bright, helpful, polite, excruciatingly out of place and uncomfortable, mimicking rituals they didn't understand, quiet and given to long, late silences spent staring out of their neatly arranged rooms at the patterns of stars in the night sky.

"The only thing that keeps him going is the visits with George," she said, pushing her plate away. "And even Candy doesn't think that's

500

such a good idea. I mean, people think we're giving him mixed messages about who his real parents are."

"Maybe she's right," Nick broke in. For a moment, Beth thought she'd imagined it; had he glanced, ever so delicately, at his watch? "Blood is blood, Bethie. And what else can you do but see him through it?"

"That's what Angelo says."

"Well, it's true. All those things, the grades and stuff — even normal kids go through that stage. I did. It sounds like he's just in a period of adjustment."

"That's what Pat thinks."

"I think Pat's right," Nick said. "Kids adapt. They're survivors."

"I hope so," she said. "Still, I wonder if — "

"Are you happy, Bethie?" he asked then, leaning forward and covering her jittering hand with his own — his small, blunt, perfectly manicured hand. It this a pass? Beth thought.

"I'm relieved," she said carefully. "But I don't know if you could say I'm happy. I don't know if it's possible for me to be happy after all this. Or if I'm just expecting too much. Or if . . . " She looked up at him, reaching up for his fingers with her own. Is *this* a pass? she thought. "Maybe what I need to be happy has nothing to do with my children."

"I've missed you," Nick said. "I thought about you so many times."

"Oh, me too," Beth said. "Me too. A million times."

"Do you want to go . . . somewhere?"

"I don't know."

They drove to a small field where someone was building a landing strip for gliders. Beth let him take her in his arms, leisurely, gently open her mouth with his tongue. She let him lift her shirt and cup her breast, feeling the shivering begin in her waist and percolate up. But her potential for lust, Beth thought, taking hold of herself forcibly, wasn't what she'd come here to measure.

What was?

"Nick," she said, breaking off, kissing his neck as she sat up. "Did you ever do . . . this before?"

"Before today?"

"No, I mean, before we did."

"Not very often," he said.

"But before? Before we did?"

"A few times, maybe." She looked at him. He had removed his sports coat and now he smoothed it, tenderly laying it on the leather of the backseat, making sure every fold was just so. Don't, she thought. Don't self-destruct in front of me, Nick. Then she reversed, sternly telling herself, Don't look for it. Don't go prospecting for grief. He wants you. He's gorgeous. He's good and kind, and the history you have with him is sweet prehistory.

But she was unable to help herself. "When?" she asked.

"Oh, when the kids were little. I don't know. It didn't mean anything."

"And with me?"

"Well, of course, Bethie. It meant something

with you. Bethie, you know how I felt about you that day. I even thought — " Okay, she breathed then, it will be okay now — "at that time, that we might . . . see each other more. That maybe we could have — "

"'See each other more'? You mean, behind people's backs?"

She couldn't believe her presumption. What had she expected him to say? 'Found the meaning of life'?

"Well, I wouldn't have put it that way," Nick smiled. "We're going to talk now, I see. I think I need a smoke."

She itched with impatience as he got out his engraved lighter, his neatly folded pack of Lights. "Nick," she asked again, "did you think that after that day we'd start being lovers?"

"Was that such a bad thing to hope?"

"And never tell anyone?"

"I didn't know. I didn't think about it."

"Even after?"

"There was no point in thinking about it after." Nick drew in on his smoke and folded his hands. "Bethie," he said then, "did you want to leave Pat? Is that what you want now?"

"No," she said. "Well, I don't know."

"When you never called me, I thought, well, it was just one of those things that happen when you're under stress. But then, when you called me today, I thought, maybe she feels her life is missing something, too."

"Is that how you feel?"

"Sure," Nick smiled. "Doesn't everybody?" He reached for her, holding her not quite

503

comfortably across the divider between the bucket seats. No wait, Beth thought. It's not just 'Doesn't everybody?' It's more than 'Doesn't everybody?'

But Nick was saying, "A long time ago, my brother Richie told me that if you put a jellybean in a jar for every time you made love during the first year of marriage, and then you took one out for every time you made love after, you'd never empty out the jar."

"What's that got to do with it?"

"Well . . . "

"So it was just sexual for you?"

"Wasn't it for you?"

"No!" she cried. "Yes, and no."

"Well, yes and no for me, too."

"And have you had other affairs, since?"

"What does it matter?"

"How often?"

"Beth, numbers are just numbers."

"No they're not."

"Okay, then. A couple of times. But not like this. Beth, they were just no big deal. I don't want you to think I'm some pig or something, Beth, but it's . . . Pat would say this . . . I mean, maybe not, because you're so . . . full of life. But for me, being bored, physically, in a marriage doesn't mean that it's not a good marriage."

Pat, thought Beth in a hot flush of loyalty, would never say that.

She asked Nick then, "Is it a good marriage? Your marriage?"

"Yes, it is," he said. "I think Trisha is happy, and the kids are great. We are good friends. We

504

respect each other. Other people rely on us. She has a full life of her own."

Beth thought, Doesn't everybody? Nick slid his hand, comfortingly, erotically, across the back of her neck, letting his fingers probe her muscles. "That doesn't mean I don't want you. That I don't want us to spend time together. Beth, a part of me will always love you. And probably even more because you've been so brave. Nobody else could have gone through this like you did. You were always that way. My ma used to say, 'Elizabeth will always get what she wants.' I used to get mad at her for it. But she was right."

Beth disentangled herself from his arm and peered out the window. She wished she could teleport, deliver herself from this seat to her kitchen in one blinked motion, without the need to taper down this conversation, smile, comb her hair, drive. From the rim of her eyes, she caught Nick tilting the mirror to re-form his hair where she had mussed it. He did it well, with the deft assurance of a woman currying her perm.

She turned to him. "It would be easy for me to make love to you. It would always have been easy for me. But it wouldn't be enough."

"I'm not saying that would be all there is to it, Beth."

"What else would there be?"

"What else do you want? Do you want to marry me, Beth? Did something change in twenty years, other than I got older and more money?"

"Yes," Beth said then, tears forming. "I

changed. I wanted . . . "

"Me? Or just something?"

"Something. I thought maybe it was you."

"And maybe it is. I'm not saying all the doors are closed, Beth. It's just . . . you call me after four years. We have lunch. You ask me if I've ever slept with anyone but my wife and you, and if I did, I'm this creep."

"Not a creep. Just not . . . "

Not Pat, she thought. Not Pat.

★ ★ ★

He was out in the yard when she got home. She had examined her face fully in the mirror; it was neither too flushed nor too wan.

It was just a little better than ordinary.

Pat was looking up at one of the bedroom windows. "Do you think a dormer would look like hell?" he asked her as she came up behind him. "I'd like to give the boys more space, but I don't want it to look like a trailer park." 'The boys.' She heard him roll the plural in his mouth, love it. She wanted to swaddle him gently, in a blanket, keep him from harm.

"Come upstairs," Beth said, surprising herself. "I want to show you something." He stared at her, then followed.

The house was hushed and cool. She locked the bedroom door behind them and walked out of the cotton pants, amazed at her own boldness — they didn't do things like this anymore. Leaning back with her palms on the wood of their dresser, planting her legs apart and rising

506

up on her toes, she coaxed Pat out of his belt. Caught between puzzlement and excitement, he tried to figure out which way to move. He kissed her, with his lips trying to draw her to the bed. Sensible. But Beth leaned back farther, her hands up under his shirt, aligning the two of them so they stood ribcage to ribcage. This had always been easy for them, because they were nearly the same height; when they were kids, they had laughed about it. All we'd ever need would be a phone booth, Pat used to say. Obligingly, he slipped out of his pants and bent his knees — Beth was surprised, as always, at how ropy and strong he always emerged from his clothes. Dressed, he looked like a little ghost.

Pat raised his face to her then, and she saw his eyes grow hooded, his jaw tense, as they always had when another element walked into the room — the harshness and urgency of a man simply hot for a woman, any woman, not necessarily his familiar wife. Those had always been the best times, even before, times when they broke out of the tight threads of emotion that surrounded them, threads of weariness and responsibility and jealousy and even love, and the nakedness was more than physical, and a cold concrete floor or six neighbors watching from a window would not have stopped her from pulling him into her.

"For an old lady," Pat said, low, almost without moving his mouth, "you are some lady. You look twenty, Bethie. You look like you did on the grass behind the fieldhouse."

She pulled him under her, into her, with her

hands along his hips, finding a place on his throat to plant her open lips and suck at him. "Paddy," she said, "Paddy. Do it. Just do it."

"Let me ... here ... " Pat cupped her breasts, awkwardly, diving between them, inhaling her.

"No, no," she shushed him, "just this way." The smell of Nick on her forearm, as it chanced to cross her face, confused her, drove her hips against Pat's with a bluntness that startled them both. "I just, I just ... "

It was infuriating. She could not dismiss Nick's movie-perfect eyes from her mind. Though she and Pat worked together gracefully, making love with the kind of concerted grace of long habit, Beth felt they were fumbling, wearing heavy gloves, taking turns at a campfire poking a single glowing coal with a stick, missing it, sending it rolling, finding it again, missing again.

They were both pouring sweat by the time Beth pushed Pat down on the bed, locking her legs around him, suddenly terrified he would let go before she caught up with him, and that this would mean something it had never meant before, not just an ordinary miss. "Wait for me," she whispered. "Wait."

He pulled her arms down then, and pinioned them with his own, so that she lay on top of him but held fast, unable to move. There was no space between them except the space Pat created with the small coring movements of his hips. And then, gratefully, Beth felt him strike the center of the coal with patient, consistent

508

friction, felt the beginning of the burn . . . and Nick's face stretched and faded and stretched until, at the instant she felt Pat buck and spill, it vanished as if punctured, popped. She could see Nick, his beauty, his style, outside her, a lovely memory. Pat, suddenly heavy and wet beneath her, smelled like soap and salt and pine: the cleanest man she'd ever known. For years, she now realized, the most she'd managed to feel was a surface sizzle when they linked, the light off a sparkler that quickly sputtered. This time, the burn had gone all through. She hadn't thought they had that left.

"You . . . you are so fine, Paddy," she said then. "You would never leave me, would you?"

Pat's voice, when it came, was remarkably calm, full of breath, not like her own postsexual rasp. "I don't know," he said. "Are you going to make me want to?"

Beth had not noticed the refrigerator chill of the air-conditioned room. She pulled a corner of the quilt over her. Sounds came back: Kerry banging in the kitchen downstairs, Vincent shouting at her to turn off the TV.

Without a word, Pat got up and began taking his suit and shirt for work out of the closet, absently selecting a tie. Beth closed her eyes. In a moment, she heard the rush of the shower across the hall. This should be the part where I have a good, hard cry, she thought. And then I'd be cleansed, and I'd know what to do. But I can never cry when I need to. Or faint when I need to. Or sleep when I need to. She lay with her eyes open, remembering a feeling from girlhood, from days when she'd come out of a movie theater, blinking into the ebbing light of a Friday afternoon, disoriented in time, sick with the sense that something had been wasted. She pulled a pillow over her face, willing the slams and muffled calls, the activity of the house, to recede.

The next sound she heard was Pat's voice, from far off, shouting to her that Sam was gone.

31

"H E'S outside," Beth, still fuddled with sleep, told Pat as she stumbled down the stairs. "What time is it? Is it morning? He went down to the school to shoot baskets." She glanced around the empty kitchen. "Is Beowulf here? Maybe he took the dog out."

Hearing his name, Beowulf obligingly slid out from under the dining room table and chuffed over to nose Beth's hand.

"It's five o'clock in the morning, Beth," said Pat. "He wouldn't go out to shoot baskets at five in the morning."

"Five o'clock in the morning?" But Pat was still dressed in creased and gravy-fragrant work clothes. "Where were you?"

He looked away. "I had a few drinks."

Ahhh, Beth thought then, her panic over Sam receding for a moment, like water off the hull of a rising submarine.

Had Pat been with . . . someone else? How many people had there been in their bed yesterday afternoon? Three, four? Not only Nick, but some lovely Claudia or Roxanne of Pat's dreams? Maybe one of the three rotating hostess-brides at Wedding, all actors or models and cute as Mediterranean buttons?

After what had happened between them yesterday?

Beth felt no stab of jealousy, only a consuming curiosity: Before yesterday, would she have cared? Or mourned? Now, she wondered if one last big, fat irony was in store: she had loved Pat all along, but thawed to the recognition of that love only just . . . too late. Months late? Days? Despite all her own digressions and frank absences, in thought and deed, in spite of the terrible words both of them had spoken over the years, she had never even considered the possibility that it would be Pat who would turn away from her.

She looked at her husband's face, shadowed with overnight stubble, shorn of the restorative balm of sleep. Her biggest fear, yesterday, had been of the reckoning, of facing with Pat the possibility that by claiming Sam, they would destroy him, and by letting him go, they would destroy their family.

Now she felt again the sinking she'd dismissed with sleep the previous day. Pat might not go the distance. Perhaps whatever reckoning was to be faced, each of them would face alone.

"It was Joey and me," Pat said then, in a hurry, as if receiving her thoughts. "And the one bride and groom, Roxanne and Dustin. We went to that hippie place on Belmont."

Beth asked, "Until five in the morning?"

The room was icy. Beth reached into the hall closet and pulled out a sweater. Why did they have to keep the air at arctic levels, anyhow? She fumbled for the thermostat.

"Then back to Joey's. We watched *The Wild Bunch*. What the fuck do you care, anyhow,

512

Bethie? You know how many times I don't come home until morning, and you don't even know? You think I was robbing a train or something? Were you waiting up or what? And where the hell is Sam?"

My God, she thought. Sam.

"He could be in the basement watching TV," she said. "Did you ask Vincent?"

"He's asleep. His door's locked. I knocked. Kerry's asleep — wasn't she going to stay over at Blythe's?"

"She got homesick. You know how she does. Georgia brought her home. I heard her come in."

"Anyhow, I looked everywhere. Jesus Christ, Beth. Jesus Christ, where is he?"

Beth reached automatically up over the coffee machine for his angina pills. "Stop now, Pat," she instructed, struggling to pop open the bottle. "Let's just think a moment. Maybe he's running. He started running . . . "

"Beth, this house has been on the news, pictures, everywhere," Pat gasped. "You don't have to have the address to cruise by and see a kid out in front . . . a kid whose face had been on every front page in the country."

"You mean," Beth asked him then, incredulous, "you think someone took Sam? Kidnapped Sam?"

"It could happen!" Pat screamed. "All the fucking publicity! Some pervert could have . . . "

The doorbell rang. Beth watched as Pat's face literally leaked color, like an ink wash in a bath, down across his cheekbones, his neck.

"Oh, Bethie, oh God, no."

It was Beth who crossed to open the door, her own heart now jerking like a cat in a sack. On the porch, in the first morning sunlight, stood Sam and George, George's arm gently propelling Sam forward. Sam's face was creased with tears and sleep. Beth could smell the milk on his breath. He half-turned back toward George, who nodded, urging him, and followed Sam inside.

"I'm sorry, Beth, Pat," George said. "I'm real sorry he did it again."

Pat was clawing at his hair. "Did what? Did what again, George?"

George looked, confused, from Beth to Pat, then back over his shoulder, where the newly risen sun's glare above the rock garden was brightest. Someone was standing just at the turn of the drive. Someone . . . Beth shaded her eyes. It was Vincent.

"What?" she asked softly. "What?"

The first time Sam climbed out of his room in the middle of the night, climbed up the rose trellis outside his old room, knocked out the screen, and got into his bed, George explained, had been another of those nights when Beth had gone to bed early and Pat had been at the restaurant. And of course, he, George, was ready to bring Sam right back — "I mean, I love my son," he said. "I'm sorry, Beth, I love Sam is what I mean. But I knew you'd be out of your mind with worry, and you'd think that I, like, let him do this." But as soon as he'd given Sam some toast and a hug and taken him outside to the front porch, well, there was Reese, hunched in his jacket, astride his bike. Reese, who gave George a worldly shrug and assured him that he'd see the wanderer home and explain everything to the folks.

That same thing had happened the second time. And the third time. And this time, too.

"Vincent never told us," Beth said, mostly to Sam.

"I know," Sam muttered. "We agreed to not tell you."

Beth turned to Pat, absurdly pointing out, "I thought you said Vincent's door was locked."

"It *was* locked," Vincent said, elbowing past George and Sam and turning toward the stairs. "You can lock a pop lock just by closing it behind you if you're a mechanical genius. There's more than one way to leave a room. Ask Sam."

"Listen, Vincent . . . " Pat clenched his teeth.

"Give it up, Dad." Vincent pulled off his slantwise Sox cap and tossed it on the banister. "I'm going to bed. He's home, right? He's home this time, anyhow."

Watching herself from without, understanding the poverty of the gesture at such a time, Beth offered George coffee. Eagerly, he accepted. Sam reached down and zipped up his jacket.

"Go up to your room, Sam," Pat said, so sternly everyone, including Sam, was visibly surprised.

"What did I do?" Sam asked, with sudden heat.

515

"You ran away! You scared the hell out of your mother and me, that's what you did! And you've done it before! You could have broken your neck, or gotten hit by a car, or worse!" Pat pushed his face close to Sam's. "Hasn't enough happened to this family? Hasn't there been enough hurt to go around for everyone?"

"Yeah," Sam answered, but as Beth watched, he seemed to gather himself, thrust forth his chest. He was nearly as tall as Pat, and broader. Oh, she thought, he is not going to back off now. He has a Cappadora's temper. He has a Kerry's stubbornness. He is going to say it. And then, ashamed of her glancing jolt of relief, she thought, Then at least I won't have to. "Yeah, there's been enough. I mean, I'm sick of this whole thing."

"What whole thing?" Pat asked quietly.

"This . . . whole thing." Tears gathered in the corners of Sam's eyes, and slowly, beautifully spilled from the fan-shaped ends of his long lashes. "I'm sick of this. I want to go home. I want my dad. I can go to court and get you to give me to my dad. I read it at school."

"Look," said Pat, "whatever you read, you can't be serious thinking you could get us to give you to the husband of the woman who stole you, who kidnapped you?"

"It's not my dad's fault!" Sam said then. "Dad, you want me to come home, right? Tell him!"

George's misery was so overwhelming, so palpable, it was like another body in the room, a sweating, laboring presence. He looked from

Sam to Pat, and then, beseechingly, at Beth, who mechanically measured out six spoons of coffee and carefully unfolded the brown paper filter.

"What?" Pat said finally. "What is he saying?"

George sat down heavily. "He's been asking me, over and over, Pat. Why he can't live with me. I keep telling him . . . what his mother did, what Cecilia did, was so wrong, and what you folks have gone through — "

"But it wasn't really her fault, either," Sam trilled. "My mom is mentally ill, Beth. She's mentally ill. You said that when we went to that little town up there. I told you all about it. She didn't know what she was doing. She really thought I was her real little boy. Right?"

Beth said, "I know."

"And no offense, Beth," Sam said then, sensing an opening, measuring it. "It's not like I hate you. I mean, I tried for three months! Three months!"

"Sam, son, come on," George said, taking Sam's arm.

"No, Dad, listen! We talked it over. Beth knows." Beth could feel Pat's scouring look along her arm. She avoided his eyes. "I told her how I don't see why I have to live here, two blocks away from my own house, with people I don't even know, because of something that happened a long time ago that I didn't even do."

"Sam," Pat said. "Sit down." Sam sat down, careful to put George between the two of them. "Sam, listen. We know how hard this has been. We know how much you miss your . . . you miss

George. But this is a fact we have to face: you're *our* son. You don't remember being our son, but the fact is, you are our son. We gave birth to you. And you belong with your own family."

"But that's just the thing!" Sam was sobbing now. "I was maybe born in your family, but I never, like, saw you before in my life. I didn't remember anything, except the . . . well, I didn't remember anything about your house or anything! You see?" Pat nodded, closing his eyes.

"But look," Sam went on, shaking, trying to smile, "it can be okay, after all. I read . . . I looked it up on the microfiche — I didn't tell you this, Beth, but there was this one kid who divorced his real parents because he wasn't happy with them, and he got to be with his foster parents from before . . . see? He was used to them, because he lived there, like, five years. Then, all of a sudden, his mom got a job or something and she's like, 'I'm taking him back.' Now, I don't think I would actually have to get a lawyer or anything — right, Dad?" He looked at George searchingly. "I could just . . . move home. And maybe sometimes, I would come over or something. Like I do with my dad now. See?"

"But that was a case where the child wasn't being taken care of," Pat said, wearily. "That mother was probably neglectful or bad to the boy. We didn't do anything wrong, Sam."

"Well, neither did I!" he shouted.

Pat continued, softer, "And, Sam, I don't

think you could do this even if we wanted it and — ”

“Yes you could,” Sam told him urgently. “I read. You could do it if you wanted to. It's all legal and everything.”

“But we don't. Sam. We love you. We wanted you back and we still want you and we'll always want you.”

Sam put his head down on his folded arms, and both Pat and George reached for him instinctively. Beth bent over the coffee pot, feeling Kerry, for once silent, come up behind her and grab hold of the tail of her shirt.

“What's the matter with him, Mom?” she asked. “What's the matter with Sam?”

“He's so sad, Ker Bear,” Beth told the girl, stroking her silky, knotted hair. “He's just so sad.”

“Go upstairs now, Sam,” George said steadily. “Lie down for a while. I'll come and see you before I go. Okay? And ball tomorrow night? Huh? Okay?” Sam lurched from the table, nearly shoving George off-balance.

“I hate you!” he screamed. “I hate you — and I hate you, too, Dad! And I hate your dumb ugly house and your dumb freako son with the peanut-butter name! I'm never coming back!” Knocking over a chair, Sam ran for the stairs and up, two at a time. Beth could hear him strike the wall, three times, in the upper hall, and then the echo of his slamming door.

“I'm so sorry,” George whispered. “The poor little sucker.”

“George, nobody blames you,” Beth said,

rushing to finish making the coffee, bringing napkins, bringing cream in a pitcher, bringing matching spoons — all things she never did.

"I want to do right by him!" George cried then, slamming his palm down, on the table. "I want him to be happy. And if you guys are the guys that can give him the family he deserves, goddamnit, then you give him that! But I got to tell you, Beth, Pat, this kid is the saddest kid in the world right now. I have never seen this kid sad more than twelve hours in his life. It's . . . it's not in Sam. I mean, even when Cecilia . . . he was *sorry* for her, Pat. He would hold her hand, and her hand was limp like a washrag, and say, 'It's okay, Mom. It's okay.' And now . . . my God. Maybe it'll get better . . . "

Pat said then, a gulp, almost a croak, "And maybe it won't."

"And maybe it won't," George said. "But I gotta tell you, it's killing me. To come in his room like I do every morning and then, once in a while, to see him curled up there in his bed. See him there, with the pillow my ma made for him tucked under his leg. Beth! Pat! Of all people on God's good earth, you know how I feel!"

Pat looked at Beth with a scalding stare. "What did he tell you, up north?"

"This, basically. But not so much," she said, lowering her eyes. "I wanted to talk to you about it . . . "

George stood up hurriedly, knocking the chair over, catching it before it hit the floor. "I'm going, you guys," he said. "I'm sorry, again."

They both made as if to rise, but George waved them down with a weary motion of his hand.

Beth and Pat sat at the table, the fresh coffee in three mugs cooling between them. I will make breakfast, Beth thought. I will get up and do that.

"Paddy," she said. "Go get some sleep, huh?" He shrugged and headed for the stairs. Beth got out a bowl and began to beat eggs. French toast, she thought. It was still a bafflement to her, cooking, after years of Pat bringing home forage from the restaurant on his dinner break for him and the children — for herself, there was always a bagel, a yogurt, a handful of crackers and cheese. But Sam seemed to expect actual meals at predictable hours — salads, side dishes, desserts. George had followed the pyramid plan religiously; Sam weirdly liked such things as bran muffins and dried apricots. Beth peeled apples and oranges and mixed them with yogurt. Fruit salad. That was a good thing for a mother to make. Beowulf slapped his fat graying tail under the bench, the scattering hairs floating in the sun's spreading glow like little slivers of glass.

Vincent came down, drawn by the scent of cinnamon and butter. Pat, now in shirtsleeves followed. In silence, one by one, they came to the table and ate. Sam collected the dishes to stack in the dishwasher.

"I'll help you," Kerry said.

"It's my day," Sam told her, carefully stacking plates and placing the silverware on the top of the heap.

521

"You want to have a catch?" Pat called to Sam.

"I said I'd mow for the Silbergs," Sam said.

"But it's not even seven o'clock," Pat told him.

"Maybe sleep a while first," Sam replied. Pat hitched his chair back so he could watch Sam at the sink. He studied Sam's hands; Pat loved Sam's capable hands on a ball, any ball. Those masterful catcher's and shooter's hands were Pat's special joy, and Beth suspected, his guilt, too. Pat had been a shortstop, all bluster and speed. Sam's baseball was different, smart and slow, all thought.

Beth emptied the coffee grounds into the trash. Kerry turned on Looney Toons. Vincent disappeared into his cave. Now I'll sit on the porch, Beth thought.

When she went outside, she found Pat watering the roses.

"I can do it," she told him, with a spurt of irritation; hadn't Angelo reminded his son a million times you had to water the roots, not the leaves, or the leaves would mold? "I thought you were going to sleep."

"I can't sleep," he said. "Can you sleep?"

"Then Paddy, I guess we'd better talk."

"If you want," he said.

"He's not happy. What happened last night, that's just the tip of it."

"I knew you were going to say that, Beth. In a situation that's almost good, you have to find the all-bad. The social worker warned us about this. She said that it was going to take a long

522

time. Remember? Confusion about his identity. All that stuff."

"That's just it, Pat. Do you think he has any confusion about his identity? I don't. He knows exactly who he is."

Pat turned his back on her and began scraping at the leaves with a hoe he found against the side of the house. "What are you getting at?"

Beth sat down on the grass. "Pat, remember when we'd read about those cases where the birth parents wanted the baby back after the adoptive parents had the kid for two or three years? And you always said that if you were the judge, you would rule in the best interests of the child? You were always the one who said it was a terrible thing to do to the child?"

"This is different."

"The effect is the same."

"The effect is not the same."

"Paddy, George is his father."

For an instant, Beth thought Pat would raise the hoe and strike her. What he did instead was drop the hoe, grab the hose and throw it hard against the trunk of a tree, so that it undulated in the air like a cobra, spraying droplets over both of them.

"Listen, Beth," he said quietly. "I'm going to say this once. I love you, Beth." He walked over to the spigot and switched off the water. "I love you, and I've probably loved you your whole life. We've been married twenty years, and I've known you your whole life. And you know what I've seen about you, your whole life?"

"What?" Beth asked.

"You have made a career out of being unhappy."

"That's not fair. When Ben was — "

"No, I mean even before Ben was kidnapped. You were always just waiting for an excuse to be miserable. I'm not a doctor, Bethie. Maybe you have some kind of head problem, a personality thing. But see, Beth, I'm not like that. If I get the chance, I'll be happy. Even before we got him back, I decided I was going to be happy. I was going to die if I didn't. And then we did get him back. My life is how I want it. I thank God for my life being how I want it. And nothing on this earth is going to make me want to change any part of it, not after what I've been through. Not after what Vincent's been through."

"You know I don't want to do anything to hurt Vincent."

"I don't think you do. I really think you believe that. But what are you suggesting, exactly? That we give Sam back to the people who stole him when he was a baby? Are you nuts, Beth? Can you imagine what people would think?"

"I don't care what people think. I care about Sam."

"Well, then be a mother to him, Beth. If you care about him, help him get better."

"I'm trying to."

"No, you're trying to figure out a way we can all be miserable again. So that you can take another nine-year powder. This is about you, Beth. It isn't about this kid."

"Pat, listen, I wasn't thinking of completely

giving him up. Lots of families, when there's a divorce or something, they share custody. We only live two blocks apart. He could have two families."

"Beth, he *has* a family! By the mercy of God, he got his family back. He's my flesh and blood, Beth, my son. And if you think I am crazy enough to go along with anything that would take my son away from me again, after all that hell, I don't want anything to do with it, Beth. Or anything to do with you. I mean it."

Beth glanced around the yard and stood up. Pat was yelling now; she was sure the Beckers could hear him through their open windows; they didn't have air conditioning. "Paddy, we don't have to decide anything right now."

"Yes, we do, Beth. This is a pattern. The restaurant's a hit because people are ghouls. So what? Maybe they are. They'll forget in time. People forget everything. My sisters hate you because they think you gave up on Ben. Well, maybe they do — they'll get over it. People get over things, Beth. Sam will get over this. People have survived worse. We're lucky, Beth. We're lucky, do you get it?"

"Pat, I can't. If I love him, I can't ignore this. Let's talk to Tom Kilgore, huh?"

"I'm not going to change my mind, Beth," said Pat.

"It's not just your decision!" she shouted at him then. "You don't just say, 'I like my life, I've got my life!' He's got a life, too!"

"Yeah, he does! And it's right here! He's my kid!"

Tell him now, Beth thought. It's too late in the day for a coward's politeness. Tell him so he can't pretend he doesn't already know. Lay out the evidence, brick on brick, so that he can't say later he never really understood — never really knew that their baby, their Ben, had been right.

There was a deep end of the ocean. Ben had gone there, and he had not come back.

They could never go there with him, or know what he had experienced, or truly understand what had made him. They could only see the result.

Ben had walked out of the waves like a sturdier Venus springing from the foam, fully grown, transformed. He had walked out Sam Karras, a fine boy any parent would be proud to have raised; but Beth and Pat had not.

The smell he remembered as parental vigilance in the night was not her soap but George's cigars. Sam was a whole sediment of accumulated beliefs and impressions that had nothing to do with the Cappadoras: The red eggs of Orthodox Easter were the ones he had held in smaller hands; Alicia Karras, not Rosie, was Sam's yaya; his nana, the patrician Sarah Lockhart. He slept in pajamas, not underwear and t-shirts, as all the Cappadoras did.

Beth wanted to tell her husband how she'd scrutinized Sam for hopeful signs of breakthrough, for the merest hints. How she had seen Sam study Angelo and wondered, Is there some connection in this? Vague, but real? How she'd waited for results after Sam spent hours with the family photo albums, poring over details with the intensity of an adult at work on a difficult jigsaw puzzle, and grieved when none seemed to come.

Pat's face was shut, truculent. Could she tell him? Or would it be wasted breath? Didn't Pat know that all of Sam's memory molecules had been altered, and not with horrors? Didn't Pat remember the day that the county social worker told them that things might have been clearer, though far more harrowing, if Sam had grown up with sexual abusers or vagrants? That then, at least, he might see his biological parents as fairy-tale heroes? Instead, she said ruefully, "I hate to say this, but he probably feels like you were the ones who stole him, from his dad." Pat had been outraged, even after the worker apologized. He'd fumed for days.

Remind him, Beth thought.

And then said, "Pat, I think there are a lot of things going on you just don't want to see. And one of them is that I'm not the enemy here. Don't you think I want the same thing you want? If I could take a pill, or Sam could, and we would all forget this ever happened, don't you think I would?"

Pat paused before he answered, then said, with care, "I don't know whether you would, Beth."

"Jesus, that's cruel. You think I enjoy this?"

"Not enjoy it. No, I wouldn't accuse you of that. But you thrive on it. I mean, what would you have to keep you going if you didn't have your . . . your holy suffering?"

"Pat!"

"Well, there it is. It's like you finally found the big misery, Bethie. The thing that made it okay to be the bleak Irish. And now you're going to look for more. Losing just one kid one time wasn't enough." He stopped.

She said, "You mean, I could accept losing him again. It wouldn't hurt me as much as it did you."

And even though Pat stood silent, Beth heard him say it again, as if he'd spoken. The words he'd used. "Losing *just* one kid once."

"'Just one'," she said. "You think that I lost them both, don't you? Sam *and* Vincent? That it was all me?"

Pat said, "No. Christ, no. I'm sorry."

"That's what you meant, though."

"I didn't, Bethie, no, and I don't." Pat looked sincerely horrified.

I could hate him now, Beth thought, and it would probably help both of us. But the only feeling she could touch, rummaging inside, was regret as soft-edged and familiar as old flannel. Regret and guilt already worn by years of touching, long before the day of the reunion ever came, the day the long-simmering virus of her mother deficiency flared into frank symptoms.

Okay.

She hadn't been the best of mothers. In her affection as well as her wrath, rough-and-tumble. Impatient. Madly loyal, but not always sympathetic. Not always willing to make enough room.

Maybe, Beth thought, and almost said, even

before the kidnapping, there were too many of them and not enough of me. I couldn't give them everything I had, the way really good mothers do, because I had to keep some for my work.

But what about you, Pat? You were in the restaurant business, for God's sake, a twenty-four-seven job your whole adult life. Why did you do it? Why didn't you sell computers instead? Did you maybe like the hours, and the life, in spite of all your bitching? Was that okay, just because you were the father? And that was how *your* father was? Because when you *were* home, you were naturally sweet, not like me?

Beth kneaded her forehead. Stop, she thought. Don't buy this. Don't use the past as a prelude to the day of the reunion and everything after as simply a reprise of the theme — Mom half-there, kids half-served, then, finally, the payoff.

No. She struggled for a single good, settling breath.

"The thing is, Pat," she said, "if it wouldn't have happened, everything would have turned out all right. For us and for the kids."

"What do you mean?"

"I mean, we'd have been happy. We were. You think Ben got lost because I was a sloppy mother. And I *was* a sloppy mother . . . "

"That wasn't — "

"Yes, it was, Pat. It was what you meant, But that didn't bother you then. Not so much. And even if I had been worse, they would have turned out okay. You want to see things in terms

529

of 'if this, then that.' That's how you are, Pat. If things go down, it's because there was a flaw in the structure. But there wasn't. Not really. When you were growing up, Angelo was always having his little phony Italian breakdowns, and Rosie was always at the shop, and you turned out. Maybe things were easier then. There was church and the Moose lodge and you lived in one place all your life. But what there wasn't when we were kids — " she paused, looking for the word — "was . . . awareness. The fact that we knew how hard it was for kids who had parents who have to hustle for everything. My parents just thought that was ordinary life. They sort of dressed you and fed you and hit you if you didn't do your homework. But *I* knew. I knew I was selfish to want lots of kids and work, too. So I tried to make it up to them, so they would understand, no matter how I failed them in little ways, I never failed them in the one big way." Beth stood up and took Pat's arms. "I knew I wanted them. They knew it, too. They knew that I was as good as I could be."

When Pat made as if to dismiss her, Beth gripped harder. "And if you want to, you can say that after Ben was lost, it was my fault that Vincent got lost, too. You can say that, because it makes it easier for you. But I was as good as I could be then, too. And the reason that my best wasn't very good wasn't just the grief. It was probably because I believed, just like you did, that it was my doing. I felt that I could easily let Vincent down simply by being his mom."

Pat was crying now. But Beth knew she could

not afford to give in to either rage or pity. She could not, would not stop. She would talk until the window slammed shut. "And you know what the only thing we still have is? Awareness. We can be aware that we have two sons and they're both strangers in our house, and if we don't pretend this isn't true, maybe we can save something out of it. You've pretended long enough, and . . . you could say I have, too. How we got here doesn't matter."

Pat looked at her then: his eyes not knowing, or full of solace, as they had been so often in years past, but, like her father's, trusting and desolate and weak.

"What does, then?" he said. "What do you want from me?"

And if Beth had ever doubted it, she was sure at that instant that there was to be no shared responsibility for the consequences of whatever happened with Sam. Even if Pat didn't hate her — and she could see that he didn't any longer dare hate her — he would still be unable to say to his family, 'We talked it over. We decided that Sam is too unhappy this way. We decided what was best for us to do.' There would be no 'we' about it. Pat would not be disloyal to her, but it would be salt plain that he was living with a choice that Beth had made.

And now she would have to make it.

32

Reese

"SO it's kind of like a joint-custody arrangement? One week here, one week there?" asked Tom, one leg thrown up over the arm of his overstuffed chair. Reese had observed that since his marriage, a few months earlier, old Tom had loosened up considerably. Perhaps getting all that regular . . . But no, he wasn't going to head down that particular path today.

"Actually, I don't know what they worked out exactly; it's only been like a few weeks. I know they went to see a judge and stuff," Reese said. "I guess there are rules about it. But he hasn't been around much." Which was overstating the case. That day when he saw Sam heading down the drive, Reese had just dived into the sounds from the luxe new CD player his father had finally allowed him to take money out of savings to buy. He didn't even go down. He could picture the scene on the porch: his dad all slumped over, probably crying, his mom standing there like she was watching the *Hindenburg* burn. And poor Kerry, holding Blythe's hand and asking, 'When's Sam coming back?' Shit, you had to be a goddamn masochist to live in the Cappadora *Days of Our Lives*. The boom box, Reese figured, was sort of a lollipop to keep Vincent from crying over the loss of his already long-lost brother; shit, this got redundant. Like he gave a damn.

The house was already about seventy percent quieter, which was fine with Reese. They had never really made it as the Cleavers, anyhow, and Mom somehow looked more normal with her eyes watching the planets spin than she'd ever looked trying to actually see what people were doing.

" . . . feel about that?" Tom was saying.

"Pardon?"

"Earth to Reese." Tom was such a card. His slang was about thirty-five years old — Reese expected him to say 'groovy' any minute — but he did his best. "I was asking you how it felt to know that Sam had made that choice. Did it feel . . . kind of tough on you?"

"On me?" Reese was surprised. "No. I thought it was kind of a kick in the butt, excuse the expression, to my parents."

"Yeah, I can see that," Tom said. "So. How'd summer go? Still training for going out for basketball?"

Reese sure as hell wasn't going to tell him about the sweet little meeting with Shit-for-Brains Teeter. "Yeah," he said. "But I might not. I mean, of course, I'm academically challenged and understimulated in the traditional high-school setting, as you know." Tom snorted with laughter. "But my dad has this idea that if I don't get into the UW I'll die young or something. So I have to book next year. Really book. I might not have the time to give to the game, you know?"

Tom made a little steeple of his fingers. After years of seeing it, Reese knew deep thoughts were on the way.

"You sleeping okay?"

"Yep, pretty fair. No problem." Actually, this was a damned lie, but there was, again, no sense getting into it. He'd been having his fucking little-kid nightmare, twice in the last week. It annoyed him to think he was probably going to always be more or less borderline nuts, over something he didn't even care about anymore, or even remember. Much, that is. He felt his heart skip and flutter. Oh, shit, no, shit no. Not that, too.

"What's wrong, Reese?" Tom swung his leg onto the floor, crouched forward in serious-shrink posture.

"Nothing, nothing. I think I'm getting the flu or something is all."

"Are you sure that's all it is? I mean, this is pretty heavy stuff, Reese. Getting him back. Figuring out that whole deal. Then having him go, and having to figure out *that* whole deal."

"I don't have to figure it out. It's got nothing to do with me."

"I think it has."

"That's your job, Tommaso. You always have to think it has, or you'd be out of work."

"True enough. But I know that shit has a way of catching up with you, too. What about your mom? You getting along?"

"Oh absolutely. With Sam gone, she has a new appreciation for my many talents. We played mixed doubles tennis on Thursdays, then there's bridge on Fridays . . . "

"That gets old, Reese."

"Well, so does the question," Reese snapped. "I mean, my mom has spoken to me like ten times in nine years, and eight of those times were in the past couple of months. It's not, like, her fault or anything, but my mom sort of generally hates my guts."

"Whoa! Whoa! Wait a minute, buddy. I know your mom has her problems with intimacy, shall we say, but I've never once had the impression that — "

"Well, look at her face once. She looks at me like something you try to scrub off the bottom of the refrigerator."

"I don't think that's true. But it's important that you feel that way."

"Tom, I've been coming here, what, four years? A little more? How often have you met my mom?"

"Once or twice."

"Well, if you gave a fuck about your kid, wouldn't you think that maybe you'd like to check in more than once or twice? Tom, I don't give a damn. I got one more year in the bosom of my family . . . "

"Make that two. At least, Reese. And what about your father, and Kerry? Are they just some kind of background scenery? Don't you care what they think?"

"Sure I do." Reese stopped for a moment and got up to look at his favorite horse picture, the one of Tom and his little sister. "Your sister, she still ride?"

"No," Tom said ruefully. "She's in middle school. And she wants to be a pompom girl. She looks like . . . like some trashy backup singer in a garage band."

"Tom, Tom, Tom — she's just expressing herself, you know." Reese waved a finger. Tom grinned.

"Well, see, what Kerry does, she rides horses now. And swims. And plays flute. And plays soccer. Kerry is going to grow up to be this one-woman vaudeville show, like riding horses while tap-dancing and playing the flute. All she ever does is take lessons."

"Maybe she feels it's a way to get some attention for herself."

"I think it's a way to get out of the house. Which I totally understand. And which is why Dad virtually lives at Wedding in the Old Neighborhood. Especially now."

"So you feel pretty left out."

"Tom! I'm sixteen. I'm not in kindergarten. It's just that . . . this isn't the family who goes bowling on Friday nights, you know? And thank God, because that would make me puke. But sure, my dad loves me and he loves Kerry."

"But your mom hates your guts. And she's the one you're around most."

"If you can call it that."

"What would you call it?"

"I'd call it, like, two people who have to live in an airport, the same airport . . . "

"And where are they going? From the airport?"

"I didn't mean they were going anywhere."

"But say they were." Tom was up to his old tricks.

"If they were, my mom would be going . . . Jesus, I have no idea . . . to Mars. And if she had her way, I'd be going to . . . Siberia. Or hell. Or something."

"Why would your mother, who's already lost one kid, twice, want her other kid to go to hell?"

The flutter-beat in his chest returned again. "I have no idea," Reese said evenly. "She resents all the shit I've caused in school. I know that. It gets in her way."

"But you said she wants you to go to hell. That's not what most people want for a maladjusted teenager, if you want to call it that."

"Call it what you want." Reese glanced at the red numbers on the clock. "Hour's up."

"Don't give it a thought, Reese. My next appointment canceled. And your dad's loaded."

"Not to hear him talk."

"Well, don't worry about it. We were talking about going to hell." And, speaking of that, why don't you? Reese muttered to himself.

"It's obvious. She blames me."

"For what?"

"For *what*?"

"You heard the question."

"For the kid going back to George is what. She was like, always, 'Pay more attention to him,' 'Don't be so hard on him' . . . "

"Were you hard on him?"

"No. I shot some hoops with him. I didn't,

537

whatever, read him bedtime. stories . . . "

"He's too old for bedtime stories."

"I mean, I treated him perfectly normal, given that I don't have much in common with a sixth grader!"

"Even a sixth-grader who happens to be your brother you haven't seen in nine years? Don't you think that might call for a little more attention, Reese? Or would that be too much effort?"

"Tom," Reese pleaded. "I think I have a fever, is what I think. I'm going."

"I think you have a bad case of the poor-little-me's, is what I think. Your dad ignores you. Your mom hates you. Even your little sister takes too many riding lessons. Sound like Oliver Twist, you know, Reese?"

"So I give, okay? All I know is, she thinks the whole fucking thing is my fault, and you don't know, because you never see her except when she's acting all . . . there, and all nice . . . "

"'The whole fucking thing'? You mean what you said, him going back to George?"

"No!" Reese caught himself, ran his hands down his forearms, so he wouldn't scream.

"What, then?"

"Nothing."

"What, Reese? I can sit here all day."

"For fucking losing Ben in the first place. Happy now?"

"No. And she does not."

"She does so."

"No one would blame a seven-year-old kid for not watching his kid brother in a crowded

538

lobby of a hotel, and anyway — "

"You don't know," Reese said miserably.
"You weren't there!"

"Neither was she."

"But she knows! She knows!"

"What does she know?"

"She knows that I . . . "

It was as if he were having the running dream
right then, having it awake. He started thinking
of that smell, the day Ben was kidnapped,
that bottle-gravy smell of that hotel kitchen,
under the scent of all the woman's powder
and cologne. And he wanted to puke on the
rug, or get up and knock Tom's glasses right
off his smug, pink-Irish face. The dick. "Look,
Tom," Reese said with an effort. "I don't know
what I meant by that. She just gives me the
creeps."

"Maybe you give *her* the creeps."

"Maybe I do."

"Maybe she was right. Maybe you did drive
the kid away. Maybe he could tell you didn't
want him around. That if he was around, maybe
you wouldn't be able to get everybody to sit up
and pay attention every time you decided to pull
some JD stunt, huh, Reese?"

Reese put his face in his hands. "Don't ask
me. I don't know."

"I think you do know, Reese," Tom said. "I
think you do know. I think you know, and you're
afraid to tell me, because that would take you to
a place you've managed to stay away from for a
real long time, wouldn't it, Reese? And it would
take a lot to go there. A lot of effort. And you

539

seem to like to take the easy way."

"The easy way?" I sound like a whistle, Reese thought. He wondered if whatever little bulimic or pyro was waiting in the outer room could hear him. Oh, right. Canceled. At least that. He lowered his voice. "If you think that living in the Addams Family has been easy, you're the one who ought to be sitting over here."

"I never said it was easy. I just said that maybe some people have enough guts to go there, and some don't."

"Guts? Look, nobody has ever called me afraid. They've called me a lot, but never chickenshit."

"I am."

"Go to hell, then."

"I thought that was your destination."

"Very cute, Tom. Highly professional."

"Reese, you might as well hang it up," Tom sighed. "You're going to be stuck where you are until you finally meet someone big enough and mean enough to beat it out of you. That's if you're lucky. I just wish you weren't so determined to take the whole family with you."

"I'm not," Reese said then. "I just want them to leave me alone."

"I thought that's what you *didn't* want. But it sounds like every time somebody tries to get close to you, you can't wait to find a way to piss in his face."

"Don't," Reese warned.

"Why, Reese? Gonna rumble with me, next? Not content with blaming your mother for all your troubles?"

"Blaming my mother? Christ, I've been trying to tell you. It's her! It's her! She knows what I did, and she hates me for it, and I don't blame her!"

"What you did? What did you do?"

"What did I do? What did I do? I let go of his hand! And you know what I said? To my sweet little kid brother? I said, 'Get lost.' I said, 'Get lost.'" Reese figured he'd cry then — it would have been a relief to cry then — but he didn't. He was boiling. Boiling dry. The top of his head would be rising like the lip of a tea kettle if Tom could see his insides.

"Reese," Tom said, far away. "Reese."

"What."

"Did you always know this? Did you remember it just now?"

"I don't know."

"You do know."

"I always knew it. And I didn't. That's the truth. It was, like it was in a box. But I remembered it when he came home. Like, first a little. Then some more. Then the words."

"Reese, think. Think a minute. There's no way on earth your mother could know you said that. And you didn't mean for him to literally get lost."

"But he did. He did."

"The fact is, you didn't mean it, and you didn't even know what it really meant. You were just a tired little kid sick of watching his little brother while your mom goofed around with all her friends. You were probably hungry, and bored . . . "

541

"Yeah, so big deal. She still hates me."

"I don't think she hates you, Reese. I think she's scared of you."

"Scared . . . of me?"

"I think she's scared you're going to find out about her, the same way you were scared she'd find out about you."

"Find out about her? What did she ever do?"

"Think about it, Reese. Think about it and we'll talk next time. It's in there, Reese. You opened the box. That's a pretty brave thing to do, Reese. Now, we have to look at whatever flies out of there, and if we have to, we'll swat it down, like a bug. Okay?"

"Okay."

"It wasn't your fault, Reese. It wasn't your fault. You don't have to believe me now. Like, people didn't used to believe there were such things as atoms, because they couldn't see them. But there are." Reese shrugged. "Listen. I told you one time about my little brother. The baby who died of SIDS. I told you I was the one who found him. But I didn't tell you the rest. My mom sent me up there to get him out of his crib." Reese looked up. Tom was looking at one of the horse pictures, directly over Reese's head. "And I was mad. I was sick of carrying around babies. There were eight of us, and we all had to take care of the little ones, and it wore you out. So I went up there, and I reached for Taylor's arm. And it was cold. It felt . . . like a little cucumber from the refrigerator. Cold and hard. And so you know what I did? Reese?"

542

Reese nodded. "I had been reading the comics, and my mom kept telling me, 'Go get the baby, go get the baby,' and all I wanted to do was finish the comics. So I did. And finally, when I went up there, and found him like that, I was still carrying that newspaper. And I spread it out, and I covered him all up with the comics. I'm sure I didn't know, or I didn't let myself know, that he was dead. But what I do know is, I wouldn't let my mother touch me for . . . really, for years. She thought it was because of what she'd done to me, exposing me to that awful thing, when I was just a little kid myself. She thought I was afraid of dying in my sleep. And I was. But that wasn't the big thing."

Reese jerked his head. "What was?"

"The big thing was, I didn't know until I was in high school, or even college . . . I thought I killed Taylor. That I messed around so long that he died from starving to death or something. That if I had just gone up there sooner, when my mom told me to, he would have been able to live, just a little longer. Reese, I thought that when I was older than you are. And you can see, I can tell by looking at you, you can already see, it simply wasn't true. It couldn't have been true."

Reese nodded again. His head was big, pulsing, like a balloon on a stick in the wind. He didn't think he'd ever had a headache this bad, so bad he almost asked Tom for some aspirin or something. But Tom would probably have had to write a prescription or some deal; doctors never just gave you anything to make you feel better. There had to be a big process.

Air, Reese thought, when Tom finally let him go, with a brotherly squeeze on his shoulder. He'd been in the fucking horse gallery for two hours. Jesus. He'd opened the box, and what for? He knew Tom was a decent guy, but that story about the dead baby — he didn't really get it; no one could really get it.

Reese steered his bike up Hollendale toward the school. It was getting dark already, summer ending, he thought. Thank Christ Dad hadn't insisted on driving him today. Maybe he would just sit in the outside bleachers for a little while. Suck some air. See if anybody was around and play a little pickup if somebody was. His neck felt like it was shrinking, pulling his head back into his shoulders.

He spun into the parking lot, pedaling hard, and then he saw it. The big old white Thunderbird, a restored '68. The vanity plates said BG COCH, which they all knew that fat bastard intended to mean 'Big Coach', but to most of the kids — except, of course, the loyal storm troopers of the varsity A squad — it was 'Big Cock' or 'Big Crotch', depending on the mood they were in.

Teeter. That fat fuck. Probably in there right now planning ways to emasculate some ninth grader into peeing himself. An old fart, gone to fat, still trying to drive his Beach Boys car around town. Teeter, thought Reese, slowing down, carefully stowing his bike in the bushes, behind a stack of railroad pilings. He put his hands in his pockets. It was almost dark now.

Which suited Reese just fine.

33

THE guard pulled the metal-armed chair out for Reese and motioned for him to sit down.

And then he left, silently, as if vaporized. Reese wouldn't even have known the guy was gone except for the eddy of deflected air from the closing door. He stared at the smeared Plexiglas partition, with its distinct prints of hands, snail trails of . . . he didn't like to think what. Reflexively, he lifted his hands into his lap and held his arms tightly against his sides. He didn't want the furniture, with its hosts of prior bacterium, to touch his body and inhabit his skin. The room was rank; it stank of hair rinsed in cigarette smoke, of dirty insoles. It was a little, little room, a narrow closet. Reese tried not to breathe, tried not to take the molecules of stink into his nose; whatever you breathed, dog fart or cinnamon bread baking, it became part of you. Oh God, I want to be clean, Reese thought. I want my bed. I want my toothbrush. He didn't have his watch anymore, and the room had no windows; but he knew it was morning. The sky had been lightening already when they drove him over from the hospital. And then it took about twelve hours to do his fingerprints and take away his normal clothes; and then they told him to go to sleep — and he did fall asleep, in spite of all the noise and crying, but only slept for like a half-hour. Then they got him up and told him his parents were there. They had been at the hospital, but he'd been so high from the shot they'd given him he couldn't remember what his mom or his dad had said, or even whether they had touched him.

Now, he wasn't much improved. If anybody asked him, Reese could not have sworn whether four hours had passed or forty. But it had to be Saturday. Just later Saturday. When he saw his mom outside the door, he suddenly had a memory flash from the hospital emergency room. Red jeans. She still had on the same red jeans.

The no-contact visiting room was supposed to be soundproof. There was a vanilla-colored telephone on his side that he would use to speak to his mother when she came in. But he could watch her already, through the long rectangle of the window of the door opposite, standing in profile as if the window were a picture frame, her head hanging down, her fuzzy dark hair shadowing her face.

She was talking to someone, and when she shifted back to pick up her shoulder bag, that someone reached for her. Candy: the swan arms and frosted fingertips unmistakable, even in a blue blazer-type thing, the kind of thing he hardly ever saw Candy wear. Candy put her arms around Reese's mom and stroked Beth's hair. Reese would have given anything, at that moment, to hear . . . He laid his head down on the Formica laminate of the counter, forcing himself not to cringe at the contact.

Soundproof — ah, yes. Another triumph of technology — not. He could hear his mother say, " . . . better off home?"

But Candy's voice was louder, good ol' Candy. Hers was a voice accustomed to giving orders to people with voices lower than hers.

Mutter, mutter, she said, and then, " . . . could kick him today even, though technically, you know, there has to be a custody proceeding for a juvenile, and we can't do that until Monday afternoon at the earliest. But Bethie . . . " They were leaning against the door now, as if they didn't realize he was sitting there at all, some three feet of air and an inch of plastic away, right there. Hello, Mom. Hello, Candy. They didn't look at him. " . . . a bad idea to let him stay the weekend." Reese could feel sweat snake down his breastbone. "There's a kind of kid you know is going to snuggle up to those little friends in there and learn some tricks . . . " Reese lost her voice for a moment as she turned briefly away, but then, " . . . scare the hell out of him. I mean, the decisions going on in there are whether to cop to the rape charge in exchange for dropping the drug charge. They got the father shooters on one side and the mother shooters on the other. It's a gamble, Bethie, but this is a kid who wrecked a stolen car, drunk, and scuffled with a cop . . . peanuts, Beth."

It's peanuts? Or not peanuts? Reese tried to slow down the thrum of his heart that interfered with his hearing. His heart rebelled, pummeling harder.

Outside, Reese's mom made a noise, tossed her head back.

"I don't mean to you," Candy went on, "but for all Reese has done in the past, you know . . . a criminal kid. This isn't a pattern. This is his first major antisocial . . . Beth, you know what I'm saying . . . In this case, reform school for this, especially with his history . . . "

Jesus God, thought Reese. Is that the best I can get, or the worst?

" . . . teach him the world doesn't owe him a living no matter how he screws up?" Mom asked then, louder.

"I don't think the world owes him a living, Beth," Candy said. "But the world owes him an apology."

" . . . to us all. And what about Sam?" True to form, Mom, Vincent thought. I'm in the can here, and we're going to find a way bring up the prodigal son. Who, like, wishes you were anywhere but here. Who literally jumped out a second-story window to get away from you. Who probably hates your guts. Yes, Mom, let's discuss Ben, alias Sam.

"Ben, too," said Candy. "That is, Sam, too. But Reese didn't do this thing because he was trying to throw his weight around . . . "

Reese heard another voice, muffled. Dad. Oh, good Christ. And Candy replied, "Well, yeah, Pat. You know all this shit. What kids do if they're hurting, kids like Reese. He's not going to come up to you and say, 'Well, Dad, I didn't really mean for Sam to leave, though I'm not entirely sorry he did. This is bothering me.'

They can't do that — Reese especially — so he has to do something crazy, something so big it draws all the attention off how he feels about this . . . "

" . . . his fault?" It was his mother.

"Oh, Beth," said Candy, her voice tangy with irritation. "You know he thinks everything is his fault. And you know, Beth, I don't want to scare you — you've been scared enough for ten people in one life — but you know how many car accidents are suicide attempts for kids? You know that? I'm not trying to lay blame on top of this, but let's think about what he's going through . . . "

Whose fault? Not yours, Mom, no way. Reese rubbed his neck. His skin felt coated with syrup; he was accreting every piece of grit in this place.

And then, all of a sudden, his Dad was yelling, " . . . pay some attention to him once in a while, he'd know you gave a shit whether he was up in his room or wrapped around a fucking tree!"

"Well, Pat, they ate last night at Wedding in the Old Neighborhood, while your son was hot-wiring a teacher's car," Beth said evenly, shrilly.

"Why not be a mother, Beth?" Reese could hear his dad's voice, tiny, but he knew Pat was yelling. He could visualize him, throwing his chest out. He hated that little rooster posture, the one that sometimes ended with a fist through a hollow-core door. "Why not just try it?"

"Pat," Candy said. "Shut up."

The door behind him whispered again. The

quiet guard. "They'll be with you in a minute, Vincent. They're talking to the chief."

The chief. A definite smile there. Reese still couldn't help it. Chief Bliss. The babe cop who found Ben Cappadora. Even though she didn't. Even though she couldn't find him, for nine years, a mile from the police station. Well, okay, Candy. Affirmative action. Go for it. He put his hands over his face. Fuck the bacteria. And then the door in front of him opened inward, and there was his mother, not much more deranged-looking than on any ordinary day, taking in the dirty window and the scummy phone and him in his lank green jail jump suit, as if all of it were furnishings, sitting down. He was so sick to his stomach, tasting the peach brandy, that looking at the raccoony way Mom rubbed the backs of her little strong hands against her cheeks as she sat down, it was so much something he could picture her doing in her robe in the kitchen or something, he almost started to cry, and then he thought he would puke. He looked away.

"Vincent," she said.

"Hi, Mom."

"How are you?"

"Okay."

They sat there. His mother breathed in through her nose and let the air escape her mouth with a long hiss. Vincent concentrated on swallowing, swallowing. Maybe, he thought, she'll give me hell. She'll tear a strip off me. Any other parent in the hemisphere would. This was, after all, a big-time jerk-off. He guessed he deserved it. Mom? He looked at her and coiled

551

in preparation. But she just sat there Momishly. Finally, she seemed to think of something.

"Well, do you need anything? I mean, anything at all from home? Because I think that you're going to have to stay here a day or so more, because it's the weekend . . . "

And learn my lesson like a good little boy, thought Reese, feeling better. Well, actually, Mom, yes, I need a couple of things. I need to get out of this shitty dump where the light's in your face no matter which way you turn and the guy in the next bed keeps looking at me as if I was a Big Mac and the little thirteen-year-old kid one room over is crying nonstop for his grandma. A little kid who cut his mother's boyfriend in the gut with a steak knife. Yeah, I need a couple of things, Mom.

"No, I'm fine," he said.

"Are you sure? You look green. Are you sick to your stomach or anything?"

Reese had to look away. It was like she could see the brandy-and-acid pluming up and down the sides of his stomach like one of those musical light fountains. Where did his goofy buddy Schaffer get that shit anyway? Did adults actually drink it? And why did he pick Schaffer up anyway? Why hadn't he just ditched the damn car and sat in a ditch to drink? No simple mistakes for you, Cappadora, he thought. He struggled again not to cry. Well, now I know. I know what people talk about to their kids in jail. Nausea. But before he could stop himself, he said, "My head aches."

"Candy says you should tell one of the officers

if you feel bad in any way, and they can get you something."

"Well, they can't get me an aspirin. I already asked. They have to have, like, a nurse. They said not for a couple hours."

"I have an aspirin," said Beth, reaching for her purse. Reese smiled and reached up to pat the Plexiglas partition. "Oh, sure. I forgot. My God, Vincent. Is your head bleeding?"

"No."

"Oh, honey. Uh . . . do you want to see Dad?"

Exit stage left, Mom, thought Vincent, that's your bit. He was about to nod when he realized, abruptly, that he did not want to see his dad, maybe ever, especially not here, did not want to see the gray crescents under Pat's eyes, and the way Pat would rake his hair and reach for the partition as if he wanted to melt through it and lift Vincent up. If he saw his dad, that would be it. He had to keep himself low and slow, low and slow. So he said, "Not now, Mom. I just want to sleep."

She said, frightened-like, "Okay." He thought she would get up to leave then, but instead she placed both her hands flat on the counter on her side and cradled the telephone on her shoulder. She reached up and touched the partition. "Vincent. There's something I want to ask you."

He was intrigued. From Mom, this much conversational initiative was the equivalent of a film festival. Panic, he thought. She knows this is the big time. She's going to ask me why

I did this — whether I was trying to kill myself or something. She's going to ask me what the hell I'm trying to do to her . . .

"Yeah?"

"Ben is here." She shook her head. "Sam is here."

"Oh, shit." Figures. "What did you bring him here for?" Turn him away from a life of crime? The existent proof?

"He asked to come."

"How in the hell did he even find out?"

"Your dad told him."

"Why?"

"He thought . . . You can imagine, Vincent. The accident was on television news. The late news. They weren't supposed to use your name, you're just a kid, but because of Ben, you know, they said it was Ben Cappadora's brother. It was a piggy thing to do. And then, of course, they were all on the lawn fifteen minutes later. By this morning, Sam saw it. He called. Well, George called and put Sam on. He thought Sam would want to know if you were hurt . . . "

"Sam," said Reese, angry now, "*Sam* wouldn't want to know if I was on fire, Ma. What is this shit?" Reese had an inspiration. "I don't even think you can bring little kids in here. That is, the little kids who aren't already in here."

"Candy said it's okay."

"Is there, like, some big therapeutic reason 'Sam' has to come in and see me? Is it, like, healing?"

"I don't care if he does or not, Vincent." His

554

mother's eyes were gone all black, no green. She laser-looked him. "I don't care if you see him or you don't. He wants to see you. I said I would tell you. He asked us to drive him over. We drove him over."

Reese thought, She knows when they say you can do whatever you want and that they couldn't care less, you always do what they want you to. There's no way out. He waved his hand at her.

"Okay," she said. "I'll go get him. He's downstairs."

"Whatever."

"Okay."

"Mom?"

"Yes?"

"Can I see Tom?"

"Tom . . . "

"Tom Kilgore Tom . . . you know, Mom?"

"Ummmm . . . I don't know, Vincent. They said only immediate family."

"But I can see Sam."

The way she looked at him then, Reese thought, She really does hate me. I knew she hated me, but she really fucking hates me. He started to apologize, to say something, but then his mother said softly, "Sam is immediate family."

"Right. I wasn't thinking."

"Well, look. I'll ask Candy if I can call Tom."

"Forget it."

"No, I will . . . And a lawyer, maybe, though I don't know if — "

555

"'Cause I don't even know if he knows."

She looked blank, so Reese reminded her: "I mean Tom."

Beth sighed. "Oh, Vincent, he knows. I think everyone in four states knows." Reese thought, I'd like to paste her, just once.

Reese stood up and tapped on the door that led back to the detention. The guard was standing right there, but he did this elaborate yawning thing, like, Oh, is that a fly I hear? Reese closed his fist and banged harder.

"Problems?" asked the guard.

"I just want a drink of water, okay?"

"No water."

"No water?"

"We got no water. You want coffee?"

"I didn't mean like bottled water . . . "

"I can't get water from here. Want coffee?"

"I'm sixteen, man. I don't even drink coffee," Reese pleaded, and then added, "Much."

"I'll see if I can find you some pop."

When the guard let the door shut, Reese felt the room suck at him. It was so very small, so small. And the patterns of dirt on the walls and floor were the only variation in all the blond-and-cream-wood-and-plaster, the only decoration. He was not claustrophobic; he remembered the box on the landing of the stairs, where all of them would hide, and snow forts . . .

Reese didn't even notice the kid. But Sam was already holding his telephone. Reese picked up. "How long have you been here?" he asked.

"A minute." The kid looked scared to death,

and he looked . . . little. Shrunken. He had on a Cubs shirt.

"Are you okay?" the kid asked.

Reese suddenly had this picture of one of the old Pat O'Brien movies his dad made him watch with him in the middle of the night, where Jimmy Cagney was this arch-criminal who was going to the chair, and Pat O'Brien was his old friend from when they were kids, a priest, and he came to the jail to beg Jimmy Cagney to act like a coward when he was going to the chair so all the little kids in the neighborhood wouldn't think this wrong guy was a hero or something. Reese started to laugh. He couldn't stop laughing.

"What's the matter?" Sam said. "What's so funny?"

"Nothing . . . I'm . . . nothing. Well, Sam man, fancy meeting you here."

"Are you okay?"

Reese automatically reached up to touch the bandage on the back of his head, where they'd stitched . . . it stung. He still couldn't figure out how the hell he'd banged the back of his head running into a light pole with the front of Teeter's car.

"I'm okay. It doesn't hurt."

"Are you going to be in here for a long time?"

"Well, five to ten years," said Vincent, and then he looked at the kid and thought, That was a shitty thing to do. "No, I don't know, Sam. I guess . . . I know guys who did stuff, and they had to go to one of these schools . . . "

"Reform school. Beth said it's not for sure."

"Yeah, well, it's like a farm, I guess. For JDs. I don't know."

"What did you do?"

"I took Teeter's car. I wasn't going to keep it. I just was going to ride around . . . "

"Teeter the coach at the high school?"

"Yeah, that asshole."

"And so why didn't you just bring it back?"

"I was going to, but this goon I know, Schaffer, and I, we were goofing around, and then when I saw the cops, I just went faster . . . "

"Were you drunk? That's what Beth said."

"I was overserved . . . yeah, Sam, I was drunk. But I never did anything this bad before . . . "

"That you got caught for."

"That . . . right. So, Sam, what do you want?"

"Nothing."

Reese could see his parents sort of scuffling to see in the skinny window, his dad waving a little. Reese waved back. He couldn't see whether his dad looked sick or not. At least Pat was wearing matching clothes; this was a sign he couldn't be too bad. Bad. Speaking of bad, he felt bad. Why am I babysitting this kid? Why wasn't one of them in here with Sam? Wasn't this against some law or something, letting a little kid go in to visit a felon?

"Well, then, why are you here? Is this, like, the alternative amusement for Saturday morning?"

"I wanted to see if you were okay."

"Well, I'm okay."

"Okay."

The kid looked around the booth.

"So? Sam?" Reese, all at once thinking he could maybe sleep, prodded the kid. The sooner this day could end, the better.

"This is pretty ugly, this place."

"It's ugly."

"How fast were you going?"

"I don't know . . . like ninety . . . "

Sam's eyes blinked and fastened on Reese. He grinned. "Ninety?"

And it occurred to Reese that maybe he should go easier here. That Sam was probably not just ordinarily fucked up, but a little more than ordinarily, just barely back with George and all. A couple of weeks at his own house after the foray into Cappadoraland. And now this shit. He was such a kid . . . Oh, Ben.

"Look, Sam. I don't know if you know . . . " Reese dropped his voice. Soundproof, my ass. "I don't know if you know how incredibly stupid what I did was."

"Well . . . " said the kid. "Yeah. I do."

"I mean really, monumentally stupid."

"Yeah?"

"Like, I'm a jerk, Sam."

"No," said Sam.

"I'm a fuck-up, and it's not funny, it's not cool." Reese was almost whispering now, leaning toward the partition.

"I just thought . . . "

"What did you think, Sam?"

"I thought we could be . . . friends."

"Friends?" Reese was glad he couldn't get his hands on the kid, "Look, you idiot. First of all, how would we be friends, Sam? I don't hang with twelve-year-olds. And second, you come back, you leave, and go in and out the window . . . I don't even know you, Sam. You're a concept, you follow me? And you don't know me!"

"That's not my fault!" The kid looked on the verge of tears. Reese could see Pat motioning for Candy to punch in the code and let him in. He quickly waved Dad off, to try to soothe him — I'm not instructing him in the finer points of car theft here, Dad. You don't have to save him.

"I know it's not your fault," he told the kid with what he thought was awesome patience, considering. "But I have a life of my own, you know? And it's unfun right at the moment. What do you want from me?"

"You're my brother. I haven't come around, because I didn't know if you guys would all be so mad at me you wouldn't want to see me. But . . . I missed you. There were even times when I thought I shouldn't have . . . whatever. You're my brother."

"I'm not your brother!" Reese gave up; the tears were running down his filthy face; he was just tired out, is all, and this fucking kid . . . "Look, if I were your brother, what would you want from me? I mean, I'm fucking going to some kind of penitentiary or something! Even Dad thinks I should be in a padded cell! I probably have, like, no future. I probably won't even graduate . . . " Reese rubbed his eyes, trying to get himself to stop. His head was filled with that pool-water smell — that drained limpness he remembered from being a little kid, when you cried and cried until your chest was hollow.

"I just thought . . . It's okay," said Sam. "I'll leave."

"Yeah, leave," said Reese. Then he winced. "Sam, I'm sorry. I know you probably feel crummy. It was nice of you to come over here. But here's the thing . . . I have to get out of this somehow . . . "

"I know, and I — "

"You don't know. Don't say you know because you don't. You never did anything wrong in your whole life! You're just a kid. And you're a real good kid. Look, when I come home, I'll come and get you and we'll go get something to eat, okay? Or shoot pool or something, okay?"

"Where?"

"What?"

"Where could we go?"

Reese sighed. "I don't know, buddy. Anywhere in walking distance. I may not be driving until, like, two thousand and ten."

"Can we go to Wedding?"

"Nah. Not there. I meant like a burger."

Then the kid sighed, too. "Okay. I just didn't want you to think I believe it when they say you're crazy."

"Well, I *am* crazy. Who says I'm crazy?"

"My dad."

"George."

"Yeah."

"He said so. In so many words?"

"Sort of."

"What do you mean 'sort of'?"

"Well, he said so."

"Okay. Come on. How?"

"He said . . . he said . . . "

"Yeah?"

"Yeah, when I was at your house, he would say, 'Watch out for that kid, Sam. Watch out for that kid. He ain't right.'"

"'Ain't right.'"

"Yeah, and I don't think . . . I mean, I love my dad, but he doesn't understand . . . He thought you would hurt me or something."

And so I would, thought Reese, and raised his arm in motion for the guard, but the kid said, "Wait a minute. Reese?"

Reese sighed again. The room would inflate.

"I got to tell you something."

Reese made a weary circular motion with one hand. So? So?

"I remembered something."

"Yeah?"

"I remembered something from when I was a kid."

Reese stiffened. He thought, Christ, no. Not today. I don't want him to remember today. And anyhow, he couldn't, he was just a baby, he couldn't remember the words . . .

"When I was at your house, Beth showed me this trunk. The trunk at the foot of your bed." The cedar chest, thought Reese. The big hope chest with the hoop top. "She took out all these baby clothes she said were mine. And she showed me some blankets and stuff. Some pictures."

"And? And?"

"And I didn't remember any of them."

"Oh." Reese's weariness was deafening. So long as the kid didn't remember the lobby, what the fuck did he care? How much, Reese thought, how much more? Isn't this enough, Mom?

"But I remembered the smell."

"The smell."

"I remembered the smell of the cedar chest. From being inside it."

Reese let the phone drop, almost. It was as if Mom, gesturing, shrugging her shoulders, outside the window, asking if Sam wanted to come out, was on film instead of real. He could feel his shorter self running up those stairs in Madison, into the little room half-made-over for baby Kerry, where they dumped everything, pulling over the boxes of diapers and clothes and whispering, "Ben, Ben, where are you, Ben?" Running back down. Thinking of the dryer. Thinking, Mommy will kill me if he's in the dryer again and turning blue. He wasn't in the dryer. A pulse thudding in his neck. He couldn't let his mother hear. She would screech. She would grab his hair.

" . . . hide-and-seek," the kid said.

"I know," Reese said, adjusting the telephone, which had gone slimy in his wet hand.

"And there was this one time I got into the big chest? Did that really happen?"

"It really happened. You let the lid shut, and it caught."

563

"I knew it! I knew it!" said the kid. "I can really remember lying in there in the dark — there were these cracks of light, so it wasn't totally dark. I was just lying there on some clothes or something, and the top was so high, I couldn't even touch it unless I sat up. And at first I tapped on the top, but nobody came, and I thought I couldn't breathe, but I could. So I just stayed there."

"And I was running all over the house, looking for you, telling you to quit fooling around, it wasn't funny anymore — "

"But I didn't hear you — "

"Because I couldn't talk loud . . . Mom would have heard me — "

"And finally you came and opened the top of the chest — "

"And you were there. You were just there. Not scared or anything. Just got up and got out."

"See, that's the thing. That's what I remember."

"What?"

"That I wasn't scared. I wasn't scared, because I knew . . . "

"Yeah?"

"I knew you would come and find me."

And Reese could see it, Ben's white freckled face, unexpected, staring up at him from the trunk, like a baby in a basket. And his relief, his huge relief, when Ben moved, sat up. He'd jerked Ben's arm, but not too hard, and called him a dork, and asked him why he didn't yell, told him to never go in the trunk again. But Ben just started jumping down the stairs, one at a time, saying he was a bunny. Reese could

564

hear him: "Bunny. Bunny. Bunny. Hop. Hop. Hop. Can you do this, Vincent?"

He tried to erase the image, cover it with anything, any picture, even last night's gaudy wash of ambulance lights. Reese wondered if this was what Pat had done when he had the coronary, willed himself to die, squeezed himself so pitilessly that his heart burst. Tried to take himself out on purpose because he couldn't stand thinking of stuff anymore. I would do it now, Reese thought, shading his eyes with one hand. If I could just die now by wanting to, I would, I'd just disappear . . . Shame was not a thought. Shame had mass and volume. Right now, thought Reese, I'd blow.

"So, Reese?"

Reese couldn't talk; he nodded.

"That's why I came. In case you were wondering. To tell you I remembered that. And see if it was real. Because then I'd know. That I was really there once. I didn't make it up or get it from pictures. And then I could figure stuff out better. Stuff I had to do, or whatever. It might not matter, but I wanted to know."

"Good," Reese mumbled, hoarse. "That's good."

"And one more thing. What did I call you?"

"What?"

"When I was a kid."

"Oh . . . uh . . . Vincent. You called me Vincent. And you could always say it right. Not like a baby."

"Vincent. So, okay. So, I'll see you, Reese, okay?"

"Okay." Reese motioned to his mother; she opened her mouth. She was telling someone to let Sam out. But as the knob turned, Reese said, quickly, "Sam?"

The kid had already put down the phone; but he grabbed it up. "Yeah?"

"You can call me it. Vincent. It's okay."

34

Beth

September 1994

BETH sat down one day in early fall and tried to think of a couple she knew well who'd been through a divorce. And after half an hour, she had to give up. She couldn't think of a single one. Surely for her age, her generation, the education level of her social circle, that was peculiar.

But unless she counted Candy — and she didn't really count Candy, that wasn't a real divorce — she didn't know anyone to compare things with. Candy's abrupt but tender parting from Chris had been more in the nature of a return to the organic nature of their friendship after an experimental grafting that had failed to take. It had been decided and was over with in a couple of weeks, decided and acted upon as suddenly, and to Beth, as surprisingly, as the marriage. Chris and Candy had dinner together after court. Surely that wasn't what most divorces were like. Beth had never seen a couple really sunder from the inside.

Eighty percent of us divorce, she remembered Penny telling the Circle meeting. Eighty percent. Penny's statistic, Beth reasoned, counted couples whose search ended in an unbearable truth. Or

567

in an endless enigma. For what had happened to her and Pat, there were no predictors.

If people knew how estranged she and Pat were becoming, they would think, Why now? Wasn't it doubly bitter, doubly unfair, after having 'been through' all that together, to split? Why not back then, if ever? Even Sam's leaving should not have accomplished what the hottest hell of fear had not managed.

But we didn't care enough to get divorced back then. Having a marriage didn't seem to matter when all you saw as a goal was staying upright for another hour.

She didn't blame Pat. When she looked at him, she felt the widest sinking. No one had decided on this. Things just happened. And once they happened, they were irrevocable. Two days after Sam 'went home' (and that was how Beth forced them all to put it) Pat had taken to sleeping downstairs. He'd done that before — on hot nights, on nights when he'd worked especially late. But those other occasions had been accidental and sometimes a relief: Pat had always been a restless spoon sleeper, and more than once she'd shoved him away and he'd left in a huff. But this time, when he'd gathered up a pillow and a blanket from Sam's fresh, abandoned bed, Pat had not done it rancorously, or with show. Next morning, he'd simply folded up his bedroll, before the children were awake, only to bring it down again the next night.

Vincent noticed Beth was sure. She couldn't look at Vincent. She was afraid to ask Pat what he thought about as he lay on the sofa. She tried not to think, as she lay upstairs, aware of Pat's wakefulness, a sort of arrhythmic blip under the deep pattern of the children's sleep. She read Jane Austen. She popped her Trazodone. She tried not to let her mind climb out of bed, glide down the stairs, and walk down the street to stand yearning in front of the red house.

Returning Sam had been a decorous procedure; only George had wept.

They'd met with the social worker and then had a brief hearing in chambers with a family court judge. The judge had asked each of them, including Sam, who sat rigid in his chair, whether this was a decision made of free will. Beth spoke first. "With a great deal of sadness," she said. "But yes, freely."

"And Mr. Cappadora?"

There was a long interval of murderous silence, and then Pat said, "Yes." He did not look at Beth, but she'd reached out and put her hand on his arm, touching the starched cotton of his long-sleeved shirt. The arm was still as marble; not even a nerve answered her touch. Asked about his willingness, George could only nod mutely. The judge then asked to speak to Samuel Karras Cappadora alone, and emerged, fifteen minutes later, slightly red about the eyes, his palms turned up. There would be, he explained, no formal custody decree granted at this time. The review of Cecilia's condition was pending; it was necessary to follow Sam in his return transition for a period of time not to exceed, say, three months.

"I think our goal should be to restore this

boy's life to as much normalcy as possible as quickly as possible," the judge told George, Beth, and Pat. "I confess that I am troubled by this, by all your suffering, and touched by all your evident concern and love for this boy. I wish all of you luck and peace."

Sam, he said, would be permitted weekly visits, unsupervised, with his natural parents, the duration of those visits to be determined by George in concordance with the Cappadoras. "I hope that he will have some interaction with his birth siblings," the judge added. "For their emotional well-being as well as his own."

Kerry reacted to the news of Sam's imminent departure with frank grief, running up to her room and sobbing into her whale puppet until the plush was soggy. "We just found him," she told Beth. "Why doesn't he like us?" Miserable as the question was, Beth was relieved. Vincent greeted the departure with his trademark frost; but Beth knew that he would talk it over with Tom.

No one, except Beth, really understood what had happened. Even Candy, who struggled to retain a shred of professional detachment, could not hide her disgust. To Beth's gratitude, Rosie and Angelo were only sad, not outraged; but she was sure she would never spend another holiday in Monica's house or in Tree's. Her brothers, sideswiped by what they considered an impulsive Beth-move, tried to counsel a wait-and-see plan. Laurie was struck speechless, and Ellen had asked, "How can you, Beth? I don't mean, how could you? I mean, how can you bring yourself to do it?"

Fortunately, nobody had the energy to alert the media, and Sam was reinstated at George's house for a full week before they got wind of it. Then, there were ponderous quotes from psychologists about the quest for identity during adolescence and the nature of memory in the constitution of family. There were stories about how rarely the 'reunions' of children adopted at birth with the parents who'd given birth to them gave rise to actual extended-family bonds. There were stray quotes from neighbors — Beth almost had to laugh at them — about how Sam had seemed quiet and content enough; they reminded her of the comments neighbors made after quiet, helpful men got up one day and shotgunned whole families.

But really, how could anyone grasp it? They had not seen Sam's face at the cedar chest. They had not seen his eyes.

It was the image that Beth kept in her mind throughout the formalities of the return. It sustained her. She could not describe it to anyone; it was like trying to describe 'yellow' to a child sightless from birth. The feel of the sun? The velvet of a daffodil? Beth could only cling to the certainty that she had known, when Sam looked up at her after the inspection of his baby clothes, that she and Pat had guardianship only over Sam's physical body. She had felt the way Cecilia, in the sad safe room of her riddled mind, could never feel, and probably had never felt — like a kidnapper holding a child against his will.

571

And was he happy now? On their few desultory visits — one outing to Great America, once to dinner at Rosie's — both she and Pat had felt keenly Sam's nearly pitiful willingness to indulge them.

On the way home from dropping him off the last time, Pat had told her suddenly, "It's like he's trying to pay us back by being glad to see us. He's grateful to us for setting him free."

There had been nothing else to say. Years ago, during their one stab at marriage counseling, the cheerful MSW had suggested that they simply try to act as if they were happy. "It has a way of becoming habitual, just as a pattern of conflict does," he'd said. Beth understood that. She'd done it for the latter half of the nine years at least. And then after Pat's illness, she'd become a method actor, a loving wife or be damned. But only during the brief sojourn of Ben's return had there been the beginnings of a renewed, real tenderness between them. A few times, before the weekend of the Fourth of July when they had lain together, after lovemaking, and Beth had actually believed they were going to be whole again, in spite of themselves. By the time she knew for sure that was what she wanted, Beth reflected now, it was probably already too late.

Even now, she sometimes caught herself hoping that the simple habit of a lifetime of Pat-and-Beth would span the gulf. But Pat had given up after Sam left. And so emotion leaked steadily out of the air between them, until there was no shape or structure that didn't have to do with Vincent's habits or Kerry's schedules.

Pat's rage on the morning after Vincent stole the car had been the most emotion he had showed toward Beth in weeks. Even anger had felt almost . . . heartening, in the sterility of their lives.

Pat's focus was now given over entirely to Vincent's rehabilitation. He drove his son to every counseling appointment with Tom, waiting for him outside; he visited the youth officer with Vincent; he closed Vincent's door behind them at night when he went in to say goodnight. Even when Beth offered to spell him, to take Vincent to see Tom on nights when she knew the session would make Pat late for opening at Wedding, Pat had refused. "I owe him, Beth," he told her. "I owe him, and even if I didn't owe him, he's the only son I have."

The day he said that, Beth sent for the catalogues, applications for the master's program in Fine Arts at the University of Wisconsin. She'd filled them out, sending her fee, not entirely certain what she was trying to accomplish. Did this mean she actually meant to leave Pat? Move away? Or was she simply trying to see if there would be a twig of pride for her to cling to if he demanded she go? And what if she did go back to school? Would she aim at teaching? Opening a studio of her own, back in Madison?

She'd left some papers lying on a coffee table, several days after they came, and caught Pat's glance on them.

"I thought," she said, stopping him in one of his headlong dashes in the door from some Vincent thing to grab his jacket for work, "I might consider taking some time, maybe a semester, so we can think things over . . . "

And she was surprised how much it cut her when Pat said, "Whatever. Do whatever you want, Bethie."

So he would not try to stop her. Why had she thought he would?

Stubbornness, the Kerry family curse, had driven her on, then, to say more, make the point harder, "I thought I could maybe rent a little place . . Kerry and Vincent could go to school at Edgewood, maybe, if we can afford it . . . "

He'd come full stop then, his look as if he were taking her by both shoulders, squaring her to face him.

"My children," he said, as slowly as if he were talking to a woman whose first language was not English, "are going noplace, Bethie. My children's home is here."

"Paddy," she began, "Kerry's still so little . . . "

And he seemed to relent, if only slightly. "Maybe . . . it's possible that Kerry would be okay. But Beth, she has friends here, and Scouts, and sports. She has Blythe, who's like her sister, and Georgia, who's like her — " He didn't, bless him, say 'like her mother'. "She might be okay, and it's something we can talk about after you make up your mind. But Vincent is not going to leave this house with you. Not ever. He is not going to leave this house until he goes to college, if, I pray to God, I can figure out how to get him out of high school in one piece, and get him to believe he can do anything except

574

screw up his life." Beth loved him then, loved him desperately, his deep, utter Pat Cappadora goodness. It was, after all, a kindness, in a sense, that she might leave. If she had ever been worthy of him, she wasn't now.

And what, after all, Beth thought that night as she listened to Pat's drawer rummaging downstairs, was a marriage really except a collection of wishes that, after years of association, took on the coloration of facts? She wondered whether she and Pat, except in the early years of their college passion — which, she reasoned, could have ignited between any two healthy young people — had ever been more than a kind of brother and sister, raised to the assumption of safety in one another. She would settle even for safety now.

Beth woke one night, shaking, from a dream of Vincent. Vincent . . . injured. Aged about five, in the hospital, a broken wrist. She'd dreamed of bursting through swinging doors — not one, or two, but an endless series — to follow the trail of wails to Vincent.

She could have her son, Beth thought, sitting up. Her lost-on-purpose son. Not the one lost by accident. If she had the guts, if she had the time, if she could find the ropes. If miracles could really happen.

If miracles could really happen.

If she didn't leave him. If she took him with her . . . but now could she do that? If she stayed . . . but how could she do that?

And from Vincent's point of view, would it make any difference?

575

Beth remembered how, in college, she'd toyed with the idea of a career in special education (Laurie called it Beth's Annie Sullivan phase). Beth had read that all children experienced to some degree the phenomenon of erased recollection. It was one of the most difficult crossroads between parents and children: adults could remember the enraptured tenderness of the early bond; children, whose job was to fracture that bond, couldn't. At six, Vincent had looked at her with flinty eyes and explained that he hated her. Beth was aghast. Where behind those eyes was her princeling, who only a year before would quiet from fear in no other arms but hers, not Rosie's, not Pat's? Where was that child, back then?

Where was he now?

Oh, Vincent, Vincent-turned-Reese, another changeling child in a house that already, impossibly, contained America's best-known changeling child. What did Vincent remember? Anything, at all, of mother love unscored by family casualties? And not remembering was the same as not knowing. If Vincent thought of her in those terms, it was probably a gauzy recollection of the amusement and affection she'd felt for Ben just before he was lost. She had, yes, given Ben more of that. Ben was easier. She'd liked him better. But love? Amusement and affection no more comprised the sum of love than sex on your honeymoon compared with going through labor and delivery — pleasure compared with the world-without-end amen. Beth was struck with a sudden, vivid

576

picture of herself, coming up the walk at night after an all-day shift at the afternoon daily in Madison where she'd worked when the boys were babies, seeing Ben dancing in his diaper on the window seat, and Vincent scooting through Jill's legs to jump on his mother. She remembered thinking, more than once, Imagine! I made them. All this beautiful, intelligent flesh I made. Actual, comical humans. And how she would think, then, aching with her abundance, I would die for them. For each of them, equally painfully, and eagerly.

If Vincent could look through her lens . . . but that was it. That picture was hers, not his. There was no way to graft it onto his heart.

Suddenly panicky, Beth thought, I'll go downstairs and wake Pat and tell him: It had gotten colossally out of hand, this notion of separating; it was just a pose. Together, they would forge a relationship with Sam, and help Vincent and Kerry do that, too. It could happen. She would go down there, and get Pat to slide over on the couch, so she could crunch in next to him, as she had in his hospital bed. She pulled back the quilt and swung her bare feet to the floor.

And then she pictured Pat's mouth, as it had looked when he told her, "Vincent is not going to leave this house with you." She pulled up her quilt and lay flat, her hands laced on her chest.

Candy dropped by one night — girlish in jeans and a paint-spattered shirt. She kissed Pat in passing as he left for work, and plopped down on the porch.

"Give me vodka," she told Beth. "I have spent all day painting my disgusting single-girl flat, in preparation for my disgusting single girl's life, and I feel old as dirt."

They sat on the porch, and Beth wondered if she only imagined Candy shooting glances down toward the corner around which Sam lived. Both of them tipped their feet up on the railing and listened to the crickets.

"How's my man Reese?" Candy asked, midway through her second drink. "Does he brag to his friends about doing time? Even though it was only two days?"

"On the contrary," said Beth. "I really think he's ashamed of it."

"That's good," Candy said. "And life on probation?"

Relieved to be able to say anything, Beth told her, "It seems better." She sketched in Vincent's evident interest, or at least his show of interest, in the basketball camp for inner-city fifth graders he'd been assigned to help coach twice each week.

"He been driving up any oak trees lately?" Candy asked.

"Vincent will probably be drawing Social Security the next time he gets behind a wheel, if Pat has his way," Beth said. "His wings are basically clipped. I mean, he goes to community service, he goes to Wedding to help out, he goes to see Tom — "

"What does Tom say?"

"I . . . I haven't talked to him. I . . . usually don't."

578

"And has Reese seen Sam? Again?"

"No."

They rocked a little longer, and Beth added, "The one thing that seems to have made the biggest impression on him is taking away the boom box."

"What?" Candy sat up.

"That was my idea. Since he was a little kid, Vincent just . . . he gets lost in music. It's way beyond a teenager thing. I stripped it all," Beth said. "Tapes. CDs. I kept them; but I donated his boom box. I gave it to Saint Vincent De Paul. I told him it was a privilege. He had to know we mean business, and after all, it's the thing he loves the most . . . "

She didn't notice, in the gathering dusk, how Candy's face had changed, so when Candy brought the chair she'd been balancing on two legs down with a crack and leveled a finger at Beth's face, Beth almost flinched.

"What he loves most," Candy said, "is right here in front of me. That's what he loves most, Beth."

Rage splashed in Beth's throat; she almost couldn't speak.

"I'm so sick of hearing it," she said finally. "I hear it even in my sleep! I'm so sick of hearing how this boy is only a delinquent because his mother didn't love him . . . Candy, forgive me, it's not so simple. Vincent never . . . even before any of this ever happened, Vincent was convinced I loved Ben better."

"Did you?"

"Jesus God! Did I? How do I know? Candy,

do you love your heart better than your brain? Your arm better than your leg? But then this happened, all of it, and Ben at the center, so there was no way I could ever convince Vincent."

"Even if you tried."

"Which I didn't, yes, mea culpa, mea maxima culpa. But anyhow, shouldn't he have known? Shouldn't a normal kid have known? Did I have to tell him every day?"

"Did he have to tell *you* every day? I mean, shouldn't you know, too?"

"What's that supposed to mean? Are you taking up Freudian analysis now, Candy?"

"Beth, I've seen this kid when he looks at you. He wants you to forgive him so bad . . . "

"Forgive him? *Forgive* him?"

"For all the shit he's pulled. Or for something, some dumb thing you don't even know about. Why don't you talk to Tom? Why don't you? I have."

"And he said?"

"He said Reese is what they call a symptom bearer. He lives out everybody's else's pain with the stuff he does. And now, with Sam gone, how do you think he feels?"

"I have no idea," Beth said wearily, and then, "You know what? I think Pat and I are separating."

Candy tossed the remains of her drink out into the bushes and slammed down the glass. "Good Christ, Beth, why?" Beth shrugged. "Isn't enough enough?"

"Candy, he wants it."

"Did he say that?"

"He didn't have to. I can tell."

"No. No. I refuse to believe that. Pat thinks the sun comes up — "

"Not anymore. Not for a long time, I guess."

"Bethie, you have to do something about this. You guys can't take another loss. Come on."

"Candy, people get divorced all the time. Most people who . . . lost a child get divorced. Look it up." Beth struggled to restore a lightness to her tone. "Even you got divorced."

"You can't sit here and compare Chris and me with . . . You were meant for each other, Bethie. You and Pat."

"Another thing I'm sick of hearing. You know? I feel like I was born with Pat's last name. Damn it. Maybe I can have a life, you know? Maybe what I need is what you have — real work, and a little place, by myself. Pat doesn't care."

"Did you ask him?"

"Yes, as a matter of fact, I did. And he said, 'Do what you want.'"

"That's just pride." Candy got up and sat on the railing. "He's just played out. You don't make these decisions after a summer like the one you had. And what about Reese? And Kerry?"

"He's going to fight to keep them here. He doesn't want me to take them back to Madison."

"To Madison?"

"Well, Candy, what's left for me here? Annual follow-ups of the many permutations and combinations of the Cappadora saga in

581

the *Tribune* magazine? Even more nasties from his sisters? My father looking at me like I shot his favorite dog? No. Shit. I'm not doing it." Beth got up and sat down on the cement stoop. "Candy, I don't know how to even think of leaving Reese or Kerry. And I know that if I move, I'll hardly ever . . . I'll lose all my contact with Sam."

"But you're played out, too, aren't you, girlfriend?" Candy kneeled next to Beth's chair. "Oh, Bethie, Bethie." Candy rocked her then, and Beth felt her tears come like the letdown of milk when she'd nursed the babies, unstoppable, purging. "Okay now, okay. Listen. I just want you to do one thing for me. One thing. Will you?" Beth nodded, and Candy said, "Don't bolt the door behind you is all. Close it partway if you have to, but don't lock it. Give him one more chance to talk. You and Pat haven't lived apart for your entire adult lives. If you go, don't forget to listen to how that really feels. Don't talk yourself into anything, Bethie. You're fully capable of talking yourself into anything, remember? Just . . . wait and see."

Beth nodded.

"When are you leaving?" Candy asked.

"I don't know . . . maybe soon," Beth murmured. "If I go at all. School starts in January. And I'd be taking classes at the university."

"Oh, my God, my God," Candy said. "Pat's going to miss you like he's lost an arm." She stood up and gathered up her mammoth bag. "And Bethie, he's not the only one. I will, too."

"You sure you don't want another drink?" asked Beth, suddenly loath for Candy to leave.

"No, I don't want to have to give myself a field sobriety test. Even though I'm now out of the fertility sweepstakes for good."

Beth said, wondering if she was going too far, "I kind of hate that, Candy. I wanted you to have your baby."

"Yeah, yeah . . . I did, too," Candy said. "I wanted it, for real. I'm sorry for Chris, too, though he'll do a lot better with the next twenty-five-year-old to come down the pike. And maybe, now that I don't have to live on slave wages, I think sometimes there's this little girl living on a mountain in Chile somewhere who wants a crazy mama who carries a gun. So maybe . . . "

"I think that would be wonderful. You'd be a wonderful mother," Beth said.

"So would you, Beth," Candy said softly, and walked down the steps.

35

Reese

IT was after eleven when Reese thought he heard the clang of a basketball on the driveway. He stopped; he'd been writing, or trying to write, something in the stupid journal Tom insisted he mess with every night.

Yeah. Definitely. It was crazy hot for September. With the air on, and the house sealed like a pie under plastic wrap, he wouldn't have heard it if he'd had even a little music on. Which he would normally have had. Even so, he wasn't sure, until he raised the window and put his head out, that he wasn't imagining it.

But no. Somebody was down there.

Reese couldn't see; his dad had told him to replace the bulbs in the floods on the garage a month ago, and of course he hadn't. The night was moonless, murky, the only light from the street lamp a block away. The ball hit again, twice, sharply. Reese had to flip the bedside lamp off to be able to tell who it was.

It was Sam.

"What the hell are you doing?" he hissed. Mom and Dad's window was next to his, and though he knew they were long gone to dreamland, and that Mom, especially, wouldn't be back until dawn, he didn't want to start anything.

"Nothing," said Sam.

"Does your dad know where you are?" asked Reese.

"Yeah," Sam replied.

"I'll just bet," said Reese, leaning out on his elbows.

"You want to play some?"

"Uh, roundhead, it's nearly midnight, in case you haven't noticed."

"Past your bedtime?"

"What I mean is, you waste, I'm in enough fucking trouble without getting Mrs. Pellicano or Mr. Becker to call me in for disturbing the peace, too."

"We could play quiet," Sam said. "Unless you're . . . like, too tired. Or too afraid."

"Fear is not in my vocabulary," Reese told him. "As you know, I could take you blindfolded. I took you every day last summer and sometimes twice on Sundays. As I recall, you had to move out to save what little lousy reputation you had left."

"I don't remember it that way," Sam said, and Reese could hear his grin. "Anyhow, that's pretty easy to say when you're up on the second floor."

"Start praying, wimp."

"I'm on my knees," Sam said.

Reese thought of putting on a shirt, but it was so damn hot anyway. He just jumped down the stairs by threes — what the hell was the kid doing hanging around their driveway at midnight? He was sure as hell George didn't know anything about this. George was probably already calling the fucking FBI or the networks or both. Jesus Christ.

He ran out the door, and Sam was standing there, sunburned, in cutoffs and Reese's White Sox jersey.

"That's my shirt," Reese said automatically.

"Awww, really?" Sam pretended to sound apologetic. "I thought it was a paint rag."

"Where'd you get it?"

"I . . . took it when I left. I'm sorry. You can have it."

"I don't need it," Reese said in a hurry, then thinking, What a complete asshole I am. "Have it. Or, have it if you beat me. So, that is, you might as well give it up now. Unless it smells." He couldn't take his eyes off the kid. It had been, like, weeks since he'd seen him at the jail. His dad and mom had taken Sam out twice, that he knew of, but Reese had been busy both times. And now, having spent two days in jail and many wonderful days and nights in the comfortable confines of his room except for the few moments they allowed him out in manacles to eat dinner did not make for easy surveillance of anything except Mr. Becker watering his hostas.

"Are you sure your dad knows where you are?" he asked again, checking the ball.

"You keep putting it off," Sam said. "I think you're scared."

"Make It — Take It, then," Reese said. "To eleven."

He had played with Sam enough to know his moves, so by rights they shouldn't have

586

fooled him. He knew that the kid hardly ever looked at you, and that was one of his tricks. Sam had these slanty eyes, Dad's eyes, and he would narrow them down to slits and fasten his gaze over your right shoulder, as if there were some giant bedbug behind you, all the while dribbling in figure eights low between his legs. You almost had to be drawn off. And he talked the whole time — "Man, you are sorry, you're so sorry, which way you want me to take you? to the right? to the left?" — but it wasn't as if his patter was directed at you, even meant to rattle you; it was just like a motor running. He made you feel like you weren't there. And the goddamn thing was, it worked.

Sam looped right around Reese and went in for the lay-up. And then walked back with his arms out, punching the air, crowing, "What's up? What's up? You asleep? You asleep?" And Reese couldn't help laughing.

But then, when he finally got the ball, he swore to God Sam had grown three inches in the last month; the kid was all over him, clapping his hands, ignoring Reese's attempts to fake him out. Reese finally drove in to the left, but Sam knocked the shot down.

"That's goaltending," Reese said sharply, though he knew it wasn't; the ball was nowhere near the descending arc. Of course, you had to object, just for form.

"If you gotta cheat, you gotta cheat — I don't care, take it over," Sam said.

"Go ahead, little boy," Reese said then.

"I'm going to go easy on you. Seeing it's late and all."

By the time the score stood seven — five, Reese ahead, both of them were gasping in the humid darkness. You could feel your lungs flap like wet gloves. "You got air inside?" Sam asked Reese.

"Full blast," said Reese. "You giving up?"

"Who's giving up?" Sam darted right and whirled, with this beautiful skyhook, which went nowhere but the bottom of the net.

"What the hell? How did you learn that?" Reese asked him. "That was your left hand."

"I'm a man of many talents," Sam laughed, checking the ball to Reese and going into his crouch.

"Call it," Reese said; then, "Keep the shirt. I pissed on it in June anyhow, that's why it was in the drawer."

"You have to stop pissing in your drawers," Sam said, and Reese reached under the ball, knocking it up so it just glanced off Sam's chin.

"You got to say 'beat', though," Sam egged him on. "You're beat, right?"

"I let you," Reese told him, "and you know it. But let's call it a night. Come back tomorrow for a rematch."

That was when Sam put his hands up and pushed the wet hair up over his forehead, so it stuck straight up, like mowed grass. And took a deep breath. He didn't move. Reese stopped, heaving and sweating, flatfooted in the driveway.

"I . . . The thing is," Sam said then, "I'm not going back."

"What do you mean?"

Sam jerked his head over his right shoulder, and there, at the end of the driveway in the dark, where Reese had not even noticed it, was a huge, battered suitcase.

"Sam," he said slowly, "man, what are you doing?"

"My dad knows," Sam answered, hurriedly. "I mean, we talked about it a lot last week, for a long time, and he said I have to do what I have to do, and he even knows why I came over here so late at night . . . "

"Which is why?"

Sam looked up at the darkened bedroom windows. "I didn't want to have this whole big number," he said. "You know. With your . . . with Beth and Pat. And, like, what if the press found out?" That killed Reese, the way he said 'the press', like he was forty years old or something. "They probably already think I'm out of my mind for going home — I mean back — I mean to George . . . "

"So he let you come out this late?"

"We walked down here before. A little while ago. I saw your light."

"Okay," Reese said, and added, almost swallowing his tongue over the words, "but, is this, like, permanent?"

Sam looked down at his feet, his mouth clamped shut, and then looked up at Reese — still, Reese thought, an inch shorter maybe — his eyes widening in the dark, as if they had no color, as

589

if they were dark little mirrors in which Reese was sure, if he could get close enough, he could see his own pale face. "I don't know," he said. "I don't know. Maybe. If I can . . . I hope — "

Reese made a motion, stopping him, and Sam stopped, turned, and went down to the end of the driveway to get his suitcase. After a beat, Reese followed. He didn't want to push him, but he had to move, to do something; he'd go crazy if he didn't.

"Loser carries," Reese said. "Fairsies fairsie." The thing weighed a ton. "What, do you collect anvils?"

Reese rounded his shoulders, strained, hefted the handle into his right hand; and then Sam reached out and closed his own hand over Reese's. Reese jerked; he felt the touch up his whole arm, as if the kid had pressure-pointed him.

"No problem. I can do it," he said.

But Sam didn't loosen his grip.

You felt like you were diving in a quarry, it was so dark. Reese had to strain to see Sam's expression in the faint cast from that corner light, the corner around which you would walk, cross one side street, and then spot the red house, the only one on that block that wasn't blue or gray or brown. Reese could picture it now clearer than he could the sweat-shaped brim of his Rockets hat, the feel of the wild goose pillow on Tom's couch. The red house that was Sam's house, now not Sam's. Maybe. He could ask again, but the answer wouldn't make any difference.

It was like everything. You just had to wait until morning and then count and see who was left. You had to keep walking until you figured out what was the right place, keep on searching until somebody found you. Reese looked up at the light, then back at the patch of darker dark that contained his brother. He could only feel him, the sweat on his palm — the kid calluses, the strength in those oversized fingers. Reese put the suitcase down; he was shivering. It was one of those times he thought he understood the way his dad felt when his heart brought down the hammer. We should just go in, is all. But fuck, thought Reese, I have to. I have to sometime. I have to now.

"I was the one," he said. "I was the one who let go of your hand."

Sam shifted his feet. Reese could hear him sigh.

"Well . . . " Sam said.

They picked up the suitcase then, even weight, like it was a mattress, and carried it between them onto the porch.

"We're locked out?" Sam asked.

"They don't make a lock that can resist the charms of Reese Cappadora," Reese said, pulling his jimmy out of his back pocket. "I get in this way half the time." Laughing, then, they struggled into the hall. Beowulf stirred on his rug, got up stretching painfully, and clicked down the hall, chuffing his graying muzzle into Sam's palm.

"Old dog," said Sam. "Good old dog." Then he noticed the stack of Beth's bags, her suitcase

591

and equipment. "Who's going on a trip?"

"My mom is maybe going to Wisconsin for . . . a job," said Reese.

Maybe. Now maybe not. Suitcases could be packed. Suitcases could be unpacked. You just had to wait. "You want to put that in here? We can take it up later." They shoved Sam's bag into the living room next to the piano.

"I could eat," Sam said.

In the kitchen, the refrigerator's glow was the only light. Reese flipped a piece of cheese to Beowulf, who gobbled it noisily. Sam reached around him to dislodge a Coke from the pyramid of stacked cans on the bottom shelf, and leaped back when all of them rolled. In the silence, they hit the linoleum like M-80s.

"Jesus Christ," hissed Reese. "Wreck the joint." They scrambled after the cans, which kept rolling out, leisurely, smoothly, one after another. One hit a corner of the baseboard, spun, and popped open. Soda geysered; Beowulf yipped. "For God's sake," Reese whispered, grinning, "shut up!"

The cans seemed endless, like a film strip of logs rolling down a chute.

"This isn't your fault," Reese gasped. "This is Dad, the master engineer of the universe. This one winter, when they were working on the restaurant, and Dad was going to save all the leftover tiles . . . so he spends all day getting them up in the rafters of the garage, and he stands there and shuts the garage door, and the rafters crack, and the whole goddamn ceiling . . . "

592

Helplessly, Sam spit his Coke, which only made Reese more determined to make him laugh. "And so every fucking tile, every single tile goes crashing down, one by one, on the floor of the — "

But they both heard her step.

"Vincent!" Beth called from the top of the stairs, her voice sleep-slurred but laced with a tang of panic. "What's that noise? Are you in the house?"

Reese put his finger to his lips. "You don't want her up," he told Sam. "Not now. Trust me on this." Sam reached silently into the refrigerator for a flat box of cold pizza, and Reese held up his palm in warning. "Wait," he ordered. Sam stopped.

Beth called, "Vincent?"

"It's okay, Mom," he yelled. "I dropped something. Go back to bed. I'm here."

Reese turned to follow Sam to the kitchen table. From the upper floor came a whoosh of water, a settling sound. He could feel Beth's urgent presence recede, down the hall. They sat down at the table, and Sam delicately opened the pizza box, grimacing disgustedly at the slabs cemented to the lid. Reese went out to the kitchen for a butter knife, and stood for a moment, his ear pitched to the creak of the floorboards overhead, the soft sponge of the bed as she lay down, and then nothing but quiet, the tick and gust of the air conditioner going on, the sounds of a house, anyone's ordinary house, at rest.

"It's pretty ickining-say," Sam said of the

593

pizza. "On the other hand, I'm pretty starving." He sat back after quickly polishing off two slices. "You think she's asleep?"

"Probably," Reese told him. "Hang on a minute more. And then, when you go up there, just sleep in my room. Just for tonight. So we don't have to get out all the sheets and stuff. The whole house will be up."

"Where will you sleep?"

"I don't know," Reese said. "Down here on the couch. With the Wulf. And I'm not even tired."

"It seems kind of crummy to come along and kick you out of your bed."

"No, really," Reese insisted. "I'll take first watch, okay?"

Sam smiled. "Okay."

"I'll walk the perimeter," said Reese, as Sam got up, rummaged in his suitcase, and extracted his toothbrush. Always the good kid.

"Look for suspicious activity," Sam whispered back.

"Right-o, sir, and have a good sleep. I won't rest until the encampment is secured," said Reese.

"Well done."

Reese sat down at the kitchen table, propping his chin on his hands. It was a lie about being wide awake; he was dogged. He felt as though he hadn't really slept in weeks. Overhead, the telltale complaint of his old bed sounded as Sam lay down. Reese looked out the big window, past his reflection, deep into the thick dark of the yard. Was it his imagination, or was there already a lightening out at the edge, where the lawn chairs were?

Out there at the perimeter?

He could just flop on the couch. It was unoccupied, for once. Not like the last few weeks. Dad was sleeping upstairs in their bed. Reese had no idea whether that meant he was trying to get her to stay or saying goodbye. But anyway, it meant that there was vacant real estate on the first floor, and Reese would wake up if anybody moved; he always did. He'd given his word, though. And it was only a few more hours, the tail end of one night. Night could only last so long.

Until the encampment is secured, Reese thought. Or until morning. Whichever comes first.

THE END